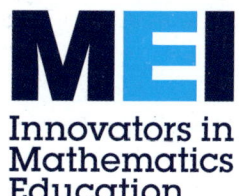

John du Feu

Series editors
Roger Porkess and
Catherine Berry

A LEVEL
FURTHER MATHEMATICS

Statistics

4th Edition

An OCR endorsed textbook

This resource is endorsed by OCR for use with specification H635 OCR AS Level Further Mathematics B (MEI) and with specification H645 OCR A Level Further Mathematics B (MEI). In order to gain OCR endorsement, this resource has undergone an independent quality check. Any references to assessment and/or assessment preparation are the publisher's interpretation of the specification requirements and are not endorsed by OCR. OCR recommends that a range of teaching and learning resources are used in preparing learners for assessment. OCR has not paid for the production of this resource, nor does OCR receive any royalties from its sale. For more information about the endorsement process, please visit the OCR website, www.ocr.org.uk.

Acknowledgements

The Publishers would like to thank the following for permission to reproduce copyright material.

Practice questions have been provided by Neil Sheldon (MEI) (pp. 165–168 and pp. 319–321).

Photo credits

p.1 © Ingram Publishing Limited/General Gold Vol 1 CD 2; **p.20** © DAVIPIX – Fotolia; **p.33** © Imagestate Media (John Foxx)/Store V3042; **p.44** © Peter Titmuss/Shutterstock; **p.49** © Ingram Publishing Limited/Occupations and Trades Vol 2 CD 4; **p.57** © rigamondis – Fotolia; **p.74** © **Cathy** Yeulet – 123RF; **p.114** © Dusan Kostic – Fotolia; **p.132** © LuckyImages/Shutterstock; **p.147** © AZP Worldwide – Fotolia.com; **p.169** © Mark Atkins – Fotolia; **p.173** © Photographee.eu – Fotolia; **p.179** © Luciano de la Rosa Gutierrez – Fotolia.com; **p.182** © Eric Isselée – Fotolia; **p.209** © Sandor Jackal – Fotolia; **p.222** © Ingram Publishing Limited/Animals Gold Vol 1 CD 3; **p.246** © 1997 Siede Preis Photography/Photodisc/Getty Images/ Eat, Drink, Dine 48; **p.259** © Anton Bogdanovich / Fotolia.com; **p.276** © S Curtis/Shutterstock; **p.289** © microgen – 123RF; **p.301** © dpa picture alliance archive/Alamy Stock Photo.

Every effort has been made to trace all copyright holders, but if any have been inadvertently overlooked, the Publishers will be pleased to make the necessary arrangements at the first opportunity.

Although every effort has been made to ensure that website addresses are correct at time of going to press, Hodder Education cannot be held responsible for the content of any website mentioned in this book. It is sometimes possible to find a relocated web page by typing in the address of the home page for a website in the URL window of your browser.

Hachette UK's policy is to use papers that are natural, renewable and recyclable products and made from wood grown in sustainable forests. The logging and manufacturing processes are expected to conform to the environmental regulations of the country of origin.

Orders: please contact Bookpoint Ltd, 130 Park Drive, Milton Park, Abingdon, Oxon OX14 4SE.
Telephone: (44) 01235 827720. Fax: (44) 01235 400454. Email education@bookpoint.co.uk
Lines are open from 9 a.m. to 5 p.m., Monday to Saturday, with a 24-hour message answering service.
You can also order through our website: www.hoddereducation.co.uk

ISBN: 978 1 4718 5302 9

© John du Feu, Roger Porkess, Catherine Berry and MEI 2017

First published in 2017 by

Hodder Education,
An Hachette UK Company
Carmelite House
50 Victoria Embankment
London EC4Y 0DZ

www.hoddereducation.co.uk

Impression number 10 9 8 7 6 5 4 3

Year 2021 2020 2019

All rights reserved. Apart from any use permitted under UK copyright law, no part of this publication may be reproduced or transmitted in any form or by any means, electronic or mechanical, including photocopying and recording, or held within any information storage and retrieval system, without permission in writing from the publisher or under licence from the Copyright Licensing Agency Limited. Further details of such licences (for reprographic reproduction) may be obtained from the Copyright Licensing Agency Limited, Saffron House, 6–10 Kirby Street, London EC1N 8TS.

Cover photo © Angela Waye/123RF.com

Typeset in Bembo Std, 11/13 pts. by Aptara®, Inc.

Printed in Italy

A catalogue record for this title is available from the British Library.

Contents

Getting the most from this book   v
Prior knowledge   vii

1 Statistical problem solving   1
1.1 The problem solving cycle   2

2 Discrete random variables   20
2.1 Notation and conditions for a discrete random variable   22
2.2 Expectation and variance   26

3 Discrete probability distributions   44
3.1 The binomial distribution   45
3.2 The Poisson distribution   49
3.3 Link between binomial and Poisson distributions   59
3.4 Other discrete distributions   64

4 Bivariate data (correlation coefficients)   74
4.1 Describing variables   76
4.2 Interpreting scatter diagrams   77
4.3 Product moment correlation   79
4.4 Rank correlation   101

5 Bivariate data (regression lines)   114
5.1 The least squares regression line (random on non-random)   115
5.2 The least squares regression line (random on random)   124

6 Chi-squared tests   132
6.1 The chi-squared test for a contingency table   133
6.2 Goodness of fit tests   147

Practice questions: Set 1   165

7 Conditional probability   169
7.1 Screening tests   170
7.2 Bayes' theorem   174

8 Continuous random variables   179
8.1 Probability density function   181
8.2 Expectation and variance   190
8.3 The median   192
8.4 The mode   193
8.5 The continuous uniform (rectangular) distribution   195
8.6 The exponential distribution   198
8.7 The expectation and variance of a function of X 203
8.8 The cumulative distribution function   209

9 Expectation algebra and the Normal distribution   222
9.1 The sums and differences of Normal variables   225
9.2 Modelling discrete situations   227
9.3 More than two independent random variables   231
9.4 The distribution of the sample mean   238
9.5 The central limit theorem   240

10 Confidence intervals   246
10.1 The theory of confidence intervals   247
10.2 Interpreting sample data using the t-distribution   259

11 Hypothesis testing — 276

- 11.1 Hypothesis testing on a sample mean using the Normal distribution — 277
- 11.2 Large samples — 280
- 11.3 Hypothesis testing on a sample mean using the t-distribution — 281
- 11.4 The Wilcoxon signed rank test on a sample median — 289

12 Simulation — 301

- 12.1 Simulating discrete uniform distributions — 304
- 12.2 Simulating continuous uniform distributions — 305
- 12.3 Simulating Normal distributions — 306
- 12.4 Simulating other distributions — 308
- 12.5 Simulation and the central limit theorem — 308

Practice questions: Set 2 — 319

Answers — 322

Index — 357

Getting the most from this book

Mathematics is not only a beautiful and exciting subject in its own right but also one that underpins many other branches of learning. It is consequently fundamental to our national wellbeing.

This book covers the Statistics elements in the MEI AS and A Level Further Mathematics specifications. Students start these courses at a variety of stages. Some embark on AS Further Mathematics in Year 12, straight after GCSE, taking it alongside AS Mathematics, and so may have no prior experience of Statistics. In contrast, others only begin Further Mathematics when they have completed the full A Level Mathematics and so have already met the Statistics covered in *MEI A Level Mathematics (Year 2)*. Between these two extremes are the many who have covered the Statistics in AS Mathematics but no more.

This book has been written with all these users in mind. So, it provides a complete course in Statistics up to the required level. Those who already know some Statistics will find some background material in the early chapters.

In the MEI specification, two Statistics papers are available at AS level, both set at AS standard and both counting for one-third of the AS qualification. Chapters 1 to 6 of this textbook cover the content of Statistics a (Y412). Chapters 8 to 12 cover the content of Statistics b (Y416). Chapter 7 covers the basic ideas of conditional probability which, although not directly examined in this specification, provide an important background for much of the work involving statistical inference in the rest of the book.

At A Level there are two Statistics papers available, both set at A Level standard. Chapters 1 to 6 of this textbook cover the content of Statistics Minor (Y432), which counts for one-sixth of the A Level qualification. Chapters 1 to 6 and Chapters 8 to 12 cover the content of Statistics Major (Y422) which counts for one-third of the A Level qualification.

Between 2014 and 2016 A Level Mathematics and Further Mathematics were very substantially revised, for first teaching in 2017. Changes that particularly affect Statistics include increased emphasis on

- Problem solving
- Mathematical rigour
- Use of ICT
- Modelling.

This book embraces these ideas. A large number of exercise questions involve elements of problem solving and require rigorous logical argument.

Throughout the book the emphasis is on understanding and interpretation rather than mere routine calculations, but the various exercises do nonetheless provide plenty of scope for practising basic techniques. The exercise questions are split into three bands. Band 1 questions (indicated by a green bar) are designed to reinforce basic understanding; Band 2 questions (yellow bar) are broadly typical of what might be expected in an examination; Band 3 questions (red bar) explore around the topic and some of them are rather more demanding. In addition, extensive online support, including further questions, is available by subscription to MEI's Integral website, http://integralmaths.org.

In addition to the exercise questions, there are two sets of Practice questions. The first of these covers Chapters 1 to 8 and the second the whole book. These include identified questions requiring problem solving **PS**, mathematical proof **MP**, use of ICT **T** and modelling **M**.

There are places where the work depends on knowledge from earlier in the book or elsewhere and this is flagged up in the Prior knowledge boxes. This should be seen as an invitation to those who have problems with the particular topic to revisit it. At the end of each chapter there is a list of key points covered as well as a summary of the new knowledge (learning outcomes) that readers should have gained.

Two common features of the book are Activities and Discussion points. These serve rather different purposes. The Activities are designed to help readers get into the thought processes of the new work that they are about to meet; having done an Activity, what follows will seem much easier. The Discussion points invite readers to talk about particular points with their fellow students and their teacher and so enhance their understanding. Another feature is a Caution icon ❗, highlighting points where it is easy to go wrong.

Answers to all exercise questions and practice questions are provided at the back of the book, and also online at www.hoddereducation.co.uk/MEIFurtherMathsStatistics

This is a 4th edition MEI textbook so much of the material is well tried and tested. However, as a consequence of the changes to A Level requirements in Further Mathematics, large parts of the book are either new material or have been very substantially rewritten.

Catherine Berry
Roger Porkess

Prior knowledge

This book is written on the assumption that readers are familiar with the statistics in GCSE Mathematics. Thus they should know a variety of elementary display techniques such as pictograms, tallies, pie charts, bar charts and scatter diagrams (including the ideas of correlation and a line of best fit). Summary measures which they are expected to know include mean, median, mode and range. Readers are also expected to be familiar with basic probability.

Chapter 1
This chapter sets up the framework in which much of statistics is carried out in everyday life. It is about statistical problem solving and so involves using display techniques and summary measures to shed light on real problems. Consequently it draws on and extends the prior knowledge for the book. In particular it introduces frequency charts and histograms, and variance and standard deviation. This chapter includes summary information about many of the terms that readers will use throughout the book, including types of data, distributions and sampling.

Chapter 2
In this chapter on discrete random variables readers use their prior knowledge of probability from GCSE, display techniques from GCSE and Chapter 1, and their knowledge of variance and standard deviation from Chapter 1.

Chapter 3
This chapter on discrete probability distributions covers the binomial, Poisson, uniform and geometric distributions all of which are particular examples of discrete random variables. Consequently it builds on and exemplifies Chapter 2. It also draws on background information from Chapter 1, for example about the idea of a distribution.

Chapter 4
This chapter is about correlation and association in bivariate data and so readers will draw on their GCSE experience of scatter diagrams. The chapter includes Spearman's rank correlation coefficient and many readers will have met this in other subjects, for example geography.

Chapter 5
This chapter is about regression lines in bivariate data. It extends the basic idea that readers met in GCSE and formalises it beyond just drawing a line by eye.

Chapter 6
In this chapter readers meet the use of χ^2 tests in several different circumstances. These include goodness of fit tests for the uniform, binomial and Poisson distributions met in Chapter 3.

Chapter 7
This chapter is about conditional probability. It builds on and extends readers' knowledge of probability from GCSE.

Chapter 8
This chapter is on continuous random variables and so it builds on and extends the ideas in Chapters 2 and 3 on discrete random variables to continuous variables. The cumulative distribution function is introduced in this chapter.

Chapter 9
The title of this chapter is *Expectation algebra and the Normal distribution*. It draws on knowledge from Chapter 8 on continuous random variables, including the extension of the use of the cumulative distribution function to the Normal distribution. It also extends work in Chapter 2 on expectation and variance. The central limit theorem is introduced in this chapter.

Chapter 10
This chapter is on confidence intervals and so it draws on the work in Chapter 8 on continuous random variables, and particularly that in Chapter 9 on the central limit theorem. It also extends the goodness of fit tests developed in Chapter 6 to tests for the Normal distribution. The t distribution is introduced in this chapter.

Chapter 11
This chapter covers hypothesis tests for a population mean using the Normal distribution and the t distribution. It builds on the work in the previous two Chapters, 9 and 10. This chapter also includes the hypothesis test for the median using the Wilcoxon signed rank test; all these tests build on the procedures for carrying out hypothesis tests developed in Chapter 6.

Chapter 12
The final chapter is on simulation and introduces the use of software to simulate various distributions. It thus builds on work throughout this book, particularly (but not exclusively) in Chapters 2, 3, 8, 9 and 10.

1 Statistical problem solving

A judicious man looks at statistics, not to get knowledge but to save himself from having ignorance foisted on him.
Thomas Carlyle (1795–1881)

Discussion point
Do you agree with the 'not to get knowledge' part of Carlyle's statement?

Think of one example where statistics has promoted knowledge or is currently doing so.

How would statistics have been different in Carlyle's time from now?

1 The problem solving cycle

Statistics provides a powerful set of tools for solving problems. While many of the techniques are specific to statistics they are nonetheless typically carried out within the standard cycle.

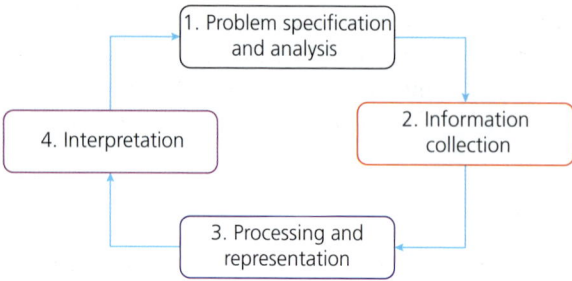

Figure 1.1

This chapter reviews the techniques that are used at the various stages, with particular emphasis on the information collection and the processing and representation elements.

Problem specification and analysis, and interpretation

The problem-solving cycle begins with a problem. That may seem like stating the obvious but it is not quite. Much of the work you do in statistics involves applying statistical techniques to statistical problems. By contrast, the problems tackled in this cycle are drawn from real life. They often require the use of statistics, but as a means to the end of providing an answer to the original problem, situation or context. Here are some examples:

- Is a particular animal in danger of extinction?
- How many coaches should a train operating company put on a particular train?
- Will a new corner shop be viable in a particular location?
- What provision of Intensive Care and High Dependency places should a hospital's neonatal unit make?

To answer questions like these you need data, but before collecting them it is essential to plan the work. Too often poor planning results in inappropriate data being collected. So, at the outset, you need to know:

- what data you are going to collect
- how you are going to collect the data
- how you are going to analyse the data
- how much data you will need
- how you are going to present the results
- what the results will mean in terms of the original problem.

Thus planning is essential and this is the work that is carried out in the first stage, problem specification and analysis, and at the end of the process interpretation is required; this includes the possible conclusion that the problem has not been addressed satisfactorily and the whole cycle must be repeated.

Both planning and interpretation depend on knowledge of how data are collected, processed and represented and so the second and third stages of the cycle are the focus of this chapter.

Information collection

The information needed in statistics is usually in the form of data so the information collection stage in the cycle is usually called **data collection**. This is an important part of statistics and this section outlines the principles involved, together with the relevant terminology and notation.

Terminology and notation

Data collection often requires you to take a sample, a set of items which are drawn from the relevant population and should be representative of it. The complete population may be too large for it to be practical, or economical, to consider every item.

A sample provides a set of data values of a random variable, drawn from all such possible values, the **parent population**. The parent population can be finite, such as all professional netball players, or infinite, such as the points where a dart can land on a dart board.

A representation of the items available to be sampled is called the **sampling frame**. This could, for example, be a list of the sheep in a flock, a map marked with a grid or an electoral register. In many situations no sampling frame exists nor is it possible to devise one, for example for the cod in the North Atlantic. The proportion of the available items that are actually sampled is called the **sampling fraction**. A 100% sample is called a **census**.

> **Note**
> Sampling fraction
> $= \dfrac{\text{Sample size}}{\text{Population size}}$

The term **random** is often used in connection with data collection. For a process to be described as random, each item in the population has a probability of being included in the sample. In many situations these probabilities are equal, but this is not essential. Most calculators give random numbers and these allow you to select an item from a list at random.

> **Note**
> Imagine you want to select a day of the year at **random**. You can number them 1 to 365. Then set your calculator to generate a three-digit number. If it is 365 or less, that gives you your day. If it is over 365, reject it and choose another number.

A parent population, often just called the population, is described in terms of its parameters, such as its mean, μ, and variance, σ^2. By convention, Greek letters are used to denote these population parameters.

A value derived from a sample is written in Roman letters, such as $\bar{x}$ and s. Such a number is the value of a sample statistic (or just statistic). When sample statistics are used to estimate the parent population parameters they are called estimates.

Thus if you take a random sample for which the mean is $\bar{x}$, you can use $\bar{x}$ to estimate the population mean, μ. Thus if in a particular sample $\bar{x} = 25.9$, you can use 25.9 as an estimate of the population mean. You would, however, expect the true value of μ to be somewhat different from 25.9.

An estimate of a parameter derived from sample data will, in general, differ from its true value. The difference is called the **sampling error**. To reduce the sampling error, you want your sample to be as representative of the parent population as you can make it. This, however, may be easier said than done.

The problem solving cycle

Sampling

There are several reasons why you might want to take a sample. These include:

- to help you understand a situation better
- as part of a pilot study to inform the design of a larger investigation
- to estimate the values of the parameters of the parent population
- to avoid the work involved in cleaning and formatting all the data in a large set
- to conduct a hypothesis test.

> **This is often the situation when you are collecting data as part of the problem.**

At the outset you need to consider how your sample data will be collected and the steps you can take to ensure their quality. You also need to plan how you will interpret your data. Here is a checklist of questions to ask yourself when you are taking a sample.

- Are the data relevant to the problem?
- Are the data unbiased?
- Is there any danger that the act of collection will distort the data?
- Is the person collecting the data suitable?
- Is the sample of a suitable size?
- Is a suitable sampling procedure being followed?
- Is the act of collecting the data destructive?

> **Discussion point**
> Give examples of cases where the answers to the first six questions are 'no'.

> **Sample size is important. The larger the sample, the more accurate will be the information it gives you.**

> **For example, bringing rare deep sea creatures to the surface for examination may result in their deaths.**

There are many sampling techniques. The list that follows includes the most commonly used. In considering them, remember that a key aim when taking a sample is that it should be **representative** of the parent population being investigated.

Simple random sampling

In a *simple random sampling procedure*, every possible sample of a given size is equally likely to be selected. It follows that in such a procedure every member of the parent population is equally likely to be selected. However, the converse is not true. It is possible to devise a sampling procedure in which every member is equally likely to be selected but some samples are not possible; an example occurs with *systematic sampling* which is described below.

Simple random sampling is fine when you can do it, but you must have a sampling frame. To carry out simple random sampling, the population must first be numbered, usually from 1 to n. Random numbers between 1 and n are then generated, and the corresponding members of the population are selected. If any repeats occur, more random numbers have to be generated to replace them. Note that, in order to carry out a hypothesis test or to construct a confidence interval (see Chapter 9), the sample taken should be a simple random sample and so some of the sampling methods below are not suitable for these purposes.

> **Example from real life**

Jury selection

The first stage in selecting a jury is to take a simple random sample from the electoral role.

Stratified sampling

Sometimes it is possible to divide the population into different groups, or strata. In *stratified sampling*, you would ensure that all strata were sampled. In *proportional stratified sampling*, the numbers selected from each of the strata are proportional to their size. The selection of the items to be sampled within each stratum is done at random, often using simple random sampling. Stratified sampling usually leads to accurate results about the entire population, and also gives useful information about the individual strata.

Example from real life

Opinion polls

Opinion polls, such as those for the outcome of an election, are often carried out online. The polling organisation collects sufficient other information to allow respondents to be placed in strata. They then use responses from the various strata in proportion to their sizes in the population.

Cluster sampling

Cluster sampling also starts with sub-groups of the population, but in this case the items are chosen from one or several of the sub-groups. The sub-groups are now called clusters. It is important that each cluster should be reasonably representative of the entire population. If, for example, you were asked to investigate the incidence of a particular parasite in the puffin population of northern Europe, it would be impossible to use simple random sampling. Rather, you would select a number of sites and then catch some puffins at each place. This is cluster sampling. Instead of selecting from the whole population you are choosing from a limited number of clusters.

Example from real life

Estimating the badger population size

An estimate of badger numbers in England, carried out between 2011 and 2013, was based on cluster sampling using 1411 1 km^2 squares from around the country. The number of badger setts in each square was counted. The clusters covered about 1% of the area of the country. There had been earlier surveys in 1985–88 and 1994–97 but with such long time intervals between them the results cannot be used to estimate the short term variability of population over a period of years rather than decades. There are two places where local populations have been monitored over many years. So the only possible estimate of short term variability would depend on just two clusters.

Systematic sampling

Systematic sampling is a method of choosing individuals from a sampling frame. If the items in the sampling frame are numbered 1 to n, you would choose a random starting point such as 38 and then every subsequent kth value, for example sample numbers 38, 138, 238 and so on. When using systematic sampling you have to beware of any cyclic patterns within the frame. For example, suppose that a school list is made up class by class, each of exactly 25 children, in order of merit, so that numbers 1, 26, 51, 76, 101, … in the frame are those at the top of their class. If you sample every 50th child starting with number 26, you will conclude that the children in the school are very bright.

The problem solving cycle

Example from real life

Rubbish on beaches

Information was collected, using systematic sampling, about the amount and type of rubbish on the high water line along a long beach.

The beach was divided up into 1m sections and, starting from a point near one end, data were recorded for every 50th interval.

Quota sampling

Quota sampling is the method often used by companies employing people to carry out opinion surveys. An interviewer's quota is always specified in stratified terms, for example how many males and how many females. The choice of who is sampled is then left up to the interviewer and so is definitely non-random.

Example from real life

If you regularly take part in telephone interviews, you may notice that, after learning your details, the interviewer seems to lose interest. That is probably because quota sampling is being used and the interviewer already has enough responses from people in your category.

Opportunity sampling

Opportunity sampling (also known as 'convenience sampling') is a very cheap method of choosing a sample where the sample is selected by simply choosing people who are readily available. For example, an interviewer might stand in a shopping centre and interview anybody who is willing to participate.

Example from real life

Credit card fraud

A barrister asked a mathematician to check that his argument was statistically sound in a case about credit card fraud. The mathematician wanted to find out more about the extent of suspected fraud. By chance, he was about to attend a teachers' conference and so he took the opportunity to ask delegates to fill in a short questionnaire about their relevant personal experience, if any. This gave him a rough idea of its extent and so achieved its aim.

Self-selected sampling

Self-selected sampling is a method of choosing a sample where people volunteer to be a part of the sample. The researcher advertises for volunteers, and accepts any that are suitable.

Example from real life

A medical study

Volunteers were invited to take part in a long-term medical study into the effects of particular diet supplements on heart function and other conditions. They would take a daily pill which might have an active ingredient or might be a placebo, but they would not know which they were taking. Potential participants were then screened for their suitability. At six-monthly intervals those involved were asked to fill in a questionnaire about their general health and lifestyle. The study was based on a self-selected sample of some 10 000 people.

Other sampling techniques

This is by no means a complete list of sampling techniques. Survey design and experimental design cover the formulation of the most appropriate sampling procedures in particular situations. They are major topics within statistics but beyond the scope of this book.

Processing and representation

At the start of this stage you have a set of raw data; by the end, you have worked them into forms that will allow people to see the information that this set contains, with particular emphasis on the problem in hand. Four processes are particularly important.

- Cleaning the data, which involves checking outliers, errors and missing items.
- Formatting the data so that they can be used on a spreadsheet or statistics package.
- Presenting the data using suitable diagrams, which is described below.
- Calculating summary measures, which is also described below.

Describing data

> **Note**
> In this example, the random variable happens to be discrete.
> Random variables can be discrete or continuous.

The data items you collect are often values of **variables** or of **random variables.** The number of goals scored by a football team in a match is a variable because it varies from one match to another; because it does so in an unpredictable manner, it is a random variable. Rather than repeatedly using the phrase 'The number of goals scored by a football team in a match' it is usual to use an upper case letter like X to represent it. Particular values of a random variable are denoted by a lower case letter; often (but not always) the same letter is used. So if the random variable X is 'The number of goals scored by a football team in a match', for a match when the team scores 5 goals, you could say $x = 5$.

The number of times that a particular value of a random variable occurs is called its **frequency**.

When there are many possible values of the variable, it is convenient to allocate the data to groups. An example of the use of **grouped data** is the way people are allocated to age groups.

The pattern in which the values of a variable occur is called its **distribution**. This is often displayed in a diagram with the variable on the horizontal scale and a measure of frequency or probability on the vertical scale. If the diagram has one peak, the distribution is **unimodal**; if the peak is to the left of the middle, the distribution has **positive skew** and if it is to the right, it has **negative skew**. If the distribution has two distinct peaks, it is **bimodal**.

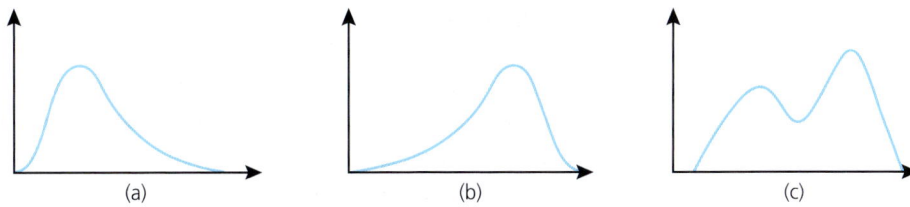

Figure 1.2 (a) Positive skew (b) negative skew (c) a bimodal distribution

The problem solving cycle

Note

Identifying outliers

There are two common tests:
- Is the item more than 2 standard deviations from the mean?
- Is the item more than 1.5 × the interquartile range beyond the nearer quartile?

A data item which is far away from the rest is called an **outlier**. An outlier may be a mistake, for example a faulty reading from an experiment, or it may be telling you something really important about the situation you are investigating. When you are cleaning your data, it is essential to look at any outliers and decide which of these is the case, and so whether to reject or accept them.

The data you collect can be of a number of different types. You always need to know what type of data you are working with as this will affect the ways you can display them and what summary measures you can use.

Categorical (or qualitative) data come in classes or categories, like types of fish or brands of toothpaste. Categorical data are also called *qualitative*, particularly if they can be described without using numbers.

Common displays for categorical data are pictograms, dot plots, tallies, pie charts and bar charts. A summary measure for the most typical item of categorical data is the modal class.

Note

A pie chart is used for showing proportions of a total.
There should be gaps between the bars in a bar chart.

Ranked data are the positions of items within their group when they are ordered according to size, rather than their actual measurements. For example the competitors in a competition could be given their positions as 1st, 2nd, 3rd, etc. Ranked data are extensively used in the branch of statistics called *Exploratory Data Analysis*; this is beyond the scope of this book, but some of the measures and displays for ranked data are more widely used and are relevant here.

The median divides the data into two groups, those with high ranks and those with low ranks. The **lower quartile** and the **upper quartile** do the same for these two groups so, between them, the two quartiles and the median divide the data into four equal-sized groups according to their ranks. These three measures are sometimes denoted by Q_1, Q_2 and Q_3. These values, with the highest and lowest value can be used to create a box plot (or box and whisker diagram).

Note

You have to be aware when working out the median as to whether n is odd or even. If it is odd, for example if $n = 9$, $\frac{n+1}{2}$ works out to be a whole number but that is not so if n is even. For example if $n = 10$, $\frac{n+1}{2} = 5\frac{1}{2}$. In that case, the data set does not have a single middle value; those ranked 5 and 6 are equally spaced either side of the middle and so the median is half way between their values.

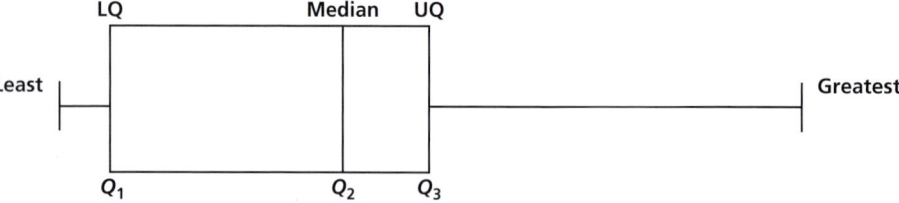

Figure 1.3 Box plot (or box and whisker diagram)

The median is a typical middle value and so is sometimes called an *average*. More formally, it is a *measure of central tendency*. It often provides a good representative value. The median is easy to work out if the data are stored on a spreadsheet since that will do the ranking for you. Notice that extreme values have little, if any, effect on the median. It is described as resistant to outliers. It is often useful when some data values are missing but can be estimated.

Interquartile range and semi interquartile range are measures of spread for ranked data, as is the range.

Drawing a stem-and-leaf diagram can be helpful when ranking data.

Numerical (or quantitative) data occur when each item has a numerical value (and not just a rank), like the number of people travelling in a car or the values of houses.

Numerical data are described as discrete if items can take certain particular numerical values but not those in between. The number of eggs a song bird lays (0, 1, 2, 3, 4, ...) the number of goals a hockey team scores in a match (0, 1, 2, 3, ...) and the sizes of women's clothes in the UK (... 8, 10, 12, 14, 16, ...) are all examples of discrete variables. If there are many possible values, it is common to group discrete data.

By contrast, **continuous** numerical data can take any appropriate value if measured accurately enough.

Distance, mass, temperature and speed are all continuous variables. You cannot list all the possible values.

If you are working with continuous data you will always need to **group** them. This includes two special cases:

- The variable is actually discrete but the intervals between values are very small. For example, cost in euros is a discrete variable with steps of €0.01 (i.e. 1 cent) but this is so small that the variable may be regarded as continuous.
- The underlying variable is continuous but the measurements of it are rounded (for example, to the nearest mm), making your data discrete. All measurements of continuous variables are rounded and, providing the rounding is not too coarse, the data should normally be treated as continuous. A particular case of rounding occurs with people's ages; this is a continuous variable but is usually rounded down to the nearest completed year.

Note

Sometimes a bar chart is used for grouped numerical data with the groups as categories, but you must still leave gaps between the bars.

Note

In frequency charts and histograms, the values of the variables go at the ends of the bars. In a bar chart, the labels are in the middle.

Note

If you are using a frequency chart, the class intervals should all be equal. For a histogram, they don't have to be equal. So, if you have continuous data grouped into classes of unequal width, you should expect to use a histogram.

Displaying numerical data

Commonly used displays for discrete data include a vertical line chart and a stem-and-leaf diagram. A frequency table can be useful in recording, sorting and displaying discrete numerical data.

A frequency chart and a histogram are the commonest ways of displaying continuous data. Both have a continuous horizontal scale covering the range of values of the variable. Both have vertical bars.

- In a frequency chart, frequency is represented by the height of a bar. The vertical scale is Frequency.
- In a histogram, frequency is represented by the area of a bar. The vertical scale is Frequency density.

Look at this frequency chart and histogram. They show the time, t minutes, that a particular train was late at its final destination in 150 journeys.

On both graphs, the interval 5–10 means $5 < t \leq 10$, and, similarly, for other intervals. A negative value of t means the train was early.

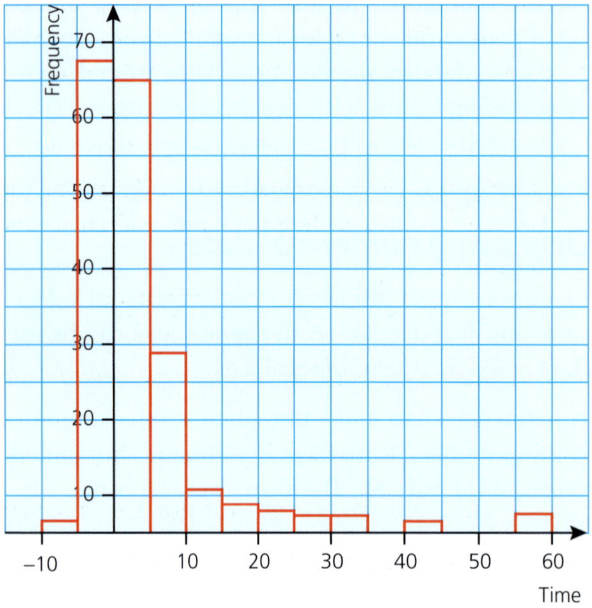

The problem solving cycle

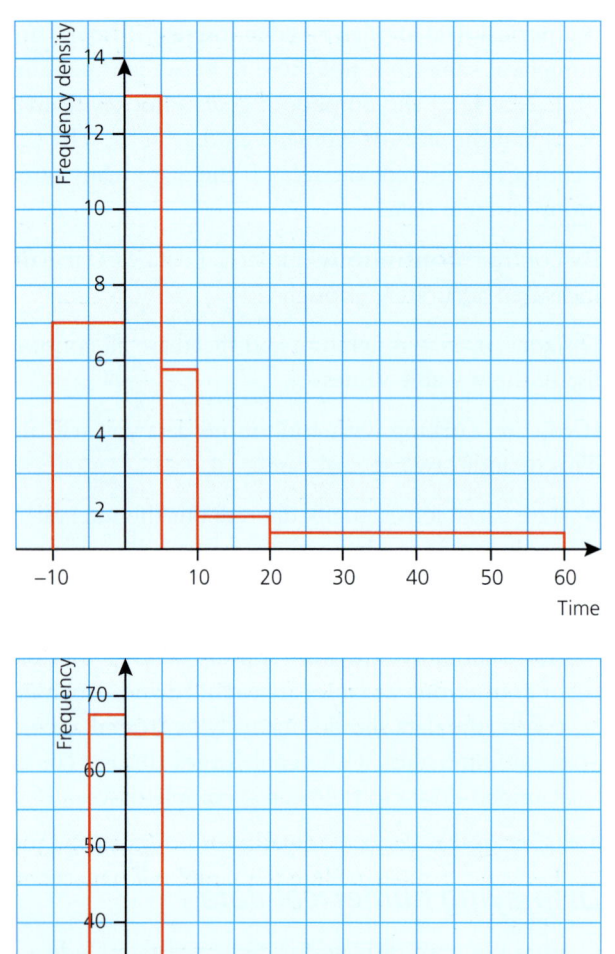

Discussion point
What is the same about the two displays and what is different?

Figure 1.4

Numerical data can also be displayed on a **cumulative frequency curve**. To draw the cumulative frequency curve, you plot the cumulative frequency (vertical axis) against the upper boundary of each class interval (horizontal axis). Then you join the points with a smooth curve. This lends itself to using the median, quartiles and other percentiles as summary measures.

Summary measures for numerical data

Summary measures for both discrete and continuous numerical data include the following.

Table 1.1

Central tendency	Spread	Position in the data
Mean	Range	Lower quartile
Weighted mean	Interquartile range	Median
Mode	Standard deviation	Upper quartile
Mid-range	Variance	Percentile
Median		
Modal class (grouped data)		

Standard deviation

Standard deviation is probably the most important measure of spread in statistics. The calculation of standard deviation, and of variance, introduce important notation which you will often come across. This is explained in the example that follows.

> **Note**
> In practice, many people would just enter the data into their calculators and read off the answer. However, it is important to understand the ideas that underpin the calculation.

Example 1.1

Alice enters dance competitions in which the judges give each dance a score between 0 and 10. Here is a sample of her recent scores.

Table 1.2

| 7 | 4 | 9 | 8 | 7 | 8 | 8 | 10 | 9 | 10 |

Calculate the mean, variance and standard deviation of Alice's scores.

Solution

Alice received 10 scores, so the number of data items, $n = 10$.

In the following table her scores are denoted by $x_1, x_2, ..., x_{10}$, with the general term x_i.

The mean score is $\bar{x}$.

The problem solving cycle

Table 1.3

	x_i	$x_i - \bar{x}$	$(x_i - \bar{x})^2$	x_i^2
x_1	7	-1	1	49
x_2	4	-4	16	16
x_3	9	1	1	81
x_4	8	0	0	64
x_5	7	-1	1	49
x_6	8	0	0	64
x_7	8	0	0	64
x_8	10	2	4	100
x_9	9	1	1	81
x_{10}	10	2	4	100
Σ	80	0	28	668

The quantity $(x_i - \bar{x})$ is the **deviation** from the mean. Notice that the total of the deviations $\Sigma(x_i - \bar{x})$ is zero. It has to be so because $\bar{x}$ is the mean, but finding it gives a useful check that you haven't made a careless mistake so far.

The value of 668 for Σx_i^2 was found in the right hand column of the table.

The mean is given by $\bar{x} = \Sigma \dfrac{x_i}{n} = \dfrac{80}{10} = 8.0$.

The variance is given by $s^2 = \dfrac{S_{xx}}{n-1}$ where $S_{xx} = \Sigma(x_i - \bar{x})^2$

In this case, $S_{xx} = 28$.

So the variance is $s^2 = \dfrac{28}{10-1} = 3.111$.

The standard deviation is $s = \sqrt{\text{variance}} = \sqrt{3.111} = 1.764$.

> **Note**
>
> An **alternative** but equivalent form of S_{xx} is given by
> $S_{xx} = \Sigma x_i^2 - n\bar{x}^2$
> In this case, $S_{xx} = 668 - 10 \times 8^2 = 668 - 640 = 28$.
> This is, as expected the same value as that found above.

ACTIVITY 1.1

Using a spreadsheet, enter the values of x in cells B2 to B11. Then, using only spreadsheet commands, and without entering any more numbers, obtain the values of $(x - \bar{x})$ in cells C2 to C11, of $(x - \bar{x})^2$ in cells D2 to D11 and of x^2 in E2 to E11. Still using only the spreadsheet commands, find the standard deviation using both of the given formulae.
Now, as a third method, use the built in functions in your spreadsheet, for example =AVERAGE and =STDEV.S to calculate the mean and standard deviation directly.

Notation

The notation in the example is often used with other variables.

So, for example, $S_{yy} = \Sigma(y_i - \bar{y})^2 = \Sigma y_i^2 - n\bar{y}^2$.

In Chapters 4 and 5, you will meet an equivalent form for bivariate data,

$$S_{xy} = \Sigma(x_i - \bar{x})(y_i - \bar{y}) = \Sigma x_i y_i - n\bar{x}\bar{y}.$$

You can also extend the notation to cases where the data are given in frequency tables.

For example, Alice's dance scores could have been written as the frequency table below.

Table 1.4

x_i	4	7	8	9	10
f_i	1	2	3	2	2

> **Note**
>
> **Bivariate data** cover two variables, such as the birth rate and life expectancy of different countries.
>
> When you are working with bivariate data you are likely to be interested in the relationship between the two variables, how this can be seen on a scatter diagram and how it can be quantified.

The number of items is then given by $n = \Sigma f_i$

The mean is $\bar{x} = \dfrac{\Sigma f_i x_i}{n}$

The sum of squared deviations is $S_{xx} = \Sigma f_i (x_i - \bar{x})^2 = \Sigma f_i x_i^2 - n\bar{x}^2$

As before, the variance is $s^2 = \dfrac{S_{xx}}{n-1}$

and the standard deviation is $s = \sqrt{\text{variance}} = \sqrt{\dfrac{S_{xx}}{n-1}}$.

Exercise 1.1

1. A club secretary wishes to survey a sample of members of his club. He uses all members present at a meeting as a sample

   (i) Explain why this sample is likely to be biased.

   Later the secretary decides choose a random sample of members. The club has 253 members and the secretary numbers the members from 1 to 253. He then generates random 3-digit numbers on his calculator. The first six random numbers are 156, 965, 248, 156, 073 and 181. The secretary uses each number, where possible, as the number of a member in the sample.

   (ii) Find possible numbers for the first four members in the sample. [OCR]

2. This stem-and-leaf diagram shows the mean GDP per person in European countries, in thousands of US$. The figures are rounded to the nearest US$ 1000.

   Table 1.5

	Europe
0	4 7 8 8 8
1	1 1 2 4 6 8 9
2	0 1 2 3 3 3 4 4 5 6 8 8
3	0 0 1 6 6 7 7 8 8
4	0 1 1 1 1 3 3 5 6
5	4 5 7
6	1 6
7	
8	0 9

   Note
   Key 3 | 7 = US$ 37 000

   (i) The mean per capita income for the UK is US$ 37 300. What is the rank of the UK among European countries (where rank 1 = largest GDP)?

   (ii) Find the median and quartiles of the data.

   (iii) Use the relevant test to identify any possible outliers.

   (iv) Describe the distribution.

   (v) Comment on whether these data can be used as a representative sample for the GDP of all the countries in the world.

3. Debbie is a sociology student. She is interested in how many children women have during their lifetimes. She herself has one sister and no brothers. She asks the other 19 students in her class 'How many children has your mother had?' Their answers follow; the figure for herself is included.

Table 1.6

1	1	2	3	1	4	2	1	2	2
2	2	2	1	0	1	2	3	8	3

Debbie says

'Thank you for your help. I conclude that the average woman has exactly 2.15 children.'

  (i)   Name the sampling method that Debbie used.

  (ii) Explain how she obtained the figure 2.15.

  (iii) State four things that are wrong with her method and her stated conclusion.

4 A supermarket chain is considering opening an out-of-town shop on a green field site. Before going any further they want to test public opinion and carry out a small pilot investigation. They employ three local students to ask people 'Would you be in favour of this development?' Each of the students is told to ask 30 adult men, 30 adult women and 40 young people who should be under 19 but may be male or female.

Their results are summarised in this table.

Table 1.7

Interviewer	Men Yes	Men No	Men Don't know	Women Yes	Women No	Women Don't know	Young people Yes	Young people No	Young people Don't know
A	5	20	5	18	12	0	12	10	18
B	12	14	4	20	8	2	11	11	18
C	9	18	3	17	9	4	10	15	15

  (i)   Name the sampling method that has been used.

  The local development manager has to give a very brief report to the company's directors and this will include his summary of the findings of the pilot survey.

  (ii) List the points that he should make.

  The directors decide to take the proposal to the next stage and this requires a more accurate assessment of local opinion.

  (iii) What sampling method should they use?

5 A certain animal is regarded as a pest. There have been two surveys, eight years apart, to find out the size of the population in the UK. After the second survey a newspaper carried an article which included these words.

> **This animal is out of control. Its numbers have doubled in just 8 years.**

The actual population, which no one knows, is shown on the following graph for 1995–2015. The unit on the vertical scale is 100 000 animals.

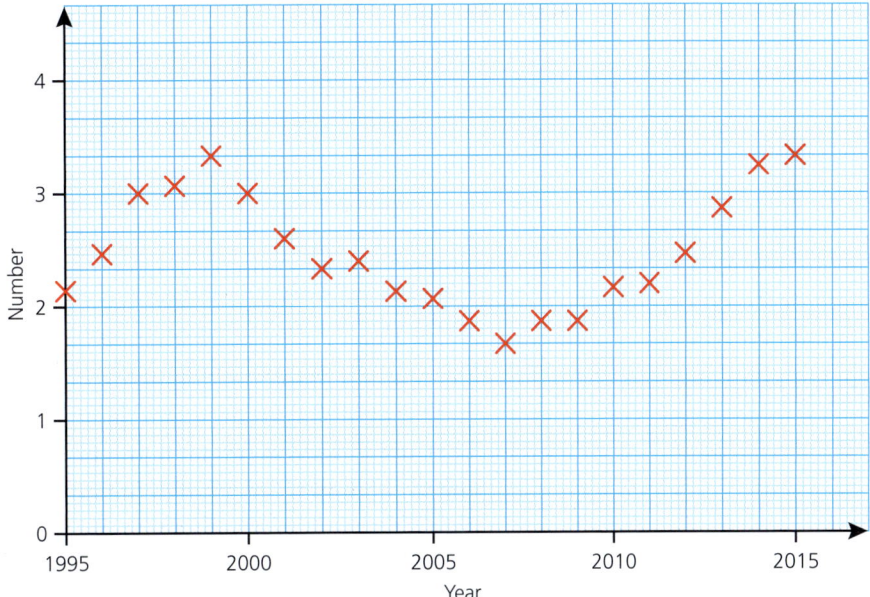

Figure 1.5 Graph of population

(i) Describe the apparent pattern of the size of the population.

(ii) In which years does it seem that the survey was carried out?

(iii) Suggest conclusions which might have been reached if the two surveys had been in (a) 1999 and 2007 (b) 1999 and 2015.

Historic data of the sale of furs of arctic mammals, such as lynx and hares, by the Hudson Bay Company indicate a 10 to 11 year cycle in their population numbers over many years.

(iv) Suppose the data are available on a spreadsheet. Describe how a systematic sample might be taken from the data on the spreadsheet. Comment on the problems that might result.

⑥ A study is conducted on the breeding success of a type of sea bird. Four islands are selected and volunteers monitor nests on them, counting the number of birds that fledge (grow up to fly away from the nest).

The results are summarised in the table below.

Table 1.8

Island	\multicolumn{5}{c	}{Number of fledglings}
	0	1	2	3	>3
A	52	105	31	2	0
B	10	81	55	6	0
C	67	33	2	0	0
D	29	65	185	11	0

(i) Describe the sample that has been used.

(ii) Explain why you are unable to give an accurate value for the sampling fraction.

(iii) Estimate the mean number of fledglings per nest and explain why this figure may not be very close to that for the whole population.

(iv) Ornithologists estimate that there are about 120 000 breeding pairs of these birds. Suggest appropriate limits within which the number of fledglings might lie, showing the calculations on which your answers are based.

The problem solving cycle

(7) The Highways Authority proposes to impose new parking restrictions on a small town. The Town Council fears that it will be bad for trade, and so for the town's prosperity. They plan to object, but first they need data so that they can estimate the cost to the town.

The council call a special meeting. Their room can only take 20 more people (in addition to the councillors) and they invite

   8 of the 41 shops

   7 of the 33 restaurants and cafes

   5 of the 27 hotels and bed and breakfasts.

(i) Describe the sort of sample they have selected. Explain how they decided on the numbers from the various groups.

(ii) They use a random selection procedure to decide who actually gets invited. Describe two possible ways they might do this.

(iii) Explain why those selected are not a simple random sample.

At the meeting, those present are asked to estimate the annual cost, to the nearest £1000, to their businesses if the parking restrictions go ahead. Their replies, in thousands of pounds, are given in the table below.

Table 1.9

Shops	2	1	5	0	12	10	8	3
Restaurants and cafes	1	2	2	1	3	2	1	-
Hotels and B&B	15	0	0	10	1	-	-	-

(iv) Use these figures to estimate the total cost of the parking restrictions to the town.

(v) Comment on the likely accuracy of the estimate and suggest measures that might be taken to improve it.

(8) A health authority takes part in a national study into the health of women during pregnancy. One feature of this is that pregnant women are invited to volunteer for a fitness programme in which they exercise every day. Their general health is monitored and the days on which their babies arrive are recorded and shown on the histogram below.

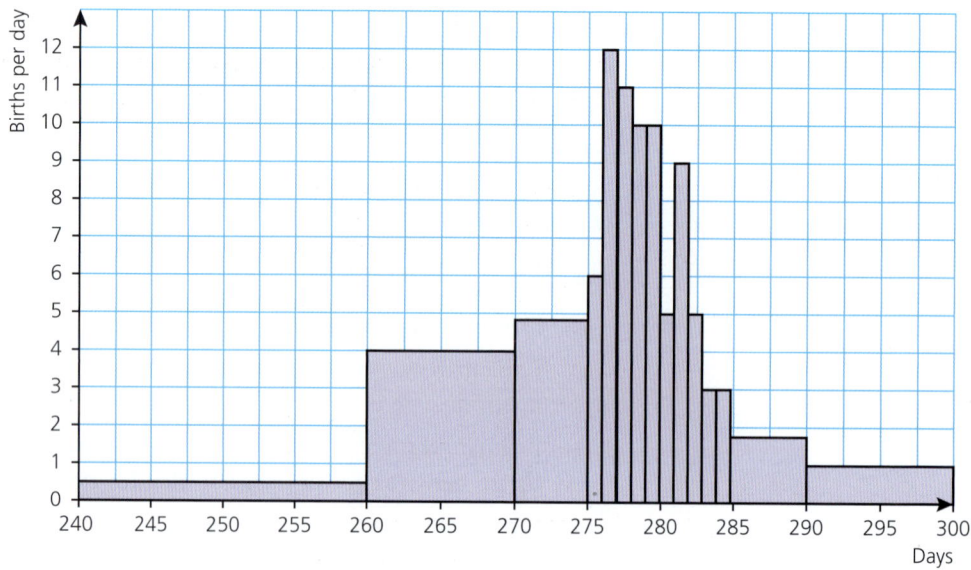

Figure 1.6

(i) The women who take part in the programme constitute a sample. What sort of sample is it?

(ii) Describe the parent population from which the sample is drawn and give one reason why it may not be completely representative. Comment on the difficulties in selecting a representative sample for this study.

(iii) Use the histogram to find how many women participated in the study.

The 'due date' of a mother to be is set at 280 days. Babies born before 260 days are described as 'pre-term'. Those born after 287 days are 'post-term'.

(iv) Give your answers to parts (a), (b) and (c) to 1 decimal place.

   (a) Find the percentage of the babies that arrived on their due dates.

   (b) Find the percentage that were pre-term.

   (c) Estimate the percentage of babies that were post-term.

   (d) Explain why your answers to parts (a), (b) and (c) do not add up to 100.

⑨ (i) Births, deaths and marriages are listed for England and Wales (and separately for other parts of the UK). As part of a pilot study, three research students, A, B and C, selected samples of the ages of women who died in 2016 from the list, using random numbers.

Summary data for their samples are:

Table 1.10

A	$n = 25$	$\Sigma x = 2038$	$\Sigma x^2 = 168545$
B	$n = 35$	$\Sigma x = 2720$	$\Sigma x^2 = 214893$
C	$n = 40$	$\Sigma x = 3230$	$\Sigma x^2 = 264936$

   (a) Describe the samples that the research students took.

   (b) Find the mean and standard deviation for each of the samples. Explain why they are not all the same.

   (c) Find the mean and standard deviation when the three samples are put together. Comment on the likely accuracy of your answer.

(ii) State the two formulae for S_{xx} and show algebraically that they are equivalent.

⑩ A local police force records the number of people arrested per day during January, February and March one year. The results are as follows.

Table 1.11

No of arrests	Frequency
0	55
1	24
2	6
3	2
4	0
5	2
6, 7	0
8	1
>8	0

The problem solving cycle

(i) Find the mean and standard deviation of the number of arrests per day.

(ii) The figure 8 is an outlier. It was the result of a fight on a train that stopped in the area. It is suggested that the data should not include that day. What percentage changes would that make to the mean and standard deviation?

(iii) Find the percentage error if the standard deviation (with the outlier excluded) is worked out using the formula

$$s = \sqrt{\frac{S_{xx}}{n}} \text{ instead of } s = \sqrt{\frac{S_{xx}}{n-1}}.$$

(iv) The standard deviation of a sample is worked out using a divisor n instead of $(n-1)$. Find the smallest value of n for which the error in doing so is less than 1%.

KEY POINTS

1. The problem solving cycle has four stages:
   - problem specification and analysis
   - information collection
   - processing and representation
   - interpretation.
2. Information collection often involves taking a sample.
3. There are several reasons why you might wish to take a sample:
   - to help you understand a situation better
   - as part of a pilot study to inform the design of a larger investigation
   - to estimate the values of the parameters of the parent population
   - to avoid the work involved in cleaning and formatting all the data in a large set
   - to conduct a hypothesis test.
4. Sampling procedures include:
   - simple random sampling
   - stratified sampling
   - cluster sampling
   - systematic sampling
   - quota sampling
   - opportunity sampling
   - self-selected sampling.
5. For processing and representation, it is important to know the type of data you are working with i.e.:
   - categorical data
   - ranked data
   - discrete numerical data
   - continuous numerical data
   - bivariate data.
6. Display techniques and summary measures must be appropriate for the type of data.

7   Notation for mean and standard deviation.

   Mean $\quad\bar{x} = \Sigma \dfrac{x_i}{n}$

   Sum of square deviations $\quad S_{xx} = \Sigma(x_i - \bar{x})^2 = \Sigma x_i^2 - n\bar{x}^2$

   Variance $\quad s^2 = \dfrac{S_{xx}}{n-1}$

   Standard deviation $\quad s = \sqrt{\text{variance}} = \sqrt{\dfrac{S_{xx}}{n-1}}.$

LEARNING OUTCOMES

When you have completed this chapter you should be able to:

- use statistics within a problem solving cycle
- explain why sampling may be necessary in order to obtain information about a population, and give desirable features of a sample, including the size of the sample
- know a variety of sampling methods, the situations in which they might be used and any problems associated with them
- explain the advantage of using a random sample when inferring properties of a population
- display sample data appropriately
- calculate and interpret summary measures for sample data.

2 Discrete random variables

Probability theory is nothing but common sense reduced to calculation.

Pierre Simon Laplace

An archery competition is held each month. In the first round of the competition, each competitor has five tries at hitting a small target. Those who hit the target at least three times get through to the next round. In April, there are 250 competitors in the first round. The frequencies of the different numbers of possible successes are as follows.

Table 2.1

Number of successes	0	1	2	3	4	5
Frequency	65	89	48	21	11	16

The numbers of successes are necessarily discrete. A discrete frequency distribution is best illustrated by a vertical line chart, as in Figure 2.1. This shows you that the distribution has positive skew, with the bulk of the data at the lower end of the distribution.

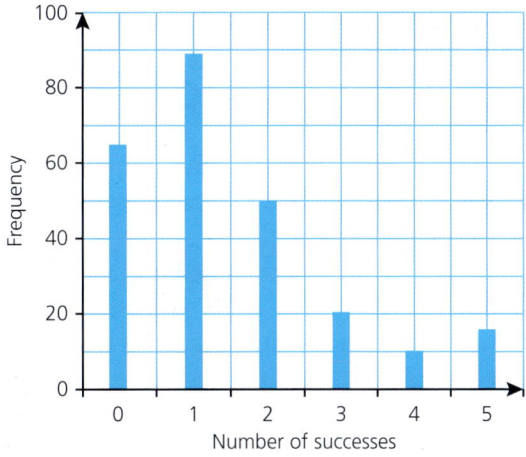

Figure 2.1

The survey involved 250 competitors. This is a reasonably large sample and so it is reasonable to use the results to estimate the *probabilities* of the various possible outcomes: 0, 1, 2, 3, 4, 5 successes. You divide each frequency by 250 to obtain the *relative frequency*, or probability, of each outcome (number of successes).

Table 2.2

Outcome (Number of successes)	0	1	2	3	4	5
Probability	0.260	0.356	0.192	0.084	0.044	0.064

> **Note**
> You can draw a diagram to show this *probability distribution*. It is identical in shape to Figure 2.1 but with probability rather than frequency on the vertical axis.

You now have a *mathematical model* to describe a particular situation. In statistics, you are often looking for models to describe and explain the data you find in the real world. In this chapter, you are introduced to some of the techniques for working with models for discrete data. Such models are called *discrete random variables*.

> For example: the number of rolls to get a six on a die.

The number of successes is a *random variable* since the actual value of the outcome is variable and can only be predicted with a given probability, i.e. the outcomes occur at random. The random variable is *discrete* since the number of successes is an integer (between 0 and 5).

In the archery competition, the maximum number of successes is five so the variable is *finite*, and so, for example, if each competitor had ten tries, then the maximum would be ten. In this case, there would be eleven possible outcomes (including zero). Two well-known examples of a finite discrete random variable are the *binomial distribution* and the *uniform distribution* which you will meet in Chapter 3.

By contrast, if you considered the number of times you need to roll a pair of dice to get a double six, there is no theoretical maximum, and so the distribution is *infinite*. Two well-known examples of infinite discrete random variables are the *geometric distribution* and the *Poisson distribution*, which you will also study in Chapter 3.

1 Notation and conditions for a discrete random variable

- A random variable is denoted by an upper case letter, such as X, Y, or Z.
- The particular values that the random variable takes are denoted by lower case letters, such as x, y, z and r.
- In the case of a discrete variable these are sometimes given suffixes such as $r_1, r_2, r_3, \ldots$
- Thus $P(X = r_1)$ means the probability that the random variable X takes a particular value r_1.
- If a finite discrete random variable can take n distinct values $r_1, r_2, \ldots, r_n$, with associated probabilities $p_1, p_2, \ldots, p_n$, then the sum of the probabilities must equal 1.
- In that case, $p_1 + p_2 + \ldots + p_n = 1$.
- This can be written more formally as

$$\sum_{k=1}^{n} p_k = \sum_{k=1}^{n} P(X = r_k) = 1.$$

- If there is no ambiguity, then

$$\sum_{k=1}^{n} P(X = r_k)$$

is often abbreviated to

$$\Sigma P(X = r).$$

> **Note**
> You will often see the expression $P(X = r)$ in a table heading.

> The various outcomes cover all possibilities; they are exhaustive.

Example 2.1

The probability distribution of a random variable X is given by

$P(X = r) = kr^2 \quad$ for $r = 3, 4, 5$

$P(X = r) = 0 \quad$ otherwise.

(i) Find the value of the constant k.

(ii) Illustrate the distribution and describe the shape of the distribution.

(iii) Two successive values of X are generated independently of each other.

Find the probability that

(a) both values of X are the same

(b) the total of the two values of X is greater than 8.

Solution

(i) Tabulating the probability distribution for X gives:

Table 2.3

r	3	4	5
$P(X = r)$	$9k$	$16k$	$25k$

Since X is a random variable,

$$\Sigma(P(X = r)) = 1$$
$$9k + 16k + 25k = 1$$
$$50k = 1$$
$$k = 0.02$$

Hence $P(X = r) = 0.02r^2$ for $r = 3, 4, 5$ which gives the following probability distribution.

Table 2.4

r	3	4	5
$P(X = r)$	0.18	0.32	0.50

(ii) The vertical line chart in Figure 2.2 illustrates this distribution. It has negative skew.

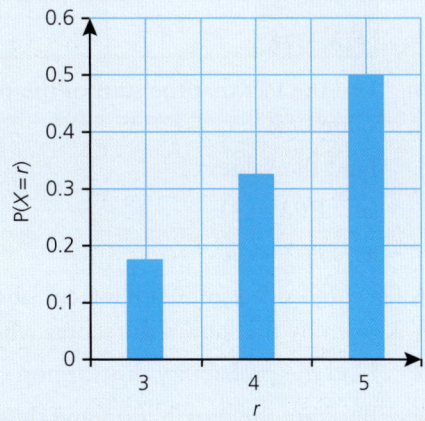

Figure 2.2

(iii) (a) P(both values of X are the same)

$$= (0.18)^2 + (0.32)^2 + (0.5)^2$$
$$= 0.0324 + 0.1024 + 0.25$$
$$= 0.3848$$

(b) P(total of the two values is greater than 8)

$$= 0.32 \times 0.5 + 0.5 \times 0.32 + 0.5 \times 0.5$$
$$= 0.16 + 0.16 + 0.25$$
$$= 0.57$$

> The ways of getting a total greater than 8 are: 4 and 5, 5 and 4, 5 and 5

Notation and conditions for a discrete random variable

Exercise 2.1

① A fair five-sided spinner has faces labelled 1, 2, 3, 4, 5. The random variable X represents the score when the spinner is spun.

   (i) Copy and complete the table below to show the probability distribution of X.

   Table 2.5

r	1	2	3		
$P(X = r)$	0.2				

   (ii) Illustrate the distribution.

   (iii) Find the values of

      (a) $P(X > 2)$

      (b) $P(X$ is even$)$

      (c) $P(X > 5)$.

② The probability distribution of a discrete random variable X is given by

$P(X = r) = kr$ for $r = 1, 2, 3, 4$

$P(X = r) = 0$ otherwise.

   (i) Copy and complete the table below to show the probability distribution of X in terms of k.

   Table 2.6

r	1	2	3	
$P(X = r)$				$4k$

   (ii) Use the fact that the sum of the probabilities is equal to 1 to find the value of k.

   (ii) Find the values of

      (a) $P(X = 4)$

      (b) $P(X < 4)$.

③ A fair three-sided spinner has faces labelled 1, 2 and 3. The random variable X is given by the sum of the scores when the spinner is spun three times.

   (i) Find the probability distribution of X.

   (ii) Illustrate the distribution and describe the shape of the distribution.

   (iii) Find the values of

      (a) $P(X > 6)$

      (b) $P(X$ is odd$)$

      (c) $P(|X - 4| < 2)$.

④ The random variable Y is given by the absolute difference when the spinner in Question 1 is spun twice.

   (i) Find the probability distribution of Y.

   (ii) Illustrate the distribution and describe the shape of the distribution.

   (iii) Find the values of

      (a) $P(Y < 2)$

      (b) $P(Y$ is even$)$.

5. Two ordinary dice are thrown. The random variable X is the product of the numbers shown on the dice.
   (i) Find the probability distribution of X.
   (ii) What is the probability that any throw of the two dice results in a value of X which is an even number?

6. The probability distribution of a discrete random variable X is given by
$$P(X = r) = \frac{kr}{4} \text{ for } r = 2, 3, 4, 5$$
$$P(X = r) = 0 \text{ otherwise.}$$
   (i) Find the value of k and tabulate the probability distribution.
   (ii) If two successive values of X are generated independently find the probability that
       (a) the two values are equal
       (b) the first value is less than the second value.

7. A curiously shaped four-faced spinner produces scores, X, for which the probability distribution is given by
$$P(X = r) = k(r^2 + 2r + 10) \text{ for } r = 0, 1, 2, 3, 4$$
$$P(X = r) = 0 \text{ otherwise.}$$
   (i) Find the value of k and illustrate the distribution.
   (ii) Show that, when this spinner is spun twice, the probability of obtaining one non-zero score which is exactly twice the other is very nearly 0.18.

8. Four fair coins are tossed.
   (i) By considering the set of possible outcomes, HHHH, HHHT, etc., tabulate the probability distribution of X, the number of heads occurring.
   (ii) Illustrate the distribution and describe the shape of the distribution.
   (iii) Find the probability that there are more heads than tails.
   (iv) Without further calculation, state whether your answer to part (iii) would be the same if five fair coins were tossed. Give a reason for your answer.

9. A doctor is investigating the numbers of children, X, which women have in a country. She notes that the probability that a woman has more than five children is negligible. She suggests the following model for X
$$P(X = 0) = 0.3$$
$$P(X = r) = k(12 + 3r - r^2) \quad \text{for } r = 1, 2, 3, 4, 5$$
$$P(X = r) = 0 \quad \text{otherwise.}$$
   (i) Find the value of k and write the probability distribution as a table.
   (ii) Find the probability that two women chosen at random both have more than three children.

10. A motoring magazine correspondent conducts a survey of the numbers of people per car travelling along a stretch of motorway. He denotes the number by the random variable X which he finds to have the following probability distribution.

Table 2.7

r	1	2	3	4	5	6+
$P(X = r)$	0.57	0.28	a	0.04	0.01	negligible

(i) Find the value of a.

He wants to find an algebraic model for the distribution and suggests the following model.

$P(X = r) = k2^{-r}$ for $r = 1, 2, 3, 4, 5$
$P(X = r) = 0$ otherwise.

(ii) Find the value of k for this model.

(iii) Compare the algebraic model with the probabilities he found, illustrating both distributions on one diagram. Do you think it is a good model?

⑪ In a game, each player throws four ordinary six-sided dice. The random variable X is the smallest number showing on the dice, so, for example, for scores of 2, 5, 3 and 4, $X = 2$.

(i) Find the probability that $X = 6$, i.e. $P(X = 6)$.

(ii) Find $P(X \geq 5)$ and deduce that $P(X = 5) = \dfrac{15}{1296}$

(iii) Find $P(X \geq r)$ and so deduce $P(X = r)$, for $r = 4, 3, 2, 1$

(iv) Illustrate and describe the probability distribution of X.

⑫ A box contains six black pens and four red pens. Three pens are taken at random from the box.

(i) Illustrate the various outcomes on a probability tree diagram.

(ii) The random variable X represents the number of black pens obtained. Find the probability distribution of X.

2 Expectation and variance

The next round of the archery competition is held in May. In this round there are 200 competitors altogether. The organisers of the competition would like to increase the number of people getting through to the next round, without changing the rules. They decide to give each of the competitors a relaxation session before their attempt. The number of successes for each competitor this time is as follows.

> **Discussion point**
>
> How would you compare the results in the competitions?

Table 2.8

Number of successes	0	1	2	3	4	5
Frequency	36	54	60	19	15	16

The competition involves 200 people. This is again a reasonably large sample and so, once again, it is reasonable to use the results to estimate the probabilities of the various possible outcomes: 0, 1, 2, 3, 4, 5 successes, as before.

Table 2.9

Outcome (Number of successes)	0	1	2	3	4	5
Probability (Relative frequency)	0.18	0.27	0.30	0.095	0.075	0.08

One way to compare the two probability distributions, in April and in May, is to calculate a measure of central tendency and a measure of spread.

Just as you can calculate the mean and variance of a frequency distribution, you can also do something very similar for a probability distribution.

- The most useful measure of central tendency for a probability distribution is the *mean* or *expectation* of the random variable. This is denoted by μ.
- The most useful measure of spread for a probability distribution is the *variance*, σ^2, or its square root the *standard deviation*, σ.

The expectation is given by $E(X) = \mu = \Sigma r P(X = r)$. Its calculation is shown below using the probability distribution for the archers in May (after the relaxation session) as an example.

Table 2.10

r	P(X = r)	rP(X = r)
0	0.18	0
1	0.27	0.27
2	0.30	0.60
3	0.095	0.285
4	0.075	0.30
5	0.08	0.4
Totals	1	1.855

> **Note**
> You will find it helpful to set your work out systematically in a table like this.

In this case:

$$E(X) = \mu = \Sigma r P(X = r)$$
$$= 0 \times 0.18 + 1 \times 0.27 + 2 \times 0.30 + 3 \times 0.095 + 4 \times 0.075 + 5 \times 0.08$$
$$= \mathbf{1.855}$$

There are two common ways of giving the variance.

Either $\text{Var}(X) = \sigma^2 = E(X^2) - [E(X)]^2$

or $E(X - \mu)^2 = \Sigma (r - \mu)^2 P(X = r)$

This version can be remembered as 'The expectation of the squares minus the square of the expectation'. It can also be written as $E(X^2) - \mu^2$.

To see how variance is calculated the same probability distribution is used as an example.

> **Note**
> You will use these statistics later to compare the distribution of numbers of successes with and without the relaxation session.

The table below shows the working for the variance in May after the relaxation session, using both of the methods above.

Table 2.11

r	P(X = r)	r²P(X = r)
0	0.18	0
1	0.27	0.27
2	0.30	1.2
3	0.095	0.855
4	0.075	1.2
5	0.08	2
Totals	1	**5.525**

r	P(X = r)	$(r-\mu)^2 P(X = r)$
0	0.18	0.6194
1	0.27	0.1974
2	0.30	0.0063
3	0.095	0.1245
4	0.075	0.3451
5	0.08	0.7913
Totals	1	**2.0840**

The mean, μ, was found above. It is **1.855**.

Expectation and variance

> **Discussion point**
> Using these two statistics, judge the success or otherwise of the relaxation session.

(a) $\text{Var}(X) = \Sigma r^2 P(X=r) - [\Sigma r P(X=r)]^2$
$= 5.525 - 1.855^2$
$= 2.084$

(b) $\text{Var}(X) = \Sigma(r-\mu)^2 P(X=r)$
$= 2.084$

The standard deviation of X is therefore $\sqrt{2.084} = 1.44$

In practice, the computation is usually easier in Method (a), especially when the expectation is not a whole number.

ACTIVITY 2.1
Show that the expectation and variance of the probability distribution in April (without the relaxation session) are 1.49 and 1.97, respectively.

Example 2.2

The discrete random variable X has the following probability distribution:

Table 2.12

r	0	1	2	3
$P(X=r)$	0.2	0.3	0.4	0.1

Find

(i) $E(X)$

(ii) $\text{Var}(X)$ using (a) $E(X^2) - \mu^2$ (b) $E\big([X-\mu]^2\big)$.

Solution

(i) **Table 2.13**

r	$P(X=r)$	$rP(X=r)$
0	0.2	0
1	0.3	0.3
2	0.4	0.8
3	0.1	0.3
Totals	1	1.4

$E(X) = \mu = \Sigma r P(X=r)$
$= 0 \times 0.2 + 1 \times 0.3 + 2 \times 0.4 + 3 \times 0.1$
$= 1.4$

> To find E(X) you simply multiply each value of r by its probability and then add.

> **Discussion point**
> Look carefully at both methods for calculating the variance. Are there any situations where one method might be preferred to the other?

(ii)
Table 2.14

r	$P(X = r)$	$r^2 P(X = r)$
0	0.2	0
1	0.3	0.3
2	0.4	1.6
3	0.1	0.9
Totals	1	2.8

r	$P(X = r)$	$(r - \mu)^2 P(X = r)$
0	0.2	0.392
1	0.3	0.048
2	0.4	0.144
3	0.1	0.256
Totals	1	0.84

(a) $\operatorname{Var}(X) = \sigma^2 = E(X^2) - \mu^2$
$= 2.8 - 1.4^2$
$= 0.84$

(b) $\operatorname{Var}(X) = \sigma^2 = E\left[[X - \mu]^2\right]$
$= \Sigma (r - \mu)^2 P(X = r)$
$= 0.84$

Notice that the two methods of calculating the variance in part (iii) give the same result, since one formula is just an algebraic rearrangement of the other. In practice, you would not need to use both methods and so only either the left-hand or the right-hand table would be needed to calculate the variance, according to which method you are using.

ACTIVITY 2.2
Use a spreadsheet to find the variance of X for the following probability distribution.

Table 2.15

r	1	2	3	4
$P(X = r)$	0.25	0.22	0.08	0.45

You should use both methods of calculating the variance and check that they give the same result.

As well as being able to carry out calculations for the expectation and variance, you often need to solve problems in context. The following example illustrates this idea.

Example 2.3

Laura has one pint of milk on three days out of every four and none on the fourth day. A pint of milk costs 40 p. Let X represent her weekly milk bill.

(i) Find the probability distribution of her weekly milk bill.

(ii) Find the mean (μ) and standard deviation (σ) of her weekly milk bill.

(iii) Find

(a) $P(X > \mu + \sigma)$

(b) $P(X < \mu - \sigma)$.

Expectation and variance

Solution

(i) The delivery pattern repeats every four weeks.

Table 2.15

M	Tu	W	T	F	Sa	Su	Number of pints	Milk bill
√	√	√	×	√	√	√	6	£2.40
×	√	√	√	×	√	√	5	£2.00
√	×	√	√	√	×	√	5	£2.00
√	√	×	√	√	√	×	5	£2.00

Tabulating the probability distribution for X gives the following.

Table 2.16

$r\ (£)$	2.00	2.40
$P(X = r)$	0.75	0.25

(ii)
$$E(X) = \mu = \Sigma r\, P(X = r)$$
$$= 2 \times 0.75 + 2.4 \times 0.25$$
$$= 2.1$$
$$\text{Var}(X) = \sigma^2 = E(X^2) - \mu^2$$
$$= 4 \times 0.75 + 5.76 \times 0.25 - 2.1^2$$
$$= 0.03$$
$$\Rightarrow \sigma = \sqrt{0.03} = 0.1732$$

Hence her mean weekly milk bill is £2.10, with a standard deviation of about 17 p.

(iii) (a) $P(X > \mu + \sigma) = P(X > 2.27) = 0.25$

   (b) $P(X < \mu - \sigma) = P(X < 1.93) = 0$

Exercise 2.2

① Find by calculation the expectation of the outcome with the following probability distribution.

Table 2.17

Outcome	1	2	3	4	5
Probability	0.1	0.2	0.4	0.2	0.1

How otherwise might you have arrived at your answer?

② The spreadsheet shows part of a discrete probability distribution, together with some calculations of $r \times P(X = r)$ and $r^2 \times P(X = r)$. Using only spreadsheet commands, and without entering any more numbers, obtain the remaining values in columns B, C and D. Hence find the mean and variance of this distribution.

	A	B	C	D
1	r	P(X=r)	r×P(X=r)	r²×P(X=r)
2	1	0.20		
3	2	0.30		
4	3	0.10	0.30	
5	4	0.05		
6	5	0.20		5.00
7	6			
8	SUM			

Figure 2.3

③ The probability distribution of the discrete random variable X is given by

$P(X = r) = \dfrac{2r-1}{16}$ for $r = 1, 2, 3, 4$

$P(X = r) = 0$ otherwise.

(i) Find $E(X) = \mu$.

(ii) Find $P(X < \mu)$.

④ (i) A discrete random variable X can take only the values 4 and 5, and has expectation 4.2.

By letting $P(X = 4) = p$ and $P(X = 5) = 1 - p$, solve an equation in p and so find the probability distribution of X.

(ii) A discrete random variable Y can take only the values 50 and 100. Given that $E(Y) = 80$, write out the probability distribution of Y.

⑤ The random variable Y is given by the absolute difference between the scores when two ordinary dice are thrown.

(i) Find $E(Y)$ and $Var(Y)$.

(ii) Find the values of the following.

(a) $P(Y > \mu)$ (b) $P(Y > \mu + 2\sigma)$

⑥ Three fair coins are tossed. Let X represent the number of tails.

(i) Find $E(X)$.

Show that this is equivalent to $3 \times \dfrac{1}{2}$.

(ii) Find $Var(X)$.

Show that this is equivalent to $3 \times \dfrac{1}{4}$.

If instead ten fair coins are tossed, let Y represent the number of tails.

(iii) Write down the values of $E(Y)$ and $Var(Y)$.

⑦ An unbiased tetrahedral die has faces labelled 2, 4, 6 and 8. If the die lands on the face marked 2, the player has to pay £5. If it lands on the face marked with a 4 or a 6, the player wins £2. If it lands on the face labelled 8, then no money changes hands.

Let X represent the amount 'won' each time the player throws the die. (A loss is represented by a negative X value.)

(i) Complete the following probability distribution for X.

Table 2.18

r	−5	0	2
P(X = r)			

31

(ii) Find E(X) and Var(X).

What does the sign of E(X) indicate?

(iii) How much less would the player have to pay, when the die lands on the face marked 2, so that he would break even in the long run?

⑧ 85% of first-class mail arrives the day after being posted, the rest takes one day longer.

For second class mail the corresponding figures are 10% and 40%, while a further 35% take three days and the remainder four days.

Two out of every five letters go by first class mail.

Let X represent the delivery time for letters.

(i) Explain why $P(X = 1) = 0.4$.

(ii) Complete the following probability distribution for X.

Table 2.19

r	1	2	3	4
$P(X = r)$	0.4			

(iii) Calculate E(X) and Var(X).

⑨ (i) A discrete random variable X can take only the values 3, 4 and 5, has expectation 4 and variance 0.6.

By letting $P(X = 3) = p$, $P(X = 4) = q$ and $P(X = 5) = 1 - p - q$, solve a pair of simultaneous equations in p and q and so find the probability distribution of X.

(ii) A discrete random variable Y can take only the values 20, 50 and 100. Given that $E(Y) = 34$ and $Var(Y) = 624$, write out the probability distribution of Y.

⑩ A random number generator in a computer game produces values which can be modelled by the discrete random variable X with probability distribution given by

$P(X = r) = kr!$ for $r = 0, 1, 2, 3, 4$

$P(X = r) = 0$ otherwise

where k is a constant and $r! = r \times (r-1) \times \cdots \times 2 \times 1$ with $0! = 1$.

(i) Show that $k = \frac{1}{34}$, and illustrate the probability distribution with a sketch.

(ii) Find the expectation and variance of X.

(iii) Two independent values of X are generated. Let these values be X_1 and X_2.

Show that $P(X_1 = X_2)$ is a little greater than 0.5.

(iv) Given that $X_1 = X_2$, find the probability that X_1 and X_2 are each equal to 4.

⑪ A traffic surveyor is investigating the lengths of queues at a particular set of traffic lights during the daytime, but outside rush hours. He counts the number of cars, X, stopped and waiting when the lights turn green on 100 occasions, with the following results.

Table 2.20

X	0	1	2	3	4	5	6	7	8	9+
f	3	10	13	16	18	17	12	9	2	0

(i) Use these figures to estimate the probability distribution of the number of cars waiting when the lights turn green.

(ii) Use your probability distribution to estimate the expectation and variance of X.

A colleague of the surveyor suggests that the probability distribution might be modelled by the expression

$P(X = r) = kr(8 - r)$ for $r = 0, 1, 2, 3, 4, 5, 6, 7, 8$
$P(X = r) = 0$ otherwise.

(iii) Find the value of k.

(iv) Find the expectation and variance of X given by this model.

(v) State, with reasons, whether it is a good model.

Expectation and variance of a linear function of a random variable

Sometimes you need to find the expectation and variance of a linear function of a random variable $E(aX + b)$ and $Var(aX + b)$.

Example 2.4

Kiara is an employee at an estate agency. The number of properties that she sells during a month is denoted by the random variable X. The probability distribution of X is as follows.

Table 2.21

Number of houses	0	1	2	3	4	5+
Probability	0.07	0.33	0.4	0.12	0.08	0

Figure 2.4

(i) Calculate $E(X)$.

Kiara earns £750 per month plus £400 for each house that she sells. The random variable Y is the amount (in £) that Kiara earns each month.

(ii) Show that $Y = 400X + 750$. Draw up a probability table for Y.

(iii) Calculate $E(Y)$.

(iv) Calculate $400E(X) + 750$ and comment on your result

Solution

(i) $E(X) = 0 \times 0.07 + 1 \times 0.33 + 2 \times 0.4 + 3 \times 0.12 + 4 \times 0.08 = 1.81$

(ii) **Table 2.22**

Earnings Y	750	1150	1550	1950	2350
Probability	0.07	0.33	0.4	0.12	0.08

(iii) $E(Y) = 750 \times 0.07 + 1150 \times 0.33 + 1550 \times 0.4$
$\qquad + 1950 \times 0.12 + 2350 \times 0.08$
$\qquad = 1474$

(iv) $400E(X) + 750 = 400 \times 1.81 + 750 = 1474$

Clearly $E(Y) = 400E(X) + 750$, both having the value 1474.

Expectation and variance

Expectation: general results

In Example 2.4 you found that $E(Y) = E(400X + 750) = 400E(X) + 750$.

The working was numerical, showing that both expressions came out to be 1474. In fact, the following rules for expectation apply to any random variable X where a, b, c and d are constants.

> **Note**
> These are very similar to the rules for the mean of a frequency distribution.

- $E(aX + b) = aE(X) + b$
- $E(cX) = cE(X)$
- $E(d) = d$

Example 2.5

The random variable X has the following probability distribution.

Table 2.23

r	1	2	3	4
$P(X = r)$	0.6	0.2	0.1	0.1

(i) Find Var(X) and the standard deviation of X.

(ii) Find Var$(3X)$ and the standard deviation of $3X$. Comment on the relationship between Var$(3X)$ and Var(X) and likewise for the standard deviations.

(iii) Find Var$(3X + 7)$ and compare this with your answer to part (ii)

Solution

(i) $E(X) = 1 \times 0.6 + 2 \times 0.2 + 3 \times 0.1 + 4 \times 0.1$
$= 1.7$

$E(X^2) = 1 \times 0.6 + 4 \times 0.2 + 9 \times 0.1 + 16 \times 0.1$
$= 3.9$

$\text{Var}(X) = E(X^2) - [E(X)]^2$
$= 3.9 - 1.7^2$
$= 1.01$

The standard deviation of $X = \sqrt{1.01} = 1.005$

(ii) $\text{Var}(3X) = E[(3X)^2] - \mu^2$
$= E(9X^2) - [E(3X)]^2$
$= 9E(X^2) - [3E(X)]^2$
$= 9 \times 3.9 - (3 \times 1.7)^2$
$= 35.1 - 26.01$
$= 9.09$

> You can use the formula for $E(aX + b)$ above to rewrite $E(9X^2)$ as $9E(X^2)$ and likewise for $E(3X)$

This shows that $\text{Var}(3X) = 9 \times \text{Var}(X)$ Note that $9 = 3^2$.

The standard deviation of $3X = \sqrt{9.09} = 3.015 = 3 \times$ s.d. of X

> **Note**
> Notice that
> $\mathrm{E}(9X^2 + 42X + 49)$
> is written as
> $\mathrm{E}(9X^2) + \mathrm{E}(42X) + \mathrm{E}(49)$.
> This illustrates the general rule that
> $\mathrm{E}(X_1 + X_2 + \cdots)$
> $= \mathrm{E}(X_1) + \mathrm{E}(X_2) + \cdots$

(iii)
$$\begin{aligned}\mathrm{Var}(3X+7) &= \mathrm{E}\left[(3X+7)^2\right] - \left[\mathrm{E}(3X+7)\right]^2 \\ &= \mathrm{E}(9X^2 + 42X + 49) - [3\mathrm{E}(X) + 7]^2 \\ &= \mathrm{E}(9X^2) + \mathrm{E}(42X) + \mathrm{E}(49) - [3 \times 1.7 + 7]^2 \\ &= 9\mathrm{E}(X^2) + 42\mathrm{E}(X) + 49 - 12.1^2 \\ &= 9 \times 3.9 + 42 \times 1.7 + 49 - 146.41 \\ &= 9.09\end{aligned}$$

This has the same value as $\mathrm{Var}(3X)$ so is also equal to $9 \times \mathrm{Var}(X)$

Variance: general results

In Example 2.5 you found that $\mathrm{Var}(3X+7) = \mathrm{Var}(3X) = 9 \times \mathrm{Var}(X)$.

As with expectation, the working was numerical, showing that both expressions came out to be 9.09. In fact, the following rules for variance apply to any random variable X where a, b, and c are constants.

- $\mathrm{Var}(aX) = a^2 \mathrm{Var}(X)$
- $\mathrm{Var}(aX + b) = a^2 \mathrm{Var}(X)$
- $\mathrm{Var}(c) = 0$ ← Notice that the variance of a constant is zero. It can only take one value so there is no spread.

It may seem surprising that $\mathrm{Var}(aX) = a^2 \mathrm{Var}(X)$ rather than simply $a\,\mathrm{Var}(X)$, but the former relationship then gives the result that the standard deviation of aX is equal to $a \times$ the standard deviation of X, as you would expect from common sense.

Notice also that adding a constant does not make any difference to the variance, which is again as you would expect.

Finally, the variance of a constant is zero. This result is obvious – a constant does not have any variation.

Sums and differences of random variables

Sometimes you may need to add or subtract a number of independent random variables. This process is illustrated in the next example.

Expectation and variance

Example 2.6

A cricket bat manufacturer makes the blades and the handles separately. The blades are made in five lengths (in cm), with a uniform discrete distribution:

38, 40, 42, 44, 46.

The lengths (in cm) of the handles of cricket bats also form a discrete uniform distribution:

22, 24, 26.

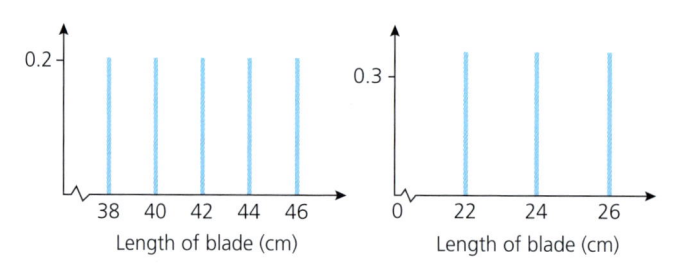

Figure 2.5

The blades and handles can be joined together to make bats of various lengths, and it may be assumed that the lengths of the two sections are independent. The different combinations occur with equal probabilities.

(i) How many different (total) bat lengths are possible?

(ii) Work out the mean and variance of random variable X_1, the length (in cm) of the blades.

(iii) Work out the mean and variance of random variable X_2, the length (in cm) of the handles.

(iv) Work out the mean and variance of random variable $X_1 + X_2$, the total length of the bats.

(v) Verify that
$$E(X_1 + X_2) = E(X_1) + E(X_2)$$
and $\text{Var}(X_1 + X_2) = \text{Var}(X_1) + \text{Var}(X_2)$.

Solution

(i) The number of different bat lengths is 7. This can be seen from the sample space diagram below.

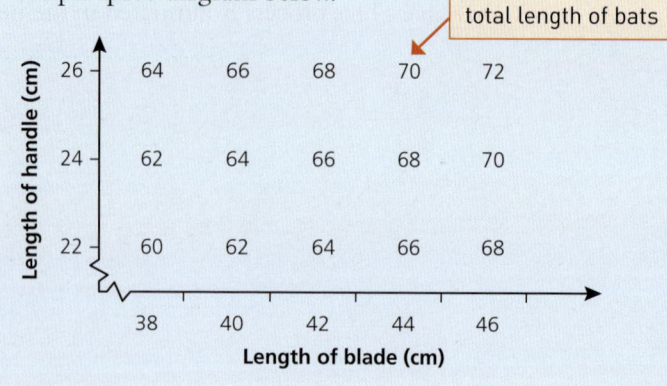

Figure 2.6

(ii) Table 2.24

Length of blade (cm)	38	40	42	44	46
Probability	0.2	0.2	0.2	0.2	0.2

$$E(X_1) = \mu_1 = \Sigma xp = (38 \times 0.2) + (40 \times 0.2) + (42 \times 0.2)$$
$$+ (44 \times 0.2) + (46 \times 0.2)$$
$$= 42\,\text{cm}$$
$$\text{Var}(X_1) = E(X_2^2) - \mu_2^2$$
$$E(X_1^2) = (38^2 \times 0.2) + (40^2 \times 0.2) + (42^2 \times 0.2)$$
$$+ (44^2 \times 0.2) + (46^2 \times 0.2)$$
$$= 1772$$
$$\text{Var}(X_1) = 1772 - 42^2 = 8$$

(iii) Table 2.25

Length of handle (cm)	2	24	26
Probability	$\frac{1}{3}$	$\frac{1}{3}$	$\frac{1}{3}$

$$E(X_2) = \mu_2 = 22 \times \frac{1}{3} + 24 \times \frac{1}{3} + 26 \times \frac{1}{3} = 24\,\text{cm}$$
$$\text{Var}(X_2) = E(X_2^2) - \mu_2^2$$
$$E(X_2^2) = \left(22^2 \times \frac{1}{3}\right) + \left(24^2 \times \frac{1}{3}\right) + \left(26^2 \times \frac{1}{3}\right) = 578.667 \text{ to 3 d.p.}$$
$$\text{Var}(X_2) = 578.667 - 24^2 = 2.667 \text{ to 3 d.p.}$$

(iv) The probability distribution of $X_1 + X_2$ can be obtained from Figure 2.5.

Table 2.26

Total length of cricket bat (cm)	60	62	64	66	68	70	72
Probability	$\frac{1}{15}$	$\frac{2}{15}$	$\frac{3}{15}$	$\frac{3}{15}$	$\frac{3}{15}$	$\frac{2}{15}$	$\frac{1}{15}$

$$E(X_1 + X_2) = \left(60 \times \frac{1}{15}\right) + \left(62 \times \frac{2}{15}\right) + \left(64 \times \frac{3}{15}\right) + \left(66 \times \frac{3}{15}\right)$$
$$+ \left(68 \times \frac{3}{15}\right) + \left(70 \times \frac{2}{15}\right) + \left(72 \times \frac{1}{15}\right)$$
$$= 66\,\text{cm}$$
$$\text{Var}(X_1 + X_2) = E\left[(X_1 + X_2)^2\right] - 66^2$$

> **Note**
> Notice that the standard deviations of X_1 and X_2 do not add up to the standard deviation of $X_1 + X_2$.
> i.e. $\sqrt{8} + \sqrt{2.667} \neq \sqrt{10.667}$
> or $2.828 + 1.633 \neq 3.266$

$$E\left[(X_1+X_2)^2\right] = \left(60^2 \times \tfrac{1}{15}\right) + \left(62^2 \times \tfrac{2}{15}\right) + \left(64^2 \times \tfrac{3}{15}\right) + \left(66^2 \times \tfrac{3}{15}\right)$$
$$+ \left(68^2 \times \tfrac{3}{15}\right) + \left(70^2 \times \tfrac{2}{15}\right) + \left(72^2 \times \tfrac{1}{15}\right)$$
$$= \frac{65500}{15} = 4366.667 \text{ to 3 d.p.}$$
$$\mathrm{Var}(X_1 + X_2) = 4366.667 - 66^2 = 10.667 \text{ to 3 d.p.}$$

(v) $\mathrm{E}(X_1 + X_2) = 66 = 42 + 24 = \mathrm{E}(X_1) + \mathrm{E}(X_2)$, as required.
$\mathrm{Var}(X_1 + X_2) = 10.667 = 8 + 2.667 = \mathrm{Var}(X_1) + \mathrm{Var}(X_2)$, as required.

General results

Example 2.6 has illustrated the following general results for the sums and differences of random variables.

For any two random variables X_1 and X_2

- $\mathrm{E}(X_1 + X_2) = \mathrm{E}(X_1) + \mathrm{E}(X_2)$
- $\mathrm{E}(X_1 - X_2) = \mathrm{E}(X_1) - \mathrm{E}(X_2)$

> Replacing X_2 by $-X_2$ in this result gives
> $\mathrm{E}(X_1 + (-X_2))$
> $= \mathrm{E}(X_1) + \mathrm{E}(-X_2)$

If the variables X_1 and X_2 are independent

- $\mathrm{Var}(X_1 + X_2) = \mathrm{Var}(X_1) + \mathrm{Var}(X_2)$
- $\mathrm{Var}(X_1 - X_2) = \mathrm{Var}(X_1) + \mathrm{Var}(X_2)$

> Replacing X_2 by $-X_2$ in this result gives
> $\mathrm{Var}(X_1 + (-X_2))$
> $= \mathrm{Var}(X_1) + \mathrm{Var}(-X_2)$
> $= \mathrm{Var}(X_1) + (-1)^2 \mathrm{Var}(X_2)$
> $= \mathrm{Var}(X_1) + \mathrm{Var}(X_2)$

Note that if X_1 and X_2 are not independent, then the relationship between $\mathrm{Var}(X_1 + X_2) = \mathrm{Var}(X_1) + \mathrm{Var}(X_2)$ does not hold. In this case, the relationship between $\mathrm{Var}(X_1 + X_2) \ldots X_2$ is beyond the scope of this book.

Linear combinations of two or more independent random variables

> A 'linear combination' of random variables is an expression of the form $a_1 X_1 + a_2 X_2 + \cdots + a_n X_n$.

These results can also be generalised to include linear combinations of random variables.

For any random variables X and Y

$$\mathrm{E}(aX + bY) = a\mathrm{E}(X) + b\mathrm{E}(Y)$$

where a and b are constants.

If X and Y are independent

$$\mathrm{Var}(aX + bY) = a^2 \mathrm{Var}(X) + b^2 \mathrm{Var}(Y)$$

These results may be extended to any number of random variables.

Exercise 2.3

① The probability distribution of random variable X is as follows.

Table 2.27

x	1	2	3	4	5
$P(X = x)$	0.1	0.2	0.3	0.3	0.1

(i) Find (a) $E(X)$ (b) $\text{Var}(X)$.
(ii) Verify that $\text{Var}(2X) = 4\text{Var}(X)$.

② The probability distribution of a random variable X is as follows.

Table 2.28

x	0	1	2
$P(X = x)$	0.5	0.3	0.2

(i) Find (a) $E(X)$ (b) $\text{Var}(X)$
(ii) Verify that $\text{Var}(5X + 2) = 25\text{Var}(X)$.

③ The expectations and variances of independent random variables A, B and C are 35 and 9, 30 and 8 and 25 and 6, respectively. Write down the expectations and variances of

(i) $A + B + C$
(ii) $5A + 4B$
(iii) $A + 2B + 3C$
(iv) $4A - B - 5C$.

④ Prove that $\text{Var}(aX - b) = a^2 \text{Var}(X)$, where a and b are constants.

⑤ A coin is biased so that the probability of obtaining a tail is 0.75. The coin is tossed four times and the random variable X is the number of tails obtained.

Find

(i) $E(2X)$
(ii) $\text{Var}(3X)$.

⑥ A discrete random variable W has the following distribution.

Table 2.29

x	1	2	3	4	5	6
$P(W = w)$	0.1	0.2	0.1	0.2	0.1	0.3

Find the mean and variance of

(i) $W + 7$
(ii) $6W - 5$

⑦ The random variable X is the number of heads obtained when four unbiased coins are tossed. Construct the probability distribution for X and find

(i) $E(X)$
(i) $\text{Var}(X)$
(i) $\text{Var}(3X + 4)$.

Expectation and variance

⑧ A mining company is prospecting for new deposits of a particular metal ore. There are five sites for which it has acquired a licence to prospect. At each site there is a probability of 0.3 of finding an amount of ore which makes it worth opening a new mine. It explores the sites, one at a time, until it finds one which has a suitable amount of ore, after which it stops exploring. The random variable X represents the number of sites explored. The probability distribution for X is as follows.

Table 2.30

r	1	2	3	4	5
$P(X = r)$	0.3	0.21	0.147	0.1029	0.2401

(i) Explain why $P(X = 2) = 0.21$.

(ii) Find $E(X)$ and $Var(X)$.

It costs £600 000 to begin prospecting, however many sites are investigated. It then costs £275 000 per site to carry out the prospecting.

(iii) Find the expectation and variance of the total cost of the exploration.

⑨ A game at a charity fair costs £1 to play. The player rolls two fair dice and receives in return 10p plus 25 times the lower of the scores on the dice.

(i) Find the probability distribution of X, the lower of the scores.

(ii) Find the expectation and the variance of the players winnings in one go at the game.

(iii) In the long run, will the game make or lose money for the charity?

⑩ The probability distributions of two independent random variables X and Y are as follows.

Table 2.31

x	1	2	3	4
$P(X = x)$	0.2	0.4	0.3	0.1

Table 2.32

y	0	1	2
$P(Y = y)$	0.2	0.3	0.5

(i) Find (a) $E(X)$ (b) $E(Y)$ (c) $Var(X)$ (d) $Var(Y)$.

(ii) Show the probability distribution of $Z = X + Y$ in a table.

(iii) Using your table, verify that (a) $E(Z) = E(X) + E(Y)$
(b) $Var(Z) = Var(X) + Var(Y)$

(iv) Show the probability distribution of $W = X - Y$ in a table.

(v) Using your table, verify that (a) $E(W) = E(X) - E(Y)$
(b) $Var(W) = Var(X) + Var(Y)$

⑪ An unbiased six-sided dice is thrown.

(i) Find the expectation and variance of the score on the dice.

(ii) The dice is thrown twice. Find the expectation and variance of the total score.

(iii) The dice is thrown twice. Find the expectation and variance of the differences in the two scores.

(iv) The dice is thrown ten times. Find the expectation and variance of the total score.

⑫ In a game at a charity fair, three coins are spun and a dice is thrown. The game costs one pound to play. The amount in pence that the player wins is ten times the score on the dice plus 20 times the number of heads that occur. Find the expectation and variance of the amount won by the player.

⑬ The random variable X represents the number of tails which occur when two fair coins are spun.
  (i) Find $E(X)$ and $Var(X)$.
  (ii) Find $E(10X - 5)$ and $Var(10X - 5)$.
  (iii) Find the expectation and variance of the total of 50 observations of X.
  (iv) Explain the similarities and differences between your answers to part (iii) and $E(50X)$ and $Var(50X)$.

⑭ At a garden centre, railway sleepers for edging a border come in three similar lengths 120 cm, 125 cm and 130 cm. If a sleeper is selected at random, the probabilities that its length is 120 cm, 125 cm and 130 cm are 0.5, 0.3 and 0.2, respectively. You can assume that there are sufficient sleepers that these probabilities do not change when a few are selected.
  (i) Find the expectation and variance of the length of a randomly selected sleeper.

  In a hurry to edge a border in her garden, Jane selects four sleepers at random.

  (ii) Her border is 5.1 m long. Find the probability that she has enough length of sleepers to edge the border.
  (iii) Find the expectation and variance of the total length of the four sleepers.

⑮ A fair five-sided spinner has faces labelled 1, 2, 3, 4, 5. Martin plays a game in which he gains or loses money according to the number that the spinner comes to rest on when it is spun. He wins £5 if it lands on a 1, loses £2 if it lands on a 2, 3 or 4 and neither gains nor loses if it lands on a 5. Let X represent the amount 'won' each time the spinner is spun.
  (i) Complete the following probability distribution for X.

  Table 2.33

r	−2	0	
$P(X = r)$			

  (ii) Find $E(X)$ and $Var(X)$.
  (iii) How much less would the player have to pay, when the die lands on the face marked 2, so that he would break even in the long run?

⑯ A family eats a lot of bread. Most days, at least one loaf of bread is bought by the family. The random variable X represents the number of loaves bought by the family on a day. The probability distribution of X is shown in the table.

Table 2.34

r	0	1	2
$P(X = r)$	0.3	0.35	0.35

Expectation and variance

(i) Find E(X) and Var (X).

The number of loaves bought on any day depends on the number of loaves bought on the previous day. The table below shows the joint distribution of the numbers of loaves X_1 and X_2 bought on two successive days.

Table 2.35

		Second day X_2			Total
		0	1	2	
First day X_1	0	0	0.05	0.25	0.3
	1	0.05	0.2	0.1	0.35
	2	0.25	0.1	0	0.35
	Total	0.3	0.35	0.35	1

(ii) Complete the following probability distribution for $Y = X_1 + X_2$, the total number bought on the two days.

Table 2.36

R	0	1	2	3	4
P(Y = r)	0	0.1	0.7		

(iii) Find E(Y), and show that Var(Y) = 0.29.

(iv) Explain why Var(Y) is not equal to $\text{Var}(X_1) + \text{Var}(X_2)$.

KEY POINTS

1. For a *discrete random variable*, X, which can take only the values $r_1, r_2, ..., r_n$, with probabilities $p_1, p_2, ..., p_n$, respectively:

    - $p_1 + p_2 + \cdots + p_n = \sum_{n=1}^{n=k} p_k = \sum_{1}^{n} P(X = r_k) = 1$ where $p_k \geq 0$

2. A discrete probability distribution is best illustrated by a *vertical line chart*.
    - The *expectation* $= E(X) = \mu = \Sigma r P(x = r)$.
    - The *variance* $= \text{Var}(X) = \sigma^2$
    $$= E(X - \mu)^2 = \Sigma(r - \mu)^2 P(X = r)$$
    or $E(X^2) - [E(X)]^2 = \Sigma r^2 P(X = r) - [\Sigma r P(X = r)]^2$.

3. For a discrete random variable, X, which can assume only the values $x_1, x_2, ..., x_n$ with probabilities $p_1, p_2, ..., p_n$, respectively:
    - $\Sigma p_i = 1$ $p_i \geq 0$
    - $E(X) = \Sigma x_i p_i = \Sigma x_i \times P(X = x_i)$
    - $\text{Var}(X) = E(X^2) - [E(X)]^2$.

4 For any random variables X and Y and constants a, b and c:
- $E(c) = c$
- $E(aX) = aE(X)$
- $E(aX + c) = aE(X) + c$
- $E(X \pm Y) = E(X) \pm E(Y)$
- $E(aX + bY) = aE(X) + bE(Y)$.

5 For two random variables X and Y, and constants a, b and c
- $\text{Var}(c) = 0$
- $\text{Var}(aX) = a^2\text{Var}(X)$
- $\text{Var}(aX + c) = a^2\text{Var}(X)$.

and, if X and Y are independent,
- $\text{Var}(X \pm Y) = \text{Var}(X) + \text{Var}(Y)$
- $\text{Var}(aX + bY) = a^2\text{Var}(X) + b^2\text{Var}(Y)$.

LEARNING OUTCOMES

When you have completed this chapter you should be able to:
- use probability functions, given algebraically or in tables
- calculate the numerical probabilities for a simple distribution
- draw and interpret graphs representing probability distributions
- calculate the expectation (mean), $E(X)$, and understand its meaning
- calculate the variance, $\text{Var}(X)$, and understand its meaning
- use the result $E(aX + b) = aE(X) + b$ and understand its meaning
- use the result $\text{Var}(aX + b) = a^2\text{Var}(X)$ and understand its meaning
- find the mean of any linear combination of random variables and the variance of any linear combination of independent random variables.

3 Discrete probability distributions

Doublethink means the power of holding two contradictory beliefs in one's mind simultaneously, and accepting both of them.
George Orwell

A learner driver has done no revision for the driving theory test. He decides to guess each answer. There are 50 questions in the test and four answers to each question. Exactly one of these answers is correct. He answers all of them.

> **Discussion point**
> How many questions on average would you expect the learner driver to get correct?

1 The binomial distribution

- The probability of getting a question correct is clearly 0.25 as there are four responses of which one is correct.
- The probability of getting a question wrong is therefore 0.75.
- If the student gets r questions correct out of 50 then he must get the remaining $50 - r$ wrong.
- You might think that the probability of getting r questions correct out of 50 is $0.25^r \times 0.75^{50-r}$.
- However, there are many possible combinations, in fact $^{50}C_r$ of them, so you need to multiply the above term by $^{50}C_r$.

So the probability of getting r questions correct out of 50 is equal to
$^{50}C_r \times 0.25^r \times 0.75^{50-r}$.

> For example the student could get the first r questions correct and the remaining ones wrong, or the first $r-1$ correct as well as the last one and the rest wrong. In all the number of possibilities is $^{50}C_r$.

This situation is an example of the binomial distribution. For a binomial distribution to be appropriate, the following conditions must apply.

- You are conducting trials on random samples of a certain size, denoted by n.
- On each trial, the outcomes can be classified as either **success** or **failure**.

> In this example, the possible outcomes are **correct** (success) and **wrong** (failure).

In addition, the following assumptions are needed if the binomial distribution is to be a good model and give reliable answers.

- The outcome of each trial is independent of the outcome of any other trial.
- The probability of success is the same on each trial.

> This is particularly true when, in contrast to answering a question involving coins, dice, cards etc., you are modelling a situation drawn from real life.

The probability that the number of success, X, has the value r, is given by

$$P(X = r) = {}^nC_r p^r q^{1-r} \text{ for } r = 0, 1, \ldots, n$$

$$P(X = r) = 0 \text{ otherwise.}$$

You can either use this formula to find binomial probabilities or you can find them directly from your calculator without using the formula.

> The probability of success is usually denoted by p and that of failure by q, so $p + q = 1$.

The notation $B(n,p)$ is often used to mean that the distribution is binomial, with n trials each with probability of success p.

Example 3.1

On average, 5% of patients do not turn up for their appointment at a dental clinic. There are 30 appointments per day.

(i) Find the probability that on a random chosen day

   (a) everybody turns up,

   (b) exactly two people do not turn up,

   (c) at least three people do not turn up.

(ii) What modelling assumption do you have to make to answer the questions in part (i)? Do you think that this assumption is reasonable?

The binomial distribution

> **Note**
>
> The distribution which you need to use is B(30, 0.05)

> **USING ICT**
>
> Notice that you can find the answers to all three parts of this example directly from your calculator without using the formula.

Solution

(i) The probabilities, to 4 s.f., are

(a) $0.95^{30} = 0.2146$

(b) $^{30}C_2 \times 0.05^2 \times 0.95^{28} = 0.2586$

(c) $1 - {}^{30}C_2 \times 0.05^2 \times 0.95^{28} - {}^{30}C_1 \times 0.05^1 \times 0.95^{29} - 0.95^{30} = 0.1878$

(ii) You have to assume that the people who miss appointments do so independently of each other. It may not be true, as perhaps two members of the same family may both have an appointment and so would probably either both attend or neither. Also fewer people may attend when the weather is bad.

Expectation and variance of the binomial distribution

> **Note**
>
> The results are:
> $E(X_1 + X_2) = E(X_1) + E(X_2)$
> $Var(X_1 + X_2)$
> $= Var(X_1) + Var(X_2)$
>
> Note that these results can be extended to any number of random variables.

In order to find the expectation and variance of X, you can sum a series, involving binomial coefficients but this is fairly awkward. However, you can instead think of X as the sum of n independent variables $X_1, X_2, \ldots, X_n$. Each of these variables is a binomial random variable which takes the value 1 with probability p and the value 0 with probability $1 - p$. To find the expectation and variance of X, you first find the expectation and variance of one of these binomial random variables. You can then use the results from the previous chapter (see note on left) to find the expectation and variance of X.

$$E(X_i) = 0 \times (1-p) + 1 \times p = p$$

$$E(X_i^2) = 0^2 \times (1-p) + 1^2 \times p = p$$

$$Var(X_i) = E(X_i^2) - [E(X_i)]^2 = p - p^2 = p(1-p) = pq \text{ where } q = 1 - p$$

You now use the results that

$$E(X_1 + X_2 + \cdots + X_n) = E(X_1) + E(X_2) + \cdots + E(X_n)$$
$$= p + p + \cdots + p = np \text{ and}$$

$$Var(X_1 + X_2 + \cdots + X_n) = Var(X_1) + Var(X_2) + \cdots + Var(X_n)$$
$$= p(1-p) + p(1-p) + \cdots + p(1-p)$$
$$= np(1-p) = npq$$

> Thus if $X \sim B(n, p)$
> $E(X) = \mu = np$ and
> $Var(X) = \sigma^2 = np(1-p) = npq$

Example 3.2

USING ICT

You can use a spreadsheet to check these formulae for a particular binomial distribution, for example B(6, 0.25). Note that using the formulae, the mean $= np = 6 \times 0.25 = 1.5$ and the variance $= npq = 6 \times 0.25 \times 0.75 = 1.125$

In order to check these results, take the following steps:

1. Enter the values of X into cells B1 to H1.

2   Enter the formula provided by your spreadsheet to find the P(X = 0), for example =BINOM.DIST(B1,6,0.25,FALSE) into cell B2.

3   Copy this formula into cells C2 to H2 to find P(X = 1) to P(X = 6).

> The number in cell G2 should come out to be 0.0044. Check that you have got this right before continuing.

	A	B	C	D	E	F	G	H	I
1	r	0	1	2	3	4	5	6	SUM
2	$P(X=r)$	0.1780	0.3560						

Figure 3.1

4   Enter the formula = B1*B2 into cell B3 to calculate $0 \times P(X = 0)$.

5   Copy this formula into cells C3 to H3 to calculate $r \times P(X = r)$ for the remaining cells.

	A	B	C	D	E	F	G	H	I
1	r	0	1	2	3	4	5	6	SUM
2	$P(X=r)$	0.1780	0.3560						
3	$r \times P(X=r)$	0.0000	0.3560						

Figure 3.2

6   Enter the formula = B1^2*B2 into cell B4 to calculate $0^2 \times P(X = 0)$.

7   Copy this formula into cells C3 to H3 to calculate $r^2 \times P(X = r)$ for the remaining cells.

	A	B	C	D	E	F	G	H	I
1	r	0	1	2	3	4	5	6	SUM
2	$P(X=r)$	0.1780	0.3560						
3	$r \times P(X=r)$	0.0000	0.3560						
4	$r^2 \times P(X=r)$	0.0000	0.3560						

Figure 3.3

8   Use the SUM function to sum the values in rows each of 2, 3 and 4. Note that the sum of row 2 should be 1 (as you would expect).

9   Enter the formula = I3 into cell B6 to find the mean (which is simply the sum of the cells B3 to H3). If you have done it correctly the answer should be 1.5.

10 Enter the formula = I4 – I3^2 into cell B7 to calculate the variance. This answer should be 1.125.

ACTIVITY 3.1

Use a spreadsheet to confirm that, for B(8, 0.625), the procedures used in the example above give the same answers as the standard binomial formulae for the mean (np) and variance (npq).

The binomial distribution

Exercise 3.1

1. A fair coin is spun ten times.
   - (i) State the distribution of the number of heads that occur.
   - (ii) Find the probability of exactly four heads occurring.
   - (iii) Find the probability of at least five heads occurring.

2. The random variable $X \sim B(15, 0.4)$
   - (i) Find $E(X)$.
   - (ii) Find $P(X = 3)$.
   - (iii) Find $P(X > 3)$.

3. Ten fair dice are rolled. The number of times that a six occurs is denoted by X.
   - (i) State the distribution of X.
   - (ii) What is the expected number of sixes?
   - (iii) Find $P(X = 1)$.
   - (iv) Find $P(X > 2)$.

4. In an airport departure lounge a stall offers the chance to win a sports car. The game is to draw a card at random from each of four normal packs. If all four cards are aces, then the car is won.
   - (i) What is the probability of winning the car?
   - (ii) How many goes would be expected before the car was won?
   - (iii) The stall charges £5 per go and the car costs £35 000. What is the expected profit per go?

5. The random variable $X \sim B(25, 0.1)$.
   - (i) State
     - (a) the number of trials
     - (b) the probability of success in any trial
     - (c) the probability of failure in any trial.
   - (ii) Find the probability of at most 4 successes.
   - (iii) Find the value of the integer a such that $P(X < a) < 0.99$ and $P(X \leq a) > 0.99$.

6. A pottery company manufactures bowls in batches of 100. The probability of a bowl being faulty is known to be 0.03.
   - (i) What is the probability that in a batch of bowls there are less than five faulty bowls?
   - (ii) What is the probability that in two batches of bowls there are at most eight faulty bowls?
   - (iii) What is the probability that in each of two batches of bowls there are at most four faulty bowls?
   - (iv) Explain why your answer to part (ii) is different from your answer to part (iii).

7. Mark travels to work by bus each morning. The probability of his bus being late is 0.25.
   - (i) What is the probability that his bus is late twice in a five-day working week?
   - (ii) What is the probability that it is late at most once in a five-day working week?

(iii) Fred buys a quarterly ticket which allows him to travel for 13 weeks. How many times would he expect the bus to be late in this thirteen-week period?

⑧ A few years ago, there were 4000 million premium bonds, costing £1 each, held by investors. Each month, 270 000 bonds were selected at random and a prize was allocated to each.

  (i) Show that the probability of a bond being allocated a prize in any particular month was about 1 in 15 000.

  (ii) Rachel held 3000 bonds. Show that the probability of her winning at least one prize in any particular month was about 0.18.

  (iii) Calculate the probability that Rachel goes without a prize for a whole year.

  (iv) If all the prizes were £50, how much would Rachel expect to win, on average, in a year? What does this represent as a percentage return on her investment?

  (v) In fact, premium bonds gave an average return of 5.2% on the money invested. Calculate the average size of a prize. [MEI]

⑨ In an election, 20% of people support the Progressive Party. A random sample of eight voters is taken.

  (i) Find the probability that at least two of them support the Progressive Party.

  (ii) Find the mean and variance of the number of Progressive Party supporters in the sample.

⑩ The random variable $X \sim B(4, 0.3)$. Prove that the mean and variance of X are 1.2 and 0.84, respectively,

  (i) using the method above just before the start of this exercise

  (ii) using the definitions of expectation and variance.

⑪ The random variable $X \sim B(n, p)$. The values of the mean and variance are 24 and 14.4, respectively.

  (i) Find $P(X = 30)$.

  (ii) Find $P(X > 30)$.

2 The Poisson distribution

Electrics Express – next day delivery

Since the new website went live, with next day delivery for all items, the number of orders has increased dramatically. We have taken on more staff to cope with the demand for our products. Orders come in from all over the place. It seems impossible to predict the pattern of demand, but one thing we do know is that currently we receive an average of 150 orders per hour.

The Poisson distribution

The appearance of this update on the Electrics Express website prompted a statistician to contact Electrics Express. She offered to analyse the data and see what suggestions she could come up with.

For her detailed investigation, she considered the distribution of the number of orders per minute. For a random sample of 1000 single-minute intervals during the last month, she collected the following data.

> There were five occasions on which there were more than seven orders. These were grouped into a single category and treated as if all five of them were eight.

Table 3.1

Number of orders per minute	0	1	2	3	4	5	6	7	> 7
Frequency	70	215	265	205	125	75	30	10	5

Summary statistics for this frequency distribution are as follows.

$$n = 1000, \quad \Sigma xf = 2525 \quad \text{and} \quad \Sigma x^2 f = 8885$$
$$\Rightarrow \bar{x} = 2.525 \quad \text{and} \quad s = 1.58 \text{ (to 3 s.f.)}$$

She also noted that:

- orders made on the website appear at random and independently of each other
- the average number of orders per minute is about 2.5 which is equivalent to 150 per hour.

She suggested that the appropriate probability distribution to model the number of orders was the Poisson distribution.

The particular Poisson distribution, with an average number of 2.5 orders per minute, is defined as an *infinite* discrete random variable given by

$$P(X = r) = e^{-2.5} \times \frac{2.5^r}{r!} \quad \text{for } r = 0, 1, 2, 3, 4, \ldots$$

where

- X represents the random variable 'number of orders per minute'
- e is the mathematical constant 2.718 ...
- $e^{-2.5}$ can be found from your calculator as 0.082
- $r!$ means r *factorial*, for example $5! = 5 \times 4 \times 3 \times 2 \times 1 = 120$.

> **USING ICT**
>
> You can find Poisson probabilities directly from your calculator, without using this formula.

You can use the formula to calculate the values of the corresponding probability distribution, together with the *expected* frequencies it would generate. For example,

$$P(X = 4) = e^{-2.5} \times \frac{2.5^4}{4!}$$
$$= 0.13360\ldots$$
$$= 0.134 \text{ (to 3 s.f.)}$$

The table shows the observed frequencies for the orders on the website, together with the expected frequencies for a Poisson distribution with a mean of 2.5.

Table 3.2

Number of orders per minute (r)	0	1	2	3	4	5	6	7	> 7
Observed frequency	70	215	265	205	125	75	30	10	5
$P(X = r)$	0.082	0.205	0.257	0.214	0.134	0.067	0.028	0.010	0.004
Expected frequency	82	205	257	214	134	67	28	10	4

> **Note**
> Note that the final probability is found by subtracting the other probabilities from 1.
> Note also that the total of the expected frequencies is 1001 due to rounding.

The closeness of the observed and expected frequencies (see Figure 3.1) implies that the Poisson distribution is indeed a suitable model in this instance.

Note also that the sample mean, $\bar{x} = 2.525$ is very close to the sample variance, $s^2 = 2.509$ (to 4 s.f.). You will see later that, for a Poisson distribution, the expectation and variance are the same. So the closeness of these two summary statistics provides further evidence that the Poisson distribution is a suitable model.

Figure 3.4

> **Note**
> As with the discrete random variables you met in Chapter 2, the Poisson distribution may be illustrated by a vertical line chart.

This is an example of the Poisson distribution. When you learnt about the binomial distribution, you needed to consider whether certain conditions and certain modelling assumptions were needed. The same is true for the Poisson distribution.

The following **conditions** are needed for the Poisson distribution to apply.

- The variable is the frequency of events that occur in a fixed interval of time or space.
- The events occur randomly.

There is rarely any doubt as to whether these conditions are satisfied. However, for the Poisson distribution to be a good model the following are also needed.

- Events occur independently of one another.
- The mean number of events occurring in each interval of the same size is the same.

There will often be doubt as to whether either or both of these are satisfied, and often the best you can say is that you must assume them to be true. So they will usually be modelling assumptions.

> So the variable takes values 0, 1, 2, 3, …

> That is, events do not occur at regular or predictable intervals.

> Whether or not one event occurs does not affect the probability of whether another event occurs.

> So the probability of an event occurring in an interval of a given size is the same. This condition can also be written as 'events occur at a constant average rate'.

> The mean number of events per interval is often denoted by λ (pronounced 'lambda'). λ is the parameter of the Poisson distribution.

So if X represents the number of events in a given interval, then

$$P(X = r) = e^{-\lambda} \times \frac{\lambda^r}{r!} \quad \text{for } r = 0, 1, 2, 3, 4, \ldots$$

The Poisson distribution has an infinite number of outcomes, so only part of the distribution can be illustrated. The shape of the Poisson distribution depends on the value of the parameter λ. If λ is small, the distribution has positive skew, but as λ increases the distribution becomes progressively more symmetrical. Three typical Poisson distributions are illustrated in Figure 3.2.

The Poisson distribution

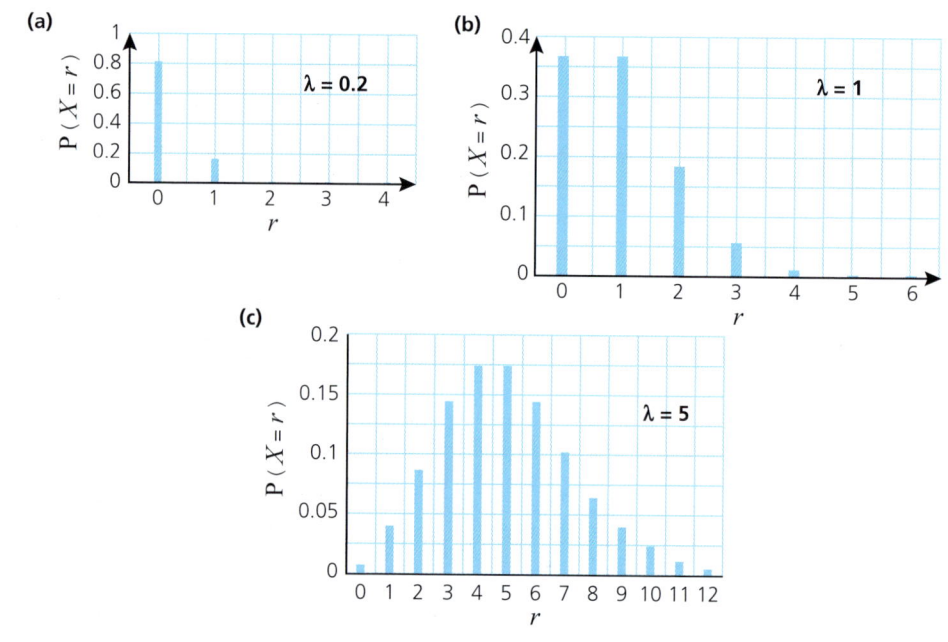

Figure 3.5 The shape of the Poisson distribution for (a) $\lambda = 0.2$ (b) $\lambda = 1$ (c) $\lambda = 5$

There are many situations in which events happen singly and the average number of occurrences per given interval of time or space is uniform and is known or can be easily found. Such events might include:

- the number of goals scored by a team in a football match
- the number of telephone calls received per minute at a call centre
- the number of accidents in a factory per week
- the number of particles emitted in a minute by a radioactive substance
- the number of typing errors per page in a document
- the number of flaws per metre in a roll of cloth
- the number of micro-organisms in 1 ml of pond water.

Modelling with the Poisson distribution

Often you will not be able to say that the conditions and assumptions for a Poisson distribution are met exactly, but you will nevertheless be able to get useful probabilities from the Poisson distribution. Sometimes it will be clear that some or all of the conditions and assumptions at not satisfied, and so you can confidently say that the Poisson distribution is not a good model.

Example 3.3

Discuss whether the Poisson distribution provides a good probability model for the variable X in each of the following scenarios.

(i) X is the number of cars that pass a point in the grandstand in a Formula 1 motor race in an interval of 3 minutes.

(ii) X is the number of coins found in $1\,m^3$ of earth during the investigation of an archaeological site.

(iii) X is the number of cars that pass a given point on a main road in a ten second period between 6 am and noon on a weekday.

(iv) X is the number of separate incidents reported to a Fire Brigade control room in a 1-hour period.

> Cars pass at a roughly constant rate, but this is not the same as 'constant *average* rate'. 'Constant rate' implies no variation.

Solution

(i) Cars in a Formula 1 race will pass the grandstand at fairly regular and predictable intervals, so the 'random' condition does not hold and a Poisson distribution is almost certainly not a good model.

(ii) It is quite likely that coins will be found in groups, or even in a hoard, and in this case the independence condition would not hold. If on the other hand you are in part of the site where single coins might have been lost on an occasional basis then independence could be assumed and the Poisson distribution might be a good model.

(iii) It is likely that the mean number of cars passing during rush hours would not be the same as the mean number passing at other times, so the 'constant average rate' assumption is unlikely to hold. This may mean that the Poisson distribution is not a good model.

(iv) In general, incidents such as these are likely to occur independently and at a uniform rate, at least within a relatively short time interval. However, circumstances might exist which negate this, for instance in the case of a series of deliberate attacks.

Discussion point

The managers of the new Avonford maternity hospital need to know how many beds are needed. At a meeting, one of the managers suggests that the number of births per day in the region covered by the hospital could be modelled by a Poisson distribution.

(i) What assumptions are needed for the Poisson distribution to be a good model?
(ii) Are these assumptions likely to hold?
(iii) What else would the managers need to consider when planning the number of beds?

> **Note**
>
> For a Poisson distribution with parameter λ,
> mean = $E(X) = \lambda$,
> variance = $Var(X) = \lambda$

The mean and variance of the Poisson distribution are both equal to the parameter λ.

You can see these results in the example about Electrics Express. The Poisson parameter was $\lambda = 2.5$, the mean of the number of orders placed per minute on the website was 2.525 and the variance was 2.512.

When modelling data with a Poisson distribution, the closeness of the mean and variance is one indication that the model fits the data well.

When you have collected the data, go through the following steps in order to check whether the data may be modelled by a Poisson distribution.

- Work out the mean and variance and check that they are roughly equal.
- Use the sample mean to work out the Poisson probability distribution and a suitable set of expected frequencies.
- Compare these expected frequencies with your observations.

The Poisson distribution

Example 3.4

The number of defects in a wire cable can be modelled by the Poisson distribution with a uniform rate of 1.5 defects per kilometre.

Find the probability that

(i) a single kilometre of wire will have exactly three defects.

(ii) a single kilometre of wire will have at least five defects.

Solution

Let X represent the number of defects per kilometre.

$$P(X=r) = e^{-1.5} \times \frac{1.5^r}{r!} \quad \text{for } r = 0, 1, 2, 3, 4, \ldots$$

> You are told that defects occur with a uniform rate of 1.5 defects per kilometre. From this, you can infer that the value of the mean, λ, is 1.5.

(i) $P(X=3) = e^{-1.5} \times \frac{1.5^3}{3!}$
$= 0.125510\ldots$
$= 0.126$ (to 3 s.f.)

(ii) $P(X \geq 5) = 1 - P(X \leq 4)$
$= 1 - 0.98142\ldots$
$= 0.0186$

You can use the term you have obtained to work out the next one. Although calculators can work out every term, sometimes you might still find it useful to understand this process. For the Poisson distribution with parameter λ

$$P(X=0) = e^{-\lambda}$$

$P(X=1) = \lambda e^{-\lambda} = \lambda P(X=0)$ Multiply the previous term by λ

$P(X=2) = e^{-\lambda} \times \frac{\lambda^2}{2!} = \frac{\lambda}{2} P(X=1)$ Multiply the previous term by $\frac{\lambda}{2}$

$P(X=3) = e^{-\lambda} \times \frac{\lambda^3}{3!} = \frac{\lambda}{3} P(X=2)$ Multiply the previous term by $\frac{\lambda}{3}$

In general, you can find $P(X=r)$ by multiplying your previous probability, $P(X=r-1)$, by $\frac{\lambda}{r}$.

> **Note**
>
> The process of finding the next term from the previous one can be described as a *recurrence relation*.

Example 3.5

Jasmit is considering buying a telephone answering machine. He has one for five days' free trial and finds that 22 messages are left on it. Assuming that this is typical of the use it will get if he buys it, find:

(i) the mean number of messages per day

(ii) the probability that on one particular day there will be exactly six messages

(iii) the probability that on one particular day there will be more than six messages.

Solution

(i) Converting the total for five days to the mean for a single day gives

$$\text{daily mean} = \frac{22}{5} = 4.4 \text{ messages per day}$$

(ii) Calling X the number of messages per day

$$P(X = 6) = e^{-4.4} \times \frac{4.4^6}{6!}$$

$$= 0.124 \text{ (3 s.f.)}$$

(iii) $P(X \leq 6) = 0.8436$

and so

$P(X > 6) = 1 - 0.8436$

$= 0.1564$ (3 s.f.)

Exercise 3.2

① If $X \sim$ Poisson (1.75), calculate
  (i) $P(X = 2)$
  (ii) $P(X > 0)$.

② If $X \sim$ Poisson (3.1), calculate
  (i) $P(X = 3)$
  (ii) $P(X < 2)$
  (iii) $P(X \leq 2)$.

③ The number of cars passing a house in a residential road between 10 a.m. and 11 a.m. on a weekday is a random variable, X. Give a condition under which X may be modelled by a Poisson distribution.

Suppose that $X \sim$ Poisson (3.4). Calculate $P(X \geq 4)$.

④ The number of wombats that are killed on a particular stretch of road in Australia in any one day can be modelled by a Poisson (0.42) random variable.
  (i) Calculate the probability that exactly two wombats are killed on a given day on this stretch of road.
  (ii) Find the probability that exactly four wombats are killed over a five-day period on this stretch of road.

⑤ A typesetter makes 1500 mistakes in a book of 500 pages. On how many pages would you expect to find (i) 0, (ii) 1, (iii) 2, (iv) 3 or more mistakes? State any assumptions in your workings.

⑥ 350 raisins are put into a mixture which is well stirred and made into 100 small buns. Estimate how many of these buns will
  (i) be without raisins
  (ii) contain five or more raisins.

In a second batch of 100 buns, exactly one has no raisins in it.
  (iii) Estimate the total number of raisins in the second mixture.

⑦ In which of the following scenarios is it likely that X can be well modelled by a Poisson distribution? For those scenarios where X is probably not a good model, give a reason.
  (i) X is the number of aeroplanes landing at Heathrow Airport in a randomly chosen period of 1 hour.
  (ii) X is the number of foxes that live in a randomly chosen urban region of area 1 km².
  (iii) X is the number of tables booked at a restaurant on a randomly chosen evening.

The Poisson distribution

(iv) X is the number of particles emitted by a radioactive substance in a period of 1 minute.

8 A ferry takes cars on a short journey from an island to the mainland. On a representative sample of weekday mornings, the numbers of vehicles, X, on the 8 a.m. sailing were as follows.

20 24 24 22 23 21 20 22 23 22
21 21 22 21 23 22 20 22 20 24

(i) Show that X does not have a Poisson distribution.

In fact 20 of the vehicles belong to commuters who use that sailing of the ferry every weekday morning. The random variable Y is the number of vehicles other than those 20 who are using the ferry.

(ii) Investigate whether Y may reasonably be modelled by a Poisson distribution.

The ferry can take 25 vehicles on any journey.

(iii) On what proportion of days would you expect at least one vehicle to be unable to travel on this particular sailing of the ferry because there was no room left and so have to wait for the next one?

9 A garage uses a particular spare part at an average rate of five per week. Assuming that usage of this spare part follows a Poisson distribution, find the probability that

(i) exactly five are used in a particular week
(ii) at least five are used in a particular week
(iii) exactly ten are used in a two-week period
(iv) at least ten are used in a two-week period
(v) exactly five are used in each of two successive weeks.
(vi) If stocks are replenished weekly, determine the number of spare parts which should be in stock at the beginning of each week to ensure that, on average, the stock will be insufficient on no more than one week in a 52-week year.

10 Small hard particles are found in the molten glass from which glass bottles are made. On average, 15 particles are found per 100 kg of molten glass. If a bottle contains one or more such particles, it has to be discarded.

Suppose bottles of mass 1 kg are made. It is required to estimate the percentage of bottles that have to be discarded. Criticise the following 'answer': Since the material for 100 bottles contains 15 particles, approximately 15% will have to be discarded.

Making suitable assumptions, which should be stated, develop a correct argument using a Poisson model, and find the percentage of faulty 1 kg bottles to three significant figures.

Show that about 3.7% of bottles of mass 0.25 kg are faulty. [MEI]

11 Weak spots occur at random in the manufacture of a certain cable at an average rate of 1 per 120 metres. If X represents the number of weak spots in 120 m of cable, write down the distribution of X.

Lengths of this cable are wound on to drums. Each drum carries 60 m of cable. Find the probability that a drum will have three or more weak spots.

A contractor buys six such drums. Find the probability that two have just one weak spot each and the other four have none.

The sum of two or more Poisson distributions

New crossing near leisure centre?

A recent traffic survey has revealed that the number of vehicles using the main road near the leisure centre has reached levels where crossing the road has become hazardous.

The survey, carried out by a leisure centre staff member, suggested that the numbers of vehicles travelling in both directions along the main road has increased so much during the past year that pedestrians are almost taking their lives into their own hands when crossing the road.

Between 2 p.m. and 3 p.m., usually one of the quietest periods of the day, the average number of vehicles travelling into town is 3.5 per minute and the average number of vehicles travelling out of town is 5.7 per minute. A new crossing is a must.

If it can be shown that there is a greater than 1 in 4 chance of more than ten vehicles passing per minute, then there is a good chance of getting a pelican crossing.

Assuming that the flows of vehicles, into and out of town, can be modelled by independent Poisson distributions, you can model the flow of vehicles in both directions as follows.

Let X represent the number of vehicles travelling into town between 2 p.m. and 3 p.m. then $X \sim$ Poisson (3.5).

Let Y represent the number of vehicles travelling out of town between 2 p.m. and 3 p.m. then $Y \sim$ Poisson (5.7).

Let T represent the number of vehicles travelling in either direction between 2 p.m. and 3 p.m. then $T = X + Y$.

You can find the probability distribution for T as follows.

$$P(T = 0) = P(X = 0) \times P(Y = 0)$$
$$= 0.0302 \times 0.0033$$
$$= 0.0001$$

$$P(T = 1) = P(X = 0) \times P(Y = 1) + P(X = 1) \times P(Y = 0)$$
$$= 0.0302 \times 0.0191 + 0.1057 \times 0.0033$$
$$= 0.0009$$

> There are two ways of getting a total of 1. They are 0 and 1, 1 and 0.

The Poisson distribution

> There are three ways of getting a total of 2. They are 0 and 2, 1 and 1, 2 and 0.

$P(T = 2) = P(X = 0) \times P(Y = 2) + P(X = 1) \times P(Y = 1) + P(X = 2) \times P(Y = 0)$

$= 0.0302 \times 0.0544 + 0.1057 \times 0.0191 + 0.1850 \times 0.0033$

$= 0.0043$

and so on.

You can see that this process is very time consuming. Fortunately, you can make life a lot easier by using the fact that if X and Y are two independent Poisson random variables, with means λ and μ, respectively, then $T = X + Y$ and T is a Poisson random variable with mean $\lambda + \mu$.

> **Note**
>
> $X \sim$ Poisson (λ) and
> $Y \sim$ Poisson (μ)
> $\Rightarrow X + Y \sim$ Poisson $(\lambda + \mu)$

Using $T \sim$ Poisson (9.2) gives the required probabilities straight away.

$$P(T = 0) = 0.0001$$
$$P(T = 1) = 0.0009$$
$$P(T = 2) = 0.0043$$

You can now use the distribution for T to find the probability that the total traffic flow exceeds ten vehicles per minute.

$$P(T > 10) = 1 - P(T \leq 10)$$
$$= 1 - 0.6820$$
$$= 0.318$$

Since there is a greater than 25% chance of more than ten vehicles passing per minute, the case for the pelican crossing has been made, based on the Poisson probability models.

Example 3.6

A rare disease causes the death, on average, of 3.8 people per year in England, 0.8 in Scotland and 0.5 in Wales. As far as is known, the disease strikes at random and cases are independent of one another.

What is the probability of 7 or more deaths from the disease on the British mainland (i.e. England, Scotland and Wales together) in any year?

Solution

Notice first that:

- $P(7$ or more deaths$) = 1 - P(6$ or fewer deaths$)$
- each of the three distributions fulfils the conditions for it to be modelled by the Poisson distribution.

You can therefore add the three distributions together and treat the result as a single Poisson distribution.

The overall mean is given by   3.8   +   0.8   +   0.5   =   5.1

                                         England   Scotland   Wales   Total

giving an overall distribution of Poisson (5.1).

The probability of 6 or fewer deaths is 0.7474.

So the probability of 7 or more deaths is given by $1 - 0.7474 = 0.2526$.

Notes

1 You may only add Poisson distributions in this way if they are independent of each other.

Example 3.7

On a lonely Highland road in Scotland, cars are observed passing at the rate of six per day and lorries at the rate of two per day. On the road, there is an old cattle grid which will soon need repair. The local works department decide that if the probability of more than 15 vehicles per day passing is less than 1%, then the repairs to the cattle grid can wait until next spring; otherwise it will have to be repaired before the winter.

When will the cattle grid have to be repaired?

Solution

Let C be the number of cars per day, L be the number of lorries per day and V be the number of vehicles per day.

Assuming that a car or a lorry passing along the road is a random event and that the two are independent

$$C \sim \text{Poisson}(6), L \sim \text{Poisson}(2)$$
and so $V \sim \text{Poisson}(6 + 2)$
$$\Rightarrow V \sim \text{Poisson}(8).$$
$$P(V \leq 15) = 0.9918.$$

The required probability is $P(V > 15) = 1 - P(V \leq 15)$
$$= 1 - 0.9918$$
$$= 0.0082.$$

This is just less than 1% and so the repairs are left until spring.

3 Link between binomial and Poisson distributions

In certain circumstances, you can use either the binomial distribution or the Poisson distribution as a model to calculate the probabilities you need. The example below illustrates this.

Example 3.8

It is known that, nationally, one person in a thousand is allergic to a particular chemical used in making a wood preservative. A firm that makes this wood preservative employs 500 people in one of its factories.

(i) Use the binomial distribution to estimate the probability that more than two people at the factory are allergic to the chemical.

(ii) What assumption are you making?

(iii) Using the fact that the mean of a binomial distribution is np, find the Poisson probability $P(Y > 2)$ where $Y \sim \text{Poisson}(np)$.

Link between binomial and Poisson distributions

Solution

(i) Let X be the number of people in a random sample of 500 who are allergic to the chemical.

$$X \sim B(500, 0.001)$$

$$P(X > 2) = 1 - P(X \leq 2)$$
$$= 1 - 0.985669\ldots$$
$$= 0.0143$$

(ii) The assumption made is that people with the allergy are just as likely to work in the factory as those without the allergy. In practice, this seems rather unlikely: you would not stay in a job that made you unwell.

(iii) The mean of the binomial is $np = 500 \times 0.001 = 0.5$.

Using $Y \sim \text{Poisson}(0.5)$

$$P(Y > 2) = 1 - P(Y \leq 2)$$
$$= 1 - 0.985612\ldots$$
$$= 0.0144.$$

These two probabilities are very similar, so this suggests that sometimes the Poisson distribution and the binomial distribution give similar results. Four comparisons of binomial and Poisson probabilities are illustrated in Figure 3.3. In each case, the binomial probabilities are shown in blue and the Poisson probabilities in red.

Examining these four charts, it seems that whatever the value of n, the value of p must be small for the two distributions to give similar results. In fact, when n is reasonably large and p is small, the binomial and Poisson probabilities are similar. The smaller the value of p and the larger the value of n, the better the two distributions agree.

> **Note**
>
> Note that if the binomial parameters are n and p then the corresponding Poisson distribution has parameter $\lambda = np$.

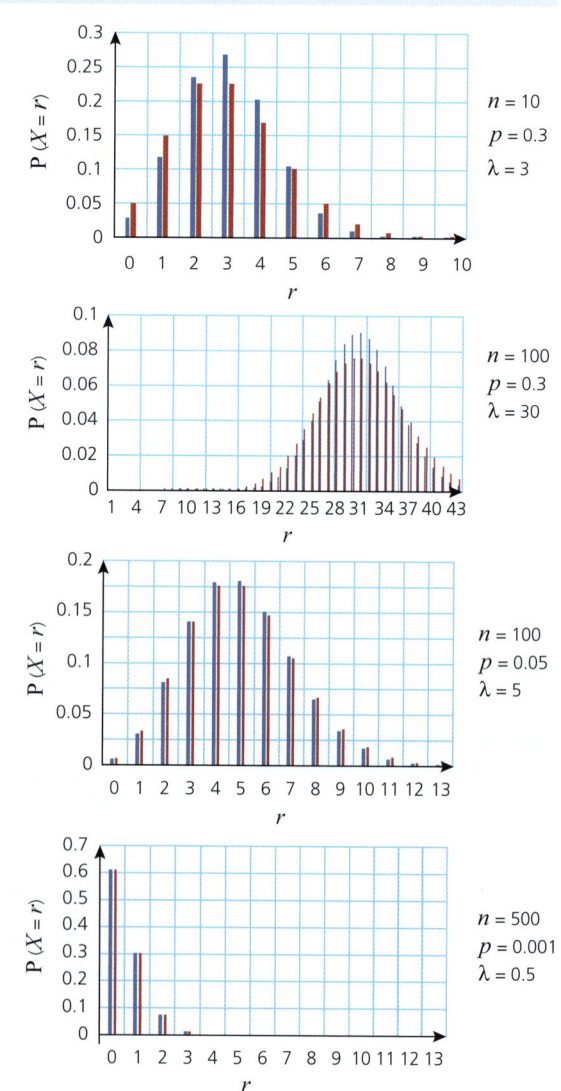

Figure 3.6 Comparison between the Poisson and binomial distributions for various values of n and p.

Exercise 3.3

① You are given that $X \sim B(200, 0.04)$.

   (i) Find $P(X = 5)$.

   (ii) State the mean of a Poisson distribution which is likely to give a similar result to the probability found in part (i).

   (iii) Use this mean to find the corresponding Poisson probability and compare it with your answer to part (i).

② The spreadsheet below shows two distributions, $B(10, 0.5)$ and Poisson(λ).

	A	B	C	D	E	F	G	H	I	J	K	L
1	r	0	1	2	3	4	5	6	7	8	9	10
2	Probability $B(10, 0.5)$	0.0010	0.0098	0.0439	0.1172	0.2051	0.2461	0.2051	0.1172	0.0439	0.0098	0.0010
3	Probability Poisson(λ)	0.0067	0.0337	0.0842	0.1404	0.1755	0.1755	0.1462	0.1044	0.0653	0.0363	0.0181

Figure 3.7

   (i) The Poisson(λ) distribution is used to approximate the $B(10, 0.5)$ distribution. Write down the value of λ.

   (ii) Plot a vertical line chart to compare the $B(10, 0.5)$ and the Poisson(λ) distributions.

   (iii) Comment on whether the Poisson distribution (λ) is a good approximation to the $B(10, 0.5)$ distribution.

   The spreadsheet shows two other distributions, $B(100, 0.05)$ and Poisson(μ).

	A	B	C	D	E	F	G	H	I	J	K	L
1	r	0	1	2	3	4	5	6	7	8	9	10
2	Probability $B(100, 0.05)$	0.0059	0.0312	0.0812	0.1396	0.1781	0.1800	0.1500	0.1060	0.0649	0.0349	0.0167
3	Probability Poisson(μ)	0.0067	0.0337	0.0842	0.1404	0.1755	0.1755	0.1462	0.1044	0.0653	0.0363	0.0181

Figure 3.8

   (iv) The Poisson(μ) distribution is used to approximate the $B(100, 0.05)$ distribution. Write down the value of μ.

   (v) Figure 3.9 shows a vertical line chart comparing the $B(100, 0.05)$ and the Poisson(μ) distributions. Compare this with the vertical line chart with the one which you have drawn for $B(10, 0.5)$ and Poisson(λ) and comment on the differences.

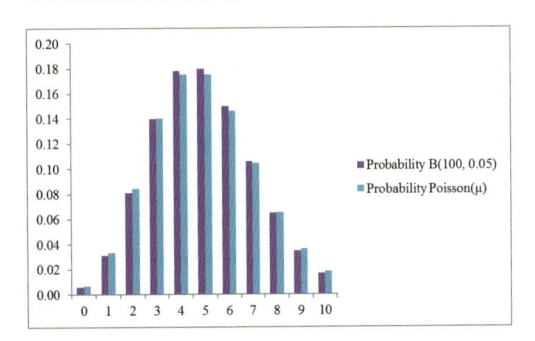

Figure 3.9

③ It is known that 0.3% of items produced by a certain process are defective. A random sample of 2000 items is selected.

   (i) Use a binomial distribution to find the probability that there are at least five defective items in the sample.

   (ii) Use a Poisson distribution to find the probability that there are at least five defective items in the sample.

   (iii) Explain why your answers are similar although you are using two different distributions.

Link between binomial and Poisson distributions

4. At a coffee shop both hot and cold drinks are sold. The number of hot drinks sold per minute may be assumed to be a Poisson variable with mean 0.7 and the number of cold drinks sold per minute may be assumed to be an independent Poisson variable with mean 0.4.

   (i) Calculate the probability that in a given one-minute period exactly one hot drink and one cold drink are sold.

   (ii) Calculate the probability that in a given three-minute period fewer than three drinks altogether are sold.

   (iii) In a given one-minute period exactly three drinks are sold. Calculate the probability that these are all hot drinks.

5. The numbers of lorry drivers and car drivers visiting an all-night transport cafe between 2 a.m. and 3 a.m. on a Sunday morning have independent Poisson distributions with means 5.1 and 3.6, respectively. Find the probabilities that between 2 a.m. and 3 a.m. on any Sunday

   (i) exactly five lorry drivers visit the café

   (ii) at least one car driver visits the café

   (iii) exactly five lorry drivers and exactly two car drivers visit the cafe.

   (iv) By using the distribution of the total number of drivers visiting the cafe, find the probability that exactly seven drivers visit the cafe between 2 a.m. and 3 a.m. on any Sunday.

   (v) Given that exactly seven drivers visit the cafe between 2 a.m. and 3 a.m. on one Sunday, find the probability that exactly five of them are driving lorries. [MEI]

6. Telephone calls reach a departmental administrator independently and at random, internal ones at a mean rate of two in any five-minute period, and external ones at a mean rate of one in any five-minute period.

   (i) Find the probability that, in a five-minute period, the administrator receives
      (a) exactly three internal calls
      (b) at least two external calls
      (c) at most five calls in total.

   (ii) Given that the administrator receives a total of four calls in a five-minute period, find the probability that exactly two were internal calls.

   (iii) Find the probability that in any one-minute interval no calls are received.

7. During a weekday, cars pass a census point on a quiet side road independently and at random times. The mean rate for westward travelling cars is two in any five-minute period, and for eastward travelling cars is three in any five-minute period.

   Find the probability

   (i) that there will be no cars passing the census point in a given two-minute period

   (ii) that at least one car from each direction will pass the census point in a given two-minute period

   (iii) that there will be exactly ten cars passing the census point in a given ten-minute period.

⑧ A ferry company has two small ferries, A and B, that run across a river. The number of times per week that ferry A needs maintenance in a week has a Poisson distribution with mean 0.5, while, independently, the number of times that ferry B needs maintenance in a week has a Poisson distribution with mean 0.3.

Find, to three decimal places, the probability that in the next three weeks

(i) ferry A will not need maintenance at all

(ii) each ferry will need maintenance exactly once

(iii) there will be a total of two occasions when one or other of the two ferries will need maintenance.

⑨ Two random variables, X and Y, have independent Poisson distributions given by $X \sim \text{Poisson}(1.4)$ and $Y \sim \text{Poisson}(3.6)$, respectively.

(i) Using the distributions of X and Y *only*, calculate

(a) $P(X+Y=0)$

(b) $P(X+Y=1)$

(c) $P(X+Y=2)$.

The random variable T is defined by $T = X + Y$.

(ii) Write down the distribution of T.

(iii) Use your distribution from part (ii) to check your results in part (i).

⑩ A boy is watching vehicles travelling along a motorway. All the vehicles he counts are either cars or lorries; the numbers of each may be modelled by two independent Poisson distributions. The mean number of cars per minute is 8.3 and the mean number of lorries per minute is 4.7.

(i) For a given period of one minute, find the probability that he sees

(a) exactly seven cars   (b) at least three lorries.

(ii) Calculate the probability that he sees a total of exactly ten vehicles in a given one-minute period.

(iii) Find the probability that he observes fewer than eight vehicles in a given period of 30 seconds.

⑪ The numbers of emissions per minute from two radioactive substances, A and B, are independent and have Poisson distributions with means 2.8 and 3.25, respectively.

Find the probabilities that in a period of one minute there will be

(i) at least three emissions from substance A

(ii) one emission from one of the two substances and two emissions from the other substance

(iii) a total of five emissions.

⑫ The number of cats rescued by an animal shelter each day may be modelled by a Poisson distribution with parameter 2.5, while the number of dogs rescued each day may be modelled by an independent Poisson distribution with parameter 3.2.

(i) Calculate the probability that on a randomly chosen day the shelter rescues

(a) exactly two cats   (b) exactly three dogs

(c) exactly five cats and dogs in total.

(ii) Given that one day exactly five cats and dogs were rescued, find the conditional probability that exactly two of these animals were cats.

13. A petrol station has service areas on both sides of a motorway, one to serve north-bound traffic and the other for south-bound traffic. The number of north-bound vehicles arriving at the station in one minute has a Poisson distribution with mean 1.4, and the number of south-bound vehicles arriving in one minute has a Poisson distribution with mean 2.3, the two distributions being independent.

(i) Find the probability that in a one-minute period
   (a) exactly three vehicles arrive
   (b) more than four vehicles arrive at this petrol station, giving your answers correct to three places of decimals.

Given that in a particular one-minute period five vehicles arrive, find

(ii) the probability that they are all from the same direction
(iii) the most likely combination of north-bound and south-bound vehicles.

14. A sociologist claims that only 3% of all suitably qualified students from inner city schools go on to university. The sociologist selects a random sample of 200 such students. Use a Poisson distribution to estimate the probability that

(i) exactly five go to university
(ii) more than five go to university.
(iii) If there is at most a 5% chance that more than n of the 200 students go to university, find the lowest possible value of n.

Another group of 100 students from inner city schools is also chosen. Find the probability that

(iv) exactly five of each group go to university
(v) exactly ten of all the chosen students go to university.

4 Other discrete distributions

You have now met the binomial distribution and the Poisson distribution. There are many other discrete distributions such as the hypergeometric distribution and the negative binomial but those that you will meet in the rest of this chapter are the uniform distribution and the geometric distribution.

The uniform distribution

When fair six-sided dice are thrown, there are only six outcomes for each of the dice, all equally likely. You can write the probability distribution for each of them formally as

$$P(X = r) = \frac{1}{6} \quad \text{for } r = 1, 2, 3, 4, 5, 6$$
$$P(X = r) = 0 \quad \text{otherwise,}$$

where X represents the score on one of the dice.

Tabulating the probability distribution for X gives

Table 3.3

r	1	2	3	4	5	6
P(X = r)	$\frac{1}{6}$	$\frac{1}{6}$	$\frac{1}{6}$	$\frac{1}{6}$	$\frac{1}{6}$	$\frac{1}{6}$

The vertical line chart in Figure 3.10 illustrates this distribution.

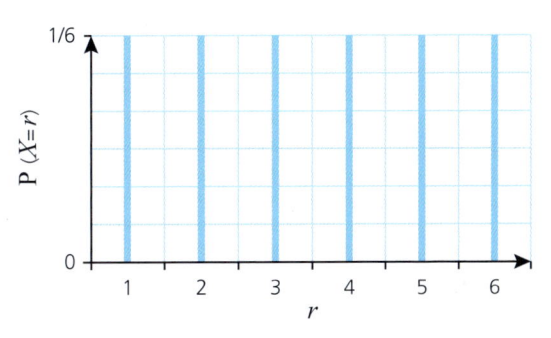

Figure 3.10

This is an example of the uniform probability distribution (sometimes also known as the rectangular distribution).

In general, the uniform probability distribution over the values $\{1, 2, \ldots, n\}$ is defined as follows:

$$P(X = r) = \frac{1}{n} \qquad \text{for } r = 1, 2, \ldots, n$$
$$P(X = r) = 0 \qquad \text{otherwise.}$$

However, the lowest value may be k rather than 1 in which case the distribution over the values $\{k, k + 1, \ldots, n + k - 1\}$ is as follows:

$$P(X = r) = \frac{1}{n} \qquad \text{for } r = k, k + 1, \ldots, n + k - 1$$
$$P(X = r) = 0 \qquad \text{otherwise.}$$

Expectation and variance of the uniform distribution

You can find the expectation and variance of the score X on one of the fair dice, using the formulae which you met in Chapter 2.

$$E(X) = \mu = \Sigma r P(X = r)$$
$$= 1 \times \frac{1}{6} + 2 \times \frac{1}{6} + \cdots + 6 \times \frac{1}{6}$$
$$= 21 \times \frac{1}{6} = \frac{21}{6} = \frac{7}{2}$$
$$\text{Var}(X) = \sigma^2 = E(X^2) - \mu^2$$
$$= 1^2 \times \frac{1}{6} + 2^2 \times \frac{1}{6} + \cdots + 6^2 \times \frac{1}{6} - \left(\frac{7}{2}\right)^2$$
$$= (1 + 4 + 9 + 16 + 25 + 36) \times \frac{1}{6} - \left(\frac{7}{2}\right)^2$$
$$= \frac{91}{6} - \frac{49}{4} = \frac{35}{12}$$

Other discrete distributions

These results can be generalised for a uniform random variable X taking the values $1, 2, \ldots, n$.

> **Note** that you are using the formula $\sum_{r=1}^{n} r = \frac{n(n+1)}{2}$.

$$E(X) = \sum_{r=1}^{n} rP(X=r)$$
$$= \sum_{r=1}^{n} \left(r \times \frac{1}{n}\right)$$
$$= \frac{1}{n} \sum_{r=1}^{n} r$$
$$= \frac{1}{n} \times \frac{n(n+1)}{2}$$
$$= \frac{n+1}{2}$$

To find the variance, you use the formula $\operatorname{Var}(X) = E(X^2) - [E(X)]^2$

> **Note** that you are using the formula $\sum_{r=1}^{n} r^2 = \frac{1}{6} n(n+1)(2n+1)$.

$$E(X^2) = \sum_{r=1}^{n} r^2 P(X=r)$$
$$= \sum_{r=1}^{n} r^2 \frac{1}{n}$$
$$= \frac{1}{n} \sum_{r=1}^{n} r^2$$
$$= \frac{1}{n} \times \frac{1}{6} n(n+1)(2n+1)$$
$$= \frac{1}{6}(n+1)(2n+1)$$

$$\operatorname{Var}(X) = E(X^2) - [E(X)]^2$$
$$= \frac{1}{6}(n+1)(2n+1) - \left(\frac{n+1}{2}\right)^2$$
$$= \frac{n+1}{12}[2(2n+1) - 3(n+1)]$$
$$= \frac{n+1}{12}(4n+2-3n-3)$$
$$= \frac{(n+1)(n-1)}{12}$$
$$= \frac{n^2-1}{12}$$

> **Note**
> For a discrete uniform distribution,
> $E(X) = \frac{n+1}{2}$, $\operatorname{Var}(X) = \frac{n^2-1}{12}$.

Example 3.9

A five-sided fair spinner has faces labelled 10, 11, 12, 13, 14. The score on the spinner when it is rolled once is denoted by Z.

(i) Prove that $E(Z) = 12$.

(ii) Prove that $\operatorname{Var}(Z) = 2$.

> **Note**
> Although it may seem obvious by symmetry that $E(Z) = 12$, the question asks for a *proof*. You therefore need to use the formula for expectation $E(X) = \sum rP(X=r)$.

Solution

(i) $E(Z) = \sum_{r=10}^{14} rP(Z=r)$.
$$= \sum_{10}^{14} \left(r \times \frac{1}{n}\right)$$
$$= 10 \times \tfrac{1}{5} + 11 \times \tfrac{1}{5} + 12 \times \tfrac{1}{5} + 13 \times \tfrac{1}{5} + 14 \times \tfrac{1}{5}$$
$$= 60 \times \tfrac{1}{5}$$
$$= 12$$

(ii) $\quad E(Z^2) = \sum_{r=1}^{n} r^2 P(Z=r)$

$= 100 \times \frac{1}{5} + 121 \times \frac{1}{5} + 144 \times \frac{1}{5} + 169 \times \frac{1}{5} + 196 \times \frac{1}{5}$

$= (100 + 121 + 144 + 169 + 196) \times \frac{1}{5}$

$= 730 \times \frac{1}{5}$

$= 146$

$Var(X) = E(X^2) - [E(X)]^2$

$= 146 - 144$

$= 2$

The geometric distribution

Asha is playing a game where you have to throw ten or more on two dice in order to start. She takes six throws to get to a score of ten or more, and says that she has always been unlucky. One of the other players was successful on her first attempt.

> There are 36 possible outcomes when two dice are thrown. Those that give a total of 10 or more are 4,6; 5,5; 5,6; 6,4; 6,5; 6,6. So the probability of a total of 10 or more is $\frac{6}{36} = \frac{1}{6}$.

- The probability that Asha is successful on any attempt is $\frac{1}{6}$.
- The probability that Asha is unsuccessful on any particular attempt is therefore $\frac{5}{6}$.

> Asha is successful on her sixth attempt so her results are F F F F F S with probabilities $\frac{5}{6} \frac{5}{6} \frac{5}{6} \frac{5}{6} \frac{5}{6} \frac{1}{6}$

- Asha has to have five failures followed by one success. So the probability that Asha is successful on her sixth attempt is $\left(\frac{5}{6}\right)^5 \times \frac{1}{6} = 0.0670$.
- So, in fact, it is about half as likely for Asha to succeed on her sixth attempt as it is on her first attempt.

The number of attempts that Asha takes to succeed, up to and including the successful attempt is an example of a *geometric* random variable. The probability distribution is an example of *geometric distribution*.

Example 3.10

Gina likes having an attempt at the coconut shy whenever she goes to the fair. From experience, she knows that the probability of her knocking over a coconut at any throw is $\frac{1}{3}$.

(i) Find the probability that Gina knocks over a coconut for the first time on her fifth attempt.

(ii) Find the probability that it takes Gina at most three attempts to knock over a coconut.

(iii) Given that Gina has already had four unsuccessful attempts, find the probability that it takes her another three attempts to succeed.

> If Gina is successful on her fifth attempt her results are F F F F S with probabilities $\frac{2}{3} \frac{2}{3} \frac{2}{3} \frac{2}{3} \frac{1}{3}$

Solution

(i) Gina has to have 4 failures followed by 1 success. The probability of this is $\left(\frac{2}{3}\right)^4 \times \frac{1}{3} = \frac{16}{243} = 0.0658$

Other discrete distributions

(ii)

Method 1

This is the probability that she is successful on her first or second or third attempt. You can do similar calculations to the above:

$$\frac{1}{3} + \left(\frac{2}{3}\right)^1 \times \frac{1}{3} + \left(\frac{2}{3}\right)^2 \times \frac{1}{3} = \frac{1}{3} + \frac{2}{9} + \frac{4}{27} = \frac{19}{27} = 0.7037.$$

Method 2

You can, instead, first work out the probability that Gina fails on all of her first three attempts and then subtract this from 1.

P(at most three attempts) = 1 − P(Fails on all of first three attempts)

$$= 1 - \left(\frac{2}{3}\right)^3 = 1 - \frac{8}{27} = \frac{19}{27} = 0.7037$$

(iii) Unfortunately for Gina, however many unsuccessful attempts she has had makes no difference to how many more attempts she will need. Thus the required probability is $\left(\frac{2}{3}\right)^2 \times \frac{1}{3} = \frac{4}{27} = 0.1481$.

> **Note**
> There is not much difference in the difficulty of these two methods if you want the probability of at most three attempts, but if we, for example, wanted the probability of at most 20 attempts, Method 2 would be far better as the calculation would take no more effort than in this case.

This is another example of a geometric random variable. Part (iii) illustrates the fact that the geometric distribution has '*no memory*'.

For a geometric distribution to be appropriate, the following conditions must apply.

- You are finding the number of trials it takes for the first success to occur.
- On each trail, the outcomes can be classified as either success or failure.

> The probability of success is usually denoted by p and that of failure by q, so $p + q = 1$.

In addition, the following assumptions are needed if the geometric distribution is to be a good model and give reliable answers.

- The outcome of each trail is independent of the outcome of any other trail.
- The probability of success is the same on each trail.

In general, the geometric probability distribution, $X \sim \text{Geo}(p)$ over the values $\{1, 2, 3,...\}$ is defined as follows:

$$P(X = r) = (1-p)^{r-1} p \text{ or } q^{r-1}p \quad \text{for } r = 1, 2, 3...$$
$$P(X = r) = 0 \quad \text{otherwise.}$$

In Method 2 of part (ii) of Example 3.8, you saw that the probability of Gina failing on all of her first three attempts is $\left(\frac{2}{3}\right)^3$. More generally, a useful feature of the geometric distribution is that $P(X > r) = (1-p)^r$, since this represents the probability that all of the first r attempts are failures.

The vertical line chart in Figure 3.11 illustrates the geometric distribution for $p = 0.3$.

> **Note**
> $P(X > r)$ is the probability that you take more than r attempts to succeed. The first r tries must therefore be failures. So $P(X > r) = (1-p)^r$.

Note

For the geometric distribution with probability of success p

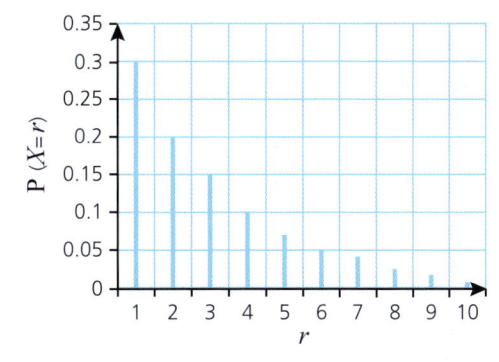

$E(X) = \dfrac{1}{p}$, $Var(X) = \dfrac{1-p}{p^2}$.

Figure 3.11

Example 3.11

In a communication network, messages are received one at a time and checked for errors. It is known that 6% of messages have an error in them. Errors in one message are independent of errors in any other message.

(i) Find the probability that the first message which contains an error is the fifth message to be checked.

(ii) Find the mean number of messages before the first that contains an error is found.

(iii) Find the probability that there are no errors in the first ten messages.

(iv) Find the most likely number of messages to be checked to find the first that contains an error.

Solution

In this situation, the distribution is geometric with probability 0.06, so Geo(0.06) so let $X \sim \text{Geo}(0.06)$.

(i) $P(X = 5) = 0.94^4 \times 0.06$

$= 0.0468$

(ii) $\text{Mean} = \dfrac{1}{0.06}$

$= 16.7$ messages

(iii) $P(X > 10) = 0.94^{10}$

$= 0.539$

(iv) Most likely number = 1 since $0.06 > 0.06 \times 0.94 > 0.06 \times 0.94^2 \ldots$

Example 3.12

The random variable $X \sim \text{Geo}(p)$. You are given that $Var(X) = 20$.

(i) Find the value of p.

(ii) Find $P(X = 7)$.

(iii) Find $P(X = 10 | X > 7)$.

Other discrete distributions

Solution

(i) $\text{Var}(X) = \dfrac{1-p}{p^2} = 20$

$\Rightarrow 1 - p = 20p^2$

$\Rightarrow 20p^2 + p - 1 = 0$

$\Rightarrow (5p-1)(4p+1) = 0$

$\Rightarrow p = 0.2$ (discard $p = -0.25$)

(ii) $P(X = 7) = 0.8^6 \times 0.2$

$= 0.0524$

(iii) $P(X = 10 | X > 7) = P(X = 3)$

$= 0.8^2 \times 0.2$

$= 0.128$

Exercise 3.4

① Two fair six-sided dice are rolled.
  (i) Find the probability that the score on the first die is at least 5.
  (ii) Find the probability that the score on at least one of the two dice is at least 5.

② A fair three-sided spinner has sectors labelled 1, 2 and 3. The spinner is spun until a 3 is scored. The number of spins required to get a 3 is denoted by X.
  (i) Find $P(X = 1)$.
  (ii) Find $P(X = 5)$.
  (iii) Find $P(X > 5)$.

③ A fair four-sided spinner has sectors labelled 2, 3, 4 and 5. The score on the spinner when it is spun once is denoted by X.
  (i) Find $P(X > 3)$.
  (ii) Find $E(X)$.
  (iii) Find $\text{Var}(X)$.

④ Five fair six-sided dice are each rolled once.
  (i) Find the expectation and variance of the score on one of the dice.
  (ii) Find the expectation and variance of the total score on the five dice.

⑤ A fair seven-sided spinner has sectors labelled 7, 8, …12 and 13. Find the expectation and variance of the score on the spinner.

⑥ The random variable X denotes the score on a fair three-sided spinner which has sectors labelled 1, 2 and 3. The random variable Y denotes the score on a fair three-sided spinner which has sectors labelled 10, 20 and 30.
  (i) Find $E(X)$ and $\text{Var}(X)$.
  (ii) Find $E(Y)$ and $\text{Var}(Y)$.
  (iii) The spinner with sectors labelled 1, 2 and 3 is spun ten times. Find the expectation and variance of the total score.
  (iv) Compare your answers to parts (ii) and (iii).

⑦ Fair four-sided dice with faces labelled 1, 2, 3 and 4 are rolled, one at a time, until a 4 is scored.
   (i) Find the probability that the first 4 is rolled on the fifth attempt.
   (ii) Find the probability that it takes at least six attempts to roll the first 4.
   (iii) Given that a four is not rolled in the first six attempts, find the probability that a four is rolled within the next two attempts.
   (iv) Write down the mean number of attempts which it takes to roll a 4.

⑧ In a game show, a player is asked questions one after another until they get one wrong, after which it is the next player's turn. The probability that they get a question correct is 0.7, independent of any other question.
   (i) Find the probability that the first player is asked a total of six questions.
   (ii) Find the probability that the first player is asked at least six questions.
   (iii) Find the average number of questions that the first player is asked.
   (iv) Find the probability that the first two players are asked a total of five questions.

⑨ An archer is aiming for the bullseye on a target. The probability of the archer hitting the target on any attempt is 0.1, independent of any other attempt.
   (i) Find the probability that the archer hits the bullseye for the first time on their tenth attempt.
   (ii) Find the probability that the archer takes at least 20 attempts to hit the bullseye.
   (iii) Find the mean and variance of the number of attempts it takes for the archer to hit the bullseye for the first time.
   (iv) The archer takes n shots at the bullseye. Find the smallest value of n for which there is a chance of 50% or more that the archer will hit the target at least once.

⑩ In order to start a board game, each player in turn rolls fair six-sided dice, one at a time, until a 6 is obtained. Let X be the number of goes a player takes to start the game.
   (i) Write down the distribution of X.
   (ii) Find (a) $P(X = 4)$, (b) $P(X < 4)$, (c) $P(X > 4)$.
   (iii) If the game has two players and they each take turns in rolling the dice, find the probability that (a) neither has started within four rolls (two rolls each), (b) both have started within four rolls (two rolls each).
   (iv) Given that $X = 3$, find the probability that the total score on all three of the dice is less than 10.

Other discrete distributions

KEY POINTS

Binomial distribution

1. The binomial distribution may be used to model situations in which these conditions hold
   - You are conducting trials on random samples of a certain size, n.
   - On each trial the outcomes can be classified as either success or failure.

   For the binomial distribution to be a good model, these assumptions are required.
   - The outcome of each trial is independent of the outcome of any other trial.
   - The probability of success is the same on each trial.

2. For a binomial random variable X, where $X \sim B(n, p)$
   - $P(X = r) = {}^nC_r q^{n-r} p^r$ for $r = 0, 1, 2, \ldots, n$.

3. For $X \sim B(n, p)$
   - $E(X) = np$
   - $Var(X) = npq$.

Poisson distribution

1. The Poisson distribution may be used in situations in which:
   - the variable is the frequency of events occurring in fixed intervals of time or space.

2. For the Poisson distribution to be a good model:
   - events occur randomly
   - events occur independently
   - events occur at a uniform average rate.

3. For a Poisson random variable X, where $X \sim \text{Poisson}(\lambda)$
   - $P(X = r) = e^{-\lambda} \times \dfrac{\lambda^r}{r!}$ for $r = 0, 1, 2, \ldots$

4. For Poisson(λ)
   - $E(X) = \lambda$
   - $Var(X) = \lambda$.

5. The sum of two independent Poisson distributions
   - If $X \sim \text{Poisson}(\lambda)$ and $Y \sim \text{Poisson}(\mu)$, then $X + Y \sim \text{Poisson}(\lambda + \mu)$.

Uniform distribution

1. The uniform distribution may be used to model situations in which:
   - all outcomes are equally likely.

2. For a uniform random variable X taking n different values
   - $P(X = r) = \dfrac{1}{n}$ for $r = 1, 2, \ldots, n$.

3. For a uniform random variable X taking values 1 to n inclusive
   - $E(X) = \dfrac{n+1}{2}$
   - $Var(X) = \dfrac{n^2 - 1}{12}$.

Geometric distribution

1 The geometric distribution may be used in situations in which:
   - there are two possible outcomes, often referred to as success and failure
   - both outcomes have fixed probabilities, p and q, and $p+q=1$
   - you are finding the number of trials up to and including the first successful trial.

2 For the geometric distribution to be a good model:
   - the probability of success is constant
   - the probability of success in any trial is independent of the outcome of any other trial.

3 For a geometric random variable X, where $X \sim \text{Geo}(p)$
   - $P(X = r) = (1-p)^{r-1} p = q^{r-1} p \qquad$ for $r = 1, 2, 3 \ldots$

4 For $\text{Geo}(p)$
   - $E(X) = \dfrac{1}{p}$
   - $\text{Var}(X) = \dfrac{1-p}{p^2}$.

LEARNING OUTCOMES

When you have completed this chapter you should be able to:
- recognise situations under which the binomial distribution is likely to be an appropriate model
- calculate probabilities using a binomial distribution
- know and be able to use the mean and variance of a binomial distribution
- recognise situations under which the Poisson distribution is likely to be an appropriate model
- calculate probabilities using a Poisson distribution
- know and be able to use the mean and variance of a Poisson distribution
- know that the sum of two or more independent Poisson distributions is also a Poisson distribution
- recognise situations in which both the Poisson distribution and the binomial distribution might be appropriate models
- recognise situations under which the discrete uniform distribution is likely to be an appropriate model
- calculate probabilities using a discrete uniform distribution
- calculate the mean and variance of any given discrete uniform distribution
- recognise situations under which the geometric distribution is likely to be an appropriate model
- calculate the probabilities using a geometric distribution, including cumulative probabilities
- know and be able to use the mean and variance of a geometric distribution.

4 Bivariate data (correlation coefficients)

It is now proved beyond doubt that smoking is one of the leading causes of statistics.

John Peers

Discussion point

1. Across the world, countries with high life expectancy tend to have low birth rates and vice-versa. How would you describe this in mathematical language? Why do you think this happens?
2. Suggest some factors that affect the proportion of new-born babies, in one country, who have all four of their grandparents still alive.

The data in this table refer to the 22 American mainland countries. They cover their population in millions, birth rate per 1000 people, life expectancy in years and mean GDP per capita in thousands of US$.

Table 4.1

Country	Population	Life expectancy	Birth rate	GDP per capita
Argentina	43.0	77.51	16.88	18.6
Belize	0.3	68.49	25.14	8.8
Bolivia	10.6	68.55	23.28	5.5
Brazil	202.7	73.28	14.72	12.1
Canada	34.8	81.67	10.29	43.1
Chile	17.4	78.44	13.97	19.1
Colombia	46.2	75.25	16.73	11.1
Costa Rica	4.8	78.23	16.08	12.9
Ecuador	15.7	76.36	18.87	10.6
El Salvador	6.1	74.18	16.79	7.5
Guatemala	14.6	71.74	25.46	5.3
Guyana	0.7	67.81	15.90	8.5
Honduras	8.6	70.91	23.66	4.8
Mexico	120.3	75.43	19.02	15.6
Nicaragua	5.8	72.72	18.41	4.5
Panama	3.6	78.3	18.61	16.5
Paraguay	6.7	76.8	16.66	6.8
Peru	3.0	73.23	18.57	11.1
Suriname	0.6	71.69	16.73	12.9
United States	318.9	79.56	13.42	52.8
Uruguay	3.3	76.81	13.18	16.6
Venezuela	28.9	74.39	19.42	13.6

This is an example of a multivariate data set. For each country, the values of four variables are given.

Multivariate analysis is an important part of statistics but is beyond the scope of this book apart for the special case of bivariate data, where just two variables are considered.

Bivariate data are usually displayed on a scatter diagram like Figure 4.1. In this, life expectancy is plotted on the horizontal axis and birth rate on the vertical axis.

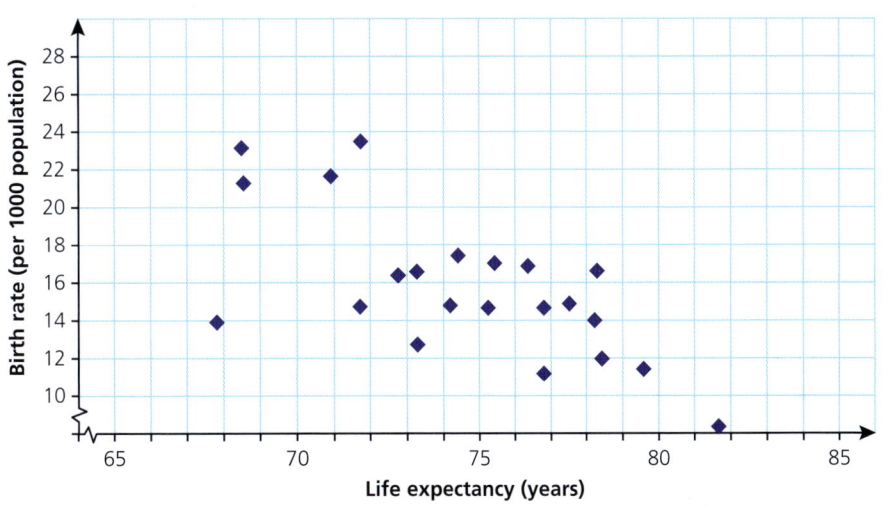

Figure 4.1

Describing variables

This diagram suggests that there is a relationship between birth rate and life expectancy. In general, such a relationship is called an **association.**

Sometimes, two special conditions apply.

- Both the variables are random.
- The relationship is linear.

> In such a case, the stronger the association, the closer the points on the scatter diagram will lie to a straight line.

Under these conditions the association is described as **correlation**. So correlation is a special case of association.

- If high values of both variables tend to occur together, and the same for low values, the correlation is **positive**.
- If, as in this example, high values of one variable are associated with low values of the other, the correlation is **negative**.

If the points on the scatter diagram lie exactly on a straight line, the correlation is described as **perfect**. However, it is much more common for the data to lie close to a straight line but not exactly on it, as in this case. The better the fit, the higher the level of correlation.

1 Describing variables

Dependent and independent variables

The scatter diagram in Figure 4.1 was drawn with the life expectancy on the horizontal axis and birth rate on the vertical axis. It could have been drawn the other way around. It is not obvious that either of the variables is dependent on the other.

By contrast, the weight of the passengers in an aeroplane is dependent on how many of them there are, but the reverse is not true; the number getting on is not determined by their weight. So, in this case, the number of passengers is described as the **independent variable** and their weight as the **dependent** variable. It is normal practice to plot the dependent variable on the vertical (y) axis and the independent variable on the horizontal (x) axis.

Here are some more examples of dependent and independent variables.

Independent variable	Dependent variable
The number of goals scored by a premier league football team in a season	The number of points the team has in the league table
The amount of rain falling on a field	The weight of a crop yielded while the crop is growing
The number of people visiting a bar	The volume of beer sold in an evening

Controlled variables

Sometimes, one or both of the variables is **controlled**, so that the variable only assumes a set of predetermined values; for example, the times at which temperature measurements are taken at a meteorological station. Controlled variables are *non-random*. Situations in which the independent variable is controlled and the dependent variable is random form the basis of *regression* analysis.

2 Interpreting scatter diagrams

You can often judge if correlation is present just by looking at a scatter diagram.

In this case, both the variables increase together.

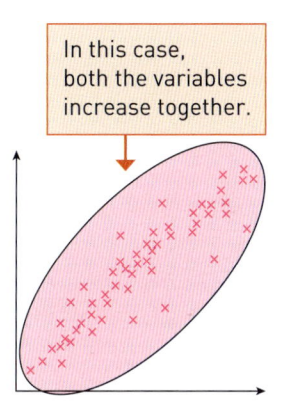

Figure 4.2 Positive correlation

Notice that in Figure 4.2 almost all of the observation points can be contained within an ellipse. This shape often arises when both variables are random. You should look for it before going on to do a calculation of Pearson's product moment correlation coefficient (see page 79). The narrower the elliptical profile, the greater the correlation.

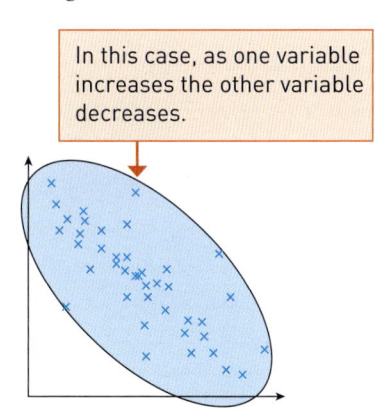

In this case, as one variable increases the other variable decreases.

Figure 4.3 Negative correlation

In Figure 4.3 the points again fall into an elliptical profile and this time there is negative correlation. The fatter ellipse in this diagram indicates weaker correlation than in the case shown in Figure 4.2.

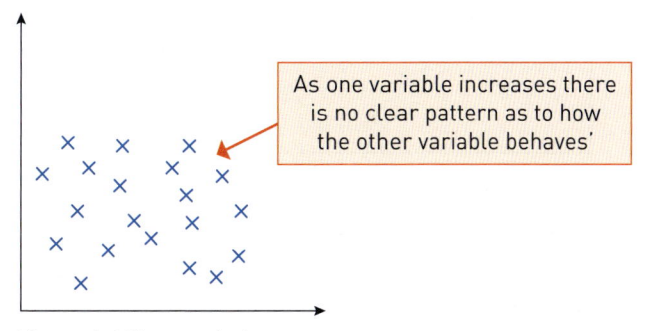

As one variable increases there is no clear pattern as to how the other variable behaves'

Figure 4.4 No correlation

In the case illustrated in Figure 4.4, the points fall randomly in the (x, y) plane and there appears to be no association between the variables.

Interpreting scatter diagrams

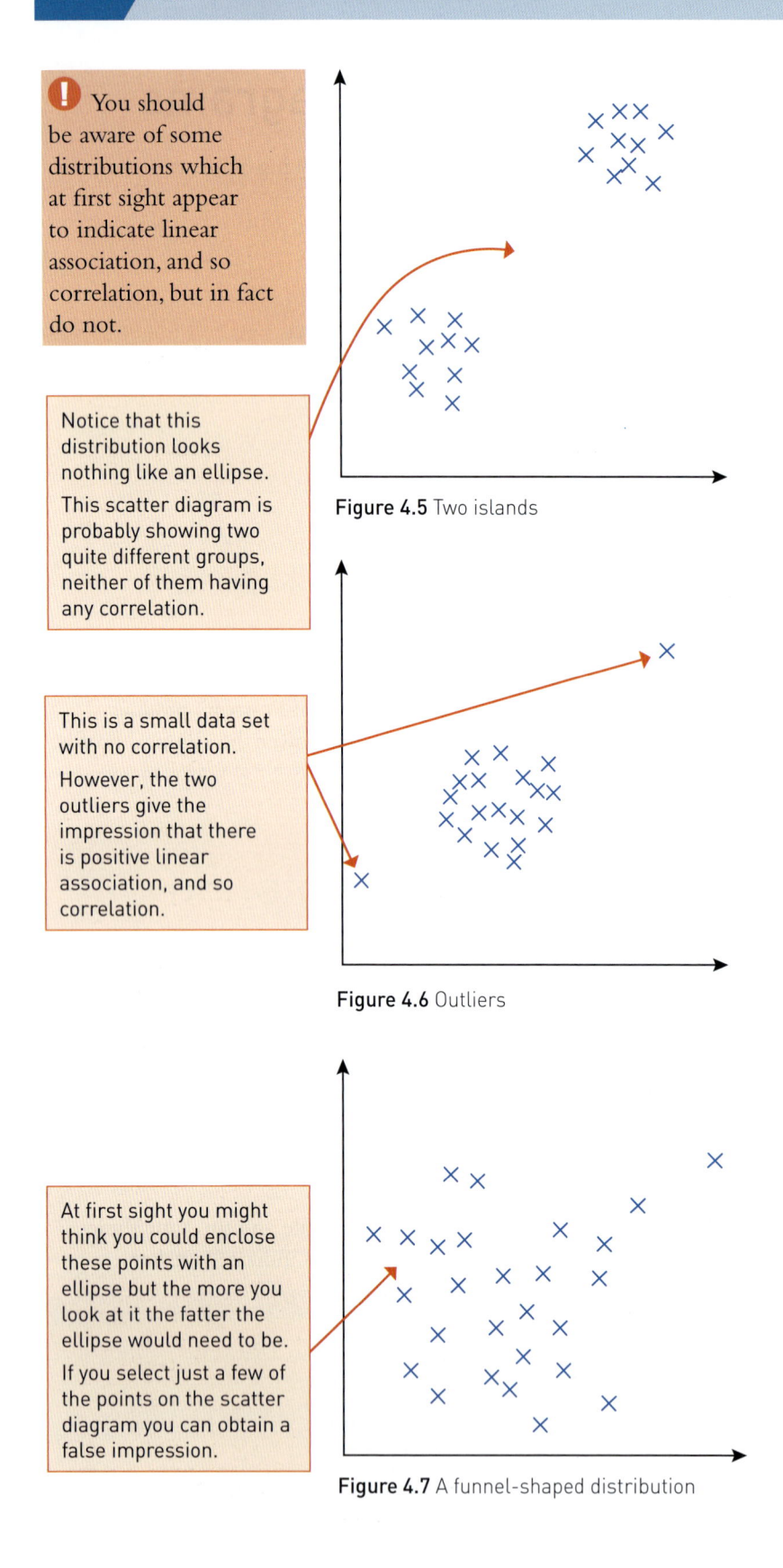

! You should be aware of some distributions which at first sight appear to indicate linear association, and so correlation, but in fact do not.

Notice that this distribution looks nothing like an ellipse.

This scatter diagram is probably showing two quite different groups, neither of them having any correlation.

Figure 4.5 Two islands

This is a small data set with no correlation.

However, the two outliers give the impression that there is positive linear association, and so correlation.

Figure 4.6 Outliers

At first sight you might think you could enclose these points with an ellipse but the more you look at it the fatter the ellipse would need to be.

If you select just a few of the points on the scatter diagram you can obtain a false impression.

Figure 4.7 A funnel-shaped distribution

Here are the scatter diagrams for some of the other pairs of variables in the data for the American countries.

Discussion point

→ Comment on any insights the diagrams give you and the presence of outliers. Say whether they show any correlation or association.

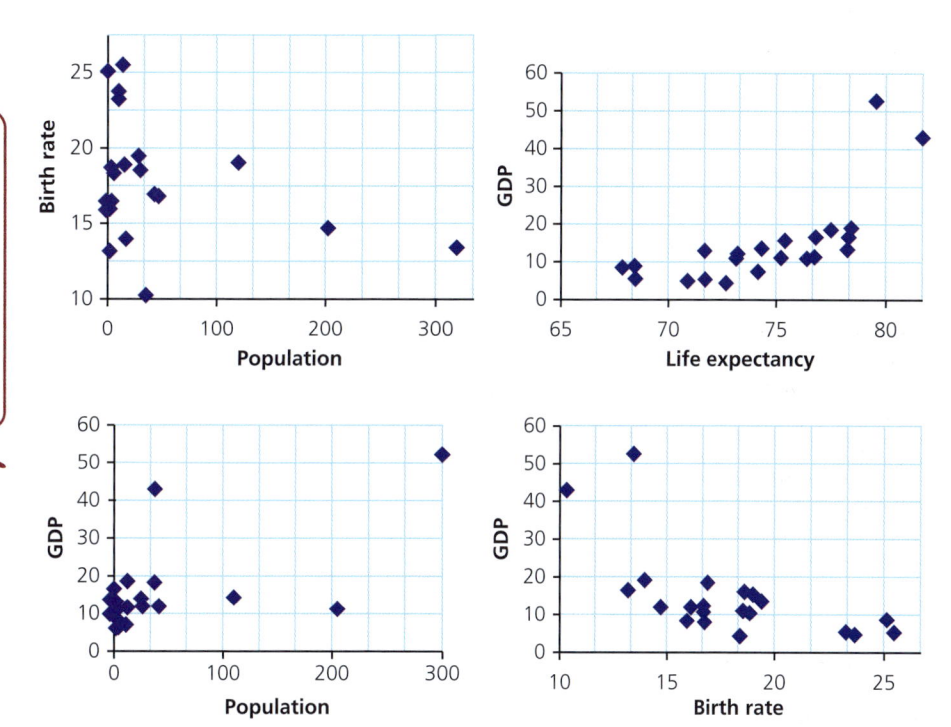

Figure 4.8

3 Product moment correlation

The scatter diagram in Figure 4.1 revealed that there may be a mutual association between life expectancy and birth rate. This section shows how such a relationship can be quantified.

Figure 4.9 shows this scatter diagram again. Life expectancy is denoted by x and birth rate by y.

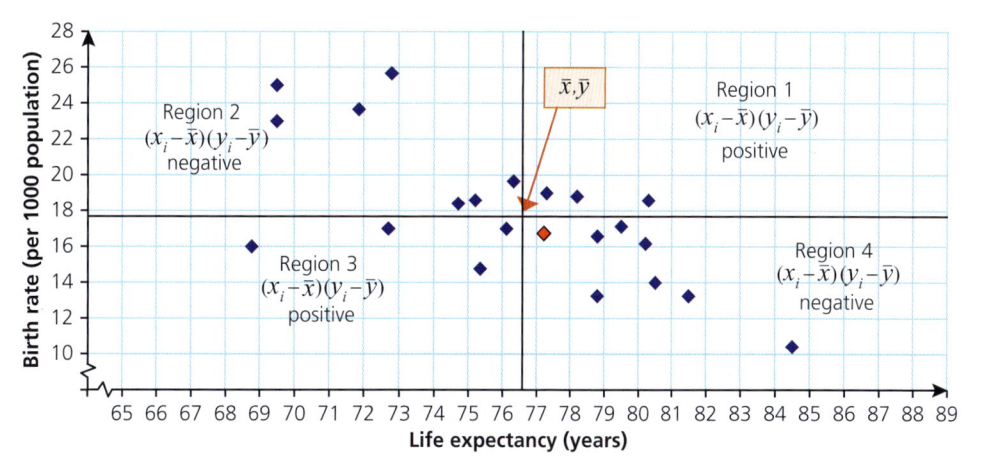

Region 2: $(x_i - \bar{x})(y_i - \bar{y})$ negative
Region 1: $(x_i - \bar{x})(y_i - \bar{y})$ positive
Region 3: $(x_i - \bar{x})(y_i - \bar{y})$ positive
Region 4: $(x_i - \bar{x})(y_i - \bar{y})$ negative

Figure 4.9

The mean life expectancy is

$$\bar{x} = \frac{\Sigma x_i}{n} = \frac{1641.35}{22} = 74.6\ldots$$

Product moment correlation

The mean birth rate is

$$\bar{y} = \frac{\Sigma y_i}{n} = \frac{391.79}{22} = 17.8\ldots$$

(x_i, y_i) are the various data points, for example (75.25, 16.73) for Colombia (marked in red); n is the number of such points, in this case 22.

You will see that the point $(\bar{x}, \bar{y})$ has also been plotted on the scatter diagram and lines drawn through this point parallel to the axes. These lines divide the scatter diagram into four regions.

You can think of the point $(\bar{x}, \bar{y})$ as the middle of the scatter diagram and so treat it as a new origin. Relative to $(\bar{x}, \bar{y})$, the co-ordinates of the various points are all of the form $(x_i - \bar{x}, y_i - \bar{y})$.

The table below gives the values of $(x_i - \bar{x})$, $(y_i - \bar{y})$ and $(x_i - \bar{x}, y_i - \bar{y})$.

Table 4.2

			$(x_i - \bar{x})$	$(y_i - \bar{y})$	$(x_i - \bar{x})(y_i - \bar{y})$
Argentina	77.51	16.88	2.903	−0.929	−2.696
Belize	68.49	25.14	−6.117	7.331	−44.845
Bolivia	68.55	23.28	−6.057	5.471	−33.139
Brazil	73.28	14.72	−1.327	−3.089	4.098
Canada	81.67	10.29	7.063	−7.519	−53.105
Chile	78.44	13.97	3.833	−3.839	−14.714
Colombia	75.25	16.73	0.643	−1.079	−0.694
Costa Rica	78.23	16.08	3.623	−1.729	−6.263
Ecuador	76.36	18.87	1.753	1.061	1.861
El Salvador	74.18	16.79	−0.427	−1.019	0.435
Guatemala	71.74	25.46	−2.867	7.651	−21.935
Guyana	67.81	15.9	−6.797	−1.909	12.973
Honduras	70.91	23.66	−3.697	5.851	−21.631
Mexico	75.43	19.02	0.823	1.211	0.997
Nicaragua	72.72	18.41	−1.887	0.601	−1.135
Panama	78.3	18.61	3.693	0.801	2.960
Paraguay	76.8	16.66	2.193	−1.149	−2.519
Peru	73.23	18.57	−1.377	0.761	−1.048
Suriname	71.69	16.73	−2.917	−1.079	3.146
United States	79.56	13.42	4.953	−4.389	−21.738
Uruguay	76.81	13.18	2.203	−4.629	−10.198
Venezuela	74.39	19.42	−0.217	1.611	−0.349
Total	1641.35	391.79	0	0	−209.54

> **Note**
>
> The point (x, y) has a moment of $(x - 74.6)$ about the vertical axis and of $(y - 17.8)$ about the horizontal axis. So $(x - 74.6)(y - 17.8)$ is called its product moment.

If you look at the data point for Colombia (shown in red in Figure 4.9), you can see that $(x_i - \bar{x})(y_i - \bar{y})$ is negative. This point is in Region 4. In fact, this will be true for all of the points in Region 4 and also Region 2. In both Region 1 and Region 3, $(x_i - \bar{x})(y_i - \bar{y})$ will be positive.

When there is positive correlation most or all of the data points will fall in Regions 1 and 3 and so you would expect the sum of these products to be positive and large.

When there is negative correlation as in this case, most or all of the points will be in Regions 2 and 4 and so you would expect the sum of these products to be negative and large.

When there is little or no correlation, the points will be scattered round all four regions. Those in Regions 1 and 3 will result in positive values of $(x_i - x)(y_i - y)$ but when you add these to the negative values from the points in Regions 2 and 4 you would expect most of them to cancel each other out. Consequently, the total value of all the terms should be small.

> **Note**
>
> In Table 4.2, S_{xy} is the total of the last column, so $S_{xy} = -209.54$.

In general, the sum of all these terms is denoted by S_{xy}.

$$S_{xy} = \Sigma(x_i - \bar{x})(y_i - \bar{y})$$

By itself the actual value of S_{xy} does not tell you very much because:

- no allowance has been made for the number of items of data
- no allowance has been made for the spread within the data
- no allowance has been made for the units of x and y.

Pearson's product moment correlation coefficient

To allow for both the number of items and the spread within the data, together with the units of x and y, the value of S_{xy} is divided by the square root of the product of S_{xx} and S_{yy}.

The sample product moment correlation coefficient is denoted by r and is given by

> **Note**
>
> You may use either formulation, since they are algebraically equivalent. Example 4.1, overleaf, gives both methods, so you may judge for yourself.

$$r = \frac{S_{xy}}{\sqrt{S_{xx}S_{yy}}} = \frac{\Sigma(x_i - \bar{x})(y_i - \bar{y})}{\sqrt{\Sigma(x_i - \bar{x})^2 \times \Sigma(y_i - \bar{y})^2}}$$

$$= \frac{\Sigma x_i y_i - n(\bar{x})(\bar{y})}{\sqrt{(\Sigma x_i^2 - n\bar{x}^2)(\Sigma y_i^2 - n\bar{y}^2)}}$$

where $S_{xx} = \Sigma(x_i - \bar{x})^2$, $S_{yy} = \Sigma(y_i - \bar{y})^2$.

The quantity, r, provides a standardised measure of correlation. Its value always lies within the range -1 to $+1$. (If you calculate a value outside this range, you have made a mistake.) A value of $+1$ means perfect positive correlation; in that case, all the points on a scatter diagram would lie exactly on a straight line with positive gradient. Similarly, a value of -1 means perfect negative correlation.

Product moment correlation

> Be careful not to confuse the quantities denoted by S_{xx}, S_{yy} and S_{xy} with those denoted by s_{xx}, s_{yy} and s_{xy} s used by some other authors.
>
> In this book S_{xx} and S_{yy} are the sums of the squares and are not divided by n. Similarly, S_{xy} is the sum of the terms $(x_i - \bar{x})(y_i - \bar{y})$ and is not divided by n.

These two cases are illustrated in Figure 4.10.

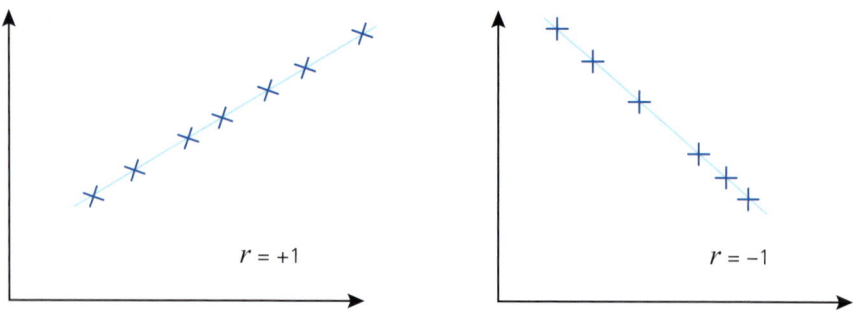

Figure 4.10 (i) Perfect positive correlation ($r = +1$) (ii) Perfect negative correlation ($r = -1$)

In cases of little or no correlation, r takes values close to zero. The nearer the value of r is to $+1$ or -1, the stronger the correlation.

Example 4.1

A gardener wishes to know if plants which produce only a few potatoes produce larger ones. He selects five plants at random, counts how many eating sized potatoes they have produced, and weighs the largest one.

Table 4.3

Number of potatoes, x	5	5	7	8	10
Weight of largest, y (grams)	240	232	227	222	215

Calculate the sample product moment correlation coefficient, r, and comment on the result.

> - In mechanics and physics the word 'weight' is used exclusively to mean the force of gravity on a body and the units of weight are those of force, such as newton. The word 'mass' is used to denote the amount of material in a body, with units such as kilogram, tonne and pound.
> - In everyday use the term 'weight' is often used where mass would be used in mechanics.
>
> In statistics the data used often come from everyday contexts or from other subjects. Consequently, it is very often the case that the word 'weight' is used to describe what would be called 'mass' in mechanics. Since statistics is a practical subject, using data to solve problems from a wide variety of contexts, this practice is accepted in this book. So the terms 'weight' and 'mass' are used interchangeably and should be interpreted according to the situation.

Solution
Method 1

Table 4.4

	x	y	$x - \bar{x}$	$y - \bar{y}$	$(x - \bar{x})^2$	$(y - \bar{y})^2$	$(x - \bar{x})(y - \bar{y})$
	5	240	-2	12.8	4	163.84	-25.6
	5	232	-2	4.8	4	23.04	-9.6
	7	227	0	-0.2	0	0.04	0
	8	222	1	-5.2	1	27.04	-5.2
	10	215	3	-12.2	9	148.84	-36.6
Totals	35	1136	0	0	18	362.80	-77.0

$$\bar{x} = \frac{\Sigma x}{n} = \frac{35}{5} = 7$$

$$S_{xx} = \Sigma(x_i - \bar{x})^2 = 18$$

$$S_{xy} = \Sigma(x_i - \bar{x})(y_i - \bar{y}) = -77.0$$

$$\bar{y} = \frac{\Sigma y}{n} = \frac{1136}{5} = 227.2$$

$$S_{yy} = \Sigma(y_i - \bar{y})^2 = 362.80$$

$$r = \frac{S_{xy}}{\sqrt{S_{xx}S_{yy}}} = \frac{\Sigma(x_i - \bar{x})(y_i - \bar{y})}{\sqrt{\Sigma(x_i - \bar{x})^2 \times \Sigma(y_i - \bar{y})^2}}$$

$$= \frac{-77}{\sqrt{18 \times 362.8}}$$

$$= -0.953 \quad \text{(to 3 s.f.)}$$

Method 2

$n = 5$

Table 4.5

	x	y	x^2	y^2	xy
	5	240	25	57600	1200
	5	232	25	53824	1160
	7	227	49	51529	1589
	8	222	64	49284	1776
	10	215	100	46225	2150
Totals	35	1136	263	258462	7875

$$S_{xy} = \Sigma xy - n(\bar{x})(\bar{y})$$
$$= 7875 - 5 \times 7 \times 227.2$$
$$= -77$$

$$S_{yy} = \Sigma y^2 - n\bar{y}^2$$
$$= 258.462 - 5 \times 227.2^2$$
$$= 362.8$$

$$\bar{x} = \frac{\Sigma x}{n} = \frac{35}{5} = 7$$

$$S_{xx} = \Sigma x^2 - n\bar{x}^2 = 263 - 5 \times 7^2 = 18$$

$$\bar{y} = \frac{\Sigma y}{n} = \frac{1136}{5} = 227.2$$

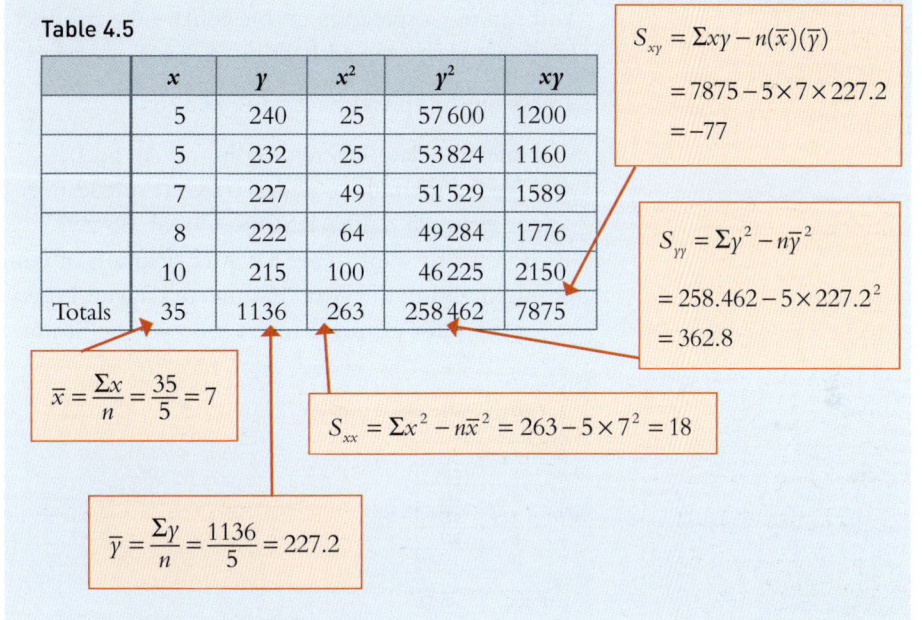

$$r = \frac{S_{xy}}{\sqrt{S_{xx}S_{yy}}} = \frac{\Sigma x_i y_i - n(\bar{x})(\bar{y})}{\sqrt{(\Sigma x_i^2 - n\bar{x}^2)(\Sigma y_i^2 - n\bar{y}^2)}}$$

$$= \frac{-77}{\sqrt{18 \times 362.8}}$$

$$= -0.953 \quad \text{(to 3 s.f.)}$$

Conclusion: There is very strong negative linear correlation between the variables. Large potatoes seem to be associated with small crop sizes.

Carrying out the calculation

Two methods of carrying out the calculation are shown here.

- Either method will give the correct value of the product moment correlation coefficient, r.
- Method 2 is generally used when the values of the data give 'awkward' values for the sample means, making the calculations in Method 1 rather unwieldy.
- Sometimes you are given summary data: $\Sigma x, \Sigma y, \Sigma x^2, \Sigma y^2, \Sigma xy$. In these cases Method 2 is the easier to use; it may be that your calculator has provided such summary data.

Product moment correlation

> However, if as in this case you are given the raw data, then the usual method of finding *r* is to use the statistical facilities on a calculator.
>
> Sometimes you are simply given summary statistics (values of Σx, Σx^2, Σxy, etc.) in which case you have to use the above formulae for S_{xx} etc.

USING ICT

A spreadsheet

You can use a spreadsheet to calculate the product moment correlation coefficient. The spreadsheet in Figure 4.11 shows the output for Example 4.1.

To set up the spreadsheet you need to:

1. Enter the data – here in columns A and B.
2. Use the formula provided by your spreadsheet to find the value of *r*, for example = PEARSON(A5:A9, B5:B9)
3. If you also want to see a scatter diagram of your data you can do this by highlighting the two columns of data and then choosing the relevant options, for example Insert followed by Scatter diagram.

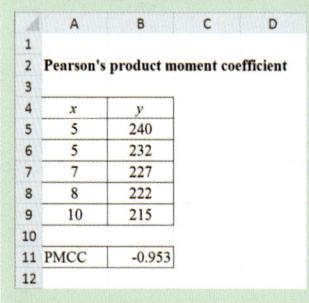

	A	B	C	D
1				
2	Pearson's product moment coefficient			
3				
4	*x*	*y*		
5	5	240		
6	5	232		
7	7	227		
8	8	222		
9	10	215		
10				
11	PMCC	-0.953		
12				

Figure 4.11

Interpreting the product moment correlation coefficient

The product moment correlation coefficient provides a measure of the correlation between the two variables. There are two different ways in which it is commonly used and interpreted: as a test statistic and as a measure of effect size.

Using *r* as a test statistic

When the data cover the whole of a population, the correlation coefficient tells you all that there is to be known about the level of correlation between the variables in the population. The population correlation coefficient is denoted by ρ.

> The symbol ρ is the Greek letter rho, pronounced 'row' as in 'row a boat'.

However, it is often the case that you do not know the level of correlation in a population and take a reasonably small sample to find out.

You use your sample data to calculate a value of the correlation coefficient, r. You know that if the value of r turns out to be close to +1 or −1, you can be reasonably confident that there is correlation, and that if r is close to 0 there is probably little or no correlation. What happens in a case such as r = 0.6?

To answer this question you have to understand what r is actually measuring. The data which you use when calculating r are actually a *sample* taken from a parent bivariate distribution, rather than the whole of a population. You have only taken a few out of a very large number of points which could, in theory, be plotted on a scatter diagram such as Figure 4.12. Each point (x_i, y_i) represents a possible pair of values corresponding to one observation of the bivariate population.

The blue crosses represent the whole population and the red dots represent the sample.

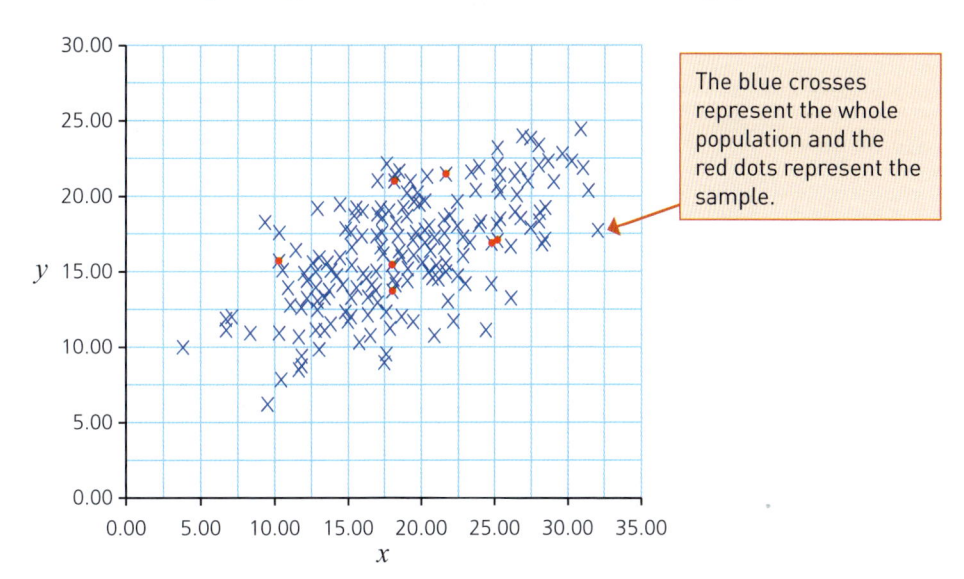

Figure 4.12 Scatter diagram showing a sample from a large bivariate population

There will be a level of correlation within the parent population and this is denoted by ρ.

The calculated value of r, which is based on the sample points, can be used as an estimate for ρ. It can also be used to carry out a hypothesis test on the value of ρ, the parent population correlation coefficient. Used in this way it is a *test statistic*.

The simplest hypothesis test which you can carry out is that there is no correlation within the parent population. This gives rise to a null hypothesis:

$H_0: \rho = 0$. There is no correlation between the two variables.

> **Note**
>
> It is also possible to test the null hypothesis that ρ has some other value, like 0.4, but such tests are beyond the scope of this book.

There are three possible alternative hypotheses, according to the sense of the situation you are investigating. These are:

1. $H_1: \rho \neq 0$. There is correlation between the variables (two-tailed test).
2. $H_1: \rho > 0$. There is positive correlation between the variables (one-tailed test).
3. $H_1: \rho < 0$. There is negative correlation between the variables (one-tailed test).

The test is carried out by comparing the value for r with the appropriate entry in a table of critical values. This will depend on the size of the sample, the significance level at which you are testing and whether your test is one-tailed or two-tailed.

Product moment correlation

Critical values

Under the null hypothesis, $H_0: \rho = 0$, i.e. when there is a complete absence of linear correlation between the variables in the *population*, it is very likely that a bivariate data set, drawn at random from the population, will produce a value of r, the *sample* product moment correlation coefficient, which is non-zero. This will be the case even if the null hypothesis is true.

The role of the significance level is that, for any sample size n, it represents the probability that the value of r will be 'further from zero' than the critical value. Three examples, using the table of critical values in Figure 4.13 (see following page) should help you to understand this concept better.

Table 4.6

Alternative hypothesis	Sample size, n	Significance level	Meaning
$H_1: \rho > 0$	11	1%	$P(r > 0.6851) = 0.01$
$H_1: \rho < 0$	6	5%	$P(r < -0.7293) = 0.05$
$H_1: \rho \neq 0$	15	10%	$P(|r| > 0.4409) = 0.1$

Example 4.2

Are students who are good at English also good at Mathematics?

A student believes that just because you are good at English, you are no more or less likely to be good at Mathematics. He obtains the results of an English examination and a Mathematics examination for eight students in his class. He then decides to carry out a hypothesis test to investigate whether he is correct.

The results of the two examinations for eight students are as follows.

Table 4.7

English, x	74	83	61	79	41	55	42	71
Mathematics, y	73	65	67	67	58	73	25	56

Solution

The relevant hypothesis test for this situation would be

$H_0: \rho = 0$. There is no correlation between English and Mathematics scores.

$H_1: \rho \neq 0$. There is correlation between English and Mathematics scores.

The student decides to use the 5% significance level.

The critical value for $n = 8$ at the 5% significance level for a two-tailed test is found from tables to be 0.7067.

	5%	2½%	1%	½%	one-tailed test
	10%	5%	2%	1%	two-tailed test

n				
1	-	-	-	-
2	-	-	-	-
3	0.9877	0.9969	0.9995	0.9999
4	0.9000	0.9500	0.9800	0.9900
5	0.8054	0.8783	0.9343	0.9587
6	0.7293	0.8114	0.8822	0.9172
7	0.6694	0.7545	0.8329	0.8745
8	0.6215	0.7067	0.7887	0.8343
9	0.5822	0.6664	0.7498	0.7977
10	0.5494	0.6319	0.7155	0.7646
11	0.5214	0.6021	0.6851	0.7348
12	0.4973	0.5760	0.6581	0.7079
13	0.4762	0.5529	0.6339	0.6835
14	0.4575	0.5324	0.6120	0.6614
15	0.4409	0.5140	0.5923	0.6411

Figure 4.13 Extract from table of values for the product moment correlation coefficient, r

The calculation of the product moment correlation coefficient, r, can be set out using *Method 2* from Example 4.1.

$n = 8$

Table 4.8

x	y	x^2	y^2	xy
74	73	5476	5329	5402
83	65	6889	4225	5395
61	67	3721	4489	4087
79	67	6241	4489	5293
41	58	1681	3364	2378
55	73	3025	5329	4015
42	25	1764	625	1050
71	56	5041	3136	3976
Totals 506	484	33838	30986	31596

$$\bar{x} = \frac{\Sigma x}{n} = \frac{506}{8} = 63.25 \quad \bar{y} = \frac{\Sigma y}{n} = \frac{484}{8} = 60.5$$

$$S_{xx} = \Sigma x^2 - n\bar{x}^2 = 33838 - 8 \times 63.25^2 = 1833.5$$

$$S_{yy} = \Sigma y^2 - n\bar{y}^2 = 30986 - 8 \times 60.5^2 = 1704$$

$$S_{xy} = \Sigma xy - n\bar{x}\bar{y} = 31596 - 8 \times 63.25 \times 60.5 = 983$$

$$r = \frac{S_{xy}}{\sqrt{S_{xx}S_{yy}}} = \frac{\Sigma x_i y_i - n(\bar{x})(\bar{y})}{\sqrt{\left(\Sigma x_i^2 - n\bar{x}^2\right)\left(\Sigma y_i^2 - n\bar{y}^2\right)}} = \frac{983}{\sqrt{1833.5 \times 1704}}$$

$$= 0.5561 \quad \text{(to 4 s.f.)}$$

Product moment correlation

> **Note**
> This example is designed just to show you how to do the calculations, and no more. A sample of size 8 is smaller than you would usually use. Also there is no indication of how the student chose the eight people in his sample. An essential requirement for a hypothesis test is that the sample is representative and usually a random sample is taken.

The critical value is 0.7067. The value of r of 0.5561 is less extreme.

So there is not enough evidence to reject the null hypothesis in favour of the alternative hypothesis.

The evidence does not suggest that the student's suggestion is wrong.

USING ICT

You can use ICT to find the correlation coefficient and also to find the p-value for the test.

Figure 4.13 shows the output from a statistical package for the data in Example 4.2. You enter the correlation coefficient, the sample size and whether the test is one- or two-tailed (and the direction if one-tailed). The software then gives you the p-value as shown in Figure 4.14.

```
From Summary Statistics                          Test Correlation
First Attribute (numeric): unassigned
Second Attribute (numeric): unassigned

Sample count: 8
The observed correlation between X and Y is 0.5561

Null hypothesis: The population correlation is 0.
Alternative hypothesis: The population correlation is not equal to 0.

The test statistic, Student's t, is 1.639. There are 6 degrees of freedom (two less
than the sample size).

If it were true that the population correlation between X and Y were equal to 0
(the null hypothesis), and the sampling process were performed repeatedly, the
probability of getting a value for Student's t with an absolute value this great
or greater would be 0.15.
```

> You can use a t test to test significance of a correlation coefficient by applying an appropriate transformation.

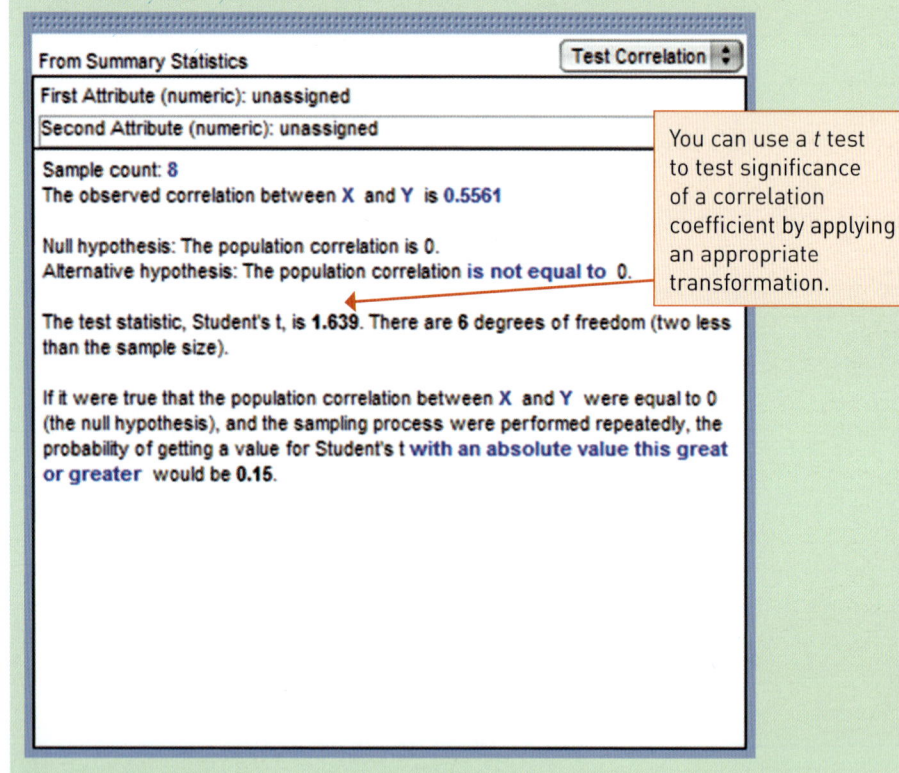

Figure 4.14

The p-value is 0.15 which is greater than 5% so there is not enough evidence to reject the null hypothesis.

> ! Hypothesis tests using Pearson's product moment correlation coefficient require modelling assumptions that both variables are *random* and that the data are drawn from a *bivariate Normal* distribution. For large data sets this is usually the case if the scatter diagram gives an approximately elliptical distribution. If one or both of the distributions is, for example, skewed or bimodal, the procedure is likely to be inaccurate.
>
> - The product moment correlation coefficient is a measure of correlation and so is only appropriate if the relationship between the variables is linear. For cases of non-linear association you should apply a test based on Spearman's correlation coefficient, which you will meet later in this chapter.
>
> - The extract from the tables gives the critical value of *r* for various values of the significance level and the sample size, *n*. You will, however, find some tables where *n* is replaced by υ, the *degrees of freedom*. Degrees of freedom are covered in the next section.

Degrees of freedom

Here is an example where you have just two data points.

Table 4.9

	Sean	Iain
Height of an adult man (m)	1.7	1.90
The mortgage on his house (£)	15 000	45 000

When you plot these two points on a scatter diagram it is possible to join them with a perfect straight line and you might be tempted to conclude that taller men have larger mortgages on their houses.

This conclusion would clearly be wrong. It is based on the data from only two men so you are bound to be able to join the points on the scatter diagram with a straight line and calculate *r* to be either +1 or −1 (providing their heights and/or mortgages are not the same). In order to start to carry out a test you need the data for a third man, say Dafyd (height 1.75 m and mortgage £37 000). When his data are plotted on the scatter diagram in Figure 4.15 you can see how close it lies to the line between Sean and Iain.

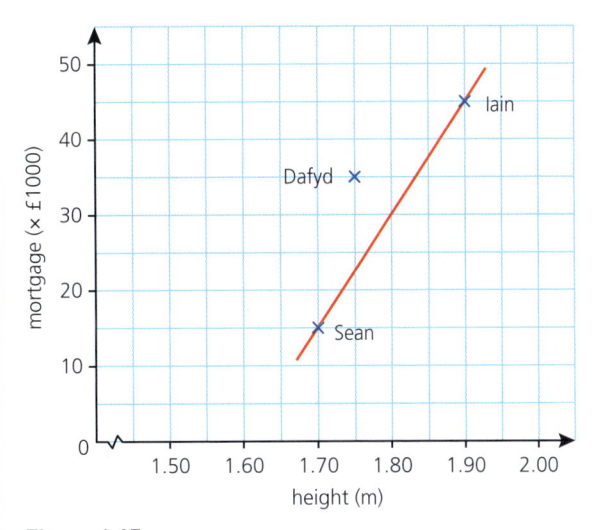

Figure 4.15

So the first two data points do not count towards a test for linear correlation. The first one to count is point number three. Similarly, if you have *n* points, only $n - 2$ of them count towards any test. $n - 2$ is called the *degrees of freedom* and denoted by υ. It is the number of free variables in the system. In this case, it is the number of points, *n*, less the 2 that have effectively been used to define the line of best fit.

In the case of the three men with their mortgages you would actually draw a line of best fit through all three, rather than join any particular two. So you cannot say that any two particular points have been taken out to draw the line of best fit, merely that the system as a whole has lost two.

Tables of critical values of correlation coefficients can be used without understanding the idea of degrees of freedom, but the idea is an important one throughout statistics. In general,

degrees of freedom = sample size − number of restrictions.

Product moment correlation

Interpreting correlation

You need to be on your guard against drawing spurious conclusions from significant correlation coefficients.

Correlation does not imply causation

Figures for the years 1995–2005 show a high correlation between the sales of laptop computers and sales of microwave ovens. There is, of course, no direct connection between the two variables. You would be quite wrong to conclude that buying a laptop computer predisposes the buyer to buying a microwave oven.

Although there may be a high level of correlation between variables A and B it does not mean that A causes B or that B causes A. It may well be that a third variable C causes both A and B, or it may be that there is a more complicated set of relationships. In the case of laptop computers and microwaves, both are clearly caused by the advance of modern technology.

Non-linear association

A low value of r tells you that there is little or no correlation. There are, however, other forms of association, including non-linear as illustrated in Figure 4.16.

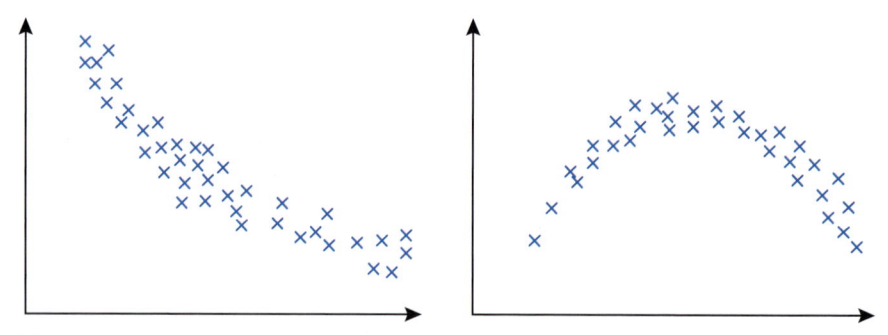

Figure 4.16 Scatter diagrams showing non-linear association

These diagrams show that there is an association between the variables, but not one that can be described as correlation.

Extrapolation

A linear relationship established over a particular domain should not be assumed to hold outside this range. For instance, there is strong correlation between the age in years and the 100 m times of female athletes between the ages of 10 and 20 years. To extend the connection, as shown in Figure 4.17, would suggest that veteran athletes are quicker than athletes who are in their prime and, if they live long enough, can even run 100 m in no time at all!

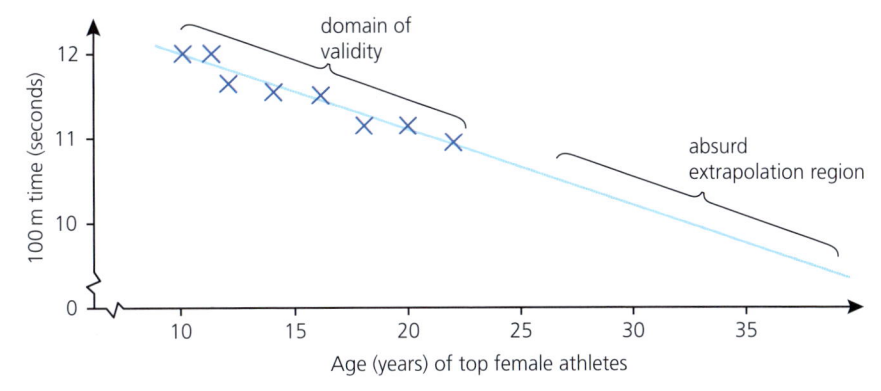

Figure 4.17

Effect size

For very large sample sizes, a very small but non-zero value of r may still be statistically significant. The null hypothesis may be rejected and the alternative hypothesis accepted. Although the result is statistically significant, there may be no real significance in terms of the use to be made of this correlation.

This is a common situation with big data where the calculation is carried out by computer and might cover millions of data items. Such data sets are often not just bivariate but multivariate covering many fields. It is quite common to find unexpected correlations but at a low level, say less than 0.1, as well as those expected at a higher level, say 0.5.

For example, suppose that there is a small but statistically significant correlation between height and intelligence. This may be of academic interest, but little use can be made of this for any practical purpose such as in selecting candidates for a job.

Effect sizes can be calculated for any significance test, but are only considered in the context of correlation in this book. One common way of judging effect size was formulated by Jacob Cohen in 1988. Cohen gave suggestions for interpreting these effect sizes, suggesting that a correlation coefficient r of 0.1 represents a small effect size, 0.3 represents a medium effect size and 0.5 represents a large effect size.

Example 4.3

The correlation matrix below shows the correlation between the four variables in the example at the start of the chapter, but for all countries in the world rather than just American countries. The four variables are population (P), life expectancy (L), birth rate (B) and GDP per capita (G).

Use Cohen's interpretation to comment on the levels of correlation.

Table 4.10

	P	L	B	G
P	1			
L	−0.017	1		
B	−0.025	−0.844	1	
G	−0.071	0.633	−0.579	1

Product moment correlation

Solution

All of the effect sizes involving population are small.

All the other effect sizes are large.

The greatest correlation is between life expectancy and birth rate. This is negative, meaning that on the whole countries with a high life expectancy tend to have a low birth rate, and vice-versa.

Exercise 4.1

①

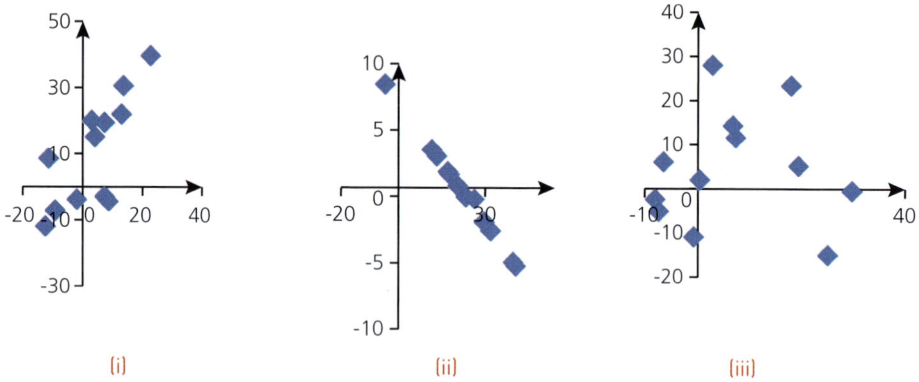

(i) (ii) (iii)

Figure 4.18

Three sets of bivariate data have been plotted on scatter diagrams, as illustrated. In each diagram the product moment correlation coefficient takes one of the values −1, −0.8, 0, 0.8, 1. Without doing any calculations, state the appropriate value of the correlation coefficient corresponding to the scatter diagrams (i), (ii) and (iii) in Figure 4.18.

② For each of the sets of data (i), (ii) and (iii) in Tables 4.11–4.13
  (a) draw a scatter diagram and comment on whether there appears to be any linear correlation.
  (b) calculate the product moment correlation coefficient and compare this with your assertion based on the scatter diagram.
  (i) The mathematics and physics test results of 14 students.

Table 4.11

Mathematics	45	23	78	91	46	27	41	62	34	17	77	49	55	71
Physics	62	36	92	70	67	39	61	40	55	33	65	59	35	40

  (ii) The wine consumption in a country in millions of litres and the years 1993 to 2000.

Table 4.12

Year	1993	1994	1995	1996	1997	1998	1999	2000
Consumption (×10^6 litres)	35.5	37.7	41.5	46.4	44.8	45.8	53.9	62.0

(iii) The number of hours of sunshine and the monthly rainfall, in centimetres, in an eight-month period.

Table 4.13

	Jan	Feb	Mar	Apr	May	Jun	Jul	Aug
Sunshine (hours)	90	96	105	110	113	120	131	124
Rainfall (cm)	5.1	4.6	6.3	5.1	3.3	2.8	4.5	4.0

③ For each of these sets of data use one or more of the following to find the product moment correlation coefficient, r (note that the data for part (iv) are given in the form of a scatter diagram).

- a scientific calculator in two variable statistics mode
- a graphics calculator in two variable statistics mode
- a spreadsheet.

(i)

Table 4.14

x	10	11	12	13	14	15	16	17
y	19	16	28	20	31	19	32	35

(ii)

Table 4.15

x	12	14	14	15	16	17	17	19
y	86	90	78	71	77	69	80	73

(iii)

Table 4.16

x	56	78	14	80	34	78	23	61
y	45	34	67	70	42	18	25	50

(iv)

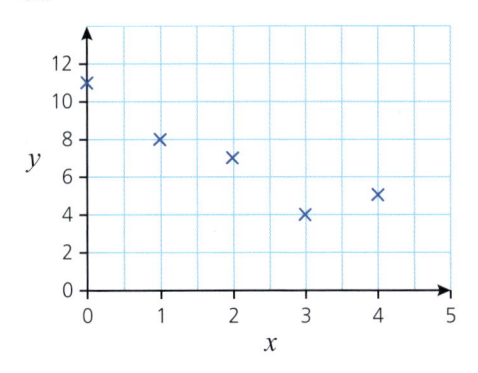

Figure 4.19

④ Find the value of r in each case below. The tables of values are not complete but, in each case, summary statistics are given for all of the data.

(i) The annual salary, in thousands of pounds, and the average number of hours worked per week by people chosen at random.

Product moment correlation

Table 4.17

Salary (× £1000)	5	7	13
Hours worked per week	18	22	35

$\Sigma x = 105, \Sigma y = 217, \Sigma x^2 = 3003, \Sigma y^2 = 7093, \Sigma xy = 3415, n = 7.$

(ii) The mean temperature in degrees Celsius and the amount of ice-cream sold in a supermarket in hundreds of litres.

Table 4.18

	Apr	May	Jun	Jul
Mean temperature (°C)	9	13	14	17
Ice-cream sold (100l)	11	15	17	20

$\Sigma x = 108, \Sigma y = 117, \Sigma x^2 = 1506, \Sigma y^2 = 1921, \Sigma xy = 1660, n = 8.$

(iii) The reaction times of women of various ages.

Table 4.19

Reaction time (×10⁻³ s)	156	165	149	180	189
Age (years)	36	40	27	50	49

$\Sigma x = 1432, \Sigma y = 337, \Sigma x^2 = 259680, \Sigma y^2 = 15089, \Sigma xy = 61717, n = 8.$

5. A language teacher wishes to test whether students who are good at their own language are also likely to be good at a foreign language. Accordingly, she collects the marks of eight students, all native English speakers, in their end of year examinations in English and French.

Table 4.20

Candidate	A	B	C	D	E	F	G	H
English	65	34	48	72	58	63	26	80
French	74	49	45	80	63	72	12	75

(i) Calculate the product moment correlation coefficient.

(ii) State the null and alternative hypotheses.

(iii) Using the correlation coefficient as a test statistic, carry out the test at the 5% significance level.

6. 'You can't win without scoring goals.' So says the coach of a netball team. Jamila, who believes in solid defensive play, disagrees and sets out to prove that there is no correlation between scoring goals and winning matches. She collects the following data for the goals scored and the points gained by 12 teams in a netball league.

Table 4.21

Goals scored, x	41	50	54	47	47	49	52	61	50	29	47	35
Points gained, y	21	20	19	18	16	14	12	11	11	7	5	2

(i) Calculate the product moment correlation coefficient.

(ii) State suitable null and alternative hypotheses, indicating whose position each represents.

(iii) Carry out the hypothesis test at the 5% significance level and comment on the result.

⑦ A medical student is trying to estimate the birth mass of babies using pre-natal scan images. The actual mass, x kg, and the estimated mass, y kg, of ten randomly selected babies are given in Table 4.22. The data are plotted in the scatter diagram.

Table 4.22

x	2.61	2.73	2.87	2.96	3.05	3.14	3.17	3.24	3.76	4.10
y	3.2	2.6	3.5	3.1	2.8	2.7	3.4	3.3	4.4	4.1

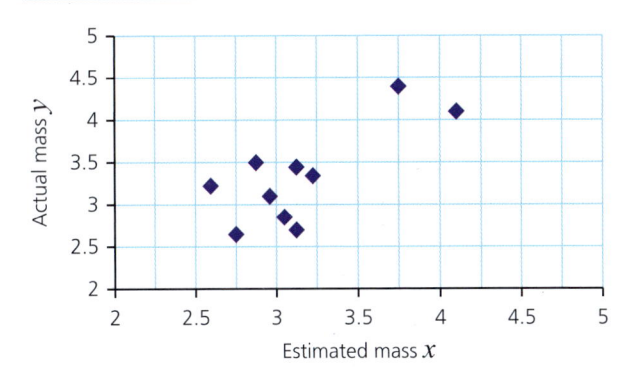

Figure 4.20

(i) The student decides to carry out a test based on the product moment correlation coefficient to investigate whether there is a positive relationship between the two variables. A friend suggests that there are two outliers so this test would not be appropriate. Explain why it may still be valid to carry out the test.

(ii) The value of the product moment correlation coefficient for these data is 0.7604. Carry out the test at the 1% significance level. [MEI]

⑧ It is widely believed that those who are good at chess are good at bridge, and vice-versa. A commentator decides to test this theory using as data the grades of a random sample of eight people who play both games.

Table 4.23

Player	A	B	C	D	E	F	G	H
Chess grade	160	187	129	162	149	151	189	158
Bridge grade	75	100	75	85	80	70	95	80

(i) Calculate the product moment correlation coefficient.

(ii) State suitable null and alternative hypotheses.

(iii) The output in Figure 4.21 over the page comes from a statistical package. Using the p-value given at the bottom of the figure, complete the hypothesis test.

Product moment correlation

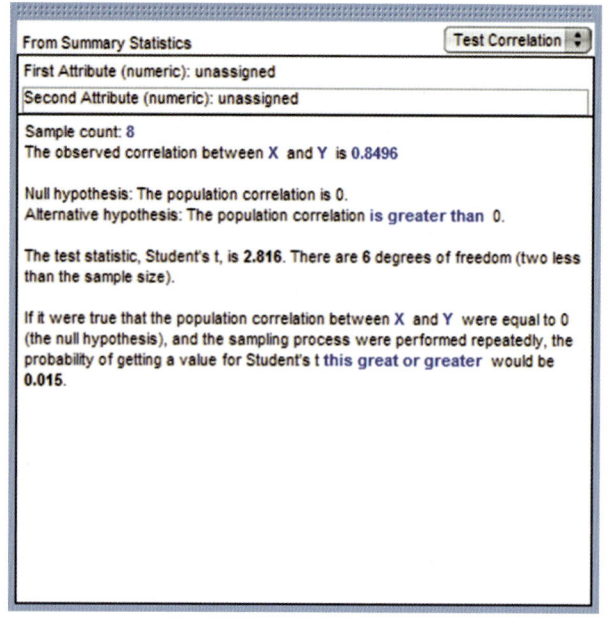

```
From Summary Statistics                    Test Correlation
First Attribute (numeric): unassigned
Second Attribute (numeric): unassigned

Sample count: 8
The observed correlation between X and Y is 0.8496

Null hypothesis: The population correlation is 0.
Alternative hypothesis: The population correlation is greater than 0.

The test statistic, Student's t, is 2.816. There are 6 degrees of freedom (two less
than the sample size).

If it were true that the population correlation between X and Y were equal to 0
(the null hypothesis), and the sampling process were performed repeatedly, the
probability of getting a value for Student's t this great or greater would be
0.015.
```

Figure 4.21

9 The correlation matrix below shows the correlation between NVR (non-verbal reasoning), VR (verbal reasoning) and Q (quantitative reasoning) scores for a large group of students. The scores are obtained from tests given to the students on each of the areas.

Table 4.24

	VR	NVR	Q
VR	1		
NVR	0.21575396	1	
Q	0.164106922	0.2393041	1

(i) Use Cohen's interpretation to comment on the levels of correlation.

(ii) A teacher at the school suggests that as there is correlation between the scores, there is no point in giving the next intake of students all three tests but just give the verbal reasoning test and predict the results of the others from that one. Comment on this suggestion.

10 A biologist believes that a particular type of fish develops black spots on its scales in water that is polluted by certain agricultural fertilisers. She catches a number of fish; for each one she counts the number of black spots on its scales and measures the concentration of the pollutant in the water it was swimming in. She uses these data to test for positive linear correlation between the number of spots and the level of pollution.

Table 4.25

Fish	A	B	C	D	E	F	G	H	I	J
Pollutant concentration (parts per million)	124	59	78	79	150	12	23	45	91	68
Number of black spots	15	8	7	8	14	0	4	5	8	8

(i) Calculate the product moment correlation coefficient.

(ii) State suitable null and alternative hypotheses.

(iii) Carry out the hypothesis test at the 2% significance level. What can the biologist conclude?

11. The correlation matrix below shows the correlation between four variables in different districts of a large city. The four variables are life expectancy (L), infant mortality (M), average income (A) and a measure of income inequality (I).

    Use Cohen's interpretation to comment on the levels of correlation.

    Table 4.26

	L	M	A	I
L	1			
M	0.37	1		
A	−0.23	0.17	1	
I	0.06	−0.19	0.46	1

12. Andrew claims that the older you get, the slower is your reaction time. His mother disagrees, saying the two are unrelated. They decide that the only way to settle the discussion is to carry out a proper test. A few days later they are having a small party and so ask their 12 guests to take a test that measures their reaction times. The results are as follows.

    Table 4.27

Age	Reaction time (s)	Age	Reaction time (s)
78	0.8	35	0.5
72	0.6	30	0.3
60	0.7	28	0.4
56	0.5	20	0.4
41	0.5	19	0.3
39	0.4	10	0.3

    Carry out the test at the 5% significance level, stating the null and alternative hypotheses. Who won the argument, Andrew or his mother?

13. The teachers at a school have a discussion as to whether girls, in general, run faster or slower as they get older. They decide to collect data for a random sample of girls the next time the school cross country race is held (which everybody has to take part in). They collect the following data, with the times given in minutes and the ages in years (the conversion from months to decimal parts of a year has already been carried out).

    Table 4.28

Age	Time	Age	Time	Age	Time
11.6	23.1	18.2	45.	13.9	29.1
15.0	24.0	15.4	23.2	18.1	21.2
18.8	45.0	14.4	26.1	13.4	23.9
16.0	25.2	16.1	29.4	16.2	26.0
12.8	26.4	14.6	28.1	17.5	23.4
17.6	22.9	18.7	45.0	17.0	25.0
17.4	27.1	15.4	27.0	12.5	26.3
13.2	25.2	11.8	25.4	12.7	24.2
14.5	26.8				

Product moment correlation

(i) State suitable null and alternative hypotheses and decide on an appropriate significance level for the test.

(ii) Calculate the product moment correlation coefficient and state the conclusion from the test.

(iii) Plot the data on a scatter diagram and identify any outliers. Explain how they could have arisen.

(iv) Comment on the validity of the test.

⑭ Apprentices joining a large company are given several tests. Two of the tests are 'Basic English' and 'Manual dexterity'. The results of these tests are labelled x and y respectively. A manager believes that there will be positive correlation between x and y.

The spreadsheet shows the first 3rd and 60th rows of data, together with the sums of each of the 5 columns.

	A	B	C	D	E	F
1		x	y	x^2	y^2	xy
2		119	118	14161	13924	14042
3		112	116	12544	13456	12992
4		116	108	13456	11664	12528
61		115	118	13225	13924	13570
62	SUM	7105	7132	846357	853620	846371

Figure 4.22

(i) Explain how you can tell that the value of n is 60.

(ii) State the formula in cell B62.

(iii) Find the values of S_{xx}, S_{yy} and S_{xy}.

(iv) Find the value of r.

(v) State suitable null and alternative hypotheses for a test to investigate the manager's belief.

(vi) Carry out the hypothesis test at the 5% significance level.

(vii) Comment on the effect size.

(viii) Do you think that this information can be of any use to the company?

⑮ The values of x and y in the table are the marks obtained in an intelligence test and a university examination, respectively, by 20 medical students. The data are plotted in the scatter diagram.

Table 4.29

x	98	51	71	57	44	59	75	47	39	58
y	85	40	30	25	50	40	50	35	25	90
x	77	65	58	66	79	72	45	40	49	76
y	65	25	70	45	70	50	40	20	30	60

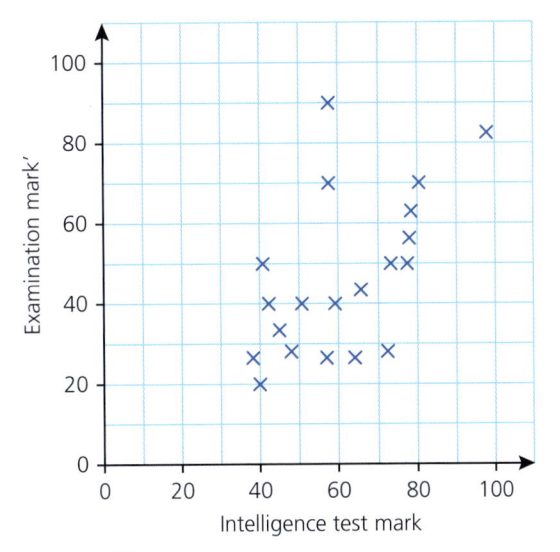

Figure 4.23

Given that $\Sigma x = 1226$, $\Sigma y = 945$, $\Sigma x^2 = 79732$, $\Sigma y^2 = 52575$ and $\Sigma xy = 61495$, calculate the product moment correlation coefficient, r, to 2 decimal places.

Referring to the evidence provided by the diagram and the value of r, comment briefly on the correlation between the two sets of marks.

Now eliminate from consideration those ten students whose values of x are less than 50 or more than 75. Calculate the new value of r for the marks of the remaining students. What does the comparison with the earlier value of r seem to indicate? [MEI]

⑯ A random sample of students who are shortly to sit an examination are asked to keep a record of how long they spend revising, in order to investigate whether more revision time is associated with a higher mark. The data are given below, with x hours being the revision time (correct to the nearest half hour) and $y\%$ being the mark scored in the examination.

Table 4.30

x	0	3	4.5	3.5	7	5.5	5	6.5	6	10.5	2
y	36	52	52	57	60	61	63	63	64	70	89

(i) Obtain the value of the product moment correlation coefficient for the data.

(ii) Specify appropriate null and alternative hypotheses, and carry out a suitable test at the 5% level of significance.

(iii) Without further calculation, state the effect of the datum $x = 2$, $y = 89$ on the value of the product moment correlation coefficient. Explain whether or not this point should be excluded when carrying out the hypothesis test. [MEI]

⑰ In order to investigate the strength of the correlation between the value of a house and the value of the householder's car, a random sample of householders was questioned. The resulting data are shown in the table, the units being thousands of pounds.

Product moment correlation

Table 4.31

x	220	212	102	188	132	52	144	102	106	266
y	24	19	4.8	8.4	8.2	0.6	6.4	12	15.6	30

(i) Represent the data graphically.

(ii) Calculate the product moment correlation coefficient.

(iii) Carry out a suitable hypothesis test, at a suitable level of significance, to determine whether or not it is reasonable to suppose that the value of a house is positively correlated with the value of the householder's car.

(iv) A student argues that when two variables are correlated one must be the cause of the other. Briefly discuss this view with regard to the data in this question.
[MEI]

⑱ The table below gives the heights, h, of six male Olympic 100m sprint winners together with the times, t, they took.

Table 4.32

h	1.80	1.83	1.87	1.88	1.85	1.76
t	10.00	9.95	10.06	9.99	9.84	9.87

(i) Draw a scatter diagram to illustrate the data.

(ii) Calculate the product moment correlation coefficient.

(iii) Carry out a suitable hypothesis test, at a suitable level of significance, to determine whether or not it is reasonable to suppose that the heights and times are positively correlated.

(iv) Rewrite the table giving just the rank of each data value, using a rank of 1 for the lowest value and 6 for the highest value. For example the rank associated with a height of 1.88 m would be 6 since it is the height of the tallest person. The rank associated with a time of 9.87 s would be 2 since it is the second lowest time.

(v) Calculate the product moment correlation coefficient of the ranked data.

(vi) Comment on the difference between the two correlation coefficients.

⑲ (i) Prove algebraically that these two formulae for S_{xx} are equivalent

$$S_{xx} = \Sigma(x_i - \bar{x})^2 \qquad S_{xx} = \Sigma x^2 - n\bar{x}^2$$

(ii) Prove algebraically these two formulae for S_{xy} are equivalent

$$S_{xy} = \Sigma(x_i - \bar{x})(y_i - \bar{y}) \qquad S_{xy} = \Sigma xy - n\bar{x}\bar{y}$$

(iii) Hence prove that these two formulae for r are equivalent

$$r = \frac{\Sigma(x_i - \bar{x})(y_i - \bar{y})}{\sqrt{\Sigma(x_i - \bar{x})^2 \times \Sigma(y_i - \bar{y})^2}} \qquad r = \frac{\Sigma x_i y_i - n(\bar{x})(\bar{y})}{\sqrt{(\Sigma x_i^2 - n\bar{x}^2)(\Sigma y_i^2 - n\bar{y}^2)}}$$

4 Rank correlation

Dance competition dispute

In the dance competition at the local fete last Saturday, the two judges differed so much in their rankings of the ten competitors that initially nobody could be declared the winner. In the end, competitor C was declared the winner as the total of her ranks was the lowest (and so the best) but several of the other entrants felt that it was totally unfair.

The judgements that caused all the trouble were as follows.

Table 4.33

Competitor	A	B	C	D	E	F	G	H	I	J
Judge 1	1	9	7	2	3	10	6	5	4	8
Judge 2	8	3	1	10	9	4	7	6	5	2
Total	9	12	⑧	12	12	14	13	11	9	10

Winner

You will see that both judges ranked the ten entrants, 1st, 2nd, 3rd, … , 10th. The winner, C, was placed 7th by one judge and 1st by the other. Their rankings look different so perhaps they were using different criteria on which to assess them. How can you use these data to decide whether that was or was not the case?

One way would be to calculate a correlation coefficient and use it to carry out a hypothesis test. However, the data you have are of a different type from any that you have used before for calculating correlation coefficients. In the point (1, 8), corresponding to competitor A, the numbers 1 and 8 are *ranks* and not scores (like marks in an examination or measurements). It is, however, possible to calculate a **rank correlation coefficient** in the same way as before. Rank correlation may be used in circumstances where ordinary correlation would not be appropriate and so is described as testing *association* rather than correlation.

The hypotheses for this test are stated as follows:

H_0: there is no association.

H_1: there is positive association.

The null hypothesis, H_0, represents the idea that the judges are using completely different unrelated criteria to judge the competitors. The alternative hypothesis represents the idea that the judges are using similar criteria to judge the competitors.

ACTIVITY 4.1

Show that the product moment correlation coefficient of the ranks in the table above is −0.794.

You probably have used the method illustrated in Example 4.1 on pages 82 and 83 to carry out the Activity above. However, the calculation is usually done in a different way, as follows.

Denoting the two sets of ranks by $x_1, x_2, …, x_n$ and $y_1, y_2, …, y_n$, the coefficient of association is given by

Rank correlation

$$r_s = 1 - \frac{6\Sigma d_i^2}{n(n^2-1)}$$

where

- r_s is called Spearman's rank correlation coefficient
- d_i is the difference in the ranks for a general data item (x_i, y_i); $d_i = x_i - y_i$
- n is the number of items of data.

The calculation of Σd_i^2 can then be set out in a table like this.

Table 4.34

Competitor	Judge 1, x_i	Judge 2, y_i	$d_i = x_i - y_i$	d_i^2
A	1	8	−7	49
B	9	3	6	36
C	7	1	6	36
D	2	10	−8	64
E	3	9	−6	36
F	10	4	6	36
G	6	7	−1	1
H	5	6	−1	1
I	4	5	−1	1
J	8	2	6	36
			Σd_i^2	296

The value of n is 10, so $r_s = 1 - \frac{6 \times 296}{10(10^2 - 1)} = -0.794$

You will see that this is the same answer as before, but the working is much shorter. It is not difficult to prove that the two methods are equivalent.

> **Note**
>
> If several items are ranked equally you give them the mean of the ranks they would have had if they had been slightly different from each other.

Hypothesis tests using Spearman's rank correlation coefficient

Spearman's rank correlation coefficient is often used as a test statistic for a hypothesis test of

H_0: there is no association between the variables

against one of three possible alternative hypotheses:

either H_1: there is association between the variables (two-tailed test)

or H_1: there is positive association between the variables (one-tailed test)

or H_1: there is negative association between the variables (one-tailed test).

The test is carried out by comparing the value of r_s with the appropriate critical value. This depends on the sample size, the significance level of the test and whether it is one-tailed or two-tailed. Critical values can be found from statistical software or tables.

Once you have found the value of r_s, this test follows the same procedure as that for correlation. However, the tables of critical values are not the same and so you need to be careful that you are using the right one.

The calculation is often carried out with the data across the page rather than in columns and this is shown in the next example.

Example 4.4

During their course two trainee tennis coaches, Rachael and Leroy, were shown videos of seven people, A, B, C, ... , G, doing a top-spin service and were asked to rank them in order according to the quality of their style. They placed them as follows.

Table 4.34

Rank order	1	2	3	4	5	6	7
Rachael	B	G	F	D	A	C	E
Leroy	F	B	D	E	G	A	C

(i) Find Spearman's coefficient of rank correlation.

(ii) Use it to test whether there is evidence, at the 5% level, of positive association between their judgements.

Solution

(i) The rankings are as follows.

Table 4.35

Person	A	B	C	D	E	F	G
Rachael	5	1	6	4	7	3	2
Leroy	6	2	7	3	4	1	5
d_i	-1	-1	-1	1	3	2	-3
d_i^2	1	1	1	1	9	4	9

$n = 7 \qquad \Sigma d_i^2 = 26$

$$r_s = 1 - \frac{6\Sigma d_i^2}{n(n^2 - 1)} = 1 - \frac{6 \times 26}{7(7^2 - 1)}$$

$$= 0.54 \text{ (2 d.p.)}$$

(ii) H_0: there is no association between their rankings.

H_1: there is positive association between their rankings.

Significance level 5%

One-tailed test.

From tables, the critical value of r_s for a one-tailed test at this significance level for $n = 7$ is 0.7143.

0.54 < 0.7143 so H_0 is accepted.

	5%	2½%	1%	½%	one-tailed test
	10%	5%	2%	1%	two-tailed test
n					
1	-	-	-	-	
2	-	-	-	-	
3	-	-	-	-	
4	1.0000	-	-	-	
5	0.9000	1.0000	1.0000	-	
6	0.8286	0.8857	0.9429	1.0000	
7	0.7143	0.7857	0.8929	0.9286	
8	0.6429	0.7381	0.8333	0.8810	
9	0.6000	0.7000	0.7833	0.8333	
10	0.5636	0.6485	0.7455	0.7939	

Figure 4.24 Extract from table of critical values for Spearman's rank correlation coefficient, r_s

There is insufficient evidence to claim positive association between Rachael's and Leroy's rankings.

Rank correlation

💻 USING ICT

You can use ICT to find the correlation coefficient and also to find the *p*-value for the test.

Figure 4.25 shows the output from a statistical package for the data in Example 4.4. You enter the data and the software produces the output shown in Figure 4.25

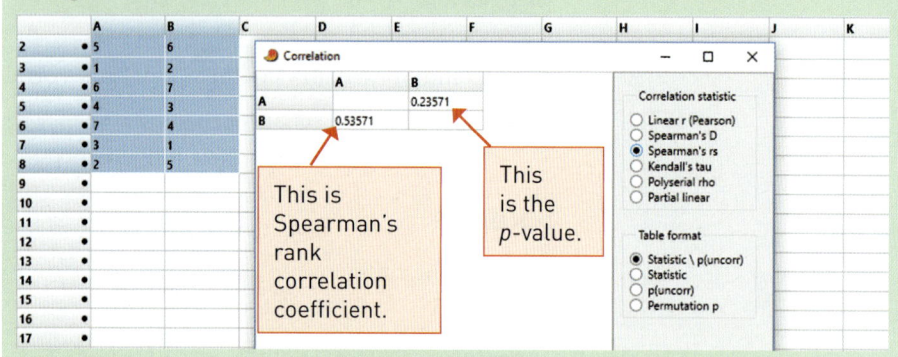

Figure 4.25

The *p*-value is 0.23571. However, because the test is one-tailed you have to divide this by 2 before comparing with the significance level. This gives approximately 0.118 which is greater than 0.05 or 5% so there is not enough evidence to reject the null hypothesis.

When to use rank correlation

Sometimes your data will be available in two forms, as values of variables or in rank order. If you have the choice you will usually work out the correlation coefficient from the variable values rather than the ranks.

It may well be the case, however, that only ranked data are available to you and, in that case, you have no choice but to use them. It may also be that, while you could collect variable values as well, it would not be worth the time, trouble or expense to do so.

Pearson's product moment correlation coefficient is a measure of correlation and so is not appropriate for non-linear data like those illustrated in the scatter diagram in Figure 4.26. You may, however, use rank correlation to investigate whether one variable generally increases (or decreases) as the other increases. The term *association* describes such a relationship.

> **Note**
>
> Spearman's rank correlation coefficient provides one among many statistical tests that can be carried out on ranks rather than variable values. Such tests are examples of *non-parametric tests*. A non-parametric test is a test on some aspect of a distribution which is not specified by its defining parameters.

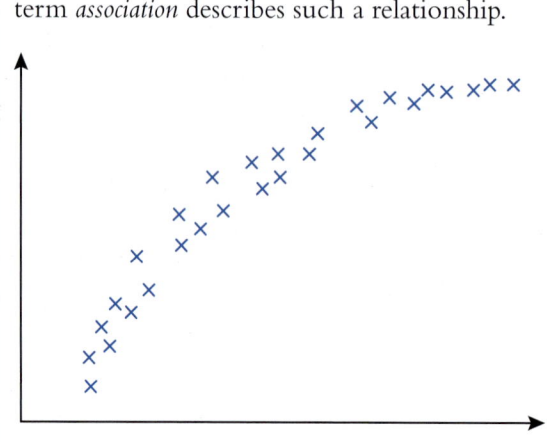

Figure 4.26 Non-linear data with a high degree of rank correlation

> **Note**
> It makes no assumptions about the population.

You should, however, always look at the sense of your data before deciding which is the more appropriate form of correlation to use.

If the value of r_s is close to 1 then in general the rankings are in agreement. If the value of r_s is close to −1 then in general the rankings are in *disagreement* – low rankings in one set correspond to high rankings in the other, and vice versa. If the value of r_s is close to 0 then the rankings have little relationship – there is neither agreement nor disagreement.

Historical note

Karl Pearson was one of the founders of modern statistics. Born in 1857, he was a man of varied interests and practised law for three years before being appointed Professor of Applied Mathematics and Mechanics at University College, London in 1884. Pearson made contributions to various branches of Mathematics but is particularly remembered for his work on the application of statistics to biological problems in heredity and evolution. He died in 1936.

Charles Spearman was born in London in 1863. After serving 14 years in the army as a cavalry officer, he went to Leipzig to study psychology. On completing his doctorate there he became a lecturer, and soon afterwards a professor also at University College, London. He pioneered the application of statistical techniques within psychology and developed the technique known as factor analysis in order to analyse different aspects of human ability. He died in 1945.

Exercise 4.2

① The order of merit of ten individuals at the start and finish of a training course were as follows.

Table 4.36

Individual	A	B	C	D	E	F	G	H	I	J
Order at start	1	2	3	4	5	6	7	8	9	10
Order at finish	5	3	1	9	2	6	4	7	10	8

Find Spearman's coefficient of rank correlation between the two orders.

② A sports coach obtained scores by nine athletes in two competitions (A and B). The maximum score in each competition was 12. The scores were as follows.

Table 4.37

Entrant	1	2	3	4	5	6	7	8	9
A score	9	2	12	5	3	7	10	6	8
B score	8	7	6	4	9	10	11	3	5

The spreadsheet shows this data together with partially completed working to calculate Spearman's coefficient of rank correlation.

	A	B	C	D	E	F	G
1	Entrant	A score	B score	Rank A	Rank B	$d_i = x_i - y_i$	d_i^2
2	1	9	8	7	6	1	1
3	2	2	7	1	5	-4	16
4	3	12	6	9	4	5	25
5	4	5	4				
6	5	3	9			-5	25
7	6	7	10				
8	7	10	11				
9	8	6	3			3	9
10	9	8	5				

Figure 4.27

Rank correlation

Complete the spreadsheet and hence find Spearman's coefficient of rank correlation between the two orders. You can use the spreadsheet to find the ranks. First you highlight rows 2 to 10. You then sort on column B. You then put the numbers 1 to 9 in column D. You again highlight rows 2 to 10 and now sort on column C. You then put the numbers 1 to 9 in column E. Finally again highlight rows 2 to 10 and sort on column A.

③ Find Spearman's coefficient of rank correlation between the two variables x and y shown in the scatter diagram.

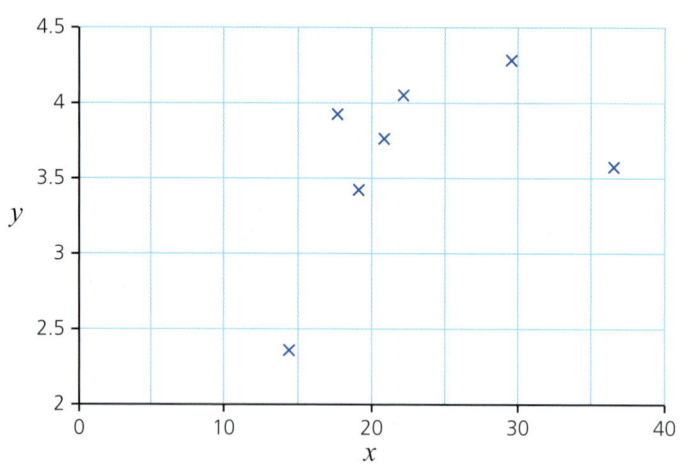

Figure 4.28

④ In a driving competition, there were eight contestants and two judges who placed them in rank order, as shown in the table below.

Table 4.38

Competitor	A	B	C	D	E	F	G	H
Judge X	2	5	6	1	8	4	7	3
Judge Y	1	6	8	3	7	2	4	5

Stating suitable null and alternative hypotheses, carry out a hypothesis test on the level of agreement of these two judges.

⑤ A coach wanted to test his theory that, although athletes have specialisms, it is still true that those who run fast at one distance are also likely to run fast at another distance. He selected six athletes at random to take part in a test and invited them to compete over 100 m and over 1500 m.

The times and places of the six athletes were as follows.

Table 4.39

Athlete	100 m time	100 m rank	1500 m time	1500 m rank
Allotey	9.8 s	1	3 m 42 s	1
Chell	10.9 s	6	4 m 11 s	2
Giles	10.4 s	2	4 m 19 s	6
Mason	10.5 s	3	4 m 18 s	5
O'Hara	10.7 s	5	4 m 12 s	3
Stuart	10.6 s	4	4 m 16 s	4

(i) Calculate the Pearson product moment and Spearman's rank correlation coefficients for these data.

(ii) State suitable null and alternative hypotheses and carry out hypothesis tests on these data.

(iii) State which you consider to be the more appropriate correlation coefficient in this situation, giving your reasons.

6. At the end of a word-processing course, the trainees are given a document to type. They are assessed on the time taken and on the quality of their work. For a random sample of 12 trainees, the following results were obtained.

Table 4.40

Trainee	A	B	C	D	E	F	G	H	I	J	K	L
Quality (%)	97	96	94	91	90	87	86	83	82	80	77	71
Time (s)	210	230	198	204	213	206	200	186	192	202	191	199

(i) Calculate Spearman's coefficient of rank correlation for the data. Explain what the sign of your association coefficient indicates about the data.

(ii) Carry out a test, at the 5% level of significance, of whether or not there is any association between time taken and quality of work for trainees who have attended this word-processing course. State clearly the null and alternative hypotheses under test and the conclusion reached. [MEI]

7. A school holds an election for parent governors. Candidates are invited to write brief autobiographies and these are sent out at the same time as the voting papers.

After the election, one of the candidates, Mr Smith, says that the more words you wrote about yourself the more votes you got. He sets out to 'prove this statistically' by calculating the product moment correlation between the number of words and the number of votes.

Table 4.41

Candidate	A	B	C	D	E	F	G
Number of words	70	101	106	232	150	102	98
Number of votes	99	108	97	144	94	54	87

(i) Calculate the product moment correlation coefficient.

Mr Smith claims that this proves his point at the 5% significance level.

(ii) State his null and alternative hypotheses and show how he came to his conclusion.

(iii) Calculate Spearman's rank correlation coefficient for these data.

(iv) Explain the difference in the two correlation coefficients and criticise the procedure Mr Smith used in coming to his conclusion.

8. To test the belief that milder winters are followed by warmer summers, meteorological records are obtained for a random sample of ten years. For each year, the mean temperatures are found for January and July. The data, in °C, are given below.

Table 4.42

January	8.3	7.1	9.0	1.8	3.5	4.7	5.8	6.0	2.7	2.1
July	16.2	13.1	16.7	11.2	14.9	15.1	17.7	17.3	12.3	13.4

(i) Rank the data and calculate Spearman's rank correlation coefficient.

(ii) Test, at the 2.5% level of significance, the belief that milder winters are followed by warmer summers. State clearly the null and alternative hypotheses under test.

(iii) Would it be more appropriate, less appropriate or equally appropriate to use the product moment correlation coefficient to analyse these data? Briefly explain why. [MEI]

Rank correlation

⑨ In a random sample of eight areas, residents were asked to express their approval or disapproval of the services provided by the local authority. A score of zero represented complete dissatisfaction, and ten represented complete satisfaction. The table below shows the mean score for each local authority together with the authority's level of community charge.

Table 4.43

Authority	A	B	C	D	E	F	G	H
Community charge (£)	485	490	378	451	384	352	420	212
Approval rating	3.0	4.0	5.0	4.6	4.1	5.5	5.8	6.1

(i) Calculate Spearman's rank correlation coefficient for the data.

(ii) State appropriate null and alternative hypotheses for a test to investigate whether there is any association between level of community charge and approval rating.

(iii) The output in Figure 4.29 below comes from a statistical package. Using the *p*-value given in the table headed 'Correlation', carry out a hypothesis test at the 5% significance level.

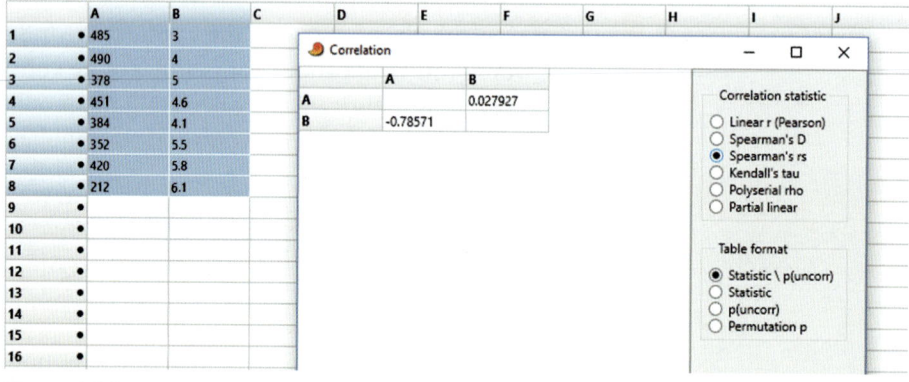

Figure 4.29 [MEI]

⑩ A fertiliser additive is claimed to enhance the growth of marrows. To test the claim statistically, a random sample of ten marrows is treated with varying levels of additive. The amounts of additive (in ounces) and the eventual weights of the marrows (in pounds) are given in the table.

Table 4.44

Amount of additive	8.2	3.5	8.8	1.6	1.9	9.9	5.8	5.5	4.4	3.9
Weight of marrow	6.6	7.2	8.4	4.7	7.4	8.7	7.5	7.3	5.9	7.0

(i) Rank the data and calculate Spearman's coefficient of rank correlation.

(ii) State appropriate null and alternative hypotheses for the test. Justify the alternative hypothesis you have given.

(iii) Carry out the test using a 5% level of significance. State clearly the conclusion reached.

(iv) Suppose it is discovered that the figures for the amounts of additive shown in the table were weights in grams rather than ounces. State, with reasons, whether this does or does not invalidate your answer. [MEI]

⑪ In order to assess whether increased expenditure in schools produces better examination results, a survey of all the secondary schools in England was conducted. Data on a random sample of 12 of these schools are shown below. The score shown is a measure of academic performance, a higher score indicating a higher success rate in examinations; expenditure is measured in thousands of pounds per student per year.

Table 4.45

Score	1.54	1.50	1.49	1.22	1.19	1.11	1.09	1.06	1.05	0.97	0.88	0.68
Expenditure	1.70	3.95	2.75	1.95	2.35	1.45	2.40	2.05	2.15	2.30	1.75	2.10

(i) Calculate the value of Spearman's rank correlation coefficient for the data.

(ii) Perform an appropriate test at the 5% level, making clear what your hypotheses are. State clearly the conclusions to be drawn from the test.

(iii) Now suppose that the value of Spearman's rank correlation coefficient, calculated for *all* the secondary schools in England, is 0.15.

(iv) What conclusion would you now reach about any association between expenditure per student and examination success, and why? [MEI]

12 In a national survey into whether low death rates are associated with greater prosperity, a random sample of 14 areas was taken. The areas, arranged in order of their prosperity, are shown in the table below together with their death rates. (The death rates are on a scale for which 100 is the national average.)

Table 4.46

most prosperous   least prosperous

Area	A	B	C	D	E	F	G	H	I	J	K	L	M	N
Death rate	66	76	84	83	102	78	100	110	105	112	122	131	165	138

(i) Calculate an appropriate correlation coefficient and use it to test, at the 5% level of significance, whether or not there is such an association. State your hypotheses and your conclusion carefully.

(ii) A newspaper carried this story under the headline 'Poverty causes increased deaths'. Explain carefully whether or not the data justify this headline.

(iii) The data include no information on the age distributions in the different areas. Explain why such additional information would be relevant. [MEI]

13 A student tests whether the amount of daily sunshine and rainfall in the UK are negatively correlated. He uses the following data.

$n = 25$, $\Sigma x = 140.6$, $\Sigma y = 77.7$,

$\Sigma x^2 = 853.76$, $\Sigma y^2 = 492.53$, $\Sigma xy = 381.15$

where x hours is the amount of daily sunshine and y mm is the daily rainfall.

(i) Calculate the product moment correlation coefficient, r.

(ii) Carry out the test at the 2.5% level of significance. State the hypotheses and conclusion carefully.

It is subsequently discovered that the student's data were taken from a newspaper, and that they all relate to UK holiday resorts on the Spring bank holiday.

(iii) Identify two distinct ways in which these data may be thought unsatisfactory.

Rank correlation

For the hypothesis test to be valid, daily amounts of sunshine and rainfall must have a particular underlying distribution.

(iv) State what this distribution is and discuss briefly whether or not it is reasonable in this case. [MEI]

14. The following data, referring to the ordering of perceived risk of 25 activities and technologies and actual fatality estimates, were obtained in a study in the United States. Use these data to test at the 5% significance level for positive correlation between

   (i) the League of Women Voters and college students
   (ii) experts and actual fatality estimates
   (iii) college students and experts.

Comment on your results and identify any outliers in the three sets of bivariate data you have just used.

Table 4.47

	League of Women Voters	College students	Experts	Actual fatalities (estimates)
Nuclear power	1	1	18	16
Motor vehicles	2	4	1	3
Handguns	3	2	4	4
Smoking	4	3	2	1
Motorcycles	5	5	6	6
Alcoholic beverages	6	6	3	2
General (private) aviation	7	12	11	11
Police work	8	7	15	18
Surgery	9	10	5	8
Fire fighting	10	9	16	17
Large construction	11	11	12	12
Hunting	12	15	20	14
Mountain climbing	13	17	24	21
Bicycles	14	19	13	13
Commercial aviation	15	13	14	20
Electric power (non-nuclear)	16	16	8	5
Swimming	17	25	9	7
Contraceptives	18	8	10	19
Skiing	19	20	25	24
X-rays	20	14	7	9
High school & college football	21	21	22	23
Railroads	22	18	17	10
Power mowers	23	23	23	22
Home appliances	24	22	19	15
Vaccinations	25	24	21	25

Source: Shwing and Albers, *Societal Risk Assessment*, Plenum

⑮ A population analyst wishes to test how death rates and birth rates are correlated in European countries.

(i) State appropriate null and alternative hypotheses for the test. Justify the alternative hypothesis you have given.

A random sample of ten countries from Europe was taken and their death rates (x) and birth rates (y), each per 1000 population for 1997, were noted.

Table 4.48

x	9	9	7	12	11	10	7	13	8	7
y	14	9	13	13	10	11	16	9	16	12

(ii) Represent the data graphically.
(iii) Calculate the product moment correlation coefficient.
(iv) Carry out the hypothesis test at the 5% level of significance. State clearly the conclusion reached.

In fact, the value of the product moment correlation coefficient for *all* the countries in Europe in 1997 was −0.555.

(v) What does this tell you about the relationship between death rates and birth rates in European countries?
(vi) State, giving a reason, whether your conclusion in part (iv) is still valid. [MEI]

⑯ Two judges give marks for artistic impression (out of a maximum of 6.0) to ten ice skaters.

Table 4.49

Skater	A	B	C	D	E	F	G	H	I	J
Judge 1	5.3	4.9	5.6	5.2	5.7	4.8	5.2	4.6	5.1	4.9
Judge 2	5.4	5.0	5.8	5.6	5.2	4.5	4.7	4.8	5.3	4.9

(i) Calculate the value of Spearman's rank correlation coefficient for the marks of the two judges.
(ii) Use your answer to part (i) to test, at the 5% level of significance, whether it appears that there is some overall agreement between the judges. State your hypotheses and your conclusions carefully.
(iii) For these marks, the product moment correlation coefficient is 0.6705. Use this to test, at the 5% level, whether there is any positive correlation between the assessments of the two judges.
(iv) Comment on which is the more appropriate test to use in this situation. [MEI]

⑰ Bird abundance may be assessed in several ways. In one long-term study in a nature reserve, two independent surveys (A and B) are carried out. The data show the number of wren territories recorded (survey A) and the numbers of adult wrens trapped in a fine mesh net (survey B) over a number of years.

Rank correlation

Table 4.50

Survey A	16	19	27	50	60	70	79	79	84	85	97
Survey B	11	12	15	18	22	35	35	71	46	53	52

(i) Plot a scatter diagram to compare results for the two surveys.

(ii) Calculate Spearman's coefficient of rank correlation.

(iii) Perform a significance test, at the 5% level, to determine whether there is any association between the results of the two surveys. Explain what your conclusion means in practical terms.

(iv) Would it be more appropriate, less appropriate or equally appropriate to use the product moment correlation coefficient to analyse these data? Explain briefly why.

[MEI]

18 Two people are interviewing eight candidates for a job. Each of the interviewers ranks each of the candidates in order, with 1 being the most preferable and 8 the least. The ranks given to each of the candidates are as follows.

Table 4.51

Interviewer A	3	7	1	2	4	8	5	6
Interviewer B	2	4	3	7	8	5	1	6

(i) Represent the data graphically.

(ii) Calculate Spearman's coefficient of rank correlation using the usual formula.

(iii) Calculate Spearman's coefficient of rank correlation using the formula for the product moment correlation coefficient.

(iv) Explain why it would not be appropriate to carry out a hypothesis on these data using the critical values for the product moment correlation coefficient.

KEY POINTS

1. A scatter diagram is a graph to illustrate bivariate data.

2. Notation for n pairs of observations (x, y)

$$S_{xx} = \Sigma(x_i - \bar{x})^2 = \Sigma x^2 - n\bar{x}^2$$

$$S_{yy} = \Sigma(y_i - \bar{y})^2 = \Sigma y^2 - n\bar{y}^2$$

$$S_{xy} = \Sigma(x_i - \bar{x})(y_i - \bar{y}) = \Sigma xy - n\bar{x}\bar{y}$$

3. Pearson's product moment correlation coefficient

$$r = \frac{S_{xy}}{\sqrt{S_{xx}S_{yy}}} = \frac{\Sigma(x_i - \bar{x})(y_i - \bar{y})}{\sqrt{\Sigma(x_i - \bar{x})^2 \times \Sigma(y_i - \bar{y})^2}} = \frac{\Sigma x_i y_i - n(\bar{x})(\bar{y})}{\sqrt{[\Sigma x_i^2 - n\bar{x}^2][\Sigma y_i^2 - n\bar{y}^2]}}$$

4. Spearman's coefficient of rank correlation

$$r_s = 1 - \frac{6\Sigma d_i^2}{n(n^2 - 1)}$$

5. Hypothesis testing based on Pearson's product moment correlation coefficient

   $H_0: \rho = 0$

   $H_1: \rho > 0$ or $\rho < 0$ (one-tailed test) or $\rho \neq 0$ (two-tailed test).

   Test the sample value, r, against the critical value, which depends on the number of pairs in the bivariate sample, n, and the significance level.

6. Hypothesis testing based on Spearman's coefficient of rank correlation

   H_0: no association

   H_1: positive association or negative association (one-tailed test) or some association (two-tailed test).

   Test the sample value, r_s, against the critical value, which depends on the number of pairs in the bivariate sample, n, and the significance level.

LEARNING OUTCOMES

When you have completed this chapter you should:

- understand what bivariate data are and know the conventions for choice of axis for variables in a scatter diagram
- be able to use and interpret a scatter diagram
- interpret a scatter diagram produced by software
- be able to calculate Pearson's product moment correlation coefficient from raw data or summary statistics
- know when it is appropriate to carry out a hypothesis test using Pearson's product moment correlation coefficient
- be able to carry out hypothesis tests using the Pearson's product moment correlation coefficient and tables of critical values or the p-value from software
- use the Pearson's product moment correlation coefficient as an effect size
- be able to calculate Spearman's rank correlation coefficient from raw data or summary statistics
- be able to carry out hypothesis tests using Spearman's rank correlation coefficient and tables of critical values or the output from software
- decide whether a test based on r or r_s may be more appropriate, or whether neither is appropriate.

5 Bivariate data (regression lines)

It is utterly implausible that a mathematical formula should make the future known to us, and those who think it can would once have believed in witchcraft.

Betrand de Jouvenel

Janice grows tomatoes in her greenhouse. Every year, she uses a liquid feed to try to get a bigger yield. One year, she wonders if there is a relationship between the amount of fertiliser she uses and the yield of the tomatoes. She does an experiment where she takes seven tomato plants and gives each of them a different amount of feed. The following table shows the amount of fertiliser, x ml, and the yield, y kg, for each of the plants.

> Notice that the amount of liquid feed is not a random variable; it is a controlled variable.
>
> You can see this from the way that the values of x go up in steps of 40. These are the doses given in ml.

Table 5.1

x	40	80	120	160	200	240	280
y	3.1	3.8	3.6	4.0	4.4	4.4	4.3

Figure 5.1 shows a scatter diagram for the data that Janice collected.

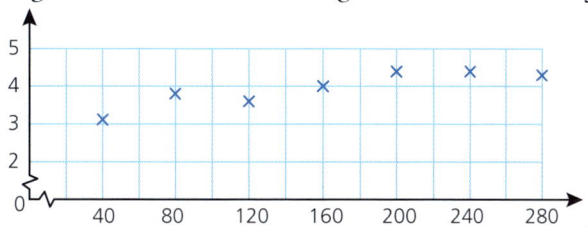

Figure 5.1

Looking at her scatter diagram, Janice thinks that there is probably a relationship between the amount of fertiliser and the yield. She considers drawing a line of best fit by eye but then a friend suggests that she should use a calculation to find the equation of a suitable line.

1 The least squares regression line (random on non-random)

A correlation coefficient provides you with a measure of the level of linear association between the two variables in a bivariate distribution.

If this indicates that there is a relationship, your question will be 'What is it?' In the case of linear correlation, it can be expressed algebraically as a linear equation or geometrically as a straight line on the scatter diagram.

Before you do any calculations, you first need to look carefully at the two variables that give rise to your data. It is normal practice to plot the *dependent variable* on the vertical axis and the *independent variable* on the horizontal axis. In the example above, the independent variable was the dose the tomatoes were given. In many situations, the independent variable is the time at which measurements are made. Notice that these are non-random variables. The procedure that follows leads to the equation of the *regression line*, the line of best fit in these circumstances.

Look at the scatter diagram (Figure 5.2) showing the n points $A(x_1, y_1)$, $B(x_2, y_2)$, ..., $N(x_n, y_n)$. On it is marked a possible line of best fit l. If the line l passed through all the points there would be no problem since there would be perfect linear correlation. It does not, of course, pass through all the points and you would be very surprised if such a line did in any real situation.

The least squares regression line (random on non-random)

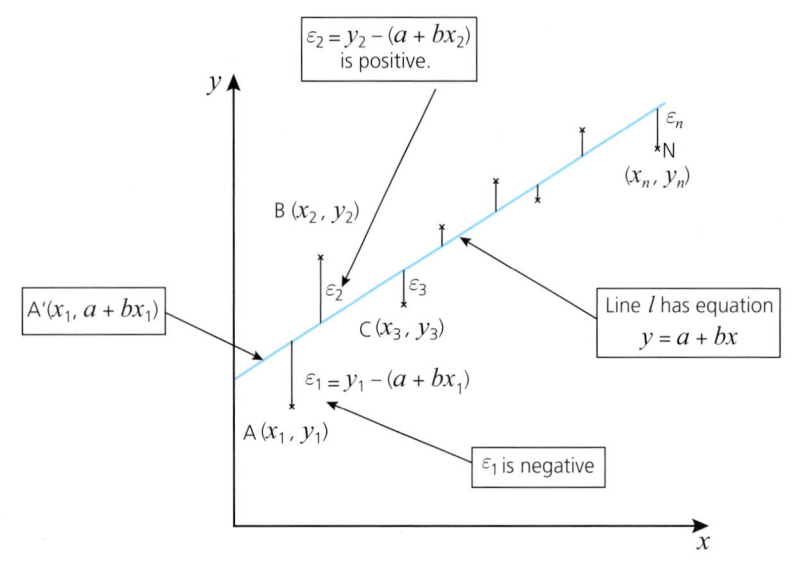

Figure 5.2 Bivariate data plotted on a scatter diagram with the regression line, l, $y = a + bx$, and the residuals $\varepsilon_1, \varepsilon_2, \cdots, \varepsilon_n$

By how much is it missing the points? The answer to that question is shown by the vertical lines from the points to the line. Their lengths $\varepsilon_1, \varepsilon_2, \cdots, \varepsilon_n^2$ are called the *residuals* and represent any variation which is not explained by the line l. The *least squares regression line* is the line which produces the least possible value of the sum of the squares of the residuals, $\varepsilon_1^2 + \varepsilon_2^2 + \cdots + \varepsilon_n^2$.

If the equation of the line l is $y = a + bx$, then it is easy to see that the point A´ on the diagram, directly above A, has co-ordinates $(x_1, a + bx_1)$ and so the corresponding residual, ε_1, is given by $\varepsilon_1 = y_1 - (a + bx_1)$. Similarly, for $\varepsilon_2, \cdots, \varepsilon_n$.

The problem is to find the values of the constants a and b in the equation of the line l which make $\varepsilon_1^2 + \varepsilon_2^2 + \cdots + \varepsilon_n^2$ a minimum for any particular set of data, that is, to minimise

$$\left[y_1 - (a + bx_1)\right]^2 + \left[y_2 - (a + bx_2)\right]^2 + \cdots + \left[y_n - (a + bx_n)\right]^2$$

The mathematics involved in doing this is not particularly difficult. The resulting equation of the regression line is given below.

$$y - \bar{y} = b(x - \bar{x})$$

$$\text{where } b = \frac{S_{xy}}{S_{xx}}$$

For Janice's data on the yield from tomato plants you can find the equation of the regression line as follows.

> **Note**
>
> You have already met S_{xx} and S_{xy} in Chapter 4. They are defined as:
>
> $S_{xx} = \Sigma(x - \bar{x})^2 = \Sigma x^2 - n\bar{x}^2$
>
> $S_{xy} = \Sigma(x - \bar{x})(y - \bar{y})$
> $= \Sigma xy - n\bar{x}\bar{y}$

Table 5.2

x	y	x^2	xy
40	3.1	1600	124
80	3.8	6400	304
120	3.6	14 400	432
160	4.0	25 600	640
200	4.4	40 000	880
240	4.4	57 600	1056
280	4.3	78 400	1204
Total	1120	27.6	224 000	4640

> As when calculating the correlation coefficient, the first step in calculating the equation of the regression line is to find the mean values of x and y.

$$\bar{x} = \frac{\Sigma x}{n} = \frac{1120}{7} = 160 \quad \bar{y} = \frac{\Sigma y}{n} = \frac{27.6}{7} = 3.94\ldots$$

$$S_{xx} = \Sigma x^2 - n\bar{x}^2 = 224\,000 - 7 \times 160^2 = 44\,800$$

$$S_{xy} = \Sigma xy - n\bar{x}\,\bar{y} = 4640 - 7 \times 160 \times 3.94\ldots = 224 \quad b = \frac{S_{xy}}{S_{xx}} = \frac{224}{44\,800} = 0.005$$

Hence the least squares regression line is given by

$$y - \bar{y} = b(x - \bar{x})$$
$$y - 3.94\ldots = 0.005(x - 160)$$
$$y = 3.14 + 0.005x$$

Notes

1. In the preceding work you will see that only variation in the y values has been considered. The reason for this is that the x values represent a non-random variable. That is why the residuals are vertical and not in any other direction. Thus $y_1, y_2, \ldots$ are values of a random variable y given by $y = a + bx + E$, where E is the residual variation, the variation that is not explained by the regression line.
2. The goodness of fit of a regression line may be judged by eye by looking at a scatter diagram. An informal measure which is often used is the coefficient of determination, r^2, which measures the proportion of the total variation in the dependent variable, Y, which is accounted for by the regression line. There is no standard hypothesis test based on the coefficient of determination.
3. This form of the regression line is often called the **y on x regression line**. If, for some reason, you had y as your independent variable, you would use the 'x on y' form obtained by interchanging x and y in the equations.

Example 5.1

A patient is given a drip feed containing a particular chemical and its concentration in his blood is measured, in suitable units, at one hour intervals for the next five hours. The doctors believe the figures to be subject to random errors, arising both from the sampling procedure and the subsequent chemical analysis, but that a linear model is appropriate.

The least squares regression line (random on non-random)

> You can see from the intervals that x is a controlled variable.

Table 5.3

Time, x (hours)	0	1	2	3	4	5
Concentration, y	2.4	4.3	5.2	6.8	9.1	11.8

(i) Find the equation of the regression line of y on x.
(ii) Illustrate the data and your regression line on a scatter diagram.
(iii) Estimate the concentration of the chemical in the patient's blood at
(a) 3½ hours,
(b) 10 hours after treatment started.
Comment on the likely accuracy of your predictions.
(iv) Calculate the residuals for each data pair. Check that the sum of the residuals is zero and find the sum of the squares of the residuals.

Solution

(i) $n = 6$

Table 5.4

x	y	x^2	xy
0	2.4	0	0.0
1	4.3	1	4.3
2	5.2	4	10.4
3	6.8	9	20.4
4	9.1	16	36.4
5	11.8	25	59.0
15	39.6	55	130.5

$$\bar{x} = \frac{\Sigma x}{n} = \frac{15}{6} = 2.5 \quad \bar{y} = \frac{\Sigma y}{n} = \frac{39.6}{6} = 6.6$$

$$S_{xx} = \Sigma x^2 - n\bar{x}^2 = 55 - 6 \times 2.5^2 = 17.5$$

$$S_{xy} = \Sigma xy - n\bar{x}\bar{y} = 130.5 - 6 \times 2.5 \times 6.6 = 31.5$$

$$b = \frac{S_{xy}}{S_{xx}} = \frac{31.5}{17.5} = 1.8$$

Hence the least squares regression line is given by

$$y - \bar{y} = b(x - \bar{x})$$
$$y - 6.6 = 1.8(x - 2.5)$$
$$y = 2.1 + 1.8x$$

(ii)

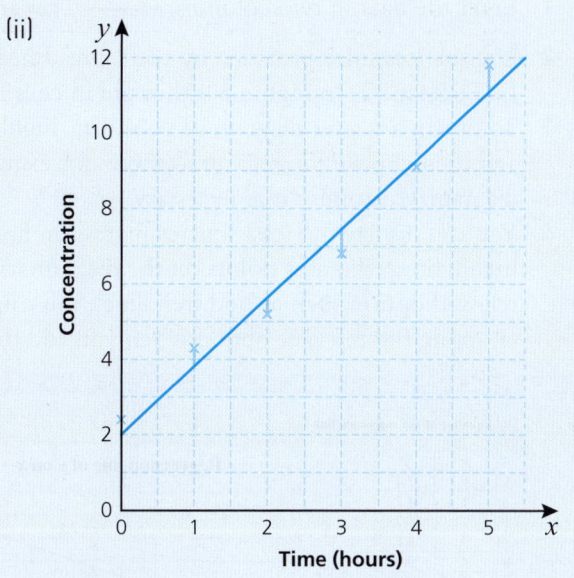

Figure 5.3

(iii) When $x = 3.5$,
$y = 2.1 + 1.8 \times 3.5$
$= 8.4$.
When $x = 10$,
$y = 2.1 + 1.8 \times 10$
$= 20.1$.

The concentration lies between the measured values of the concentration at a time between 3 hours and 4 hours, so the prediction seems quite reasonable.

The time ten hours is a long way outside the set of data times; there is no indication that the linear relationship can be extrapolated to such a time, even though there seems to be a good fit, so the prediction is probably unreliable.

(iv) For each pair of data, (x, y), the corresponding point on the regression line is denoted by $(x, \hat{y})$. So the predicted value is $\hat{y} = 2.1 + 1.8x$. Corresponding values of y and $\hat{y}$ are tabulated below, together with the residuals and their squares.

Table 5.5

x	y	$\hat{y}$	$y - \hat{y}$	$(y - \hat{y})^2$
0	2.4	2.1	0.3	0.09
1	4.3	3.9	0.4	0.16
2	5.2	5.7	−0.5	0.25
3	6.8	7.5	−0.7	0.49
4	9.1	9.3	−0.2	0.04
5	11.8	11.1	0.7	0.49
15	39.6	39.6	0.0	1.52

You can see that the sum of the residuals, $\Sigma(y - \hat{y})$ is zero, and that the sum of the squares of the residuals, $\Sigma(y - \hat{y})^2$, is 1.52.

> In this case, the value of x from which you want to predict the value of y lies within the range of data values.
> This is an example of *interpolation* (meaning within the points).

> In this second case, the value of x from which you want to predict the value of y lies outside the range of data values.
> This is an example of *extrapolation* (meaning outside the points).

> **Note**
> If the same procedure were carried out using the same data with any other line, the sum of the squares of the residuals would work out to be greater than 1.52.

> **Note**
> So the actual data point (x,y) is in the same vertical line as $(x,\hat{y})$ on scatter diagram.

The least squares regression line (random on non-random)

USING ICT

A spreadsheet

Setting up a spreadsheet to work out the coefficients a and b of the least squares regression line, $y = a + bx$, is fairly straightforward; it will also display a scatter diagram. This is illustrated in Figure 5.4 using the data from the previous example. It is obtained by carrying out these steps.

1. Enter the data in two columns. ← They are columns A and B in Figure 5.4.
2. Use the formulae provided by your spreadsheet, for example SLOPE and INTERCEPT. In Figure 5.4 they are in cells B12 and B13.
3. To obtain a scatter diagram of your data, highlight the two columns of data and then choose the relevant options, for example Insert followed by scatter diagram. Customise it as necessary.
4. You can display the least squares regression line on the scatter diagram by highlighting the data points on the diagram, right-clicking and choosing the relevant option such as 'add trendline'. You can also display the equation by choosing the relevant option when you add the 'trendline'.

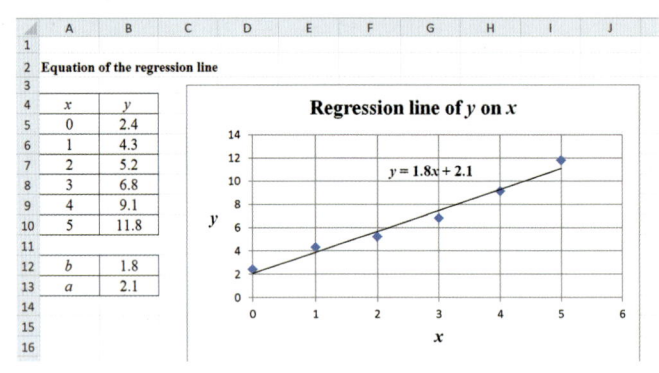

Figure 5.4

Exercise 5.1

① For the following bivariate data
  (i) Find the mean values of x and y.
  (ii) Find the values of S_{xx} and S_{xy}.
  (iii) Find the equation of the least squares regression line of y on x.

Table 5.6

x	5	10	15	20	25
y	30	28	27	27	21

② Calculate the equation of the regression line of y on x for the following distribution and use it to estimate the value of y when $x = 42$.

Table 5.7

x	25	30	35	40	45	50
y	78	70	65	58	48	42

③ The 1980 and 2000 catalogue prices, in pence, of five British postage stamps are as follows.

Table 5.8

1980 price, x	10	20	30	40	50
2000 price, y	100	215	280	360	450

  (i) Plot these data on a scatter diagram.
  (ii) Calculate the equation of the regression line and draw it accurately on your scatter diagram.

(iii) Another stamp was valued at £5 in 1980 and £62 in 2000. Comment.

(iv) Calculate the values of the five residuals and illustrate them on your graph.

(v) Find the sum of the squares of the residuals and relate this to the least squares regression line. [MEI]

④ The speed of a car, $v\,\mathrm{m\,s^{-1}}$, at time t s after it starts to accelerate is shown in the table below, for $0 \leq t \leq 10$.

Table 5.9

t	0	1	2	3	4	5	6	7	8	9	10
v	0	3.0	6.8	10.2	12.9	16.4	20.0	21.4	23.0	24.6	26.1

($\Sigma t = 55$, $\Sigma v = 164.4$, $\Sigma t^2 = 385$, $\Sigma v^2 = 3267.98$, $\Sigma tv = 1117.0$.)

The relationship between t and v is initially modelled by using all the data above and calculating a single regression line.

(i) Plot a scatter diagram of the data, with t on the horizontal axis and v on the vertical axis.

(ii) Using all the data given, calculate the equation of the regression line of v on t. Give numerical coefficients in your answers correct to 3 significant figures.

(iii) Calculate the product moment correlation coefficient for the given data.

(iv) Comment on the validity of modelling the data by a single straight line and on the answer obtained in part (iii).

⑤ The results of an experiment to determine how the percentage sand content of soil, y, varies with the depth in cm below ground level, x, are given in the following table.

Table 5.10

x	0	6	12	18	24	30	36	42	48
y	80.6	63.0	64.3	62.5	57.5	59.2	40.8	46.9	37.6

(i) Illustrate the data by a scatter diagram.

(ii) Calculate the equation of the regression line and plot it on your graph.

(iii) Use your regression equation to predict the values of y for $x = 50$ and $x = 100$. Comment on the validity of your predictions.

(iv) Calculate the residuals and explain why their sum is zero. [MEI]

⑥ Observations of a cactus graft were made under controlled environmental conditions. The table gives the observed heights, y cm, of the graft at x weeks after grafting. Also given are the values of $z = \ln(y)$.

Table 5.11

x	1	2	3	4	5	6	8	10
y	2.0	2.4	2.5	5.1	6.7	9.4	18.3	35.1
$z = \ln(y)$	0.69	0.88	0.92	1.63	1.90	2.24	2.91	3.56

(i) Draw two scatter diagrams, one for y and x, and one for z and x.

The least squares regression line (random on non-random)

(ii) It is desired to estimate the height of the graft seven weeks after grafting. Explain why your scatter diagrams suggest the use of the line of regression of z on x for this purpose, but not the line of regression of y on x.

(iii) Obtain the required estimate given that $\Sigma x = 39$, $\Sigma x^2 = 255$, $\Sigma z = 14.73$, $\Sigma z^2 = 34.5231$, $\Sigma xz = 93.55$. [MEI]

7. In an experiment on memory, five groups of people (chosen randomly) were given varying lengths of time to memorise the same list of 40 words. Later, they were asked to recall as many words as possible from the list. The table below shows the average number of words recalled, y, and the time given, t s.

Table 5.12

t	20	40	60	80	100
y	12.1	18.5	22.8	24.6	24.0

(i) Plot the data on a scatter diagram.

(ii) Calculate the equation of the regression line for y on t.

(iii) Use your regression line to predict y when $t = 30$ and $t = 160$. Comment on the usefulness or otherwise of these results.

(iv) Discuss briefly whether the regression line provides a good model or whether there is a better way of modelling the relationship between y and t. [MEI]

8. A farmer is investigating the relationship between the density at which a crop is planted and the quality. By using more seed per hectare (x) he can increase the yield, but he suspects that the percentage of high-quality produce (y) may fall. The farmer collects data which he enters into the spreadsheet below. He also uses the spreadsheet to produce a scatter diagram.

	A	B	C	D	E	F	G	H
1								Sum
2	x	120	130	140	150	160	170	870
3	y	31.3	28.9	25.4	21.3	21	10.1	138
4	x^2	14400	16900	19600	22500	25600	28900	127900
5	xy	3756	3757	3556	3195	3360	1717	19341

Figure 5.5

(i) Discuss how suitable a straight line model would be for the relationship between y and x.

(i) Use the sums in the spreadsheet to help you calculate the equation of the regression line of y on x.

(i) Obtain from your regression line the predicted values of y at $x = 145$ and $x = 180$. Comment, with reasons, on the likely accuracy of these predictions.

⑨ A car manufacturer is testing the braking distance for a new model of car. The table shows the braking distance, y m, for different speeds, x km h^{-1}, when the brakes were applied.

Table 5.13

Speed of car, x km h^{-1}	30	50	70	90	110	130
Braking distance, y m	25	50	85	155	235	350

(i) Plot a scatter diagram on graph paper.

(ii) Calculate the equation of the regression line of y on x. Draw the line on your scatter diagram, together with the residuals.

(iii) Use your regression equation to predict values of y when $x = 100$ and $x = 150$. Comment, with reasons, on the likely accuracy of these predictions.

(iv) Discuss briefly whether the regression line provides a good model or whether there is a better way of modelling the relationship between y and x. [MEI]

⑩ The authorities in a school are concerned to ensure that their students enter appropriate mathematics examinations. As part of a research project into this they wish to set up a performance-prediction model. This involves the students taking a standard mid-year test, based on the syllabus and format of the final end-of-year examination.

The school bases its model on the belief that in the final examination students will get the same things right as they did in the mid-year test and, in addition, a proportion, p, of the things they got wrong.

Consequently, a student's final mark, y%, can be predicted on the basis of his or her test mark, x%, by the relationship

$$y = x + p \times (100 - x)$$

Final mark = test mark + $p \times$ (the marks the student did not get on the test)

Investigate this model, using the following bivariate data. Start by finding the y on x regression line and then rearrange it to estimate p.

Table 5.14

x	y
40	55
22	40
10	25
46	68
66	75
8	32
48	69
58	66
50	51
80	85

x	y
27	44
32	50
26	49
68	76
54	66
68	70
88	92
48	59
82	90
66	76

x	y
60	72
50	70
90	95
30	50
64	80
100	100
44	50
58	62
54	60
24	31

x	y
46	70
70	85
33	63
40	60
56	57
45	55
78	85
68	80
78	85
89	91

2 The least squares regression line (random on random)

Note

The y on x regression line estimates the expectation of y as a linear function of the value of x (and the equivalent for any pair of variables).

Although the approach so far is only true for a random variable on a non-random variable, it happens that, for quite different reasons, the same form of the regression line applies if both variables are random and have a bivariate Normal distribution. If this is the case, the scatter diagram will show an approximately elliptical distribution. Since this is a common situation, this form of the regression line may be used more widely than might at first have seemed to be the case. Because both variables are random, there are, in fact, two regression lines, y on x and x on y. If a value of y is to be estimated from a value of x, then the regression line of y on x must be used. If, however, a value of x is to be estimated from a value of y, then the regression line of x on y must be used.

The equation of the regression line of y on x is the same as that for the random on non-random case:

$$y - \bar{y} = \frac{S_{xy}}{S_{xx}}(x - \bar{x})$$

The equation of the regression line of y on x follows the same form with x and y interchanged:

$$x - \bar{x} = \frac{S_{xy}}{S_{yy}}(y - \bar{y})$$

The goodness of fit of the regression line can be judged by examining the scatter diagram. As in the random on non-random case, an additional method is to find the coefficient of determination. This is the square of the value of Pearson's product moment correlation coefficient. This value gives an estimate of the proportion of variation in one variable that is explained by the variation in the other variable. Other factors are responsible for the remainder of the variation.

Example 5.2

The VR (verbal reasoning) and NVR (non-verbal reasoning) scores for a group of 60 students were obtained from tests given to the students on the two areas; these variables are labelled x and y respectively.

Summary figures are as follows:

$\Sigma x = 7105$, $\Sigma y = 7132$, $\Sigma x^2 = 846357$, $\Sigma y^2 = 853620$, $\Sigma xy = 846371$, $n = 60$.

The correlation coefficient between x and y is 0.337.

The following scatter diagram illustrates the data.

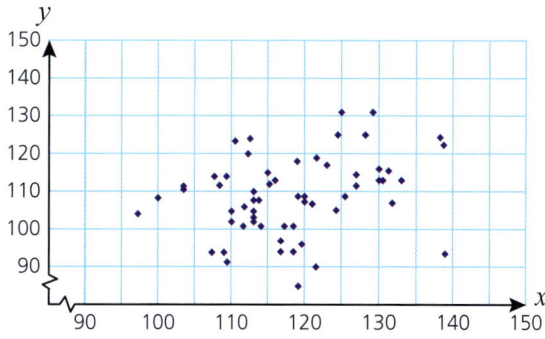

Figure 5.6

(i) Explain why it may be appropriate to calculate the equation of a regression line, despite the fact that both variables are random.

(ii) Calculate the equation of a regression line which is suitable to estimate the value of the VR score for a student who missed the VR test but whose NVR score is known.

(iii) Estimate the VR score for a student whose NVR score is 125.

(iv) Comment on how reliable your estimate is likely to be.

Solution

(i) Although both variables are random, the scatter diagram appears to have a roughly elliptical shape and so the distribution is of the variables may be bivariate Normal.

(ii) Since you are trying to estimate the value of x you need to use the regression line of x on y:

$$x - \bar{x} = \frac{S_{xy}}{S_{yy}}(y - \bar{y})$$

$$S_{xy} = \Sigma xy - \frac{\Sigma x \Sigma y}{n} = 846371 - \frac{7105 \times 7132}{60} = 1823.333$$

$$S_{yy} = \Sigma y^2 - \frac{(\Sigma y)^2}{n} = 853620 - \frac{7132^2}{60} = 5862.933$$

The equation of the regression line is

$$x - \frac{7105}{60} = \frac{1823.333}{5862.933}\left(y - \frac{7132}{60}\right)$$

So $x - 118.417 = 0.310993(y - 118.867)$

So $x = 0.311y + 81.4$

(iii) The estimate is $x = 0.311 \times 125 + 81.4 = 120.3$.

(iv) • The scatter diagram shows that the points do not lie very close to a straight line.
 • The correlation coefficient r is 0.337 which is not very high.
 • The value of the coefficient of determination r^2 is only 0.113 so only roughly 11% of the variation in the values of x is explained by the variation in the values of y.

All of these indicators suggest that the estimate is not likely to be very reliable.

> Roughly 11% of the variation in the values of x are explained by the variation in the values of y. So, 89% of the variation in x is explained by other factors.

The least squares regression line (random on random)

Exercise 5.2

① Use a spreadsheet to find the equation of the line of regression for these bivariate data.

Table 5.15

x	6.3	8.7	4.2	3.7	6.5
y	24.7	39.2	19.6	20.3	26.2

② Calculate the equation of the line of regression for these bivariate data.

Table 5.16

x	69.0	66.5	71.5	63.6	98.8	52.4	64.0	79.9
y	297.9	310.5	300.5	296.7	416.3	261.1	285.9	321.8

③ The bivariate sample illustrated in the scatter diagram shows the heights, x cm, and masses, y kg, of a random sample of 20 students.

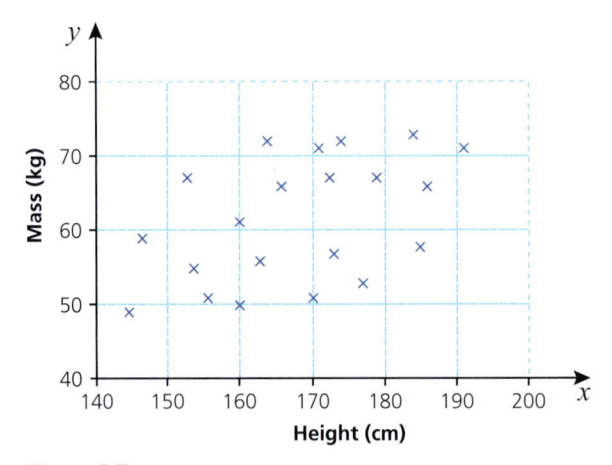

Figure 5.7

$\Sigma x = 3358$, $\Sigma x^2 = 567\,190$, $\Sigma y = 1225$, $\Sigma y^2 = 76\,357$, $\Sigma xy = 206\,680$.

(i) Calculate the equation of a regression line which is suitable to estimate the weight of a student whose height is known.

(ii) Estimate the weight of a student whose height is 180 cm.

(iii) Comment, with reasons, on the likely accuracy of your estimate in part (ii).

(iv) Explain why it might not be sensible to use the equation which you calculated in part (i) to predict the weight of a student whose height is 210 cm. [MEI]

④ A student thinks that the amount of daily sunshine and rainfall in the UK are negatively correlated. He uses the following data.

$n = 25$, $\Sigma x = 140.6$, $\Sigma y = 77.7$, $\Sigma x^2 = 853.76$, $\Sigma y^2 = 492.53$, $\Sigma xy = 381.15$

where x hours is the amount of daily sunshine and y mm is the daily rainfall.

(i) Use a suitable regression line to estimate the number of hours of sunshine on a day when there is 4 mm of rain.

(ii) Calculate the value of the product moment correlation coefficient.

(iii) Comment with reasons on the likely accuracy of your estimate in part (i). [MEI]

⑤ A medical statistician wishes to carry out a hypothesis test to see if there is any correlation between the head circumference and body length of newly born babies.

(i) State appropriate null and alternative hypotheses for the test.

A random sample of 20 newly born babies have their head circumference, x cm, and body length, y cm, measured. This bivariate sample is illustrated in the scatter diagram.

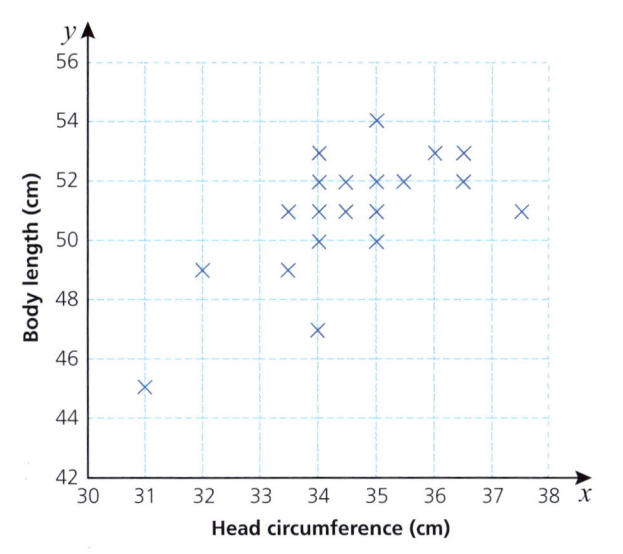

Figure 5.8

Summary statistics for this data set are as follows.

$n = 20$, $\Sigma x = 691$, $\Sigma y = 1018$, $\Sigma x^2 = 23\,917$, $\Sigma y^2 = 51\,904$, $\Sigma xy = 35\,212.5$

(ii) Calculate the product moment correlation coefficient for the data. Carry out the hypothesis test at the 1% significance level, stating the conclusion clearly. What assumption is necessary for the test to be valid?

(iii) Use a suitable regression line to estimate the body lengths of babies whose head circumferences are 36.0 cm and 29.0 cm.

(iv) Comment, with reasons, on the likely accuracy of these estimates. [MEI]

⑥ A fruit grower is investigating a crop of plums. She measures the lengths and circumferences in mm of ten randomly selected plums. She uses a spreadsheet to analyse the results. The spreadsheet below shows her analysis.

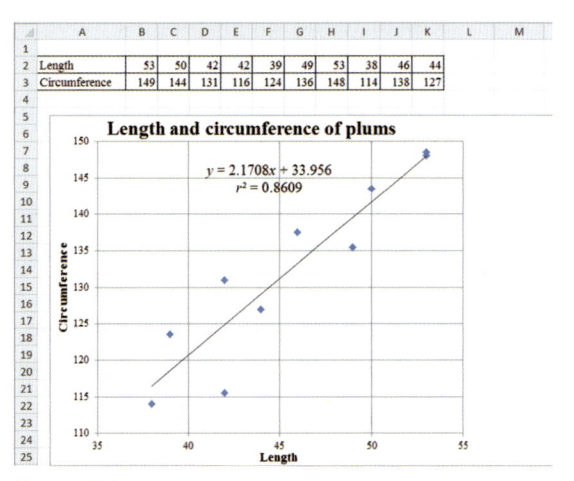

Figure 5.9

The least squares regression line (random on random)

(i) The equation given is for the regression line of y on x. Estimate the circumference of a plum of length 40 mm.

(ii) Comment, giving two different reasons, on the likely accuracy of this estimate.

(iii) Give a reason why it would not be sensible to use this equation to estimate the circumference of a plum of length 70 mm.

(iv) Give a reason why it would not be sensible to use this equation to estimate the length of a plum of circumference 130 mm.

⑦ An investment analyst thinks that there may be correlation between the cost of oil, $\$x$ dollars per barrel, and the price of a particular share, y p. The analyst selects 50 days at random and records the values of x and y. Summary statistics for these data are shown below, together with the output from a spreadsheet for these 50 days.

$\Sigma x = 2331.3$, $\Sigma y = 6724.3$, $\Sigma x^2 = 111\,984$, $\Sigma y^2 = 921\,361$, $\Sigma xy = 316\,345$, $n = 50$

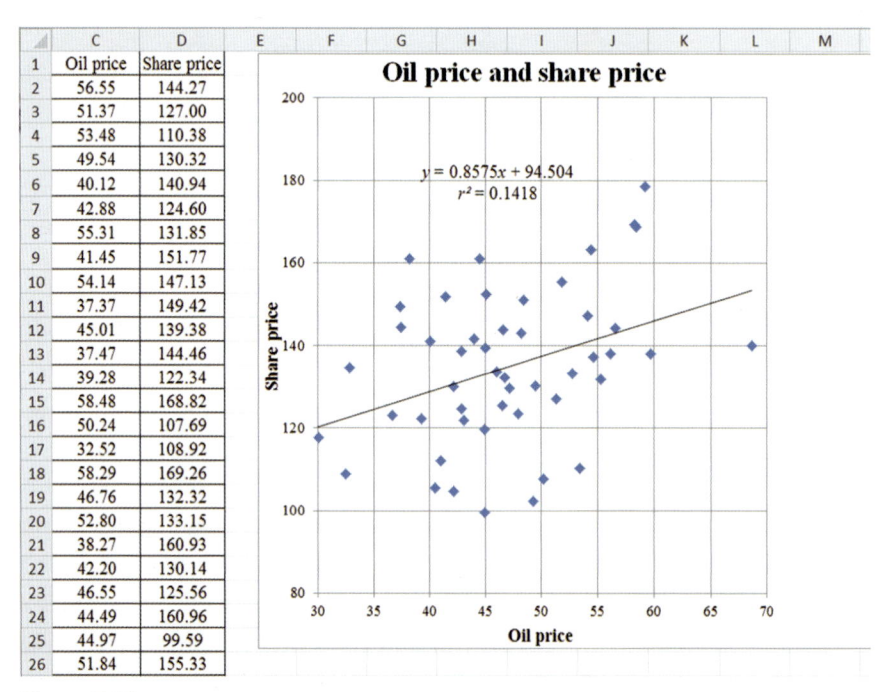

	C	D
1	Oil price	Share price
2	56.55	144.27
3	51.37	127.00
4	53.48	110.38
5	49.54	130.32
6	40.12	140.94
7	42.88	124.60
8	55.31	131.85
9	41.45	151.77
10	54.14	147.13
11	37.37	149.42
12	45.01	139.38
13	37.47	144.46
14	39.28	122.34
15	58.48	168.82
16	50.24	107.69
17	32.52	108.92
18	58.29	169.26
19	46.76	132.32
20	52.80	133.15
21	38.27	160.93
22	42.20	130.14
23	46.55	125.56
24	44.49	160.96
25	44.97	99.59
26	51.84	155.33

Scatter plot titled "Oil price and share price" with $y = 0.8575x + 94.504$, $r^2 = 0.1418$.

Figure 5.10

(i) Calculate the sample product moment correlation coefficient.

(ii) Carry out a hypothesis test at the 5% significance level to investigate the analyst's belief. State your hypotheses clearly, defining any symbols which you use.

(iii) An assumption that there is a bivariate Normal distribution is required for this test to be valid. State whether it is the sample or the population which is required to have such a distribution. State, with a reason, whether, in this case, the assumption appears to be justified.

(iv) Explain why a two-tailed test is appropriate even though it is clear from the scatter diagram that the sample has a positive correlation coefficient.

(v) The regression equation of share price on oil price is given on the spreadsheet. Estimate the share price when the oil price is $\$65$.

(vi) Comment, giving two different reasons, on the likely accuracy of this estimate. [MEI]

⑧ The best times for a 400 m race in ten 'Olympic' years are as follows.

Table 5.17

Years after 1900, x	60	64	68	72	76	80	84	88	92	96
Time, y	55.5	54.2	54.3	52.9	52.3	52.6	50.7	51.0	49.6	48.9

(i) Plot the data on a scatter diagram.

(ii) Calculate the equation of the regression line of y on x.

(iii) Identify an important point through which a regression line must pass, marking this point on your diagram. Draw the regression line on the scatter diagram and indicate the residuals.

(iv) Use your regression equation to predict the best times for the race in the years 2000 and 2020. Comment on the likely accuracy of these predictions. [MEI]

⑨ An experiment was conducted to determine the mass, y g, of a chemical that would dissolve in 100 ml of water at $x\,°C$. The results of the experiment were as follows.

Table 5.18

Temperature, x (°C)	10	20	30	40	50
Mass, y (g)	61	64	70	73	75

(i) Represent the data on graph paper.

(ii) Calculate the equation of the regression line of y on x. Draw this line on your graph.

(iii) Calculate an estimate of the mass of the chemical that would dissolve in the water at 35 °C.

(iv) Suggest a range of temperatures for which such estimates are reliable. Give a reason for your answer.

(v) Calculate the residuals for each of the temperatures. Illustrate them on your graph.

(vi) The regression line is often referred to as 'the least squares regression line'. Explain what this means in relation to the residuals. [MEI]

⑩ A science student took the temperature of a cup of coffee for ten one-minute intervals with the following results.

Table 5.19

Time, x (minutes)	0	1	2	3	4	5	6	7	8	9	10
Temperature, y (°C)	96	84	73	64	55	49	44	40	36	33	31

$n = 11, \Sigma x = 55, \Sigma y = 605, \Sigma x^2 = 385, \Sigma xy = 2326$

(i) The science student calculates the equation of the least squares regression line of y on x and uses it to predict the temperatures after 4.3 mins and after 15 mins. Obtain the regression line and the predictions. Show that *both* of these predictions are unsatisfactory.

The least squares regression line (random on random)

(ii) Plot a scatter diagram on graph paper to illustrate the data. Draw the regression line and the residuals on your diagram. By considering the pattern of the residuals, discuss whether there is a better way of modelling the relationship between temperature and time. [MEI]

11. A car manufacturer is introducing a new model. The car is tested for fuel economy three times at each of four different speeds. The values of the fuel economy, y miles per gallon (mpg), at each of the speeds, x miles per hour (mph), are displayed in the following table.

Table 5.20

x	40	40	40	50	50	50	60	60	60	70	70	70
y	52.7	53.8	54.5	48.1	49.7	51.3	43.3	41.1	48.0	37.5	42.0	44.7

$n = 12, \Sigma x = 660, \Sigma y = 566.7, \Sigma x^2 = 37\,800, \Sigma xy = 30\,533$

(i) Explain which of the variables is controlled and how you can tell that it is.

(ii) Represent the data by a scatter diagram, drawn on graph paper.

(iii) Calculate the equation of the regression line of y on x and plot it on your scatter diagram.

(iv) Hence predict the fuel economy of the car at speeds of
  (a) 45 mph
  (a) 65 mph.

(v) Use your scatter diagram to compare the reliability of your predictions in part (iv).

What do your comments suggest about the validity of a least squares regression line for this data set? [MEI]

12. The approximate population of the world in billions from the year 1900 to 2000 is displayed in the following table.

Table 5.21

Year, x	1900	1910	1920	1930	1940	1950	1960	1970	1980	1990	2000
Population, y	1.67	1.75	1.86	2.07	2.30	2.56	3.04	3.71	4.45	5.28	6.08

(i) Draw a scatter diagram to illustrate the data.

(ii) Explain why it would not be sensible to find the equation of the regression line of Population on Year.

(iii) Let $z = x - 1900$. Display the values of z and of z^2, together with y in a new table.

(iv) Draw a scatter diagram with z^2 on the horizontal axis and y on the vertical axis.

(v) Calculate the equation of the regression line of y on z^2 and plot it on your scatter diagram.

(vi) Hence estimate the population of the world in
  (a) the year 1995
  (b) the year 2100.

(vii) Comment on the reliability of each of your estimates.

KEY POINTS

Random on non-random regression lines

1. The equation of the y on x regression line $y = a + bx$ is given by
$$y - \bar{y} = b(x - \bar{x}), \text{ where } b = \frac{S_{xy}}{S_{xx}} = \frac{\Sigma(x-\bar{x})(y-\bar{y})}{\Sigma(x-\bar{x})^2} = \frac{\Sigma xy - n\bar{x}\bar{y}}{\Sigma x^2 - n\bar{x}^2}$$
$$\Rightarrow a = \bar{y} - b\bar{x}$$

2. For any data pair (x, y) the predicted value of y is
$$\hat{y} = a + bx \Rightarrow \text{ the residual is } \varepsilon = y - \hat{y}$$

3. The sum of the residuals $\Sigma\varepsilon = 0$.
4. The least squares regression line minimises the sum of the squares of the residuals, $\Sigma\varepsilon^2$.
5. When using a regression line for prediction, a value within the data values (interpolation) is more likely to be predicted reliably than a value beyond the data values (extrapolation).

Random on random regression lines

6. If a value of y is to be predicted from a value of x, then the y on x regression line $y = a + bx$ needs to be used. The equation of this regression line is exactly the same as for the random on non-random regression line.

7. If a value of x is to be predicted from a value of y, then the x on y regression line $x = a + by$ needs to be used. The equation for this line is given by
$$x - \bar{x} = b(y - \bar{y}), \text{ where}$$
$$b = \frac{S_{xy}}{S_{yy}} = \frac{\Sigma(x-\bar{x})(y-\bar{y})}{\Sigma(y-\bar{y})^2} = \frac{\Sigma xy - n\bar{x}\bar{y}}{\Sigma y^2 - n\bar{y}^2}$$
$$\Rightarrow a = \bar{x} - b\bar{y}$$

8. Both of these lines pass through the point $(\bar{x}, \bar{y})$.
9. The goodness of fit of the regression line can be judged by the coefficient of determination. This is the square of the value of Pearson's product moment correlation coefficient.

LEARNING OUTCOMES

When you have completed this chapter you should be able to:
- obtain the equation of the least squares regression line for a random variable on a non-random variable, using raw data or summary statistics
- use the regression line as a model to estimate a value of the random variable and know when it is appropriate to do so
- know the meaning of the term residual and be able to calculate and interpret residuals
- obtain the equations of the two least squares regression lines, y on x and x on y, where both variables are random, using raw data or summary statistics
- use either regression line to estimate the expected value of one variable for a given value of the other and know when it is appropriate to do so
- check how well the model fits the data
- know the relationship between the two regression lines and when to use one rather than the other.

6 Chi-squared tests

The fact that the criterion which we happen to use has a fine ancestry of statistical theorems does not justify its use. Such justification must come from empirical evidence that it works.

W. A. Shewhart

What kind of films do you enjoy?

To help it decide when to show trailers for future programmes, the management of a cinema asks a sample of its customers to fill in a brief questionnaire saying which type of film they enjoy. It wants to know whether there is any relationship between people's enjoyment of horror films and action movies.

Discussion point
How do you think the management should select the sample of customers?

1 The chi-squared test for a contingency table

The management of the cinema takes 150 randomly selected questionnaires and records whether those patrons enjoyed or did not enjoy horror films and action movies.

Table 6.1

Observed frequency f_o	Enjoyed horror films	Did not enjoy horror films
Enjoyed action movies	51	41
Did not enjoy action movies	15	43

This method of presenting data is called a 2 × 2 *contingency table*. It is used where two variables (here 'attitude to horror films' and 'attitude to action movies') have been measured on a sample, and each variable can take two different values ('enjoy' or 'not enjoy').

The values of the variables fall into one or other of two categories. You want to determine the extent to which the variables are *related*.

It is conventional, and useful, to add the row and column totals in a contingency table: these are called the *marginal totals* of the table.

> **Note**
> You will meet larger contingency tables later in this chapter.

Table 6.2

Observed frequency f_o	Enjoyed horror films	Did not enjoy horror films	Total
Enjoyed action movies	51	41	92
Did not enjoy action movies	15	43	58
Total	66	84	150

A formal version of the cinema management's question is, 'Is enjoyment of horror films independent of enjoyment of action movies?'. You can use the sample data to investigate this question.

You can estimate the probability that a randomly chosen cinema-goer will enjoy horror films as follows. The number of cinema-goers in the sample who enjoyed horror films is 51 + 15 = 66.

So the proportion of cinema-goers who enjoyed horror films is $\frac{66}{150}$.

In a similar way, you can estimate the probability that a randomly chosen cinema-goer will enjoy action movies. The number of cinema-goers in the sample who enjoyed action movies is 51 + 41 = 92.

So the proportion of cinema-goers who enjoyed action movies is $\frac{92}{150}$.

> Notice how you use the marginal totals 66 and 92 which were calculated previously.

If people enjoyed horror films and action movies independently with the probabilities you have just estimated, then you would expect to find, for instance:

The chi-squared test for a contingency table

Number of people enjoying both types

$= 150 \times$ P(a random person enjoying both types)

$= 150 \times$ P(enjoying horror) $\times$ P(enjoying action)

$= 150 \times \dfrac{66}{150} \times \dfrac{92}{150}$

$= \dfrac{6072}{150}$

$= 40.48.$

In the same way, you can calculate the number of people you would expect to correspond to each cell in the table.

Table 6.3

Expected frequency f_e	Enjoyed horror films	Did not enjoy horror films	Total
Enjoyed action movies	$150 \times \dfrac{66}{150} \times \dfrac{92}{150} = 40.48$	$150 \times \dfrac{84}{150} \times \dfrac{92}{150} = 51.52$	92
Did not enjoy action movies	$150 \times \dfrac{66}{150} \times \dfrac{58}{150} = 25.52$	$150 \times \dfrac{84}{150} \times \dfrac{58}{150} = 32.48$	58
Total	66	84	150

Note that it is an inevitable consequence of this calculation that these expected figures have the same marginal totals as the sample data.

You are now in a position to test the original hypotheses, which you can state formally as:

H_0: enjoyment of the two types of film is independent.

H_1: enjoyment of the two types of film is not independent.

The expected frequencies were calculated assuming the null hypothesis is true. You know the actual sample frequencies and the aim is to decide whether those from the sample are so different from those calculated theoretically that the null hypothesis should be rejected.

A statistic which measures how far apart a set of observed frequencies is from the set expected under the null hypothesis is the χ^2 (chi-squared) statistic. It is given by the formula:

The value of the χ^2 test statistic is denoted by X^2.

$$X^2 = \sum \dfrac{(f_o - f_e)^2}{f_e} = \sum \dfrac{(\text{observed frequency} - \text{expected frequency})^2}{\text{expected frequency}}$$

You can use this here: the observed and expected frequencies are summarised below.

Table 6.4

Observed frequency f_o	Enjoyed horror	Did not enjoy horror
Enjoyed action	51	41
Did not enjoy action	15	43

Expected frequency f_e	Enjoyed horror	Did not enjoy horror
Enjoyed action	40.48	51.52
Did not enjoy action	25.52	32.48

The χ^2 statistic is:

$$X^2 = \sum \frac{(f_o - f_e)^2}{f_e} = \frac{(51-40.48)^2}{40.48} + \frac{(41-51.52)^2}{51.52} + \frac{(15-25.52)^2}{25.52} + \frac{(43-32.48)^2}{32.48}$$

$$= \frac{(10.52)^2}{40.48} + \frac{(10.52)^2}{51.52} + \frac{(10.52)^2}{25.52} + \frac{(10.52)^2}{32.48} = 12.626$$

> Note that the four numbers on the top lines (numerators) in this calculation are equal. This is not by chance; it will always happen with a 2 × 2 table. It provides you with a useful check and short cut when you are working out X^2.

Following the usual hypothesis-testing methodology, you want to know whether a value for this statistic at least as large as 12.626 is likely to occur by chance when the null hypothesis is true. The critical value at the 10% significance level for this test statistic is 2.706.

> You will see how to find critical values for a χ^2 test later in this chapter.

Since 12.626 > 2.706, you reject the null hypothesis, H₀, and conclude that people's enjoyment of the two types of film is not independent or that the enjoyment of the two is *associated*.

> **Note**
> Notice that you cannot conclude that enjoying one type of film *causes* people to enjoy the other. The test is of whether enjoyment of the two types is associated. It could be that a third factor, such as bloodthirstiness, causes both, but you do not know. The test tells you nothing about causality.

The diagram below shows you the relevant χ^2 distribution for this example, the critical region and the test statistic.

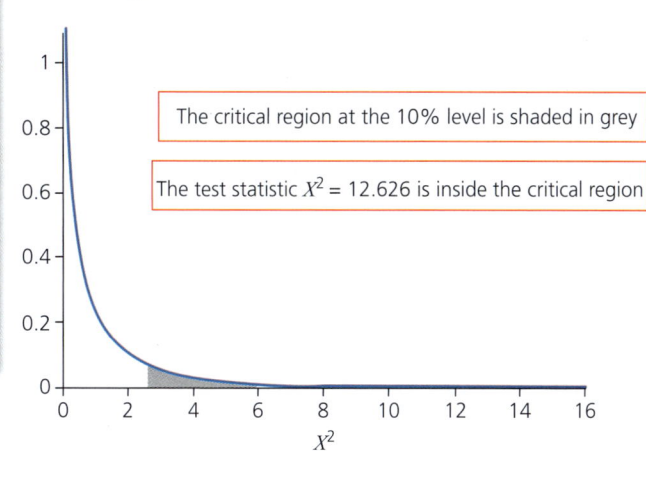

The critical region at the 10% level is shaded in grey

The test statistic $X^2 = 12.626$ is inside the critical region

Figure 6.1

> The information about the χ^2 distribution is for your interest – you do not need to use it to carry out the tests in this chapter.
>
> A standard Normal variable is drawn from a Normal population with mean 0 and variance 1.

The chi-squared distribution

The χ^2 distribution with n degrees of freedom is the distribution of the sum of the squares of n independent standard Normal random variables.

You can use it to test how well a set of data matches a given distribution. Many examples of such tests are covered in this chapter.

These tests include that used in the example of the cinema-goers: that is, whether the two classifications used in a contingency table are independent of one another. The hypotheses for such a test are:

H₀: The two variables whose values are being measured are independent in the population.

H₁: The two variables whose values are being measured are not independent in the population.

In order to carry out this test, you need to know more about the χ^2 distribution.

The chi-squared test for a contingency table

Figure 6.1 is an example of a χ^2 distribution. The shape of the χ^2 distribution curve depends on the number of free variables involved, the degrees of freedom, v. To find the value for v in this case, you start off with the number of cells which must be filled and then subtract one degree of freedom for each restriction, derived from the data, which is placed on the frequencies. In the cinema example above, you are imposing the requirements that the total of the frequencies must be 150, and that the overall proportions of people enjoying horror films and action movies are $\frac{66}{150}$ and $\frac{92}{150}$, respectively.

Hence $v = 4$ (number of cells)

$\quad\quad\quad - 1$ (total of frequencies is fixed by the data)

$\quad\quad\quad - 2$ (proportions of people enjoying each type are estimated from the data)

$\quad\quad = 1$.

So Figure 6.1 shows the shape of the χ^2 distribution for 1 degree of freedom.

In general, for an $m \times n$ contingency table, the degrees of freedom is:

$v = m \times n$ (number of cells)

$\quad - (m + n - 1)$ (Row and column totals are fixed but row totals and column totals have the same sum.)

$= mn - m - n + 1$

$= (m - 1)(n - 1)$.

As you will see later in the chapter, the calculation of the degrees of freedom varies from one χ^2 test to another.

Figure 6.2 shows the shape of the chi-squared distribution for $v = 1, 2, 3, 6,$ and 10 degrees of freedom.

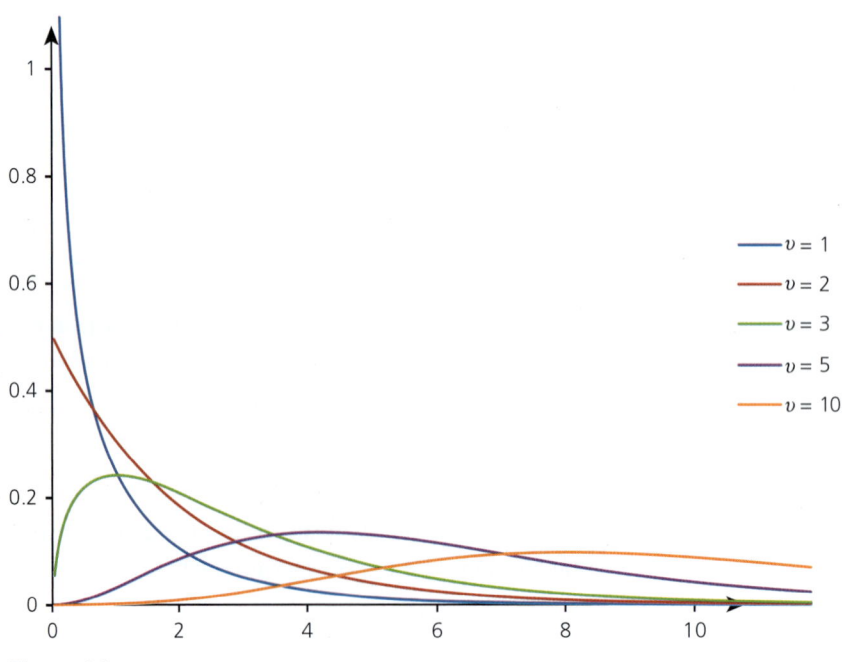

> **Note**
>
> As you can see, the shape of the chi-squared distribution depends very much on the number of degrees of freedom. So the critical region also depends on the number of degrees of freedom.

Figure 6.2

You can see in Figure 6.3 a typical χ^2 distribution curve together with the critical region for a significance level of $p\%$. An extract from a table of critical values of the χ^2 distribution for various degrees of freedom is also shown. The possible use of the left-hand tail probabilities (99%, 95% etc.) is discussed later in this chapter.

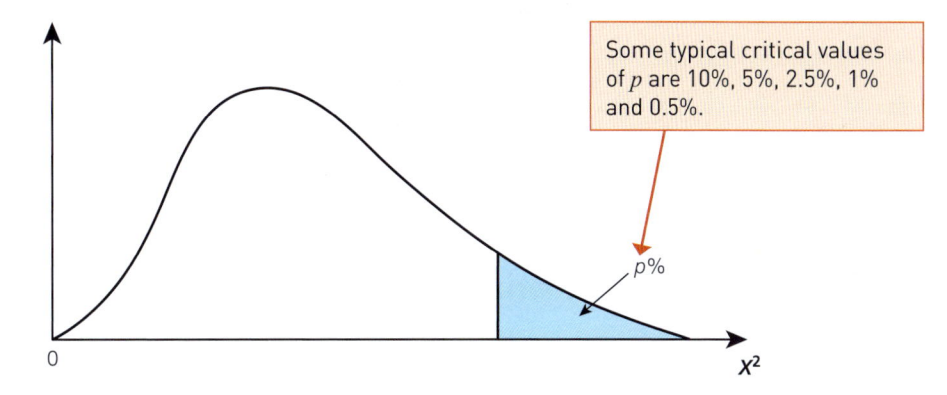

Some typical critical values of p are 10%, 5%, 2.5%, 1% and 0.5%.

$p\%$	99	97.5	95	90	10	5.0	2.5	1.0	0.5
$v = 1$	.0001	.0010	.0039	.0158	2.706	3.841	5.024	6.635	7.879
2	.0201	.0506	0.103	0.211	4.605	5.991	7.378	9.210	10.60
3	0.115	0.216	0.352	0.584	6.521	7.815	9.348	11.34	12.84
4	0.297	0.484	0.711	1.064	7.779	9.488	11.14	13.28	14.86
5	0.554	0.831	1.145	1.610	9.236	11.07	12.83	15.09	16.75
6	0.872	1.237	1.635	2.204	10.64	12.59	14.45	16.81	18.55
7	1.239	1.690	2.167	2.833	12.02	14.07	16.01	18.48	20.28
8	1.646	2.180	2.733	3.490	13.36	15.51	17.53	20.09	21.95
9	2.088	2.700	3.325	4.168	14.68	16.92	19.02	21.67	23.59

Figure 6.3

Properties of the test statistic X^2

You have seen the test statistic is given by

$$X^2 = \sum_{\text{All classes}} \frac{(f_o - f_e)^2}{f_e}$$

> **Note**
> An alternative notation which is often used is to call the expected frequency in the ith class E_i and the observed frequency in the ith class O_i.
> In this notation
> $$X^2 = \sum_i \frac{(O_i - E_i)^2}{E_i}$$

Here are some points to notice.

- It is clear that as the difference between the expected values and the observed values increases then so will the value of this test statistic. Squaring the top gives due weight to any particularly large differences. It also means that all values are positive.
- Dividing $(f_e - f_o)^2$ by f_e has the effect of standardising that element, allowing for the fact that, the larger the expected frequency within a class, the larger will be the difference between the observed and the expected.
- The usual convention in statistics is to use a Greek letter for a parent population parameter and the corresponding Roman letter for the equivalent sample statistic. Unfortunately, when it comes to χ^2, there is no Roman

equivalent to the Greek letter χ since it translates into CH. Since X looks rather like χ a sample statistic from a χ^2 population is denoted by X^2. (In the same way Christmas is abbreviated to χmas but written Xmas.)

For example:

Population parameters	Sample statistics
Greek letters	Roman letters
μ	m
σ	s
ρ	r

Continuing with tests on contingency tables

Example 6.1

The 4 × 3 contingency table below shows the type of car (saloon, sports, hatchback or SUV) owned by 360 randomly chosen people, and the age category (under 30, 30–60, over 60) into which the owners fall.

Note

The marginal totals are not essential in a contingency table, but it is conventional – and convenient – to add them. They are very helpful for subsequent calculations.

Table 6.5

Observed frequency f_o	Age of driver under 30	Age of driver 30–60	Age of driver over 60	Total
Saloon	10	67	57	134
Sports car	19	14	3	36
Hatchback	32	47	34	113
SUV	7	56	14	77
Total	68	184	108	360

(i) Write down appropriate hypotheses for a test to investigate whether type of car and owner's age are independent.

(ii) Calculate expected frequencies assuming that the null hypothesis is true.

(iii) Calculate the value of the test statistic X^2.

(iv) Find the critical value at the 5% significance level.

(v) Complete the test.

(vi) Comment on how the ownership of different types of car depends on the age of the owner.

> You need to calculate the expected frequencies in the table assuming that the null hypothesis is true.
>
> Use the probability estimates given by the marginal totals.
>
> For instance the expected frequency for hatchback and owner's age is over 60 is given by
>
> $360 \times \dfrac{113}{360} \times \dfrac{108}{360}$
>
> $= \dfrac{113 \times 108}{360} = 33.900$

Solution

(i) H_0: Car type is independent of owner's age.

H_1: Car type is not independent of owner's age.

(ii) Table 6.6

Expected frequency f_e	Age of driver — under 30	30–60	over 60	Total
Saloon	25.311	68.489	40.200	134
Sports car	6.800	18.400	10.800	36
Hatchback	21.344	57.756	33.900	113
SUV	14.544	39.356	23.100	77
Total	68	184	108	360

> **Note**
>
> This illustrates the general result for contingency tables:
>
> Expected frequency for a cell
>
> $= \dfrac{\text{product of marginal totals for that cell}}{\text{number of observations}}$

> **Note**
>
> You need to check that all the frequencies are large enough to make the χ^2 distribution a good approximation to the distribution of the X^2 statistic. The usual rule of thumb is to require all the expected frequencies to be at least 5.
>
> This requirement is (just) satisfied here. However, you might be cautious in your conclusions if the X^2 statistic is very near the relevant critical value. If some of the cells have small expected frequencies, you should either collect more data or amalgamate some of the categories if it makes sense to do so. For instance, two adjacent age ranges could reasonably be combined, but two car types probably could not.

(iii) The value of the X^2 statistic is $X^2 = \sum \dfrac{(f_o - f_e)^2}{f_e}$

The contributions of the various cells to this are shown in the table below.

Table 6.7

Contribution to test statistic	Age of driver — under 30	30–60	over 60
Saloon	9.262	0.032	7.021
Sports car	21.888	1.052	5.633
Hatchback	5.319	2.003	0.000
SUV	3.913	7.039	3.585

Total = 9.262 + 0.032 + 7.021 + 21.888 + … + 3.585

$X^2 = 66.749$

> An example of the calculation is
>
> $\dfrac{(10 - 25.311)^2}{25.311} = 9.262$
>
> for the top left cell.

The chi-squared test for a contingency table

> The number of rows, m, is 4
> The number of columns, n, is 3

(iv) The degrees of freedom are given by $v = (m-1)(n-1)$.

$v = (4-1) \times (3-1) = 6$

From the χ^2 tables, the critical value at the 5% level with six degrees of freedom is 12.59.

(v) The observed X^2 statistic of 66.749 is greater than the critical value of 12.59. So the null hypothesis is rejected and the alternative hypothesis is accepted at the 5% significance level:

that car type is not independent of owner's age,

or that car type and owner's age are associated.

(vi) In this case, the under-30 age group own fewer saloon cars and SUVs, more hatchbacks and many more sports cars than expected. Other cells with relatively large contributions to the X^2 statistic correspond to SUVs being owned more often than expected by 30–60-year-olds, and less often than expected by older or younger drivers, and over-60s owning more saloon cars and fewer sports cars than expected.

> **Note**
> You reject the null hypothesis if the test statistic is *greater* than the critical value.

> **Note**
> You should always refer to the size of the contributions when commenting on the way that one variable is associated with the other (assuming, of course, that the conclusion to your test is that there is association).

USING ICT

Statistical software

You can use statistical software to carry out a χ^2 test for a contingency table. In order for the software to process the test, you need to input the information in the table of observed frequencies. This consists of category names and the observed frequencies, so, in this case, it is the information in this table.

Table 6.8

	Age of driver		
Observed frequency f_o	under 30	30–60	over 60
Saloon	10	67	57
Sports car	19	14	3
Hatchback	32	47	34
SUV	7	56	14

The software then carries out all the calculations. Here is a typical output.

ChiSquared test

	under 30	30–60	over 60
Saloon	25.3111 9.2619 10	68.4889 0.0324 67	40.2 7.0209 57
Sports car	6.8 21.8882 19	18.4 1.0522 14	10.8 5.633 3
Hatchback	21.3444 5.3195 32	57.7556 2.003 47	33.9 0.0003 34
SUV	14.5444 3.9134 7	39.3556 7.0394 56	23.1 3.5848 14

Result
ChiSquared test
df 6
X^2 .... 66.7493
p 0.0000

Figure 6.4

> **Discussion points**
> The output includes the following information.
> → the expected frequencies
> → the contributions to the X^2 statistic
> → the degrees of freedom
> → the value of the X^2 statistic
> → the p-value for the test
>
> Identify where each piece of information is displayed.
>
> What other information is contained in the output box?

> Notice that the *p*-value is stated to be 0.0000. This requires some interpretation.
> - The other output figures are given either to 4 decimal places or as whole numbers.
> - So you can conclude that *p* = 0.0000 to 4 decimal places and therefore that *p* < 0.000 05.
> - So the result is significant even at the 0.01% significance level.

A spreadsheet

You can also use a spreadsheet to do the final stages of this test. To set it up, you would need to take the following steps.

- Enter the same information as before: the variable categories and the observed frequencies.
- Use a suitable formula to calculate the expected frequencies.
- Combine classes as necessary if any expected frequencies are below 5.
- Use a suitable formula to calculate the contributions to the test statistic.
- Find the sum of the contributions.
- Find the *p*-value using the formula provided with the spreadsheet, for example =CHISQ.DIST.RT(H1,6).

Cell H1 contains the value of the test statistic, X^2.

There are 6 degrees of freedom.

In this case, a typical spreadsheet gives the value of *p* as 1.894E-12, ie 1.894×10^{-12}, so much less than the upper bound of 0.000 05 inferred from the statistical software.

Exercise 6.1

① A group of 330 students, some aged 13 and the rest aged 16 is asked 'What is your usual method of transport from home to school?' The frequencies of each method of transport are shown in the table.

Table 6.9

	Age 13	Age 16
Walk	43	35
Cycle	24	42
Bus	64	49
Car	41	32

(i) Find the total of each row and each column.

A student is going to carry out a test to determine whether method of transport is independent of age.

(ii) Show that the expected frequency for age 16 students who walk is 37.35.

(iii) Show that the expected frequency for age 13 students who cycle is 34.40.

(iv) Would you expect the method of transport to be independent of age?

The chi-squared test for a contingency table

② A random sample of 80 students studying for a first aid exam was selected. The students were asked how many hours of revision they had done for the exam. The results are shown in the table, together with whether or not they passed the exam.

Table 6.10

	Pass	Fail
Less than 10 hours	13	18
At least 10 hours	42	7

(i) Find the expected frequency for each cell for a test to determine whether the number of hours of revision is independent of passing or failing.

(ii) Find the corresponding contributions to the chi-squared test statistic.

③ A group of 281 voters is asked to rate how good a job they think the Prime Minister is doing. Each is also asked for the highest educational qualifications they have achieved. The frequencies with which responses occurred are shown in the table.

Table 6.11

Rating of PM	Highest qualifications achieved			
	None	GCSE or equivalent	A-level or equivalent	Degree or equivalent
Very poor	11	37	13	6
Poor	12	17	22	8
Moderate	7	11	25	10
Good	10	17	17	9
Very good	19	16	8	6

Use these figures to test whether there is an association between rating of the Prime Minister and highest educational qualification achieved.

④ A medical insurance company office is the largest employer in a small town. When 37 randomly chosen people living in the town were asked where they worked and whether they belonged to the town's health club, 21 were found to work for the insurance company, of whom 15 also belonged to the health club, while 7 of the 16 not working for the insurance company belonged to the health club.

Test the hypothesis that health club membership is independent of employment by the medical insurance company.

⑤ In a random sample of 163 adult males, 37 suffer from hay-fever and 51 from asthma, both figures including 14 men who suffer from both. Test whether the two conditions are associated.

⑥ In a survey of 184 London residents brought up outside the south-east of England, respondents were asked whether, job and family permitting, they would like to return to their area of origin. Their responses are shown in the table.

Table 6.12

Region of origin	Would like to return to	Would not like to return to
South-west	16	28
Midlands	22	35
North	15	31
Wales	8	6
Scotland	14	9

Test the hypothesis that desire to return is independent of region of origin.

7. A sample of 80 men and 150 women selected at random are tested for colour-blindness. Twelve of the men and five of the women are found to be colour-blind. Is there evidence at the 1% level that colour-blindness is sex-related?

8. Depressive illness is categorised as type I, II or III. In a group of depressive psychiatric patients, the length of time for which their symptoms are apparent is observed. The results are shown below.

Table 6.13

Length of depressive episode	Type of symptoms I	II	III
Brief	15	22	12
Average	30	19	26
Extended	7	13	21
Semi-permanent	6	9	11

Is the length of the depressive episode independent of the type of symptoms?

9. The personnel manager of a large firm is investigating whether there is any association between the length of service of the employees and the type of training they receive from the firm. A random sample of 200 employee records is taken from the last few years and is classified according to these criteria. Length of service is classified as short (meaning less than 1 year), medium (1–3 years) and long (more than 3 years). Type of training is classified as being merely an initial 'induction course', proper initial on the job training but little, if any, more, and regular and continuous training. The data are as follows.

Table 6.14

Type of training	Length of service Short	Medium	Long
Induction course	14	23	13
Initial on-the-job	12	7	13
Continuous	28	32	58

The chi-squared test for a contingency table

The output from a statistical package for these data is shown below.

ChiSquared test

	Short	Medium	Long
Induction course	13.5000 0.018519 14	15.500 3.6290 23	21.000 3.0476 13
Initial on-the-job	8.6400 1.3067 12	9.9200 0.85952 7	13.440 0.01440 13
Continuous	313.860 0.46766 28	36.580 0.57344 32	49.560 1.4373 58

Result
ChiSquared test
df 4
X^2 .... 11.354
p 0.022859

Figure 6.5

Use the output to examine at the 5% level of significance whether these data provide evidence of association between length of service and type of training, stating clearly your null and alternative hypotheses.

Discuss your conclusions.

(10) In the initial stages of a market research exercise to investigate whether a proposed advertising campaign would be worthwhile, a survey of newspaper readership was undertaken. 100 people selected at random from the target population were interviewed. They were asked how many newspapers they read regularly. They were also classified as to whether they lived in urban or rural areas. The results were as follows.

Table 6.15

Number of newspapers read regularly	Urban	Rural
None	15	11
One	22	18
More than one	27	7

The output from a statistical package for these data is shown below.

ChiSquared test

	Urban	Rural
None	16.64 0.1616 15	9.36 0.2874 11
One	25.6 0.5063 22	14.4 0.9 18
More than one	21.76 1.2618 27	12.24 2.2433 7

Result
ChiSquared test
df 2
X^2 .... 5.3603
p 0.0686

Figure 6.6

(i) Use the output to examine at the 10% level of significance whether these data provide evidence of an association between the categories. State clearly the null and alternative hypotheses you are testing.

(ii) Justify the degrees of freedom for the test.

(iii) Discuss the conclusions reached from the test.

11. Public health officers are monitoring air quality over a large area. Air quality measurements using mobile instruments are made frequently by officers touring the area. The air quality is classified as poor, reasonable, good or excellent. The measurement sites are classified as being in residential areas, industrial areas, commercial areas or rural areas. The table shows a sample of frequencies over an extended period. The row and column totals and the grand total are also shown.

Table 6.16

Measurement site	Poor	Reasonable	Good	Excellent	Row totals
Residential	107	177	94	22	400
Industrial	87	128	74	19	308
Commercial	133	228	148	51	560
Rural	21	71	24	16	132
Column totals	348	604	340	108	1400

Examine at the 5% level of significance whether or not there is any association between measurement site and air quality, stating carefully the null and alternative hypotheses you are testing. Report briefly on your conclusions.

12. In an investigation of small business development in England, researchers are examining whether there is any association between the geographical area where such a business is located and the lifespan of the business. A random sample of records has been obtained from a national database. The geographical areas are classified very broadly as South-east, Midlands, North and 'Rest'. Lifespans are classified as short, medium and long. The table shows the frequencies obtained in the sample; row and column totals and the grand total are also shown.

Table 6.17

Geographical area	Short	Medium	Long	Row totals
South-east	140	72	56	268
Midlands	104	53	45	202
North	71	51	48	170
Rest	57	48	59	164
Column totals	372	224	208	804

Examine at the 1% level of significance whether or not there is any association between geographical area and lifespan, stating carefully the null and alternative hypotheses you are testing. Report briefly on your conclusions.

[MEI]

The chi-squared test for a contingency table

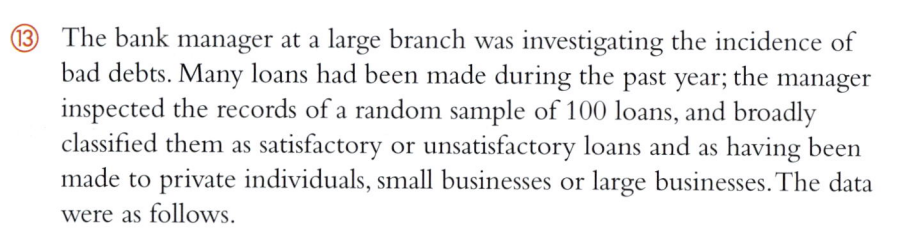

⑬ The bank manager at a large branch was investigating the incidence of bad debts. Many loans had been made during the past year; the manager inspected the records of a random sample of 100 loans, and broadly classified them as satisfactory or unsatisfactory loans and as having been made to private individuals, small businesses or large businesses. The data were as follows.

Table 6.18

	Satisfactory	Unsatisfactory
Private individual	22	5
Small business	34	11
Large business	21	3

(i) Discuss any problems which could occur in carrying out a χ^2 test to examine if there is any association between whether or not the loan was satisfactory and the type of customer to whom the loan was made.

(ii) State suitable null and alternative hypotheses for the test described in part (i).

(iii) Carry out a test at the 5% level of significance without combining any groups.

(iv) Explain which groups it might be best to combine and carry out the test again with these groups combined.

⑭ A survey of a random sample of 44 people is carried out. Their musical preferences are categorised as pop, classical or jazz. Their ages are categorised as under 20, 20 to 39, 40 to 59 and 60 or over. A test is to be carried out to examine whether there is any association between musical preference and age group. The results are as follows.

Table 6.19

		Musical preference		
		Pop	Classical	Jazz
Age group	Under 20	8	4	1
	20–39	3	3	0
	40–59	2	4	3
	60 or over	1	7	8

(i) Calculate the expected frequencies for 'Under 20' and '60 or over' for pop music.

(ii) Explain why the test would not be valid using these four age categories.

(iii) State which categories it would be best to combine in order to carry out the test.

(iv) Using this combination, carry out the test at the 5% significance level.

(v) Discuss briefly how musical preferences vary between the combined age groups, as shown by the contributions to the test statistic.

[MEI ADAPTED]

2 Goodness of fit tests

The χ^2 test is commonly used to see if a proposed model fits observed data.

Goodness of fit test for the uniform distribution

> **Discussion point**
> Why is it the model that should fit the data and not the other way round?

The extraordinary world of Roald Drysdale and the dice that Roald rolled

Roald Drysdale claims to be able to influence the world around him by mind alone.

One demonstration of this is his influence over throwing dice. 'You must realise that objects we take to be inanimate do in fact have a spirit,' he explained. 'Take these dice. At the moment their spirits are willing them to produce a certain result. I can't change that, but by concentrating my thought field on the dice, I can enhance their spirits and help them to produce the outcome that they are seeking.'

The power of the mind – Roald Drysdale claims to have psychic influence

One evening the spirits of the dice were clearly willing them to show 1, as you can see from these remarkable results from 120 throws.

Table 6.20

Score	6	5	4	3	2	1
Frequency	12	16	15	23	24	30

> **Discussion point**
> Do you think that Roald Drysdale actually used biased dice to fool people?

Do these figures provide evidence that Roald had influenced the outcomes, or is this just the level of variation you would expect to occur naturally? Clearly, a formal statistical test is required.

If Roald's claim had been that he could make a particular number, say 6, turn up more often than the other numbers, you could use a binomial test.

However, all he said was that he could 'enhance the spirits of the dice' by making some number come up more than the others. So all six outcomes are involved and a different test is needed.

The expected distribution of the results, based on the null hypothesis that the outcomes are not biased, is easily obtained. The probability of each outcome is $\frac{1}{6}$ and so the expectation for each number $120 \times \frac{1}{6} = 20$.

Table 6.21

Outcome	1	2	3	4	5	6
Expected frequency, f_e	20	20	20	20	20	20

You would not, however, expect exactly this result from 120 throws. Indeed, you would be very suspicious if somebody claimed to have obtained it, and might well disbelieve it. You expect random variation to produce small differences in the frequencies. The question is whether the quite large differences in Roald's case can be explained in this way or not.

Goodness of fit tests

When this is written in the formal language of statistical tests, it becomes:

$H_0: p = \frac{1}{6}$ for each outcome.

$H_1: p \neq \frac{1}{6}$ for each outcome.

> Notice that these are the same hypotheses that you would use for a test on whether the dice are biased.

The expected frequencies are denoted by f_e and the observed frequencies by f_o. To measure how far the observed data are from the expected, you clearly need to consider the difference between the observed frequencies, f_o, and the expected, f_e. The measure which is used as a test statistic for this is denoted by X^2 and given by:

$$X^2 = \sum_{\text{All classes}} \frac{(f_o - f_e)^2}{f_e}$$

You have already met this statistic when carrying out tests involving contingency tables earlier in this chapter. In this case, the calculation of X^2 is as follows.

Table 6.22

Outcome	6	5	4	3	2	1
Observed frequency, f_o	12	16	15	23	24	30
Expected frequency, f_e	20	20	20	20	20	20
Difference, $f_o - f_e$	−8	−4	−5	3	4	10
$(f_o - f_e)^2$	64	16	25	9	16	100
$(f_o - f_e)^2 / f_e$	3.2	0.8	1.25	0.45	0.8	5

$X^2 = 3.2 + 0.8 + 1.25 + 0.45 + 0.8 + 5 = 11.5$

The test statistic X^2 has the χ^2 (chi-squared) distribution. Critical values for this distribution are given in tables but, before you can use them, you have to think about two more points.

What is to be the significance level of the test?

> This means that it is unlikely that the null hypothesis (that the dice scores really are random) would not be rejected without very strong evidence.

This should really have been set before any data were collected. Because many people will be sceptical about Roald's claim, it would seem advisable to make the test rather strict, and so the 1% significance level is chosen.

How many degrees of freedom are involved?

As mentioned in the section on contingency tables, the shape of the χ^2 distribution curve depends on the number of free variables involved, the degrees of freedom, ν. To find the value for ν you start off with the number of cells which must be filled and then subtract one degree of freedom for each restriction, derived from the data, which is placed on the frequencies.

In this case, there are six classes (corresponding to scores of 1, 2, 3, 4, 5 and 6) but since the total number of throws is fixed (120) the frequency in the last class can be worked out if you know those of the first five classes.

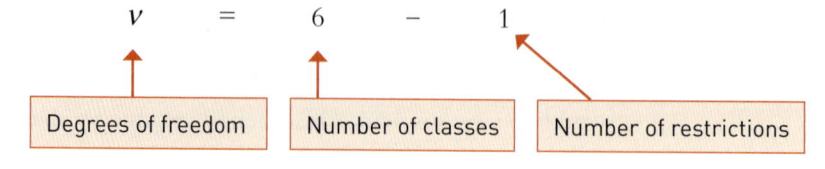

$$\nu \quad = \quad 6 \quad - \quad 1$$

Degrees of freedom | Number of classes | Number of restrictions

Looking in the tables for the 1% significance level and $v = 5$ gives a critical value of 15.09; see Figure 6.7.

Since $11.5 < 15.09$, there is no evidence to reject H_0.

There is no reason at this significance level to believe that any number was any more likely to come up than any other. Roald's powers are not proved.

> **Note**
>
> As with the test for a contingency table, the expected frequency of any class must be at least five. If a class has an expected frequency of less than five, then it must be grouped together with one or more other classes until their combined expected frequency is at least five.
>
> When a particular distribution is fitted to the data, it may be necessary to estimate one or more parameters of the distribution. This, together with the restriction on the total, will reduce the number of degrees of freedom:
>
> v = number of classes – number of estimated parameters – 1

$p\%$	99	97.5	95	90	10	5.0	2.5	1.0	0.5
$v = 1$	.0001	.0010	.0039	.0158	2.706	3.841	5.024	6.635	7.879
2	.0201	.0506	0.103	0.211	4.605	5.991	7.378	9.210	10.60
3	0.115	0.216	0.352	0.584	6.521	7.815	9.348	11.34	12.84
4	0.297	0.484	0.711	1.064	7.779	9.488	11.14	13.28	14.86
5	0.554	0.831	1.145	1.610	9.236	11.07	12.83	15.09	16.75
6	0.872	1.237	1.635	2.204	10.64	12.59	14.45	16.81	18.55
7	1.239	1.690	2.167	2.833	12.02	14.07	16.01	18.48	20.28
8	1.646	2.180	2.733	3.490	13.36	15.51	17.53	20.09	21.95
9	2.088	2.700	3.325	4.168	14.68	16.92	19.02	21.67	23.59

critical region, 1%

The test statistic $X^2 = 11.5$ is outside the critical region.

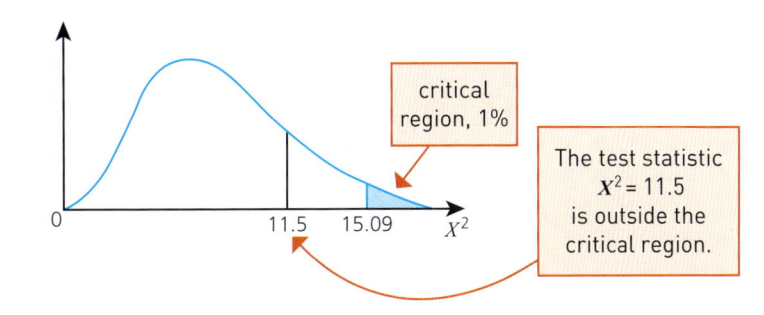

Figure 6.7

Notes

This is a one-tailed test with only the right-hand tail under consideration. The interpretation of the left-hand tail (where the agreement seems to be too good) is discussed later in the chapter.

Goodness of fit test for the Poisson distribution

Example 6.2

The number of telephone calls made to a counselling service is thought to be modelled by the Poisson distribution. Data are collected on the number of calls received during one-hour periods, as shown in the table. Use these data to test at the 5% significance level whether a Poisson model is appropriate.

Table 6.23

No. of calls per hour	0	1	2	3	4	5	6	Total
Frequency	6	13	26	14	7	4	0	70

Goodness of fit tests

Solution

H_0: the number of calls can be modelled by the Poisson distribution.
H_1: the number of calls cannot be modelled by the Poisson distribution.

Nothing is known about the form of the Poisson distribution, so the data must be used to estimate the Poisson parameter.

From the data, the mean number of calls per hour is

$$\frac{0 \times 6 + 1 \times 13 + 2 \times 26 + 3 \times 14 + 4 \times 7 + 5 \times 4}{70} = \frac{155}{70} = 2.214$$

The Poisson distribution with parameter $\lambda = 2.214$ is as follows.

Table 6.24

x	$P(X = x)$	$70 \times P(X = x)$	Expected frequency
0	$P(X = 0) \times e^{-2.214}$	70×0.1093	7.65
1	$P(X = 1) \times \frac{2.214}{1}$	70×0.2419	16.93
2	$P(X = 2) \times \frac{2.214}{2}$	70×0.2678	18.74
3	$P(X = 3) \times \frac{2.214}{3}$	70×0.1976	13.84
4	$P(X = 4) \times \frac{2.214}{4}$	70×0.1094	7.66
5	$P(X = 5) \times \frac{2.214}{5}$	70×0.0484	3.39
≥ 6	$1 - P(X < 6)$	70×0.0256	1.79

> The expected frequencies are not rounded to the nearest whole number. To do so would invalidate the test. Expected frequencies do not need to be integers.

> The expected frequency for the last class is worked out as $1 - P(X < 6)$ and not as $P(X = 6)$, which would have cut off the right-hand tail of the distribution. The classes need to cover all *possible* outcomes, not just those that occurred in your survey.

The expected frequencies for the last two classes are both less than 5 but if they are put together to give an expected value of 5.2, the problem is overcome.

The table for calculating the test statistic is shown below.

Table 6.25

No. of calls, X	0	1	2	3	4	5+	Total
Observed frequency, f_o	6	13	26	14	7	4	70
Expected frequency, f_e	7.65	16.93	18.74	13.84	7.66	5.18	
$(f_o - f_e)$	−1.65	−3.93	7.26	0.16	−0.66	−1.18	
$(f_o - f_e)^2/f_e$	0.3544	0.9126	2.8080	0.0020	0.0567	0.2702	4.4040

$X^2 = 0.3544 + 0.9126 + 2.8080 + 0.0020 + 0.0567 + 0.2702 = 4.4040$

The degrees of freedom are

v = number of classes − number of estimated parameters − 1

Table 6.26

No. of calls, X	0	1	2	3	4	5+	Total
Observed frequency, f_o	6	13	26	14	7	4	70

$v \quad = \quad 6 \quad - \quad 1 \quad - \quad 1 \quad = 4$

- The number of classes is 6 because 2 of the original 7 classes have been combined.
- λ was estimated as 2.214, one restriction.
- The total frequency (70) is one restriction.

From the tables, the critical value for a significance level of 5% and 4 degrees of freedom is 9.488.

The calculated test statistic, $X^2 = 4.404$. Since $4.404 < 9.488$, H_0 is accepted.

The data are consistent with a Poisson distribution for the number of calls.

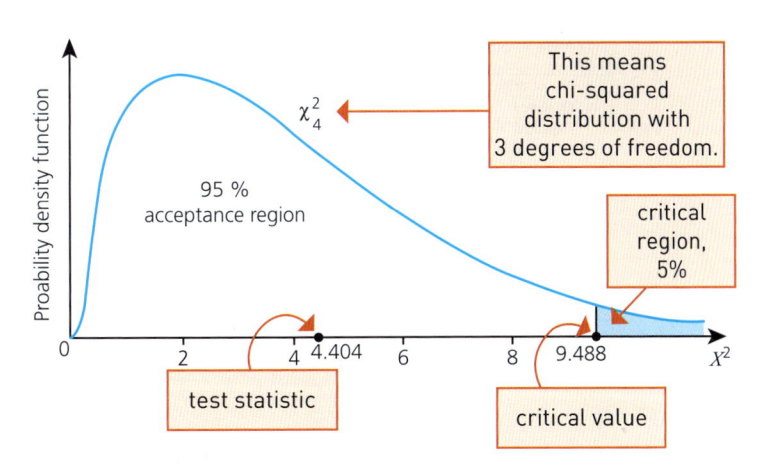

Figure 6.8

Goodness of fit tests

USING ICT

A spreadsheet

You can also use a spreadsheet to carry out the steps for a goodness of fit test for the Poisson model. To set it up, you would need to take the following steps.

- Enter the variable categories and the observed frequencies. In this example they are:

Table 6.27

No. of calls, X	0	1	2	3	4	5+
Observed frequency, f_o	6	13	26	14	7	4

- Find the mean value. *(In this case, the mean works out to be 2.21429.)*
- Calculate the Poisson probabilities and use them to work out the expected frequencies. *(This includes the final class which is open-ended.)*
- Combine classes as necessary if any expected frequencies are below 5.
- Calculate the individual contributions to the test statistic.
- Find the sum of the contributions.
- Find the degrees of freedom.
- Find the p-value using the formula provided with the spreadsheet, for example = CHISQ.DIST.RT.

A typical display for this example is shown below.

	A	B	C	D	E	F	G	H
1	No. of calls.	0	1	2	3	4	5	>=6
2	Observed	6	13	26	14	7	4	0
3	Expected	7.646	16.931	18.745	13.836	7.659	3.392	1.792
4								
5	Mean	2.21429						
6								
7	No. of calls.	0	1	2	3	4	>=5	Sum
8	Observed	6	13	26	14	7	4	70
9	Expected	7.65	16.93	18.74	13.84	7.66	5.18	70.00
10	Contribution	0.354423	0.912643	2.808036	0.001955	0.056694	0.270227	4.403979
11	d of freedom	4						
12	p-value	0.3541						

Figure 6.9

You can adapt these steps to use a spreadsheet to test for goodness of fit of other distributions.

Goodness of fit test for the binomial distribution

Example 6.3

An egg packaging firm has introduced a new box for its eggs. Each box holds six eggs. Unfortunately, it finds that the new box tends to mark the eggs. Data on the number of eggs marked in 100 boxes are collected.

Table 6.28

No. of marked eggs	0	1	2	3	4	5	6	Total
No. of boxes, f_o	3	3	27	29	10	7	21	100

It is thought that the distribution may be modelled by the binomial distribution. Carry out a test on the data at the 0.5% significance level to determine whether the data can be modelled by the binomial distribution.

Solution

H_0: The number of marked eggs can be modelled by the binomial distribution.

H_1: The number of marked eggs cannot be modelled by the binomial distribution.

The binomial distribution has two parameters, n and p. The parameter n is clearly 6, but p is not known and so must be estimated from the data.

From the data, the mean number of marked eggs per box is

$$\frac{0\times3+1\times3+2\times27+3\times29+4\times10+5\times7+6\times21}{100} = 3.45$$

Since the population mean is np you may estimate p by putting $6p = 3.45$

estimated $p = 0.575$ and estimated $q = 1 - p = 0.425$.

These parameters are now used to calculate the expected frequencies of $0, 1, 2, \ldots, 6$ marked eggs per box in 100 boxes.

Table 6.29

x	$P(X = x)$		Expected frequency, f_e $100 \times P(X = x)$
0	0.425^6	0.0059	0.59
1	$6 \times 0.575^1 \times 0.425^5$	0.0478	4.78
2	$15 \times 0.575^2 \times 0.425^4$	0.1618	16.18
3	$20 \times 0.575^3 \times 0.425^3$	0.2919	29.19
4	$15 \times 0.575^4 \times 0.425^2$	0.2962	29.62
5	$6 \times 0.575^5 \times 0.425^1$	0.1603	16.03
6	0.575^6	0.0361	3.61

In this case, there are three classes with an expected frequency of less than 5. The class for $x = 0$ is combined with the class for $x = 1$, bringing the expected frequency just over 5, and the class for $x = 6$ is combined with that for $x = 5$.

Table 6.30

No. of marked eggs, x	0, 1	2	3	4	5, 6	Total
Observed frequency, f_o	6	27	29	10	28	100
Expected frequency, f_e	5.37	16.18	29.19	29.62	19.64	100
$(f_o - f_e)$	0.68	10.82	−0.19	−19.62	8.36	
$(f_o - f_e)^2/f_e$	0.07	7.24	0.00	13.00	3.56	

The test statistic, $X^2 = 0.07 + 7.24 + 0.00 + 13.00 + 3.56 = 23.87$

Goodness of fit tests

The degrees of freedom

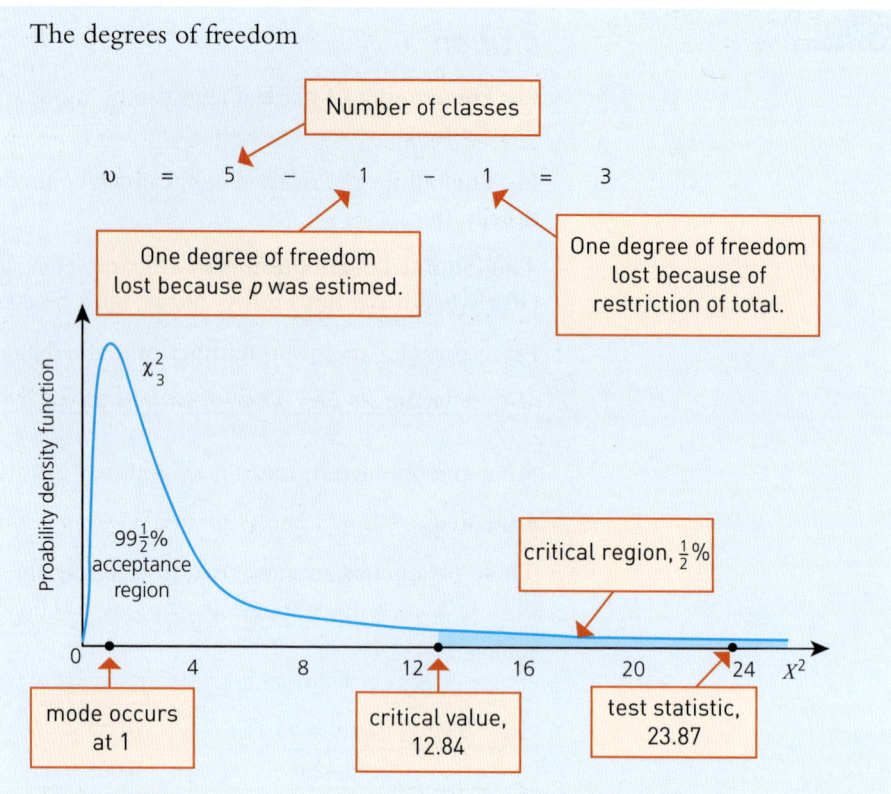

$$\upsilon = 5 - 1 - 1 = 3$$

- Number of classes
- One degree of freedom lost because *p* was estimated.
- One degree of freedom lost because of restriction of total.

[Chi-squared distribution graph with χ^2_3, showing mode occurs at 1, 99½% acceptance region, critical value 12.84, critical region ½%, test statistic 23.87]

Figure 6.10

From the tables, for the 0.5% significance level and $\nu = 3$, the critical value of χ^2_3 is 12.84.

Since 23.87 > 12.84, H₀ is rejected.

The data indicate that the binomial distribution is not an appropriate model for the number of marked eggs. If you look at the distribution of the data, as illustrated in Figure 6.11, you can easily see why, since it is bimodal.

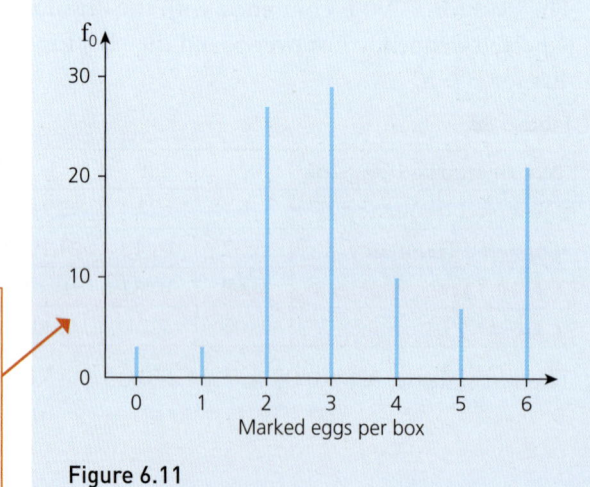

[Bar chart of f_0 vs Marked eggs per box, showing bimodal distribution with peaks at 2 and 3, and another at 6]

You can see that the distribution has two peaks. They are not both exactly the same height, but the second peak is sufficiently high to suggest bimodality.

Figure 6.11

Example 6.4

It is generally believed that a particular genetic defect is carried by 10% of people. A new and simple test becomes available to determine whether somebody is a carrier of this defect, using a blood specimen. As part of a research project, 100 hospitals are asked to carry out this test anonymously on the next 30 blood samples they take. The results are as follows.

Table 6.31

Number of positive tests	0	1	2	3	4	5	6	7+
Frequency, f_o	11	29	26	20	9	3	1	1

Do these figures support the model that 10% of people carry this defect, independently of any other condition, at the 5% significance level?

Solution

H_0: the model that 10% of people carry this defect is appropriate.

H_1: the model that 10% of people carry this defect is not appropriate.

The expected frequencies may be found using the binomial distribution $B(30, 0.1)$.

Table 6.32

Number of positive tests	0	1	2	3	4	5	6	7+
Expected frequency, f_e	4.24	14.13	22.77	23.61	17.71	10.23	4.74	2.58

Since the expected frequencies for 6 and 7+ positive tests are less than 5, you need to combine these two classes.

The calculation then proceeds as follows.

Table 6.33

No. of positive tests	0, 1	2	3	4	5	6+	Total
Observed frequency, f_o	40	26	20	9	3	2	100
Expected frequency, f_e	18.37	22.77	23.61	17.71	10.23	7.32	
$(f_o - f_e)$	21.63	3.23	−3.61	−8.71	−7.23	−5.32	
$(f_o - f_e)^2 / f_e$	25.47	0.46	0.55	4.28	5.11	3.87	

The test statistic $X^2 = 25.47 + 0.46 + 0.55 + 4.28 + 5.11 + 3.87$

$= 39.74$

The degrees of freedom,

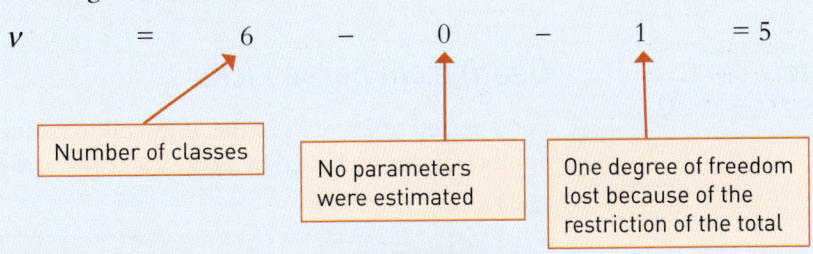

$\nu \quad = \quad 6 \quad - \quad 0 \quad - \quad 1 \quad = 5$

- Number of classes (6)
- No parameters were estimated (0)
- One degree of freedom lost because of the restriction of the total (1)

Goodness of fit tests

> **Note**
> 1. Although this example is like the previous one in that both used the binomial distribution as a model, the procedure is different. In this case, the given model included the information $p = 0.1$ and so you did not have to estimate the parameter p. Consequently, a degree of freedom was not lost from doing so.
> 2. The value of X^2 was very large in comparison with the critical value. What went wrong with the model?
>
> You will find that if you use the data to estimate p, it does not work out to be 0.1 but a little under 0.07. Fewer people are carriers of the defect than was believed to be the case. If you work through the example again with the model $p = 0.07$, you will find that the fit is good enough for you to start looking at the left-hand tail of the distribution.

[Figure 6.12: A chi-squared distribution χ^2_5 curve showing the 95% acceptance region, mode occurring at 3, critical value of 11.07, critical region of 5%, and test statistic of 39.74 well into the critical region.]

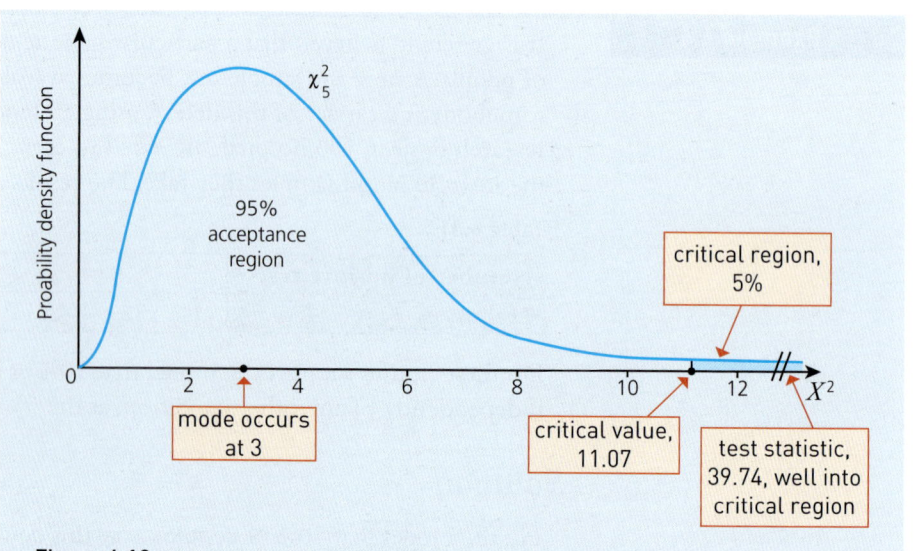

Figure 6.12

From the tables, for 5% significance level and $\nu = 5$, the critical value of χ^2_5 is 11.07. Since $39.74 > 11.07$, H_0 is rejected.

The data indicate that the binomial distribution with $p = 0.1$ is not an appropriate model.

ACTIVITY 6.1

Carry out a goodness of fit test for the data in Example 6.4 using the p-value estimated from the data in the previous example.

The left-hand tail

The χ^2 test is conducted as a one-tailed test, looking to see if the test statistic gives a value to the right of the critical value, as in the previous examples.

However, examination of the left-hand tail also gives information. In any modelling situation you would expect there to be some variability. Even when using the binomial to model a clear binomial situation, like the number of heads obtained in throwing a coin a large number of times, you would be very surprised if the observed and expected frequencies were identical. The left-hand tail may lead you to wonder whether the fit is too good to be credible. The following very famous example was one of the first published examples that brought the Poisson distribution to public notice.

Death from horse kicks

For a period of 20 years in the 19th century data were collected of the annual number of deaths caused by horse kicks per army corps in the Prussian army.

Table 6.34

No. of deaths	0	1	2	3	4
No. of corps, f_o	109	65	22	3	1

These data give a mean of 0.61. The variance of 0.6079 is almost the same, suggesting that the Poisson model may be appropriate.

The Poisson distribution (0.61) gives these figures.

Table 6.35

No. of deaths	0	1	2	3	4 or more
No. of corps, f_e	108.7	66.3	20.2	4.1	0.7

This looks so close that there seems little point in using a test to see if the data will fit the distribution. However, proceeding to the test, and remembering to combine classes to give expected values of at least 5, the null and alternative hypotheses are as follows.

H_0: Deaths from horse kick can be modelled by a Poisson distribution.

H_1: Deaths from horse kick cannot be modelled by a Poisson distribution.

Table 6.36

No. of deaths	0	1	2 or more
Observed frequency, f_o	109	65	26
Expected frequency, f_e	108.7	66.3	25
$(f_o - f_e)$	0.3	−1.3	1
$(f_o - f_e)^2/f_e$	0.001	0.025	0.040

The test statistic $X^2 = 0.001 + 0.025 + 0.040$

$\qquad\qquad\qquad\ = 0.066$

The degrees of freedom are given by

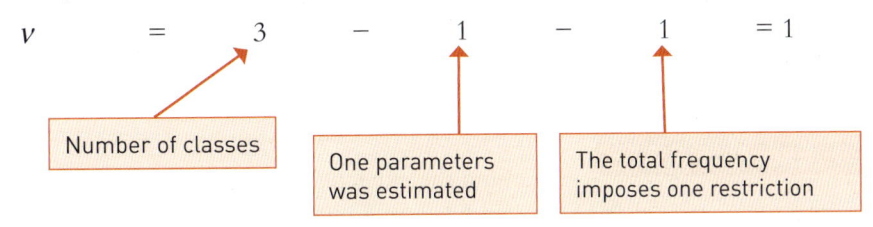

$\nu\ =\ 3\ -\ 1\ -\ 1\ =\ 1$

- Number of classes
- One parameters was estimated
- The total frequency imposes one restriction

> **Discussion point**
> Looking at the expected values of the Poisson distribution in comparison with the observed values suggests that the fit is very good indeed. Is it perhaps suspiciously good? Might the data have been fixed?

The critical value of χ^2 for 1 degree of freedom at the 5% significance level is 3.841.

As 0.066 < 3.841 it is clear that the null hypothesis, that the Poisson distribution is an appropriate model, should be accepted.

The tables relating to the left-hand tail of the χ^2 distribution give critical values for this situation. For example, the value for 95% significance level for $\nu = 1$ is 0.0039. This means that if the null hypothesis is true, you would expect a value for X^2 less than 0.0039 from no more than 5% of samples.

In this case, the test statistic is $X^2 = 0.066$. This is greater than the 95% critical value, and so you can conclude that a fit as good as this will occur with more than 1 sample in 20. That may well help allay your suspicions.

If your test statistic does lie within the left-hand critical region, you should check the data to ensure that the figures are genuine and that all the procedures have been carried out properly. There are three situations you should particularly watch out for.

Goodness of fit tests

- The model was constructed to fit a set of data. It is then being tested by seeing how well it fits the same data. Once the model is determined, new data should be used to test it.
- Some of the data have been omitted in order to produce a better fit.
- The data are not genuine.

Although looking at the left-hand tail of the χ^2 distribution may make you suspicious of the quality of the data, it does not provide a formal hypothesis test that the data are not genuine. Thus the term *critical region* is not really appropriate to this tail: *warning region* would be better.

The χ^2 test is a **distribution-free test;** this means that there are no modelling assumptions associated with the test itself. This has the advantage that the test can be widely used, but, on the other hand, it is not a very sensitive test. The test for rank correlation which you met in Chapter 4 is another example of a distribution-free test: one can test for rank correlation without knowing anything about the underlying bivariate distribution, but one frequently finds there is no significant evidence of correlation.

> ❗ If you obtain a p-value for a goodness of fit test, you need to take a little care interpreting it. The lower the p-value, the less likely it is that the sample could have been drawn from a distribution for which the null hypothesis is true; conversely, the higher the p-value, the more likely it is that that the sample could have been drawn from such a distribution.
>
> Quite often you will want to show that a certain distribution is appropriate and so you will associate a high p-value with a successful outcome. By contrast, in many other hypothesis tests, you are hoping to show that the null hypothesis is false, and so something special has happened; in such cases, a low p-value can be regarded as a successful outcome.

Exercise 6.2

① Find the expected frequencies of 0, 1, 2, 3, ≥ 4 successes if 80 observations are taken of a binomial random variable with $n = 20$ and $p = 0.09$.

② You are given that $X \sim$ Poisson (1.6). Find the expected frequencies of $x = 0, 1, 2, 3, 4, \geq 5$ if 60 observations of X are taken.

③ Part of a large simulation study requires the provision of many simulated observations that can be taken as coming from the Poisson distribution with parameter 2. There is a suspicion that this part of the simulation is not working properly.

Two hundred of the simulated observations are recorded in the form of a frequency table as follows.

Table 6.37

Number of simulated observations	0	1	2	3	4	≥ 5
Frequency	20	40	52	49	27	12

Carry out a χ^2 test, at the 5% level of significance, to examine whether the required Poisson distribution can be assumed for the simulated observations.

[MEI, PART]

④ A typist makes mistakes from time to time in a 200-page book. The number of pages with mistakes are as follows.

Table 6.38

Number of mistakes	0	1	2	3	4	5
Number of pages	18	62	84	30	5	1

(i) Test at the 5% significance level whether the Poisson distribution is an appropriate model for these data.

(ii) What factors would make it other than a Poisson distribution?

⑤ A biologist crosses two pure varieties of plant, one with pink flowers, the other white. The pink is dominant so that the flowers of the second generation should be in the ratio pink : white = 3 : 1.

He plants the seeds in batches of 5 in 32 trays and counts the numbers of plants with pink and with white flowers in each tray.

Table 6.39

Number of white flowers	0	1	2	3	4	5
Number of frequency	9	12	7	2	1	1

(i) What distribution would you expect for the number of plants with white flowers in each tray?

(ii) Use these figures to test at the 2.5% significance level whether the distribution is that which you expected.

⑥ As part of a survey, a railway company took a sample of 80 people, each of whom had recently travelled three times on a particular route, and asked them on how many of these three occasions they were generally satisfied with their journeys. The results were as follows.

Table 6.40

Number of occasions generally satisfied	0	1	2	3
Number of people	4	20	44	12

The company is considering fitting a binomial model to these data, with p taken as the probability of being generally satisfied on a journey.

(i) Estimate the value of p.

(ii) Use a suitable statistical procedure and 10% significance level to assess the goodness of fit of a binomial model.

(iii) What assumption is required about the sample? Discuss briefly whether this assumption is likely to hold. [MEI]

⑦ An examination board is testing a multiple-choice question. They get 100 students to try the question and their answers are as follows.

Table 6.41

Choice	A	B	C	D	E
Frequency	32	18	10	28	12

Are there grounds, at the 10% significance level, for the view that the question was so hard that the students guessed the answers at random?

Goodness of fit tests

⑧ A student on a geography field trip has collected data on the size of rocks found on a scree slope. The student counts the number of large rocks (that is, heavier than a stated weight) found in a 2 m square at the top, middle and bottom of the slope.

Table 6.42

	Top	Middle	Bottom
Number of large rocks	5	10	18

(i) Test at the 5% significance level whether these data are consistent with the hypothesis that the size of rocks is distributed evenly on the scree slope.

(ii) What does your test tell the student about the theory that large rocks will migrate to the bottom of the slope?

⑨ A researcher is investigating the feeding habits of bees. She sets up a feeding station some distance from a beehive and, over a long period of time, records the numbers of bees arriving each minute. For a random sample of 100 one-minute intervals she obtains the following results.

Table 6.43

Number of bees	0	1	2	3	4	5	6	7	≥ 8
Number of intervals	6	16	19	18	17	14	6	4	0

(i) Show that the sample mean is 3.1 and find the sample variance. Do these values support the possibility of a Poisson model for the number of bees arriving each minute? Explain your answer.

(ii) Show that, if a Poisson model with the mean in part (i) fits the data, the expected frequency for two bees arriving is 21.65.

(iii) Use the spreadsheet below to complete a test of the goodness of fit of a Poisson model to the data.

	A	B	C	D	E	F	G	H	I	J
1	Number of bees	0	1	2	3	4	5	6	7	>=8
2	Number of intervals	6	16	19	18	17	14	6	4	0
3	Probability		0.0450	0.1397	0.2165	0.2237	0.1733	0.1075	0.0555	0.0246
4	Expected frequency		4.505	13.97	21.65	22.37	17.33	10.75	5.553	2.459
5										
6	Attempts		<=1	2	3	4	5	>=6	Sum	
7	Observed frequency		22	19	18	17	14	10	100	
8	Probability		0.1847	0.2165	0.2237	0.1733	0.1075	0.0943	1.0000	
9	Expected frequency		18.47	21.65	22.37	17.33	10.75	9.433	100	
10	Contribution		0.6746	0.3235	0.8529	0.0065	0.9842	0.0340	2.8756	
11										
12	Mean		3.1							
13	X^2 statistic		2.8756							
14	d of f		4							
15	p-value		0.5789							

Figure 6.13

[MEI, PART]

⑩ A university student working in a small seaside hotel in the summer holidays looks at the records for the previous holiday season of 30 weeks. She records the number of days in each week on which the hotel had to turn away visitors because it was full. The data she collects are as follows.

Table 6.44

Number of days visitors turned away	0	1	2	3	4	5+	Total
Number of weeks	11	13	4	1	1	0	30

(i) Calculate the mean and variance of the data.

(ii) The student thinks that these data can be modelled by the binomial distribution. Carry out a test at the 5% significance level to see if the binomial distribution is a suitable model.

(iii) What other distribution might be used to model these data? Give your reasons.

11. Morag is writing a book. Every so often she uses the spell check facility in her word processing software, and, for interest, records the number of mistakes she has made on each page. In the first 20 pages, the results were as follows.

Table 6.45

Number of mistakes/page	0	1	2	3	4+	Total
Frequency	9	6	4	1	0	20

(i) Explain why it is not possible to use the χ^2 test on these data to decide whether the occurrence of spelling mistakes may be modelled by the Poisson distribution.

In the next 30 pages Morag's figures are as follows.

Table 6.46

Number of mistakes/page	0	1	2	3	4+	Total
Frequency	14	7	7	0	2	30

(ii) Use the combined figures, covering the first 50 pages, to test whether the occurrence of Morag's spelling mistakes may be modelled by the Poisson distribution. Use the 5% significance level.

(iii) If the distribution really is Poisson, what does this tell you about the incidence of spelling mistakes? Do you think this is realistic?

12. In a survey of five towns, the population of the town and the number of petrol-filling stations were recorded as follows.

Table 6.47

Town	Population (to nearest 10 000)	Number of filling stations
A	4	22
B	3	16
C	7	35
D	6	27
E	12	60
Totals	32	160

An assistant researcher, who wanted to find out whether the petrol stations were evenly distributed between the towns, performed a χ^2 test on the number of filling stations, with a null hypothesis that there was no difference in the number of filling stations in each town. She found that her X^2 value was 36.69. Without repeating her calculation, state with reasons what her conclusion was.

Goodness of fit tests

13 A local council has records of the number of children and the number of households in its area. It is therefore known that the average number of children per household is 1.40. It is suggested that the number of children per household can be modelled by the Poisson distribution with parameter 1.40. In order to test this, a random sample of 1000 households is taken, giving the following data.

Table 6.48

Number of children	0	1	2	3	4	5+
Number of households	273	361	263	78	21	4

(i) Find the corresponding expected frequencies obtained from the Poisson distribution with parameter 1.40.

(ii) Carry out a χ^2 test, at the 5% level of significance, to determine whether or not the proposed model should be accepted. State clearly the null and alternative hypotheses being tested and the conclusion which is reached. [MEI]

14 Properties where people live are placed in one of eight bands for council tax assessment. Band A represents the lowest-value properties (up to £40 000) and band H represents the highest-value properties (over £320 000).

It is desired to investigate whether the distribution of properties within the eight bands in the city of Trumpton matches the national distribution.

A random sample of 500 properties in Trumpton is taken. The percentage of properties in each band nationally and the number of properties in each band in the sample are as follows.

Table 6.49

Band	Percentage of properties nationally	Number of properties in sample
A	14.2%	53
B	22.6%	105
C	20.8%	111
D	14.3%	80
E	11.4%	63
F	9.8%	49
G	5.9%	36
H	1.0%	3
Total	100.0%	500

(i) Find the expected frequency within each band in Trumpton based on the national proportions.

(ii) Carry out an appropriate hypothesis test, at the 10% significance level. State your hypotheses and conclusions carefully.

(iii) If a random sample of 1000 properties had been taken and there had been precisely *twice* as many properties in each band, what effect would this have on your conclusions in part (ii)? [MEI]

15 (i) A random sample of supermarkets were sent a questionnaire on which they were asked to report the number of cases of shoplifting they had dealt with in each month of the previous year. The totals for each month were as follows.

Table 6.50

J	F	M	A	M	J	J	A	S	O	N	D
16	12	10	17	6	18	16	17	10	22	14	16

Carry out a χ^2 test at an appropriate level of significance to determine whether or not shoplifting is more likely to occur in some months than others. (You may take all months to be of the same length.) Make clear your null and alternative hypotheses, the level of significance you are using, and your conclusion.

You may, if you wish, use the fact that, when all the values of f_e are equal, the usual X^2 test statistic may be written as

$$\frac{1}{f_e}\Sigma f_0^2 - \Sigma f_e$$

(ii) Prove the result given at the end of part (i). [MEI]

16. A man accuses a casino of having two loaded dice. He throws them 360 times with the following outcomes for their sum at each throw.

Table 6.51

Total	2	3	4	5	6	7	8	9	10	11	12
Frequency	5	15	30	35	45	61	53	45	31	24	16

(i) State null and alternative hypotheses for a test to investigate whether the dice are fair.

(ii) Show that the expected frequency for totals of 2 and 5 are 10 and 40, respectively.

(iii) Does the man have grounds for his accusation at the 5% significance level?

17. The manager of a large supermarket has recently moved from one store to another. At the previous store, it was known from surveys that 42% of the customers lived within 5 miles of the store, 35% lived between 5 and 10 miles from the store and the remaining 23% lived more than 10 miles from the store. The manager wishes to test whether the same proportions apply at the new store.

One Saturday morning, the first 100 customers to enter the store after 11.00 am were asked how far from the store they lived. The results, grouped into the same categories as for the previous store, were as follows.

Table 6.52

Distance (miles)	0–5	5–10	more than 10
Number of customers	34	48	18

(i) Assuming that this is a random sample of all the customers at the store, test at the 5% level of significance whether the proportions at the manager's new store may be taken to be the same as those at the previous store. Discuss your conclusions briefly.

(ii) Discuss whether this is likely to be a random sample. [MEI]

18. In Question 12, the senior researcher decided to use the hypothesis that the number of filling stations was directly proportional to the size of the town's population. Show that, on this basis, the expected number of garages for town A would be 20, and test the hypothesis at the 10% significance level stating your conclusions clearly. [MEI]

Goodness of fit tests

KEY POINTS

1 Contingency tables

To test whether the variables in an $m \times n$ contingency table are independent the steps are as follows.

(i) The null hypothesis is that the variables are independent, the alternative is that they are not.

(ii) Calculate the marginal (row and column) totals for the table.

(iii) Calculate the *expected frequency* in each cell.

(iv) The χ^2 statistic is given by $X^2 \sum \dfrac{(f_o - f_e)^2}{f_e}$ where f_o is the observed frequency and f_e is the expected frequency in each cell.

(v) The number of *degrees of freedom*, v, for the test is $(m-1)(n-1)$ for an $m \times n$ table.

(vi) Read the critical value from the χ^2 tables (alternatively, use suitable software) for the appropriate degrees of freedom and significance level. If X^2 is less than the significance level, the null hypothesis is accepted; otherwise it is rejected.

(vii) If two variables are not independent, you say that there is an *association* between them.

2 Goodness of fit tests

To test whether a distribution models a situation, the steps are as follows.

(i) Select your model, binomial, Poisson, etc.

(ii) Set up null and alternative hypotheses and choose the significance level.

(iii) Collect data. Record the observed frequency for each outcome.

(iv) Calculate the expected frequencies arising from the model.

(v) Check that the expected frequencies are all at least 5. If not, combine classes.

(vi) Calculate the test statistic.

The χ^2 statistic is given by $X^2 \sum \dfrac{(f_o - f_e)^2}{f_e}$.

(vii) Find the degrees of freedom, v, for the test using the formula.
v = number of classes − number of estimated parameters − 1
where the number of classes is counted *after* any necessary combining has been done.

(viii) Read the critical value from the χ^2 tables for the appropriate degrees of freedom and significance level. If X^2 is less than the significance level, the null hypothesis is accepted; otherwise it is rejected.

(ix) Draw conclusions from the test – state what the test tells you about the model.

LEARNING OUTCOMES

When you have completed this chapter you should be able to:

► interpret bivariate categorical data in a contingency table
► apply the χ^2 test to a contingency table
► carry out a χ^2 test for goodness of fit of a uniform, binomial, geometric or Poisson model
► interpret the results of a χ^2 test using tables of critical values or the output from software.

Practice questions: Set 1

1. The scatter diagrams below were constructed from data on 248 adult patients at a clinic in the United States. Weights are in kg, heights are in cm and ages are in completed years.

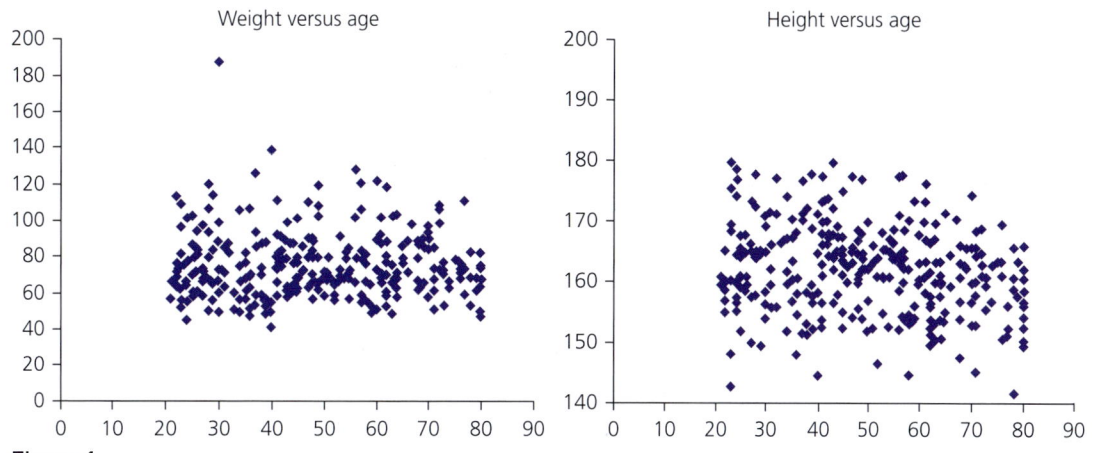

Figure 1

(i) Aster says that the average weight is much the same for patients of all ages, but the spread of weights is less for older patients. State what features of the weight versus age scatter diagram support these conclusions.

Comment in similar terms on the relationship between height and age for these patients. [4 marks]

(ii) Describe the skewness, if any, in (A) the distributions of these patients' weights, and (B) the distribution of their heights. [2 marks]

(iii) Estimate the mean weight and the mean height for these patients. Hence, given that all the patients are of the same sex, state with a reason whether they are men or women. [4 marks]

(iv) For these data it is possible to calculate three product moment correlation coefficients: weight and age, height and age, weight and height. The values of these three coefficients, in random order, are -0.17, -0.05, and 0.31. State, with justification, which correlation has the value 0.31. [2 marks]

(v) Explain why, without further information, it would not be advisable to regard these data as representative of the population in the area where the clinic is situated. [2 marks]

2. A primatologist was investigating whether there is any relationship between the ages of the female and the male in chimpanzee mating pairs. For a random sample of 10 chimpanzee births, she estimated the ages, in years, of the parents. The raw data and a scatter diagram are shown on the following page.

165

Practice questions: Set 1

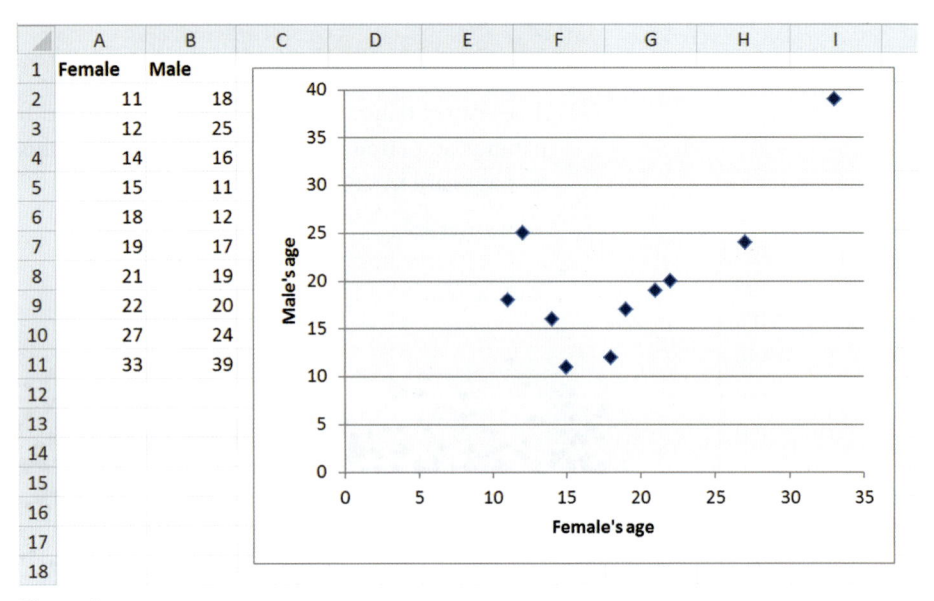

	A	B	C	D	E	F	G	H	I
1	Female	Male							
2	11	18							
3	12	25							
4	14	16							
5	15	11							
6	18	12							
7	19	17							
8	21	19							
9	22	20							
10	27	24							
11	33	39							

Figure 2

- (i) Explain why it would not be appropriate to use the product moment correlation coefficient with these data. [1 mark]
- (ii) Calculate the Spearman rank correlation coefficient for the data. [2 marks]
- (iii) Complete the hypothesis test that the primatologist should carry out, using a 5% significance level. [4 marks]

3 Esperanza buys a large number of Premium Bonds. These bonds are entered into a monthly draw and may win a prize. Esperanza calculates that her probability of winning one or more prizes in any month is 0.4.

- (i) Find the probability that Esperanza wins
    - (A) her first prize in the third month, [1 mark]
    - (B) no prizes in the first six months, [1 mark]
    - (C) no prizes in the first six months but at least one prize in the first year. [2 marks]
- (ii) Esperanza wins her first prize in month X. State the distribution of X. State also the expected value of X. [2 marks]
- (iii) Esperanza calculates that, in a month when she wins one or more prizes, her average winnings will be £27. Find the expected value of Esperanza's winnings in one year. [2 marks]

4 In human beings, body fat has a lower density than muscle, bone and other tissues. Overall body density can therefore be used to calculate the proportion of fat in a person's body. Body mass index (BMI) is calculated as M/H^2, for a person of mass M kg and height H m.

The following scatter diagram shows, for a sample of 240 adults, BMI (x) and body density (y). The scatter diagram also shows the linear regression line of y on x. The value shown as R^2 is the square of the product moment correlation coefficient for these data.

Figure 3

$y = -0.00404125x + 1.1579$
$R^2 = 0.501149$

Figure 3

(i) Explain how the scatter diagram suggests that the analysis of the data carried out here is appropriate. [2 marks]

(ii) Calculate the product moment correlation coefficient for the data. [2 marks]

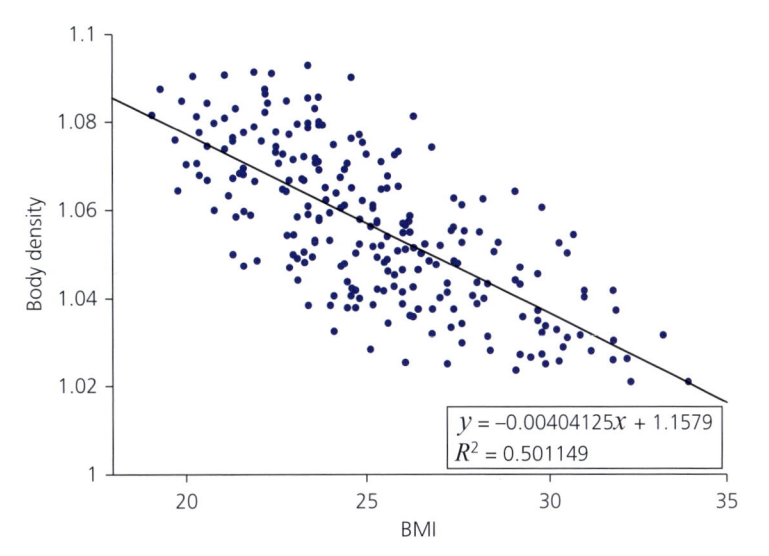

(iii) Use the given regression line to calculate the value of y when $x = 25$. Explain carefully what this value of y represents. [2 marks]

(iv) Explain why it would not be appropriate to use the given regression line to calculate the value of x when $y = 1.08$ [2 marks]

5 A research project investigated whether there was any association between the 'birth order' of students and the subject they chose to study at university. Birth order divides students into four groups as follows.

- only child (someone having no siblings)
- first born (the oldest of a set of siblings)
- middle born (someone having both older and younger siblings)
- last born (the youngest of a set of siblings)

The subjects that students study are classified as Science, Humanities and Other.

A random sample of students at a large university were surveyed and the results were summarised as shown in the following screenshot of a spreadsheet.

	A	B	C	D	E
1		Science	Humanities	Other	Total
2	Only child	8	5	6	19
3	First born	35	54	61	150
4	Middle born	8	21	8	37
5	Last born	31	26	33	90
6	Total	82	106	108	296

Figure 4

Practice questions: Set 1

(i) Explain what these figures suggest about the numbers of children per family in this sample. [2 marks]

(ii) What does a comparison of the figures in cells E3 and E5 suggest? [1 mark]

(iii) State the null and alternative hypotheses for a chi-squared test on these data. [1 mark]

The spreadsheet is used to calculate the expected frequencies and the contributions to the test statistic, as shown in the following screenshot.

7				
8	Exp freq	Science	Humanities	Other
9	Only child	5.26	6.80	6.93
10	First born	41.55	53.72	54.73
11	Middle born	10.25	13.25	13.50
12	Last born	24.93	32.23	32.84
13				
14	Contribs	Science	Humanities	Other
15	Only child	1.42	0.48	0.13
16	First born	1.03	0.00	0.72
17	Middle born	0.49	4.53	2.24
18	Last born	1.48	1.20	0.00

Figure 5

(iv) Give spreadsheet formulae for cells B9 and B15. [2 marks]

(v) Given that the sum of the contributions to the test statistic is 13.73, complete the test using a 5% significance level. [3 marks]

(vi) Discuss briefly what the two largest contributions to the test statistic indicate. [2 marks]

⑥ LCD display panels consist of a very large number, typically many millions, of pixels. A very small proportion of pixels will be faulty. Let X denote the number of faulty pixels on a newly manufactured LCD panel of a particular size and type.

(i) State two assumptions required to justify modelling X using a Poisson distribution. [2 marks]

You are now given that the required assumptions hold and that the average number of faulty pixels per panel at the time of manufacture is 1.2.

(ii) Find the probability that a newly manufactured panel has (A) no faulty pixels, (B) fewer than 4 faulty pixels. [2 marks]

Newly manufactured panels are checked before sale, and those with 4 or more faulty pixels are not sold. Let Y be the number of faulty pixels on a panel that is sold.

(iii) Show that $P(Y = 0) = 0.3117$ correct to 4 decimal places. [1 mark]

(iv) Copy and complete the table for the distribution of Y.

r	0	1	2	3
$P(Y = r)$	0.3117			

[3 marks]

(v) Calculate the mean and standard deviation of Y. [4 marks]

7 Conditional probability

The consequences of an act affect the probability of its occurring again.

B.F. Skinner

This picture shows a tropical lightning storm.

Typically, about two people die per year in the UK from being struck by lightning.

→ How would you estimate the probability that a particular person will be killed by lightning strike in the UK on Wednesday next week?

Screening tests

You might give an argument along these lines.

There are about 60 million people in the UK.

So the probability of any individual being killed by lightning strike in the next year is

$$\frac{2}{60\,000\,000}$$

There are 365 days in a year so the probability of this happening on any particular day is

$$\frac{2}{60\,000\,000} \times \frac{1}{365} \approx 9 \times 10^{-11}$$

or a little under 1 in 10 billion.

The problem with this argument is that it assumes that all people are equally likely to be victims of lightning strike and that it is equally likely to happen on any day of the year. Neither of these is true.

- Lightning is much more common over the summer months.
- Relevant data show that men are much more likely to be the victims than women.

So the figure of 1 in 10 billion is actually meaningless. The probability is conditional upon other circumstances such as the time of year and the gender and lifestyle of the person.

This chapter is about **conditional probability**.

Notation

In standard notation

- A and B are events.
- The event *not-A* is denoted by A'. $P(A') = 1 - P(A)$.
- $P(A|B)$ means the probability of event A occurring, given that event B has occurred.

You can see the meaning of $P(A|B)$ in this Venn diagram. The fact that event B has already occurred restricts the possibilities to the red region. If event A also occurs the event must be in the overlap region $A \cap B$.

So the probability is given by

$$P(A|B) = \frac{P(A \cap B)}{P(B)}$$

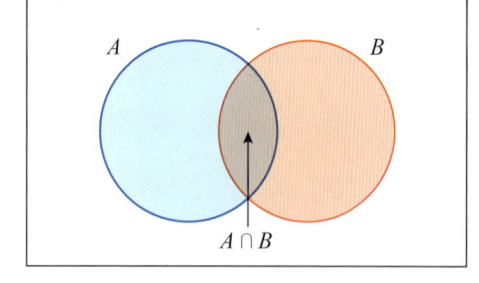

Figure 7.1 Venn diagram

This is a fundamental result in conditional probability.

> **Note**
>
> A false positive occurs when a person tests positive but has not got the condition. A false negative occurs when a person tests negative but has actually got the condition.

1 Screening tests

Another example of conditional probability arises with medical screening tests.

For many medical conditions, a *screening test* is given to large parts of the population to check if they have the condition. These tests are never 100% reliable and it is often the case that the test suggests that a person has the condition being screened for when in fact they do not. Such a case is called a *'false positive'*. On other occasions, the test suggests that a person does not have the condition when in fact they do have it. This type of case is known as a *'false negative'*. It may at first seem strange that screening tests do not give the correct result 100% of the time, but the human body is a very complex system and screening tests are useful. They provide early diagnosis of conditions that would later become difficult or impossible to treat.

Example 7.1

This contingency table shows the probabilities for the outcomes of a screening test for a medical condition on a randomly selected person.

The following letters describe the sets involved.

C Has the condition C' Does not have the condition

Y Tests positive N Tests negative

Table 7.1

	C	C'
Y	0.20	0.15
N	0.05	0.60

(i) Copy the table and add in the marginal totals.

(ii) Find the probabilities that a randomly selected person

(a) has the condition and tests positive, (b) has the condition, (c) tests positive.

Use set notation as well as giving the values of your answers.

(iii) Find the probability that a person who has the condition tests positive.

(iv) Find the percentages of false positives and false negatives given by the test. Hence state the percentage of incorrect results it gives.

Solution

(i) The marginal totals are given in **red**.

Table 7.2

	C	C'	
Y	0.20	0.15	**0.35**
N	0.05	0.60	**0.65**
	0.25	**0.75**	**1**

(ii) (a) $P(C \cap Y) = 0.20$ (b) $P(C) = 0.25$ (c) $P(Y) = 0.35$.

(iii) $P(Y|C) = \dfrac{P(Y \cap C)}{P(C)} = \dfrac{0.2}{0.25} = 0.8$.

(iv) False positives $P(C' \cap Y) = 0.15 = 15\%$

False negatives $P(C \cap N) = 0.05 = 5\%$

Incorrect results $15\% + 5\% = 20\%$

Discussion point

In this example, set notation was used to describe most of the events. You will find it helpful to relate these to a Venn diagram below.

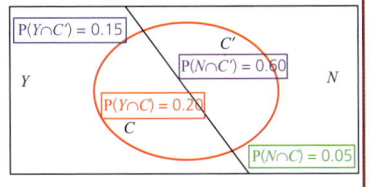

$P(Y \cap C') = 0.15$
$P(N \cap C') = 0.60$
$P(Y \cap C) = 0.20$
$P(N \cap C) = 0.05$

Figure 7.2

What sets do the various regions represent? What probabilities are associated with them?

Screening tests

Another way to represent conditional probabilities is to use a tree diagram, as in the next example.

Example 7.2

This contingency table, together with the marginal totals, shows the probabilities for the outcomes of a screening test for a medical condition on a randomly selected person.

This is the same table as in Example 7.1.

Table 7.3

	C	C'	
Y	0.20	0.15	**0.35**
N	0.05	0.60	**0.65**
	0.25	**0.75**	**1**

(i) Draw a tree diagram to illustrate the same information, marking in all the relevant probabilities.

(ii) Using appropriate notation, describe the numbers that appear vertically above and below each other in the tree diagram.

(iii) Show that $P(Y) = P(Y|C) \times P(C) + P(Y|C') \times P(C')$.

Discussion point

Identify which of the numbers in the table in the question feature in the tree diagram, and where they appear.

State which numbers in the table do not feature in the tree diagram.

Would your answers be the same if you drew the tree diagram with Y and N for the left-hand branches and C and C' for the right-hand branches?

Solution

(i)

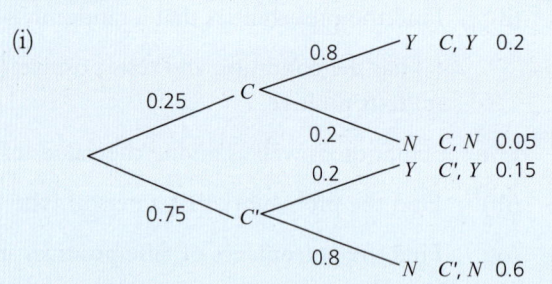

```
            0.8      Y   C, Y   0.2
      0.25 ─ C ─
                0.2  N   C, N   0.05
                0.2  Y   C', Y  0.15
      0.75 ─ C' ─
            0.8      N   C', N  0.6
```

Figure 7.3

(ii) Left-hand branches $0.25 = P(C), 0.75 = P(C')$

Right-hand branches $0.8 = P(Y|C), 0.2 = P(N|C)$

$0.2 = P(Y|C'), 0.8 = P(N|C')$

Right-hand line $0.2 = P(C \cap Y), 0.05 = P(C \cap N),$

$0.15 = P(C' \cap Y), 0.6 = P(C' \cap N)$

Multiplying along the branches and adding the two cases where Y occurs.

(iii) In numbers $P(Y) = 0.25 \times 0.8 + 0.75 \times 0.2$

In symbols $P(Y) = P(C) \times P(Y|C) + P(C') \times P(Y|C')$
$= P(Y|C) \times P(C) + P(Y|C') \times P(C')$

as required.

Note

You will meet this result later in the chapter in connection with Bayes' theorem.

It will be given for events A and B in the form

$P(B) = P(B|A) \times P(A) + P(B|A') \times P(A')$

The next example shows how important it is to specify the prior conditions correctly when using conditional probability.

Figure 7.4

Example 7.3

A robbery has taken place on one of the UK's islands. When carrying out the crime, the robber suffered from a cut and left a sample of blood at the scene. A test shows that it is group AB−; this is the rarest group in the UK, occurring in about 1% of people.

The police have the blood groups of a few of the island's 800 residents on record, including Tom who is AB−. On this evidence alone, he is arrested for the crime.

- The arresting officer says 'The national figures for this blood group mean that the probability that you are innocent is 1% and so that you are guilty is 99%'.
- Tom's solicitor says 'About eight people on the island will have this blood group, so, in the absence of any other evidence, the probability that my client is guilty is only $12\frac{1}{2}$% and that he is innocent is $87\frac{1}{2}$%'.

(i) Which one of these two statements is correct?

(ii) How would you explain the fault in the other statement?

> **Note**
>
> Explaining why the other statement is wrong requires some thought. The arresting officer has, in fact, made a well-known error called *the prosecutor's fallacy*.
>
> In order to use probability in the analysis of a situation like this, you have to be very careful to ask the right question.

Solution

(i) The solicitor's statement is correct.

The expected number of people on the island with AB− blood is $800 \times 1\% = 8$.

So the probability that the blood is from Tom is $\frac{1}{8} = 0.125$ or 12.5%.

Bayes' theorem

> **Discussion point**
>
> This example was set on an island with a small population. This allowed the solicitor's statement to be fairly obviously correct. If it had been set in, say, somewhere in London it would not have been possible to quantify the probability that the accused person was innocent and so the prosecutor's fallacy might have seemed more plausible, even though it was still completely false.
>
> Is there a danger of the prosecutor's fallacy being used in cases where identification is carried out on the basis of DNA?

(ii) There are three relevant events.

R A blood sample selected at random is AB–,

T The blood sample came from Tom,

I Tom is innocent.

The arresting officer asked

'What is the probability that a random blood sample is AB–?'

i.e. 'What is the value of $P(R)$?'

The officer has made the reasonable assumption that people's criminal tendencies and their blood groups are independent. So the question he asked is equivalent to

'What is the probability that an innocent person has blood group AB–?'

i.e. 'What is the value of $P(R \mid I)$?'

However, this is the wrong question because it is known that event R has occurred but it is not known that event I has occurred.

The correct question is

'Given that an AB– sample has been found, what is the probability that it came from Tom?'

i.e. 'What is the value of $P(T \mid R)$?'

If the sample did come from Tom, then he is guilty. So the probability that he is innocent is given by

$P(I) = 1 - P(T \mid R)$.

2 Bayes' theorem

The last example involved the prosecutor's fallacy. It showed that, without clear thinking, it is all too easy to go wrong with conditional probability, with potentially serious consequences. The rest of this chapter shows how Bayes' theorem can be used to place the analysis of such situations on a more formal basis.

Example 7.4

A screening test for a particular condition is not 100% reliable. In fact, the probability that a person who has the condition tests positive is 0.97. The probability that a person who does not have the condition tests positive is 0.01. The proportion of the population which has the condition is 1.5%.

A person is selected at random and tested for the condition.

(i) Using A for the event that the person does not have the condition and B for the event that the person tests positive, illustrate this situation on a tree diagram.

(ii) Find the probability that the person tests positive.

(iii) The person tests positive. Find the probability that the person does not have the condition.

(iv) In the light of your answer to part (iii), comment briefly on the effectiveness of the test.

Solution

(i)

Figure 7.5

Tree diagram:
- 0.985 to A, then 0.01 to B (Does not have the condition, tests positive) and 0.99 to B' (Does not have the condition, tests negative)
- 0.015 to A', then 0.97 to B (Has the condition, tests positive) and 0.03 to B' (Has the condition, tests negative)

0.015 is the probability that a person has the condition so 0.985 is the probability that the person does not

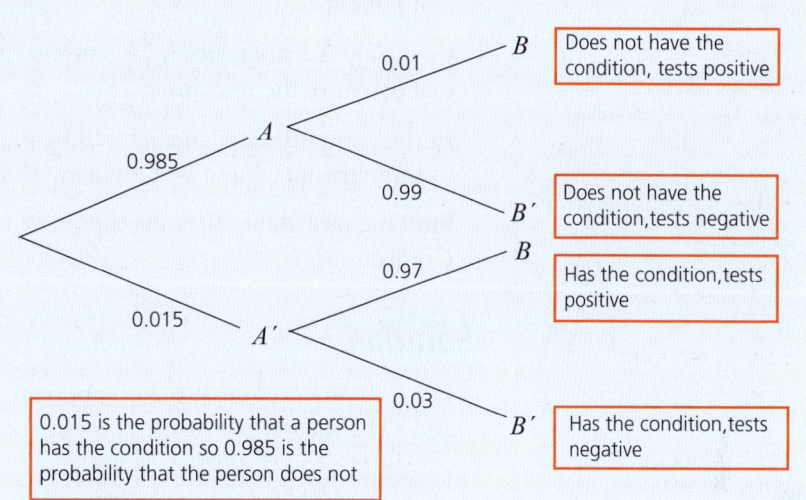

> To find the probability that the person tests positive, you need to include both those who have the condition and those who do not.

(ii) $P(B) = 0.985 \times 0.01 + 0.015 \times 0.97$

$= 0.00985 + 0.01455$

$= 0.0244$

(iii) To find the probability that someone who tested positive (event B) does not have the condition (Event A), use the conditional probability formula

$$P(A\mid B) = \frac{P(A \cap B)}{P(B)}.$$

From part (ii) you know that $P(B) = 0.0244$.

From the tree diagram $P(A \cap B) = 0.985 \times 0.01 = 0.00985$

So $P(A' \mid B) = \dfrac{0.00985}{0.0244} = 0.404$.

> $P(A \cap B)$ is the probability that the person does not have the condition and tests positive.
> You can find this by multiplying along the A and B branches of the tree diagram.

(iv) The test has a false positive rate of just over 40%. This does seem rather high. The false positives would need further tests to determine whether they actually have the condition and would be unnecessarily worried. On the other hand, under 1% of the population would be in this situation so the screening test may still be worthwhile. Also over half of the positives would actually have the condition.

Note
The event $A\mid B$ is an example of a false positive

This example illustrates Bayes' theorem which states that:

$$P(A\mid B) = \frac{P(A \cap B)}{P(B\mid A)P(A) + P(B\mid A')P(A')}.$$

Substituting the numbers for the previous example, gives

$$P(A\mid B) = \frac{0.01 \times 0.985}{0.01 \times 0.985 + 0.97 \times 0.015} = 0.403\,688\ldots$$

Bayes' theorem

When you are solving problems like this, you can either work out the probability from first principles, as in the example above, or you can use Bayes' theorem, as in the next example.

Example 7.5

Two different companies manufacture a particular type of electrical component.

Company A manufactures 75% of the components and Company B manufactures the remaining 25%.

In the components manufactured by Company A, 1% fail early, whereas 2% of those manufactured by Company B fail early.

Find the probability that a component which fails early was manufactured by Company A.

Solution

Let A be the event that the component was manufactured by Company A and D be the event that the component is defective.

Using Bayes' theorem to find $P(A|D)$,

$$P(A|D) = \frac{P(A \cap D)}{P(D|A)P(A) + P(D|A')P(A')}$$

$P(A) = 0.75, P(A') = 0.25, P(D|A) = 0.01, P(D|A') = 0.02$

$P(A \cap D) = 0.75 \times 0.01 = 0.0075$

$$P(A|D) = \frac{0.0075}{0.01 \times 0.75 + 0.02 \times 0.25} = 0.6$$

> **Note**
>
> Note that A' is the event that the component was not manufactured by Company A.
>
> So A' is the event that it was manufactured by Company B.

Exercise 7.1

1. It is given that $P(A) = 0.25$, $P(B) = 0.13$ and $P(A \cap B) = 0.05$.
   (i) Find $P(A \cup B)$.
   (ii) Find $P(A|B)$.
   (iii) Find $P(B|A)$.

2. Steve is going on holiday. The probability that he is delayed on his outward flight is 0.3. The probability that he is delayed on his return flight is 0.2, independently of whether or not he is delayed on the outward flight.
   (i) Find the probability that Steve is delayed on his outward flight but not on his return flight.
   (ii) Find the probability that he is delayed on at least one of the two flights
   (iii) Given that he is delayed on at least one flight, find the probability that he is delayed on both flights. [MEI]

3. In the 2001 census, people living in Wales were asked whether or not they could speak Welsh. A resident of Wales is selected at random.
   - W is the event that this person speaks Welsh.
   - C is the event that this person is a child.
   You are given that $P(W) = 0.20$, $P(C) = 0.17$ and $P(W \cap C) = 0.06$.

(i) Determine whether the events W and C are independent.

(ii) Draw a Venn diagram, showing the events W and C, and mark in the probability corresponding to each region of your diagram.

(iii) Find $P(W|C)$.

(iv) Given that $P(W|C') = 0.169$, use this information and your answer to part (iii) to comment very briefly on how the ability to speak Welsh differs between children and adults. [MEI]

④ When it is reasonably dry, I cycle to work. Otherwise I take the bus. On one day in ten, on average, it is too wet for me to cycle. If I cycle, the probability that I am late for work is 0.02. If I take the bus, the probability that I am late for work is 0.15.

(i) Find the probability that I am late on a randomly chosen day.

(ii) Given that I am late, find the probability that I cycled.

⑤ A screening test for a particular disease has a probability of 0.99 of giving a positive result for somebody who has the disease and of 0.05 for somebody who does not have the disease. It is thought that 0.35% of the population have the disease.

(i) Find the probability that a randomly selected person tests positive.

(ii) Find the probability that a randomly selected person has the disease given that they test positive.

(iii) Write down the probability that a randomly selected person does not have the disease given that they test positive.

(iv) In the light of your answers to parts (ii) and (iii), comment briefly on the effectiveness of the test.

⑥ A machine which makes gear wheels has two settings, fast and slow. On the fast setting, 10% of the gear wheels are faulty. On the slow setting, 1% of them are faulty. One day, 1000 gear wheels are made using the fast setting and 500 using the slow setting.

(i) Find the probability that a randomly selected gear wheel from the day's production is faulty.

(ii) Given that a gear wheel is faulty, find the probability that the machine was on the slow setting when it was manufactured.

⑦ Two thirds of the trains which I catch on my local railway line have four coaches and the rest have eight coaches (the eight coach trains are run during busy periods). If I catch a four coach train, the probability of me getting a seat is 0.7. If I catch an eight coach train, the probability of me getting a seat is 0.9. Given that I get a seat on a train, find the probability that it is a train with four coaches.

⑧ A company which runs a large fleet of HGVs (heavy goods vehicles) regularly tests its employees for consumption of illegal drugs. The test is not 100% reliable, so if somebody is found to be positive, further testing is carried out. The false positive rate is 0.5% and the false negative rate is 3%. You should assume that 1% of employees have taken drugs preceding the test.

(i) Find the probability that a randomly selected person tests positive.

(ii) Find the probability that a randomly selected person has consumed illegal drugs, given that they test positive.

Bayes' theorem

⑨ Three machines, A, B and C are used to make dress fabric. Machine A makes 50% of the fabric, Machine B makes 30% and Machine C makes the remainder. Each piece of fabric is checked for defects. The percentages of defective fabric for Machines A, B and C are 2, 4 and 1.5, respectively.

(i) Find the probability that a randomly selected piece of fabric is defective.

(ii) Given that a piece of fabric is defective, find the probability that it was produced on Machine A.

⑩ Onions often suffer from a disease called white rot. This disease stays in the soil for several years, and when onions are planted in infected ground, they can get the disease. A gardener grows onions in four separate plots Q, R, S and T, so that there is less risk of most of her onions getting white rot. She grows an equal number of onions in each plot.

The percentages of onions in each plot which get white rot are as follows

- Plot Q 2%
- Plot R 3%
- Plot S 60%
- Plot T 8%.

(i) Find the probability that a randomly selected onion has white rot.

(ii) Given that a randomly selected onion has white rot, find the probability that it came from plot S.

KEY POINTS

1 The conditional probability of event A given the event B has occurred is given by

$$P(A|B) = \frac{P(A \cap B)}{P(B)}$$

2 It is often helpful to use a tree diagram or a contingency table to illustrate a situation involving conditional probability.

3 Bayes' theorem states that

$$P(A|B) = \frac{P(A \cap B)}{P(B|A)P(A) + P(B|A')P(A')}$$

4 Bayes' theorem is used to find conditional probabilities.

5 In contexts such as a medical screening test:
- a false positive occurs when a person tests positive but has not got the condition
- a false negative occurs when a person tests negative but actually has got the condition.

LEARNING OUTCOMES

When you have completed this chapter you should be able to:
➤ understand and use the notation associated with conditional probability
➤ use tree diagrams and contingency tables to illustrate situations involving conditional probability
➤ understand and use Bayes' theorem to solve problems involving conditional probability.

8 Continuous random variables

A theory is a good theory if it satisfies two requirements: It must accurately describe a large class of observations on the basis of a model that contains only a few arbitrary elements, and it must make definite predictions about the results of future observations.

Stephen Hawking,
A Brief History of Time

Lucky escape for local fisherman

Local fisherman George Sutherland stared death in the face yesterday as he was plucked from the deck of his 56 ft boat, the *Belle Star*, by a freak wave. Only the quick thinking of his brother James, who grabbed hold of his legs, saved George from a watery grave.

'It was a bad day and suddenly this lump of water came down on us,' said George. 'It was a wave in a million, higher than the mast of the boat, and it caught me off guard'.

Hero James is a man of few words. 'All in a day's work' was his only comment.

Continuous random variables

> **Note**
>
> The data are historical. The last weather ship, the Polarfront, was withdrawn from service in 2010.

Freak waves do occur and they can have serious consequences in terms of damage to shipping, oil rigs and coastal defences, sometimes resulting in loss of life. It is important to estimate how often they will occur, and how high they will be. Was George Sutherland's one in a million estimate for a wave higher than the mast of the boat (11 m) at all accurate?

Before you can answer this question, you need to know the *probability density* of the heights of waves at that time of the year in the area where the *Belle Star* was fishing. The graph in Figure 8.1 shows this sort of information; it was collected in the same season of the year as the Sutherland accident by the Offshore Weather Ship *Juliet* in the North Atlantic.

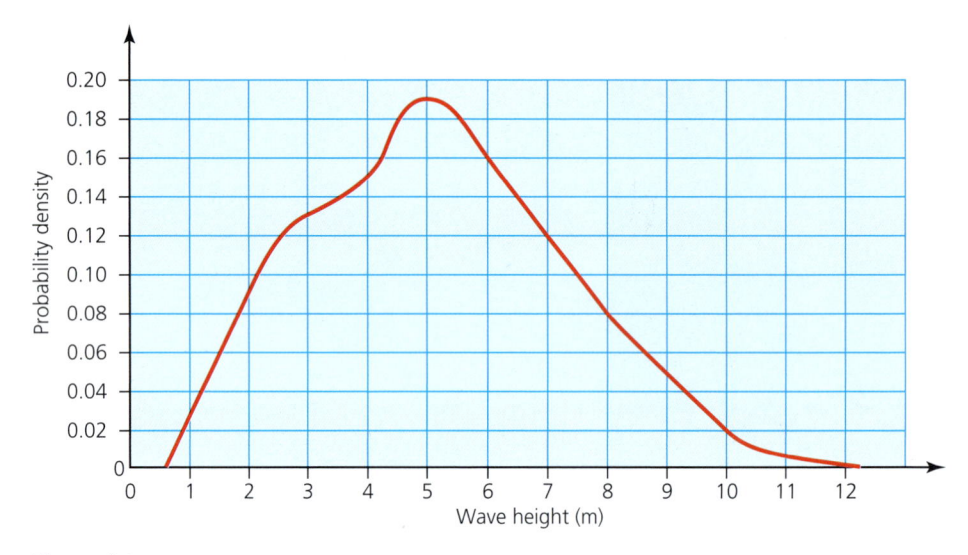

Figure 8.1

To obtain Figure 8.1 a very large amount of wave data had to be collected. This allowed the class interval widths of the wave heights to be sufficiently small for the outline of the curve to acquire this shape. It also ensured that the sample data were truly representative of the population of waves at that time of the year.

In a graph such as Figure 8.1, the vertical scale is a measure of probability density. Probabilities are found by estimating the area under the curve. The total area is 1.0, meaning that, effectively, all waves at this place have heights between 0.6 and 12.0 m (see Figure 8.2).

If this had been the place where the *Belle Star* was situated, the probability of encountering a wave at least 11 m high would have been 0.003, about 1 in 300. Clearly, George's description of it as 'a wave in a million' was not justified purely by its height. The fact that he called it a 'lump of water' suggests that perhaps it may have been more remarkable for its steep sides than its height.

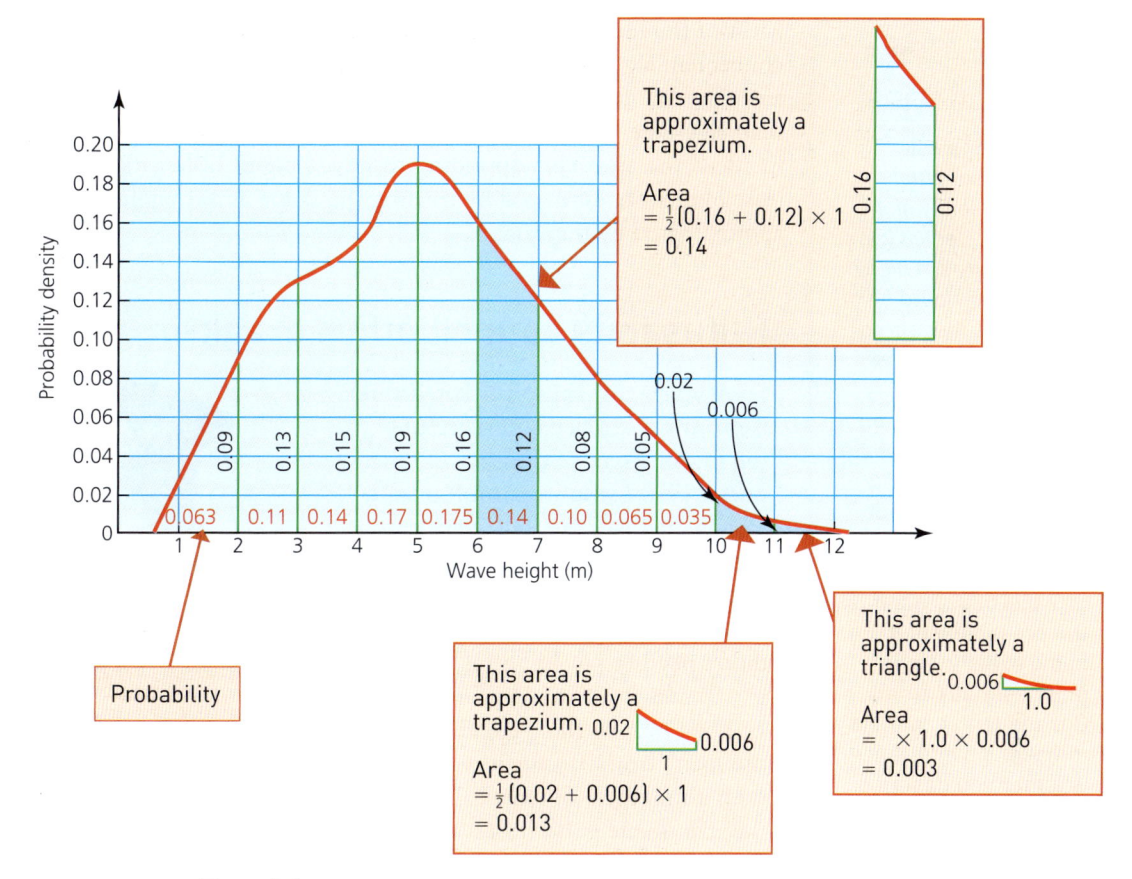

Figure 8.2

1 Probability density function

Discussion point

Is it reasonable to describe the height of a wave as *random*?

In the wave height example, the curve was determined experimentally, using equipment on board the Offshore Weather Ship *Juliet*. The curve is continuous because the random variable, the wave height, is continuous and not discrete. The possible heights of waves are not restricted to particular steps (say every 0.5 m), but may take any value within a range.

A function represented by a curve of this type is called a *probability density function*, often abbreviated to p.d.f. The probability density function of a continuous random variable, X, is usually denoted by $f(x)$. If $f(x)$ is a p.d.f. it follows that:

Note

In the wave heights example, the probability density function has quite a complicated curve and so it is not possible to find a simple algebraic expression with which to model it.

- $f(x) \geq 0$ for all x You cannot have negative probabilities.

- $\displaystyle\int_{\text{All values of } x} f(x)\,dx = 1$ The total area under the curve is 1.

For a continuous random variable with probability density function $f(x)$, the probability that X lies in the interval $[a, b]$ is given by

$$P(a \leq X \leq b) = \int_a^b f(x)\,dx$$

181

Probability density function

> **Note: Class boundaries**
>
> If you were to ask the question 'What is the probability of a randomly selected wave being exactly 2 m high?' the answer would be zero. If you measured a likely looking wave to enough decimal places (assuming you could do so), you would eventually come to a figure which was not zero. The wave height might be 2.01...m or 2.000 003...m but the probability of it being exactly 2 m is infinitesimally small. Consequently, in theory, it makes no difference whether you describe the class interval from 2 to 2.5 m as $2 < h < 2.5$ or as $2 \leq h \leq 2.5$.
>
> However, in practice, measurements are always rounded to some extent. The reality of measuring a wave's height means that you would probably be quite happy to record it to the nearest 0.1 m and get on with the next wave. So, in practice, measurements of 2.0 m and 2.5 m probably will be recorded, and intervals have to be defined so that it is clear which class they belong to. You would normally expect < at one end of the interval and ≤ at the other: either $2 \leq h < 2.5$ or $2 < h \leq 2.5$. In either case, the probability of the wave being within the interval would be given by $\int_{2}^{2.5} f(x) dx$

Most of the techniques in this chapter assume that you do, in fact, have a convenient algebraic expression with which to work. However, the methods are still valid if this is not the case, but you would need to use numerical, rather than algebraic, techniques for integration and differentiation. In the high-wave incident, the areas corresponding to wave heights of less than 2 m and of at least 11 m were estimated by treating the shape as a triangle: other areas were approximated by trapezia.

Rufus foils council office break-in

Somewhere an empty-pocketed thief is nursing a sore leg and regretting the loss of a pair of trousers. Council porter Fred Lamming, and Rufus, a wiry haired Jack Russell, were doing a late-night check round the Council head office when they came upon the intruder on the ground floor. 'I didn't need to say anything,' Fred told me; 'Rufus went straight for him and grabbed him by the leg.' After a tussle, the man's trousers tore, leaving Rufus with a mouthful of material while the man made good his escape out of a window.

Following the incident, the local Council are looking at an electronic security system. 'Rufus won't live for ever,' explained Council leader Sandra Martin.

Example 8.1

The local Council are thinking of fitting an electronic security system inside head office. They have been told by manufacturers that the lifetime, X years, of the system they have in mind has the p.d.f.:

$$f(x) = \frac{3x(20-x)}{4000} \quad \text{for } 0 \leq x \leq 20.$$
$$\text{and } f(x) = 0 \quad \text{otherwise.}$$

(i) Show that the manufacturers' statement is consistent with f(x) being a probability density function.

(ii) Find the probability that:
   (a) it fails in the first year
   (b) it lasts ten years but then fails in the next year.

Solution

(i) The condition $f(x) \geq 0$ for all values of x between 0 and 20 is satisfied, as shown by the graph of f(x), Figure 8.3.

> **Note**
>
> The general rule is:
> $F(x) = P(X \leq x) = \int_{-\infty}^{x} f(u) \, du$.
> However, in practice the lower limit of the integral is replaced by the lower limit of the non-zero part of the probability density function (except when this is itself equal to $-\infty$).

This area gives the probability it fails in the first year, part **(ii)(a)**

This area gives the probability that it lasts 10 years but then fails in the next year, part **(ii)(b)**

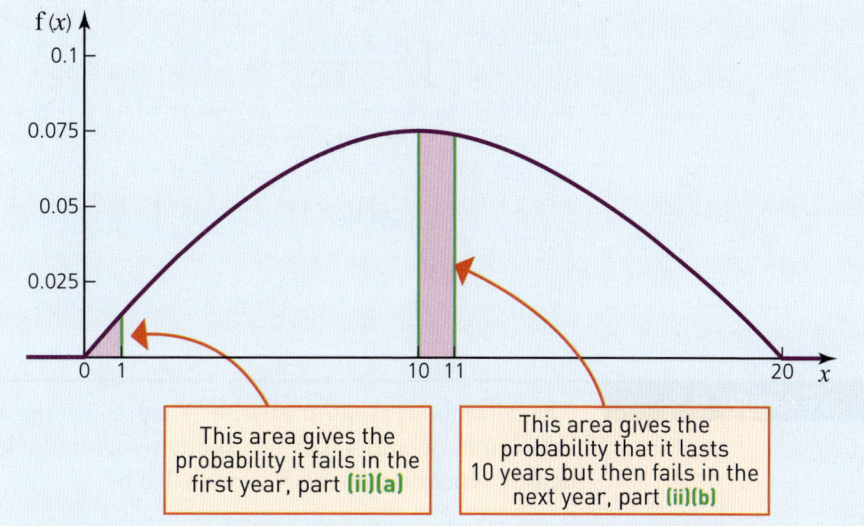

Figure 8.3

The other condition is that the area under the curve is 1.

$$\text{Area} = \int_{-\infty}^{\infty} f(x) \, dx = \int_{0}^{20} \frac{3x(20-x)}{4000} \, dx$$

$$= \frac{3}{4000} \int_{0}^{20} (20x - x^2) \, dx$$

$$= \frac{3}{4000} \left[10x^2 - \frac{x^3}{3} \right]_{0}^{20}$$

$$= \frac{3}{4000} \left[10 \times 20^2 - \frac{20^3}{3} \right]$$

$$= 1, \text{ as required.}$$

(a)   *It fails in the first year.*

This is given by $P(X < 1) = \int_{0}^{1} \frac{3x(20-x)}{4000} \, dx$

$$= \frac{3}{4000} \int_{0}^{1} (20x - x^2) \, dx$$

$$= \frac{3}{4000} \left[10x^2 - \frac{x^3}{3} \right]_{0}^{1}$$

$$= \frac{3}{4000} \left(10 \times 1^2 - \frac{1^3}{3} \right)$$

$$= 0.0725$$

(b)   *It fails in the 11th year.*

This is given by $P(10 \leq X < 11)$

Probability density function

$$= \int_{10}^{11} \frac{3x(20-x)}{4000} dx$$

$$= \frac{3}{4000}\left[10x^2 - \frac{1}{3}x^3\right]_{10}^{11}$$

$$= \frac{3}{4000}\left(10 \times 11^2 - \frac{1}{3} \times 11^3\right) - \frac{3}{4000}\left(10 \times 10^2 - \frac{1}{3} \times 10^3\right)$$

$$= 0.07475$$

Example 8.2

The continuous random variable X represents the amount of sunshine in hours between noon and 4 p.m. at a skiing resort in the high season. The probability density function, $f(x)$, of X is modelled by

$$f(x) = \begin{cases} kx^2 & \text{for } 0 \leq x \leq 4 \\ 0 & \text{otherwise.} \end{cases}$$

(i) Find the value of k.

(ii) Find the probability that on a particular day in the high season there are more than two hours of sunshine between noon and 4 p.m.

Solution

(i) To find the value of k you must use the fact that the area under the graph of $f(x)$ is equal to 1.

$$\int_{-\infty}^{\infty} f(x) dx = \int_0^4 kx^2 dx = 1$$

Therefore $\left[\dfrac{kx^3}{3}\right]_0^4 = 1$

$$\frac{64k}{3} = 1$$

So $k = \dfrac{3}{64}$

(ii)

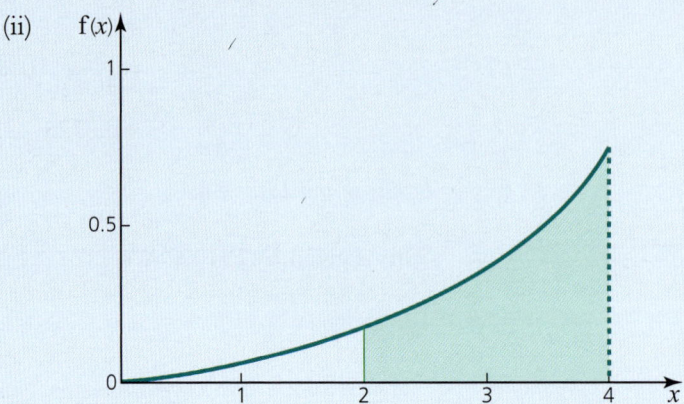

Figure 8.4

The probability of more than 2 hours of sunshine is given by

$$P(X > 2) = \int_2^\infty f(x)\,dx = \int_2^4 \frac{3x^2}{64}\,dx$$

$$= \left[\frac{x^3}{64}\right]_2^4$$

$$= \frac{64-8}{64}$$

$$= \frac{56}{64}$$

$$= 0.875$$

Example 8.3

The number of hours Darren spends each day working in his garden is modelled by the continuous random variable X, with p.d.f. $f(x)$ defined by

$$f(x) = \begin{cases} kx & \text{for } 0 \le x < 3 \\ k(6-x) & \text{for } 3 \le x < 6 \\ 0 & \text{otherwise.} \end{cases}$$

(i) Find the value of k.

(ii) Sketch the graph of $f(x)$.

(iii) Find the probability that Darren will work between 2 and 5 hours in his garden on a randomly selected day.

Solution

(i) To find the value of k you must use the fact that the area under the graph of $f(x)$ is equal to 1. You may find the area by integration, as shown below.

$$\int_{-\infty}^\infty f(x)\,dx = \int_0^3 kx\,dx + \int_3^6 k(6-x)\,dx = 1$$

$$\left[\frac{kx^2}{2}\right]_0^3 + \left[6kx - \frac{kx^2}{2}\right]_3^6 = 1$$

Therefore $\quad \dfrac{9k}{2} + (36k - 18k) - \left(18k - \dfrac{9k}{2}\right) = 1$

$$9k = 1$$

So $\quad k = \dfrac{1}{9}$

Probability density function

> In this case, you could have found k without integration because the graph of the p.d.f. is a triangle, with area given by ½ × base × height, resulting in the equation
>
> $\frac{1}{2} \times 6 \times k(6-3) = 1$
>
> hence $9k = 1$
>
> and $k = \frac{1}{9}$.

(ii) Sketch the graph of f(x).

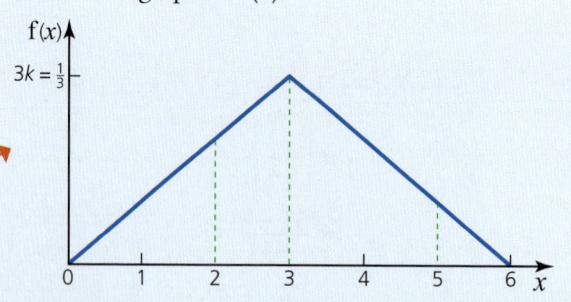

$3k = \frac{1}{3}$

Figure 8.5

(iii) To find P($2 \leq X \leq 5$), you need to find both P($2 \leq X < 3$) and P($3 \leq X \leq 5$) because there is a different expression for each part.

$$P(2 \leq X \leq 5) = P(2 \leq X < 3) + P(3 \leq X \leq 5)$$
$$= \int_2^3 \frac{1}{9}x \, dx + \int_3^5 \frac{1}{9}(6-x) \, dx$$
$$= \left[\frac{x^2}{18}\right]_2^3 + \left[\frac{2x}{3} - \frac{x^2}{18}\right]_3^5$$
$$= \frac{9}{18} - \frac{4}{18} + \left(\frac{10}{3} - \frac{25}{18}\right) - \left(2 - \frac{1}{2}\right)$$
$$= 0.72 \text{ to two decimal places.}$$

The probability that Darren works between 2 and 5 hours in his garden on a randomly selected day is 0.72.

Exercise 8.1

① The continuous random variable X has probability density function f(x) where

$$f(x) = \begin{cases} kx & \text{for } 1 \leq x < 6 \\ 0 & \text{otherwise.} \end{cases}$$

(i) Find the value of the constant k.
(ii) Sketch $y = f(x)$.
(iii) Find P($X > 5$).
(iv) Find P($2 \leq X \leq 3$).

② The continuous random variable X has p.d.f. f(x) where

$$f(x) = \begin{cases} k(5-x) & \text{for } 0 \leq x \leq 4 \\ 0 & \text{otherwise.} \end{cases}$$

(i) Find the value of the constant k.
(ii) Sketch $y = f(x)$.
(iii) Find P($1.5 \leq X \leq 2.3$).

③ The continuous random variable X has p.d.f. f(x) where

$$f(x) = \begin{cases} c & \text{for } -3 \leq x \leq 5 \\ 0 & \text{otherwise.} \end{cases}$$

(i) Find c.
(ii) Sketch $y = f(x)$.
(iii) Find $P(X < -1)$.
(iv) Find $P(X > 2)$.

④ The continuous random variable X has p.d.f. $f(x)$ where

$$f(x) = \begin{cases} kx & \text{for } 0 \leq x \leq 2 \\ 4k - kx & \text{for } 2 < x \leq 4 \\ 0 & \text{otherwise.} \end{cases}$$

(i) Find the value of the constant k.
(ii) Sketch $y = f(x)$.
(iii) Find $P(1 \leq X \leq 3.5)$.

⑤ The continuous random variable X has p.d.f. $f(x)$ where

$$f(x) = \begin{cases} ax^3 & \text{for } 0 \leq x \leq 3 \\ 0 & \text{otherwise.} \end{cases}$$

(i) Find the value of the constant a.
(ii) Sketch $y = f(x)$.
(iii) Find $P(X \leq 2)$.

⑥ A continuous random variable X has p.d.f.

$$f(x) = \begin{cases} k(x-1)(6-x) & \text{for } 1 \leq x \leq 6 \\ 0 & \text{otherwise.} \end{cases}$$

(i) Find the value of k.
(ii) Sketch $y = f(x)$.
(iii) Find $P(2 \leq X \leq 3)$.

⑦ A random variable X has p.d.f.

$$f(x) = \begin{cases} (x-1)(2-x) & \text{for } 1 \leq x < 2 \\ a & \text{for } 2 \leq x < 4 \\ 0 & \text{otherwise.} \end{cases}$$

(i) Find the value of the constant a.
(ii) Sketch $y = f(x)$.
(iii) Find $P(1.5 \leq X \leq 2.5)$.
(iv) Find $P(|X - 2| < 1)$.

⑧ A random variable X has p.d.f.

$$f(x) = \begin{cases} kx(3-x) & \text{for } 0 \leq x \leq 3 \\ 0 & \text{otherwise.} \end{cases}$$

(i) Find the value of k.
(ii) The lifetime (in years) of an electronic component is modelled by this distribution. Two such components are fitted in a radio which will only function if both devices are working. Find the probability that the radio will still function after two years, assuming that their failures are independent.

Probability density function

⑨ The planning officer in a council needs information about how long cars stay in the car park, and asks the attendant to do a check on the times of arrival and departure of 100 cars. The attendant provides the following data.

Table 8.1

Length of stay	Under 1 hour	1–2 hours	2–4 hours	4–10 hours	More than 10 hours
Number of cars	20	14	32	34	0

The planning officer suggests that the length of stay in hours may be modelled by the continuous random variable X with probability density function of the form

$$f(x) = \begin{cases} k(20-2x) & \text{for } 0 \leq x \leq 10 \\ 0 & \text{otherwise.} \end{cases}$$

(i) Find the value of k.

(ii) Sketch the graph of $f(x)$.

(iii) According to this model, how many of the 100 cars would be expected to fall into each of the four categories?

(iv) Do you think the model fits the data well?

(v) Are there any obvious weaknesses in the model? If you were the planning officer, would you be prepared to accept the model as it is, or would you want any further information?

⑩ A fish farmer has a very large number of trout in a lake. Before deciding whether to net the lake and sell the fish, she collects a sample of 100 fish and weighs them. The results (in kg) are as follows.

Table 8.2

Weight, W	Frequency
$0 < W \leq 0.5$	2
$0.5 < W \leq 1.0$	10
$1.0 < W \leq 1.5$	23
$1.5 < W \leq 2.0$	26

Weight, W	Frequency
$2.0 < W \leq 2.5$	27
$2.5 < W \leq 3.0$	12
$3.0 < W$	0

(i) Illustrate these data on a histogram, with the number of fish on the vertical scale and W on the horizontal scale. Is the distribution of the data symmetrical, positively skewed or negatively skewed?

A friend of the farmer suggests that W can be modelled as a continuous random variable and proposes four possible probability density functions.

$$f_1(w) = \frac{2}{9}w(3-w) \qquad f_2(w) = \frac{10}{81}w^2(3-w)^2$$

$$f_3(w) = \frac{4}{27}w^2(3-w) \qquad f_4(w) = \frac{4}{27}w(3-w)^2$$

in each case for $0 \leq w \leq 3$.

(ii) Using your calculator (or otherwise), sketch the curves of the four p.d.f.s and state which one matches the data most closely in general shape.

(iii) Use this p.d.f. to calculate the number of fish which that model predicts should fall within each group.

(iv) Do you think it is a good model?

⑪ During a war, the crew of an aeroplane has to destroy an enemy railway line by dropping bombs. The distance between the railway line and where the bomb hits the ground is X m, where X has the following p.d.f.

$$f(x) = \begin{cases} 10^{-4}(a+x) & \text{for } -a \le x < 0 \\ 10^{-4}(a-x) & \text{for } 0 \le x \le a \\ 0 & \text{otherwise.} \end{cases}$$

(i) Find the value of a.
(ii) Find $P(50 \le X \le 60)$.
(iii) Find $P(|X| < 20)$. [MEI]

⑫ A random variable X has a probability density function f given by

$$f(x) = \begin{cases} cx(5-x) & 0 \le x \le 5 \\ 0 & \text{otherwise.} \end{cases}$$

Show that $c = \dfrac{6}{125}$.

The lifetime X (in years) of an electric light bulb has this distribution. Given that a standard lamp is fitted with two such new bulbs and that their failures are independent, find the probability that neither bulb fails in the first year and the probability that exactly one bulb fails within two years. [MEI]

⑬ This graph shows the probability distribution function, $f(x)$, for the heights, X, of waves at the point with Latitude 44°N Longitude 41°W.

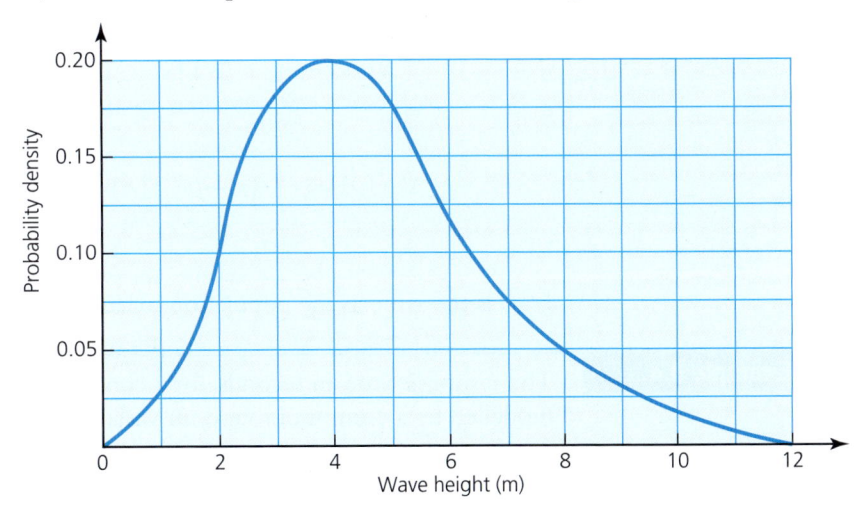

Figure 8.6

(i) Write down the values of $f(x)$ when $x = 0, 2, 4, \ldots, 12$.

(ii) Hence estimate the probability that the height of a randomly selected wave is in the interval

(a) 0–2 m
(b) 2–4 m
(c) 4–6 m
(d) 6–8 m
(e) 8–10 m
(f) 10–12 m.

A model is proposed in which

$$f(x) = \begin{cases} kx(12-x)^2 & \text{for } 0 \leq x \leq 12 \\ 0 & \text{otherwise.} \end{cases}$$

(iii) Find the value of k.

(iv) Find, according to this model, the probability that a randomly selected wave is in the interval

(a) 0–2 m (b) 2–4 m (c) 4–6 m
(d) 6–8 m (e) 8–10 m (f) 10–12 m.

(v) By comparing the figures from the model with the real data, state whether you think it is a good model or not.

2 Expectation and variance

You will recall that, for a discrete random variable, expectation and variance are given by:

$$E(X) = \sum_i x_i p_i$$

$$Var(X) = \sum_i (x_i - \mu)^2 p_i = \sum_i x_i^2 p_i - [E(X)]^2$$

> **Note**
>
> You met these formulae in Chapter 2.
>
> Notice that p_i is another way of writing $P(X = x_i)$.

where μ is the mean and p_i is the probability of the outcome x_i for $i = 1, 2, 3, \ldots$, with the various outcomes covering all possibilities.

The expressions for the expectation and variance of a continuous random variable are equivalent, but with summation replaced by integration.

> $\int_{\text{All values of } x}$ can also be written as $\int_{-\infty}^{x}$

$$E(X) = \int_{\text{All values of } x} x f(x) \, dx$$

$$Var(X) = \int_{\text{All values of } x} (x - \mu)^2 f(x) \, dx = \int_{\text{All values of } x} x^2 f(x) \, dx - [E(X)]^2$$

$E(X)$ is the same as the population mean, μ, and is often called the mean of X.

Example 8.4

The response time, in seconds, for a contestant in a general knowledge quiz is modelled by a continuous random variable X whose p.d.f. is

$$f(x) = \frac{x}{50} \quad \text{for } 0 < x \leq 10.$$

The rules state that a contestant who makes no answer is disqualified from the whole competition. This has the consequence that everybody gives an answer, if only a guess, to every question. Find

(i) the mean time in seconds for a contestant to respond to a particular question

(ii) the standard deviation of the time taken.

The organiser estimates the proportion of contestants who are guessing by assuming that they are those whose time is at least one standard deviation greater than the mean.

(iii) Using this assumption, estimate the probability that a randomly selected response is a guess.

Solution

(i) Mean time:

$$E(X) = \int_0^{10} x \frac{x}{50} dx$$

$$= \left[\frac{x^3}{150}\right]_0^{10} = \frac{1000}{150} = \frac{20}{3}$$

$$= 6\frac{2}{3}$$

(ii) Variance:

$$\text{Var}(X) = \int_0^{10} x^2 f(x) dx - [E(X)]^2$$

$$= \int_0^{10} \frac{x^3}{50} dx - \left(6\frac{2}{3}\right)^2$$

$$= \left[\frac{x^4}{200}\right]_0^{10} - \left(6\frac{2}{3}\right)^2$$

$$= 5\frac{5}{9}$$

Standard deviation $= \sqrt{\text{variance}} = \sqrt{5\frac{5}{9}}$

The standard deviation of the times is 2.357 seconds (to 3 d.p.).

(iii) All those with response times greater than $6.667 + 2.357 = 9.024$ seconds are taken to be guessing. The longest possible time is 10 seconds.

The probability that a randomly selected response is a guess is given by

$$= \int_{9.024}^{10} \frac{x}{50} dx$$

$$= \left[\frac{x^2}{100}\right]_{9.024}^{10}$$

$$= 0.185$$

so just under 1 in 5 answers are deemed to be guesses.

> **Note**
> Although the intermediate answers have been given rounded to three decimal places, more figures have been carried forward into subsequent calculations.

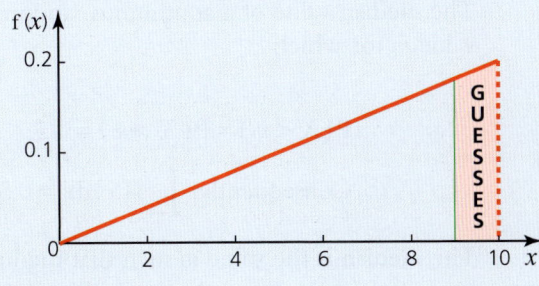

Figure 8.7

The median

Example 8.5

This is a continuation of Example 8.3 from page 185.

The number of hours per day that Darren spends in his garden is modelled by the continuous random variable X, the p.d.f. of which is

$$f(x) = \begin{cases} \frac{1}{9}x & \text{for } 0 \leq x \leq 3 \\ \frac{6-x}{9} & \text{for } 3 < x \leq 6 \\ 0 & \text{otherwise.} \end{cases}$$

Find $E(X)$, the mean number of hours per day that Darren spends in his garden.

Solution

$$E(X) = \int_{-\infty}^{\infty} x f(x) \, dx$$

$$= \int_{0}^{3} x \cdot \frac{1}{9} x \, dx + \int_{3}^{6} x \cdot \frac{6-x}{9} \, dx$$

$$= \left[\frac{x^3}{27} \right]_0^3 + \left[\frac{x^2}{3} - \frac{x^3}{27} \right]_3^6$$

$$= 1 - 0 + (12 - 8) - (3 - 1)$$

$$= 3$$

Darren spends a mean of 3 hours per day in his garden.

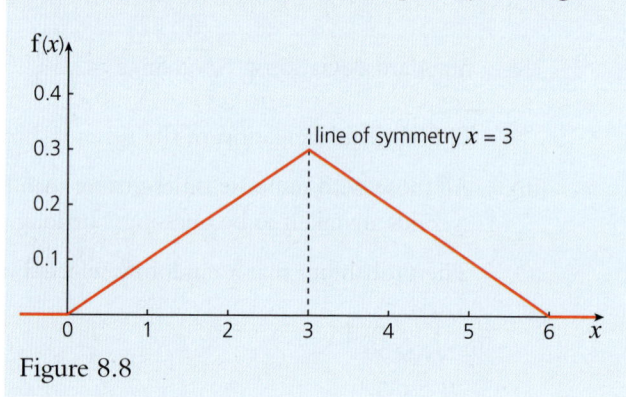

> **Note**
> Notice that, in this case, $E(X)$ can be found from the line of symmetry of the graph of $f(x)$. This situation often arises and you should be alert to the possibility of finding $E(X)$ by symmetry as shown in Figure 8.8.

Figure 8.8

3 The median

The median value of a continuous random variable X with p.d.f. $f(x)$ is the value m for which

$$P(X < m) = P(X > m) = 0.5.$$

Consequently, $\int_{-\infty}^{m} f(x) \, dx = 0.5$ and $\int_{m}^{\infty} f(x) \, dx = 0.5$.

The median is the value m such that the line $x = m$ divides the area under the curve $f(x)$ into two equal parts. In Figure 8.9, a is the smallest possible value of

X, b the largest. The line $x = m$ divides the shaded region into two regions A and B, both with area 0.5.

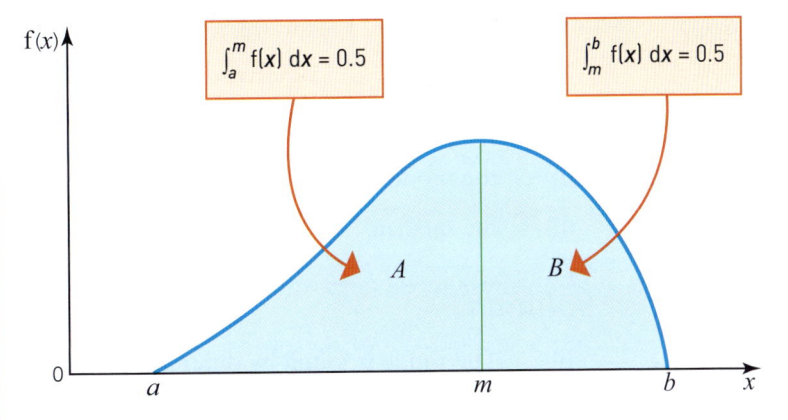

$\int_a^m f(x)\, dx = 0.5$ 　　　 $\int_m^b f(x)\, dx = 0.5$

> ❗ In general, the *mean* does not divide the area into two equal parts but it will do so if the curve is symmetrical about it because, in that case, it is equal to the median.

Figure 8.9

4 The mode

The mode of a continuous random variable X whose p.d.f. is $f(x)$ is the value for which $f(x)$ has the greatest value. Thus the mode is the value of X where the curve is at its highest.

If the mode is at a local maximum of $f(x)$, then it may often be found by differentiating $f(x)$ and solving the equation

$$f'(x) = 0.$$

> **Discussion point**
> For which of the distributions in Figure 8.10 could the mode be found by differentiating the p.d.f.?

(a) The exponential distribution $f(x) = \lambda e^{-\lambda x}$

(b) A distribution with negative skew

(c) A triangular distribution

(d) A bimodal distribution

(e) Pascal's distribution $f(x) = \tfrac{1}{2} e^{-|x|}$

(f) A uniform (rectangular) distribution

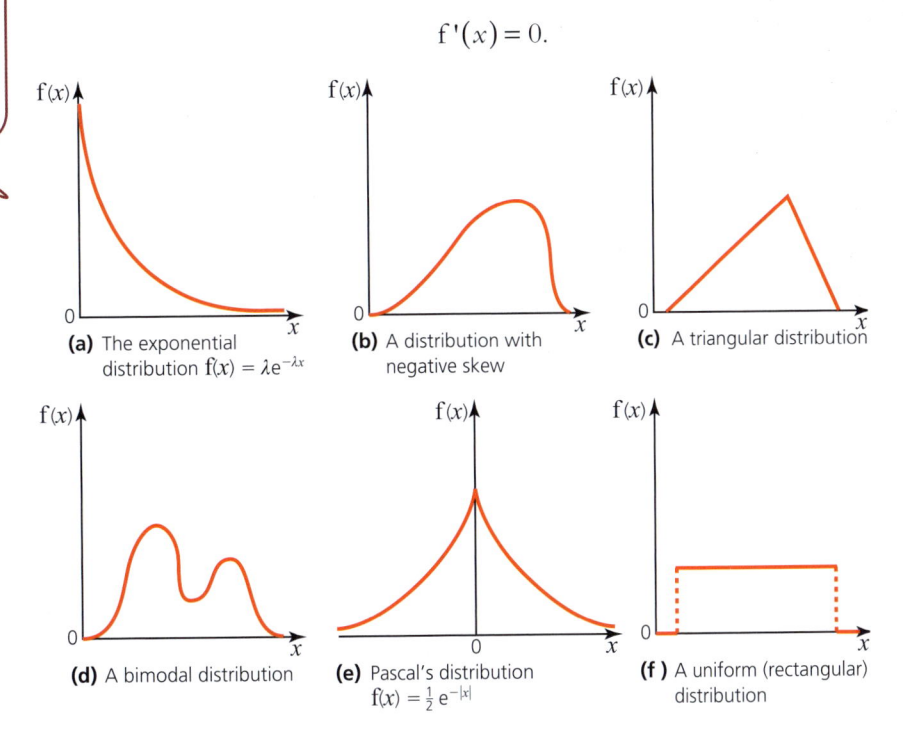

Figure 8.10

The mode

Example 8.6

The continuous random variable X has p.d.f. $f(x)$ where

$$f(x) = \begin{cases} 4x(1-x^2) & \text{for } 0 \leq x \leq 1 \\ 0 & \text{otherwise.} \end{cases}$$

Find

(i) the mode

(ii) the median.

Solution

(i) The mode is found by differentiating $f(x) = 4x - 4x^3$

$$f'(x) = 4 - 12x^2$$

Solving $f'(x) = 0$

$$x = \frac{1}{\sqrt{3}} = 0.577 \text{ to 3 decimal places.}$$

> $x = -0.577$ is also a root of $f'(x) = 0$ but is outside the range $0 \leq x \leq 1$.

It is easy to see from the shape of the graph (see Figure 8.11 below) that this must be a maximum, and so the mode is 0.577.

(ii) The median, m, is given by

$$\int_{-\infty}^{m} f(x)\,dx = 0.5$$

$$\Rightarrow \int_{0}^{m}(4x - 4x^3)\,dx = 0.5$$

> Since $x \geq 0$

$$\left[2x^2 - x^4\right]_{0}^{m} = 0.5$$

$$2m^2 - m^4 = 0.5$$

$$2m^4 - 4m^2 + 1 = 0.$$

> This equation is a quadratic in m^2. You can solve it using the quadratic formula and then taking the square root of the answer.

$m = 0.541$ or 1.307 to 3 decimal places.

$m = \pm 0.541$ or ± 1.307

The median is 0.541 (3 s.f.)

> Since 1.307 is outside the domain of X, the median is 0.541.

> Since -0.541 and ± 1.307 are all outside the domain of X, the median is 0.541.

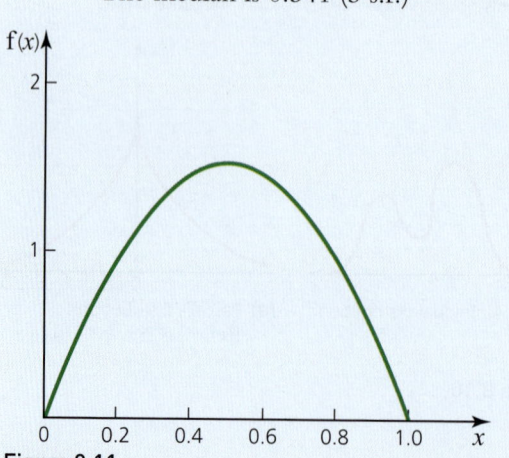

Figure 8.11

5 The continuous uniform (rectangular) distribution

> **Note**
> It is common to describe distributions by the shapes of the graphs of their p.d.f.s: U-shaped, J-shaped, etc.

You will recall having studied the discrete uniform distribution in Chapter 3. You will now meet the continuous uniform distribution. Since the term uniform distribution can be applied to both discrete and continuous variables, in the continuous case it is often written as uniform (rectangular).

The *continuous uniform (rectangular) distribution* is particularly simple since its p.d.f. is constant over a range of values and zero elsewhere.

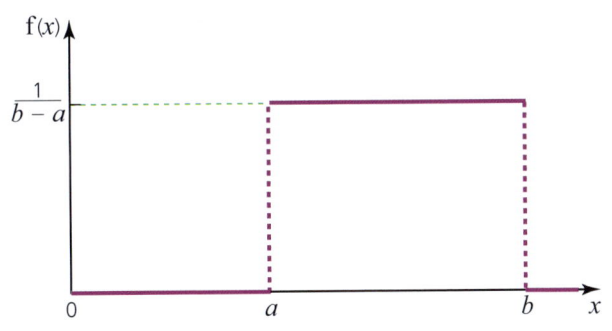

Figure 8.12

In Figure 8.12, X may take values between a and b, and is zero elsewhere. Since the area under the graph must be 1, the height is $\frac{1}{b-a}$.

Example 8.7

A junior gymnastics league is open to children who are at least five years old but have not yet had their ninth birthday. The age, X years, of a member is modelled by the uniform (rectangular) distribution over the range of possible values between five and nine. Age is measured in years and decimal parts of a year, rather than just completed years. Find

(i)   the p.d.f. $f(x)$ of X

(ii) $P(6 \leq X \leq 7)$

(iii) $E(X)$

(iv) $Var(X)$

(v)   the percentage of the children whose ages are within one standard deviation of the mean.

Solution

(i) The p.d.f. $f(x) = \begin{cases} \dfrac{1}{9-5} = \dfrac{1}{4} & \text{for } 5 \leq x < 9 \\ 0 & \text{otherwise.} \end{cases}$

The continuous uniform (rectangular) distribution

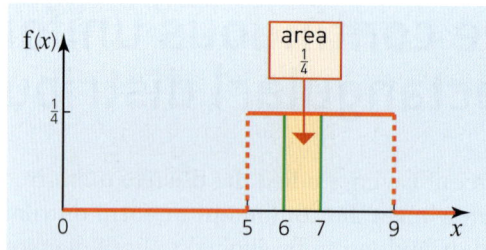

Figure 8.13

(ii) $P(6 \leq X \leq 7) = \frac{1}{4}$ by inspection of the rectangle above.

Alternatively, using integration

$$P(6 \leq X \leq 7) = \int_6^7 f(x)\,dx = \int_6^7 \frac{1}{4}\,dx$$

$$= \left[\frac{x}{4}\right]_6^7$$

$$= \frac{7}{6} - \frac{6}{4}$$

$$= \frac{1}{4}.$$

(iii) By the symmetry of the graph $E(X) = 7$. Alternatively, using integration

$$E(X) = \int_{-\infty}^{\infty} x f(x)\,dx = \int_5^9 \frac{x}{4}\,dx$$

$$= \left[\frac{x^2}{8}\right]_5^9$$

$$= \frac{81}{8} - \frac{25}{8} = 7.$$

$$\text{Var}(X) = \int_{-\infty}^{\infty} x^2 f(x)\,dx - [E(X)]^2 = \int_5^9 \frac{x^2}{4}\,dx - 7^2$$

$$= \left[\frac{x^3}{12}\right]_5^9 - 49$$

$$= \left(\frac{729}{12} - \frac{125}{12}\right) - 49$$

$$= 1.333 \text{ to 3 decimal places.}$$

(v) Standard deviation $\sqrt{\text{variance}} = \sqrt{1.333} = 1.155$.

So the percentage within 1 standard deviation of the mean is

$$\frac{2 \times 1.155}{4} \times 100\% = 57.7\%.$$

> Those within 1 standard deviation of the mean are those whose ages lie between 7 − 1.155 and 7 + 1.155. So the total range of ages is 2 × 1.155.

The mean and variance of the uniform (rectangular) distribution

In the previous example the mean and variance of a particular uniform distribution were calculated. This can easily be extended to the general uniform distribution given by:

$$f(x) = \begin{cases} \dfrac{1}{b-a} & \text{for } a \leq x \leq b \\ 0 & \text{otherwise.} \end{cases}$$

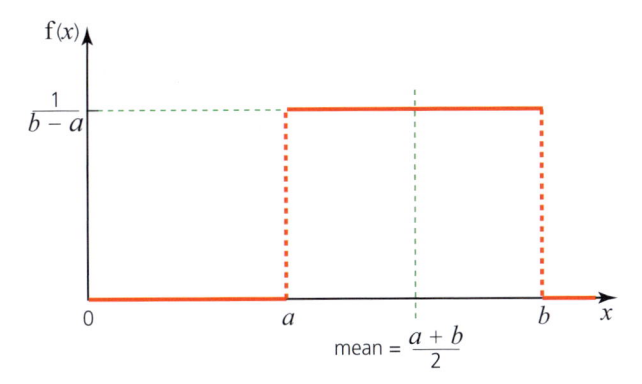

Figure 8.14

Mean: By symmetry the mean is $\dfrac{a+b}{2}$.

Variance:
$$\begin{aligned}
\mathrm{Var}(X) &= \int_{-\infty}^{\infty} x^2 f(x)\,dx - [E(X)]^2 \\
&= \int_a^b x^2 f(x)\,dx - [E(X)]^2 \\
&= \int_a^b \frac{x^2}{b-a}\,dx - \left(\frac{a+b}{2}\right)^2 \\
&= \left[\frac{x^3}{3(b-a)}\right]_a^b - \frac{1}{4}\left(a^2 + 2ab + b^2\right) \\
&= \frac{b^3 - a^3}{3(b-a)} - \frac{1}{4}\left(a^2 + 2ab + b^2\right) \\
&= \frac{(b-a)}{3(b-a)}\left(b^2 + ab + a^2\right) - \frac{1}{4}\left(a^2 + 2ab + b^2\right) \\
&= \frac{1}{12}\left(b^2 - 2ab + a^2\right) \\
&= \frac{1}{12}(b-a)^2
\end{aligned}$$

6 The exponential distribution

This distribution is often used to model the waiting times between events, such as earthquakes, radioactive emissions, telephone calls, etc. when the events being counted occur at random, singly and independently, at a constant overall rate.

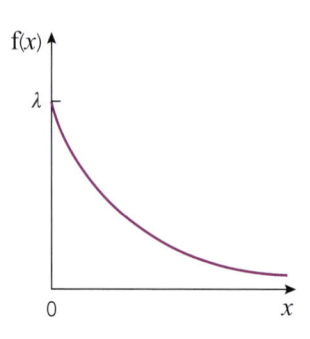

Figure 8.15

The random variable X has p.d.f. $f(x)$ as shown in Figure 8.15, given by:

$$f(x) = \begin{cases} \lambda e^{-\lambda x} & \text{for } x \geq 0 \\ 0 & \text{otherwise.} \end{cases}$$

where λ is a constant and $\lambda > 0$.

The mean is $\dfrac{1}{\lambda}$ and the variance is $\dfrac{1}{\lambda^2}$.

Proof

(i) Show that, for $x \geq 0$, $f(x)$ satisfies the requirements for a p.d.f., that is,

$f(x) \geq 0$ for all x

> This is true because both λ and $e^{-\lambda}$ are positive

and

$$\int_{\text{All values of } x} f(x)\,dx = \int_0^\infty \lambda e^{-\lambda x}\,dx$$

> Since x may take only positive or zero values, the lower limit is 0 rather than $-\infty$.

$$= \left[-e^{-\lambda x}\right]_0^\infty$$
$$= (0) - (-1)$$
$$= 1, \text{ as required.}$$

The graph in Figure 8.15 shows that $f(x) \geq 0$ for all x.

(ii) Show that $E(X) = \dfrac{1}{\lambda}$.

$$E(X) = \int_0^\infty x f(x)\,dx = \int_0^\infty \lambda x e^{-\lambda x}\,dx$$

Integrating by parts gives

$$E(X) = \left[-x e^{-\lambda x}\right]_0^\infty + \int_0^\infty e^{-\lambda x}\,dx$$

$$= 0 - \left[\frac{e^{-\lambda x}}{\lambda}\right]_0^\infty$$

$$= -\left(-\frac{1}{\lambda}\right)$$

$$= \frac{1}{\lambda}, \text{ as required.}$$

> **Note**
>
> Since it has been shown in part (ii) that
>
> $$\int_0^\infty \lambda x e^{-\lambda x}\, dx = \frac{1}{\lambda}$$
>
> it follows that
>
> $$2\int_0^\infty x e^{-\lambda x}\, dx = \frac{2}{\lambda^2}$$

(iii) Show that $\text{Var}(X) = \dfrac{1}{\lambda^2}$.

$$\text{Var}(X) = \int_0^\infty x^2 f(x)\, dx - [E(X)]^2 = \int_0^\infty x^2 \lambda e^{-\lambda x}\, dx - \left(\frac{1}{\lambda}\right)^2$$

Integrating by parts gives

$$\text{Var}(X) = \left[-x^2 e^{-\lambda x}\right]_0^\infty + \int_0^\infty e^{-\lambda x} 2x\, dx - \frac{1}{\lambda^2}$$

$$= 0 + 2\int_0^\infty x e^{-\lambda x}\, dx - \frac{1}{\lambda^2}$$

and so $\quad \text{Var}(X) = \dfrac{2}{\lambda^2} - \dfrac{1}{\lambda^2}$

$$= \frac{1}{\lambda^2}, \text{ as required.}$$

Exercise 8.2

① The continuous random variable X has p.d.f. $f(x)$, where

$$f(x) = \begin{cases} \dfrac{1}{8}x & \text{for } 0 \leq x \leq 4 \\ 0 & \text{otherwise.} \end{cases}$$

Find

(i) $E(X)$

(ii) $\text{Var}(X)$

(iii) the median value of X.

② The continuous random variable T has p.d.f. defined by

$$f(t) = \begin{cases} \dfrac{6-t}{18} & \text{for } 0 \leq t \leq 6 \\ 0 & \text{otherwise.} \end{cases}$$

Find

(i) $E(T)$

(ii) $\text{Var}(T)$

(iii) the median value of T.

③ The random variable X has p.d.f.

$$f(x) = \begin{cases} \dfrac{1}{6} & \text{for } -2 \leq x \leq 4 \\ 0 & \text{otherwise.} \end{cases}$$

(i) Sketch the graph of $f(x)$.

(ii) Find $P(X < 2)$.

(iii) Find $E(X)$.

(iv) Find $P(X < 1)$.

④ The continuous random variable Y has p.d.f. $f(y)$ defined by

$$f(y) = \begin{cases} 12y^2(1-y) & \text{for } 0 \leq y \leq 1 \\ 0 & \text{otherwise.} \end{cases}$$

The exponential distribution

   (i) Find E(Y).

   (ii) Find Var(Y).

   (iii) Show that, to 2 decimal places, the median value of Y is 0.61.

5. The continuous random variable X has p.d.f. f(x) defined by

$$f(x) = \begin{cases} \frac{2}{9}x(3-x) & \text{for } 0 \leq x \leq 3 \\ 0 & \text{otherwise.} \end{cases}$$

   (i) Find E(X).

   (ii) Find Var(X).

   (iii) Find the mode of X.

   (iv) Find the median value of X.

   (v) Draw a sketch graph of f(x) and comment on your answers to parts (i), (iii) and (iv) in the light of what it shows you.

6. The random variable X has a uniform (rectangular) distribution over the interval (−2, 5). Find

   (i) the p.d.f. of X

   (ii) E(X)

   (iii) Var(X)

   (iv) P(X is positive).

7. The function $f(x) = \begin{cases} k(3+x) & \text{for } 0 \leq x \leq 2 \\ 0 & \text{otherwise.} \end{cases}$

   is the probability density function of the random variable X.

   (i) Show that $k = \frac{1}{8}$.

   (ii) Find the mean and variance of X.

   (iii) Find the probability that a randomly selected value of X lies between 1 and 2.

8. A continuous random variable X has a uniform (rectangular) distribution over the interval (4, 7). Find

   (i) the p.d.f. of X

   (ii) E(X)

   (iii) Var(X)

   (iv) $P(4.1 \leq X \leq 4.8)$.

9. The distribution of the lengths of adult Martian lizards is uniform between 10 cm and 20 cm. There are no adult lizards outside this range.

   (i) Write down the p.d.f. of the lengths of the lizards.

   (ii) Find the mean and variance of the lengths of the lizards.

   (iii) What proportion of the lizards have lengths within

      (a) one standard deviation of the mean

      (b) two standard deviations of the mean?

⑩ The p.d.f. of the lifetime, X hours, of a brand of electric light bulb is modelled by

$$f(x) = \begin{cases} \dfrac{1}{60\ 000}x & \text{for } 0 \le x \le 300 \\ \dfrac{1}{50} - \dfrac{1}{20\ 000}x & \text{for } 300 < x \le 400 \\ 0 & \text{for } x > 400. \end{cases}$$

(i) Sketch the graph of $f(x)$.
(ii) Show that $f(x)$ fulfils the conditions for it to be a p.d.f.
(iii) Find the expected lifetime of a bulb.
(iv) Find the variance of the lifetimes of the bulbs.
(v) Find the probability that a randomly selected bulb will last less than 100 hours.

⑪ The marks of candidates in an examination are modelled by the continuous random variable X with p.d.f.

$$f(x) = \begin{cases} kx(x-50)^2(100-x) & \text{for } 0 \le x \le 100 \\ 0 & \text{otherwise.} \end{cases}$$

(i) Find the value of k.
(ii) Sketch the graph of $f(x)$.
(iii) Describe the shape of the graph and give an explanation of how such a graph might occur, in terms of the examination and the candidates.
(iv) Is it permissible to model a mark, which is a discrete variable going up in steps of 1, by a continuous random variable like X, as defined in this question?

⑫ The municipal tourism officer at a Mediterranean resort on the Costa Del Sol wishes to model the amount of sunshine per day during the holiday season. She denotes by X the number of hours of sunshine per day between 8 am and 8 pm and she suggests the following probability density function for X:

$$f(x) = \begin{cases} k\left[(x-3)^2 + 4\right] & \text{for } 0 \le x \le 12 \\ 0 & \text{otherwise.} \end{cases}$$

(i) Show that $k = \dfrac{1}{300}$ and sketch the graph of the p.d.f. $f(x)$.
(ii) Assuming that the model is accurate, find the mean and standard deviation of the number of hours of sunshine per day. Find also the probability of there being more than eight hours of sunshine on a randomly chosen day.
(iii) Obtain a cubic equation for m, the median number of hours of sunshine, and verify that m is about 9.74 to 2 decimal places.

⑬ The continuous random variable X has p.d.f. $f(x)$ defined by

$$f(x) = \begin{cases} ae^{-kx} & \text{for } x \ge 0 \\ 0 & \text{otherwise.} \end{cases}$$

The exponential distribution

Find, in terms of k,

(i) a

(ii) $E(X)$

(iii) Var(X)

(iv) the median value of X.

(v) There are many situations where this random variable might be used as a model. Describe one such situation. [MEI]

14. A statistician is also a keen cyclist. He believes that the distance which he cycles between punctures may be modelled by the random variable, X km, with p.d.f. $f(x)$ given by

$$f(x) = \begin{cases} 0.005e^{-0.005x} & \text{for } x > 0 \\ 0 & \text{otherwise.} \end{cases}$$

(i) Find the mean distance he cycles between punctures.

(ii) He has just repaired one puncture. What is the probability that he will travel at least 500 km before having another one?

(iii) He has just repaired one puncture. What is the probability that he will travel less than 30 km before having another one?

On one occasion he starts a race with new tyres but then has a puncture after 30 km. When he starts again, he has another puncture after k km. He says that according to his model the combined probability of first a puncture within 30 km and then one within k km is 0.005.

(iv) What is the value of k?

15. The continuous random variable X has p.d.f. $f(x)$ defined by

$$f(x) = \begin{cases} \dfrac{a}{x} & \text{for } 1 \leq x \leq 2 \\ 0 & \text{otherwise.} \end{cases}$$

(i) Find the value of a.

(ii) Sketch the graph of $f(x)$.

(iii) Find the mean and variance of X.

(iv) Find the proportion of values of X between 1.5 and 2.

(v) Find the median value of X.

16. An examination is taken by a large number of candidates. The marks scored are modelled by the continuous random variable X with probability density function

$$f(x) = kx^3(120 - x) \qquad 0 \leq x \leq 100.$$

(You should assume throughout this question that marks are on a continuous scale. Hence there is no need to consider *continuity corrections* which you will meet in Chapter 9.)

(i) Sketch the graph of this probability density function. What does the model suggest about the abilities of the candidates in relation to this examination?

(ii) Show that $k = 10^{-9}$.

(iii) The pass mark is set at 50. Find what proportion of candidates fail the examination.

(iv) The top 20% of candidates are awarded a distinction. Determine whether a mark of 90 is sufficient for a distinction. Find the least whole number mark which is sufficient for a distinction. [MEI]

7 The expectation and variance of a function of X

There are times when one random variable is a function of another random variable. For example:

- as part of an experiment, you are measuring temperatures in Celsius but then need to convert them to Fahrenheit: $F = 1.8C + 32$
- you are measuring the lengths of the sides of square pieces of material and deducing their areas: $A = L^2$
- you are estimating the ages, A years, of hedgerows by counting the number, n, of types of shrubs and trees in 30 m lengths: $A = 100n - 50$.

In fact, in any situation where you are entering the value of a random variable into a formula, the outcome will be another random variable which is a function of the one you entered. Under these circumstances, you may need to find the expectation and variance of such a function of a random variable.

For a discrete random variable, X, the expectation of a function $g[X]$ is given by:

$$E(g[X]) = \sum g[x_i] p_i$$
$$\text{Var}(g[X]) = \sum (g[x_i])^2 p_i - \{E(g[X])\}^2$$

The equivalent result for a continuous random variable, X, with p.d.f. $f(x)$ are:

$$E(g[X]) = \int_{\text{All values of } x} g[x] f(x) \, dx$$

$$\text{Var}(g[X]) = \int_{\text{All values of } x} (g[x])^2 f(x) \, dx - \{E(g[X])\}^2$$

Example 8.8

The continuous random variable X has p.d.f. $f(x)$ given by:

$$f(x) = \begin{cases} \dfrac{x}{50} & \text{for } 0 < x \leq 10 \\ 0 & \text{otherwise.} \end{cases}$$

(This random variable was used to model response times in Example 8.4.)

(i) Find $E(3X + 4)$.

(ii) Find $3E(X) + 4$.

(iii) Find $\text{Var}(3X + 4)$.

(iv) Verify that $\text{Var}(3X + 4) = 3^2 \text{Var}(X)$.

The expectation and variance of a function of X

Solution

> Here you are using
> $$E(g[X]) = \int_{\text{All values of } x} g[x]f(x)dx$$

(i) $E(3X+4) = \int_0^{10} (3x+4)\frac{x}{50}dx$

$= \int_0^{10} \frac{1}{50}(3x^2 + 4x)dx$

$= \left[\frac{x^3}{50} + \frac{x^2}{25}\right]_0^{10}$

$= 20 + 4$

$= 24$

(ii) $3E(X) + 4 = 3\int_0^{10} x\frac{x}{50}dx + 4$

$= \left[\frac{3}{150}x^3\right]_0^{10} + 4$

$= 20 + 4$

$= 24$

Notice here that $E(3X+4) = 24 = 3E(X) + 4$.

(iii) To find $\text{Var}(3X+4)$, use

$$\text{Var}(g[X]) = \int [g(x)]^2 f(x)dx - \{E(g[X])\}^2$$

with $g(x) = 3X + 4$.

$\text{Var}(3X+4) = \int_0^{10} (3x+4)^2 \frac{1}{50}x \, dx - 24^2$

$= \int_0^{10} \frac{1}{50}(9x^3 + 24x^2 + 16x)dx - 576$

$= \frac{1}{50}\left[\frac{9x^4}{4} + 8x^3 + 8x^2\right]_0^{10} - 576$

$= 50$

(iv) $\text{Var}(X) = E(X^2) - [E(X)]^2$

$E(X^2) = \int_0^{10} x^2 \frac{1}{50}x \, dx$ and $E(X) = \int_0^{10} x \frac{1}{50}x \, dx$

$E(X^2) = \int_0^{10} \frac{1}{50}x^3 \, dx$ and $E(X) = \int_0^{10} \frac{1}{50}x^2 \, dx$

$E(X^2) = \left[\frac{1}{200}x^4\right]_0^{10}$ and $E(X) = \left[\frac{1}{150}x^3\right]_0^{10}$

$E(X^2) = 50$ and $E(X) = 6.\dot{6}$

so $\text{Var}(X) = 50 - 6.\dot{6}^2 = 5.\dot{5}$

and $3^2 \text{Var}(X) = 9 \times 5.\dot{5} = 50$

From part (iii), $\text{Var}(3X+4) = 50$

So $\text{Var}(3X+4) = 3^2 \text{Var}(X)$, as required.

> **Note**
> You have of course already met these results for discrete random variables in Chapter 2.

General results

This example illustrates a number of general results for random variables, continuous or discrete.

$E(c) = c$ $\quad\quad\quad$ $\text{Var}(c) = 0$

$E(aX) = aE(X)$ $\quad\quad$ $\text{Var}(aX) = a^2\text{Var}(X)$

$E(aX + b) = aE(X) + b$ $\quad$ $\text{Var}(aX + b) = a^2\text{Var}(X)$

$$E[g(X) \pm h(X)] = E[g(X)] \pm E[h(X)]$$

where a, b and c are constants and $g(X)$ and $h(X)$ are functions of X.

In Chapter 2, you met results for the expectation and variance of linear combinations of discrete independent random variables, X and Y.

$$E(aX \pm bY) = aE(X) \pm bE(Y) \text{ and } \text{Var}(aX \pm bY) = a^2\text{Var}(X) + b^2 E(Y)$$

The same results hold if the variables are continuous, but they must still be independent.

> **Note**
> The result $\text{Var}(aX) = a^2\text{Var}(X)$ should not surprise you. It follows from the fact that if the standard deviation of a set of data is k, then the standard deviation of the set formed by multiplying all the data by a positive constant, a, is ak. That is,
>
> standard deviation(aX)
> $= a \times$ standard deviation(X)
>
> Since variance
> $=$ (standard deviation)^2
> then $\text{Var}(aX)$
> $=$ [standard deviation(aX)]^2
> $=$ [$a \times$ standard deviation(X)]^2
> $= a^2$[standard deviation(X)]^2
> $= a^2 \text{Var}(X)$.

Example 8.9

The continuous random variable X has p.d.f. $f(x)$ given by

$$f(x) = \begin{cases} \dfrac{3}{125}x^2 & \text{for } 0 \leq x \leq 5 \\ 0 & \text{otherwise.} \end{cases}$$

Find

(i) $E(X)$ $\quad$ (ii) $\text{Var}(X)$ $\quad$ (iii) $E(7X - 3)$ $\quad$ (iv) $\text{Var}(7X - 3)$.

Solution

(i) $\displaystyle E(X) = \int_{-\infty}^{\infty} x f(x)\,dx$

$\displaystyle = \int_0^5 x \frac{3}{125}x^2\,dx$

$\displaystyle = \left[\frac{3}{500}x^4\right]_0^5$

$= 3.75$

(ii) $\displaystyle \text{Var}(X) = \int_{-\infty}^{\infty} x^2 f(x)\,dx - [E(X)]^2$

$\displaystyle = \int_0^5 x^2 \frac{3}{125}x^2\,dx - 3.75^2$

$\displaystyle = \left[\frac{3}{625}x^5\right]_0^5 - 14.0625$

$= 15 - 14.0625$

$= 0.9375$

The expectation and variance of a function of X

(iii) $E(7X-3) = 7E(X) - 3$
$= 7 \times 3.75 - 3$
$= 23.25$

(iv) $Var(7X - 3) = 7^2 Var(X)$
$= 49 \times 0.9375$
$= 45.94$ to 2 decimal places

Exercise 8.3

1. A continuous random variable X has the p.d.f.:
$$f(x) = \begin{cases} k & \text{for } 0 \leq x \leq 5 \\ 0 & \text{otherwise.} \end{cases}$$

   (i) Find the value of k.
   (ii) Sketch the graph of $f(x)$.
   (iii) Find $E(X)$.
   (iv) Find $E(4X - 3)$ and show that your answer is the same as $4E(X) - 3$.

2. The continuous random variable X has p.d.f.
$$f(x) = \begin{cases} 4x^3 & \text{for } 0 \leq x \leq 1 \\ 0 & \text{otherwise.} \end{cases}$$

   (i) Find $E(X)$.
   (ii) Find $E(X^2)$.
   (iii) Find $Var(X)$.
   (iv) Verify that $E(5X + 1) = 5E(X) + 1$.

3. The number of kilograms of metal extracted from 10 kg of ore from a certain mine is modelled by a continuous random variable X with probability density function $f(x)$, where
$$f(x) = \begin{cases} cx(2-x)^2 & \text{for } 0 \leq x \leq 2 \\ 0 & \text{otherwise,} \end{cases}$$
where c is a constant.

   Show that c is $\frac{3}{4}$, and find the mean and variance of X.

   The cost of extracting the metal from 10 kg of ore is £10x. Find the expected cost of extracting the metal from 10 kg of ore.

4. A continuous random variable Y has p.d.f.
$$f(y) = \begin{cases} \frac{2}{9}y(3-y) & \text{for } 0 \leq y \leq 3 \\ 0 & \text{otherwise.} \end{cases}$$

   (i) Find $E(Y)$.
   (ii) Find $E(Y^2)$.
   (iii) Find $E(Y^2) = [E(Y)]^2$.
   (iv) Find $E(2Y^2 + 3Y + 4)$.
   (v) Find $\int_0^3 (y - E(Y))^2 f(y) dy$.

   Why is the answer the same as that for part (iii)?

⑤ A continuous random variable X has p.d.f. $f(x)$, where
$$f(x) = \begin{cases} 12x^2(1-x) & \text{for } 0 \leq x \leq 1 \\ 0 & \text{otherwise.} \end{cases}$$

(i) Find μ, the mean of X.

(ii) Find $E(6X - 7)$ and show that your answer is the same as $6E(X) - 7$.

(iii) Find the standard deviation of X.

(iv) What is the probability that a randomly selected value of X lies within one standard deviation of μ?

⑥ The continuous random variable X has p.d.f.
$$f(x) = \begin{cases} \frac{2}{25}(7-x) & \text{for } 2 \leq x \leq 7 \\ 0 & \text{otherwise.} \end{cases}$$

The function $g(X)$ is defined by $g(x) = 3x^2 + 4x + 7$.

(i) Find $E(X)$.

(ii) Find $E[g(X)]$.

(iii) Find $E(X^2)$ and hence find $3E(X^2) + 4E(X) + 7$.

(iv) Use your answers to parts (ii) and (iii) to verify that $E[g(X)] = 3E(X^2) + 4E(X) + 7$.

⑦ A toy company sells packets of coloured plastic equilateral triangles. The triangles are actually offcuts from the manufacture of a totally different toy, and the length, X, of one side of a triangle may be modelled as a random variable with a uniform (rectangular) distribution for $2 \leq x \leq 8$.

(i) Find the p.d.f. of X.

(ii) An equilateral triangle of side x has area a. Find the relationship between a and x.

(iii) Find the probability that a randomly selected triangle has area greater than $15\,\text{cm}^2$. (Hint: What does this imply about x?)

(iv) Find the expectation and variance of the area of a triangle.

⑧ The continuous random variable X has probability density function
$$f(x) = \begin{cases} \frac{3}{1024} x(x-8)^2 & 0 \leq x \leq 8 \\ 0 & \text{otherwise} \end{cases}$$

A sketch of $f(x)$ is shown in the diagram.

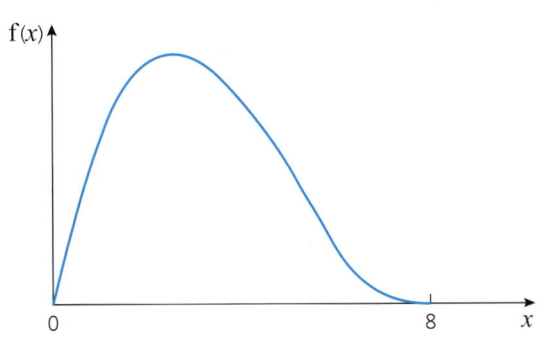

Figure 8.16

Find $E(X)$ and show that $Var(X) = 2.56$.

The times, in minutes, taken by a doctor to see her patients are modelled by the continuous random variable $T = X + 2$.

(i) Sketch the distribution of T and describe in words what this model implies about the lengths of the doctor's appointments. [MEI]

9. A continuous random variable has probability density function f defined by

$$f(x) = \begin{cases} kx(6-x) & \text{for } 0 \leq x \leq 6 \\ 0 & \text{otherwise.} \end{cases}$$

Evaluate k and the mean of the distribution.

A particle moves along a straight line in such a way that during the first six seconds of its motion its displacement at time t seconds is s m, where $s = 2(t + 1)$.

The particle is observed at time t seconds, where t denotes a random value from a distribution whose probability density function is the function f defined above. Calculate the probability that at the time of observation the displacement of the particle is less than 5 m.

10. Every day, I travel to and from work on the local shuttle bus, which runs every 10 minutes. The time I have to wait for the bus is modelled by the random variable T, which has a uniform (rectangular) distribution on the interval [0, 10].

(i) Write down the probability density function for T, and state its mean and variance.

The *total* time I have to wait for a bus, going to and coming from work, is modelled by the random variable X whose probability density function is given by

$$f(x) = \begin{cases} 0.01x & \text{for } 0 \leq x \leq 10 \\ 0.01(20 - x) & \text{for } 10 < x \leq 20 \\ 0 & \text{otherwise.} \end{cases}$$

(ii) Sketch the graph of the probability density function for X.

(iii) State $E(X)$ and use integration to find $Var(X)$.

The times I wait for the bus when going to work and coming home from work are represented by independent random variables T_1 and T_2, respectively, so that $X = T_1 + T_2$.

(iv) Find $P(X \geq 14)$. Give a reason why you would expect $P(X \geq 14)$ to be greater than $P(T_1 \geq 7) \times P(T_2 \geq 7)$. [MEI]

8 The cumulative distribution function

500 enter community half-marathon

There was a record entry for this year's Community half-marathon, including several famous names who were treating it as a training run in preparation for the London marathon. Overall winner was Reuben Mhango in 1 hour 4 minutes and 2 seconds; the first woman home was 37-year-old Lynn Barber in 1 hour 20 minutes exactly. There were many fun runners but everybody completed the course within 4 hours.

Record numbers, but no record times this year

£150 prize to be won

Mike Harrison, chair of the Half Committee, says: 'This year we restricted entries to 500 but this meant disappointing many people. Next year we intend to allow everybody to run and expect a much bigger entry. In order to allow us to marshall the event properly we need a statistical model to predict the flow of runners, and particularly their finishing times. We are offering a prize of £150 for the best such model submitted.'

Time (hours)	Finished (%)
1¼	3
1½	15
1¾	33
2	49
2¼	57
2½	75
3	91
3½	99
4	100

An entrant for the competition proposed a model in which a runner's time, X hours, is a continuous random variable with p.d.f.

$$f(x) = \begin{cases} \frac{4}{27}(x-1)(4-x)^2 & 1 \leq x \leq 4 \\ 0 & \text{otherwise.} \end{cases}$$

According to this model, the mode is at 2 hours, and everybody finishes in between 1 hour and 4 hours; see Figure 8.17.

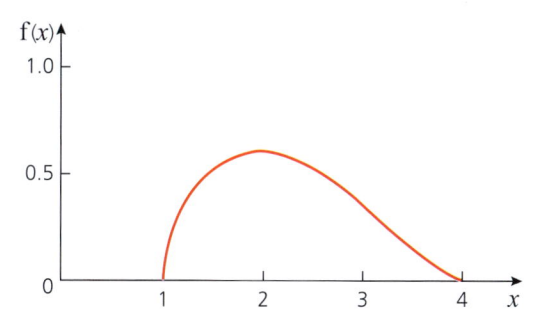

Figure 8.17

The cumulative distribution function

How does this model compare with the figures you were given for the actual race?

Those figures gave the *cumulative distribution*, the total numbers (expressed as percentages) of runners who had finished by certain times. To obtain the equivalent figures from the model, you must find the relevant area under the graph in Figure 8.18.

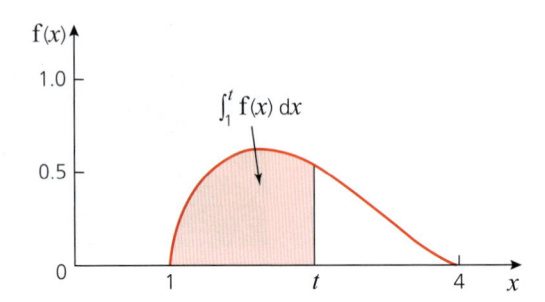

Figure 8.18

In this model, the proportion finishing by time t hours is given by

$$\int_1^t f(x)\,dx = \int_1^t \frac{4}{27}(x-1)(4-x)^2\,dx$$

$$= \frac{4}{27}\int_1^t (x^3 - 9x^2 + 24x - 16)\,dx$$

$$= \frac{4}{27}\left[\frac{1}{4}x^4 - 3x^3 + 12x^2 - 16x\right]_1^t$$

$$= \frac{4}{27}\left(\frac{1}{4}t^4 - 3t^3 + 12t^2 - 16t\right) - (-1)$$

$$= \frac{1}{27}t^4 - \frac{4}{9}t^3 + \frac{16}{9}t^2 - \frac{64}{27}t + 1$$

This is called the *cumulative distribution function* (c.d.f.) and denoted by $F(t)$. In this case,

$$F(t) = \begin{cases} 0 & \text{for } t < 1 \\ \frac{1}{27}t^4 - \frac{4}{9}t^3 + \frac{16}{9}t^2 - \frac{64}{27}t + 1 & \text{for } 1 \leq t \leq 4 \\ 1 & \text{for } t > 4. \end{cases}$$

To find the proportions of runners finishing by any time, substitute that value for t; so when $t = 2$

$$F(2) = \frac{1}{27} \times 2^4 - \frac{4}{9} \times 2^3 + \frac{16}{9} \times 2^2 - \frac{64}{27} \times 2 + 1$$

$$= 0.41 \text{ to two decimal places.}$$

Here is the complete table, with all the values worked out.

Table 8.3

Time (hours)	Model	Runners
1.00	0.00	0.00
1.25	0.04	0.03
1.50	0.13	0.15
1.75	0.26	0.33
2.00	0.41	0.49
2.25	0.55	0.57
2.50	0.69	0.75
3.00	0.89	0.91
3.50	0.98	0.99
4.00	1.00	1.00

> **Discussion point**
>
> Do you think that this model is worth the £150 prize? If you were on the organising committee what more might you look for in a model?

Notice the distinctive shape of the curves of these functions (Figure 8.19), sometimes called an *ogive*.

> **Note**
>
> You have probably met this shape already when drawing cumulative frequency curves.

Figure 8.19

Properties of the cumulative distribution function, F(x)

The graphs, Figure 8.20, show the probability density function f(x) and the cumulative distribution function F(x) of a typical continuous random variable X. You will see that the values of the random variable always lie between a and b.

> **Note**
>
> These graphs illustrate the probability density function of a function that can take a limited range of values. The lower limit is a and the upper limit is b. You could look at it a different way and say, for example, that the lower limit is 0; in that case the two graphs would have line segments along the x axis joining 0 to a. Some distributions, for example the Normal distribution, have no limits and so the range of possible values is from $-\infty$ to $+\infty$.

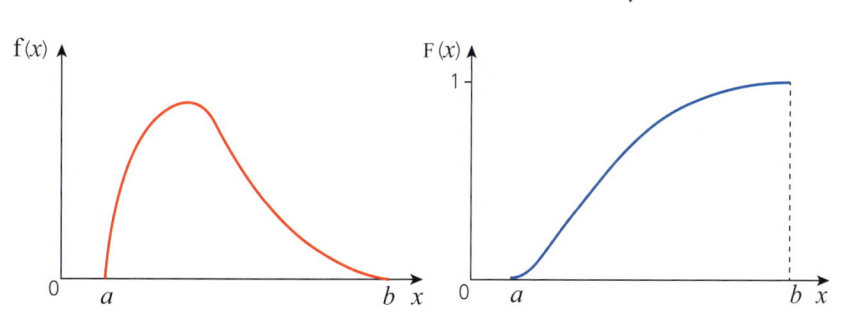

Figure 8.20

The cumulative distribution function

> **Notes**
>
> 1 Notice the use of lower and upper case letters here. The probability density function is denoted by the lower case f, whereas the cumulative distribution function is given the upper case F.
>
> 2 F was derived here as a function of t rather than x, to avoid using the same variable in the expression to be integrated. In this case, t was a natural variable to use because time was involved, but that is not always the case.
>
> It is more usual to write F as a function of x, F(x), but you would not be correct to write down an expression like
>
> $$F(x) = \int_1^x \frac{4}{27}(x-1)(4-x)^2 \, dx$$
>
> **INCORRECT**
>
> since x would then be both a limit of the integral and the variable used within it. To overcome this problem, a dummy variable, u, is used in the rest of this section, so that F(x) is now written,
>
> $$F(x) = \int_1^x \frac{4}{27}(u-1)(4-u)^2 \, du$$
>
> **CORRECT**
>
> You may of course use another symbol, like y or p, rather than u; anything except x.
>
> 3 The term cumulative distribution function is often abbreviated to c.d.f.

These graphs illustrate a number of general results for cumulative distribution functions.

1 F(x) = 0   for $x \leq a$, the lower limit of x.

The probability of X taking a value less than or equal to a is zero; the value of X must be greater than or equal to a.

2 F(x) = 1 for $x \geq b$, the upper limit of x. X cannot take values greater than b.

3 P($c \leq X \leq d$) = F(d) − F(c)

P($c \leq X \leq d$) = P($X \leq d$) − P($X \leq c$)

This is very useful when finding probabilities from a p.d.f. or a c.d.f.

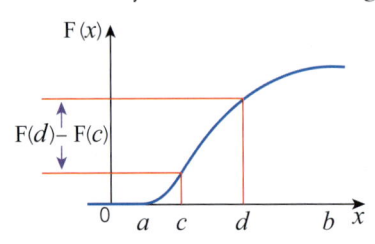

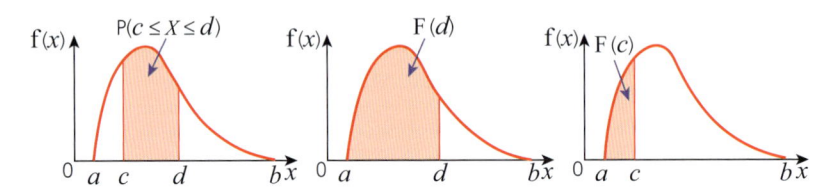

Figure 8.21

4 The median, m, satisfies the equation F(m) = 0.5.
P($X \leq m$) = 0.5 by definition of the median.

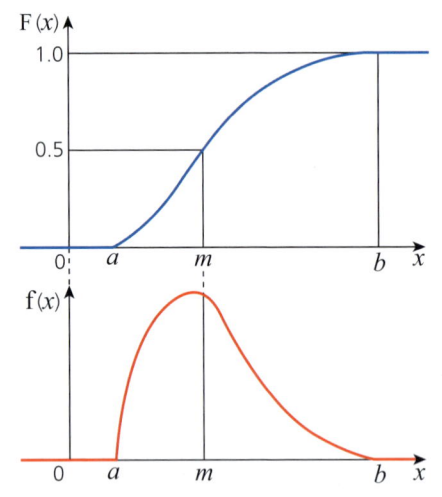

Figure 8.22

5 $f(x) = \dfrac{d}{dx} F(x) = F'(x)$

Since you integrate $f(x)$ to obtain F(x), the reverse must also be true: differentiating F(x) gives $f(x)$.

6 F(x) is a continuous function: the graph of y = F(x) has no gaps.

Example 8.10

A machine saws planks of wood to a nominal length. The continuous random variable X represents the error in millimetres of the actual length of a plank coming off the machine. The variable X has p.d.f. $f(x)$, where

$$f(x) = \begin{cases} \dfrac{10-x}{50} & \text{for } 0 \leq x \leq 10 \\ 0 & \text{otherwise.} \end{cases}$$

(i) Sketch $f(x)$.

(ii) Find the cumulative distribution function $F(x)$.

(iii) Sketch $F(x)$ for $0 \leq x \leq 10$.

(iv) Find $P(2 \leq X \leq 7)$.

(v) Find the median value of X.

A customer refuses to accept planks for which the error is greater than 8 mm.

(iv) What percentage of planks will he reject?

Solution

(i)

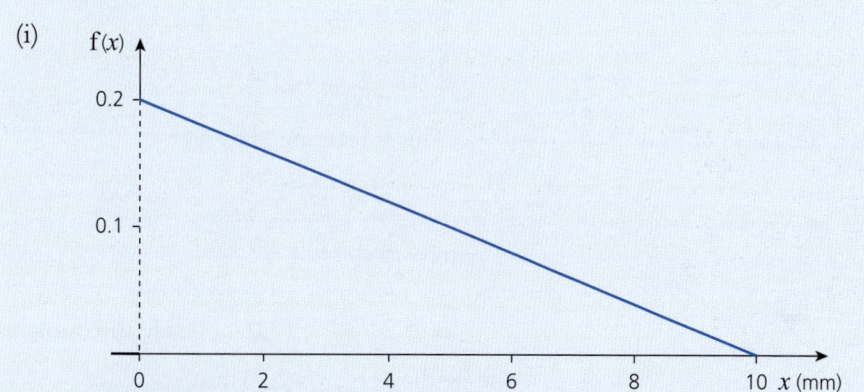

Figure 8.23

(ii) $F(x) = \displaystyle\int_0^x \dfrac{(10-u)}{50} du$

$= \dfrac{1}{50}\left[10u - \dfrac{u^2}{2} \right]_0^x$

$= \dfrac{1}{5}x - \dfrac{1}{100}x^2$

The full definition of $F(x)$ is:

$$F(x) = \begin{cases} 0 & \text{for } x < 10 \\ \dfrac{1}{5}x - \dfrac{1}{100}x^2 & \text{for } 0 \leq x \leq 10 \\ 1 & \text{for } x > 10. \end{cases}$$

The cumulative distribution function

(iii) The graph F(x) is shown in Figure 8.24.

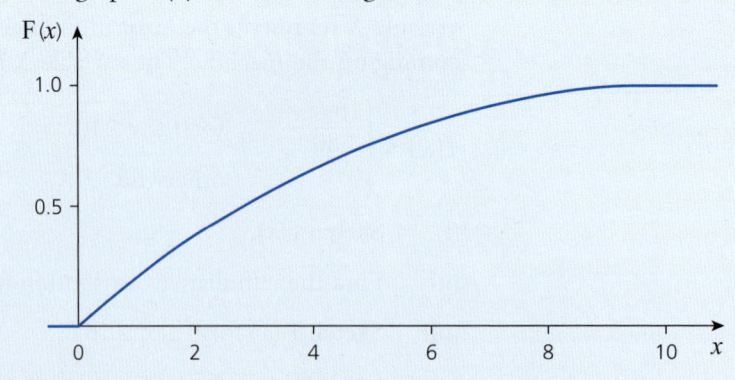

Figure 8.24

(iv) $P(2 \leq X \leq 7) = F(7) - F(2)$

$= \left[\frac{7}{5} - \frac{49}{100}\right] - \left[\frac{2}{5} - \frac{4}{100}\right]$

$= 0.91 - 0.36$

$= 0.55.$

(v) The median value of X is found by solving the equation

$F(m) = 0.5$

$\frac{1}{5}m - \frac{1}{100}m^2 = 0.5.$

This is rearranged to give

$m^2 - 20m + 50 = 0$

$m = \frac{20 \pm \sqrt{20^2 - 4 \times 50}}{2}$

$m = 2.93$ (or 17.07, outside the domain for X).

The median error is 2.93 mm.

(vi) The customer rejects those planks for which $8 \leq X \leq 10$.
$P(8 \leq X \leq 10) = F(10) - F(8)$

$= 1 - 0.96$

so 4% of planks are rejected.

Example 8.11

The p.d.f. of a continuous random variable X is given by:

$$f(x) = \begin{cases} \dfrac{x}{24} & \text{for } 0 \leq x \leq 4 \\ \dfrac{(12-x)}{48} & \text{for } 4 \leq x \leq 12 \\ 0 & \text{otherwise.} \end{cases}$$

(i) Sketch $f(x)$.

(ii) Find the cumulative distribution function $F(x)$.

(iii) Sketch $F(x)$.

Solution

(i) The graph of f(x) is shown in Figure 8.25

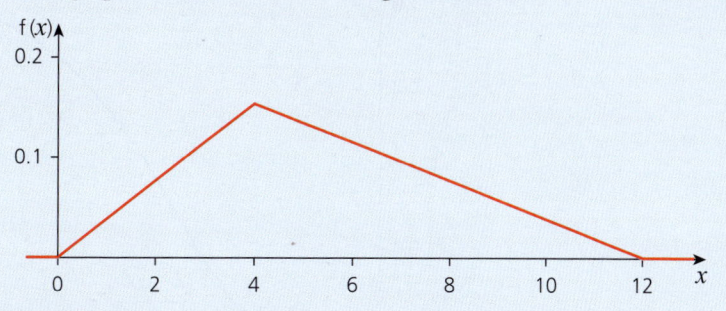

Figure 8.25

(ii) For $0 \leq x \leq 4$, $F(x) = \int_0^x \dfrac{u}{24} \, du$

$$= \left[\dfrac{u^2}{48}\right]_0^x$$

$$= \dfrac{x^2}{48}$$

and so $F(4) = \dfrac{1}{3}$

For $4 \leq x \leq 12$, a second integration is required:

$$F(x) = \int_0^4 \dfrac{u}{24} \, du + \int_4^x \left(\dfrac{12-u}{48}\right) du$$

$$= F(4) + \left[\dfrac{u}{4} - \dfrac{u^2}{96}\right]_4^x$$

$$= \dfrac{1}{3} + \dfrac{x}{4} - \dfrac{x^2}{96} - \dfrac{5}{6}$$

$$= -\dfrac{1}{2} + \dfrac{x}{4} - \dfrac{x^2}{96}$$

So the full definition of $F(x)$ is

$$F(x) = \begin{cases} 0 & \text{for } x < 0 \\ \dfrac{x^2}{48} & \text{for } 0 \leq x \leq 4 \\ -\dfrac{1}{2} + \dfrac{x}{4} - \dfrac{x^2}{96} & \text{for } 4 \leq x \leq 12 \\ 1 & \text{for } x > 12. \end{cases}$$

The cumulative distribution function

(iii) The graph of F(x) is shown in Figure 8.26.

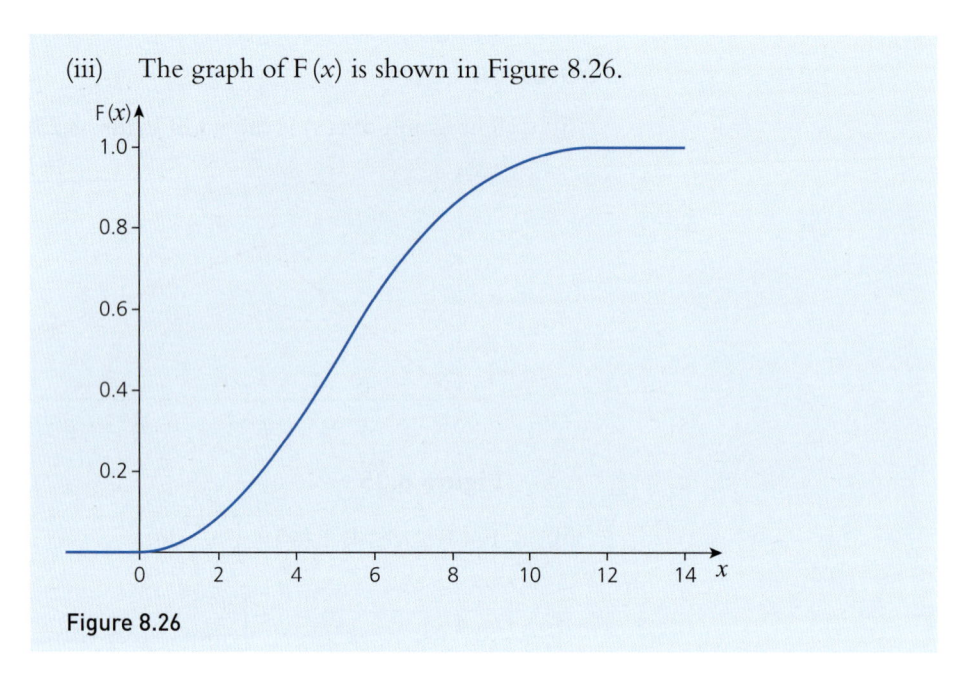

Figure 8.26

Example 8.12

The continuous random variable X has cumulative distribution function $F(x)$ given by:

$$F(x) = \begin{cases} 0 & \text{for } x < 2 \\ \dfrac{x^2}{32} - \dfrac{1}{8} & \text{for } 2 \leq x \leq 6 \\ 1 & \text{for } x > 6. \end{cases}$$

Find the p.d.f. $f(x)$.

Solution

$f(x) = \dfrac{d}{dx} F(x)$

$$f(x) = \begin{cases} \dfrac{d}{dx} F(x) = 0 & \text{for } x < 2 \\ \dfrac{d}{dx} F(x) = \dfrac{x}{16} & \text{for } 2 \leq x \leq 6 \\ \dfrac{d}{dx} F(x) = 0 & \text{for } x > 6. \end{cases}$$

Exercise 8.4

① The continuous random variable X has p.d.f. $f(x)$ where

$$f(x) = \begin{cases} 0.2 & \text{for } 0 \leq x \leq 5 \\ 0 & \text{otherwise.} \end{cases}$$

(i) Find $E(X)$.

(ii) Find the cumulative distribution function, $F(x)$.

(iii) Find $P(0 \leq x \leq 2)$ using

(a) F(x)

(b) f(x) and show your answer is the same by each method.

② The continuous random variable U has p.d.f. f(u)

where $f(u) = \begin{cases} ku & \text{for } 5 \leq u \leq 8 \\ 0 & \text{otherwise.} \end{cases}$

(i) Find the value of k.

(ii) Sketch f(u).

(iii) Find F(u).

(iv) Sketch the graph of F(u).

③ A continuous random variable X has p.d.f. f(x)

where $f(x) = \begin{cases} cx^2 & \text{for } 1 \leq x \leq 4 \\ 0 & \text{otherwise.} \end{cases}$

(i) Find the value of c.

(ii) Find F(x).

(iii) Find the median of X.

(iv) Find the mode of X.

④ The continuous random variable X has p.d.f. f(x) given by

$f(x) = \begin{cases} \dfrac{k}{(x+1)^4} & \text{for } x \geq 0 \\ 0 & \text{otherwise.} \end{cases}$

where k is a constant.

(i) Show that $k = 3$, and find the cumulative distribution function.

(ii) Find also the value of x such that $P(X < x) = \dfrac{7}{8}$.

⑤ The continuous random variable X has c.d.f. given by

$F(x) = \begin{cases} 0 & \text{for } x < 0 \\ 2x - x^2 & \text{for } 0 \leq x \leq 1 \\ 1 & \text{for } x > 1. \end{cases}$

(i) Find P($X > 0.5$).

(ii) Find the value of q such that $P(X < q) = \dfrac{1}{4}$.

(iii) Find the p.d.f. f(x) of X, and sketch its graph.

⑥ The continuous random variable X has p.d.f. f(x) given by

$f(x) = \begin{cases} k(9 - x^2) & \text{for } 0 \leq x \leq 3 \\ 0 & \text{otherwise} \end{cases}$

where k is a constant.

Show that $k = \dfrac{1}{18}$ and find the values of E(X) and Var(X).

Find the cumulative distribution function for X, and verify by calculation that the median value of X is between 1.04 and 1.05.

⑦ A random variable X has p.d.f. f(x) where

$f(x) = \begin{cases} 12x^2(1-x) & \text{for } 0 \leq x \leq 1 \\ 0 & \text{otherwise} \end{cases}$

Find μ, the mean of X, and show that σ, the standard deviation of X, is $\frac{1}{5}$.

Show that $F(x)$, the probability that $X \leq x$ (for any value of x between 0 and 1), satisfies

$$F(x) = \begin{cases} 0 & \text{for } x < 0 \\ 4x^3 - 3x^4 & \text{for } 0 \leq x \leq 1 \\ 1 & \text{for } x > 1. \end{cases}$$

Use this result to show that $P(|X - \mu| < \sigma) = 0.64$. [MEI]

What would this probability be if, instead, X were Normally distributed?

⑧ The temperature in degrees Celsius in a refrigerator which is operating properly has probability density function given by

$$f(t) = \begin{cases} kt^2(12 - t) & 0 < t < 12 \\ 0 & \text{otherwise.} \end{cases}$$

(i) Show that the value of k is $\frac{1}{1728}$.

(ii) Find the cumulative distribution function $F(t)$.

(iii) Show, by substitution, that the median temperature is about 7.37 °C.

(iv) The temperature in a refrigerator is too high if it is over 10 °C. Find the probability that this occurs. [MEI]

⑨ A random variable X has p.d.f. $f(x)$, where

$$f(x) = \begin{cases} k \sin 2x & \text{for } 0 \leq x \leq \frac{\pi}{2} \\ 0 & \text{otherwise.} \end{cases}$$

By integration find, in terms of x and the constant k, an expression for the cumulative distribution function of X for $0 \leq x \leq \frac{\pi}{2}$.

Hence show that $k = 1$ and find the probability that $X < \frac{\pi}{8}$. [MEI]

⑩ The time, T minutes, between customer arrivals at a country store, from Monday to Friday, can be modelled, for $t \geq 0$, by the probability density function $f(t)$ defined by illustrating these probabilities on a sketch of the graph of $f(t)$.

$f(t) = 0.1 \, e^{-0.1t}$.

(i) Find the probability that the time between arrivals is

(a) less than 5 minutes

(b) more than 15 minutes.

(ii) Obtain the cumulative distribution function for T. Hence find the median time between arrivals. The time, x minutes, between customer arrivals at the country store on Saturdays can be modelled by the probability density function $g(x)$ defined by $g(x) = \lambda e^{-\lambda t}$ for $x \geq 0$ where λ is a positive constant.

(iii) On Saturdays, the probability of the time between customer arrivals exceeding 5 minutes is 0.4. Estimate the value of λ.

⑪ A firm has a large number of employees. The distance in miles they have to travel each day from home to work can be modelled by a continuous random variable X whose cumulative distribution function is given by

$$F(x) = \begin{cases} 0 & \text{for } x < 1 \\ k\left(1 - \dfrac{1}{x}\right) & \text{for } 1 \leq x \leq b \\ 1 & \text{for } x > b \end{cases}$$

where b represents the farthest distance anybody lives from work.

The diagram below shows a sketch of this cumulative distribution function.

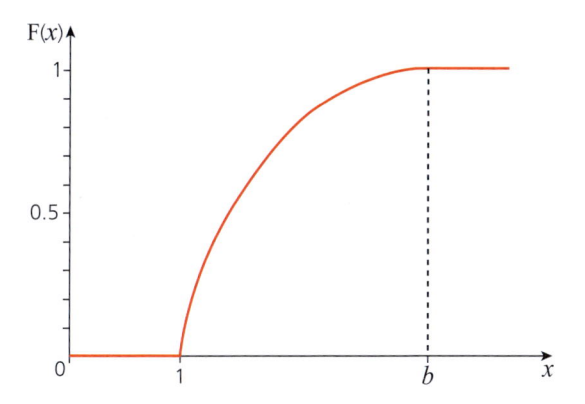

Figure 8.27

A survey suggests that $b = 5$. Use this parameter for parts (i) to (iv).

(i) Show that $k = 1.25$.

(ii) Write down and solve an equation to find the median distance travelled to work.

(iii) Find the probability that an employee lives within half a mile of the median.

(iv) Derive the probability density function for X and illustrate it with a sketch.

(v) Show that, for any value of b greater than 1, the median distance travelled does not exceed 2. [MEI]

⑫ The wages department of a large company models the incomes of the employees by the continuous random variable X with cumulative distribution function

$$F(x) = 1 - \left(\dfrac{3}{x}\right)^4 \quad 3 \leq x < \infty$$

where X is measured in an arbitrary currency unit. (X is said to have a Pareto distribution.)

(i) Find the median income. Find also the smallest income of an employee in the top 10% of incomes.

(ii) Find the probability density function of X and hence show that the mean income is 4.

(iii) Find the probability that a randomly chosen employee earns more than the mean income. [MEI]

The cumulative distribution function

13 A continuous random variable X has probability density function $f(x)$. The probability that $X \leq x$ is given by the function $F(x)$.

Explain why $F'(x) = f(x)$.

A rod of length $2a$ is broken into two parts at a point whose position is random. State the form of the probability distribution of the length of the smaller part, and state also the mean value of this length.

Two equal rods, each of length $2a$, are broken into two parts at points whose positions are random. X is the length of the shortest of the four parts thus obtained. Find the probability, $F(x)$, that $X \leq x$, where $0 < x \leq a$.

Hence, or otherwise, show that the probability density function of X is given by

$$f(x) = \begin{cases} \dfrac{2(a-x)}{a^2} & \text{for } 0 < x \leq a \\ 0 & \text{for } x \leq 0,\ x > a \end{cases}$$

Show that the mean value of X is $\frac{1}{3}a$.

Write down the mean value of the sum of the two smaller parts and show that the mean values of the four parts are in the proportions $1:2:4:5$. [JMB]

14 (i) Explain the significance of the results:

(a) $\displaystyle\int_{-\infty}^{\infty} \frac{1}{\sqrt{2\pi}} e^{-\frac{1}{2}z^2} \, dz = 1$ (b) $\displaystyle\int_{-\infty}^{\infty} \frac{1}{\sqrt{2\pi}} z e^{-\frac{1}{2}z^2} \, dz = 0$

The random variable Y is given by $Y = Z^2$ (where Z is the standardised Normal variable).

(ii) Using the results in part (i), find

(a) $E(Y)$ (b) $Var(Y)$.

(You will need to use integration by parts.)

KEY POINTS

1 A continuous random variable

If X is a continuous random variable with probability density function $f(x)$

- $\displaystyle\int_{-\infty}^{\infty} f(x) \, dx$
- $f(x) \geq 0$ for all x
- $P(c \leq x \leq d) = \displaystyle\int_{c}^{d} f(x) \, dx$
- $E(X) = \displaystyle\int_{-\infty}^{\infty} x f(x) \, dx$
- $Var(X) = \displaystyle\int_{-\infty}^{\infty} x^2 f(x) \, dx - [E(X)]^2$
- The mode of X is the value of x for which $f(x)$ is greatest.

2. **A function of a continuous random variable**
   If g[X] is a function of X then
   - $E[g(X)] = \int_{-\infty}^{\infty} g(x) f(x) \, dx$
   - $Var[g(X)] = \int_{-\infty}^{\infty} [g(x)]^2 f(x) \, dx - [E[g(X)]]^2$

3. **A linear combination of continuous random variables**
   - $E(aX \pm bY) = aE(X) \pm bE(Y)$
   - if x and y are independent, $Var(aX \pm bY) = a^2 Var(X) + b^2 E\, Var(Y)$

4. **The cumulative distribution function**
   - $F(x) = \int_a^x f(u) \, du$ where the constant a is the lower limit of X.
   - $f(x) = \dfrac{d}{dx} F(x)$
   - For the median, m, $F(m) = 0.5$
   - For the pth percentile p, $F(p) = \dfrac{p}{100}$

5. **The uniform (rectangular) distribution over the interval (a, b)**
   - $f(x) = \dfrac{1}{b-a}$
   - $E(x) = \dfrac{1}{2}(a+b)$
   - $Var(X) = \dfrac{(b-a)^2}{12}$

6. **The exponential distribution**
   - $f(x) = \lambda e^{-\lambda x}$ for $x \geq 0$
   - $E(X) = \dfrac{1}{\lambda}$
   - $Var(X) = \dfrac{1}{\lambda^2}$

LEARNING OUTCOMES

When you have completed this chapter, you should:
- be able to use a simple continuous random variable as a model
- know and be able to use the results for the expectation and variance of a linear combination of independent continuous random variables
- understand the meaning of a p.d.f. and be able to use one to find probabilities
- know and use the properties of a p.d.f.
- be able to sketch the graph of a p.d.f.
- be able to find the mean and variance from a given p.d.f.
- understand the meaning of a c.d.f. and be able to obtain one from a given p.d.f.
- be able to sketch a c.d.f.
- be able to obtain a p.d.f. from a given c.d.f.
- use a c.d.f. to calculate the median and other percentiles.

9 Expectation algebra and the Normal distribution

To approach zero defects, you must have statistical control of processes.

David Wilson

Florence is an Airedale terrier. People say that she is exceptionally heavy for a female. She weighs 26 kg.

It is true that the majority of female Airedale terriers do weigh quite a lot less than this, but how rare is it for a female to weigh this much? To answer that question you need to know the distribution of weights of female Airedale terriers. Of course, the distribution is continuous, so if you knew the probability density function for this distribution, you could work out the probability of a weight which is at least 26 kg.

> **Note**
>
> As you saw in Chapter 8 for a continuous random variable such as this, the probability that a dog's weight is exactly 26 kg is zero. Instead, you need to specify a range of values, in this case at least 26 kg.

> **Note**
>
> The mean μ and standard deviation σ (or variance σ^2), are the two parameters used to define the distribution. Once you know their values, you know everything there is to know about the distribution.

Like many other naturally occurring variables, the weights of female Airedale terriers may be modelled by a Normal distribution, shown in Figure 9.1. You will see that this has a distinctive bell-shaped curve and is symmetrical about its middle. The curve is continuous as weight is a continuous variable.

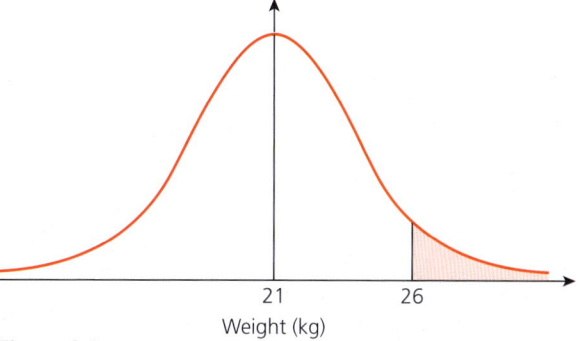

Figure 9.1

> In this case, the lower limit is 26 kg and the upper limit is infinite. Of course, you cannot enter infinity into your calculator, so instead you have to enter a very large positive number for the upper limit.

Before you can start to find this area, you must know the mean and standard deviation of the distribution, in this case, roughly 21 kg and 2.5 kg, respectively.

You can find the probability of a weight which is at least 26 kg directly from your calculator. You need to enter the mean, standard deviation and lower and upper limits.

This probability is 0.02275, so roughly 2.3% of female Airedale terriers will weigh at least 26 kg.

> **Note**
>
> Note that this is a model so the probability that you have calculated is unlikely to be exactly correct.
>
> - The distribution of the weights is unlikely to be exactly Normal.
> - The mean and standard deviation are not exactly 21 kg and 2.5 kg, respectively.

Notation

- The mean of a population is denoted by μ.
- The standard deviation is denoted by σ and the variance by σ^2.
- The curve for the Normal distribution with mean μ and standard deviation σ (i.e. variance σ^2) is given by the function $\phi(x)$, where

$$\phi(x) = \frac{1}{\sigma\sqrt{2\pi}} e^{-\frac{1}{2}\left(\frac{x-\mu}{\sigma}\right)^2}$$

- The notation $X \sim N(\mu, \sigma^2)$ is used to describe this distribution.
- The number of standard deviations the value of a variable x is beyond the mean, μ, is denoted by the letter z.
- So $z = \frac{x - \mu}{\sigma}$. This is called standardised form.
- So the equation for the standardised Normal distribution, $Z \sim N(0,1)$ is

$$\phi(z) = \frac{1}{\sqrt{2\pi}} e^{-\frac{z^2}{2}}$$

- The function $\Phi(z)$ gives the area under the Normal distribution curve to the left of the value z, that is, the shaded area in Figure 9.2. It is the cumulative distribution function. The total area under the curve is 1, and the area given by $\Phi(z)$ represents the probability of a value smaller than z.

> **Note**
>
> Be careful using the notation $X \sim N(\mu, \sigma^2)$. The notation uses the variance not the standard deviation. So you need to take the square root the second value to find the standard deviation.

USING ICT

In the past, values of $\Phi(z)$ were found from tables but advances in technology have made these tables no longer necessary.

Expectation algebra and the Normal distribution

> **Note**
>
> In the example on page 222, Florence's weight is 26 kg. The mean is 21 kg and the standard deviation is 2.5 kg.
> So $x = 26$, $\mu = 21$ and $\sigma = 2.5$,
> and $z = \dfrac{26 - 21}{2.5} = 2$.
> Florence's weight is 5 kg above the mean, and that is $\dfrac{5}{2.5} = 2$ standard deviations above the mean.

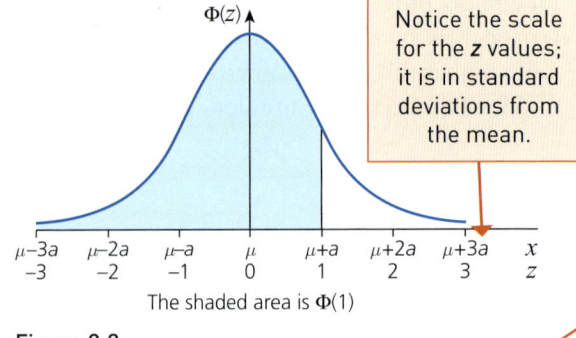

Figure 9.2 (The shaded area is $\Phi(1)$)

Notice the scale for the z values; it is in standard deviations from the mean.

Notice how lower case letters, x and z, are used to indicate particular values of the random variables, whereas upper case letters, X and Z, are used to describe or name those variables.

- So $P(Z < z) = \Phi(z) = \dfrac{1}{\sqrt{2\pi}} \displaystyle\int_{-\infty}^{z} e^{-\frac{1}{2}u^2} \, du$.

- Unfortunately, the integration cannot be carried out algebraically and so there is no neat expression for $\Phi(z)$. Instead, the integration can be performed numerically and, as you have seen, you can find the values directly from a calculator, both for the standardised Normal distribution and for $N(\mu, \sigma^2)$.

- The area to the right of z is $1 - \Phi(z)$.

> **Note**
>
> In the example of Florence, the Airedale terrier, you calculated
> $P(Z > 2) = 1 - P(Z < 2)$.
> $P(Z < 2) = \Phi(2)$ so the probability which you calculated is $1 - \Phi(2)$.

Example 9.1

The volume of cola in a can is modelled by a Normal distribution with mean 332 ml and standard deviation 4 ml.

(i) Find the probability that a can contains
    (a) at least 330 ml
    (b) less than 340 ml
    (c) between 325 ml and 335 ml.

(ii) 95% of cans contain at least a ml of cola. Find the value of a.

> **A word of caution**
>
> The symbols for phi Φ, ϕ (or φ) look very alike and are easily confused.
>
> - Φ is used for the cumulative distribution and is the symbol you will often use.
> - ϕ and φ are used for the equation of the actual curve; you won't actually need to use them in this book.
>
> These symbols are the Greek letter phi. Φ is upper case and ϕ is lower case.

> **USING ICT**
>
> In these calculations, 1000 is just a typically large number and 0 a typically small number.

Solution

(i) You need to enter the mean and standard deviation into your calculator and then the lower and upper limits.

    (a) Lower limit 300, upper limit e.g. 1000
        P(at least 330 ml) = 0.6914

    (b) Lower limit e.g. 0, upper limit 340
        P(less than 340 ml) = 0.9772

    (c) Lower limit 325, upper limit 335
        P(between 325 ml and 335 ml) = 0.7333

(ii) You can use your calculator to work out the value of a. You know that 95% of cans contain at least a ml. Therefore 5% of cans contain less than a ml. You need to use the inverse Normal function (often

The inverse Normal function on your calculator gives $P(X \leq x)$ for $X \sim N(\mu, \sigma^2)$.

labelled invNormal on a calculator). You enter the mean and standard deviation and then the maximum probability, which in this case is 5% or 0.05.

Using your calculator gives $a = 325.42$.

You can, instead, use the table of percentage points of the Normal distribution.

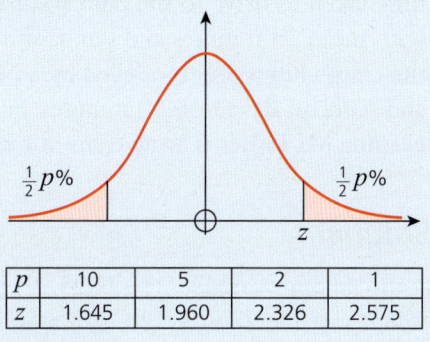

p	10	5	2	1
z	1.645	1.960	2.326	2.575

Figure 9.3

You know that 5% of cans contain less than $a$ml. The left-hand tail which is labelled $\frac{1}{2}p\%$ is therefore 5%. Thus $p = 10\%$. The z-value for is 1.645. However, you need the lower tail and so the z-value which you need is actually -1.645.

The standardised value $z = \dfrac{x - \mu}{\sigma}$

$$\Rightarrow -1.645 = \frac{x - 332}{4}$$

$$\Rightarrow x = 332 + 4 \times (-1.645) = 325.42$$

1 The sums and differences of Normal variables

In Chapter 2, you were given general results for discrete random variables. These results are also true for continuous random variables, as you saw in Chapter 8. Here are these results.

For any two random variables X_1 and X_2

- $E(X_1 + X_2) = E(X_1) + E(X_2)$
- $E(X_1 - X_2) = E(X_1) - E(X_2)$

If the variables X_1 and X_2 are independent then

- $Var(X_1 + X_2) = Var(X_1) + Var(X_2)$
- $Var(X_1 - X_2) = Var(X_1) + Var(X_2)$

If the variables X_1 and X_2 are Normally distributed, then the distributions of $(X_1 + X_2)$ and $(X_1 - X_2)$ are also Normal. The means of these distributions are $E(X_1) + E(X_2)$ and $E(X_1) - E(X_2)$.

The sums and differences of Normal variables

You must, however, be careful when you come to their variances, since you may only use the result that $\text{Var}(X_1 \pm X_2) = \text{Var}(X_1) + \text{Var}(X_2)$ to find the variances of these distributions if the variables X_1 and X_2 are independent.

This is the situation in the next two examples.

Example 9.2

Robert Fisher, a keen chess player, visits his local club most days. The total time taken to drive to the club and back is modelled by a Normal variable with mean 25 minutes and standard deviation 3 minutes. The time spent at the chess club is also modelled by a Normal variable with mean 120 minutes and standard deviation 10 minutes. Find the probability that on a certain evening Mr Fisher is away from home for more than 2½ hours.

Solution

$E(X_1 + X_2) = E(X_1) + E(X_2)$
$= 25 + 120 = 145$
$\text{Var}(X_1 + X_2) = \text{Var}(X_1) + \text{Var}(X_2) = 3^2 + 10^2 = 109$, so the standard deviation of $(X_1 + X_2) = \sqrt{109}$. It is NOT $3 + 10$.

Let the random variable $X_1 \sim N(25, 3^2)$ represent the driving time, and the random variable $X_2 \sim N(120, 10^2)$ represent the time spent at the chess club.

Then the random variable T, where $T = X_1 + X_2 \sim N\left(145, \left(\sqrt{109}\right)^2\right)$, represents his total time away.

You can use your calculator to find the probability that Mr Fisher is away for more than 2½ hours (150 minutes).

Alternatively it is given by

$$P(T > 150) = 1 - \Phi\left(\frac{150 - 145}{\sqrt{109}}\right)$$
$$= 1 - \Phi(0.479)$$
$$= 0.316$$

required area

145 150 $X_1 + X_2$
Standard deviation = $\sqrt{109}$

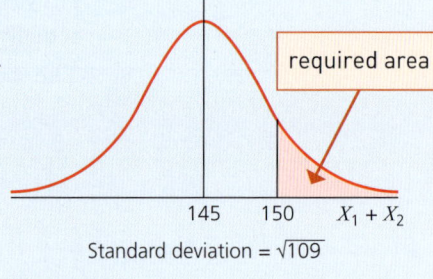

Figure 9.4

Note

You need to assume that X_1 and X_2 are independent. In other words, the time to drive to and from the chess club does not affect the time spent at the club. This assumption seems very reasonable.

Example 9.3

In the manufacture of a bridge made entirely from wood, circular pegs have to fit into circular holes. The diameters of the pegs are Normally distributed with mean 1.60 cm and standard deviation 0.01 cm, while the diameters of the holes are Normally distributed with mean 1.65 cm and standard deviation of 0.02 cm. What is the probability that a randomly chosen peg will not fit into a randomly chosen hole?

Solution

Let the random variable X be the diameter of a hole:

$X \sim N(1.65, 0.02^2) = N(1.65, 0.0004)$.

Let the random variable Y be the diameter of a peg:

$Y \sim N(1.60, 0.01^2) = N(1.6, 0.0001)$.

Let $F = X - Y$. F represents the gap remaining between the peg and the hole and so the sign of F determines whether or not a peg will fit in a hole.

$E(F) = E(X) - E(Y) = 1.65 - 1.60 = 0.05$

$Var(F) = Var(X) + Var(Y) = 0.0004 + 0.0001 = 0.0005$

$F \sim N(0.05, 0.0005)$

If, for any combination of peg and hole, the value of F is negative, then the peg will not fit into the hole.

You can use your calculator to find the probability that the peg will not fit into the hole, $P(F < 0)$.

The probability that $F < 0$ is given by

$$\Phi\left(\frac{0 - 0.05}{\sqrt{0.0005}}\right) = \Phi(-2.326)$$

$= 1 - 0.9873$

$= 0.0127$.

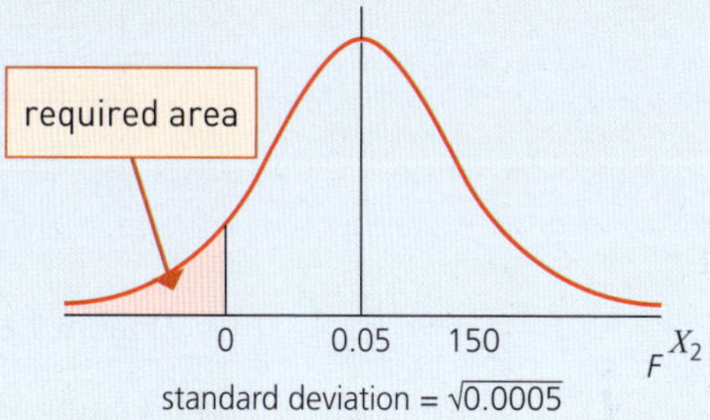

> Note that $Var(X_1 - X_2) = Var(X_1) + Var(X_2)$ and not as you might at first imagine $Var(X_1) - Var(X_2)$.

Figure 9.5

2 Modelling discrete situations

Although the Normal distribution applies strictly to a continuous variable, it is also common to use it in situations where the variable is discrete providing that:

- the distribution is approximately Normal; this requires that the steps in its possible values are small compared with its standard deviation
- *continuity corrections* are applied where appropriate.

The meaning of the term continuity correction is explained in the following example.

Example 9.4

The heights X cm of adult males living in a particular country are known to be Normally distributed with mean 174 and standard deviation 10. What proportion of adult males in this country would you expect to have heights between 176 and 180 cm inclusive (measured to the nearest cm)?

Solution

Although the random variable X is continuous, you are asked for heights measured to the nearest cm. In effect, this is a discrete variable which can be called Y. If you draw the probability distribution function for the discrete variable Y it looks like Figure 9.6. The area you require is the total of the five bars representing 176, 177, 178, 179 and 180.

Modelling discrete situations

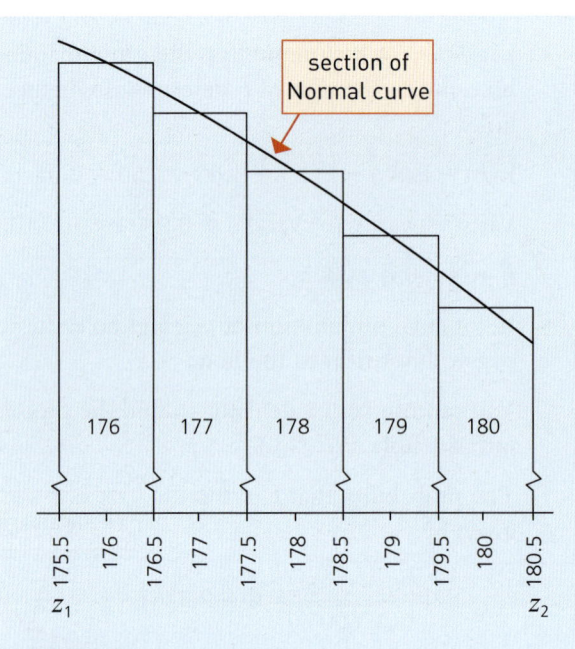

Figure 9.6

The equivalent section of the Normal curve would run not from 176 to 180 but from 175.5 to 180.5, as you can see in Figure 9.6. When you change from the discrete scale to the continuous scale, the numbers 176, 177, etc. no longer represent the whole intervals, just their centre points.

So the area you require under the Normal curve is given by $\Phi(z_2) - \Phi(z_1)$

where $z_1 = \dfrac{175.5 - 174}{10}$ and $z_2 = \dfrac{180.5 - 174}{10}$

Using a calculator this probability is 0.1825.

Answer: The proportion of adult males with heights between 176 and 180 cm (inclusive) should be approximately 18%.

In this calculation, both end values needed to be adjusted to allow for the fact that a continuous distribution was being used to approximate a discrete one. These adjustments, 176 → 175.5 and 180 → 180.5, are called continuity corrections. Whenever a discrete distribution is approximated by a continuous one, a continuity correction may need to be used.

You must always think carefully when applying a continuity correction. Should the corrections be added or subtracted? In this case, 176 and 180 are inside the required area and so any value (like 175.7 or 180.4) which would round to them must be included. It is often helpful to draw a sketch to illustrate the region you want, like the one in Figure 9.6.

If the region of interest is given in terms of inequalities, you should look carefully to see whether they are inclusive ($\leq$ or $\geq$) or exclusive ($<$ or $>$). For example, $40 \leq X \leq 50$ becomes $39.5 \leq X < 50.5$ whereas $40 < X < 50$ becomes $40.5 \leq X < 49.5$.

Exercise 9.1

① X is a random variable with distribution N(20, 25). Find
   (i) $P(X < 25)$ (ii) $P(X > 28)$ (iii) $P(12 \leq X \leq 24)$.

② The weights in grams of a variety of apple can be modelled as Normally distributed with mean 124 and standard deviation 15. Find the probability that the weight of a randomly selected apple will be
   (i) less than 100 g, (ii) at least 120 g, (iii) between 110 and 140 grams.

③ The menu at a cafe is shown below.

Table 9.1

Main course		Dessert	
Fish and chips	£3	Ice cream	£1
Bacon and eggs	£3.50	Apple pie	£1.50
Pizza	£4	Sponge pudding	£2
Steak and chips	£5.50		

The owner of the cafe says that all the main-course dishes sell equally well, as do all the desserts, and that customers' choice of dessert is not influenced by the main course they have just eaten.

The variable M denotes the cost of the items for the main course, in pounds, and the variable D the cost of the items for the dessert. The variable T denotes the total cost of a two-course meal: $T = M + D$.

   (i) Find the mean and variance of M.
   (ii) Find the mean and variance of D.
   (iii) List all the possible two-course meals, giving the price for each one.
   (iv) Use your answer to part (iii) to find the mean and variance of T.
   (v) Hence verify that for these figures
      mean (T) = mean (M) + mean (D)
      and
      variance (T) = variance (M) + variance (D).

④ X_1 and X_2 are independent random variables with distributions N(50, 16) and N(40, 9), respectively. Write down the distributions of
   (i) $X_1 + X_2$ (ii) $X_1 - X_2$ (iii) $X_2 - X_1$.

⑤ A play is enjoying a long run at a theatre. It is found that the performance time may be modelled as a Normal variable with mean 130 minutes and standard deviation 3 minutes, and that the length of the intermission in the middle of the performance may be modelled by a Normal variable with mean 15 minutes and standard deviation 5 minutes. Find the probability that the performance is completed in less than 140 minutes.

Modelling discrete situations

6 The time Melanie spends on her history assignments may be modelled as being Normally distributed, with mean 40 minutes and standard deviation 10 minutes. The times taken on assignments may be assumed to be independent. Find

  (i) the probability that a particular assignment takes longer than an hour
  (ii) the time in which 95% of all assignments can be completed
  (iii) the probability that two assignments will be completed in less than 75 minutes.

7 The weights of full cans of a particular brand of pet food may be taken to be Normally distributed, with mean 260 g and standard deviation 10 g. The weights of the empty cans may be taken to be Normally distributed, with mean 30 g and standard deviation 2 g. Find

  (i) the mean and standard deviation of the weights of the contents of the cans
  (ii) the probability that a full can weighs more than 270 g
  (iii) the probability that two full cans together weigh more than 540 g.

8 In a vending machine, the capacity of cups is Normally distributed, with mean 200 cm^3 and standard deviation 4 cm^3. The volume of coffee discharged per cup is Normally distributed, with mean 190 cm^3 and standard deviation 5 cm^3. Find the percentage of drinks which overflow.

9 On a distant island the heights of adult men and women may both be taken to be Normally distributed, with means 173 cm and 165 cm and standard deviations 10 cm and 8 cm, respectively.

  (i) Find the probability that a randomly chosen woman is taller than a randomly chosen man.
  (ii) Do you think that this is equivalent to the probability that a married woman is taller than her husband?

10 The lifetimes of a certain brand of refrigerator are approximately Normally distributed, with mean 2000 days and standard deviation 250 days.

Mrs Chudasama and Mr Poole each buy one on the same date.

What is the probability that Mr Poole's refrigerator is still working one year after Mrs Chudasama's refrigerator has broken down?

11 A random sample of size 2 is chosen from a Normal distribution N(100, 10).

Find the probability that

  (i) the sum of the sample numbers exceeds 225
  (ii) the first observation is at least 12 more than the second observation.

12 An examination has a mean mark of 80 and a standard deviation of 12. The marks are assumed to be Normally distributed.

  (i) Find the probability that a randomly selected candidate scores a mark between 75 and 85 inclusive (note that you will need to include a continuity correction in your calculation).
  (ii) The bottom 5% of candidates are to be given extra help. Find the maximum mark required for extra help to be given.
  (iii) Three candidates are selected at random. Find the probability that at least one of them is given extra help (you should assume that the examination is taken by a very large group of candidates).

⑬ In a reading test for eight-year-old children, it is found that a reading score X is Normally distributed with mean 5.0 and standard deviation 2.0.

(i) What proportion of children would you expect to score between 4.5 and 6.0?

(ii) There are about 700 000 eight-year-olds in the country. How many would you expect to have a reading score of more than twice the mean?

(iii) Why might educationalists refer to the reading score X as a *score out of 10*?

The reading score is often reported, after scaling, as a value Y which is Normally distributed, with mean 100 and standard deviation 15. Values of Y are usually given to the nearest integer.

(iv) Find the probability that a randomly chosen eight-year-old gets a score, after scaling, of 103.

(v) What range of Y scores would you expect to be attained by the best 20% of readers? [MEI]

⑭ Scores on an IQ test are modelled by the Normal distribution with mean 100 and standard deviation 15. The scores are reported to the nearest integer.

(i) Find the probability that a person chosen at random scores

   (a) exactly 105   (b) more than 110.

(ii) Only people with IQs in the top 2.5% are admitted to the organisation *BRAIN*. What is the minimum score for admission?

(iii) Find the probability that, in a random sample of 20 people, exactly 6 score more than 110.

(iv) Find the probability that, in a random sample of 200 people, at least 60 score more than 110.

3 More than two independent random variables

The results in Section 9.1 may be generalised to give the mean and variance of the sums and differences of n random variables, $X_1, X_2, \ldots, X_n$.

$$E(X_1 \pm X_2 \pm \cdots \pm X_n) = E(X_1) \pm E(X_2) \pm \cdots \pm E(X_n)$$

and, provided $X_1, X_2, \ldots, X_n$ are independent,

$$\text{Var}(X_1 \pm X_2 \pm \cdots \pm X_n) = \text{Var}(X_1) + \text{Var}(X_2) + \cdots + \text{Var}(X_n).$$

If $X_1, X_2, \ldots, X_n$ is a set of Normally distributed variables, then the distribution of $(X_1 \pm X_2 \pm \cdots \pm X_n)$ is also Normal.

More than two independent random variables

Example 9.5

The mass, X, of a suitcase at an airport is modelled as being Normally distributed, with mean 15 kg and standard deviation 3 kg. Find the probability that a random sample of ten suitcases weighs more than 154 kg.

Solution

The mass X of one suitcase is given by $X \sim N(15, 9)$.

Then the mass of each of the ten suitcases has the distribution of X; call them $X_1, X_2, \ldots, X_{10}$.

Let the random variable T be the total weight of ten suitcases.

$$T = X_1 + X_2 + \cdots + X_{10}.$$
$$E(T) = E(X_1) + E(X_2) + \cdots + E(X_{10})$$
$$= 15 + 15 + \cdots + 15$$
$$= 150$$

Similarly

$$\text{Var}(T) = \text{Var}(X_1) + \text{Var}(X_2) + \cdots + \text{Var}(X_{10})$$
$$= 9 + 9 + \cdots + 9$$
$$= 90$$

So $T \sim N(150, 90)$

The probability that T exceeds 154 is given by

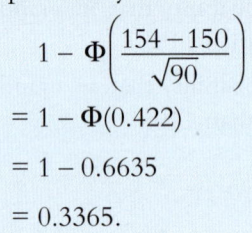

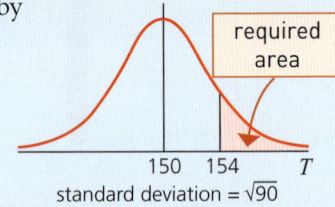

$$1 - \Phi\left(\frac{154 - 150}{\sqrt{90}}\right)$$
$$= 1 - \Phi(0.422)$$
$$= 1 - 0.6635$$
$$= 0.3365.$$

Figure 9.7

Example 9.6

The running times of the four members of a 4×400 m relay race may all be taken to be Normally distributed, as follows.

Table 9.2

Member	Mean time (s)	Standard deviation (s)
Adil	52	1
Brian	53	1
Colin	55	1.5
Dexter	51	0.5

Assuming that no time is lost during changeovers, find the probability that the team finishes the race in less than 3 minutes 28 seconds.

Solution

Let the total time be T.

$$E(T) = 52 + 53 + 55 + 51 = 211$$
$$\text{Var}(T) = 1^2 + 1^2 + 1.5^2 + 0.5^2$$
$$= 1 + 1 + 2.25 + 0.25 = 4.5$$

So $T \sim N(211, 4.5)$.

The probability of a total time of less than 3 minutes 28 seconds (208 seconds) is given by

$$\Phi\left(\frac{208-211}{\sqrt{4.5}}\right) = \Phi(-1.414)$$
$$= 1 - 0.9213$$
$$= 0.0787$$

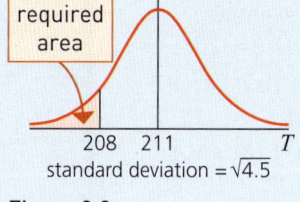

Figure 9.8

Linear combinations of two or more independent random variables

The results given in Section 9.1 can also be generalised to include linear combinations of random variables.

For any random variables X and Y,

- $E(aX + bY) = aE(X) + bE(Y)$, where a and b are constants.

If X and Y are independent

- $\text{Var}(aX + bY) = a^2\text{Var}(X) + b^2\text{Var}(Y)$.

If the distributions of X and Y are Normal, then the distribution of $(aX + bY)$ is also Normal.

These results may be extended to any number of random variables.

Example 9.7

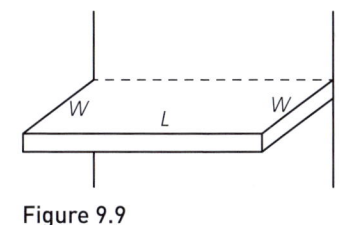

In a workshop, joiners cut out rectangular sheets of laminated board, of length L cm and width W cm, to be made into work surfaces. Both L and W may be taken to be Normally distributed with standard deviation 1.5 cm. The mean of L is 150 cm, that of W is 60 cm, and the lengths of L and W are independent. Both of the short sides and one of the long sides have to be covered by a protective strip (the other long side is to lie against a wall and so does not need protection).

What is the probability that a protecting strip 275 cm long will be too short for a randomly selected work surface?

Figure 9.9

More than two independent random variables

> **Note**
>
> You have to distinguish carefully between the random variable $2W$, which means twice the size of one observation of the random variable W, and the random variable $W_1 + W_2$, which is the sum of two independent observations of the random variable W.
> In the last example $E(2W) = 2E(W) = 120$ and $Var(2W) = 2^2 Var(W) = 4 \times 2.25 = 9$.
> In contrast, $E(W_1 + W_2) = E(W_1) + E(W_2) = 60 + 60 = 120$ and $Var(W_1 + W_2) = Var(W_1) + Var(W_2) = 2.25 + 2.25 = 4.5$

Solution

Denoting the length and width by the independent random variables L and W and the total length of strip required by T:

$$T = L + 2W$$

$$E(T) = E(L) + 2E(W)$$
$$= 150 + 2 \times 60$$
$$= 270$$

$$Var(T) = Var(L) + 2^2 Var(W)$$
$$= 1.5^2 + 4 \times 1.5^2$$
$$= 11.25$$

The probability of a strip 275 cm long being too short is given by

$$1 - \Phi\left(\frac{275 - 270}{\sqrt{11.25}}\right) = 1 - \Phi(1.491)$$
$$= 1 - 0.932$$
$$= 0.068$$

Example 9.8

A machine produces sheets of paper the thicknesses of which are Normally distributed with mean 0.1 mm and standard deviation 0.006 mm.

(i) State the distribution of the total thickness of eight randomly selected sheets of paper.

(ii) Single sheets of paper are folded three times (to give eight thicknesses). State the distribution of the total thickness.

Solution

Denote the thickness of one sheet (in mm) by the random variable W, and the total thickness of eight sheets by T.

(i) *Eight separate sheets*

In this situation $T = W_1 + W_2 + W_3 + W_4 + W_5 + W_6 + W_7 + W_8$

where $W_1, W_2, \ldots, W_8$ are eight independent observations of the variable W. The distribution of W is Normal with mean 0.1 and variance 0.006^2.

So the distribution of T is Normal with

mean $= 0.1 + 0.1 + \cdots + 0.1 = 8 \times 0.1 = 0.8$

variance $= 0.006^2 + 0.006^2 + \cdots + 0.006^2 = 8 \times 0.006^2$
$= 0.000\,288$

standard deviation = $\sqrt{0.000288} = 0.017$.

The distribution is $N(0.8, 0.017^2)$.

(ii) *Eight thicknesses of the same sheet*

In this situation $T = W_1 + W_2 + W_3 + W_4 + W_5 + W_6 + W_7 + W_8 = 8W_1$ where W_1 is a single observation of the variable W.

So the distribution of T is Normal with

mean $= 8 \times E(W) = 0.8$

variance $= 8^2 \times \text{Var}(W) = 8^2 \times 0.006^2 = 0.002304$

standard deviation $= \sqrt{0.002304} = 0.048$.

The distribution is $N(0.8, 0.048^2)$.

! Notice that, in both cases, the mean thickness is the same but for the folded paper the variance is greater. Why is this?

Exercise 9.2

① The random variable Y is Normally distributed with mean μ and variance σ^2.

Write down the distribution of

(i) $5Y$ (ii) the sum of five independent observations of Y.

② The distributions of two independent random variables X and Y are $N(10, 5)$ and $N(20, 10)$, respectively.

Find the distributions of

(i) $X + Y$ (ii) $10X$ (iii) $3X + 4Y$.

③ A random sample of 15 items is chosen from a Normal population with mean, 30 and variance, 9. Find the probability that the sum of the variables in the sample is less than 440.

④ A company manufactures floor tiles of mean length 20 cm with standard deviation 0.2 cm. Assuming that the distribution of the lengths of the tiles is Normal, find the probability that, when 12 randomly selected floor tiles are laid in a row, their total length exceeds 241 cm.

⑤ The masses of Christmas cakes produced at a bakery are independent and may be modelled as being Normally distributed with mean 4 kg and standard deviation 100 g. Find the probability that a set of eight Christmas cakes has a total mass between 32.3 kg and 32.7 kg.

⑥ The distributions of four independent random variables X_1, X_2, X_3 and X_4 are $N(7, 9)$, $N(8, 16)$, $N(9, 4)$ and $N(10, 1)$, respectively.

Find the distributions of

(i) $X_1 + X_2 + X_3 + X_4$ (ii) $X_1 + X_2 - X_3 - X_4$ (iii) $X_1 + X_2 + X_3$.

⑦ The distributions of X and Y are $N(100, 25)$ and $N(110, 36)$, and X and Y are independent. Find

(i) the probability that $8X + 2Y < 1000$

(ii) the probability that $8X - 2Y > 600$.

⑧ The distributions of the independent random variables A, B and C are $N(35, 9)$, $N(30, 8)$ and $N(35, 9)$. Write down the distributions of

(i) $A + B + C$ (ii) $5A + 4B$ (iii) $A + 2B + 3C$ (iv) $4A - B - 5C$.

More than two independent random variables

⑨ The distributions of the independent random variables X and Y are $N(60, 4)$ and $N(90, 9)$. Find the probability that

   (i) $X - Y < -35$ (ii) $3X + 5Y > 638$ (iii) $3X > 2Y$.

⑩ Given that $X \sim N(60, 4)$ and $Y \sim N(90, 9)$ and that X and Y are independent, find the probability that

   (i) when one item is sampled from each population, the one from the Y population is more than 35 greater than the one from the X population

   (ii) the sum of a sample consisting of three items from population X and five items from population Y exceeds 638

   (iii) the sum of a sample of three items from population X exceeds that of two items from population Y.

⑪ Given that $X_1 \sim N(600, 400)$ and $X_2 \sim N(1000, 900)$ and that X_1 and X_2 are independent, write down the distributions of

   (i) $4X_1 + 5X_2$

   (ii) $7X_1 - 3X_2$

   (iii) $aX_1 + bX_2$, where a and b are constants.

⑫ The quantity of fuel used by a coach on a return trip of 200 km is modelled as a Normal variable with mean 45 litres and standard deviation 1.5 litres.

   (i) Find the probability that in nine return journeys the coach uses between 400 and 406 litres of fuel.

   (ii) Find the volume of fuel which is 95% certain to be sufficient to cover the total fuel requirements for two return journeys.

⑬ Assume that the weights of men and women may be taken to be Normally distributed, men with mean 75 kg and standard deviation 4 kg, and women with mean 65 kg and standard deviation 3 kg.

At a village fair, tug-of-war teams consisting of either five men or six women are chosen at random. The competition is then run on a knock-out basis, with teams drawn out of a hat. If in the first round a women's team is drawn against a men's team, what is the probability that the women's team is the heavier?

State any assumptions you have made and explain how they can be justified.

⑭ A petrol company issues a voucher with every 12 l of petrol that a customer buys. Customers who send 50 vouchers to Head Office are entitled to a 'free gift'. After this promotion has been running for some time, the company receives several hundred bundles of vouchers in each day's post. It would take a long time, and so be costly, for somebody to count each bundle and so they weigh them instead. The weight of a single voucher is a Normal variable with mean 40 mg and standard deviation 5 mg.

   (i) What is the distribution of the weights of bundles of 50 vouchers?

   (ii) Find the weight W mg which is exceeded by 95% of bundles.

   The company decides to count only the number of vouchers in those bundles which weigh less than W mg. A man has only 48 vouchers but decides to send them in, claiming that there are 50.

   (iii) What is the probability that the man is detected?

15. Jim Longlegs is an athlete whose specialist event is the triple jump. This is made up of a *hop*, a *step* and a *jump*. Over a season, the lengths of the *hop*, *step* and *jump* sections, denoted by H, S and J, respectively, are measured, from which the following models are proposed:

    $H \sim N(5.5, 0.5^2)$, $S \sim N(5.1, 0.6^2)$, $J \sim N(6.2, 0.8^2)$

    where all distances are in metres. Assume that H, S and J are independent.

    (i) In what proportion of his triple jumps will Jim's total distance exceed 18 metres?

    (ii) In six successive independent attempts, what is the probability that at least one total distance will exceed 18 m?

    (iii) What total distance will Jim exceed 95% of the time?

    (iv) Find the probability that, in Jim's next triple jump, his step will be greater than his hop. [MEI]

16. A country baker makes biscuits whose masses are Normally distributed with mean 30 g and standard deviation 2.3 g. She packs them by hand into either a small carton (containing 20 biscuits) or a large carton (containing 30 biscuits).

    (i) State the distribution of the total mass, S, of biscuits in a small carton and find the probability that S is greater than 615 g.

    (ii) Six small and four large cartons are placed in a box. Find the probability that the total mass of biscuits in the ten cartons lies between 7150 g and 7250 g.

    (iii) Find the probability that three small cartons contain at least 25 g more than two large ones.

    The label on a large carton of biscuits reads 'Net mass 900 g'. A trading standards officer insists that 90% of such cartons should contain biscuits with a total mass of at least 900 g.

    (iv) Assuming the standard deviation remains unchanged, find the least value of the mean mass of a biscuit consistent with this requirement. [MEI]

17. The weights of pamphlets are Normally distributed with mean 40 g and standard deviation 2 g. What is the distribution of the total weight of

    (i) a random sample of two pamphlets?

    (ii) a random sample of n pamphlets?

    Pamphlets are stacked in piles nominally containing 25. To save time, the following method of counting is used. A pile of pamphlets is weighed and is accepted (i.e. assumed to contain 25 pamphlets) if its weight lies between 980 g and 1020 g. Assuming that each pile is a random sample, determine, to three decimal places, the probabilities that

    (iii) a pile actually containing 24 pamphlets will be accepted

    (iv) a pile actually containing 25 pamphlets will be rejected.

    Justify the choice of the limits as 980 g and 1020 g. [MEI]

18. Bricks of a certain type are meant to be 65 mm in height, but, in fact, their heights are Normally distributed with mean 64.4 mm and standard deviation 1.4 mm. A warehouse keeps a large stock of these bricks, stored on shelves. The bricks are stacked one on top of another. The heights of the bricks may be regarded as statistically independent.

The distribution of the sample mean

(i) Find the probability that an individual brick has height greater than 65 mm.

(ii) Find the probability that the height of a stack of six bricks is greater than 390 mm.

(iii) Find the vertical gap required between shelves to ensure that, with probability 0.99, there is room for a stack of six bricks.

(iv) The vertical gap between shelves is Normally distributed with a mean of 400 mm and standard deviation 7 mm. Find the probability that such a gap has room for a stack of six bricks.

(v) A workman buys ten bricks which can be considered to be a random sample from all the bricks in the warehouse. Find the probability that the average height of these bricks is between 64.8 mm and 65.2 mm. [MEI]

4 The distribution of the sample mean

In many practical situations you do not know the true value of the mean of a variable that you are investigating, that is, the parent population mean (usually just called the *population mean*). Indeed, that may be one of the things you are trying to establish.

In such cases, you will usually take a random sample, $x_1, x_2, \ldots, x_n$, of size n from the population and work out the sample mean $\bar{x}$, given by

$$\bar{x} = \frac{x_1 + x_2 + \cdots + x_n}{n}$$

to use as an estimate for the true population mean μ.

How accurate is this estimate likely to be and how does its reliability vary with n, the sample size?

Each of the sample values $x_1, x_2, \ldots, x_n$ can be thought of as a value of an independent random variable $X_1, X_2, \ldots, X_n$. The variables $X_1, X_2, \ldots, X_n$ have the same distribution as the population and so $E(X_1) = \mu$, $\text{Var}(X_1) = \sigma^2$, etc.

So the sample mean is a value of the random variable $\bar{X}$ given by

$$\bar{X} = \frac{1}{n}(X_1 + X_2 + \cdots + X_n)$$

$$= \frac{1}{n}X_1 + \frac{1}{n}X_2 + \cdots + \frac{1}{n}X_n$$

and so

$$E(\bar{X}) = \frac{1}{n}E(X_1) + \frac{1}{n}E(X_2) + \cdots + \frac{1}{n}E(X_n)$$

$$= \frac{1}{n}\mu + \frac{1}{n}\mu + \cdots + \frac{1}{n}\mu$$

> **Note**
>
> The derivation has required no assumptions about the distribution of the parent population, other than that μ and σ are finite. If, in fact, the parent distribution is Normal, then the sampling distribution will also be Normal, whatever the size of n.
>
> If the parent population is not Normal, the sampling distribution will still be approximately Normal, and will be more accurately so for larger values of n.
>
> This result is called the central limit theorem and will be developed after Example 9.9.
>
> The derivation does require that the sample items are independent (otherwise the result for Var(X) would not have been valid).

$$= n\left(\frac{1}{n}\mu\right)$$

$$= \mu, \text{ the population mean.}$$

Further, using the fact that $X_1, X_2, \ldots, X_n$ are independent,

$$\text{Var}(\bar{X}) = \text{Var}\left(\frac{X_1}{n}\right) + \text{Var}\left(\frac{X_2}{n}\right) + \cdots + \text{Var}\left(\frac{X_n}{n}\right)$$

$$= \frac{1}{n^2}\text{Var}(X_1) + \frac{1}{n^2}\text{Var}(X_2) + \cdots + \frac{1}{n^2}\text{Var}(X_n)$$

$$= \frac{1}{n^2}\sigma^2 + \frac{1}{n^2}\sigma^2 + \cdots + \frac{1}{n^2}\sigma^2$$

$$= n\left(\frac{1}{n^2}\sigma^2\right)$$

$$= \frac{\sigma^2}{n}$$

Thus the distribution of the means of samples of size n, drawn from a parent population with mean μ and variance σ^2, has mean μ and variance $\frac{\sigma^2}{n}$. The distribution of the sample means is called the *sampling distribution of the means*, or often just the *sampling distribution*.

Notice that $\text{Var}(\bar{X}) = \frac{\sigma^2}{n}$ means that as n increases the variance of the sample mean decreases. In other words, the value obtained for $\bar{X}$ from a large sample is more reliable as an estimate for μ than one obtained from a smaller sample. This result, simple though it is, lies at the heart of statistics: it says that you are likely to get more accurate results if you take a larger sample.

The standard deviation of sample means of size n is $\frac{\sigma}{\sqrt{n}}$ and this is called the *standard error of the mean*, or often just the *standard error*. It gives a measure of the degree of accuracy of $\bar{X}$ as an estimate for μ.

Example 9.9

The discrete random variable X has a probability distribution as shown.

Table 9.3

X	1	2	3
Probability	0.5	0.4	0.1

A random sample of size 2 is chosen, with replacement after each selection.

(i) Find μ and σ^2.

(ii) Verify that $\text{E}(\bar{X}) = \mu$ and $\text{Var}(\bar{X}) = \frac{\sigma^2}{2}$

The central limit theorem

Solution

(i) $\mu = E(X) = 1 \times 0.5 + 2 \times 0.4 + 3 \times 0.1$

$= 1.6$

$E(X^2) = 1^2 \times 0.5 + 2^2 \times 0.4 + 3^2 \times 0.1$

$= 3$

$\sigma^2 = \text{Var}(X) = E(X^2) - [E(X)]^2$

$= 3 - 1.6^2 = 0.44$

(ii) The table below lists all the possible samples of size 2, their means and probabilities.

Table 9.4

Sample	1,1	1,2	1,3	2,1	2,2	2,3	3,1	3,2	3,3
Mean	1	1.5	2	1.5	2	2.5	2	2.5	3
Probability	0.25	0.2	0.05	0.2	0.16	0.04	0.05	0.04	0.01

This gives the following probability distribution of the sample mean.

For example P(1, 2) = 0.5 × 0.4 = 0.2

Table 9.5

X	1	1.5	2	2.5	3
Probability	0.25	0.4	0.26	0.08	0.01

Using this table gives

$E(\overline{X}) = 1 \times 0.25 + 1.5 \times 0.4 + 2 \times 0.26 + 2.5 \times 0.08 + 3 \times 0.01$

$= 1.6 = \mu$, as required.

$E(\overline{X}^2) = 1^2 \times 0.25 + 1.5^2 \times 0.4 + 2^2 \times 0.26 + 2.5^2 \times 0.08 + 3^2 \times 0.01$

$= 2.78$

$\text{Var}(\overline{X}) = E(\overline{X}^2) - [E(\overline{X})]^2$

$= 2.78 - (1.6)^2$

$= 0.22$

$= \dfrac{0.44}{2} = \dfrac{\sigma^2}{2}$ as required.

5 The central limit theorem

This theorem is fundamental to much of statistics and so it is worth pausing to make sure you understand just what it is saying.

It deals with the distribution of the sample mean. This is called the *sampling distribution of the mean*. There are three aspects to it.

1. The expected value of the sample mean is μ, the population mean of the original distribution. That is not a particularly surprising result but it is extremely important.

For samples of size n drawn from a distribution with mean μ and finite variance σ^2, the distribution of the sample mean is approximately $N\left(\mu, \dfrac{\sigma^2}{n}\right)$ for sufficiently large n.

2 The standard deviation of the sample mean is $\dfrac{\sigma}{\sqrt{n}}$. This is often called the *standard error of the mean*. Within a sample, you would expect some values above the population mean, others below it, so that overall the deviations would tend to cancel each other out, and the larger the sample the more this would be the case. Consequently, the standard deviation of the sample means is smaller than that of individual items, by a factor of $\sqrt{n}$.

3 The distribution of the sample mean is approximately Normal.
This last point is the most surprising part of the theorem. Even if the underlying parent distribution is not Normal, the distribution of the mean of samples of a particular size drawn from it is approximately Normal. The larger the sample size, n, the closer this distribution is to the Normal. For any given value of n, the sampling distribution will be closest to Normal when the parent distribution is not unlike the Normal.

In many cases, the value of n does not need to be particularly large. For most parent distributions, you can rely on the distribution of the sample mean being Normal if n is about 20 or 25 (or more).

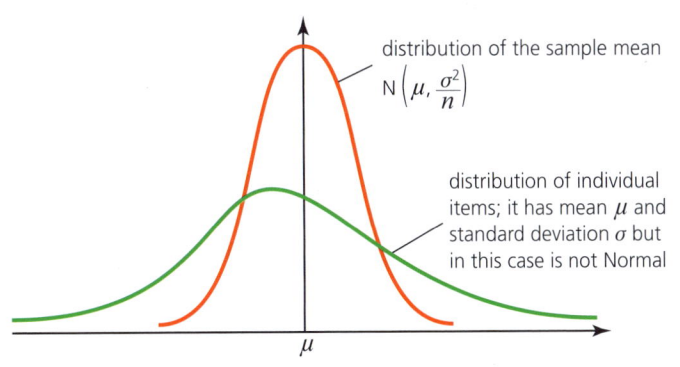

Figure 9.10

Example 9.10

It is known that the mean length of a species of fish is 40.5 cm with standard deviation 3.2.

(i) A random sample of five fish is taken. Explain why you cannot find the probability that the mean of this sample is at least 40.

(ii) A random sample of 50 fish is taken. Calculate an estimate of the probability that the mean of this sample is at least 40.

(iii) If the lengths of individual fish could only be measured to the nearest 1 cm, make a new estimate of the probability calculated in part (ii).

Solution

(i) Because you are told nothing about the distribution of the parent population (the distribution of the length of this species of fish), you cannot carry out any probability calculations.

The central limit theorem

(ii) Although you do not know the distribution of the parent population, the sample size of 50 is large enough to apply the central limit theorem. This states that for a large sample, the distribution of the sample mean is approximately Normal. The distribution is therefore $N(40.5, \frac{3.2^2}{50})$. Using a calculator P(sample mean > 40) = 0.8654.

(iii) If the lengths are only measured to the nearest 1 cm, then the sample mean can only take values ... 39.96, 39.98, 40.00, 40.02, 40.04 ... You therefore need to calculate P(sample mean > 39.99) rather than P(sample mean > 40). Using a calculator P(sample mean > 39.99) = 0.8701.

Distribution of the sample means is $N\left(\mu, \frac{\sigma^2}{n}\right)$ and you are given that $\mu = 40.5$ and $\sigma = 3.2$

For example, if all except one of the fish were 40 cm long and the last was 41 cm long the sample mean would be 40.02. If instead the last was 39 cm long the sample mean would be 39.98.

> **Note**
> This is an example of a continuity correction which you met earlier in the chapter. As you can see, it requires some careful thought to work out the value needed, particularly when it involves a sample mean.

Exercise 9.3

① The random variable X is Normally distributed with mean 30 and variance 4. Write down the distribution of a random sample of
   (i)   2
   (ii) 10
   (iii) 100
   observations of X.

② The random variable X is has mean 200 and standard deviation of 30. Write down if possible the approximate distribution of a random sample of
   (i)   10
   (ii) 30
   (iii) 100
   observations of X.
   If you cannot write down the distribution, explain why you cannot.

③ At a men's hairdresser, haircuts take an average of 18 minutes with standard deviation 3 minutes. Find the distribution of the total time taken for 30 haircuts at the hairdresser. State any assumption which you make.

④ A random sample of 40 items is chosen from a population with mean 60 and variance 25. Find the probability that the mean of the sample is less than 59.

⑤ A company manufactures paving slabs of mean length 45.5 cm with standard deviation 0.5 cm. Find the probability that the mean length of a random sample of 100 slabs is at least 45.4 cm.

⑥ A certain type of low energy light bulb is claimed to have a lifetime of 8000 hours, with standard deviation 600 hours. A random sample of 25 bulbs is selected. Assuming that the claim is true:
   (i)   write down the standard error of the sample mean
   (ii) find the probability that the sample mean is greater than 7900 hours.
   (iii) The mean is measured and found to be 7450 hours. Comment on this result.

⑦ In a certain city, the heights of women have mean 164 cm and standard deviation 8.5 cm.
   (i)   Find the probability that the mean height of a random sample of 50 women will be within 1 cm of the mean.

(ii) Find the sample size required so that the probability that a random sample of this size will be within 0.5 cm of the mean is the same as your answer to part (i).

⑧ A random sample of n items is chosen from a population with mean 200 and standard deviation 15. You are given that n is large. The probability that the sample mean is greater than 201 is 0.2755 to 4 significant figures. Find the value of n.

⑨ Wooden sleepers for use in landscape gardening are available in two lengths 1.2 m and 1.8 m. The smaller ones actually have mean length 1.23 m with standard deviation 0.05 m. The larger ones have mean length 1.84 m with standard deviation 0.10 m. Find the probability that:

(i) 30 of the smaller sleepers have mean length less than 1.22 m

(ii) 40 of the longer sleepers have mean length more than 1.85 m.

(iii) The mean length of 45 smaller sleepers is greater than two thirds of the mean length of 30 longer sleepers.

⑩ Scores in an IQ test are modelled by a Normal distribution with mean 100 and standard deviation 15. The scores are reported to the nearest integer. The test is taken by a large number of children. Find the probability that

(i) the score of an individual child is greater than 110

(ii) the mean score of random sample of ten children is greater than 110.

⑪ The mean weight of the contents of a jar of jam produced in a factory is 353 g with standard deviation 8 g. The weights of the contents are recorded to the nearest gram. A random sample of 25 jars is selected.

(i) Write down the standard error of the mean.

(ii) Find the probability that the sample mean is

(a) at least 353

(b) less than 350

(c) between 352 and 354 inclusive.

Note that a continuity correction is required for part (ii).

KEY POINTS

1. The Normal distribution with mean μ and standard deviation σ is denoted by $N(\mu, \sigma^2)$.
2. This may be given in standardised form by using the transformation
$$z = \frac{x - \mu}{\sigma}$$
3. In the standardised form, $N(0, 1)$, the mean is 0, the standard deviation and variance both 1.
4. The standardised Normal curve is given by
$$\phi(z) = \frac{1}{\sqrt{2\pi}} e^{-\frac{1}{2}z^2}.$$

The central limit theorem

5 Probabilities may be found directly from a calculator by entering the mean, standard deviation and lower and upper limits. Alternatively, the area to the left of the value z in the diagram below, representing the probability of a value less than z, is denoted by Φ(z) and can be found using tables.

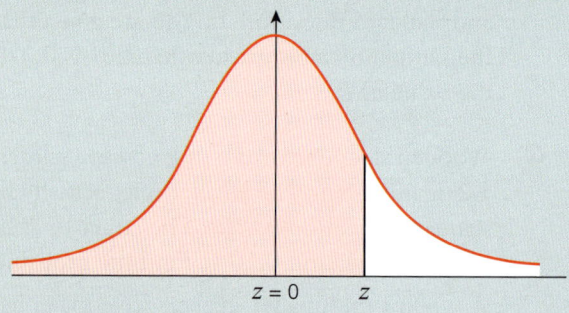

Figure 9.11

6 The Normal distribution may be used to approximate suitable discrete variables but continuity corrections are then required.

7 For two random variables X and Y, whether independent or not, and constants a and b,

- $E(X \pm Y) = E(X) \pm E(Y)$
- $E(aX + bY) = aE(X) + bE(Y)$

and, if X and Y are independent,

- $\text{Var}(X \pm Y) = \text{Var}(X) + \text{Var}(Y)$
- $\text{Var}(aX + bY) = a^2 \text{Var}(X) + b^2 \text{Var}(Y)$.

8 For a set of n random variables $X_1, X_2, ..., X_n$

- $E(X_1 \pm X_2 \pm \cdots \pm X_n) = E(X_1) \pm E(X_2) \pm \cdots \pm E(X_n)$

and, if the variables are independent,

- $\text{Var}(X_1 \pm X_2 \pm \cdots \pm X_n) = \text{Var}(X_1) + \text{Var}(X_2) + \cdots + \text{Var}(X_n)$.

9 If random variables are Normally distributed, then so are the sums, differences and other linear combinations of them.

10 For samples of size n drawn from an infinite (or large) population with mean μ and variance σ^2, or for sampling with replacement

- $E(\bar{X}) = \mu$
- $\text{Var}(\bar{X}) = \dfrac{\sigma^2}{n}$
- The standard deviation of the sample mean is $\dfrac{\sigma}{\sqrt{n}}$ called the standard error of the mean or just the standard error.

11 For samples of size n drawn from a distribution with mean μ and variance σ^2, the distribution of the sample mean is approximately $N(\mu, \dfrac{\sigma^2}{n})$ for sufficiently large n.

LEARNING OUTCOMES

When you have completed this chapter you should:

- be able to use the Normal distribution as a model, and to calculate and use probabilities from a Normal distribution
- be able to use linear combinations of independent Normal random variables in solving problems
- be able to find the mean of any linear combination of random variables and the variance of any linear combination of independent random variables
- understand that the sample mean is a random variable with a probability distribution
- be able to calculate and interpret the standard error of the mean
- know that if the underlying distribution is Normal, then the sample mean is Normally distributed
- understand how and when the central limit theorem may be applied to the distribution of sample means and use this result in probability calculations, using a continuity correction where appropriate
- be able to apply the central limit theorem to the sum of identically distributed independent random variables.

10 Confidence intervals

> When we spend money on testing an item, we are buying confidence in its performance.
>
> Tony Cutler

The perfect apple grower

From our farming correspondent Tom Smith

Fruit grower, Angie Fallon, believes that, after years of trials, she has developed trees that will produce the perfect supermarket apple. 'There are two requirements', Angie told me, 'The average weight of an apple should be 100 grams and they should all be nearly the same size. I have measured hundreds of mine and the standard deviation is a mere 5 grams.'

Angie invited me to take any ten apples off the shelf and weigh them for myself. It was quite uncanny; they were all so close to the magic 100 g: 98, 107, 105, 98, 100, 99, 104, 93, …, 105, 103.

> **Discussion point**
> What can you conclude from the weights of the reporter's sample of ten apples?

Before going any further, it is appropriate to question whether the reporter's sample was random. Angie invited him to 'take any ten apples off the shelf'. That is not necessarily the same as taking any ten off the tree. The apples on the shelf could all have been specially selected to impress the reporter. So what follows is based on the assumption that Angie has been honest and the ten apples really do constitute a random sample.

The sample mean is

$$\bar{x} = \frac{98 + 107 + 105 + 98 + 100 + 99 + 104 + 93 + 105 + 103}{10} = 101.2$$

> **Discussion point**
> What does that tell you about the population mean, μ?

To answer this question, you need to know something about the distribution of the sample mean and also about the spread of the data. The usual measure of spread is the standard deviation, σ; in the article you are told that $\sigma = 5$.

You would estimate the population mean to be the same as the sample mean, namely 101.2.

You can express this by saying that you estimate μ to lie within a range of values, an interval, centred on 101.2:

101.2 − a bit < μ < 101.2 + a bit.

Such an interval is called a *confidence interval*.

Imagine that you take a large number of samples and use a formula to work out the interval for each of them. Sometimes the true population mean will be in your confidence interval and sometimes it will not be. If you catch the true population mean in 90% of your intervals, the confidence interval is called a 90% confidence interval. Other percentages are also used and the confidence intervals are named accordingly.

The width of the interval is clearly twice the 'bit'.

Finding a confidence interval involves a fairly simple calculation but the reasoning behind it is somewhat subtle and requires clear thinking. It is explained in the next section.

> **Note**
> Commonly used confidence intervals are 90%, 95% and 99%.

1 The theory of confidence intervals

> **Note**
> A word of advice: read through this section twice, lightly first time and then more thoroughly when you have tried a few questions. That will help you to gain a good understanding of the meaning of confidence intervals.

To understand confidence intervals you need to look not at the particular sample whose mean you have just found, but at the parent population from which it was drawn. For the data on Angie Fallon's apples this does not look very promising. All you know about it is its standard deviation σ (in this case, 5). You do not know its mean, μ, which you are trying to estimate, or even its shape.

It is now that the strength of the central limit theorem becomes apparent. This states that the distribution of the means of samples of size n drawn from any population is approximately Normal with mean, μ, and standard deviation $\frac{\sigma}{\sqrt{n}}$ for large values on n.

The theory of confidence intervals

In Figure 10.1, the central 90% region has *been shaded leaving the two 5% tails,* corresponding to z-values of ±1.645, unshaded. So if you take a large number of samples, all of size n, and work out the sample mean $\overline{X}$ for each one, you would expect that in 90% of cases the value of $\overline{X}$ would lie in the shaded region between A and B.

> **USING ICT**
>
> The value 1.645 is the 95% point of the cumulative Normal distribution, $\Phi(z)$. You can find this from your calculator or from a table of percentage points of the Normal distribution.

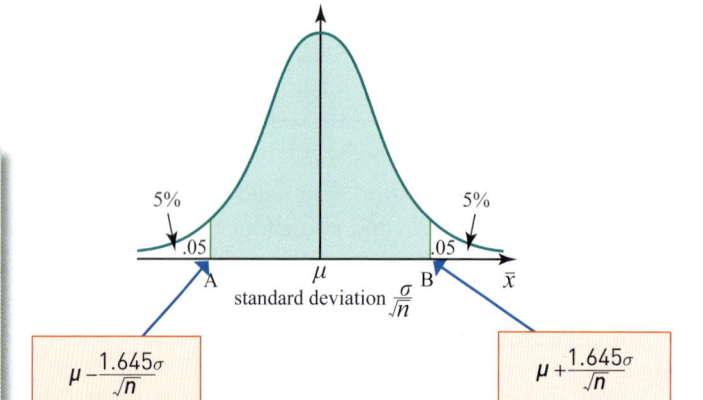

Figure 10.1

For such a value of $\overline{X}$ to be in the shaded region.

- it must be to the right of A: $\quad \overline{x} > \mu - 1.645 \dfrac{\sigma}{\sqrt{n}}$

- it must be to the left of B: $\quad \overline{x} < \mu + 1.645 \dfrac{\sigma}{\sqrt{n}}$

Putting these two inequalities together gives the result that, in 90% of cases,

$$\overline{x} - 1.645 \dfrac{\sigma}{\sqrt{n}} < \mu < \overline{x} + 1.645 \dfrac{\sigma}{\sqrt{n}}$$

and this is the 90% confidence interval for μ.

The numbers corresponding to the points A and B are called the 90% *confidence limits* and 90% is the *confidence level*. If you want a different confidence level, you use a different z value from 1.645.

This number is often denoted by k; commonly used values are:

Table 10.1

> **USING ICT**
>
> You can find all of these values of k from your calculator or from a table of percentage points of the Normal distribution.

Confidence level	k
90%	1.645
95%	1.96
99%	2.58

and the confidence interval is given by

$$\overline{x} - k\dfrac{\sigma}{\sqrt{n}} \text{ to } \overline{x} + k\dfrac{\sigma}{\sqrt{n}}.$$

The *P*% confidence interval for the mean is an interval constructed from sample data in such a way that *P*% of such intervals will include the true population mean. Figure 10.2 shows a number of confidence intervals constructed from different samples, one of which fails to catch the population mean.

> **Note**
> Notice that this is a two-sided symmetrical confidence interval for the mean, μ. Confidence intervals do not need to be symmetrical and can be one-sided. The term confidence interval is a general one, applying not just to the mean but to other population parameters, like variance and skewness, as well. All those cases, however, are outside the scope of this book.

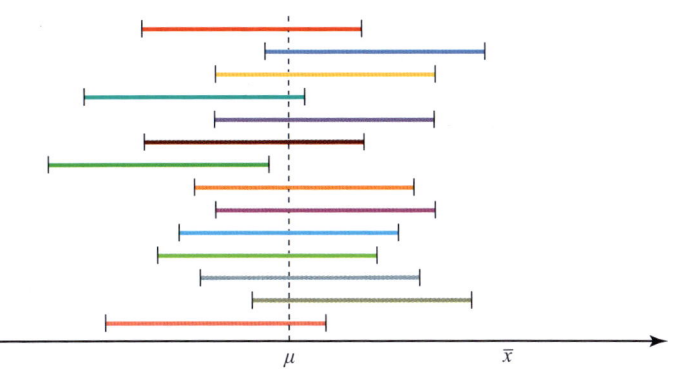

Figure 10.2

In the case of the data on the Angie Fallon's apples,

$\bar{x} = 101.2$, $\sigma = 5$, $n = 10$

and so the 90% confidence interval is

$$101.2 - 1.645 \times \frac{5}{\sqrt{10}} \text{ to } 101.2 + 1.645 \times \frac{5}{\sqrt{10}}$$

98.6 to 103.8.

Since this interval includes 100, this suggests that Angie's claim that the mean weight of her apples is 100 grams may be correct.

> **Note**
> Note that this confidence interval assumes that the sample mean is Normally distributed. This seems at first to be a rather risky assumption. However, even though you do not know the distribution of the parent population (the weight of an individual apple), you can use the central limit theorem. The value of n is rather small but, assuming that the parent population distribution is not too skewed, your confidence interval should give a good estimate of the true confidence interval

USING ICT

Statistical software

You can use statistical software to find a confidence interval.

In order for the software to find the interval, you need to input the values of the sample mean, the variance, the value of n and the confidence level. Here is a typical output using the data on Angie Fallon's apples.

Table 10.2

Z Estimate of a Mean	
Confidence Level	0.90

	Sample
Mean	101.2
σ	5
n	10

	Result
Mean	101.2
σ	5
SE	1.5811
N	10
Lower Limit	98.6
Upper Limit	103.8
Interval	101.2 ± 2.60

> **USING ICT**
> The software gives the interval as 101.2 ± 2.60 as well as giving the lower and upper limit.

The theory of confidence intervals

Known and estimated standard deviation

Notice that you can only use this procedure if you already know the value of the standard deviation of the parent population, σ. In this example, Angie Fallon said that she knew from hundreds of measurements of her apples, that its value is 5.

It is more often the situation that you do not know the population standard deviation or variance, and have to estimate it from your sample data. If that is the case, the procedure is different in that you use the t-distribution rather than the Normal distribution, provided that the parent population is Normally distributed, and this results in different values of k. The use of the t-distribution will be developed later in this chapter.

However, if the sample is large, for example over 50, confidence intervals worked out using the Normal distribution will be reasonably accurate even though the standard deviation used is an estimate from the sample. So it is quite acceptable to use the Normal distribution for large samples whether the standard deviation is known or not.

Paired samples

Very often you want to find an estimate of the difference between the means of two populations, as in the following example.

Example 10.1

The senior tutor at a flying school is interested to see if there is a difference between the percentage marks achieved on Paper 1 and Paper 2 of the theory examination. She considers that her 200 students are sufficiently typical for them to be regarded as a random sample of all those taking the examination.

For each student, she calculates the difference, d = Paper 1 mark − Paper 2 mark. She then finds

- the mean of d: $\bar{d} = 5.62$
- the standard deviation of d: $s = 16.45$.

(i) Find a 95% confidence interval for the mean value of d.

(ii) Interpret your answer.

Solution

(i) This is a large enough sample for an assumption that the differences are distributed Normally to be unnecessary for the calculation of a 95% confidence interval for their mean value.

For a 2-sided 95% confidence interval the value of k is 1.96 and so the interval is

$$5.62 - 1.96 \times \frac{16.45}{\sqrt{200}} \text{ to } 5.62 + 1.96 \times \frac{16.45}{\sqrt{200}}$$

3.34 to 7.90.

Note that, as the sample size of 200 is large, it is reasonable to use s as an estimate for σ.

(ii) This whole interval is positive, so she concludes that Paper 1 appears to be easier.

You can see that the process here is exactly the same as for finding a confidence interval for the mean of a population with the extra initial step of finding the differences.

The situation in this example in which the data are paired (there are two marks for each student) is best for comparisons if you can obtain a suitable sample.

Such a sample is called a *paired sample* or a *matched sample*. In practice, however, it is often impossible to obtain paired data. Instead, you have to resort to taking a random sample from each population with no link between members of each sample. This is called a *two-sample* experiment; the design is described as unpaired. It involves slightly more complicated procedures which are beyond the scope of this book.

EXPERIMENT 10.1

This experiment is designed to help you understand confidence intervals, rather than to teach you anything new about dice.

Imagine that you have a large number of dice. When each of them is thrown, the possible outcomes, 1, 2, 3, 4, 5, 6, are all equally likely with probability $\frac{1}{6}$. Consequently, the expectation or mean score from throwing one of the dice is

$$\mu = 1 \times \frac{1}{6} + 2 \times \frac{1}{6} + \cdots + 6 \times \frac{1}{6} = 3.5.$$

Similarly, the standard deviation is

$$\sigma = \sqrt{\left(1^2 \times \frac{1}{6} + 2^2 \times \frac{1}{6} + \cdots + 6^2 \times \frac{1}{6}\right) - 3.5^2} = 1.708.$$

Imagine that you know σ but don't know μ and wish to construct a 90% confidence interval for it.

Converging confidence intervals

Imagine that you throw one of the dice just once. Suppose you get a 5. You have a sample of size 1, namely {5}, which you could use to work out a sort of 90% confidence interval (but see the warning below).

This confidence interval is given by

$$5 - 1.645 \times \frac{1.708}{\sqrt{1}} \text{ to } 5 + 1.645 \times \frac{1.708}{\sqrt{1}}$$

2.19 to 7.81.

> So far the procedure is not valid. The sample is small and the underlying distribution is not Normal. However, things will get better. The more dice you throw, the larger the sample size and so the more justifiable the procedure. This is because you can make use of the central limit theorem which tells you that for reasonable large samples, the sample mean will be approximately Normally distributed.

Now imagine that you throw two dice. Suppose that this time you get a 5 and a 3. You now have a sample of size 2, namely {5, 3}, with mean 4, and can work out another confidence interval.

The confidence interval is given by

$$4 - 1.645 \times \frac{1.708}{\sqrt{2}} \text{ to } 4 + 1.645 \times \frac{1.708}{\sqrt{2}}$$

2.79 to 5.21.

> Again the procedure is not valid. The sample is still far too small and the underlying distribution is not Normal. You need a much larger sample.

Instead of actually throwing more and more dice, you can use a spreadsheet to simulate throwing any number of dice. You will study simulation in more detail in Chapter 12.

The theory of confidence intervals

USING ICT

A spreadsheet

You can use a spreadsheet to simulate throwing as many dice as you choose. You can then work out a 90% confidence interval for the population mean. Figure 10.3 illustrates a simulation using 25 dice.

In order to find the find the confidence interval, take the following steps.

1. Enter the formula provided by your spreadsheet, for example = RANDBETWEEN(1,6) in cell A1 to simulate throwing one of the dice.
2. Copy this formula into cells A2 to A25 to simulate throwing the remaining 24 dice.
3. Enter the formula provided by your spreadsheet, for example = AVERAGE(A1:A25) in cell A26 to find the sample mean.

The confidence interval will then be

$$\bar{x} - 1.645 \times \frac{1.708}{\sqrt{25}} \text{ to } \bar{x} + 1.645 \times \frac{1.708}{\sqrt{25}}$$

This can be simplified to

$$\bar{x} - 0.562 \text{ to } \bar{x} + 0.562$$

4. Enter the formula = A26 − 0.562 into cell A27 to find the lower confidence limit.
5. Enter the formula = A26 + 0.562 into cell A28 to find the upper confidence limit.

Catching the population mean

If you now copy the whole of column A into columns B to CV inclusive, you will have 100 simulated values of the sample mean. You know that the real value of μ is 3.5 and it should be that this is caught within 9 out of 10 of 90% confidence intervals. Therefore you should find that approximately 90 of your intervals catch the true value of 3.5.

> **Note**
> Of course you would not expect <u>exactly</u> 90 of your intervals catch the true value of 3.5.

	A	B	C	D	E	F	G	H	I
1		3	2	4	3	5	1	6	3
2		1	5	6	3	3	6	4	2
3		3	6	4	5	4	4	4	4
4		5	6	4	1	3	1	5	6
5		1	1	4	5	6	6	3	6
6		2	4	2	3	2	4	3	2
7		3	5	5	4	4	5	4	6
8		4	6	2	3	3	4	2	1
9		4	3	6	2	2	5	3	1
10		3	6	5	5	3	4	2	2
11		1	2	6	6	4	1	6	4
12		2	3	5	2	3	5	6	3
13		5	1	4	6	5	2	5	1
14		2	2	2	1	4	6	2	3
15		4	4	3	1	1	2	6	4
16		2	4	6	2	2	6	2	4
17		1	3	6	2	5	1	1	1
18		1	6	4	2	2	5	6	5
19		6	1	6	6	4	2	1	5
20		1	2	4	6	3	6	3	5
21		2	3	6	2	4	6	4	1
22		4	6	3	5	1	6	2	6
23		5	3	4	5	4	6	1	1
24		4	1	1	1	2	1	1	5
25		2	6	6	6	2	4	3	2
26	Sample mean	2.84	3.64	4.32	3.48	3.24	3.96	3.4	3.32
27	Lower limit	2.278	3.078	3.758	2.918	2.678	3.398	2.838	2.758
28	Upper limit	3.402	4.202	4.882	4.042	3.802	4.522	3.962	3.882

The lower limit is above 3.5

The upper limit is below 3.5

Figure 10.3

For this particular simulation, you can see that the first confidence limit has not caught the true population mean, nor has the third, but all of the others shown have caught it. You can only see the first eight simulations but there are actually in fact 100 columns, each with a simulated sample mean and corresponding 90% confidence interval. When the author carried out this particular simulation, 88 of the 100 confidence intervals actually contained the true population mean, which is quite close to the 90 which you expect on average. Try it for yourself and see how many of your confidence intervals catch the population mean of 3.5.

How large a sample do you need?

You are now in a position to start to answer the question of how large a sample needs to be. The answer, as you will see in Example 10.2, depends on the precision you require, and the confidence level you are prepared to accept.

Example 10.2

A trading standards officer is investigating complaints that a coal merchant is giving short measure. Each sack should contain 25 kg but some variation will inevitably occur because of the size of the lumps of coal; the officer knows from experience that the standard deviation should be 1.5 kg.

The officer plans to take, secretly, a random sample of n sacks, find the total weight of the coal inside them and thereby estimate the mean weight of the coal per sack. He wants to present this figure correct to the nearest kilogram with 95% confidence. What value of n should he choose?

Note

This example illustrates that a larger sample size leads to a narrower confidence interval. In fact three things affect the width of the confidence interval; sample size, confidence level and population variability. Increasing the sample size results in a decrease in the width of the confidence interval. Increasing the confidence level and/or population variability results in an increase in the width of the confidence interval.

Solution

The 95% confidence interval for the mean is given by

$$\bar{x} - \frac{1.96\sigma}{\sqrt{n}} \text{ to } \bar{x} + \frac{1.96\sigma}{\sqrt{n}}$$

and so, since $\sigma = 1.5$, the inspector's requirement is that

$$\frac{1.96 \times 1.5}{\sqrt{n}} \leq 0.5$$

The officer wants the mean weight to be correct to the nearest kg, so ± 0.5 kg.

$$\Rightarrow \frac{1.96 \times 1.5}{0.5} \leq \sqrt{n}$$

$$\Rightarrow n \geq 34.57$$

So the inspector needs to take 35 sacks.

Large samples

Given that the width of a confidence interval decreases with sample size, why is it not standard practice to take very large samples?

The answer is that the cost and time involved has to be balanced against the quality of information produced. Because the width of a confidence interval depends on $\frac{1}{\sqrt{n}}$ and not on $\frac{1}{n}$, increasing the sample size does not produce a proportional reduction in the width of the interval. You have, for example, to increase the sample size by a factor of 4 to halve the width of the interval. In

The theory of confidence intervals

the previous example the inspector had to weigh 35 sacks of coal to achieve a class interval of 2 × 0.5 = 1 kg with 95% confidence. That is already quite a daunting task; does the benefit from reducing the interval to 0.5 kg justify the time, cost and trouble involved in weighing another 105 sacks?

Exercise 10.1

1. The mean of a random sample of ten observations of a random variable X is 27.2. It is known that X is Normally distributed and that the standard deviation of X is 2.9. Show that a 95% confidence interval for the mean μ of X is 25.40 to 29.00.

2. Weights in grams of eight bags of sugar are as follows.

   1023   1016   1027   1014   1023   1029   1022   1018

   It is known that the weights of such bags of sugar are Normally distributed with standard deviation 5.5 grams.

   (i) Find the sample mean.

   (ii) Write down the standard error.

   (iii) Show that a 90% confidence interval for the mean weights of bags of sugar is 1018.3 to 1024.7.

3. A delivery company has a fleet of 120 lorries. The company manager wishes to switch from conventional diesel fuel to a blend of biodiesel fuel. Before switching, he decides to check whether using biodiesel will affect the fuel consumption of the lorries. He selects 8 lorries and checks their fuel consumption using conventional diesel and then again using biodiesel. The results, measured in litres per 100 km, are as follows.

   Table 10.3

Lorry	A	B	C	D	E	F	G	H
Conventional diesel	36.5	34.4	28.6	25.0	27.8	31.9	33.6	38.7
Biodiesel	38.7	36.0	29.2	25.3	27.8	32.6	33.9	39.3

   The manager knows from previous data that fuel consumption is Normally distributed with standard deviation 4.61 litres per 100 km.

   (i) Assuming that the standard deviation for biodiesel lorries is also 4.61, show the standard deviation of the difference in fuel consumption between lorries using each type of fuel is 6.520 to 3 decimal places.

   (ii) Using the value found in part (i) for the population standard deviation of the differences, calculate 90% confidence limits for the mean difference in fuel consumption.

   (iii) Does the confidence interval that you have calculated suggest that there is any difference between fuel consumption using each type of fuel? [MEI]

4. The management of a large chain of shops has introduced an incentive bonus scheme. A statistician who works for the chain wonders whether the scheme has made any difference to the level of absenteeism among its workforce. In order to investigate this, the statistician measures the percentage of working days lost before and after its introduction for each of a random sample of 60 shops.

For each shop, the difference d = absentee rate before incentive scheme − absentee rate after incentive scheme. She then finds:

- the mean of d: $\bar{d} = 0.436$
- the standard deviation of d: $s = 1.150$

(i) Find a 99% confidence interval for the mean value of d.

(ii) Do you think that the scheme has made any difference to the rate? [MEI]

5. A biologist studying a colony of beetles selects and weighs a random sample of 20 adult males. She knows that, because of natural variability, the weights of such beetles are Normally distributed with standard deviation 0.2 g. Their weights, in grams, are as follows.

5.2 5.4 4.9 5.0 4.8 5.7 5.2 5.2 5.4 5.1
5.6 5.0 5.2 5.1 5.3 5.2 5.1 5.3 5.2 5.2

(i) Find the mean weight of the beetles in this sample.

(ii) Find 95% confidence limits for the mean weight of such beetles.

6. An aptitude test for deep-sea divers has been designed to produce scores which are approximately Normally distributed on a scale from 0 to 100 with standard deviation 25. The scores from a random sample of people taking the test were as follows.

23 35 89 35 12 45 60 78 34 66

(i) Find the mean score of the people in this sample.

(ii) Construct a 90% confidence interval for the mean score of people taking the test.

(iii) Construct a 99% confidence interval for the mean score of people taking the test. Compare this confidence interval with the 90% confidence interval.

7. In a large city the distribution of incomes per family has a standard deviation of £5200.

(i) For a random sample of 400 families, what is the probability that the sample mean income per family is within £500 of the actual mean income per family?

(ii) Given that the sample mean income was, in fact, £8300, calculate a 95% confidence interval for the actual mean income per family. [MEI]

8. A manufacturer of women's clothing wants to know the mean height of the women in a town (in order to plan what proportion of garments should be of each size). She knows that the standard deviation of their heights is 5 cm. She selects a random sample of 50 women from the town and finds their mean height to be 165.2 cm.

(i) Use the available information to estimate the proportion of women in the town who were

(a) over 170 cm tall

(b) less than 155 cm tall.

(ii) Construct a 95% confidence interval for the mean height of women in the town.

(iii) Another manufacturer in the same town wants to know the mean height of women in the town to within 0.5 cm with 95% confidence. What is the minimum sample size that would ensure this?

The theory of confidence intervals

⑨ An examination question, marked out of 10, is answered by a very large number of candidates. A random sample of 400 scripts is taken and the marks on this question are recorded.

Table 10.4

Mark	0	1	2	3	4	5	6	7	8	9	10
Frequency	12	35	11	12	3	20	57	87	20	14	129

(i) Calculate the sample mean and the sample standard deviation.

(ii) Assuming that the population standard deviation has the same value as the sample standard deviation, find 90% confidence limits for the population mean.

⑩ An archaeologist discovers a short manuscript in an ancient language which he recognises but cannot read. There are 30 words in the manuscript and they contain a total of 198 letters. There are two written versions of the language. In the *early* form of the language, the mean word length is 6.2 letters with standard deviation 2.5; in the *late* form, certain words were given prefixes, raising the mean length to 7.6 letters but leaving the standard deviation unaltered. The archaeologist hopes the manuscript will help him to date the site.

(i) Construct a 95% confidence interval for the mean word length of the language.

(ii) What advice would you give the archaeologist?

⑪ The distribution of measurements of thicknesses of a random sample of yarns produced in a textile mill is shown in the following table.

Table 10.5

Yarn thickness in microns (mid-interval value)	Frequency
72.5	6
77.5	18
82.5	32
87.5	57
92.5	102
97.5	51
102.5	25
107.5	9

Illustrate these data on a histogram. Estimate, to 2 decimal places, the mean and standard deviation of yarn thickness.

Hence estimate the standard error of the mean to 2 decimal places, and use it to determine approximate symmetrical 95% confidence limits, giving your answer to 1 decimal place. [MEI]

⑫ In a game of patience, which involves no skill, the player scores between 0 and 52 points. The standard deviation is known to be 8; the mean is unknown but thought to be about 12.

(i) Explain why players' scores cannot be Normally distributed if the mean is indeed about 12.

A casino owner wishes to make this into a gambling event but needs to know the mean score before he can set the odds profitably. He employs a student to play the game 500 times. The student's total score is 6357.

(ii) Find 99% confidence limits for the mean score.

The student recorded all her individual scores and finds, on investigation, that their standard deviation is not 8 but 6.21.

(iii) What effect would accepting this value for the standard deviation have on the 99% confidence interval?

The casino owner wants to know the mean score to the nearest 0.1 with 99% confidence.

(iv) Using the value of 6.21 for the standard deviation, find the smallest sample size that would be needed to achieve this.

⑬ The label on a particular size of milk bottle states that it holds 1.136 l of milk. In an investigation at the bottling plant, the contents, x litres, of 100 such bottles are carefully measured. The data are summarised by

$$\Sigma x = 112.4, \Sigma x^2 = 126.80.$$

(i) Estimate the variance of the underlying population.

(ii) Provide a 90% confidence interval for the mean of the underlying population, stating the assumptions you have made.

(iii) A manager states that 'the probability that the population mean lies in the calculated interval is 90%'. Explain why this interpretation is wrong. Give the correct interpretation of the interval.

(iv) Use the calculated interval to explain whether it appears that the target of 1.136 l in a bottle is being met. [MEI]

⑭ The manager of a supermarket is investigating the queuing situation at the check-outs. At busy periods, customers usually have to queue for some time to reach a check-out and then a further amount of time to be served.

(i) At an initial stage of the investigation, the time Q, in minutes, spent queuing to reach a check-out is modelled by a random variable having mean 5.6 and standard deviation 3.8. Similarly, the time R, in minutes, spent being served is modelled by a random variable having mean 1.8 and standard deviation 1.4. It is assumed that Q and R are independent. The total time for a customer to pass through the system is $Q + R$. Find the mean and standard deviation of $Q + R$.

100 customers, selected at random, are timed passing through the system. Their times, t minutes, are summarised by

$$\Sigma t = 764, \Sigma t^2 = 12\,248.$$

(ii) Estimate the mean and variance of the underlying population and hence comment informally on the adequacy of the model for $Q + R$ in part (i).

(iii) Provide a 90% confidence interval for the mean of the underlying population.

(iv) Explain why the confidence interval calculated in part (iii) is only approximate. Give two reasons why, with sample of size 100, the approximation is good. [MEI]

The theory of confidence intervals

15. In an investigation concerning acid rain, a large number of specimens of rain water were collected at different times over a wide area. These may be considered as a large random sample. They were analysed for acidity and the readings for a standard measure of acidity are summarised by

    number of specimens = 75, $\Sigma x = 282.6$, $\Sigma x^2 = 1096.42$.

    (i) Estimate the mean and variance of the underlying population.

    (ii) Provide a 90% two-sided confidence interval for the population mean acidity of the rain water.

    (iii) Explain carefully the interpretation of the interval in part (ii).

    Now let $X_1, X_2, \ldots, X_n$ represent a random sample from a distribution with mean μ and variance σ^2, where n is large. Let $\bar{X} = \frac{1}{n}\Sigma X_i$ and let $V = \frac{1}{n-1}\Sigma(X_i - \bar{X})^2$

    (iv) State the approximate distribution of $\dfrac{\bar{X} - \mu}{\frac{\sigma}{\sqrt{n}}}$

    (v) Suppose that σ^2 is unknown and is estimated by v, where v is the value of V as calculated from observations on the X_i. Explain whether the approximation in part (iv) is still good when σ is replaced by $\sqrt{v}$. [MEI]

16. A football boot manufacturer did extensive testing on the wear of the front studs of its Supa range. It found that, after 30 hours use, the wear (i.e. the amount by which the length was reduced) was Normally distributed with standard deviation 1.3 mm. However, the mean wear on the studs of the boot on the dominant foot of the player was 4 mm more than on the studs of the other boot.

    (i) Using the manufacturer's figure, find the standard deviation of the differences in wear between a pair of boots after 30 hours use.

    The coach of a football team accepted the claim for the standard deviation but was suspicious of the claim about the mean difference. He chose ten of his squad at random. He fitted them with new boots and measured the wear after 30 hours of use with the following results.

    Table 10.6

Player	1	2	3	4	5	6	7	8	9	10
Dominant foot	6.5	8.3	4.5	6.7	9.2	5.3	7.6	8.1	9.0	8.4
Other foot	4.2	4.6	2.3	3.8	7.0	4.7	1.4	3.8	8.4	5.7

    (ii) Using the value found in part (i) for the population standard deviation of the differences, calculate 95% confidence limits for the mean difference in wear based on the sample data.

    (iii) Use these limits to explain whether or not you consider the coach's suspicions were justified.

17. An education authority decided to introduce a new P.E. programme for all 11-year-old children to try to improve the fitness of the students. In order to see whether the programme was effective, several tests were done. For one of these, the students were timed on a run of 1 km in their first week

in the school and again ten weeks later. A random sample of 100 of the students did both runs. The differences of their mean times, subtracting the time of the second run from that of the first, were calculated. The mean and standard deviation were found to be 0.75 minutes and 1.62 minutes, respectively.

Calculate a 90% confidence interval for the population mean difference. You may assume that the differences are distributed Normally. What assumption have you made in finding this confidence interval?

The organiser of the programme considers that it should lead to an improvement of at least half a minute in the average times. Explain whether or not this aim has been achieved.

2 Interpreting sample data using the *t*-distribution

Students find new bat

Two students and a lecturer have found their way into the textbooks. On a recent field trip they discovered a small colony of a previously unknown bat living in a cave.

'Somewhere in Britain' is all that Shakila Mahadavan, 20, would say about its location. 'We don't want the general public disturbing the bats or worse still catching them for specimens,' she explained.

The other two members of the group, lecturer Alison Evans and 21-year-old Iain Scott, showed scores of photographs of the bats as well as pages of measurements that they had gently made on the few they had caught before releasing them back into their cave.

At a mystery location, students have pushed forward the frontiers of science

The measurements referred to in the article include the weights (in g) of eight bats which were identified as adult males.

156   132   160   142   145   138   151   144

From these figures, the team want to estimate the mean weight of an adult male bat, and 95% confidence limits for their figure.

It is clear from the newspaper report that these are the only measurements available. All that is known about the parent population is what can be inferred from these eight measurements. You know neither the mean nor the standard deviation of the parent population, but you can estimate both.

Interpreting sample data using the *t*-distribution

The mean is estimated to be the same as the sample mean:

$$\frac{156+132+160+142+145+138+151+144}{8} = 146.$$

When it comes to estimating the standard deviation, start by finding the sample variance

$$s^2 = \frac{S_{xx}}{n-1} = \sum_i \frac{(x_i - \bar{x})^2}{(n-1)}$$

and then take the square root to find the standard deviation, *s*.

The use of ($n-1$) as divisor illustrates the important concept of degrees of freedom.

The deviations of the eight numbers are as follows.

$156 - 146 = 10$

$132 - 146 = -14$

$160 - 146 = 14$

$142 - 146 = -4$

$145 - 146 = -1$

$138 - 146 = -8$

$151 - 146 = -5$

$144 - 146 = -2$

> **Note**
> The deviation is the difference (+ or −) of the value from the mean. In this example the mean is 146.

> **Note**
> You need to know the degrees of freedom in many situations where you are calculating confidence intervals or conducting hypothesis tests. You may recall meeting the idea in earlier chapters.

These eight deviations are not independent: they must add up to zero because of the way the mean is calculated. This means that when you have worked out the first seven deviations, it is inevitable that the final one has the value it does (in this case −2). Only seven values of the deviation are independent, and, in general, only ($n-1$) out of the *n* deviations from the sample mean are independent.

Consequently, there are $n-1$ **free variables** in this situation. The number of free variables within a system is called the **degrees of freedom** and denoted by ν.

> **Note**
> A particular value of the sample variance is denoted by s^2, the associated random variable by S^2.

So the sample variance is worked out using divisor ($n-1$). The resulting value is very useful because it is an **unbiased estimate of the parent population variance**

In the case of the bats, the estimated population variance is

$$s^2 = \frac{(100 + 196 + 196 + 16 + 1 + 64 + 25 + 4)}{7} = 86$$

> The numbers on the top line, 100, 196 and so on, are the squares of the deviations.

and the corresponding value of the standard deviation is $s = \sqrt{86} = 9.27$.

Calculating the confidence intervals

Returning to the problem of estimating the mean weight of the bats, you now know that:

$$\bar{x} = 146, \quad s^2 = 86, \quad s = 9.27 \quad \text{and} \quad \nu = 8 - 1 = 7.$$

Before starting on further calculations, there are some important and related points to notice.

1. This is a small sample. It would have been much better if they had managed to catch and weigh more than eight bats.
2. The true parent standard deviation, σ, is unknown and, consequently, the standard deviation of the sampling distribution given by the central limit theorem, $\frac{\sigma}{\sqrt{n}}$, is also unknown.
3. In situations where the sample is small and the parent standard deviation or variance is unknown, there is little more that can be done unless you can assume that the parent population is Normal. (In this case that is a reasonable assumption, the bats being a naturally occurring population.) If you can assume Normality, then you may use the t-distribution, estimating the value of σ from your sample.
4. It is possible to test whether a set of data could reasonably have been taken from a Normal distribution by using Normal probability graph paper. The method involves making a cumulative frequency table and plotting points on a graph with specially chosen axes. If the graph obtained is approximately a straight line, then the data could plausibly have been drawn from a Normal population. Otherwise a Normal population is unlikely. Alternatively, you can use a spreadsheet to produce a Normal probability plot as you will see later in this chapter.

The t-distribution looks very like the Normal distribution, and, indeed, for large values of ν is little different from it. The larger the value of ν, the closer the t-distribution is to the Normal. Figure 10.4 shows the Normal distribution and t-distributions $\nu = 2$ and $\nu = 10$.

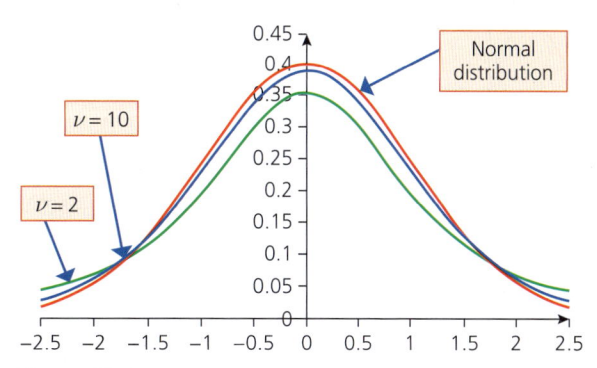

Figure 10.4

Interpreting sample data using the *t*-distribution

> **Historical note**
>
> William S. Gosset was born in Canterbury in 1876. After studying both mathematics and chemistry at Oxford, he joined the Guinness breweries in Dublin as a scientist. He found that an immense amount of statistical data was available, relating the brewing methods and the quality of the ingredients, particularly barley and hops, to the finished product. Much of this data took the form of samples, and Gosset developed techniques to handle them, including the discovery of the *t*-distribution. Gosset published his work under the pseudonym 'Student' and so the *t* test is often called Student's *t* test.
>
> Gosset's name has frequently been misspelt as Gossett (with a double t), giving rise to puns about the *t*-distribution.

Confidence intervals using the *t*-distribution are constructed in much the same way as those using the Normal, with the confidence limits given by:

$$\bar{x} \pm k \frac{s}{\sqrt{n}}$$

where the values of k are found from a spread sheet or from tables. For instance, to find the value of K at the 5% significance level with 7 degrees of freedom, you can use the formula provided by your spread sheet, for example $= \text{T.INV.2T}(0.05, 7)$.

2T means that we are using the two-tailed t-distribution

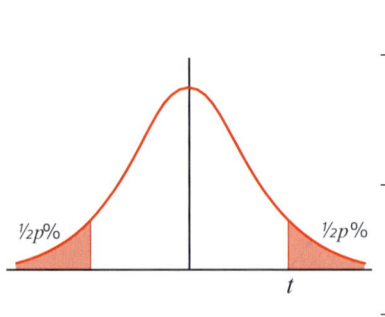

$p\%$	10	5	2	1
$v = 1$	6.314	12.71	31.82	63.66
2	2.920	4.303	6.965	9.925
3	2.353	3.182	4.541	5.841
4	2.132	2.776	3.747	4.604
5	2.015	2.571	3.365	4.032
6	1.943	2.447	3.143	3.707
7	1.895	2.365	2.998	3.499
8	1.860	2.306	2.896	3.355
9	1.833	2.262	2.821	3.250
10	1.812	2.228	2.764	3.169
11	1.796	2.201	2.718	3.106
12	1.782	2.179	2.681	3.055
13	1.771	2.160	2.650	3.012
14	1.761	2.145	2.624	2.977
15	1.753	2.131	2.602	2.947
20	1.725	2.086	2.528	2.845
30	1.697	2.042	2.457	2.750
50	1.676	2.009	2.403	2.678
100	1.660	1.984	2.364	2.626
∞	1.645	1.960	2.326	2.576

$v = 7, p = 5\%$ gives $k = 2.365$

= Percentage points of the Normal distribution $N(0, 1)$

Figure 10.5

To construct a 95% confidence interval for the mean weight of the bats, you look under $p = 5\%$ and $v = 7$, to get $k = 2.365$; see Figure 5.2. This gives a 95% confidence interval of

$$146 - 2.365 \times \frac{9.27}{\sqrt{8}} \text{ to } 146 + 2.365 \times \frac{9.27}{\sqrt{8}}$$

138.2 to 153.8.

Another bat expert suggests that these bats are not, in fact, a new species, but from a known species. The average weight of adult males of this species is 160 grams. However, because the maximum value in the confidence interval is less than 160, in fact, only 153.8, this suggests that the expert may not be correct. Even if you use a 99% confidence interval, the upper limit is $146 + 3.499 \times \frac{9.27}{\sqrt{8}} = 157.5$. Therefore, it seems very unlikely that these bats are of the same species, based simply on their weights.

Example 10.3

A bus company is about to start a scheduled service between two towns some distance apart. Before deciding on an appropriate timetable, they do nine trial runs to see how long the journey takes. The times, in minutes, are:

89 92 95 94 88 90 92 93 91

(i) Use these data to set up a 95% confidence interval for the mean journey time. You should assume that the journey times are Normally distributed.

The company regards its main competition as the railway service, which takes 95 minutes.

(ii) Does your confidence interval provide evidence that the journey time by bus is different from that by train?

Solution

(i) For the given data,

$n = 9$, $v = 9 - 1 = 8$, $\bar{x} = 91.56$, $s = 2.297$.

For a 95% confidence interval, with $v = 9$, $k = 2.306$ (from tables). The confidence limits are given by

$$\bar{x} \pm k \frac{s}{\sqrt{n}} = 91.56 \pm 2.306 \times \frac{2.297}{\sqrt{9}}.$$

So the 95% confidence interval for μ is 89.79 to 93.33.

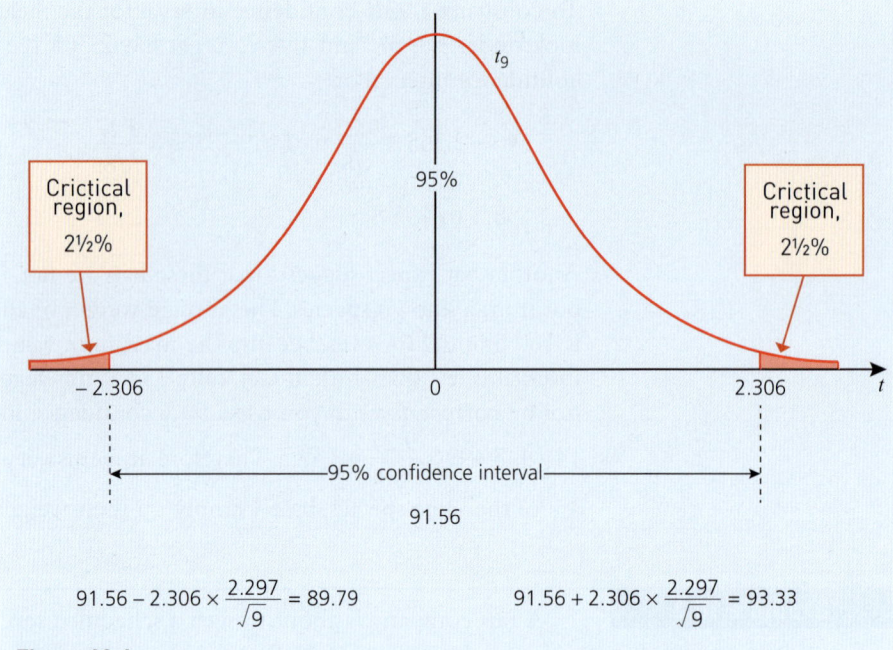

Interpreting sample data using the t-distribution

Figure 10.6

$$91.56 - 2.306 \times \frac{2.297}{\sqrt{9}} = 89.79 \qquad 91.56 + 2.306 \times \frac{2.297}{\sqrt{9}} = 93.33$$

(ii) The confidence interval does not contain 95 minutes (the time taken by the train). Therefore there is sufficient evidence to suggest that the journey time by bus is different from that by train, and that it is, in fact, less.

Using the t-distribution for paired samples

The ideas developed in the last few pages can also be used in constructing confidence intervals for the difference in the means of paired data. This is shown in the next example.

Example 10.4

In an experiment on group behaviour, 12 subjects were each asked to hold one arm out horizontally while supporting a 2 kg weight, under two conditions:

- while together in a group
- while alone with the experimenter.

The times, in seconds, for which they were able to support the weight under the two conditions were recorded as follows.

Table 10.7

Subject	A	B	C	D	E	F	G	H	I	J	K	L
'Group' time	61	71	72	53	71	43	85	72	82	54	70	73
'Alone' time	43	72	81	35	56	39	63	66	38	60	74	52
Difference	18	−1	−9	18	15	4	22	6	44	−6	−4	21

Find a 90% confidence interval for the true difference between 'group' times and 'alone' times. You may assume that the differences are Normally distributed. Does your result provide evidence that there is any difference in the times in the population as a whole?

Solution

The sample comprises the 12 differences.

Mean, $\bar{d} = 10.67$

Standard deviation, $s = 15.24$.

Degrees of freedom $v = 12 - 1 = 11$

Given the assumption that the differences are Normally distributed, you may use the *t*-distribution.

For $v = 11$, the two-tailed critical value from the *t*-distribution at the 10% level of significance is 1.796.

The 90% symmetrical confidence interval for the mean difference between the 'group' and 'alone' times is

$$\bar{d} - 1.796 \times \frac{s}{\sqrt{12}} \text{ to } \bar{d} + 1.796 \times \frac{s}{\sqrt{12}}$$

2.77 to 8.57.

Since the confidence interval does not contain zero, there is evidence that there is a difference in the times in the population as a whole.

Checking the goodness of fit of a Normal distribution

When you use a *t*-distribution, a basic assumption is that the data come from a Normal distribution. This assumption can be checked in a number of ways. In an earlier chapter you looked at chi-squared tests of goodness of fit for discrete distributions, but you did not look at them for any continuous distributions. You can, in fact, do these tests for continuous distributions, including the Normal distribution, but this is beyond the scope of this book. There are, however, other tests for Normality which you can use. These include:

- drawing a histogram
- Normal probability plots
- various hypothesis tests which are usually carried out using software.

> The theory behind these tests is beyond the scope of this book.

If the data set is fairly large, then a histogram can be used to look for a symmetrical bell shaped distribution which would suggest that the Normal distribution is a good fit to the data. However, with smaller data sets, a histogram is not very useful. Other methods can be used in this case.

Normal probability plots

Normal probability plots can be used to check whether a Normal distribution model is appropriate for a dataset. They can be drawn on Normal probability graph paper or by using software such as a spreadsheet.

On Normal probability graph paper, the horizontal scale is a standard linear scale and the data values are plotted on this in order from lowest to highest. The vertical axis has a probability scale, transformed to a theoretical

Interpreting sample data using the *t*-distribution

cumulative Normal distribution. If a Normal model fits the data perfectly, the data points lie on a straight line. The closer the points lie to a straight line, the better the model.

When using software, the vertical axis usually consists of *z*-values. Some software have the axes the other way round but the interpretation is the same: the straighter the line, the more likely it is that a Normal model is appropriate.

Figure 10.8 shows four histograms and their related Normal probability plots. The first shows a Normal distribution, the second shows a bimodal distribution, and the third and fourth show positively and negatively skewed distributions, respectively.

Example 10.5

The lengths in cm of a random sample of ten fish of a particular species are given below. Use a Normal probability plot to investigate whether the distribution of the population may be Normal.

Table 10.8

| 49.6 | 47.8 | 52.4 | 65.3 | 61.8 | 41.6 | 75.1 | 57.6 | 62.0 | 59.1 |

The output from two different spreadsheets is shown in Figure 10.8.

Solution

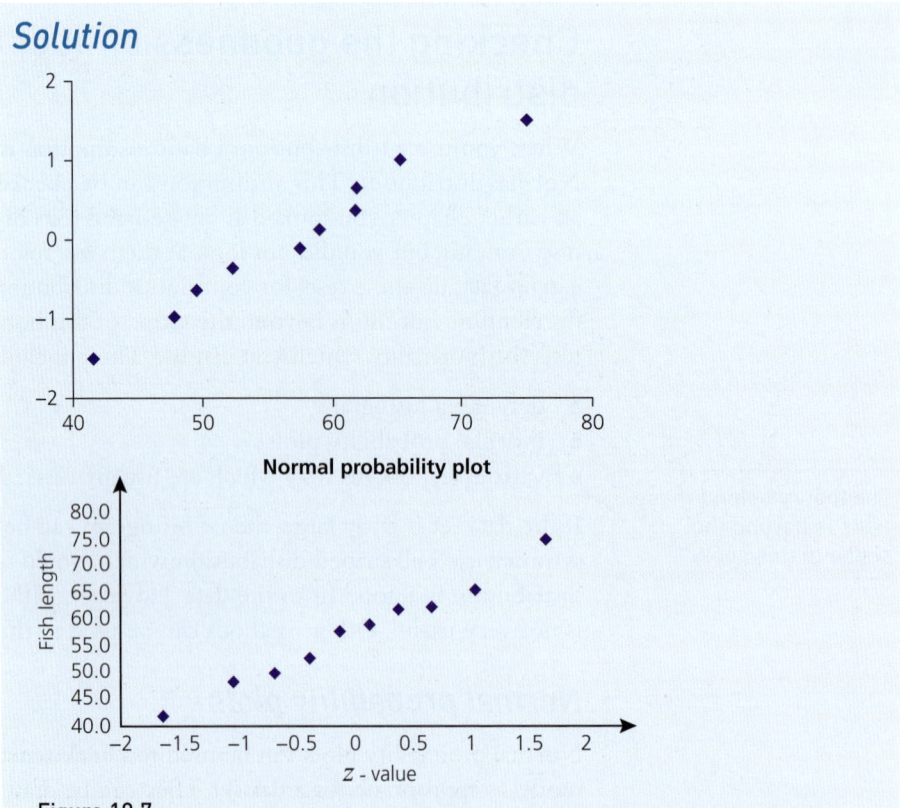

Figure 10.7

The first of these plots has the *z*-values on the vertical axis and the data values on the horizontal axis. The second is the other way round. Both plots suggest that a Normal model may be appropriate for these data.

Figure 10.8

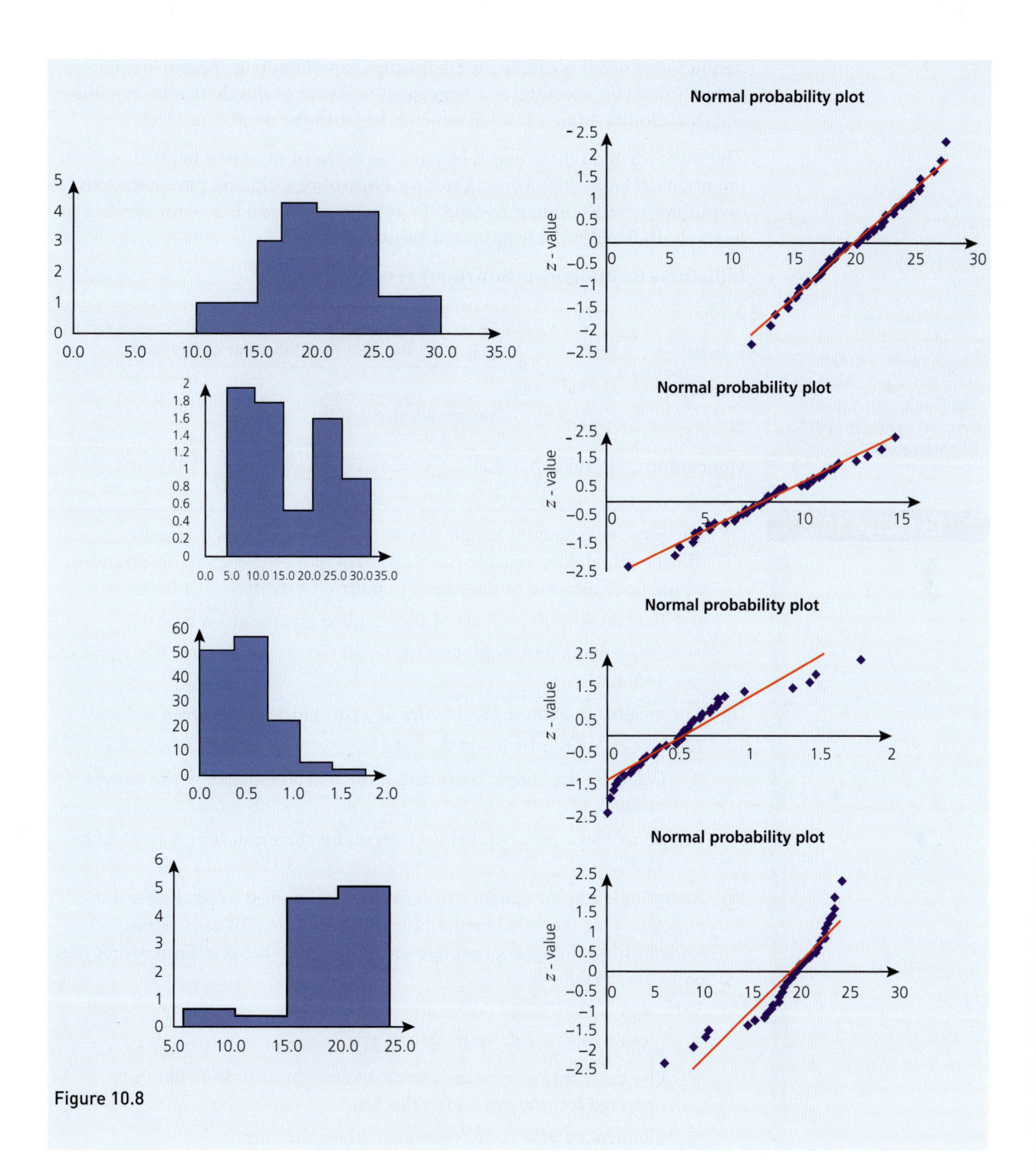

Other tests for Normality

In addition to Normal probability plots, there are many other tests of Normality. These include the chi-squared test of goodness of fit and the Lilliefors (Kolmogorov–Smirnov) test.

These tests all have the null hypothesis that the data are drawn from a Normal population. Consequently, accepting the null hypothesis may be regarded as a positive result and this is indicated by a p-value which is greater than the

Interpreting sample data using the t-distribution

significance level. By contrast, in many other hypothesis tests, a positive result occurs when you reject the null hypothesis in favour of the alternative hypothesis and this is indicated by a p-value which is less than the significance level.

The theory behind these tests is beyond the scope of this book but it is important to know how you can test for Normality, including interpreting the output from the Kolmogorov–Smirnov test. This is shown below for the data in Example 10.5 about the lengths of a sample of fish.

Lilliefors (Kolmogorov–Smirnov) test

Alpha   0.05
p-value   0.97
Statistic   0.11
N   10
Conclusion   Possibly Normal

The significance level is denoted by α

The p-value is greater than the significance level suggesting that a Normal model may be appropriate

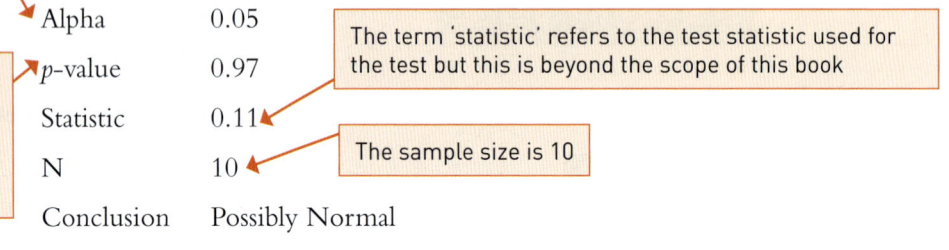

The term 'statistic' refers to the test statistic used for the test but this is beyond the scope of this book

The sample size is 10

Exercise 10.2

① The mean of a random sample of seven observations of a Normally distributed random variable X is 132.6. Based on these seven observations, an unbiased estimate of the parent population variance s^2 is 148.84.

  (i) Explain why an estimate of the standard error is given by 4.61.

  (ii) Show that a 95% confidence interval for the mean μ of X is 121.3 to 143.9.

② The weights in grams of six beetles of a particular species are as follows
  12.3   9.7   11.8   10.1   11.2   12.4

  (i) Calculate the sample mean and show that an estimate of the sample variance is 1.291.

  (ii) Show that a 90% confidence interval for the mean μ of X is 10.32 to 12.18.

③ An aptitude test for entrance to university is designed to produce scores which may be modelled by the Normal distribution. In early testing, 15 students from the appropriate age group are given the test. Their scores (out of 500) are as follows.

  321   445   219   378   317   407   289   345
  276   463   265   165   340   298   315

  (i) Use these data to estimate the mean and standard deviation to be expected for students taking this test.

  (ii) Construct a 95% confidence interval for the mean.

④ A fruit farmer has a large number of almond trees, all of the same variety and of the same age. One year, he wishes to estimate the mean yield of his trees. He collects all the almonds from eight trees and records the following weights (in kg).

  36   53   78   67   92   77   59   66

  (i) Use these data to estimate the mean and standard deviation of the yields of all the farmer's trees.

  (ii) Construct a 95% confidence interval for the mean yield.

(iii) What statistical assumption is required for your procedure to be valid?

(iv) How might you select a sample of eight trees from those growing in a large field?

5. A forensic scientist is trying to decide whether a man accused of fraud could have written a particular letter. As part of the investigation, she looks at the lengths of sentences used in the letter. She finds them to have the following numbers of words.

17 18 25 14 18 16 14 16 16 21 25 19

(i) Use these data to estimate the mean and standard deviation of the lengths of sentences used by the letter writer.

(ii) Construct a 90% confidence interval for the mean length of the letter writer's sentences.

(iii) What assumptions have you made to obtain your answer?

(iv) A sample of sentences written by the accused has mean length 26 words. Does this mean he is in the clear?

6. A large company is investigating the number of incoming telephone calls at its exchange, in order to determine how many telephone lines it should have. During March one year, the number of calls received each day was recorded and written down, across the page, as follows.

Table 10.9

623	584	598	701	656	210	23	655	661	599
634	681	197	25	592	643	642	698	659	201
19	588	672	612	706	650	212	29	681	642
677									

(i) What day of the week was 1 March?

(ii) Which of the data do you consider relevant to the company's research and why?

(iii) Construct a 95% confidence interval for the number of incoming calls per weekday.

(iv) Your calculation is criticised on the grounds that your data are discrete and so the underlying distribution cannot possibly be Normal. How would you respond to this criticism?

7. A tyre company is trying out a new tread pattern which it is hoped will result in the tyres giving greater distance. In a pilot experiment, 12 tyres are tested; the mileages (×1000 miles) at which they are condemned are as follows.

65 63 71 78 65 69 59 81 72 66 63 62

(i) Construct a 95% confidence interval for the mean distance that a tyre travels before being condemned.

(ii) What assumptions, statistical and practical, are required for your answer to part (i) to be valid?

8. A history student wishes to estimate the life expectancy of people in Lincolnshire villages around 1750. She looks at the parish registers for five villages at that time and writes down the ages of the first ten people buried after the start of 1750. Those less than one-year-old were recorded as 0. The data were as follows.

Interpreting sample data using the *t*-distribution

Table 10.10

2	6	72	0	0	18	45	91	6	2
0	12	56	4	25	1	1	5	0	7
8	65	12	63	2	76	70	0	1	0
9	15	3	49	54	0	2	71	6	8
6	0	67	55	2	0	1	54	1	5

(i) Use these data to estimate the mean life expectancy at that time.

(ii) Explain why it is not possible to use these data to construct a confidence interval for the mean life expectancy.

(iii) Is a confidence interval a useful measure in this situation anyway?

A friend tells the student that she could construct a confidence interval for the mean life expectancy of those who survive childhood (age ≥ 15).

(iv) Construct a 95% confidence interval for the mean life expectancy of this group, and comment on whether you think your procedure is valid.

⑨ A large fishing-boat made a catch of 500 mackerel from a shoal. The total mass of the catch was 320 kg. The standard deviation of the mass of individual mackerel is known to be 0.06 kg.

(i) Find a 99% confidence interval for the mean mass of a mackerel in the shoal.

An individual fisherman caught ten mackerel from the same shoal. These had masses (in kg) of

1.04   0.94   0.92   0.85   0.85   0.70   0.68   0.62   0.61   0.59

(ii) From these data only, use your calculator to estimate the mean and standard deviation of the masses of mackerel in the shoal.

(iii) Assuming that the masses of mackerel are Normally distributed, use your results from part (ii) to find another 99% confidence interval for the mean mass of a mackerel in the shoal.

(iv) Give two statistical reasons why you would use the first limits you calculated in preference to the second limits.

⑩ A farmer has a large field of sunflowers. He wishes to know the average height of these sunflowers. The output from statistical software below shows the calculations for a 95% confidence interval for the heights. All figures are in metres.

Table 10.11

t estimate of a mean	

Confidence Level	0.95

		Sample
	Mean	2.153
	s	0.263
	n	12

	Result
Mean	2.153
σ	0.263
SE	0.07592
N	12
Lower limit	1.9859
Upper limit	2.32018
Interval	2.153 ± 0.1671

(i) Write down the confidence interval in the form $a < \mu < b$.

(ii) State the sample size.

(iii) State any assumptions required for the construction of this confidence interval.

(iv) Check that this is the same confidence interval as you obtain using the relevant value of k given in the table in Figure 10.6.

⑪ A rail commuter suspects that the train he travels to work by arrives late regularly. On five such journeys, he noted the times, T minutes, by which the train was late. The data were summarised by

$$\sum t = 11.8, \quad \sum t^2 = 65.3.$$

(i) Find the mean and standard deviation of the data, and use them to find a and b, the lower and upper limits for the 90% confidence interval for μ, the mean time by which the train is late. State clearly two important assumptions you need to make.

(ii) The commuter interprets the result in part (i) as 'the probability that μ lies between a and b is 0.9'. Comment on this interpretation.

(iii) Use your result in part (i) to comment on whether the commuter's suspicions are justified.

(iv) The railway management notes the value of T on a further 40 occasions. State, with reasons, how you might expect its confidence interval for μ to differ from the one calculated in part (i). [MEI]

⑫ When a darts player aims at the centre of the dart board the distance from the centre to the point where the dart lands is R, which is modelled as a continuous random variable. A suggested probability density function for R is as shown in the diagram.

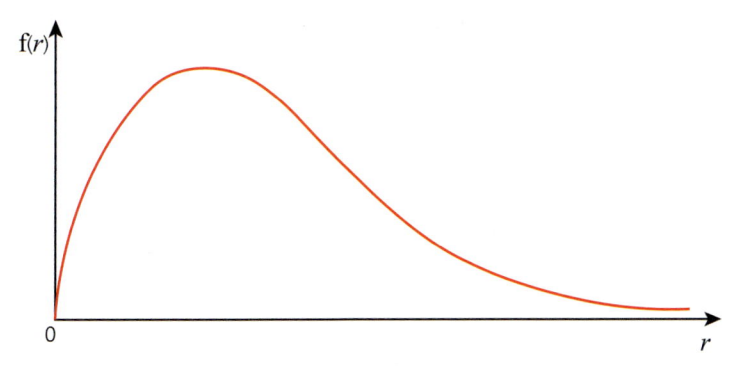

Figure 10.9

(i) Copy the diagram and show the position of the mode. Show also the approximate position of the mean in relation to the mode.

Interpreting sample data using the t-distribution

The mean value of R will vary for players of different ability. The famous darts player Willy Jackson aims 50 darts at the centre of the board. The distances from the centre are summarised as follows.

$$\Sigma r = 35.5, \quad \Sigma r^2 = 33.2$$

(ii) Construct a 90% confidence interval for the mean value of R. What assumption(s) have you made about the set of 50 throws?

(iii) Estimate the number of throws required if the 90% confidence interval for the mean of R for Willy Jackson is to be of width 0.1. Explain why your answer is only an estimate.

(iv) A second darts player records the results for ten throws. Explain carefully why it would not be possible to obtain an accurate confidence interval for the mean value of R for this player. [MEI]

13. A youth club has a large number of members (referred to as the *population* in the remainder of the question). In order to find the distribution of weekly allowances of the members, a random sample of ten is questioned.

(i) Describe a method of producing the random sample.

Such a random sample produced the following weekly allowances:

£5.20, £4.40, £3.00, £2.00, £3.30,
£7.50, £5.00, £6.50, £4.80, £5.70

(ii) Estimate the population mean and variance.

(iii) Find a 95% confidence interval for the population mean. State any assumptions on which your method is based.

(iv) Explain how the width of the confidence interval may be reduced. Assuming the same variance as in part (ii) what must the sample size be to reduce the width to £2?

14. A tax inspector is carrying out an audit survey of firms located in a certain city.

From the list of all N such firms, a random sample of size n is selected for detailed study.

(i) Define what is meant by a random sample.

(ii) Explain why a sample, even though random, might nevertheless be biased, explaining also the meaning of the word 'biased' in this context.

(iii) For a random sample of size $n = 14$, the values of a particular financial indicator are found to be

8.6 9.1 9.3 8.2 8.9 9.2 9.9 9.2 9.4 8.7 9.1 10.2 9.2 9.1.

Obtain a two-sided 99% confidence interval for the mean value of this indicator in the underlying population. State any required assumption and explain carefully the interpretation of the interval. [MEI]

15. An aggregate material used for road building contains gravel and stones. The average size of the stones is supposed to be 55 mm. Each batch of this material is checked to ensure that the stones are of the correct size. For each batch, a random sample of eight stones is selected and a 95% confidence interval is found for the size of the stones.

(i) Explain why it would not be sensible to simply discard a batch if the confidence interval does not contain 55 mm.

(ii) Suggest what should be done instead if the confidence interval for a particular batch does not contain 55 mm.

For a particular batch, the eight observations are:

46.21 51.67 48.60 47.34 50.93 49.60 60.97 55.17

A Normal probability plot for these data is shown below:

Normal probability plot

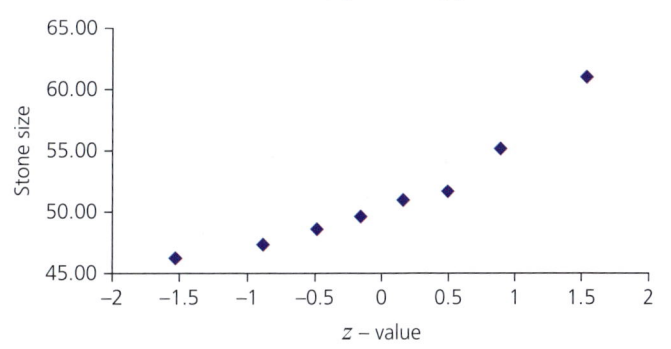

(scatter plot: Stone size vs z-value)

Figure 10.10

(iii) Explain why it seems that the assumption necessary for a *t* test may not be justified?

(iv) If, in fact, the data do come from a Normal distribution, construct a 95% confidence interval for the population mean.

⑯ A new computerised job-matching system has been developed which finds suitably-skilled applicants to fit notified vacancies. It is hoped that this will reduce unemployment rates, and a trial of the system is conducted in seven areas.

The unemployment rates in each area just before the introduction of the system and after one month of its operation are recorded in the table below.

Table 10.12

Area	1	2	3	4	5	6	7
Rate before new system (%)	10.3	3.6	17.8	5.1	4.6	11.2	7.7
Rate after new system (%)	9.3	4.1	15.2	5.0	3.3	10.3	8.1

(i) Find a 90% confidence interval for the true difference between the two rates of unemployment.

(ii) Does your confidence interval provide evidence that there is a difference in the rates after the new system is introduced?

(iii) Do you think that the assumptions required to construct the confidence interval are justified here?

⑰ Two timekeepers at an athletics track are being compared. They each time the nine sprints one afternoon.

(i) Find a 99% confidence interval for the true difference between the times recorded by the two timers. The times they record are listed below.

Table 10.13

Race	1	2	3	4	5	6	7	8	9
Timer 1	9.65	10.01	9.62	21.90	20.70	20.90	42.30	43.91	43.96
Timer 2	9.66	9.99	9.44	22.00	20.82	20.58	42.39	44.27	44.22

(ii) Do you think that the two timers are equivalent on average?

(iii) Are the assumptions appropriate for a confidence interval based on the *t* test justified in this case?

Interpreting sample data using the *t*-distribution

⑱ Fourteen marked rats were timed twice as they ran through a maze. In one condition, they had just been fed; in the other they were hungry.

(i) Find a 95% confidence interval for the true difference between the rats' times when they are fed and when they are hungry. The data below give the rats' times in each condition.

Table 10.14

Rat	A	B	C	D	E	F	G	H	I	J	K	L	M	N
Fed time (seconds)	30	31	25	23	50	26	14	27	31	39	38	39	44	30
Hungry time (seconds)	29	18	14	27	37	34	15	22	29	18	20	10	30	32

(ii) Do you think that the assumptions required to construct the confidence interval are justified here?

(iii) Half of the rats were made to run the maze first when hungry and half ran it first when fed. Why did the experimenter do this?

⑲ An experiment to determine the acceleration due to gravity, $g\,\mathrm{m\,s^{-2}}$, involves measuring the time, T seconds, taken by a pendulum of length l m to perform complete swings. T is regarded as a random variable.

Thirty measurements are made on T, and they are summarised by

$$\Sigma t = 59.8, \quad \Sigma t^2 = 119.7.$$

Construct a two-sided 98% confidence interval for μ, the mean value of T. Determine the corresponding range of values of g, using the formula

$$g = \frac{4\pi^2}{\mu^2}$$

This result for g is not precise enough, so a longer series of measurements of T is made. Assuming that the sample mean and standard deviation remain about the same, how many measurements will be required in total to halve the width of the 98% confidence interval for μ? What will be the corresponding effect on the range of values for g? [MEI]

KEY POINTS

1. When the population standard deviation, σ, is known and the distribution is Normal, confidence intervals for μ are found using the Normal distribution.
2. Two-sided confidence intervals based on the Normal distribution are given by $\bar{x} - k\frac{\sigma}{\sqrt{n}}$ to $\bar{x} + k\frac{\sigma}{\sqrt{n}}$.
3. The value of k for any confidence level can be found using Normal distribution tables.

Table 10.15

Confidence level	k
90%	1.645
95%	1.96
99%	2.58

4 For large values of n, the requirement that the distribution is Normal may be relaxed.

5 Confidence intervals for paired samples are formed in the same way but the variable is now the difference between the paired values.

6 When the population standard deviation, σ, is not known and is estimated as being the sample standard deviation, s, and the distribution is Normal, confidence intervals for μ are found using the t-distribution.

7 Two-sided confidence intervals for μ based on the t-distribution are given by
$$\bar{x} - k\frac{s}{\sqrt{n}} \text{ to } \bar{x} + k\frac{s}{\sqrt{n}}.$$

8 The value of k for any confidence level can be found using t-distribution tables.

9 The value of s can be found using the formula
$$s^2 = \frac{S_{xx}}{n-1} = \sum_i \frac{(x_i - \bar{x})^2}{(n-1)}.$$

10 As with confidence intervals based on the Normal distribution, confidence intervals for paired samples are formed in the same way but the variable is now the difference between the paired values.

11 The goodness of fit of a Normal distribution can be checked using a Normal probability plot.

12 Alternatively, the goodness of fit of a Normal distribution can be checked using a statistical test such as the Lilliefors (Kolmogorov–Smirnov) test.

LEARNING OUTCOMES

When you have completed this chapter you should:

- know the meaning of the term confidence interval for a parameter and associated language
- understand the factors which affect the width of a confidence interval
- be able to construct and interpret a confidence interval for a single population mean using the Normal or t-distributions and know when it is appropriate to do so
- know when samples from two populations should be considered as paired
- be able to construct and interpret a confidence interval for the difference in means of two paired populations using a paired sample and a Normal or t-distribution and know when it is appropriate to do so
- interpret confidence intervals given by software
- use a confidence interval for a population parameter to make a decision about a hypothesised value of that parameter
- interpret a Normal probability plot, and the output from other tests, using software, to decide whether a Normal model might be appropriate.

11 Hypothesis testing

Every experiment may be said to exist only to give the facts a chance of disproving the null hypothesis.

R. A. Fisher

Seagulls getting heavier?

In the last few years, the numbers of seagulls living on roofs in towns has been increasing. It is known that in the past, before the advent of scavenging, the mean weight of adult female seagulls was 1015 grams, with standard deviation 110. Many of the gulls scavenge food discarded by patrons of takeaway restaurants. A reporter for a local paper says that as a result of the 'easy pickings' from these restaurants, the seagulls in the town where she lives are heavier now than they were in the past, before they discovered free takeaway food. She enlists the help of an ornithologist to capture and weigh ten adult female seagulls in the town, before releasing them so that they can continue to take advantage of the free food.

The weights of the ten seagulls measured in grams are

1050   1145   1205   985   1015   1100   890   940   1290   1080

You will recall that you have already met hypothesis testing in Chapter 4 when testing for correlation and in Chapter 6 when testing for goodness of fit. You can also test whether a sample mean has a particular value, using a Normal distribution or a *t* distribution, provided that certain conditions are satisfied.

Hypotheses for a test for a mean

The null hypothesis is always:

- $H_0: \mu = a$, where *a* is the specified 'original' value of the mean. In other words, *a* is the mean if nothing has changed.

The alternative hypothesis has one of three forms.

- $H_1: \mu \neq a$ ← This is two-tailed
- $H_1: \mu < a$
- $H_1: \mu > a$ ← These are one-tailed

> Since the weight of a seagull is a naturally occurring variable, it is reasonable to assume its distribution is Normal

> You have no information about how the sample was collected but it is reasonable to assume that it was random

> **Note**
> The significance level is the probability of rejecting the null hypothesis when it is actually true. This is called a **Type 1 error**.
> Accepting the null hypothesis when it is false is called a **Type 2 error**.

> **Note**
> You are investigating whether the weights of seagulls have increased. The test is therefore one-tailed because the alternative hypothesis is $\mu > 1015$ and so is one sided.
> If you had instead been investigating whether the weights of seagulls had changed, then it would have been a two-tailed test and the alternative hypothesis would have been $\mu \neq 1015$.

1 Hypothesis testing on a sample mean using the Normal distribution

You can carry out a hypothesis test based on the Normal distribution to investigate whether it is likely that the scavenging seagulls are heavier than seagulls used to be. Two requirements for this test to be valid are that:

- the population from which the sample is drawn has a sample that comes from a Normal distribution
- the sample is representative of the population; this is usually ensured by having a random sample.

To use the Normal distribution, you also have to know the standard deviation of the parent population. You do not know this for the scavenging seagulls, but you do know that in the past it was 110 g. You have to assume that it is still 110 g.

To carry out the test, you to decide the significance level; in this case 5% is chosen. You also need to state the null and alternative hypotheses; the alternative hypothesis will tell you whether it is a one- or two-tailed test. In this case,

Null hypothesis: $H_0: \mu = 1015$
Alternative hypothesis: $H_1: \mu > 1015$
Significance level: 5%
Test: one-tailed.

There are three slightly different methods used to carry out a hypothesis test based on the Normal distribution. They are all based on the central limit theorem; that is, that the distribution of the sample means is given by

$$\overline{X} \sim N\left(\mu, \frac{\sigma^2}{n}\right)$$

Hypothesis testing on a sample mean using the Normal distribution

for large values of the sample size, n.

Start by calculating the sample mean.

$$\left(\frac{1050 + 1145 + 1205 + 985 + 1015 + 1100 + 890 + 940 + 1290 + 1080}{10}\right)$$

$$= \frac{10700}{10} = 1070$$

Method 1: Using critical regions

> **Note**
> For a one-tailed test rather than the symbol ± in the critical values, you either have + or − according to whether you are interested in the upper or lower tail.

Since the distribution of sample means is $N\left(\mu, \frac{\sigma^2}{n}\right)$, critical values for a test on the sample mean are given by

$$\mu \pm k \times \frac{\sigma}{\sqrt{n}}.$$

In this case, if H_0 is true: $\mu = 1015$; $\sigma = 110$; $n = 10$.

The test is one-tailed, for $\mu > 1015$, so only the right-hand tail applies.

k is the critical value for the standardised value, z.

Using the inverse Normal function on a calculator, the value of k is 1.645.

> Make sure that you know how to get this value from your calculator
> For some calculators, you may need to calculate $1 - 0.05 = 0.95$

For a one-tailed test at the 5% significance level, the critical value is

$$1015 + 1.645 \times \frac{110}{\sqrt{10}} = 1072.2, \text{ as shown in the diagram below.}$$

[Diagram: Normal distribution curve with critical value 1072.2, critical region shaded in right tail, marks at 1015, 1070, and $\bar{x} = 1070$]

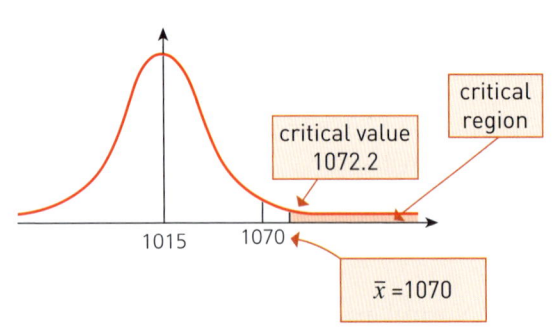

Figure 11.1

However, the sample mean $\bar{x} = 1070$, and $1070 < 1072.2$.

Therefore the sample mean lies outside the critical region and so there is insufficient evidence to reject the null hypothesis.

> This does not mean that the null hypothesis is definitely true but that the evidence suggests, at this significance level, that this is the case.

There is insufficient evidence to suggest that the mean weight of scavenging gulls is greater than before the advent of scavenging.

Method 2: Using probabilities

The distribution of sample means, $\bar{x}$, is $N\left(\mu, \frac{\sigma^2}{n}\right)$.

According to the null hypothesis, $\mu = 1015$ and it is known that $\sigma = 110$ and $n = 10$.

So this distribution is $N\left(1015, \frac{110^2}{10}\right)$, see following diagram.

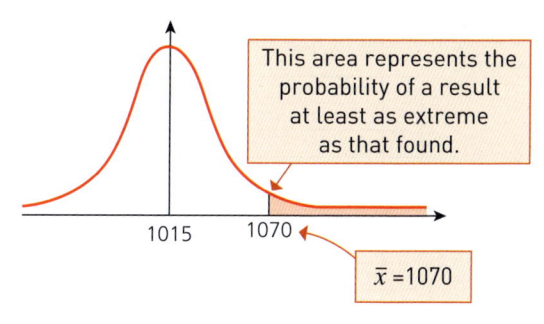

[Figure 11.2: Normal distribution curve with mean 1015, showing $\bar{x} = 1070$ in the tail. Annotation: "This area represents the probability of a result at least as extreme as that found."]

Figure 11.2

The probability of the mean, $\bar{X}$, of a randomly chosen sample being greater than the value found, i.e. 1070, is given by

$$P(\bar{X} \geq 1070) = 1 - \phi\left(\frac{1070 - 1015}{\frac{110}{\sqrt{10}}}\right)$$

$$= 1 - \phi(1.581)$$
$$= 1 - 0.9431$$
$$= 0.0569.$$

Since $0.0569 > 0.05$, there is insufficient evidence to reject the null hypothesis. [0.05 is the significance level]

There is insufficient evidence to suggest that the mean weight of scavenging gulls is greater than before the advent of scavenging.

Method 3: Using the test statistics (or critical ratios)

The *test statistic* (or *critical ratio*) is given by $z = \left(\dfrac{\bar{x} - \mu}{\frac{\sigma}{\sqrt{n}}}\right)$

In this case, $z = \left(\dfrac{1070 - 1015}{\frac{110}{\sqrt{10}}}\right) = 1.581.$

This is now compared with the critical value for z, in this case, $z = 1.645$. [This is the value of k in Method 1]

Since $1.581 < 1.645$, H_0 is not rejected. There is insufficient evidence to reject the null hypothesis.

There is insufficient evidence to suggest that the mean weight of scavenging gulls is greater than before the advent of scavenging.

> **Note**
> The calculated probability is often called the *p*-value.
> If the *p*-value is smaller than the significance level, then you reject H_0 and accept H_1. Otherwise you accept H_0, as in this case.

USING ICT

Statistical software

You can use statistical software to do all of the calculations for this test. In order for the software to process the test, you need to input the following information:
- the population mean if H_0 is true
- the form of the alternative hypothesis ($<$, $>$ or $\neq$)
- the population standard deviation
- the sample mean
- the sample size.

Large samples

> ⚠ You need to be careful when interpreting the *p*-value. In many tests, like this one, rejecting the null hypothesis, H_0, means that you have found an interesting result, expressed as the alternative hypothesis, H_1; it is sometimes summarised as 'The test is significant'. So a *p*-value that is less than the significance level might be seen as desirable.
>
> By contrast, in goodness of fit tests, the interesting result, that you have found a suitable distribution to use as a model, is given by the null hypothesis. So, in such tests, a *p*-value that is higher than the significance level can be seen as desirable.

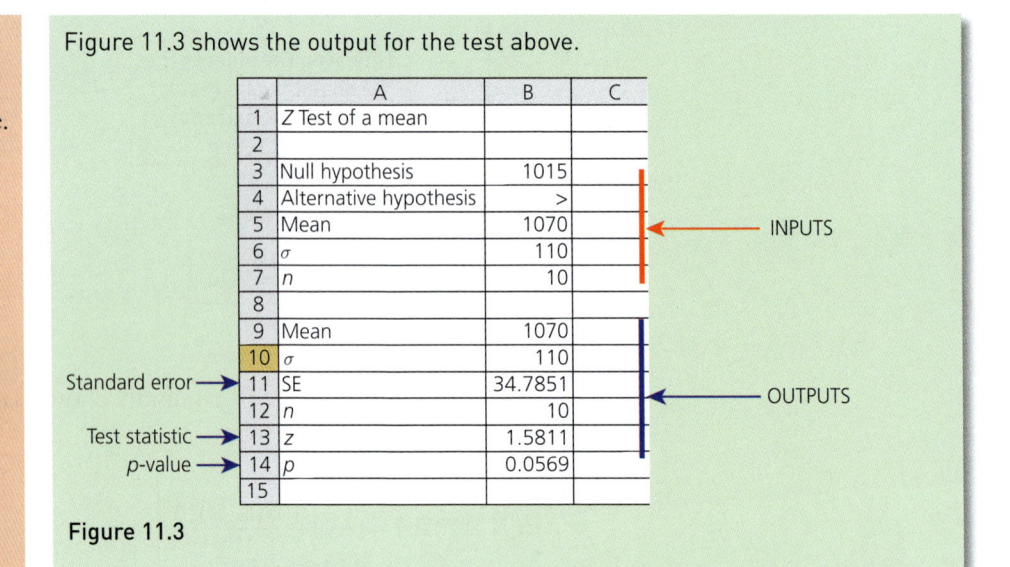

Figure 11.3 shows the output for the test above.

	A	B	C
1	Z Test of a mean		
2			
3	Null hypothesis	1015	
4	Alternative hypothesis	>	
5	Mean	1070	
6	σ	110	
7	n	10	
8			
9	Mean	1070	
10	σ	110	
11	SE	34.7851	
12	n	10	
13	z	1.5811	
14	p	0.0569	
15			

Rows 3–7 are INPUTS. Row 11 is Standard error. Row 13 is Test statistic. Row 14 is *p*-value. Rows 9–14 are OUTPUTS.

Figure 11.3

You can see that the output from the software gives both the *p*-value of 0.0569 and the test statistic of 1.5811.

2 Large samples

If you have a large sample, then you do not need to know the standard deviation in order to carry out a hypothesis test for the mean. This is because, if your sample is large, the sample standard deviation may be used as an estimate of the population standard deviation. Theoretically, it can be shown that the sample variance, s^2, is an unbiased estimate of the population variance, σ^2. Furthermore, if you have a large sample, then the central limit theorem implies that the distribution of the sample mean will be approximately Normal even though the parent population distribution is not. Therefore, if your sample is large, you can carry out a test for the mean based on the Normal distribution when you do not know either the distribution or the standard deviation of the parent population. The example below illustrates a situation where you know neither of these.

Example 11.1

A psychologist is investigating reaction times. From many previous experiments, she knows that the mean reaction time for an adult to respond to a stimulus provided by a computer is 0.650 seconds. She thinks that the reaction time of 12-year-old children will be quicker. She selects a sample of 60 of these children and measures their reaction times, xs, to the stimulus. The results are summarised by

$$\Sigma x = 38.24 \qquad \Sigma x^2 = 25.18$$

(i) State any conditions necessary for a hypothesis test to investigate whether the reaction times of 12-year olds are lower.

(ii) Carry out the test described in part (i) at the 10% significance level.

Notes

1. A hypothesis test should be formulated before the data are collected and not after. In this case, the reporter thought that the gulls might be larger and so data was collected to test this hypothesis. If sample data had led the reporter to form a hypothesis, then a new set of data would have been required in order to carry out a suitable test.

2. If the data were not collected properly, any test carried out on them may be worthless. So if the seagulls did not form a random sample from the population, then the test would be invalid.

Note

This is a large sample and so you do not need to know the standard deviation of the parent population. Instead, you can use the sample standard deviation as an estimate for it.

Also, you do not need to know anything about the distribution of the parent population since the central limit theorem tells you that the distribution of the sample mean will be approximately Normal.

Solution

(i) The sample of children must be random.

(ii) You can use any of the three methods given above. *Method 3* is used here.

First, you must state the null and alternative hypotheses.

Null hypothesis: $H_0: \mu = 0.650$

Alternative hypothesis: $H_1: \mu < 0.650$

Significance level: 10%

Test: one-tailed

You are investigating whether the reaction times of children are quicker. The test is therefore one-tailed.

To estimate the population standard deviation σ, find the sample standard deviation, s. The general form of this is

$$s = \sqrt{\text{Variance}} = \sqrt{\frac{S_{xx}}{n-1}}, \text{ where } S_{xx} = \Sigma x^2 - n\bar{x}^2$$

$$\bar{x} = \frac{\Sigma x}{n} = \frac{38.24}{60} = 0.6373\ldots$$

and so $S_{xx} = \Sigma x^2 - n\bar{x}^2 = 25.18 - 60 \times 0.6373\ldots^2 = 0.80837\ldots$

$$s = \sqrt{\frac{0.80837\ldots}{59}} = 0.117\ldots$$

The *test statistic* is given by

$$z = \frac{\bar{x} - \mu}{\frac{\sigma}{\sqrt{n}}} = \frac{0.6373\ldots - 0.650}{\frac{0.117\ldots}{\sqrt{60}}} = -0.838\ldots$$

This is now compared with the critical value for z, in this case $z = -1.282$.

Since $-0.838 > -1.282$, H_0 is not rejected. There is insufficient evidence to reject the null hypothesis.

There is insufficient evidence to suggest that the 12-year-old children have quicker reaction times to the stimulus compare to adults.

3 Hypothesis testing on a sample mean using the *t*-distribution

In Chapter 10, you met the *t* distribution. This is the distribution of a sample mean when the parent population is Normally distributed but the standard deviation of the parent population is unknown and has to be estimated using the sample standard deviation, s. In addition to finding a confidence interval, you can also carry out a hypothesis test based on the *t* distribution.

Hypothesis testing on a sample mean using the *t*-distribution

Example 11.2

> **ACTIVITY 11.1**
> Use *Methods 1 and 2* to carry out the test. You should of course come to the same conclusion.

Tests are being carried out on a new drug designed to relieve the symptoms of the common cold. One of the tests is to investigate whether the drug has any effect on the number of hours that people sleep.

The drug is given in tablet form one evening to a random sample of 16 people who have colds. The number of hours they sleep may be assumed to be Normally distributed and is recorded as follows.

| 8.1 | 6.7 | 3.3 | 7.2 | 8.1 | 9.2 | 6.0 | 7.4 |
| 6.4 | 6.9 | 7.0 | 7.8 | 6.7 | 7.2 | 7.6 | 7.9 |

There is also a large control group of people who have colds but are not given the drug. The mean number of hours they sleep is 6.6.

(i) Use these data to set up a 95% confidence interval for the mean length of time somebody with a cold sleeps after taking the tablet.

(ii) Carry out a test, at the 1% significance level, of the hypothesis that the new drug has an effect on the number of hours a person sleeps.

> **Note**
> The critical value in this case is negative since you are carrying out a lower tail test. You can either give the comparison as shown above $-0.838 > -1.282$ or use the absolute values (moduli) in which case the comparison would be $|-0.838| < |-1.282|$. You should **not** compare -0.838 with $+1.282$.

Solution

(i) For the given data, $n = 16$, $\upsilon = 16 - 1 = 15$, $\bar{x} = 7.094$, $s = 1.276$.

For a 95% confidence interval, with $\upsilon = 15$, $k = 2.131$ (from tables).

The confidence limits are given by $\bar{x} \pm k \dfrac{s}{\sqrt{n}} = 7.094 \pm 2.131 \times \dfrac{1.276}{\sqrt{16}}$,

So the 95% confidence interval for μ is 6.41 to 7.77.

t_{15}

95%

critical region, $2\frac{1}{2}\%$ critical region, $2\frac{1}{2}\%$

−2.131   0   2.131

95% confidence interval

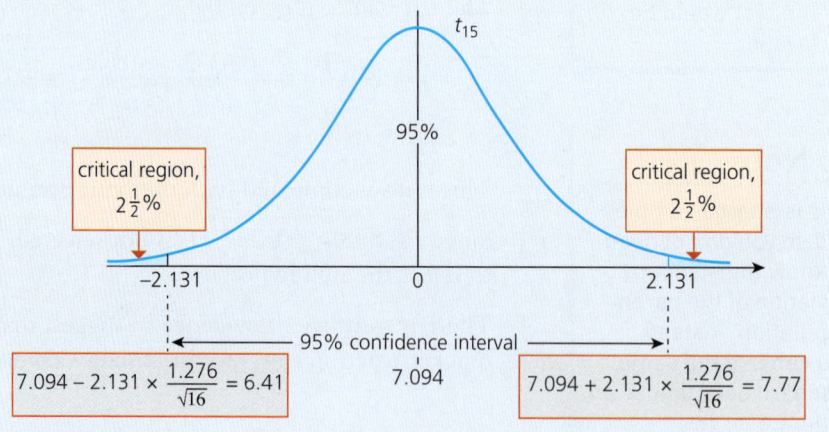

$7.094 - 2.131 \times \dfrac{1.276}{\sqrt{16}} = 6.41$ 7.094 $7.094 + 2.131 \times \dfrac{1.276}{\sqrt{16}} = 7.77$

Figure 11.4

(ii) H_0: there is no change in the mean number of hours sleep. $\mu = 6.6$
H_1: there is a change in the mean number of hours sleep. $\mu \neq 6.6$
Two-tailed test at the 1% significance level.

For this sample, $n = 16$, $\upsilon = 16 - 1 = 15$, $\bar{x} = 7.094$, $s = 1.276$.

The critical value for t, for $\upsilon = 15$, at the 1% significance level, is found from tables to be 2.947.

The test statistic $t = \left(\dfrac{\bar{x} - \mu}{\frac{s}{\sqrt{n}}}\right) = \left(\dfrac{7.094 - 6.6}{\frac{1.276}{\sqrt{16}}}\right) = 1.55$.

This is to be compared with 2.947, the critical value, for the 1% significance level.

Since 1.55 < 2.947, there is no reason at the 1% significance level to reject the null hypothesis.

There is insufficient evidence to suggest that the mean number of hours sleep is different when people take the drug.

USING ICT

Using a spreadsheet

You can use a spreadsheet (see Figure 11.5) to do all of the calculations for this test using the following steps:

1. Enter the data (in this case into cells B2 to B17)
2. Use the spreadsheet functions provided by your spreadsheet, for example = AVERAGE and = STDEV to find the mean and sample standard deviation.
3. Calculate the t value using the formula = (B18-6.6)/(B19/SQRT(16))
4. Use the spreadsheet function provided by your spreadsheet, for example = T.INV.2T(0.01,15) to calculate the critical value.
5. You can also find the p-value using the spreadsheet function provided by your spreadsheet, for example = T.DIST.2T(1.5482,15)

	A	B
1		Data
2		8.1
3		6.7
4		3.3
5		7.2
6		8.1
7		9.2
8		6.0
9		7.4
10		6.4
11		6.9
12		7.0
13		7.8
14		6.7
15		7.2
16		7.6
17		7.9
18	Mean	7.0938
19	Sample sd	1.2757
20	n	16
21	t value	1.5482
22	Critical t	2.9467
23	p-value	0.1424

In this case, the values of $\bar{x}$ and s are given in cells B18 and B19.

Figure 11.5

Hypothesis testing on a sample mean using the *t*-distribution

Exercise 11.1

1. A hypothesis test is to be carried out at the 5% level on a Normally distributed population with standard deviation 2.7. The null hypothesis is $H_0: \mu = 25$, and the alternative hypothesis is $H_1: \mu > 25$. A random sample of size 9 is selected and the sample mean is 26.71.

   (i) Find the standard error of the mean.

   (ii) Calculate the test statistic.

   (iii) Write down the critical value.

   (iv) Explain whether the null hypothesis should be rejected.

2. Bags of flour are supposed to weigh at least 1.5 kg. Sampling is carried out at the factory where the bags are filled to check that the bags are not underweight. On a particular day, the sample mean of a random sample of 40 bags is 1.4972 kg with sample standard deviation 0.009 kg. A hypothesis test is carried out at the 1% significance level to check whether the bags are satisfactory.

   (i) Explain why you do not need to know the distribution of the parent population in order to carry out the test.

   (ii) Write down suitable null and alternative hypotheses.

   (iii) Find the standard error of the mean.

   (iv) Calculate the test statistic.

   (v) Write down the critical value.

   (vi) Explain whether the null hypothesis should be rejected.

3. The spreadsheet below shows the output for a *t* test to investigate the hypotheses

   $H_0: \mu = 180$ and $H_1: \mu \neq 180$.

   (i) State whether the test is one-tailed or two-tailed and use the 'Critical *t*' in cell B13 to find the significance level of the test.

   (ii) State the result of the test relating it to the content of cells B12 and B13.

   (iii) State the result of the test, this time relating it to the content of cell B14.

	A	B
1		Data
2		172.24
3		198.79
4		167.81
5		192.23
6		183.81
7		178.49
8		183.27
9	Mean	182.37
10	Sample sd	10.80
11	n	7
12	*t* value	0.8796
13	Critical t	2.3646
14	*p*-value	0.4082

   Figure 11.6

④ A farmer grows onions. The weight in kilograms of the variety of onions which he usually grows is Normally distributed with mean 0.155 and variance 0.005. He is trying out a new variety, which he hopes will yield a higher mean weight. In order to test this, he takes a random sample of 25 onions of the new variety and finds that their total weight is 4.77 kg. You should assume that the weight in kilograms of the new variety is Normally distributed with variance 0.005.

(i) Write down suitable null and alternative hypotheses for the test in terms of μ. State the meaning of μ in this case.

(ii) Carry out the test at the 1% level. [MEI]

⑤ It is known that the diameter of marigold flowers is Normally distributed with mean 47 mm and standard deviation 8.5 mm. A certain fertiliser is expected to cause flowers to have a larger mean diameter, but without affecting the standard deviation. A large number of marigolds are grown using this fertiliser. The diameters of a random sample of ten of the flowers are measured and the mean diameter is found to be 49.2 mm. Carry out a hypothesis test at the 5% significance level to check whether flowers grown with this fertiliser appear to be larger on average. [MEI]

⑥ A council is investigating the weight of rubbish in domestic dustbins. It has recently started a recycling initiative and wishes to determine whether there has been a reduction in the weight of rubbish. Before the initiative, the mean weight was 33.5 kg. A random sample of 60 domestic dustbins is selected and the weight x kg of rubbish in each bin is recorded. The results are summarised as follows.

$$\Sigma x = 1801.2 \qquad \Sigma x^2 = 56963$$

Carry out a hypothesis test at the 1% level to investigate whether the mean weight has been reduced.

⑦ Over a long period, it has been found that the time that it takes for an underground train to complete a particular journey is 18.6 minutes. New signalling equipment is introduced which might affect the journey time. The times t taken for a random sample of 30 journeys after the change are summarised as follows.

$$\Sigma t = 548.0 \qquad \Sigma t^2 = 10055$$

(i) Carry out a test at the 10% significance level using the Normal distribution to investigate whether there has been any change in journey time since the introduction of the new signalling equipment. You should use an estimate of the population standard deviation.

(ii) It is suggested that, because the sample size is only 30, the estimate of population standard deviation may not be very reliable. Carry out an alternative test and state an assumption necessary for this test.

⑧ Freeze drying is often used in the production of coffee. For best results, the drying rate (measured in suitable units) should be 72.0. It is thought that the drying rate in a particular batch may be higher than this. In order to test this, a sample of 12 observations was selected and the drying rates were as follows.

75   73   81   88   75   79   69   91   82   76   73   72

Hypothesis testing on a sample mean using the *t*-distribution

(i) Carry out a test at the 0.5% significance level to determine whether the drying rates in this batch are greater than the ideal. State clearly your null and alternative hypotheses and your conclusion.

(ii) What assumptions are required for your answer to part (i) to be valid?

9 A fisherman claims that pollack are not as big as they used to be. 'They used to average three quarters of a kilogram each', he says. When challenged to prove his point, he catches 20 pollack from the same shoal. Their masses (in kg) are as follows.

| 0.65 | 0.68 | 0.77 | 0.71 | 0.67 | 0.75 | 0.69 | 0.72 | 0.73 | 0.69 |
| 0.70 | 0.70 | 0.72 | 0.76 | 0.73 | 0.78 | 0.75 | 0.69 | 0.70 | 0.71 |

(i) State the null and alternative hypotheses for a test to investigate whether the fisherman's claim is true.

(ii) Carry out the test at the 5% significance level and state the conclusion.

(iii) State any assumptions underlying your procedure and comment on their validity.

10 In the game of bridge, a standard pack of 52 playing cards is dealt into four hands of 13 cards each. Players usually assess the value of their hands by counting 4 points for an ace, 3 for a King, 2 for a Queen, 1 for a Jack and nothing for any other card. The total points available from the four suits are $(4 + 3 + 2 + 1) \times 4 = 40$. So the mean number of points per hand is $\frac{40}{4} = 10$. Helene claims that she never gets good cards. One day, she is challenged to prove this and agrees to keep a record of the number of points she gets on each hand next time she plays, with the following results.

| 5 | 16 | 7 | 1 | 11 | 2 | 8 | 9 | 14 | 12 |
| 21 | 10 | 0 | 7 | 12 | 7 | 6 | 8 | 13 | 4 |

(i) What assumption underlies the use of the *t* test in this situation? To what extent do you think the assumption is justified?

(ii) State null and alternative hypotheses relating to Helene's claim.

(iii) Carry out the test at the 5% significance level and comment on the result.

(This question is set in memory of a lady called Helene who claimed that bridge hands had not been the same since the Second World War.)

11 At a bottling plant, wine bottles are filled automatically by a machine. The bottles are meant to hold 75 cl. Under-filling leads to contravention of regulations and complaints from customers. Over-filling prevents the bottles being sealed securely.

The contents of ten bottles are carefully measured and found to be as follows, in centilitres.

75.6   76.2   74.3   74.8   75.3   76.3   75.9   74.2   75.6   76.7

(i) State appropriate null and alternative hypotheses for the usual *t* test for examining whether the bottles are being filled correctly.

(ii) State the conditions necessary for correct application of this test.

(iii) Carry out the test, using a 5% significance level. [MEI]

⑫ Sugar is automatically packed by a machine into bags of nominal weight 1000 g. Due to random fluctuations and the set up of the machine, the weights of bags are, in fact, Normally distributed with mean 1020 g and standard deviation 25 g. Two bags are selected at random.

(i) Find the probability that the total weight of the two bags is less than 2000 g.

(ii) Find the probability that the weights of the two bags differ by less than 20 g.

Another machine is also in use for packing sugar into bags of nominal weight 1000 g. It is assumed that the distribution of the weights for this machine is also Normal. A random sample of nine bags packed by this machine is found to have the following weights (in grams).

1012   996   984   1005   1008   994   1003   1017   1002

(iii) Test at the 5% level of significance whether it may be assumed that the mean weight for this machine is 1000 g. [MEI]

⑬ A trial is being made of a new diet for feeding pigs. Ten pigs are selected and their increases in weight (in kilograms) are measured, over a certain period, using the new diet. The data are as follows.

15.2   13.8   14.6   15.8   13.1   14.9   17.2   15.1   14.9   15.2

The underlying population can be assumed to be Normally distributed.

(i) Using an established diet, the mean increase in weight of pigs over the period is known to be 14.0 kg. Test at the 5% level of significance whether the new diet is an improvement, stating carefully your null and alternative hypotheses and your conclusion.

(ii) Find a 95% confidence interval for the mean increase in weight using the new diet.

(iii) Little information about the conduct of the trial is given in the opening paragraph of the question. Comment on *two* aspects of how the trial should have been conducted. [MEI]

⑭ A notional allowance of 9 minutes has been given for the completion of a routine task on a production line. The operatives have complained that it appears usually to be taking slightly longer.

An inspector took a sample of 12 measurements of the time required to undertake this task. The results (in minutes) were as follows.

9.4   8.8   9.3   9.1   9.4   8.9   9.3   9.2   9.6   9.3   9.3   9.1

Hypothesis testing on a sample mean using the *t*-distribution

Stating carefully your null and alternative hypotheses and the assumptions underlying your analysis, test at the 1% level of significance whether the task is indeed taking on average longer than 9 minutes. [MEI]

15. A chemical is packed into bags by a machine. The mean weight of the chemical in the bags is controlled by the machine operator, but the standard deviation is fixed at 0.96 kg. The mean weight should be 50 kg, but it is suspected that the machine has been set to give underweight bags. You may assume that the weight of chemical in the bags is Normally distributed. The mean weight of a random sample of 36 bags is $\bar{x}$ kg.

   (i) If $\bar{x} = 49.7$, is there evidence at the 5% significance level to support the suspicion? You must state the null and alternative hypotheses.

   (ii) Find the maximum value of $\bar{x}$ for which the null hypothesis would be accepted at the 5% level.

   (iii) If, in fact, the population mean $\mu = 49.9$, then

      (a) state whether the null or alternative hypothesis should be accepted

      (b) state the distribution of the sample mean $\bar{X}$,

      (c) Hence find the probability that the sample mean $\bar{X}$ is greater than the value found in part (ii),

      (d) State the probability that the test comes to a correct conclusion.
   [MEI ADAPTED]

16. Archaeologists have discovered that all skulls found in excavated sites in a certain country belong either to racial Group A or to racial Group B. The mean lengths of skulls from Group A and Group B are 190 mm and 196 mm, respectively. The standard deviation for each group is 8 mm, and skull lengths are distributed Normally and independently.

   A new excavation produced 12 skulls of mean length x and there is reason to believe that all these skulls belong to Group A. It is required to test this belief statistically with the null hypothesis (H_0) that all the skulls belong to Group A and the alternative hypothesis (H_1) that all the skulls belong to Group B.

   (i) State the distribution of the mean length of 12 skulls when H_0 is true.

   (ii) Explain why a test of H_0 versus H_1 should take the form: 'Reject H_0 if $\bar{x} > c$', where c is some critical value.

   (iii) Calculate this critical value c to the nearest 0.1 mm when the probability of rejecting H_0 when it is, in fact, true is chosen to be 0.05.

   (iv) Perform the test, given that the lengths (in mm) of the 12 skulls are as follows.

      204.1   201.1   187.4   196.4   202.5   185.0

      192.6   181.6   194.5   183.2   200.3   202.9   [MEI]

4 The Wilcoxon signed rank test on a sample median

Local M.P.'s popularity plummets

Following her controversial remarks about people being replaced by robots in our new society, local M.P. Glenda Sykes has seen her approval rating drop from 52% to a mere 29%.

In the past, a politician's popularity was measured by the size of the crowds she or he drew. These days, it is more common for opinion pollsters to ask us questions like the one below.

'The Prime Minister is doing the best possible job, in the circumstances.' Please choose one of the following responses.

Table 11.1

agree strongly	agree	inclined to agree	have no opinion	inclined to disagree	disagree	disagree strongly

You will probably recognise this as the sort of question that is asked by opinion pollsters. However, surveys of people's attitudes are not just undertaken on political issues: market researchers for businesses, local authorities, psychologists and pressure groups, for instance, are all interested in what we think about a very wide variety of issues.

You are going to test the hypothesis:

The Prime Minister's performance is generally disapproved of.

The question above was asked of a group of twelve 17-year-olds and each reply recorded as a number from 1 to 7, where 1 indicates 'agree strongly', and 7 indicates 'disagree strongly'. This method of recording responses gives a *rating scale* of attitudes to the Prime Minister's performance. The data obtained are shown below.

3   6   7   4   3   4   7   3   5   6   5   6

The Wilcoxon signed rank test on a sample median

What do these data indicate about the validity of the hypothesis in the population from which the sample was drawn?

You should recognise this question as similar to those you asked when conducting *t* tests. You want to know whether attitudes in the population as a whole are centred around the neutral response of '4' or show lower approval in general. That is, you want a **test of location** of the sample: one which decides what values are taken, on average, in the population.

You could not use a *t* test here to decide whether the mean of the underlying distribution equals 4 because the response variable is clearly not Normally distributed: it only takes discrete values from 1 to 7 (and the sample size is small).

This chapter looks at the Wilcoxon single sample test (also called the Wilcoxon signed rank test), a test of location which is valid even for small samples. It does not require the strict distributional assumptions needed for the *t* test, and so is more widely applicable.

> **Note**
>
> Tests such as the Wilcoxon test are known as *'non-parametric'* since they do not rely on the parameters of a probability distribution. You may recall that you met such a test in Chapter 4 for Spearman's rank correlation coefficient.

Suppose that, despite your hypothesis, there is no tendency to approve or disapprove of the Prime Minister. Then it would seem plausible that in the population from which the data are drawn the response variable should be modelled as follows.

- It has a median value of 4: that is, half approve and half disapprove.
- It is symmetrically distributed about this median value: so, for example, you do not have half strongly approving and half slightly disapproving.

The strategy you adopt, therefore, is to test the following hypotheses, on the assumption that responses are symmetrically distributed about the median.

H_0: the median response is 4.

H_1: the median response is greater than 4.

Note the form of the alternative hypothesis which reflects the fact that the original question was one-tailed ('is the Prime Minister generally disapproved of?').

The Wilcoxon test, like Spearman's rank correlation test (see Chapter 4), is based on ranks. In the Wilcoxon case, however, you do not rank the actual data themselves, but their distances from the hypothesised median of the population, in this case, 4.

For these data this gives the following results.

> **Note**
> Notice that the two people who gave a rating of 4 (equal to the median) have been omitted. This has reduced the sample size from 12 to 10.

> **Note**
> Where two or more ratings have the same difference, they are given the appropriate 'average rank', i.e. the mean.
> In this case, there are five rankings of 1 so they should occupy the ranks 1, 2, 3, 4 and 5; instead, they are all given the average rank of 3.
> Similarly, the two rankings of 3 should occupy ranks 9 and 10 so both are given the mean rank of 9.5.

> **Note**
> You will probably have met the formula which states that the sum of the first n natural numbers is $\frac{1}{2}n(n+1)$

Table 11.2

Rating, r	$r - 4$	$|r - 4|$	Rank
3	−1	1	3
6	2	2	7
7	3	3	9.5
3	−1	1	3
7	3	3	9.5
3	−1	1	3
5	1	1	3
6	2	2	7
5	1	1	3
6	3	2	7

- The ratings are ranked according to their absolute differences from the median
- The rating with the smallest difference is given the lowest ranking
- Similarly, the rating with the highest difference is given the highest ranking

Suppose that the assumption of symmetry is correct, and the null hypothesis that the median is 4 is true. Then you would expect a rating of 5 to come up as often as a rating of 3, a rating of 6 to come up as often as a rating of 2 and a rating of 7 to come up as often as a rating of 1. In other words, ratings at each distance from the supposed median of 4 should be equally likely to be above or below that median.

To test whether the data support this, the next step is to calculate the sum of the ranks of the ratings above 4 and below 4 and compare these with the total sum of the ranks. Here:

sum of ranks of ratings above $4 = 7 + 9.5 + 9.5 + 3 + 7 + 3 + 7 = 46$

sum of ranks of ratings below $4 = 3 + 3 + 3 = 9$
total sum of ranks $= 9 + 46 = 55.$

Note that, because of the way in which the ratings were ranked, the total sum of ranks must be equal to the sum of the numbers from 1 to 10:

$1 + 2 + \cdots + 10 = \frac{1}{2} \times 10 \times (10 + 1) = 55.$

If the null hypothesis is true, you may expect the sum of the ranks of ratings above 4 to be approximately equal to the sum of the ranks of ratings below 4. This means that each would be about half of 55, i.e. 27.5. The fact that for these data the sum of ranks of ratings above 4 is considerably more than this, and the sum of ranks of ratings below 4 correspondingly less, implies either that more people disapproved than approved or that those who disapproved tended to disapprove more, so that the larger rank sum is associated with disapproval.

Actually, both of these are true of the data.

In order to conduct a hypothesis test, you need to know the critical values of the test statistic. Tables of the critical values for the Wilcoxon test are available, and a section of one is shown in Table 11.3. Later in the chapter, you will see how these tables are calculated.

The Wilcoxon signed rank test on a sample median

Table 11.3 Critical values for the Wilcoxon single sample test

One-tailed Two-tailed	5% 10%	2½% 5%	1% 2%	½% 1%
n				
2				
3				
4				
5	0			
6	2	0		
7	3	2	0	
8	5	3	1	0
9	8	5	3	1
10	10	8	5	3
11	13	10	7	5
12	17	13	9	7
13	21	17	12	9
14	25	21	15	12
15	30	25	19	15

The test you are conducting is one-tailed because you are trying to decide whether your data indicate disapproval; that is, whether the sum of ranks corresponding to approval is significantly smaller and, equivalently, whether the sum of ranks corresponding to disapproval is significantly larger than chance would suggest. The table is constructed to give the largest value of the rank sum that can be regarded as significantly smaller than chance would suggest, so it is the sum of ranks corresponding to approval (those ratings below 4) that provide the test statistic; it is often denoted by W. In this case, its value is 9 and so this is the number to be compared with the critical value.

Once the two subjects with no opinion are excluded, you have a sample size of 10, and, for a one-tailed test at the 5% significance level, the table gives a critical value of 10. This means that any value less than or equal to 10 for the sum of the ranks of the ratings below 4 lies in the critical region. In this example, the data give a test statistic $W = 9$, so you can reject the null hypothesis in favour of the alternative hypothesis that the median is greater than 4.

Formal procedure for the Wilcoxon ranked sum test

The work in the previous example may be stated more formally.

- The hypotheses to be tested are as follows.

H_0: the population median of a random variable is equal to a given value M.

H_1: either (a) the population median $\neq M$ ← two-tailed test

or (b) the population median > M ← one-tailed tests
or (c) the population median < M. ←

- The null hypothesis is based on the assumption that the random variable is symmetrically distributed about its median.
- The data are the values $x_1, x_2, \ldots, x_n$ of the random variable from a sample of size n. If any of these is equal to M, it is removed from the list and the value of n is reduced accordingly.
- To calculate the test statistic you take the following steps.

1. Calculate the absolute differences between each sample value and the hypothesised median M, i.e.
$x_1 - M, x_2 - M, \ldots, x_n - M$.
2. Rank these values from 1 to n, giving the lowest rank to the smallest absolute difference. If two or more absolute differences are equal, each is given the rank which is the mean of the ranking positions they occupy together.
3. Calculate the sum W_+ of the ranks of the sample values which are greater than M, and the sum W_- of the ranks of the sample values which are less than M.
4. Check that $W_+ + W_- = \frac{1}{2}n(n+1)$; this must work because the right-hand side is the formula for the sum of the numbers from 1 to n, i.e. the total of all the ranks.
5. The test statistic W is then found as follows:

- for the two-tailed alternative hypothesis (a), take the test statistic W to be the smaller of W_- and W_+
- for the one-tailed alternative hypothesis (b), take $W = W_-$
- for the one-tailed alternative hypothesis (c), take $W = W_+$.
  - Reject the null hypothesis is rejected if W is *less than or equal to* the appropriate critical value found in the tables which depends on the sample size, the chosen significance level and whether the test is one- or two-tailed.

> **Note**
> Note that if the assumption of symmetry of the distribution about its median is true then this median is also the mean.

> **Discussion points**
> This test is sometimes called the Wilcoxon single sample test and at other times the Wilcoxon signed rank test. Explain these two names.

Rationale for the Wilcoxon test

As you have seen, the sum of W_+ and W_- is determined by the sample size, so that the criterion for rejecting the null hypothesis is that the difference between W_+ and W_- is large enough. What makes this difference large?

Take the case where W_+ is much larger than W_-. (The rationale is just the same if it is W_- that is much larger.) This requires W_+ to contain *more* ranks, or *larger* ranks than W_-. This will occur if *most* of the sample or the *more extreme* values (those furthest from the hypothesised median) in the sample are above the median rather than below. The largest difference between W_+ and W_- will therefore occur if the sample contains only a few values just below the hypothesised median and many values well above the hypothesised median. This is exactly the situation which would cast most doubt on the claim that the suggested median is the true one.

The Wilcoxon signed rank test on a sample median

Figure 11.7 shows the frequency distribution of a representative sample of size 15 drawn from a population which has median 1. The distribution is not symmetrical; it has strong positive skew.

Discussion point

What happens if you apply the Wilcoxon two-tailed test to this sample using a 10% significance level?

Do you come to the correct conclusion? If not, why not?

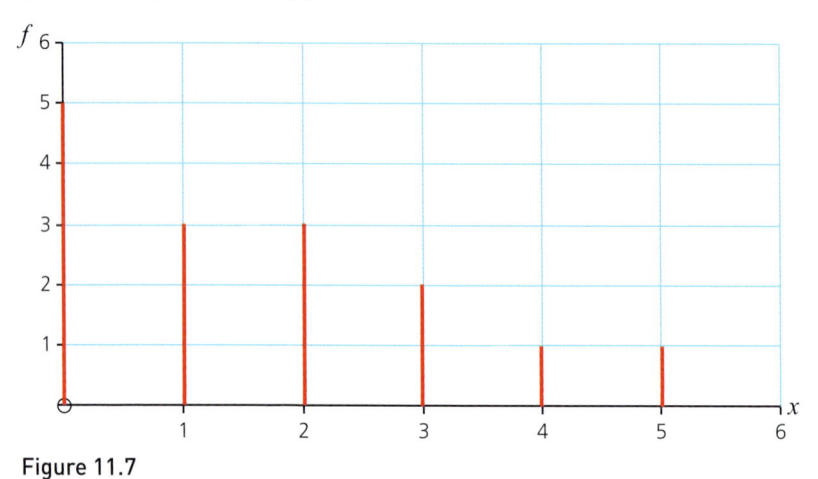

Figure 11.7

Example 11.3

A railway Customer Service Division knows from long experience that if passengers are asked to rate a railway company's buffet car service on a scale from 1 to 10 their responses are symmetrically distributed about a median of 4.5.

After an experimental trolley service is introduced on a particular route, passengers are asked to rate this service on a scale from 1 to 10. The ratings of a sample of 16 passengers were as follows.

2   4   1   4   9   3   3   5
6   2   1   2   5   6   2   4

Is there evidence at the 5% level that passengers rate this service differently?

Solution

The test can be specified as follows.

Null hypothesis: H_0: the ratings are symmetrically distributed about a median of 4.5.

Alternative hypothesis: H_1: the ratings are symmetrically distributed about a median different from 4.5.

Significance level: 5%

Test: two-tailed.

When placed in order the ratings are as follows.

1   1   2   2   2   2   3   3
4   4   4   5   5   6   6   9

The first step in calculating W_+ and W_- is to draw up a table giving the absolute differences of the ratings from the hypothesised median.

Table 11.4

Rating, r	Frequency	r − 4.5	|r − 4.5|
1	2	−3.5	3.5
2	4	−2.5	2.5
3	2	−1.5	1.5
4	3	−0.5	0.5
5	2	0.5	0.5

The ranks are found from these data as follows.

The smallest absolute difference that you are ranking is 0.5. This corresponds to ratings of 4 and 5 and occurs with frequency 3 + 2 = 5; so the ranks, 1, 2, 3, 4 and 5 are associated with 0.5. The mean of these ranks is 3.

The next absolute difference being ranked is 1.5, which occurs with frequency 2 + 2 = 4, so the ranks 6, 7, 8 and 9 are associated with 1.5. The mean of these ranks is 7.5.

A complete list of ranks can now be drawn up by the same method and added to the table.

Table 11.5

Rating, r	Frequency	r −4.5	|r −4.5|	Rank
1	2	−3.5	3.5	14.5
2	4	−2.5	2.5	11.5
3	2	−1.5	1.5	7.5
4	3	−0.5	0.5	3
5	2	0.5	0.5	3
6	2	1.5	1.5	7.5
9	1	4.5	4.5	16

The sum of the ranks for the ratings below the median of 4.5 is:

$W_- = 14.5 \times 2 + 11.5 \times 4 + 7.5 \times 2 + 3 \times 3 = 99$

and the sum of the ranks for the ratings above the median is:

$W_+ = 3 \times 2 + 7.5 \times 2 + 16 \times 1 = 37$.

Check: $W_- + W_+ = 99 + 37 = 136 = \frac{1}{2} \times 16 \times 17$.

This is a two-tailed test, so the test statistic, W, is taken to be the smaller of W_+ and W_- which in this case is $W_+ = 37$.

From the tables, the critical value for a two-tailed test on a sample of size 16, using the 5% significance level, is 29. But 37 > 29 so there is no significant evidence that the rankings of the trolley service are different from those of the buffet car and you accept the null hypothesis.

The Wilcoxon signed rank test on a sample median

Why Wilcoxon?

Both the Wilcoxon test and the *t* test are testing whether the distribution of a random variable in a population has a given value of a **location parameter**. A location parameter is any parameter which, when it varies, shifts the position of all the values taken by the random variable but not the shape of the distribution. For instance, in the family of Normal distributions, the mean is a location parameter but the variance is not; in the family of rectangular distributions, the mid-range is a location parameter but the range is not.

The value of the Wilcoxon test is that it does not make the rather strict distributional assumption of the *t* test that the distribution of the random variable is Normal. It is therefore very useful when this assumption is not thought to be justified, and when the sample size is not large enough for the sample means, nevertheless, to be Normally distributed.

In fact, although the Wilcoxon test places a less severe restriction than the *t* test on the family of distributions which the underlying variable might possess, it is nonetheless of comparable power when compared to the *t* test under a wide range of conditions. This means that it is a sensible choice for testing location, even when a *t* test might also be justifiable.

Exercise 11.2

① A two-tailed Wilcoxon test is carried out on a sample of size 15. The values of W_- and W_+ are 84 and 36, respectively.
   (i) Write down the critical value for the test at the 5% level.
   (ii) State whether the null hypothesis should be accepted or rejected.

② A Wilcoxon test is carried out to investigate hypotheses as follows.
   H_0: the ratings are symmetrically distributed about a median of 25.
   H_1: the ratings are symmetrically distributed about a median greater than 25.
   The values of W_- and W_+ are 8 and 37, respectively
   (i)   Find the sample size (assuming that none of the values in the sample is equal to 25).
   (ii) Write down the critical value for the test at the 5% level.
   (iii) Complete the test.

③ Gerry runs 5000 m races for his local athletics club. His coach has been monitoring his practice times for several months and he believes that their median is 15.3 minutes. The coach suggests that Gerry should try running with a pacemaker in order to see if this can improve his times. Subsequently, a random sample of ten of Gerry's times with the pacemaker is collected to see if any reduction has been achieved. A test is carried out using the hypotheses below to investigate whether the times have reduced.
   H_0: the times are symmetrically distributed about a median of 15.3.
   H_1: the times are symmetrically distributed about a median less than 15.3.
   The spreadsheet output below shows the calculations for a Wilcoxon test to investigate this.

	A	B	C	D	E	F
1	Time	Time - 15.3	|Time - 15.3|	Rank	Negative	Positive
2	14.86	-0.44	0.44	7	7	
3	15.00	-0.30	0.30	4	4	
4	15.62	0.32	0.32	5		5
5	14.44	-0.86	0.86	9	9	
6	15.27	-0.03	0.03	1	1	
7	15.64	0.34	0.34	6		6
8	14.58	-0.72	0.72	8	8	
9	14.30	-1.00	1.00	10	10	
10	15.08	-0.22	0.22	2.5	2.5	
11	15.08	-0.22	0.22	2.5	2.5	
12				Sum	44	11

Figure 11.8

(i) Write down the values of W_- and W_+.

(ii) Explain why the sum of W_- and W_+ must be equal to 55.

(iii) Carry out the test at the 5% level of significance.

④ An ancient human settlement site in the Harz mountains has been explored by archaeologists over a long period. They have established by a radio-carbon method that the ages of bones found at the site are approximately uniformly distributed between 3250 and 3100 years. A new potassium–argon method of dating has now been developed and 11 samples of bone randomly selected from finds at the site are dated by this new method. The ages, in years, determined by the new method are as listed below.

3115   3234   3247   3198   3177   3226
3124   3204   3166   3194   3220

Is there evidence at the 5% level that the potassium–argon method is producing different dates, on average, for bones from the site?

⑤ A local education authority sets a reasoning test to all eleven-year-olds in the borough. The scores of the whole borough on this test have been symmetrically distributed around a median of 24 out of 40 over many years. One year, a primary school's 33 leavers have the following scores out of 40.

21   11   34   32   19   23   26   35   21   35   40
13   15   28   31   26   21   16   24   22   29   36
38   37   27   22   20   18   32   37   29   28   33

Is there evidence at the 5% level to support the headteacher's claim that her leavers score better on the reasoning test than average?

When must this claim have been made if the hypothesis test is to be valid?

⑥ An investigator stopped a sample of 50 city workers and checked the time shown by their watches against an accurate timer. The number of minutes fast (+) or slow (−) is recorded for each watch, and the data are shown.

+2   0   +4   0   −1   −7   +1   +2   +2
−1   −3   +2   −4   −1   0   +3   +2   +3
+1   −1   +8   +4   −2   −4   +5   +1   −2
−3   +2   0   +2   +4   +2   0   +3   −1
−2   −4   +1   +3   +6   +2   0   −6   0
−1   −2   +1   +2   +2

Is there evidence at the 5% level that city workers tend to keep their watches running fast?

The Wilcoxon signed rank test on a sample median

7. Becotide inhalers for asthmatics are supposed to deliver 50 mg of the active ingredient per puff. In a test in a government laboratory, 17 puffs from randomly selected inhalers in a batch were tested and the amount of active ingredient that was delivered was determined. The results, in milligrams, are given below.

43	47	52	51	44	50	51	41	48
46	52	50	47	45	49	46	42	

    Is there evidence at the 2% level that the inhalers are not delivering the correct amount of active ingredient per puff?

8. (i) Under what circumstances might one use a Wilcoxon single sample test in order to test a hypothesis about the median of a population? What distributional assumption is needed for the test?

    (ii) On a stretch of road leading out of the centre of a town, highways officials have been monitoring the speed of the traffic in case it has increased. Previously, it was known that the median speed on this stretch was 28.7 miles per hour. For a random sample of 12 vehicles on the stretch, the following speeds were recorded.

    32.0 29.1 26.1 35.2 34.4 28.6 32.3 28.5 27.0 33.3 28.2 31.9

    Carry out a test, with a 5% significance level, to see whether the speed of the traffic on this stretch of road seems to have increased on the whole. [MEI]

9. At a large secondary school, the median number of half days absent per pupil per year (based on several years' records) was known to be 23. Last year, the school carried out a drive to lower the number of absences. A random sample of 12 pupils had been absent for the following numbers of half days during the year.

    14 10 15 13 35 9 24 19 30 26 29 8

    (i) Why might a Wilcoxon test be appropriate?

    (ii) What distributional assumption is needed for the test?

    (iii) Carry out the test, using a 5% level of significance. [MEI]

10. When a consignment of grain arrives at Rotterdam docks the percentage of moisture in 11 samples is measured. It is claimed that when the ship left Ontario, the percentage of moisture in the grain was 2.353%, on average. The percentages found in the samples were as follows

5.294	0.824	3.353	1.706	3.765	3.235
8.235	0.760	3.412	6.471	3.471	

    (i) Test at the 5% level whether the median percentage of moisture in the grain is greater than 2.353, using the Wilcoxon single sample test. What assumptions are you making about the distribution of the percentage of moisture in the grain?

    (ii) Test at the 5% level whether the mean percentage of moisture in the grain is greater than 2.353, using the t test. What assumption are you making about the distribution of the percentage of moisture in the grain?

    (iii) Compare your two conclusions and comment.

⑪ Check the claim in the tables that the critical value for the Wilcoxon single sample test, at the 5% level, for a sample of size nine is 8.

Hint: There are $2^9 = 512$ different sets of ranks that, under the null hypothesis, are equally likely to make up W_+ but it is only necessary to write down those with the smallest rank sums – the sets giving rank sums up to and including 9 are sufficient to verify the result. For example, the sets $\{1\}, \{2, 3\}, \{1, 3, 6\}$ all have sums of 9 or less.

⑫ An estate agent claims that the median price of detached houses in a certain area is £230 000. An advertising standards officer takes a random sample of ten such houses that have recently been sold and finds that their prices (in £) are:

| 276 000 | 220 000 | 235 000 | 260 000 | 243 800 |
| 212 000 | 330 000 | 268 000 | 259 000 | 250 000. |

(i) Suggest why a Normal distribution might not be a suitable model for the underlying population of prices.

(ii) Calculate the value of the Wilcoxon single sample test statistic for examining the estate agent's claim.

(iii) Taking the alternative hypothesis to be that the median price is not £230 000, and using suitable tables, state the critical region for a test at

(a) the 5% level of significance
(b) the 1% level of significance.

(iv) What is your conclusion in respect of the estate agent's claim?

(v) Find the level of significance of the data as given by the approximation

$$N\left(\frac{n(n+1)}{4}, \frac{n(n+1)(2n+1)}{24}\right)$$

to the distribution of the test statistic if the null hypothesis is true. Comment on the accuracy of the approximation in the light of your answers to part (iii).

KEY POINTS

1 **Hypothesis test for the mean using a Normal distribution**

- Sample data may be used to carry out a hypothesis test on the null hypothesis that the population mean has some particular value μ_0, i.e. $H_0: \mu = \mu_0$.
- The alternative hypothesis takes one of the three forms.
  - $H_1: \mu \neq \mu_0$
  - $H_1: \mu < \mu_0$
  - $H_1: \mu > \mu_0$
- The test statistic $z = \dfrac{\bar{x} - \mu_0}{\frac{\sigma}{\sqrt{n}}}$ is used.
- If the sample is large, you can use the sample standard deviation s as an estimate of the population standard deviation σ if the latter is not known.

The Wilcoxon signed rank test on a sample median

- If the sample is large, then using the central limit theorem, you can carry out a test using a Normal distribution even is the distribution of the parent population is not known.

2 **Hypothesis test for the mean using a t distribution**
   - If the population is Normally distributed but the population standard deviation σ is not known then, whatever the sample size, you can carry out a hypothesis test using a t distribution.
   - The null hypothesis is the same as for the Normal distribution $H_0: \mu = \mu_0$.
   - You estimate the population standard deviation using the sample standard deviation s.
   - The test statistic $t = \dfrac{\bar{x} - \mu_0}{\dfrac{s}{\sqrt{n}}}$ is used.

3 **Hypothesis test for the median using the Wilcoxon signed rank test**
   - This is used for testing the null hypothesis that the population median of a random variable is equal to a given value M, under the assumption that the variable is symmetrically distributed about its median.
   - Given a sample, remove any element equal to M. Let n be the size of the reduced sample.
   - To calculate the test statistic:
     - Find the absolute differences between each sample value and M.
     - Rank these values giving the lowest rank to the smallest difference.
     - W_+ and W_- are the sums of ranks of sample values, respectively greater or less than M.
     - Take the test statistic W to be the smaller of W_- and W_+ for a two-tailed test, or make the appropriate choice for a one-tailed test.
   - The null hypothesis is rejected if W is less than or equal to the appropriate critical value.

LEARNING OUTCOMES

When you have completed this chapter you should be able to:

▶ carry out a hypothesis test for a single population mean using the Normal or t distributions and know when it is appropriate to do so

▶ carry out a hypothesis test for a single population median using the Wilcoxon signed rank test and know when it is appropriate to do so.

12 Simulation

But to us, probability is the very guide of life.
Bishop Joseph Butler (1756)

In a game at a charity fair, five dice are rolled. In order to win a small prize, the total score has to be at least 21. What is the probability of winning? You could actually roll five dice many times to find an estimate of the probability. Alternatively, you can use a spreadsheet to estimate the probability.

In fact, it would not be too difficult to calculate this particular probability. However, many situations that you would like to analyse may well be too complicated even for sophisticated mathematical techniques.

Simulation

> There are several different types and versions of spreadsheet and the commands are not exactly the same on all of them. When a command is required in this chapter, it is written as 'for example, …'. The command given may work on your spreadsheet but it may not. If it does not, check the function help on your spreadsheet to find the equivalent.

Example 12.1

How would you use a spreadsheet to simulate throwing five dice?

How would this allow you to find the probability of getting a winning total score of at least 21?

Solution

You can generate random numbers between 1 and 6 using a spreadsheet formula.

- Use the command provided by your spreadsheet, for example =RANDBETWEEN(1,6).
- Then find the sum of the five scores using the =SUM formula, as shown in Figure 12.1.

	A	B	C	D	E	F	G
1							Sum
2	Score on dice	2	1	4	1	2	10

Figure 12.1

Clearly, this single simulation gives you no idea of what the probability of winning actually is. It needs to be repeated many times. You can simply highlight cells A2 to G2 and copy them down to produce something like the spreadsheet in Figure 12.2.

	A	B	C	D	E	F	G
1							Sum
2	Scores on dice	1	2	1	2	6	12
3	Scores on dice	2	6	2	6	1	17
4	Scores on dice	1	5	6	3	4	19
5	Scores on dice	3	1	5	1	4	14
6	Scores on dice	5	5	3	3	4	20
7	Scores on dice	4	5	5	4	3	21
8	Scores on dice	6	1	3	3	4	17
9	Scores on dice	5	6	3	5	1	20
10	Scores on dice	5	1	1	3	3	13
11	Scores on dice	2	6	6	6	5	25
12	Scores on dice	4	6	6	5	2	23
13	Scores on dice	6	4	2	6	3	21
14	Scores on dice	3	1	4	2	3	13
15	Scores on dice	3	1	3	1	3	11
16	Scores on dice	5	5	3	3	4	20
17	Scores on dice	5	6	4	1	6	22
18	Scores on dice	2	2	4	4	5	17
19	Scores on dice	1	1	1	3	1	7
20	Scores on dice	5	1	1	6	6	19
21	Scores on dice	3	6	6	6	4	25

Figure 12.2

In this particular simulation, there are 6 out of the 20 simulated values which give a sum of at least 21, so you would estimate the probability to be 6 out of 20 or 0.3.

You can, in fact, use the command provided by your spreadsheet, for example =COUNTIF(G2:G21,">20"), to count the number of values which are 21 or more, rather than having to count them one by one for yourself.

However, this is only one simulation and the result will probably be different if you carry out another simulation. To repeat the simulation, you need to recalculate the formulae in the spreadsheet, for example by pressing the function key F9, which recalculates all of the values with new random numbers. Alternatively, you could copy down for many more rows in the spreadsheet. Figure 12.3 shows the start of 500 trials, together with the number of times that the score is at least 21 and the estimated probability.

	A	B	C	D	E	F	G	H	I	J
1							Sum			
2	Scores on dice	1	2	1	2	6	12		Number at least 21	113
3	Scores on dice	2	6	2	6	1	17		Probability	0.226
4	Scores on dice	1	5	6	3	4	19			
501	Scores on dice	2	3	1	6	6	18			

Figure 12.3

You might think that with 500 trials, the estimate of the probability would be very close to the true value. However, if you repeatedly recalculate the formulae (for example, by pressing the F9 key) the probabilities have quite a large range of values. For two recalculations of this simulation, the probabilities obtained were 0.192 and 0.256, so to get a more accurate estimate, you would have to have many more rows and/or repeat the simulation many times. In fact, simply using many more rows and performing just one simulation is not a good way to proceed since it does not give you any idea of variation. It is far better to repeat the simulation many times (preferably with more rows than 500) and then you will have a much better idea of the variation in the different simulated values.

SPREADSHEET INVESTIGATIONS 12.1

1   Carry out the above simulation many times with 500 rows. Record the probabilities on a new page of your spreadsheet. Now make a final estimate of the probability of getting a score of at least 21. Examine also the variation in your individual estimates.
2   Repeat Number 1 above but using 5000 rows in your spreadsheet. How good do you think your estimate in Number 1 was?
3   Set up a spreadsheet to estimate the probability that the total score on 20 dice is less than 50, using 500 rows. Is there any difference in the likely accuracy of your estimate when you are using 20 dice instead of 5?
4   Repeat Number 3 above but using 5000 rows in your spreadsheet.

1 Simulating discrete uniform distributions

The situation above is an example of the discrete uniform distribution which you met in Chapter 3. It is easy to simulate any discrete uniform distribution using the command provided by your spreadsheet, for example =RANDBETWEEN(a, b), where a and b are the minimum and maximum values. Example 12.2 below is another illustration of this.

Example 12.2

An eight-sided fair spinner has sectors labelled {10, 11, … 17}. The spinner is spun ten times.

Estimate the probability that the difference between the lowest and highest scores on the spinner is less than 4.

Solution

Set up a spreadsheet using the command provided by your spreadsheet, for example =RANDBETWEEN(10,17).

Then use the commands provided by your spreadsheet, for example MAX and MIN to find the maximum and minimum values.

Then count the number of differences which are less than four. Use, for example, the =COUNTIF command.

Finally, estimate the probability by dividing the number of values less than 4 by the total number of trials.

In a simulation with 50 trials, the probability worked out to 0.06. Figure 12.4 shows the first 12 rows of this simulation (with columns C to H hidden) together with the probability calculation.

> **Note**
>
> This example and the one above are fairly simple to express in words, but to calculate the probabilities would be fairly difficult. Simulation offers a much easier way of obtaining an estimate of these probabilities.

	A	B	J	K	L	M	N	O
1			Min	Max	Difference			
2	Score on spinner	10	10	17	7			
3	Score on spinner	13	10	14	4		Number less than 4	3
4	Score on spinner	12	11	15	4		Probability	0.06
5	Score on spinner	14	10	17	7			
6	Score on spinner	11	11	17	6			
7	Score on spinner	17	10	17	7			
8	Score on spinner	10	10	17	7			
9	Score on spinner	15	10	17	7			
10	Score on spinner	14	13	17	4			
11	Score on spinner	15	10	17	7			
12	Score on spinner	10	10	17	7			
13	Score on spinner	10	10	17	7			

Figure 12.4

Figure 12.5 shows the formulae used in the spreadsheet in Figure 12.4.

	A	B	J	K	L	M	N	O
1			Min	Max	Difference			
2	Score on spinner	=RANDBETWEEN(10,17)	=MIN(B2:I2)	=MAX(B2:I2)	=K2-J2			
3	Score on spinner	=RANDBETWEEN(10,17)	=MIN(B3:I3)	=MAX(B3:I3)	=K3-J3		Number less than 4	=COUNTIF(L2:L51,"<4")
4	Score on spinner	=RANDBETWEEN(10,17)	=MIN(B4:I4)	=MAX(B4:I4)	=K4-J4		Probability	=O3/50
5	Score on spinner	=RANDBETWEEN(10,17)	=MIN(B5:I5)	=MAX(B5:I5)	=K5-J5			
6	Score on spinner	=RANDBETWEEN(10,17)	=MIN(B6:I6)	=MAX(B6:I6)	=K6-J6			
7	Score on spinner	=RANDBETWEEN(10,17)	=MIN(B7:I7)	=MAX(B7:I7)	=K7-J7			
8	Score on spinner	=RANDBETWEEN(10,17)	=MIN(B8:I8)	=MAX(B8:I8)	=K8-J8			
9	Score on spinner	=RANDBETWEEN(10,17)	=MIN(B9:I9)	=MAX(B9:I9)	=K9-J9			
10	Score on spinner	=RANDBETWEEN(10,17)	=MIN(B10:I10)	=MAX(B10:I10)	=K10-J10			
11	Score on spinner	=RANDBETWEEN(10,17)	=MIN(B11:I11)	=MAX(B11:I11)	=K11-J11			
12	Score on spinner	=RANDBETWEEN(10,17)	=MIN(B12:I12)	=MAX(B12:I12)	=K12-J12			
13	Score on spinner	=RANDBETWEEN(10,17)	=MIN(B13:I13)	=MAX(B13:I13)	=K13-J13			

Figure 12.5

> **Note**
>
> In this situation as in most simulations, you need to have a fairly large number of repetitions of the situation. Once you have this, you then need to recalculate the spreadsheet many times in order to both find the required value (in this case, the probability that the difference is less than 4) and to find out how much variation there is in the simulated probability.

You must then repeat the simulation many times to give a good estimate of the required probability. The average number of times that the difference is less than 4 in a total of 100 simulations is 1.80. This means that an estimate of the required probability is 0.018. Figure 12.6 is a vertical line graph showing the number of times that the number of differences is less than 4. As you can see, the most common value is 1, but 2 and 3 occur fairly frequently too.

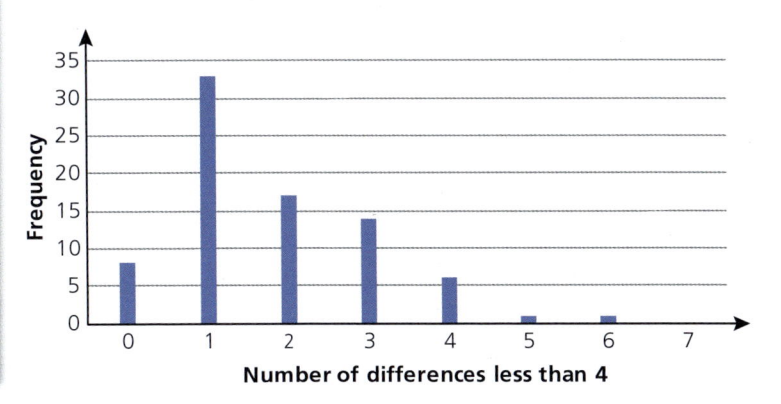

Figure 12.6

2 Simulating continuous uniform distributions

Just as discrete uniform distributions can be simulated using the commands provided by your spreadsheet, for example =RANDBETWEEN, continuous uniform distributions can be simulated using, for example, the =RAND spreadsheet command. The =RAND command gives a random number between 0 and 1. To simulate a random variable between a and b, you can use the formula $= a + (b - a) \star \text{RAND}()$.

Example 12.3

X and Y are independent random variables.

X is uniformly distributed over the interval (10, 50), Y is uniformly distributed over the interval (0, 10). Estimate the probability that $X - 4Y > 0$.

> **Note**
>
> RAND() gives a random number between 0 and 1. Multiplying by $(b - a)$ gives a random number with the correct range of values, but starting at zero. Finally, adding a to this gives a random number in the range from a to b.

Solution

You need to take the following steps

- Set up a spreadsheet using two RAND formulae:
  - For X you need $= 10 + 40 \star \text{RAND}()$.
  - For Y you need $= 10 \star \text{RAND}()$.
- Then find $X - 4Y$.
- Then copy down a number of rows.

Simulating Normal distributions

- Find the number of values of $X - 4Y$ which are greater than zero, using, for example, the =COUNTIF command.
- Finally, estimate the probability by dividing the number of values of $X - 4Y$ which are greater than zero by the total number of trials.

Figure 12.7 below shows a simulation with 1000 trials.

	A	B	C	D	E	F	G	H
1	X	Y	X - 4Y					Estimated probabilities
2	41.4996	3.29809	28.3073					0.735
3	11.7708	6.64511	-14.81		Number > 0	713		0.724
4	31.548	2.44607	21.7637		Estimated probability	0.713		0.739
5	18.9578	6.58669	-7.3889					0.733
6	13.2481	5.32213	-8.0404					0.724
7	42.1605	7.24517	13.1798					0.694
8	42.0609	4.01712	25.9924					0.709
9	39.5089	7.23313	10.5764					0.705
10	32.6192	5.2062	11.7944					0.716
11	27.7012	2.53016	17.5805					0.713
12	43.0868	4.00937	27.0493					
13	20.5624	7.74684	-10.425				Average	0.7193
14	31.4812	6.62041	4.99955					
15	41.4301	0.22243	40.5404					
16	42.4697	9.58281	4.13848					
17	32.0749	7.3886	2.52052					
991	23.2617	9.3464	-14.124					
992	35.3335	9.37893	-2.1822					
993	40.7136	9.22927	3.79649					
994	21.2714	4.67656	2.56513					
995	40.2288	9.01125	4.18375					
996	15.4144	7.81915	-15.862					
997	17.6517	3.70688	2.82416					
998	35.5909	6.23464	10.6524					
999	38.6513	0.55228	36.4421					
1000	24.5697	6.95819	-3.2631					
1001	12.5986	9.93924	-27.158					

Figure 12.7

The column on the right of the spreadsheet shows the results of ten simulations, each of 1000 trials. You can see that the estimated probabilities all lie between 0.694 and 0.739. Their average is 0.7192. You can be fairly certain, therefore, that the true probability lies between 0.71 and 0.73.

3 Simulating Normal distributions

You can simulate a Normal random variable on a spreadsheet, using, for example, the =NORM.INV command. This has three inputs: the probability, the mean and the standard deviation. The probability is a random variable between 0 and 1 and this can be simulated using =RAND().

So, for example, to simulate a Normal variable with mean 10 and standard deviation 5, you can use =NORM.INV(RAND(), 10, 5), 10, 5). Copying this formula down will give as many examples as you want.

Example 12.4

A particular type of drink is sold in bottles of two sizes. Bottles of the larger size are Normally distributed with mean volume $2006 \, cm^3$ and standard deviation $7 \, cm^3$. Bottles of the smaller size are Normally distributed with mean $1004 \, cm^3$ and standard deviation $5 \, cm^3$. Sandy buys one large bottle and two small ones.

(i) Use a spreadsheet to estimate the probability that the larger bottle contains more than the two smaller bottles in total.

(ii) Use a calculation to find the exact value of this probability.

Solution

(i) Set up a spreadsheet using $\boxed{=\text{NORM.INV}}$ formulae.

- For the large bottle, you need to use $\boxed{=\text{NORM.INV}(\text{RAND}(), 2006, 7)}$.
- For the two small bottles, use two examples of $\boxed{=\text{NORM.INV}(\text{RAND}(), 1004, 5)}$.
- Then find the difference in contents between the large bottle and the two smaller bottles.
- Finally, find the number of times that the difference is positive, using, for example, the $\boxed{=\text{COUNTIF}}$ command, and divide this number by the total number of trials.

	A	B	C	D	E	F	G
1	Large bottle	First small	Second small	L −2S			
2	2008.54	1002.22	1008.83	−2.51		Number > 0	22
3	2024.3	1004.15	1002.83	17.33		Estimated probability	0.44
4	1996.68	1005.83	1004.64	−13.79			
5	2016.71	996.55	1005.1	15.07		Estimates	
6	2001.42	998.33	1006.92	−3.83		0.44	
7	2000.81	1002.41	1001.77	−3.37		0.4	
8	2003.04	1009.12	1012.43	−18.51		0.56	
9	2005.38	993.46	1006.68	5.25		0.54	
10	1996.39	1006.15	996.93	−6.69		0.56	
11	1998.75	1003.86	1006.3	−11.41		0.36	
12	2003.93	1002.42	1001.63	−0.12		0.36	
43	2009.96	1007.71	1006.34	−4.09		0.62	
44	2010.76	996.31	1002.38	12.07		0.36	
45	2019.46	1004.01	1003.28	12.17		0.44	
46	2012.69	1004.56	1008.91	−0.51	Mean	0.4485	
47	1996.24	994.07	998.33	3.85			
48	2011.72	1007.88	1013.96	−10.13			
49	2001.26	1010.59	1010.81	−20.15			
50	2001.84	1008.18	1004.19	−10.52			
51	1996.37	1003.41	1009.78	−16.83			

Figure 12.8

> The window in Figure 12.8 has been split so that you can see the results of the first eleven and the last eight simulations, together with some of the probability estimates and the overall average probability estimate from the 40 simulations.

> L is the volume of the large bottle.
> S_1 and S_2 are the volumes of the two small bottles.

Figure 12.8 above illustrates a simulation with 50 trials. On the right of the spreadsheet there are the results of 40 simulations, each of 50 trials. The average of these results is approximately 0.45 so this is an estimate of the probability.

(ii) An alternative to using simulation is to use the Normal distribution to calculate the probability.

$L \sim N(2007, 49)$, $S_1 \sim N(1004, 25)$, $S_2 \sim N(1004, 25)$

$L - S_1 - S_2 \sim N(2007 - 1004 - 1004, 49 + 25 + 25)$

So $L - S_1 - S_2 \sim N(-1, 99)$

Using a calculator, $P(L - S_1 - S_2) = 0.460$.

Thus the simulation gives you a fairly accurate result. You could, of course, increase the number of trials in each simulation, or increase the total number of simulations, or both, to improve the likely accuracy of the result.

Simulation and the central limit theorem

4 Simulating other distributions

Any distribution can be simulated using a spreadsheet. Different spreadsheet packages have different ways of simulating specific distributions, for example the uniform, binomial, Poisson and Normal distributions.

For such distributions, you can generate an array of random variables for a specific distribution. As an example, to simulate a geometric distribution with parameter 0.4 on one spreadsheet, you use the spreadsheet command =RANDGEOM(0.3).

5 Simulation and the central limit theorem

> **Note**
> You met the central limit theorem in Chapter 9. It states that the distribution of the sample mean is approximately Normal for sufficiently large n.

You can use simulation to investigate how closely a Normal distribution approximates the distribution of the sum of n independent random variables drawn from another distribution (such the uniform distribution or the geometric distribution). In the next example, this is done for the Poisson distribution. Notice that this distribution is far from Normal; it has strong positive skew (it is actually J-shaped) and is discrete.

Example 12.5

> **Note**
> This example concerns the sum of n independent observations of X rather than the mean of n independent observations of X. However, the central limit theorem implies that the sum will also be Normally distributed for sufficiently large values of n.

> **Solution**
> The approach in this example is first to simulate a number of trials for each of $n = 5$, 20 and 100 and then to investigate how well the resulting distribution is modelled by the Normal distribution.

Let $X \sim$ Poisson(0.5). X_n is the sum of n independent observations of X.

Investigate whether X_n is well modelled by a Normal distribution for (i) $n = 5$ (ii) $n = 20$ (iii) $n = 100$.

You can simulate the distribution of X_n using a suitable spreadsheet with a command such as =RANDPOISSON.

(i) Figure 12.9 shows a spreadsheet simulation of 30 trials with $n = 5$, together with a Kolmogorov–Smirnov test of Normality and a Normal probability plot.

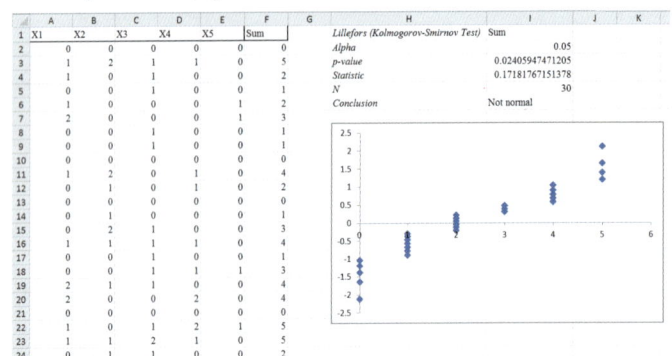

Figure 12.9

In this case, both the Kolmogorov–Smirnov test and the Normal probability plot suggest that X_n is not well modelled by a Normal distribution in the case when $n = 5$. However, this is only one simulation. Several more need to be carried out to be more certain. In fact, repeating this several times, most of the p-values are well below 0.01 so you can be confident that this conclusion is correct.

(ii) Figure 12.10 shows a spreadsheet simulation of 30 trials with $n = 20$, together with a Kolmogorov–Smirnov test of Normality and a Normal probability plot. It also shows the p-values from ten simulations.

Note

This particular example has a p-value of below 0.05 so the conclusion is 'not Normal'. However, seven of the p-values are above 0.05 which leads to the conclusion 'possibly Normal'.

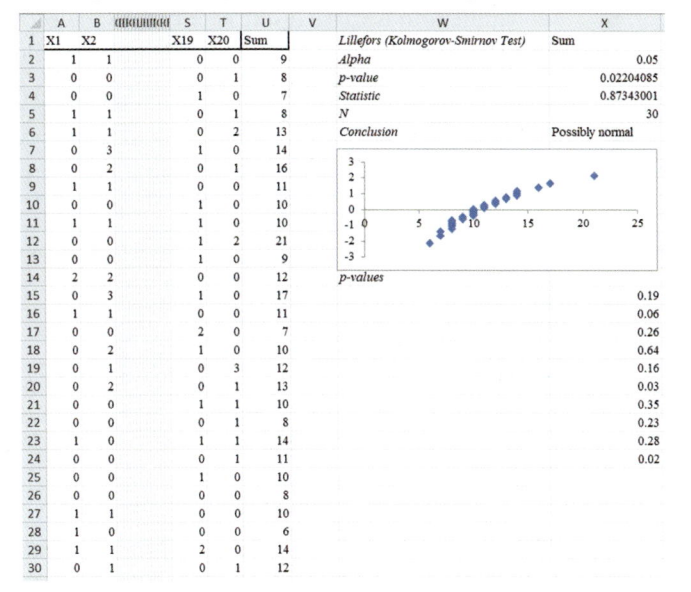

Figure 12.10

The simulation suggests that X_n is moderately well modelled by a Normal distribution in the case when $n = 20$, since most of the p-values are above 0.05. This is despite the highly skewed nature of the parent distribution.

(iii) Figure 12.11 shows a spreadsheet simulation of 30 trials with $n = 100$, together with a Kolmogorov–Smirnov test of Normality and a Normal probability plot. It again also shows the p-values from ten simulations.

The conclusion of the test is not 'definitely Normal', but instead 'possibly Normal'. This is because, as with any hypothesis test, you cannot know for certain that the distribution is Normal, only that there is insufficient evidence to suggest that it is not Normal.

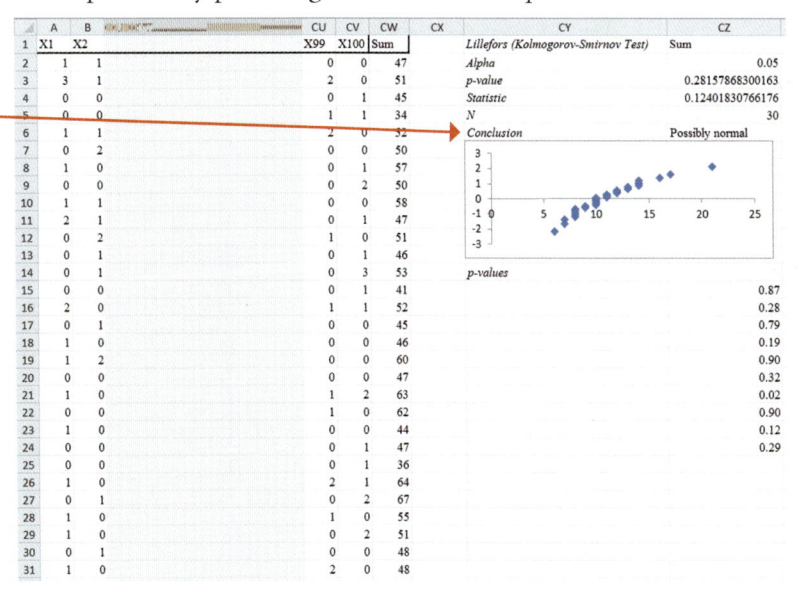

Figure 12.11

The simulation suggests that X_n is very well modelled by a Normal distribution in the case when $n = 100$ since all but one of the p-values are well above 0.05.

According to the central limit theorem, as n increases, the distribution of X_n should become closer and closer to a Normal distribution. The spreadsheet simulations above bear this out.

Simulation and the central limit theorem

Exercise 12.1

1. A three-sided spinner has faces labelled 1, 2, 3. The probabilities that the spinner lands on each of these faces are 0.5, 0.3 and 0.2, respectively. A simulation is carried out to estimate the probability that the total of ten spins will be at least 20. The spreadsheet below shows the simulation.

	A	B	C	D	E	F	G	H	I	J	K
1	X1	X2	X3	X4	X5	X6	X7	X8	X9	X10	SUM
2	1	2	3	1	2	1	1	1	2	1	15
3	3	3	1	1	2	2	3	1	1	2	19
4	1	3	2	2	2	1	1	1	3	1	17
5	3	2	1	2	2	2	1	1	2	1	17
6	1	1	3	2	2	2	3	1	3	1	19
7	2	3	1	3	3	1	1	1	3	3	21
8	2	1	1	2	1	1	1	1	1	3	14
9	2	1	1	3	1	1	2	1	2	3	17
10	1	1	1	2	3	1	3	1	2	1	16
11	2	2	3	2	2	2	1	3	1	2	20

Figure 12.12

   (i)   Write down the formula in cell K2.

   (ii) Write down the estimate of the probability that the total of ten spins will be at least 20.

   (iii) Comment briefly on how good an estimate this is likely to be.

   (iv) Explain how you could improve this estimate.

2. A student wants to know the probability of getting at least six heads when eight fair coins are spun. She sets up the spreadsheet below to simulate spinning eight coins. She uses 0 to denote a tail and 1 to denote a head.

	A	B	C	D	E	F	G	H	I
1	X1	X2	X3	X4	X5	X6	X7	X8	SUM
2	1	0	1	0	0	0	0	0	2
3	1	0	1	1	0	1	1	1	6
4	1	1	1	1	0	0	0	1	5
5	0	0	1	0	1	0	0	0	2
6	0	1	1	1	1	1	0	1	6
7	1	0	0	0	0	1	1	1	4
8	1	1	1	1	1	0	0	0	5
9	0	1	1	0	1	0	0	1	4
10	0	1	1	1	0	0	1	1	5
11	0	0	1	0	1	0	0	0	2
12	0	1	1	0	0	1	0	1	4
13	1	0	1	1	0	0	1	0	4
14	0	1	0	0	0	0	0	0	1
15	1	1	0	0	1	1	1	0	5
16	0	1	0	0	0	1	0	0	2
17	1	1	0	1	0	1	1	1	6
18	0	0	1	0	1	1	0	1	4
19	1	0	1	1	1	0	1	1	6
20	1	1	1	1	1	1	1	1	8
21	0	1	0	1	1	0	1	1	5

Figure 12.13

   (i)   Write down a suitable formula for cell I2.

   (ii) Write down an estimate of the probability of getting at least six heads, based on the simulation.

   (iii) Calculate the theoretical value of this probability and compare it with your answer to part (ii).

3. In a game, Player A has 6 four-sided fair dice with faces labelled 1, 2, 3, 4 and Player B has 4 six-sided fair dice with faces labelled 1, 2, 3, 4, 5, 6. In every round of the game, each of the dice is rolled once. The random variables X and Y represent the total score for Player A and Player B, respectively, in one round. The spreadsheet below shows a simulation of 20 plays of the game.

	A	B	C	D	E	F	G	H	I	J	K	L
1			Player A				X		Player B			Y
2	1	2	1	1	3	4	12	4	4	2	6	16
3	3	4	3	4	3	2	19	1	5	2	1	9
4	3	3	1	1	4	2	14	4	3	3	3	13
5	2	1	3	3	4	1	14	6	5	2	2	15
6	4	4	3	4	4	2	21	2	4	6	1	13
7	4	3	4	4	1	3	19	4	2	6	5	17
8	3	4	2	4	2	4	19	2	6	4	4	16
9	2	4	4	2	1	2	15	5	5	4	3	17
10	4	2	2	1	3	1	13	6	1	2	5	14
11	4	3	4	1	4	3	19	3	5	4	3	15
12	2	1	4	4	1	2	14	5	4	4	3	16
13	1	3	4	3	4	4	19	6	4	4	3	17
14	3	1	4	1	4	1	14	2	1	1	5	9
15	1	3	1	4	3	4	16	1	1	4	5	11
16	1	2	1	2	1	1	8	3	6	4	3	16
17	2	2	3	1	4	2	14	1	6	3	4	14
18	4	2	1	2	2	3	14	4	3	1	4	12
19	2	4	2	2	1	4	15	6	5	4	3	18
20	4	2	3	2	2	3	16	6	1	2	2	11
21	4	4	1	2	1	4	16	5	5	1	5	16

Figure 12.14

(i) Write down the formulae in cells A2 and G2.

(ii) Use the spreadsheet to estimate $P(X > Y)$.

(iii) Explain why this estimate may not be very accurate.

(iv) Explain how you could improve this estimate.

4. An unbiased four-sided spinner has sectors labelled 3, 6, 9, 12. The spinner is spun n times. The random variable X represents the difference between the highest and second highest scores.

(i) For $n = 2$, find $P(X > 0)$.

(ii) For $n = 3$, find $P(X = 9)$.

(iii) Without doing any calculation, explain whether for $n = 3$ you would expect the value of $P(X > 0)$ to be less than, equal to, or greater than the value which you found in part (i).

Simulation and the central limit theorem

The spreadsheet below shows 25 simulated values of X for $n = 10$.

(iv) Estimate $P(X > 0)$.

	A	B	C	D	E	F	G	H	I	J	K	L	M
1	X1	X2	X3	X4	X5	X6	X7	X8	X9	X10	Max	Second max	$\bar{X}$
2	3	9	12	6	12	3	6	3	9	3	12	12	0
3	9	3	3	6	6	9	12	3	9	3	12	9	3
4	6	6	9	6	12	12	6	6	12	9	12	12	0
5	9	9	3	9	6	12	12	6	3	3	12	12	0
6	3	3	3	9	6	9	12	12	6	3	12	12	0
7	9	6	12	12	3	6	12	9	3	6	12	12	0
8	9	12	9	12	3	6	12	6	3	12	12	12	0
9	12	3	3	12	3	9	12	12	6	12	12	12	0
10	6	6	6	12	12	9	6	3	3	9	12	12	0
11	3	6	6	12	3	6	12	3	9	12	12	12	0
12	9	6	6	3	3	6	12	3	6	6	12	9	3
13	9	12	6	3	9	9	3	3	3	6	12	9	3
14	9	9	3	3	12	12	9	12	6	9	12	12	0
15	3	9	9	9	12	9	3	3	12	3	12	12	0
16	12	9	6	9	9	12	3	3	9	6	12	12	0
17	3	3	9	3	9	3	9	12	12	3	12	12	0
18	12	9	6	6	3	6	3	9	9	6	12	9	3
19	3	12	9	3	12	6	6	12	12	9	12	12	0
20	9	3	6	12	3	6	9	6	12	3	12	12	0
21	3	9	9	9	6	9	3	3	9	3	9	9	0
22	12	12	9	9	6	3	3	3	9	9	12	12	0
23	6	12	12	12	12	3	6	6	6	9	12	12	0
24	3	12	6	6	9	9	9	3	6	3	12	9	3
25	3	3	9	6	9	6	12	6	6	3	12	9	3
26	12	9	12	3	6	12	6	6	9	3	12	12	0

Figure 12.15

⑤ Every weekday I catch a bus to work. The buses do not run to their timetable but their arrival times at my bus stop are instead modelled by a uniform distribution over the interval (0, 10).

(i) Find the probability that I have to wait at least 4 minutes for a bus.

(ii) Find the probability that each day for five working days, I have to wait at least 4 minutes for a bus.

I want to know the probability that I have to wait at least 20 minutes in total in a five-day working week. The spreadsheet below illustrates a simulation of 50 five-day weeks.

(iii) Give an estimate of the above probability.

(iv) Explain how you would improve the likely accuracy of this estimate.

(v) Discuss how you would modify the spreadsheet for somebody who caught the same bus every day of the week including Saturdays and Sundays.

(vi) State the formulae you would need for Saturdays and Sundays if arrival times on these days were instead modelled by a uniform distribution over the interval (0, 15).

	A	B	C	D	E	F	G	H
1	Mon	Tue	Wed	Thur	Fri	Total	Summary of totals	Frequency
2	8.26	0.13	1.23	0.47	9.60	19.69	<10	0
3	8.66	4.41	6.02	0.82	8.62	28.53	<20	12
4	7.61	0.05	4.27	1.65	7.39	20.97	<30	42
5	9.84	7.18	8.47	1.82	9.67	36.98	<40	48
6	4.95	5.42	2.57	4.98	4.48	22.40	<=50	50
7	8.82	2.82	9.24	9.12	5.99	35.99		
8	9.26	6.94	4.81	0.63	8.20	29.84		
9	9.83	6.45	2.17	5.22	5.36	29.03		
10	6.39	4.12	3.27	1.22	1.42	16.42		
11	5.41	1.26	4.82	5.84	9.85	27.18		
12	1.72	5.76	5.02	5.04	6.67	24.21		
13	6.04	9.28	0.79	6.09	0.45	22.65		
14	9.73	0.54	7.20	6.37	0.27	24.11		
15	5.99	7.89	7.84	0.25	2.53	24.50		

Figure 12.16

⑥ Three independent random variables, X, Y and Z are uniformly distributed over the intervals $(0, 20)$, $(0, 30)$ and $(10, 50)$, respectively.

(i) State the mean value of $2X + Y - Z$.

(ii) Find the variance of $2X + Y - Z$.

The spreadsheet below shows 100 simulated values of X, Y and Z together with $2X + Y - Z$. It also shows how many times $2X + Y - Z$ is less than some particular values.

(iii) Use the spreadsheet to estimate

a) $P(2X + Y - Z) < 20$
b) $P(2X + Y - Z) > 40$
c) $-20 \leq P(2X + Y - Z) < 20$.

	A	B	C	D	E	F
1	X	Y	Z	2X + Y - Z	Number of values less than	Frequency
2	11.83	6.90	27.88	2.68	-40.00	1
3	4.87	26.64	34.31	2.07	-20.00	10
4	1.35	24.48	14.30	12.88	0.00	36
5	18.96	24.64	31.52	31.04	20.00	75
6	9.09	12.96	13.37	17.77	40.00	95
7	12.64	22.69	14.02	33.95	60.00	100
8	18.45	15.52	39.26	13.16		
9	8.13	11.88	13.06	15.08		
10	4.39	0.31	33.65	-24.56		
11	6.09	5.89	15.48	2.59		
12	0.51	28.15	45.38	-16.21		
13	19.14	4.05	23.52	18.81		
14	11.34	25.26	31.49	16.45		
15	17.81	19.60	35.21	20.01		
16	3.56	11.00	21.47	-3.35		
17	6.05	4.92	22.02	-5.00		

Figure 12.17

⑦ An underground train leaves from my local station every 8 minutes. The time in minutes taken for my journey to work on the train is Normally distributed with mean 21 and standard deviation 3. It takes me 7 minutes to walk to my local station and 6 minutes to walk from the train to work. I arrive at my local station at a random time between trains.

(i) Find the probability that my train journey takes at least 25 minutes.

(ii) Write down a spreadsheet formula which would generate the time that I have to wait for a train to arrive at the station.

(iii) Write down a spreadsheet formula which would generate the journey time on the train.

The spreadsheet on the following page shows 25 simulated journeys to work.

(iv) Estimate the probability that it takes me at least 40 minutes to get to work.

Simulation and the central limit theorem

	A	B	C	D	E
1	To station	Wait for train	Train journey	Walk to work	Total
2	7	2.14	18.12	6	33.26
3	7	7.20	15.34	6	35.54
4	7	2.43	18.34	6	33.77
5	7	4.36	26.81	6	44.17
6	7	4.38	19.49	6	36.87
7	7	2.73	24.93	6	40.66
8	7	5.22	19.21	6	37.43
9	7	7.27	21.77	6	42.04
10	7	4.55	25.10	6	42.65
11	7	5.38	17.77	6	36.15
12	7	2.91	23.32	6	39.23
13	7	6.52	15.80	6	35.32
14	7	1.55	15.36	6	29.91
15	7	3.87	28.25	6	45.12
16	7	5.36	17.00	6	35.36
17	7	2.96	22.49	6	38.45
18	7	6.52	19.80	6	39.32
19	7	2.42	19.80	6	35.22
20	7	4.48	23.18	6	40.66
21	7	4.64	22.59	6	40.23
22	7	4.78	20.51	6	38.29
23	7	2.02	17.76	6	32.78
24	7	3.64	13.22	6	29.86
25	7	7.04	21.72	6	41.76
26	7	6.87	21.79	6	41.66

Figure 12.18

⑧ The random variable X is Normally distributed with mean 50 and variance 100. A student thinks that the distribution of the sum, Y, of five independent observations of X, $Y = X_1 + X_2 + X_3 + X_4 + X_5$ will be same as the distribution as $Z = 5X$. In order to test this, he uses a simulation to find $P(Y > 250)$ and $P(Z > 250)$.

(i) Explain why this will not provide a satisfactory check on his conjecture.

His lecturer advises him to use a simulation instead to find $P(Y > 275)$ and $P(Z > 275)$. The spreadsheet below shows 10 simulated values of Y and Z, together the numbers of values of Y and Z, which are greater than 275.

(ii) Write down a spreadsheet formula which would generate a value of X.

(iii) Use the spreadsheet to estimate $P(Y > 275)$ and $P(Z > 275)$.

The student says that the two probabilities are fairly similar so his conjecture is probably correct.

(iv) Comment on why this conclusion does not follow from the simulation that has been carried out.

(v) Calculate the exact values of $P(Y > 275)$ and $P(Z > 275)$.

	A	B	C	D	E	F	G	H	I	J
1	X1	X2	X3	X4	X5	Y	X	Z = 5X	Number of Y > 275	2
2	39.91	76.06	68.09	32.17	24.85	241.08	41.21	206.04	Number of Z > 275	3
3	47.12	40.25	48.29	54.53	48.83	239.02	33.99	169.94		
4	52.23	64.21	46.23	48.01	49.67	260.35	56.11	280.55		
5	61.55	49.61	51.11	56.82	41.66	260.75	33.3	166.51		
6	37.05	52.36	49.2	52.38	52.79	243.78	57.83	289.17		
7	54.12	44.56	59.45	63.13	66.03	287.29	48.04	240.22		
8	43.93	64.26	32.35	50.59	75.06	266.19	56.93	284.67		
9	56.16	55.56	24.66	50.03	51.87	238.28	39.35	196.73		
10	53.74	61.27	56.32	59.83	47.19	278.35	35.21	176.05		
11	42.91	42.47	26.94	53.6	35.05	200.97	53.65	268.27		
12										

Figure 12.19

⑨ The spreadsheets below show simulations of ten sample means for n independent random variables distributed over the interval $(0, 10)$. The value of n for the first spreadsheet is 4 and for the second spreadsheet is 15. For each spreadsheet, there is a Normal probability plot and also a Kolmogorov–Smirnov test of Normality.

(i) What would the central limit theorem suggest about the distribution of these two sample means?

(ii) Comment on the conclusions which you can draw from the two probability plots and tests.

	A	B	C	D	E	F	G
1	X1	X2	X3	X4	Mean	Kolmogorov-Smirnov Test	Column 1
2	4.285145	0.57249	4.029817	6.742293	3.907436	Alpha	0.05
3	4.491723	4.865048	4.145813	4.132843	4.408857	p-value	0.003405127
4	3.352152	7.933718	4.403454	1.833882	4.380802	Statistic	0.32607064
5	3.716375	2.974345	0.247939	9.425246	4.090976	N	10
6	2.797732	6.354465	1.030241	4.846914	3.757338		
7	6.319134	8.313829	6.50768	2.527969	5.917153		
8	3.360974	3.313456	4.713218	8.503854	4.972875		
9	8.833739	2.248589	2.995169	1.373269	3.862692		
10	9.716025	2.971337	9.569268	1.874168	6.032699		
11	1.423506	9.265326	8.749393	3.903456	5.83542		

Normal probability plot

	A	B	...	N	O	P	Q	R
1	X1	X2	...	X14	X15	Mean	Kolmogorov-Smirnov test	Column 1
2	4.796397	1.211888		8.423683642	1.517113	3.965891	Alpha	0.05
3	8.04591	9.285166		5.805695114	9.876356	4.715494	p-value	0.632476
4	4.724627	8.632884		9.517562808	4.330791	4.85136	Statistic	0.163234
5	2.45591	1.964194		1.151547836	6.786123	4.893335	N	10
6	5.925184	4.445599		8.264891041	3.414507	4.931902		
7	7.993854	5.670953		2.230906145	5.793585	5.054006		
8	7.19724	7.79728		7.543942205	6.068751	5.336226		
9	4.884732	4.115068		6.990927613	1.467027	5.482756		
10	6.421051	5.379973		2.615229	2.594376	5.884338		
11	3.802455	9.421445		6.893405119	0.616614	6.539805		

Normal probability plot

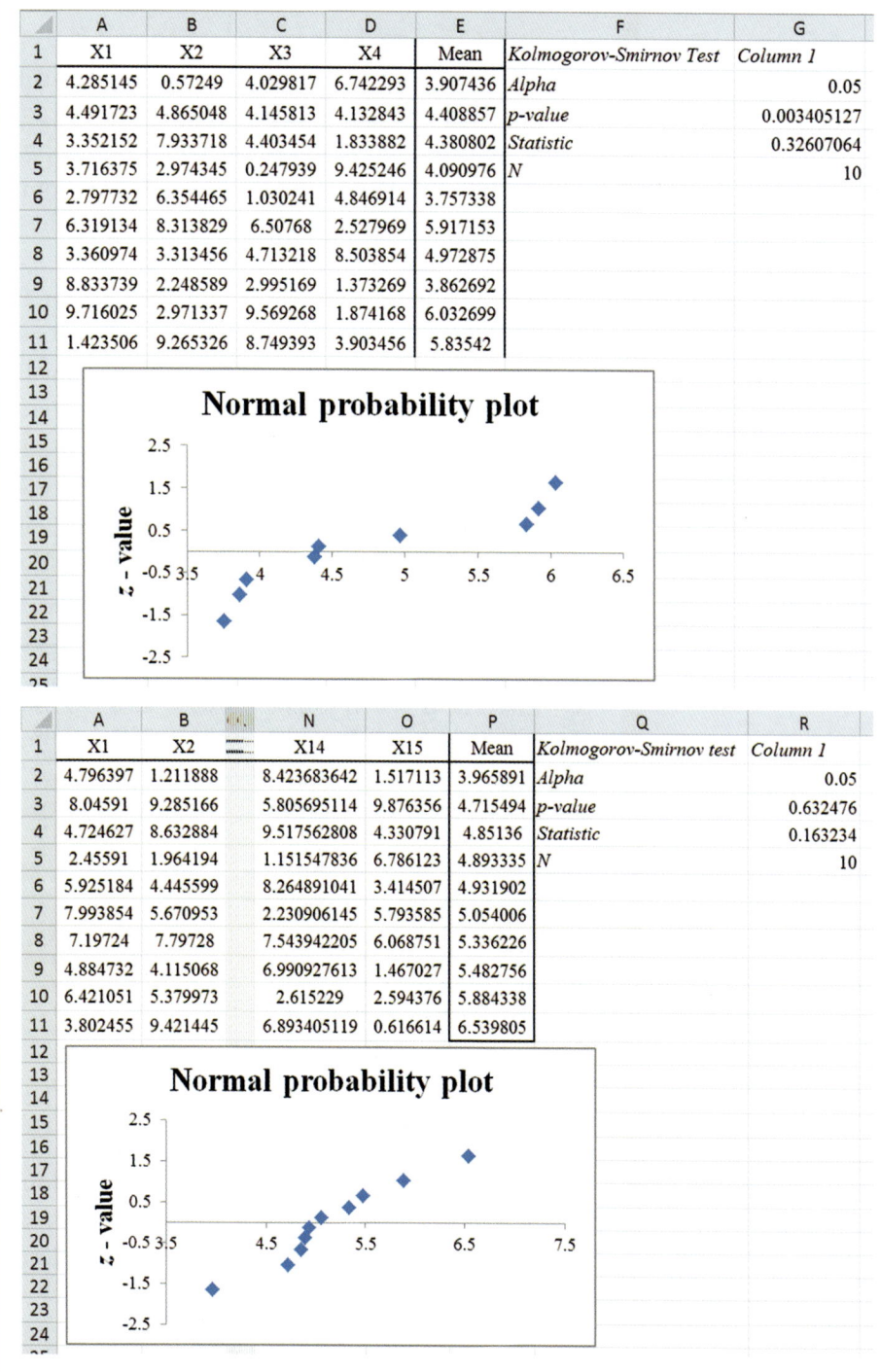

Figure 12.20

Simulation and the central limit theorem

⑩ The random variable X is uniformly distributed over the interval $(0, 1)$. The random variable S is the sum of six independent observations of X.

  (i) State the mean and variance of X.

  (ii) Calculate the mean and variance of S.

  (iii) The random variable U is Normally distributed with the same mean and variance as S. Find $P(U > 3.5)$, $P(U > 4)$, and $P(U > 4.5)$.

The random variable Y has a discrete uniform distribution over the values $\{0, 1\}$. The random variable T is the sum of six independent observations of Y.

  (iv) State the mean and variance of Y.

  (v) Calculate the mean and variance of T.

  (vi) The random variable V is Normally distributed with the same mean and variance as T. Find $P(V > 3.5)$ and $P(V > 4.5)$.

A student wants to investigate whether S and T can be well modelled by the Normal distribution. The two extracts from a spreadsheet below show 10 000 simulations of S and T. It also shows how many trials of S and T are greater than various values.

  (vii) Use the spreadsheet to find estimates for $P(S > 3.5)$, $P(S > 4)$ and $P(S > 4.5)$ and compare these with your earlier estimates.

  (viii) Use the spreadsheet to find estimates for $P(T > 3)$ and $P(T > 4)$ and compare these with your earlier estimates.

  (ix) Explain why you were asked to calculate $P(V > 3.5)$ and $P(V > 4.5)$ rather than $P(V > 3)$ and $P(V > 4)$.

  (x) Do your calculations in parts (vii) and (viii) provide evidence that S and T cannot be well modelled by the Normal distribution?

	A	B	C	D	E	F	G	H	I	J
1	X1	X2	X3	X4	X5	X6	S		Number of $S > 3.5$	2422
2	0.510	0.577	0.315	0.507	0.779	0.381	3.069		Number of $S > 4$	779
3	0.264	0.511	0.415	0.491	0.456	0.800	2.937		Number of $S > 4.5$	160
4	0.413	0.795	0.144	0.146	0.479	0.236	2.213			
5	0.883	0.308	0.299	0.166	0.305	0.955	2.916			
6	0.621	0.778	0.828	0.813	0.767	0.588	4.395			
7	0.646	0.712	0.521	0.127	0.683	0.896	3.585			
8	0.290	0.533	0.467	0.004	0.081	0.419	1.794			
9	0.318	0.806	0.260	0.287	0.990	0.814	3.475			
10										
11	Y1	Y2	Y3	Y4	Y5	Y6	T		Number of $T > 3$	3433
12	1	1	0	0	1	0	3		Number of $T > 4$	1086
13	1	0	1	0	1	0	3		Number of $T > 5$	166
14	1	1	1	0	1	0	4			
15	0	1	1	1	1	0	4			
16	0	0	0	0	0	1	1			
17	0	0	1	0	1	0	2			
18	1	0	1	1	0	1	4			
19	0	0	1	0	0	1	2			

Figure 12.21

⑪ IQ test scores are modelled by the Normal distribution with mean 100 and standard deviation 15. The scores are reported to the nearest integer.

  (i) Find the probability that a randomly selected person will have an IQ greater than 130.

(ii) A random sample of ten people is selected. Their mean IQ is calculated. The spreadsheet below illustrates 10 000 simulations of this mean together with the number of times that the mean is greater than 103. Estimate the probability that the mean is greater than 103.

(iii) Use calculation to find this probability and compare it with your answer to part (ii). (Note that you will need to use a continuity correction.)

	A	B	C	D	E	F	G	H	I	J	K
1	X1	X2	X3	X4	X5	X6	X7	X8	X9	X10	Mean
2	82	108	111	69	100	91	100	119	118	108	100.60
3	72	123	98	83	94	90	112	103	98	108	98.10
4	106	85	103	99	107	91	99	104	123	94	101.10
5	118	96	110	109	89	90	100	124	109	103	104.80
6	114	89	121	93	94	85	122	85	123	96	102.20
7	121	119	97	94	59	74	106	65	98	99	93.20
8	93	96	111	102	89	121	94	85	110	112	101.30
9	91	108	93	71	102	110	103	93	95	76	94.20
10	86	87	130	96	118	83	91	99	100	89	97.90
11	70	103	116	91	102	84	95	123	96	113	99.30
12	108	82	107	112	100	97	101	105	109	124	104.50
13	119	110	99	109	97	117	91	109	93	106	105.00
14	91	109	112	119	96	118	138	106	77	100	106.60
15	105	105	105	73	96	95	90	96	121	98	98.40
16	129	114	102	98	88	77	98	106	128	80	102.00
17	104	100	73	95	99	99	75	97	90	66	89.80
18	103	104	110	104	103	106	139	105	110	114	109.80

Figure 12.22

12 Five fair four-faced dice with faces labelled 1, 2, 3, 4 are each rolled once. The spreadsheet below shows the first 13 rows of 100 simulations, together with the sample mean for each simulation. It also shows the number of times for which the sample mean is at least 3.

	C	D	E	F	G	H	I
1	X3	X4	X5	Mean			
2	4	4	2	2.8			
3	3	2	2	2		Number of means ≥ 3	24
4	1	3	2	2.2			
5	2	4	3	3.2			
6	4	2	4	3			
7	2	4	3	3.4			
8	4	4	4	3.4			
9	3	4	1	2.8			
10	4	4	2	2.8			
11	2	1	3	2.2			
12	4	2	3	3			
13	2	3	1	2.2			
14	3	3	3	2.4			

Figure 12.23

(i) Estimate the probability that the sample mean is at least three.

A further simulation is done with 30 dice rather than five. The spreadsheet below shows the first 13 rows of 500 simulations, the sample mean for each simulation and the number of times for which the sample mean is at least 2.6.

Simulation and the central limit theorem

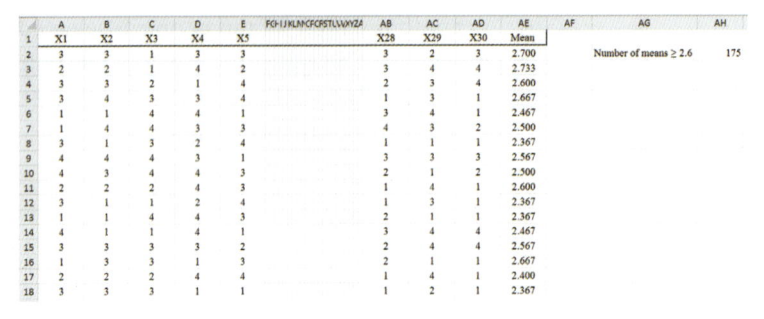

Figure 12.24

(ii) Estimate the probability that the sample mean is at least 2.6.

(iii) Use the central limit theorem to calculate an estimate of the probability in part (ii).

(iv) Explain why you cannot calculate an estimate of the probability in part (i).

KEY POINTS

1. Spreadsheets can be used to simulate probability distributions.
2. To simulate a discrete uniform distribution on the interval (a, b), you can use the formula provided by your spreadsheet, for example =RANDBETWEEN (a, b).
3. To simulate a continuous uniform distribution on the interval (a, b), you can use the formula provided by your spreadsheet, for example $=a + (b - a) *$ RAND().
4. To simulate a Normal distribution with mean μ and variance σ^2, you can use the formula provided by your spreadsheet, for example =NORM.INV(RAND(), μ, σ).
5. You can use simulation to estimate probabilities when the theoretical probabilities are difficult to find.
6. When you repeat sampling, there will be some variation in the results.
7. You can use simulation to investigate the central limit theorem.

LEARNING OUTCOMES

When you have completed this chapter you should:
- know that spreadsheets can be used to simulate probability distributions, and be able to do so for discrete and continuous uniform distributions, including Normal distributions
- know that simulations can be used to approximate probability distributions and to estimate probabilities, including in situations where the theory may be technically difficult
- be able to interpret the output from spreadsheet simulations.

Practice questions: Set 2

① A group of 12 patients were given an experimental treatment for calcium deficiency. One side-effect of the treatment was thought to be reduced appetite and hence weight loss. Over a three month period of treatment, the mean weight lost by the 12 patients was 2.4 kg with a standard deviation of 1.3 kg.

(i) Construct a 95% confidence interval from these data. [4 marks]

(ii) State the assumptions made in constructing the confidence interval. [2 marks]

(iii) Explain carefully how to interpret the confidence interval. [1 mark]

② A website allows people to give approval ratings to restaurants by moving a slider on a scale from 0 to 10.

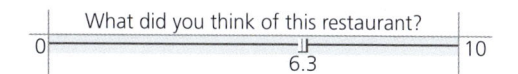

What did you think of this restaurant?
0 ———————— 6.3 ———————— 10

Figure 1

From having eaten there, I think that Paulo's Pizza Parlour should get an average rating of 5, and I want to test that hypothesis. The 10 most recent scores for Paulo's Pizza Parlour on the website are as follows.

3.3   2.2   0.0   4.6   2.8   9.9   8.7   4.9   4.3   8.2

(i) Explain why it would not be appropriate to use a t-test. [1 mark]

(ii) Identify two assumptions required for a Wilcoxon signed rank test to be valid. [2 marks]

(iii) Carry out the Wilcoxon signed rank test, using a 5% significance level. [4 marks]

③ James has a medical condition which results in episodes when he is unwell. Between episodes he is fine.

Research, covering many people with the condition over a long time, has shown that the time in days, between episodes is well modelled by a continuous random variable T with cumulative distribution function

$$F(t) = 1 - e^{-0.02t},\ t \geq 0$$

(i) James has just had an episode. Use this model to find the probability that

(a) his next episode will be within 50 days

(b) that his next episode will occur between 20.2 and 30.4 days from now. [2 marks]

(ii) Find the median time between James's episodes according to this model. [2 marks]

A possible new treatment for the condition is being trialled. The mean time between episodes for those on the trial is 109.3 days.

(iii) Investigate whether the new treatment seems to be effective. [3 marks]

Practice questions: Set 2

④ At a weather station, daily records are kept of the proportion of daylight hours for which the Sun is visible. (So a value of 0.7 on a particular day means that the Sun was visible for 70% of the daylight hours.) For a randomly chosen day in the spring months (March, April and May), this proportion, X, is modelled by the following probability density function (pdf).

$$f(x) = k(x^2 - 0.8x + 0.3) \qquad 0 \leq x \leq 1$$

(i) Show that $k = \dfrac{30}{7}$. [2 marks]

(ii) Sketch the pdf. Explain what its shape indicates about the proportion of daylight hours for which the Sun is visible. [3 marks]

(iii) Find the expectation and variance of X. [5 marks]

For a random sample of 25 days in spring, Y denotes the mean proportion of daylight hours for which the Sun is visible.

(iv) Find the expectation and standard deviation of Y. State, with a reason, the approximate shape of the pdf of Y. [4 marks]

⑤ It is sometimes claimed that the 'ideal' body shape in humans has the height equal to the arm span. In order to investigate this, data were obtained from the *CensusAtSchool* website. A random sample of 50 sixth form students was taken. The data, in cm and sorted by arm span, start and finish as follows.

(i) Explain why it would be sensible to eliminate the first three data points from the sample. What seems to have happened here? [2 marks]

It seems likely that the fourth data point is an error too, and there is some doubt about the fifth. So the subsequent investigation is based on just 45 data points. Three students analyse the data.

(ii) Annabel finds that the correlation coefficient for the data is 0.85 and she states that this provides strong evidence that height and arm span are almost equal. Explain why Annabel is wrong. [2 marks]

(iii) Boris finds the regression line of height (y) on arm span (x) to be as follows.

$$y = 1.017x - 3.989$$

Discuss briefly whether or not Boris could argue that height and arm span are nearly equal. [3 marks]

(iv) Clarissa constructs the set of differences (*height − arm span*) for the 45 data points in order to test whether the mean difference in the underlying population is zero. The sample differences have a mean of 1.178 cm and a standard deviation of 6.231 cm.

Carry out, at the 5% level of significance, the hypothesis test that Clarissa could perform and determine the conclusion she should reach. [5 marks]

(v) Annabel and Boris point out that Clarissa did not check that the differences were Normally distributed. Explain whether or not this invalidates Clarissa's conclusion. [2 marks]

	A	B
1	Height	Arm span
2	170	50
3	170	50
4	164	67
5	165	100
6	162	132
7	158	151
8	164	152
9	153	153
10	167	154
42	180	175
43	173	177
44	178	178
45	173	179
46	174	183
47	181	183
48	183	183
49	187	189
50	190	196
51	205	207

Figure 2

6 A spreadsheet is being used to investigate tests for Normality. The screenshot below gives the output when the Lilliefors (Kolmogorov–Smirnov) test is used on the values in column A. These values are a random sample of size 50 from a distribution that is known to be Normal. (The screenshot does not show all 50 values.)

	A	B	C	D
1	6.16712		Lilliefors (Kolmogoroc-Smirnov) Test	Column A
2	2.06141		Alpha	0.05
3	2.60491		p-Value	0.0111
4	6.04970		Statistic	0.1441
5	2.98491		N	50
6	7.55101		Conclusion	Reject null hypothesis
7	7.50361			
8	5.49196			
9	5.43799			
10	3.22318			
11	7.12870			
12	2.01225			
13	5.59205			
14	3.52848			
15	3.07595			
16	4.81548			
17	4.38537			
18	3.42120			
19	3.97845			
20	3.75781			

Figure 3

(i) State what the null and alternative hypotheses of the test are.

Explain what *Alpha* (0.05) and *p-value* (0.0111) represent.

Explain how the conclusion 'Reject null hypothesis' is reached. How should this conclusion be interpreted? [5 marks]

(ii) A fresh random sample from the same Normal distribution is generated and this time the *p*-value is 0.9914. Explain what the conclusion would be and what you would expect the graph to look like on this occasion. [3 marks]

(iii) Many random samples are now generated from the same Normal distribution by repeatedly pressing the F9 key. Each of these samples is tested for Normality with *Alpha* equal to 0.05. For what proportion of these samples will the conclusion be 'Reject null hypothesis'?

Explain whether or not your answer would change if the samples were now of size 100 rather than 50.

Why is a sample of size 100 better than a sample of size 50 when testing for Normality? [3 marks]

Answers

Chapter 1

Discussion point, page 1
Statistics often points the way to new knowledge, for example the health dangers in smoking. In Carlyle's time much of the statistics that you will meet in this book had not yet been discovered. There were no calculators or computers, making it almost impossible to analyse data sets of any size. So what could be achieved was distinctly limited.

Discussion point, page 4
- Are the data relevant to the problem? In an investigation into accidents involving cyclists, collecting data on accidents involving pedestrians would be of no use.
- Are the data unbiased? In an investigation into average earnings, taking a sample consisting only of householders would give a biased sample.
- Is there any danger that the act of collection will distort the data? When measuring the temperature of very small objects, the temperature probe might itself heat up or cool down the object.
- Is the person collecting the data suitable? In a survey into the incidence of drug use, a policeman would not be a suitable person to carry out interviews with individuals since people who use drugs would be unlikely to give truthful answers and so the sample obtained would not be representative.
- Is the sample of a suitable size? In an opinion poll for an election, a sample of size 500 is too small to give a reliable result.
- Is a suitable sampling procedure being followed? In an investigation into the weight of individual carrots from a large crop in a field, sampling 50 carrots from the edge of the field would not be appropriate as those at the edge of the field might grow larger or smaller than in the middle of the field.

Discussion point, page 10

Same	They are illustrating the same data	
Different	**Labels**	
	Frequency chart	The vertical scale is labelled 'Frequency'
	Histogram	The vertical scale is labelled 'Frequency density'
	Scales on the vertical axes	
	Frequency chart	The vertical scale is the frequency
	Histogram	The vertical scale is such that the areas of the bars represent frequency. The frequency density is Trains per minute
	Class intervals	
	Frequency chart	The class intervals are all the same, 5 minutes
	Histogram	The class intervals are not all the same; some are 5 minutes, others 10 minutes and one is 40 minutes.

Exercise 1.1

1. (i) E.g. Members who attend may be of a particular type.
   E.g. Absent members cannot be included.
   (ii) 156, 248, 73, 181

2. (i) Either 19th or 20th
   (ii) $Q_2 = 30$, $Q_1 = 19.5$, $Q_3 = 41$
   (iii) $1.5 \times IQR = 32.25$; $19.5 - 32.25 < 0$ so no low outliers; $41 + 32.25 = 73.24$ so 80 and 89 are both outliers.
   (iv) Positively skewed.
   (v) No. There is no reason to believe it would be representative. (As European countries tend to be affluent it is unlikely to be representative.)

3. (i) Opportunity
   (ii) The total number of children is 43 and there were 20 mothers. $\frac{43}{20} = 2.15$
   (iii)
   - The sample is not representative of all women because all the women are mothers; those who have had no children have been excluded.
   - The answer 0 looks like a mistake and needs to be investigated.
   - The word 'exactly' should not be used. At best it is an estimate.
   - Debbie has given her answer to 3 significant figures which implies an unrealistic level of accuracy.

4. (i) Quota
   (ii)
   - Opinion is almost equally divided for and against.
   - There is a strong difference of opinion between men and women with most men against the scheme and most women in favour.
   - Most adults have made up their minds but many young people don't know.
   (iii) Proportional stratified.

5. (i) The population size appears to be cyclic with period 16 years.
   (ii) 2007 and 2015
   (iii) (a) The population is decreasing sharply.
   (b) The population is steady at about 330 000 animals.
   (iv) A systematic sample is very unsuitable for data with a cyclic pattern. It may select items at about the same points in the cycle and so give misleading information.

6. (i) Cluster
   (ii) The total number of the birds is unknown.
   (iii) $\frac{887}{734} = 1.21$ (2 d.p.)
   There is considerable variability between the clusters and with only four of them it would be surprising if the mean was very close to the true value.
   (iv) The highest rate is D with $1.613\ldots$ fledglings per nest.
   The lowest rate is C with $0.362\ldots$ fledglings per nest.
   These figures suggest outer limits of about 43 000 and 194 000 fledglings.

7. (i) Proportional stratified
   (ii) Writing the names on sheets of paper and drawing them from a hat.
   Listing and numbering the three groups and then using random numbers to make the selections.
   (iii) Not all samples can be selected, for example one with 20 shops.
   (iv) £407 000
   (v) There are major differences within two of the groups; these need to be understood and addressed in the stratified sampling.

8. (i) Self-selected or opportunity
   (ii) All pregnant women, or all pregnant women in the UK.
   It may well be that only the fitter women agreed to take part.
   People taking part must be volunteers otherwise it would be unethical.
   (iii) 167
   (iv) (a) 3.0% (b) 6.0% (c) About 9.2%
   (d) The categories are not exhaustive as there are others which are not counted in (e.g. day 276).

9. (i) (a) Simple random samples
   (b) A $\bar{x} = 81.52$, $s = 10.02$,
   B $\bar{x} = 77.71$, $s = 10.16$,
   C $\bar{x} = 80.75$, $s = 10.27$
   Statistical variability
   (c) Overall $\bar{x} = 79.88$, $s = 10.20$. Should be more accurate with the larger total sample size.

(ii) $\Sigma(x-\bar{x})^2$ and $\Sigma x^2 - n\bar{x}^2$

$$= \Sigma x^2 - 2(\Sigma x)\bar{x} + n\bar{x}^2$$
$$= \Sigma x^2 - 2(n\bar{x}) \times \bar{x} + n\bar{x}^2$$
$$= \Sigma x^2 - n\bar{x}^2$$

10 (i) 0.667, 1.25
(ii) Mean is reduced by 13.3%, standard deviation by 21.52%
(iii) 0.56%
(iv) 51

Chapter 2

Discussion point, page 26
By comparing the mean scores in each competition (and perhaps also the standard deviation to get an idea of variation).

Discussion point, page 28
The mean score after the relaxation session is 1.855 as compared with 1.49 before, which suggests that the relaxation session has helped the archers to achieve higher scores. The variance after the relaxation session is 2.084 as compared with 1.97 before, which suggests that the relaxation session has made very little difference to the variation in performance.

Discussion point, page 29
The first method is preferable if the mean is not a round number, since in that case all of the values $(r - \mu)$ will be decimals resulting in a lot of work in the calculations. However, if the mean is a round number the second method may be a little quicker than the first.

Exercise 2.1

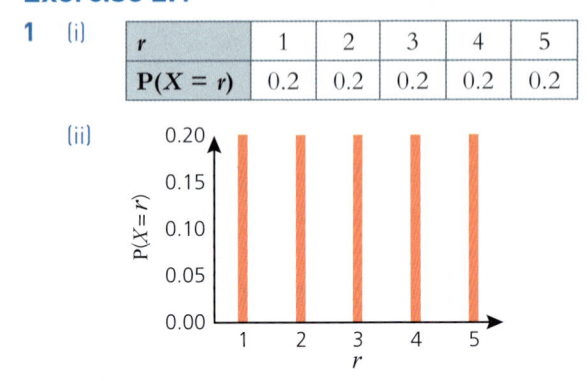

1 (i)

r	1	2	3	4	5
P(X = r)	0.2	0.2	0.2	0.2	0.2

(ii) [bar chart of uniform distribution]

(iii) (a) 0.6 (b) 0.4 (c) 0

2 (i)

r	1	2	3	4
P(X = r)	k	2k	3k	4k

(ii) $k = 0.1$
(iii) (a) 0.4 (b) 0.6

3 (i)

r	3	4	5	6	7	8	9
P(X = r)	$\frac{1}{27}$	$\frac{1}{9}$	$\frac{2}{9}$	$\frac{7}{27}$	$\frac{2}{9}$	$\frac{1}{9}$	$\frac{1}{27}$

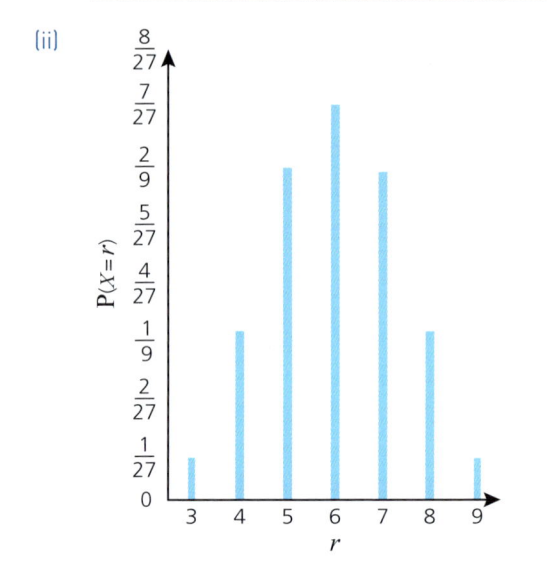

(ii) [bar chart]

Symmetrical

(iii) (a) $\frac{10}{27}$ (b) $\frac{14}{27}$ (c) $\frac{10}{27}$

4 (i)

r	0	1	2	3	4
P(Y = r)	$\frac{1}{5}$	$\frac{8}{25}$	$\frac{6}{25}$	$\frac{4}{25}$	$\frac{2}{25}$

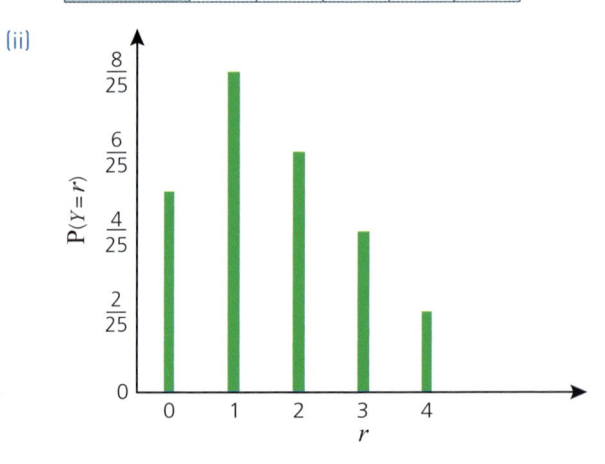

(ii) [bar chart]

Positive skewed

(iii) (a) $\frac{13}{25}$ (b) $\frac{13}{25}$

5 (i)

r	1	2	3	4	5	6	8	9	10	12	15	16	18	20	24	25	30	36
P(X = r)	$\frac{1}{36}$	$\frac{1}{18}$	$\frac{1}{18}$	$\frac{1}{12}$	$\frac{1}{18}$	$\frac{1}{9}$	$\frac{1}{18}$	$\frac{1}{36}$	$\frac{1}{18}$	$\frac{1}{9}$	$\frac{1}{18}$	$\frac{1}{36}$	$\frac{1}{18}$	$\frac{1}{18}$	$\frac{1}{18}$	$\frac{1}{36}$	$\frac{1}{18}$	$\frac{1}{36}$

(ii) $\frac{3}{4}$

6 (i) $k = \frac{2}{7}$

r	2	3	4	5
P(X = r)	$\frac{1}{7}$	$\frac{3}{14}$	$\frac{2}{7}$	$\frac{5}{14}$

(ii) (a) $\frac{27}{98}$ (b) $\frac{71}{196}$

7 (i) $k = \frac{1}{100}$

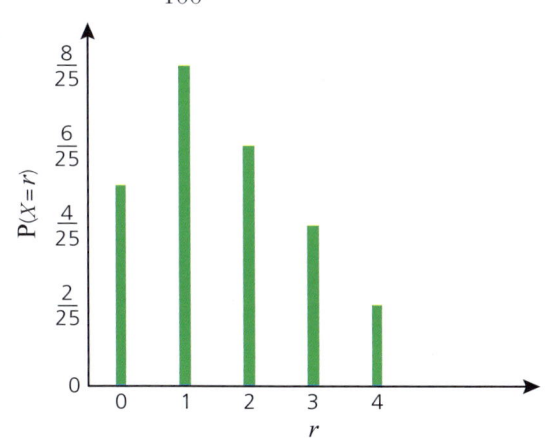

8 (i)

r	0	1	2	3	4
P(X = r)	$\frac{1}{16}$	$\frac{1}{4}$	$\frac{3}{8}$	$\frac{1}{4}$	$\frac{1}{16}$

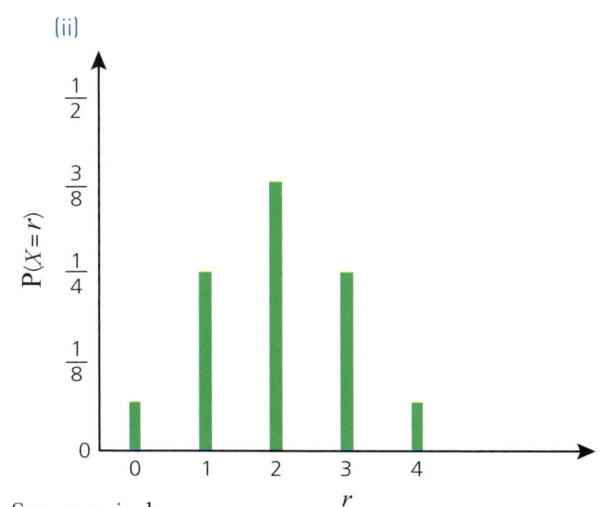

(ii) Symmetrical

(iii) $\frac{5}{16}$

(iv) Greater because you cannot have equal numbers of heads and tails, so the probability of more heads than tails will be equal to the probability of less heads than tails and both will be equal to $\frac{1}{2}$.

9 (i) $k = 0.014$

r	0	1	2	3	4	5
P(X = r)	$\frac{3}{10}$	$\frac{49}{250}$	$\frac{49}{250}$	$\frac{21}{125}$	$\frac{14}{125}$	$\frac{7}{250}$

(ii) $\frac{1}{25}$

10 (i) $a = 0.1$

(ii) $k = \frac{32}{31}$

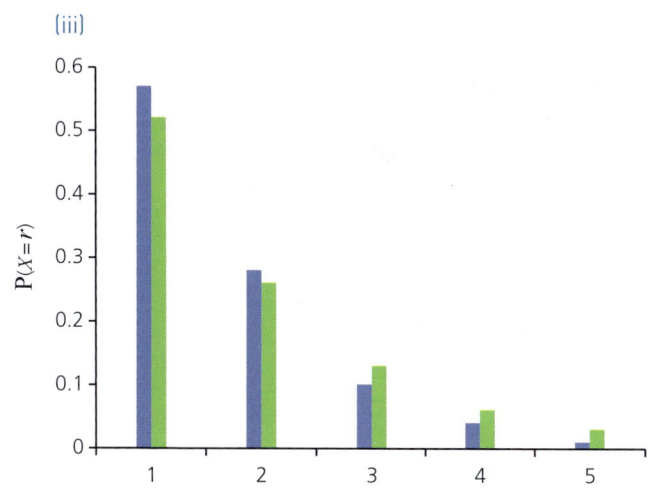

(iii)

Note: actual values in blue, Model in green.
The model is fairly good although it suggests that there are rather fewer cars with 1 or 2 people and rather more with 3, 4 or 5 people.

11 (i) $\frac{1}{1296}$

(ii) $\frac{16}{1296}$ or $\frac{1}{81}$

(iii)

r	1	2	3	4	5	6
P(X ≥ r)	1	625/1296	256/1296	81/1296	16/1296	1/1296
P(X = r)	671/1296	369/1296	175/1296	65/1296	15/1296	1/1296

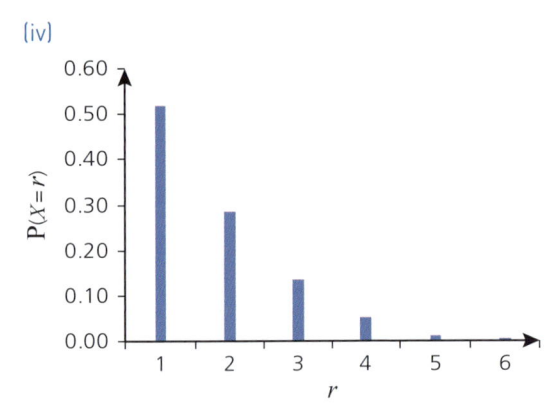

(iv) Highly positively skewed

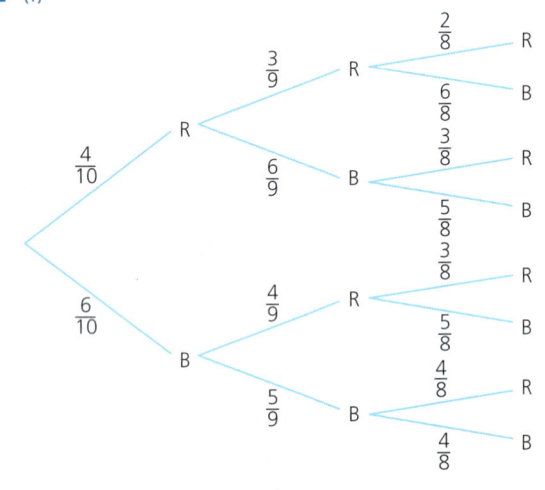

12 (i) [tree diagram]

(ii)

r	0	1	2	3
P(X = r)	$\frac{1}{30}$	$\frac{3}{10}$	$\frac{1}{2}$	$\frac{1}{6}$

Exercise 2.2

1 $E(X) = 3$;
Because the distribution is symmetrical so take the mid-range value.

2 Mean = 3.2, Variance = 3.26

	A	B	C	D
1	r	P(X = r)	r × P(X = r)	r² × P(X = r)
2	1	0.20	0.20	0.20
3	2	0.30	0.60	1.20
4	3	0.10	0.30	0.90
5	4	0.05	0.20	0.80
6	5	0.20	1.00	5.00
7	6	0.15	0.90	5.40
8	SUM	1.00	3.20	13.50

3 (i) $E(X) = 3.125$
(ii) $P(X < 3.125) = 0.5625$

4 (i) $p = 0.8$

r	4	5
P(Y = r)	0.8	0.2

(ii)

r	50	100
P(Y = r)	0.4	0.6

5 (i) $E(Y) = 1.944; \text{Var}(Y) = 2.052$
(ii) (a) $\frac{5}{9}$ (b) $\frac{1}{18}$

6 (i) $E(X) = 1.5$
(ii) $\text{Var}(X) = 0.75$
(iii) $E(Y) = 5, \text{Var}(Y) = 2.5$

7 (i)

r	−5	0	2
P(X = r)	0.25	0.25	0.5

(ii) $E(X) = -0.25, \text{Var}(X) = 8.188$;
Negative expectation means a loss
(iii) £1 less

8 (i) $P(X = 1) = 0.4 \times 0.85 + 0.6 \times 0.1$
(ii)

r	1	2	3	4
P(X = r)	0.4	0.3	0.21	0.09

(iii) $E(X) = 1.99, \text{Var}(X) = 0.97$

9 (i) $p = 0.3, q = 0.4$

r	3	4	5
P(X = r)	0.3	0.4	0.3

(ii)

r	20	50	100
P(Y = r)	0.7	0.2	0.1

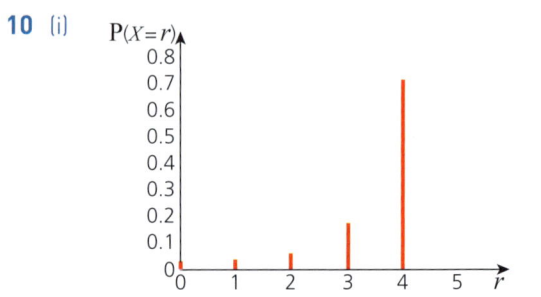

10 (i) [bar chart]
(ii) $E(X) = 3.5, \text{Var}(X) = 0.897$ (to 3 s.f.)
(iii) $P(X_1 = X_2) = 0.535$ (to 3 s.f.)
(iv) 0.932 (to 3 s.f.)

11 (i)

r	P(X = r)
0	0.03
1	0.10
2	0.13
3	0.16
4	0.18
5	0.17
6	0.12
7	0.09
8	0.02

(ii) $E(X) = 3.92, \text{Var}(X) = 3.83$ (to 3 s.f.)

(iii) $k = \dfrac{1}{84}$

(iv) $E(X) = 4, \text{Var}(X) = 3$

(v) The expectations are almost the same and the theoretical variance is only slightly less than the experimental variance, so the model is quite good.

Exercise 2.3

1 (i) (a) $E(X) = 3.1$
   (b) $\text{Var}(X) = 1.29$
2 (i) (a) $E(X) = 0.7$
   (b) $\text{Var}(X) = 0.61$
3 (i) $E(A + B + C) = 90, \text{Var}(A + B + C) = 23$
   (ii) $E(5A + 4B) = 295, \text{Var}(5A + 4B) = 353$
   (iii) $E(A + 2B + 3C) = 170,$
   $\text{Var}(A + 2B + 3C) = 95$
   (iv) $E(4A - B - 5C) = -15,$
   $\text{Var}(4A - B - 5C) = 302$
5 (i) $E(2X) = 6$
   (ii) $\text{Var}(3X) = 6.75$
6 (i) 10.9, 3.09
   (ii) 18.4, 111.24
7 (i) 2
   (ii) 1
   (iii) 9
8 (i) $P(X = 2) = 0.7 \times 0.3 = 0.21$
   (ii) $E(X) = 2.77 \quad \text{Var}(X) = 2.42$
   (iii) $E(X) = £1.36$ million $\text{Var}(X) = 1.83 \times 10^{11}$
9 (i)

r	1	2	3	4	5	6
P(X = r)	$\dfrac{11}{36}$	$\dfrac{1}{4}$	$\dfrac{7}{36}$	$\dfrac{5}{36}$	$\dfrac{1}{12}$	$\dfrac{1}{36}$

(ii) $E(X) = 73.2p \quad \text{Var}(X) = 1232$

(iii) Make money since cost £1 and average winnings 73.2p.

10 (i) (a) $E(X) = 2.3$ (b) $E(Y) = 1.3$

(c) $\text{Var}(X) = 0.81$ (d) $\text{Var}(Y) = 0.61$

(ii)

r	1	2	3	4	5	6
P(Z = r)	0.04	0.14	0.28	0.31	0.18	0.05

(iii) (a) $E(Z) = 3.6 = 2.3 + 1.3$
   (b) $\text{Var}(Z) = 1.42 = 0.81 + 0.61$

(iv)

r	−1	0	1	2	3	4
P(W = r)	0.1	0.26	0.31	0.22	0.09	0.02

(v) (a) $E(W) = 1 = 2.3 - 1.3$
   (b) $\text{Var}(W) = 1.42 = 0.81 + 0.61$

11 (i) $E(\text{Score}) = 3.5 \quad \text{Var}(\text{Score}) = 2.917$
   (ii) $E(\text{Total Score}) = 7.0 \quad \text{Var}(\text{Total Score}) = 5.833$
   (iii) $E(\text{Difference}) = 0 \quad \text{Var}(\text{Difference}) = 5.833$
   (iv) $E(\text{Total Score}) = 35 \quad \text{Var}(\text{Total Score}) = 29.17$
12 $E(\text{Amount}) = 65 \quad \text{Var}(\text{Amount}) = 591.7$
13 (i) $E(X) = 1 \quad \text{Var}(X) = 0.5$
   (ii) $E(10X - 5) = 5 \quad \text{Var}(10X - 5) = 50$
   (iii) $E(50 \text{ obs of } X) = 50 \quad \text{Var}(50 \text{ obs of } X) = 25$
   (iv) $E(50X) = E(50 \text{ obs of } X) = 50$
   but $\text{Var}(50X) = 1250 = 50 \times \text{Var}(50 \text{ obs of } X)$
14 (i) $E(\text{Length}) = 123.5 \quad \text{Var}(\text{Length}) = 15.25$
   (ii) $4 \times 0.5 \times 0.2^3 + 4 \times 0.3 \times 0.2^3 + 6 \times 0.3^2 \times 0.2^2 + 0.2^4 = 0.0488$
   (iii) $E(\text{Length}) = 494 \quad \text{Var}(\text{Length}) = 61$
15 (i)

r	−2	0	5
P(X = r)	0.6	0.2	0.2

(ii) $E(X) = -0.2 \quad \text{Var}(X) = 7.36$

(iii) Pay 0.33 pounds less, so pay £1.67.

16 (i) $E(X) = 1.05 \quad \text{Var}(X) = 0.6475$

(ii)

r	0	1	2	3	4
P(Y = r)	0	0.1	0.7	0.2	0

(iii) $E(Y) = 2.1$

(iv) Because X_1 and X_2 are not independent.

Chapter 3

Discussion point, page 44

On average, you would expect $0.25 \times 50 = 12.5$ questions.

Discussion point, page 53

(i) Births would need to occur independently of one another and at a constant average rate throughout the day.

(ii) The 'independence' condition would seem to be reasonable. There is some evidence that more births occur in the morning than at other times of the day.

(iii) This is a complex question and there are many issues to consider. They include:
- Does the expected number of births differ from one month to another?
- For how long is each bed needed?
- How many births are likely to take place at home?
- Is the expected number of births in Avonford likely to change much during the period for which the decisions are being made?
- What happens if there are too few beds, or too many beds?

You may well be able to think of other issues.

Exercise 3.1

1 (i) B(10, 0.5) (ii) 0.2051 (iii) 0.6230
2 (i) 6 (ii) 0.0634 (iii) 0.9095
3 (i) B(10, $\frac{1}{6}$) (ii) $\frac{5}{3}$
  (iii) 0.3230 (iv) 0.2248
4 (i) 3.501×10^{-5}
  (ii) 28 560 (iii) £3.77
5 (i) (a) 25 (b) 0.1 (c) 0.9
  (ii) 0.9020 (iii) $a = 6$
6 (i) 0.8178 (ii) 0.8504 (iii) 0.6689
  (iv) Because in part (ii) you can put 0 in first and 8 in second, 1 and 7, ... whereas in (iii) you can only have 4 and 4
7 (i) 0.2637 (ii) 0.6328 (iii) 16.25 times
8 (i) $\frac{270\,000}{4\,000\,000\,000}$ is approx. $\frac{1}{15\,000}$
  (ii) $1 - \left(1 - \frac{1}{15\,000}\right)^{3000} = 0.181$ approx 0.18
  (iii) $(1 - 0.18)^{12} = 0.088$ (using exact figures gives 0.0907)
  (iv) £121.50 (using exact figures gives £120)
  (v) £64.19 (using exact figures gives £65)
9 (i) 0.4967 (ii) mean 1.6, variance 1.28
11 (i) 0.0301 (ii) 0.0445

Exercise 3.2

1 (i) 0.266
  (ii) 0.826
2 (i) 0.2237
  (ii) 0.1847
  (iii) 0.4012
3 X may be modelled by a Poisson distribution when cars arrive singly and independently and at a known overall average rate; 0.4416

4 (i) 0.058
  (ii) 0.099
5 (i) 25
  (ii) 75
  (iii) 112
  (iv) 288
  Errors occur randomly and independently.
6 (i) 3
  (ii) 27.5
  (iii) 460
7 (i) Aeroplanes land at Heathrow at an almost constant rate (zero at some times of the night), so the event 'an aeroplane lands' is not a random event.
  (ii) Foxes may well occur in pairs, in which case the events would not be independent. (The fact that some regions of area 1 km² will be less popular for foxes than others may be an issue but it is at least partially dealt with by choosing the region randomly.)
  (iii) Bookings are likely not to be independent of one another, as there may be groups requiring more than one table.
  (iv) This should be well modelled by a Poisson distribution (although it would be necessary to assume that the rate of emission was not so high that the total mass was likely to be substantially reduced during a period of 1 minute – i.e. that the half-life of substance is substantially larger than 1 minute).
8 (i) The mean is much greater than the variance therefore X does not have a Poisson distribution.
  (ii) Yes, because now the values of the mean and variance are similar.
  (iii) 0.012
9 (i) 0.175
  (ii) 0.560
  (iii) $\lambda = 10$ 0.1251
  (iv) 0.5421
  (v) 0.0308
  (vi) 10
10 Some bottles will contain two or more hard particles. This will decrease the percentage of bottles that have to be discarded.
   13.9%
   Assume the hard particles occur singly, independently and randomly.
11 $X \sim \text{Poisson}(1)$; 0.014; 0.205

Exercise 3.3

1. (i) 0.0906
   (ii) 8
   (iii) 0.0916; This is very similar to the binomial probability.
2. (i) $\lambda = 5$
   (ii)

   (iii) The probabilities in the chart showing B(10, 0.5) and Poisson(5) are not very similar at all for each value of X and so the Poisson distribution (λ) is a not good approximation to the B(10, 0.5) distribution.
   (iv) $\mu = 5$
   (v) The probabilities in the chart showing B(100, 0.05) and Poisson(5) are very similar for each value of X. The probabilities in the chart showing B(10, 0.5) and Poisson(5) are not very similar at all for each value of X. This is to be expected because in the former case n is large and p is small whereas in the latter case n is small and p is not small.
3. (i) 0.7153
   (ii) 0.7149
   (iii) Because if n is large and p is small then a Poisson distribution with mean np is a good approximation to a binomial distribution.
4. (i) 0.102
   (ii) 0.3586
   (iii) 0.2545
5. (i) 0.175
   (ii) 0.973
   (iii) 0.031
   (iv) 0.125
   (v) 0.248
6. (i) (a) 0.180
       (b) 0.264
       (c) 0.916
   (ii) 0.296
   (iii) 0.05
7. (i) 0.135
   (ii) 0.5947
   (iii) 0.125
8. (i) 0.233
   (ii) 0.123
   (iii) 0.262
9. (i) (a) 0.007
       (b) 0.034
       (c) 0.084
   (ii) $T \sim$ Poisson (5.0)
10. (i) (a) 0.134
        (b) 0.848
    (ii) 0.086
    (iii) 0.673
11. (i) 0.531
    (ii) 0.065
    (iii) 0.159
12. (i) (a) 0.257
        (b) 0.223
        (c) 0.168
    (ii) 0.340
13. (i) (a) 0.209   (b) 0.313
    (ii) 0.454
    (iii) North-bound 2, south-bound 3
14. (i) 0.161
    (ii) 0.554
    (iii) 10
    (iv) 0.016
    (v) 0.119

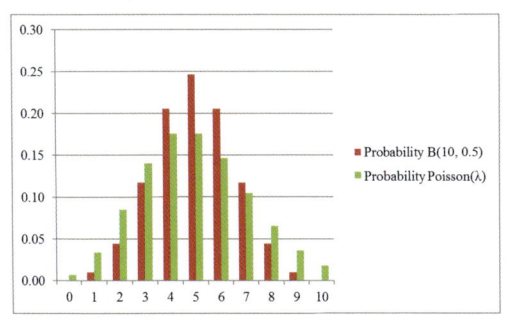

Exercise 3.4

1. (i) $\frac{1}{3}$
   (ii) $\frac{5}{9}$
2. (i) $\frac{1}{3}$
   (ii) $\frac{16}{243}$
   (iii) $\frac{32}{243}$
3. (i) $\frac{1}{2}$
   (ii) $E(X) = 3.5$
   (iii) $Var(X) = 1.25$
4. (i) $E(X) = 3.5$, $Var(X) = \frac{35}{12}$
   (ii) $E(X) = 17.5$, $Var(X) = \frac{175}{12}$
5. $E(X) = 10$, $Var(X) = 4$
6. (i) $E(X) = 2$, $Var(X) = \frac{2}{3}$
   (ii) $E(Y) = 20$, $Var(Y) = \frac{200}{3}$
   (iii) $E(Z) = 20$, $Var(Z) = \frac{20}{3}$
   (iv) Means are equal but variance of Y is larger because it is $10^2 \times Var(X)$ rather than $10 \times Var(X)$

7 (i)   0.0791
   (ii) 0.2373
   (iii) 0.4375
   (iv) 4
8 (i)   0.0504
   (ii) 0.1681
   (iii) 3⅓
   (iv) 0.1235
9 (i)   0.0387
   (ii) 0.1351
   (iii) Mean = 10, Variance = 90
   (iv) n = 7
10 (i)   Geo (⅙)
   (ii) (a) 0.0965 (b) 0.4213 (c) 0.4822
   (iii) (a) 0.4923 (b) 0.0934
   (iv) 0.12

Chapter 4

Discussion point, page 74

1 There is a negative association (or correlation) between life expectancy and birth rate. This is a situation where correlation does not imply causation. Neither directly causes the other but there are other factors that influence both, such as the level of economic development in a country.
2 • The life expectancy in that country
   • The average age of mothers and fathers when they have their first child
   • The number of children that people have

Exercise 4.1

1 (i)   0.8
   (ii) −1
   (iii) 0
2 (i)   (a)

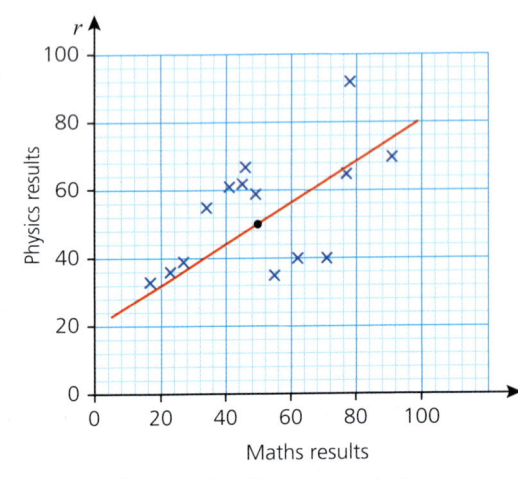

There appears to be positive linear correlation.

   (b) 0.560; This confirms there is a positive linear correlation.
   (ii) (a)

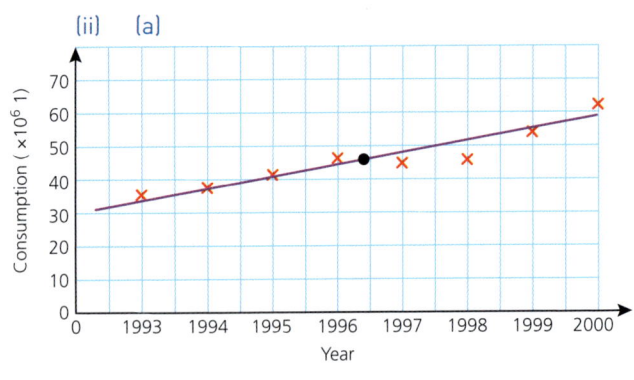

There appears to be strong positive linear correlation.

   (b) 0.940; This confirms there is strong positive linear correlation.
   (iii)

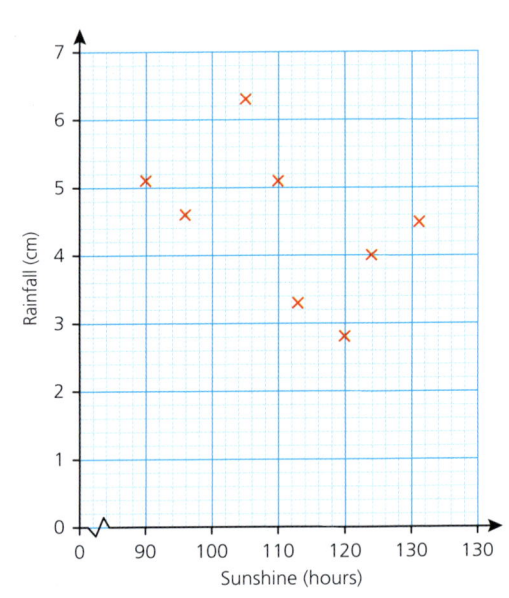

There appears to be no linear correlation (or very weak negative linear correlation).

   (b) −0.461; This confirms there is weak negative linear correlation.
3 (i)   0.704
   (ii) −0.635
   (iii) −0.128
   (iv) −0.924
4 (i)   0.221
   (ii) 0.802
   (iii) 0.806
5 (i)   0.913
   (ii) $H_0: \rho = 0, H_1: \rho > 0$
   (iii) Accept H_1
6 (i)   0.380
   (ii) $H_0: \rho = 0$ (Jamila), $H_1: \rho > 0$ (coach)

(iii) Accept H₀; there is not enough evidence to reject H₀. r needs to be > 0.4973 to reject H₀ at the 5% significance level.

7 (i) Although these data items are a little way from the rest of the data, the sample is very small and with more data it could be that the distribution is bivariate Normal.

(ii) H₀: $\rho = 0$, H₁: $\rho > 0$
Accept H₀; there is not enough evidence to reject H₀. r needs to be > 0.7155 to reject H₀ at the 1% significance level.

8 (i) 0.850
(ii) H₀: $\rho = 0$, H₁: $\rho > 0$
(iii) 0.015 < 0.05 so reject H₀. There is sufficient evidence to suggest that there is positive correlation between chess grade and bridge grade.

9 (i) The effect size involving VR and Q is small. The other two effect sizes are medium and positive, suggesting that students with higher NVR scores tend to have both higher VR scores and higher Q scores.
(ii) This is a very poor suggestion. The correlation coefficients are much closer to 0 than to 1 and so predicting one score from another will be very unreliable.

10 (i) 0.946
(ii) H₀: $\rho = 0$, H₁: $\rho > 0$
(iii) Accept H₁; there is very strong positive correlation.

11 (i) The effect size involving A and I is large and positive suggesting that districts with higher values of A have higher values of I. The effect size involving L and M is medium and positive suggesting that districts with higher values of L have higher values of M. The effect size involving A and L is medium and negative, suggesting that districts with higher values of A have lower values of L and vice versa. The other effect sizes are all small.

12 H₀: $\rho = 0$, H₁: $\rho > 0$; r = 0.901; Andrew

13 (i) H₀: $\rho = 0$, H₁: $\rho \neq 0$. 5% sig. level
(ii) 0.491, accept H₁

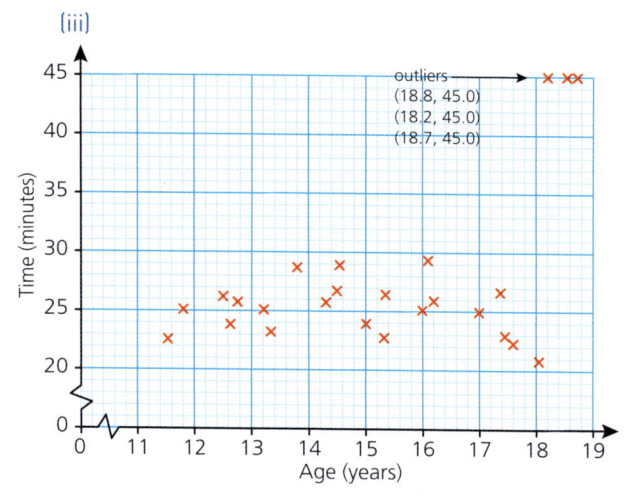

(iii)

[Scatter diagram: Time (minutes) vs Age (years), with outliers labelled (18.8, 45.0), (18.2, 45.0), (18.7, 45.0)]

Outliers: (18.8, 45), (18.2, 45), (18.7, 45), it seems as though these girls stopped for a rest.

(iv) The scatter diagram should have been drawn first and the outliers investigated before calculating the product moment correlation coefficient. With the three outliers removed, r = −0.1612, accept H₀.

14 (i) The data starts in row 2 and finishes in row 61, so there are 60 rows of data.
(ii) =SUM(B2:B61)
(iii) S_{xx} = 5006.6 S_{yy} = 5862.9 and S_{xy} = 1823.3
(iv) r = 0.3365
(v) H₀: $\rho = 0$, H₁: $\rho > 0$;
(vi) 0.3365 > 0.2144 so reject H₀; there is sufficient evidence to reject H₀.
(vii) The effect size is medium.
(viii) It suggests that the two scores are somewhat related. This suggests that the things they are measuring, although not identical, have some similarities. The company should therefore carry on giving both tests as the effect size is only medium.

15 r = 0.59. Diagram suggests moderate positive correlation which is confirmed by the fairly high positive value of r.
After eliminating the high and low values, r = −0.145. Discarding high and low values of x seems to produce an uncorrelated test.

16 (i) 0.3377
(ii) H₀: $\rho = 0$, H₁: $\rho > 0$; 0.3377 < 0.5214 so accept H₀.
(iii) It reduces the value of the product moment correlation coefficient. It should be included, unless there is any reason to suppose it is an error, as it is as valid as any other point.

17 (i)

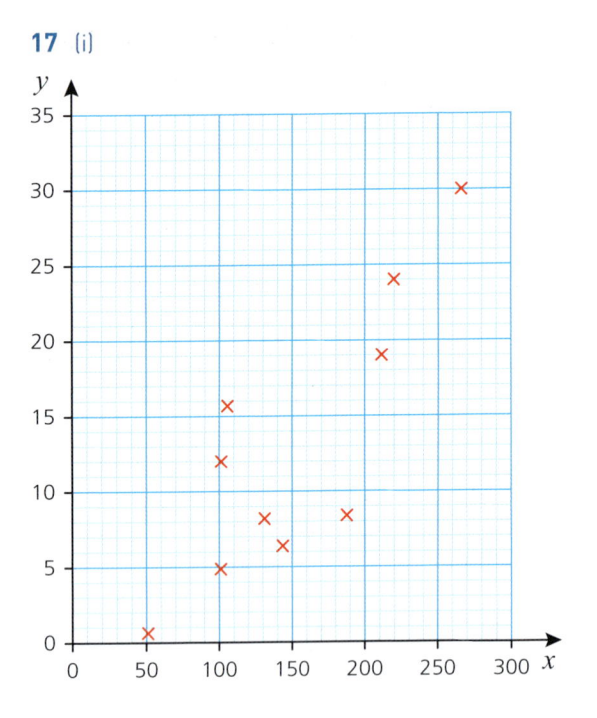

[Scatter plot with y-axis 0–35 and x-axis 0–300]

(ii) 0.834

(iii) $H_0: \rho = 0, H_1: \rho > 0$; critical values: 0.5494 (5%), 0.7155 (1%); 0.834 > 0.7155 so reject H_0.

(iv) The student's view is wrong; correlation does not imply causation. In this case, a common underlying cause, such as wealth, seems plausible.

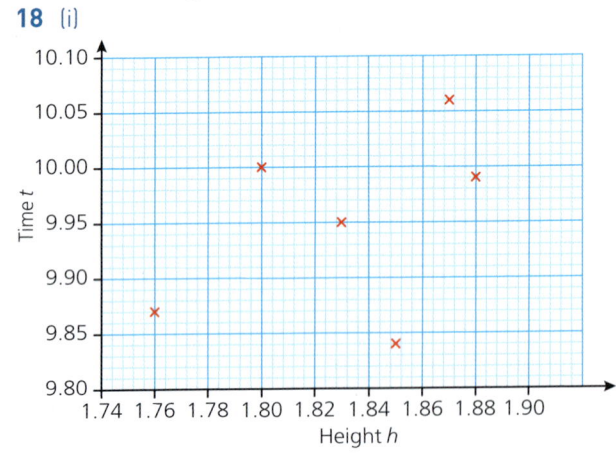

18 (i)

[Scatter plot of Time t against Height h]

(ii) 0.4386

(iii) $H_0: \rho = 0, H_1: \rho > 0$; 0.4386 < 0.7293 so accept H_0; there is not sufficient evidence to reject H_0.

(iv)
Rank h	2	3	5	6	4	1
Rank t	5	3	6	4	1	2

(v) 0.3143

(vi) the correlation coefficient for the ranked data is quite a bit lower than for the unranked. This is probably because ranking loses information.

Exercise 4.2

1 0.576

2 0.20

3 0.50

4 H_0: no association between judges' scores, H_1: positive association between judges' scores. $r_s = 0.6667 > 0.6429$ accept H_1 at 5% significance level. There is positive association between judges' scores.

5 (i) 0.766, −0.143

(ii) $H_0: \rho = 0, H_1: \rho > 0$, accept H_1.

(iii) Product moment correlation coefficient is more suitable here because it takes into account the magnitude of the variables.

6 (i) 0.636. Positive sign indicates possible positive correlation.

(ii) H_0: no association between time and quality, H_1: some association between time and quality. Accept H_1; there is some association between time taken and quality of work.

7 (i) 0.680

(ii) $H_0: \rho = 0, H_1: \rho > 0$, 0.680 > 0.6694 so accept H_1.

(iii) 0.214

(iv) The two correlation coefficients measure different quantities. The product moment correlation coefficient measures linear correlation using the actual data values. Spearman's coefficient measures rank correlation using the data ranks. Mr Smith ought to have used Spearman's coefficient.

8 (i)

January	July
1	1
3	2
8	3
2	4
4	5
5	6
9	7
10	8
7	9
6	10

0.636

(ii) H₀: no association between January and July temperatures, H₁: positive association between January and July temperatures. Accept H₀

(iii) It is more appropriate to use the product moment correlation coefficient since it utilises the actual data values.

9 (i) −0.7857

(ii) H₀: no association between level of community charge and approval rating. H₁: some association between level of community charge and approval rating.

(iii) 0.0279 < 0.05 so reject H₀. There is sufficient evidence to suggest that there is some association between level of community charge and approval rating.

10 (i)

Rank for additive	Rank for weight
3	8
8	6
2	2
10	10
9	4
1	1
4	3
5	5
6	9
7	7

0.612

(ii) H₀: no association between amount of additive and weight of marrow, H₁: positive association between amount of additive and weight of marrow. The alternative hypothesis is one-sided because the additive is claimed to enhance growth.

(iii) 0.612 > 0.5636 so reject H₀. There appears to be positive association between amount of additive and weight of marrow.

(iv) This does not change the rankings so does not affect the conclusions.

11 (i) 0.1608

(ii) H₀: no association between expenditure and score, H₁: positive association between expenditure and score. 0.5035 > 0.1608 so accept H₀. There is insufficient evidence to suggest positive association between expenditure and score.

(iii) If r_s = 0.15 for the whole population then there is an association but it is weak.

12 (i) r_s = 0.952; H₀: no association between prosperity and death rate, H₁: positive association between prosperity and death rate. 0.952 > 0.4637 so reject H₀. There is insufficient evidence to suggest positive association between prosperity and death rate.

(ii) It is not justified; a strong association exists but this does not imply that poverty causes a higher death rate.

(iii) Death rates depend on age distributions, for example an area with many old people will have a higher death rate.

13 (i) −0.44 (2 s.f.)

(ii) $H_0: \rho = 0, H_1: \rho < 0$; −0.44 < −0.3961 0.1608 so reject H₀.

(iii) The sample is not representative in time or space.

(iv) The distribution must be bivariate Normal. It may not be reasonable as the distribution of rainfall is likely to be positive skewed.

14 (i) 0.881

(ii) 0.888

(iii) 0.622

There is significant correlation at the 5% level in all three cases. There are outliers in (i) contraceptives, (ii) contraceptives and (iii) nuclear power.

15 (i) $H_0: \rho = 0, H_1: \rho \neq 0$; two-tailed test is used because the analyst does not specify a positive or a negative correlation.

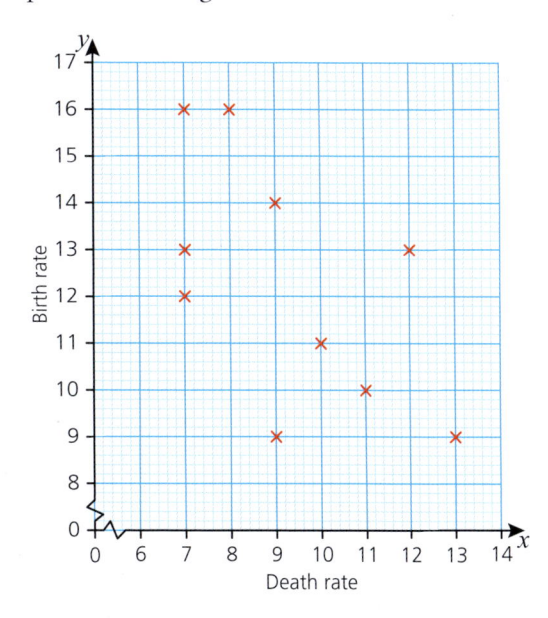

(ii)

(iii) -0.574

(iv) Since $-0.574 > -0.6319$, accept H_0; the death rates and birth rates are not correlated.

(v) There is weak negative correlation between death rates and birth rates.

(vi) No, the additional evidence shows that H_0 should be rejected.

16 (i) 0.66

(ii) H_0: no association between judges' scores, H_1: positive association between judges' scores. c.v. (critical value) = 0.5636, reject H_0 implying the judges are in broad agreement

(iii) c.v. = 0.5494, reject H_0 implying the judges are in broad agreement.

(iv) The rank correlation hypothesis test is more appropriate since the data gives rank order and the sample is unlikely to come from a bivariate Normal population.

17 (i)

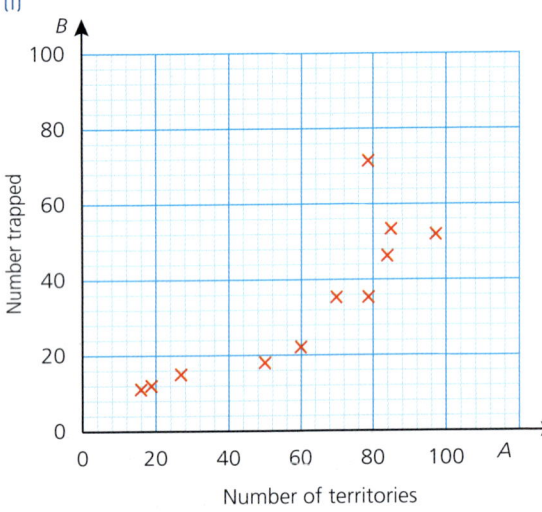

(ii) 0.916 (3 s.f.)

(iii) H_0: no association between the results of the two surveys, H_1: some association between the results of the two surveys. c.v. = 0.6182, 0.916 > 0.6182 so reject H_0, generally, the greater the number of territories recorded, the greater the number trapped.

(iv) It would be less appropriate; the data do not seem to conform to a linear pattern and there is no real evidence of an elliptical scatter.

18 (i)

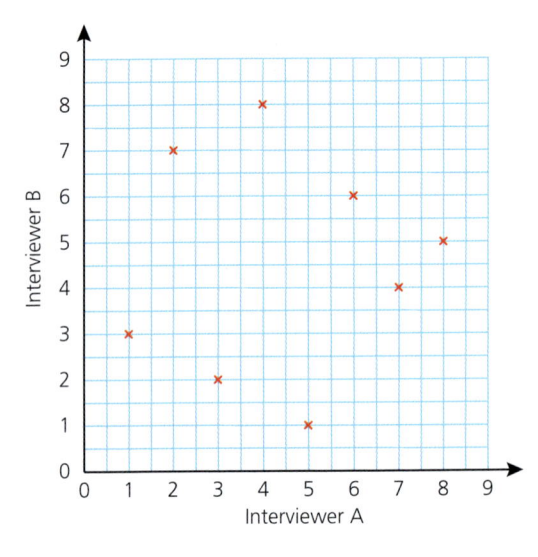

(ii) 0.0476

(iii) 0.0476

(iv) Because the data are ranked.

Chapter 5

Exercise 5.1

1 (i) 15, 26.6

(ii) 250, -95

(iii) $y = 0.38x + 32.3$

2 $1.446x + y = 114.38$, 53.7

3 (i), (ii), (iv)

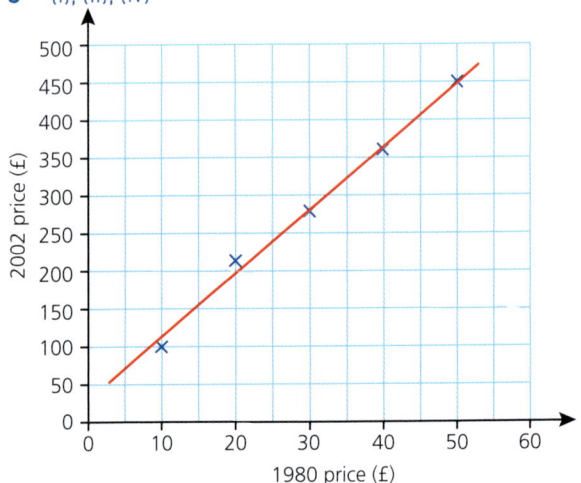

(ii) $y = 8.45x + 27.5$

(iii) This is roughly in line with the rest of the data. It is below the line, so the price increase is slightly below average.

(iv) $-12, 18.5, -1, -5.5, 0$

(v) 517.5; the least squares regression line gives the minimum value of the sum of the squares of the residuals. Altering the line would increase the sum.

$$= \sum_{r=1}^{n} y_r - n\bar{y} - \frac{S_{xy}}{S_{xx}}\left(\sum_{r=1}^{n} x_r - n\bar{x}\right) = 0$$

4 (i) [scatter diagram of y vs t, points from (0,0) rising to about (9,26)]

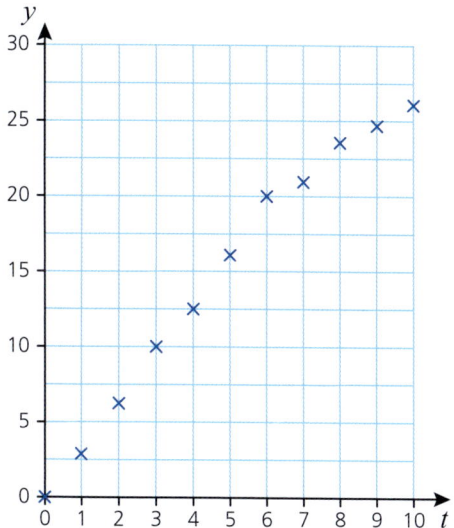

(ii) $v = 2.68t + 1.54$
(iii) 0.988
(iv) Modelling data by a single straight line assumes that the correlation is linear. However, looking at the scatter diagram there is a possibility that r is proportional to a power of t thus making the correlation non-linear.

5 (i), (ii) [scatter diagram of percentage sand content vs depth below ground level (cm), with regression line]

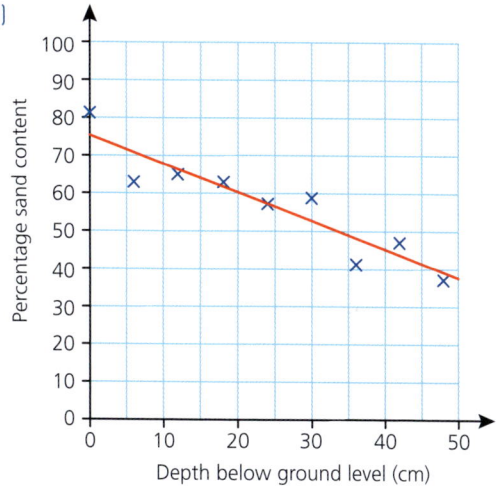

(ii) $y = -0.752x + 75.0$
(iii) When $x = 50$, $y = 37.4$; this is slightly outside the range of data values and so may not be reliable. When $x = 100$, $y = -0.2$; this is further outside the range of data values and there is no evidence that the linear correlation can be extrapolated.
(iv) 5.63, −7.46, −1.65, 1.06, 0.576, 6.78, −7.11, 3.50, −1.29;
$$\sum_{r=1}^{n}\left(y_r - \left(\bar{y} + \frac{S_{xy}}{S_{xx}}(x - \bar{x})\right)\right)$$

6 (i) [scatter diagram of y vs x]

[scatter diagram of $z = \ln y$ vs x]

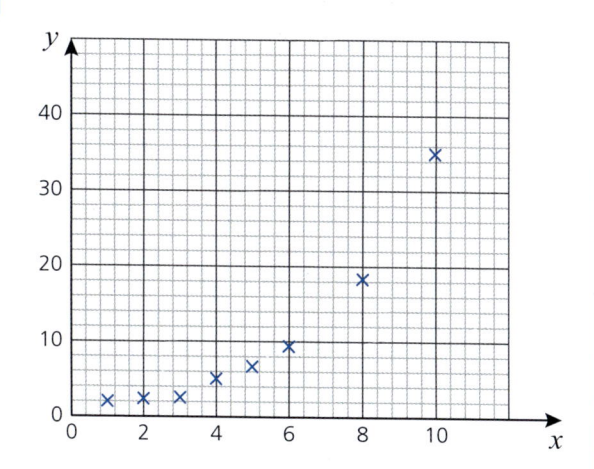

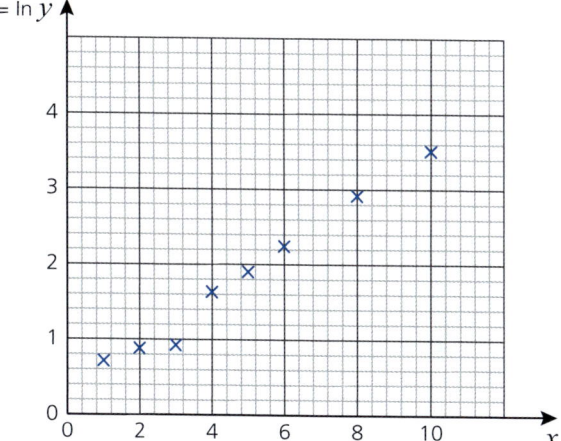

(ii) The line of regression of y is not very accurate because the correlation is not linear. The line of regression of z is much more accurate.
(iii) 12.8

7 (i) [scatter diagram of y vs t]

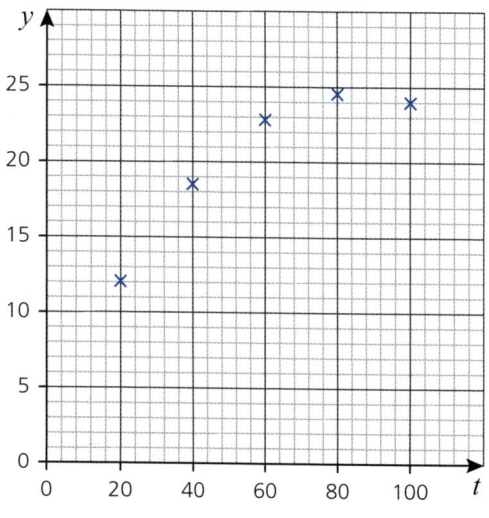

(ii) $y = 0.1495t + 11.43$

(iii) When $t = 30$, $y = 15.915$; likely to be accurate.
When $t = 160$, $y = 35.35$; extrapolation very unlikely to be accurate.

(iv) The regression line does not provide a good model; the data appear to be distinctly non-linear. Perhaps there is a curved relationship or perhaps a levelling off in y.

8 (i) A straight line seems good for x at the low end of the range, but is suspect at the high end of the range.

(ii) $y = 77.289 - 0.374x$

(iii) When $x = 145$, $y = 23.06$; likely to be accurate as it is within the range of the data.
When $x = 180$, $y = 9.97$; may not be accurate as it is beyond the range of the data.

9 (i)

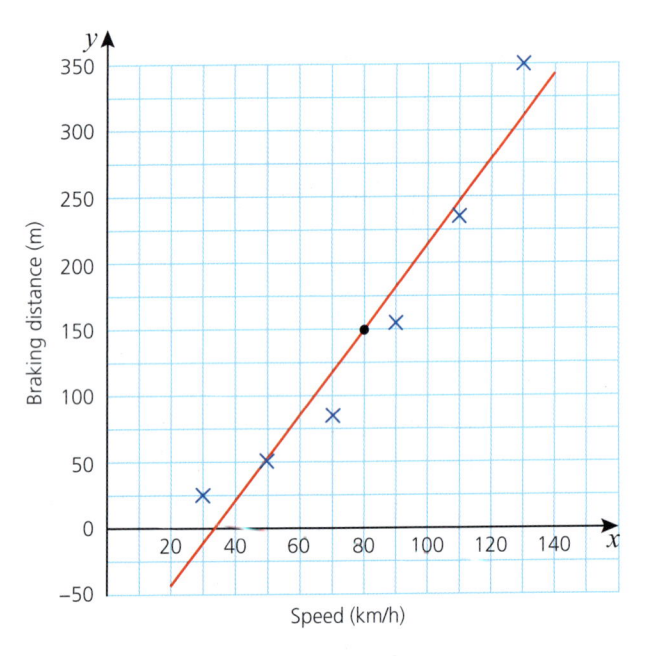

[Scatter plot: Speed (km/h) on x-axis, Braking distance (m) on y-axis, with regression line]

(ii) $y = 3.124x - 107.1$

(iii) When $x = 100$, $y = 241$; seems reasonable since it is within the data range and fits with the neighbouring points.
When $x = 150$, $y = 375$; probably unreliable since the value $x = 150$ lies outside the data range and there is no indication that the linear relationship can be extrapolated.

(iv) The regression line does not seem to provide a good model; a curve may fit the data better.

10 Regression line of y on x: $y = 0.78x + 24.0$ or approx. $y = x + \frac{1}{4}(100 - x)$, thus $\rho \approx \frac{1}{4}$.

Exercise 5.2

1 $y = 3.728x + 4.078$
2 $y = 3.209x + 84.44$
3 (i) $y = 0.2964x + 11.48$
  (ii) $64.8\,\text{kg}$
  (iii) Not very accurate as, although found by interpolation, the points are quite scattered.
  (iv) Because this would be extrapolation (well beyond the range of the data).

4 (i) Regression line is $x = -0.2224y + 6.315$. Estimate is 5.43 hours.
  (ii) $r = -0.444$
  (iii) The estimate is not very reliable since the value of r^2 is only 0.197. The value is, however, probably within the range of the data as the mean value of y is 3.1.

5 (i) $H_0: \rho = 0, H_1: \rho \neq 0$
  (ii) $r = 0.661$ (3 s.f.), c.v. $= 0.5614$, reject H_0; the population must be bivariate Normal
  (iii) Regression line is $y = 0.9453x + 18.24$. Estimates are is 52.3 cm and 45.7 cm.
  (iv) The first is likely to be fairly accurate as interpolation and the value of r^2 is 0.437. The second is less likely to be accurate as the head circumference is well below any occurring in the data (extrapolation).

6 (i) 120.8 mm
  (ii) Fairly accurate because interpolation and r^2 is fairly close to 1.
  (iii) Because it is extrapolation.
  (iv) Because you should use the line of regression of x on y.

7 (i) 0.377
  (ii) $H_0: \rho = 0, H_1: \rho \neq 0$ where ρ is the population correlation coefficient.
  $0.377 > 0.2787$ reject H_0.
  (iii) Population
  Yes since the scatter diagram has a roughly elliptical shape.
  (iv) Because the alternative hypothesis should be decided without referring to the sample data and there is no suggestion that the correlation should be positive rather than negative.
  (v) 150.2
  (vi) There is only one point beyond this value so it is nearly extrapolation so not too likely to be accurate. Also the value of r^2 is only 0.1418 so again not too likely to be accurate.

The value of r^2 is 0.1418 so only 14% of the variation in share price is explained by the variation in oil price, so again the estimate is not too likely to be accurate.

8 (i)

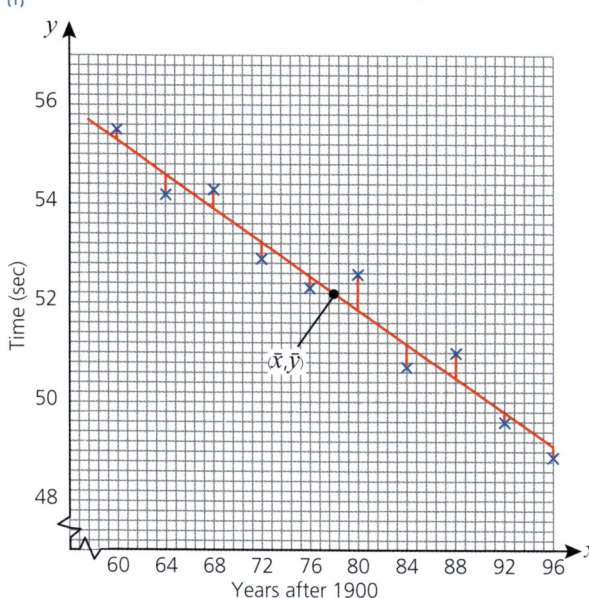

(ii) $y = 65.72 - 0.1733x$
(iii) See graph
(iv) When $x = 100$, $y = 48.39$; this is slightly outside the range of data values so may not be reliable.
When $x = 120$, $y = 44.92$; this is further outside the range of data values and there is no evidence that the linear correlation can be extrapolated.

9 (i)

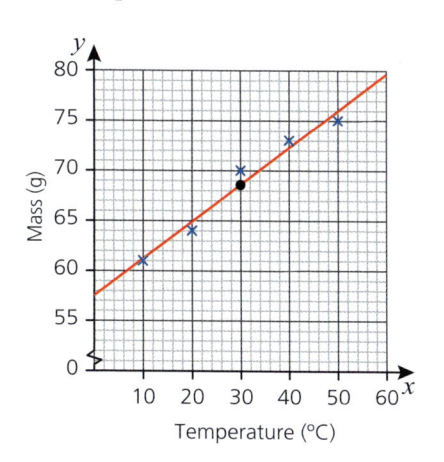

(ii) $y = 0.37x + 57.5$
(iii) 70.45 g;
(iv) 10 °C to 50 °C; unwise to extrapolate outside the data set.
(v) $-0.2, -0.9, 1.4, 0.7, -1.0$
(vi) The equation of the regression line is found by minimising the sum of the squares of the residuals.

10 (i) $y = 86.77 - 6.35x$
When $x = 4.3$, $y = 59.4$; fairly inaccurate since, although it is within the range of the data, the fit does not look good.
When $x = 15$, $y = -8.5$; unsatisfactory since not only is it outside the range of the data but it also implies that the coffee will freeze.

(ii)

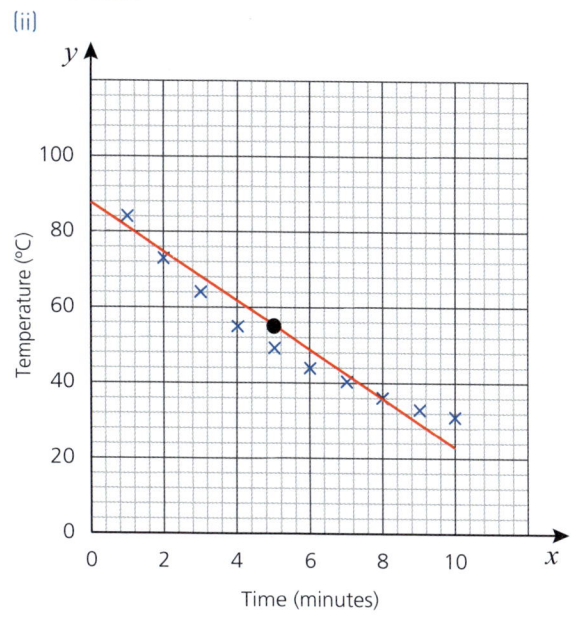

Since the residuals are first positive, then negative and finally positive, a linear regression line does not seem to be appropriate; a curve may be a better fit.

11 (i) Speed is the controlled variable. You can tell this because the speeds are clearly chosen in advance of the test.

(ii)

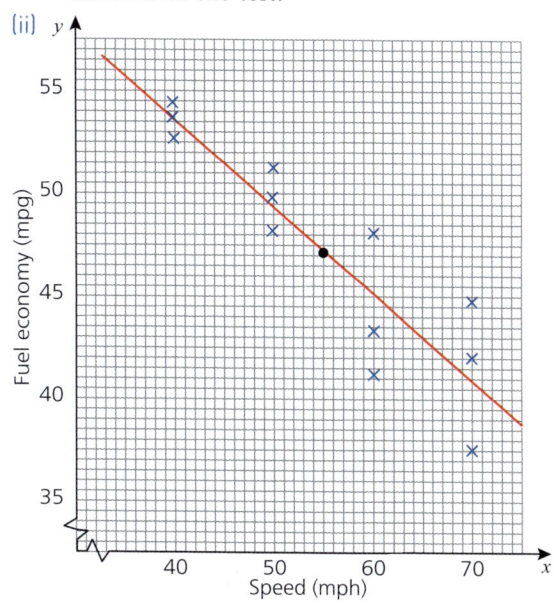

337

(iii) $y = 70.527 - 0.424x$
(iv) (a) 51.45 mpg
(b) 43.0 mpg
(v) The prediction for 45 mph is more reliable than that for 65 mph since the regression line is a better fit at lower speeds; as the speeds increase, the values for the fuel economy have a wider spread and so the use of the regression line to make predictions, especially at the upper end, is dubious.

12 (i)

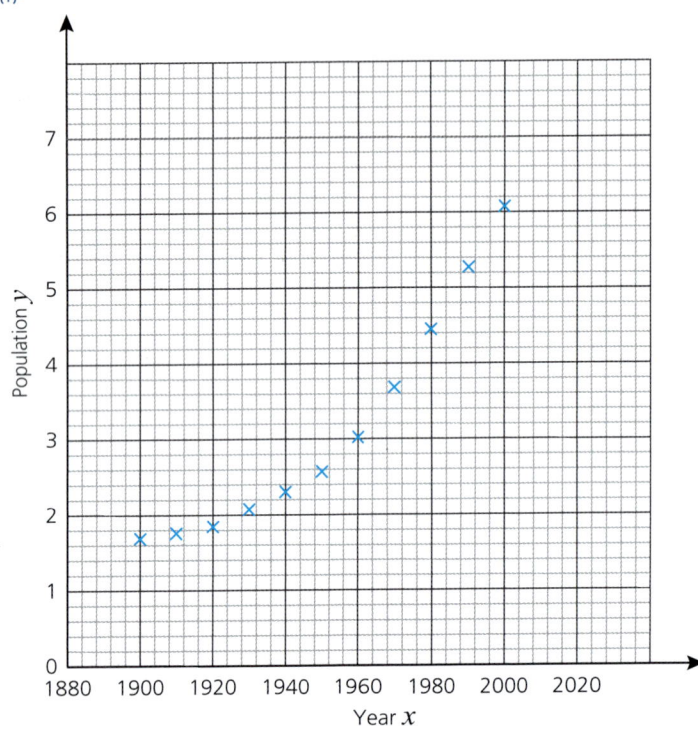

(ii) Because the scatter diagram suggests that there is a relationship but that it should be modelled by a curve.

(iii)

z	0	10	20	30	40	50	60	70	80	90	100
z^2	0	100	400	900	1600	2500	3600	4900	6400	8100	10000
y	1.67	1.75	1.86	2.07	2.30	2.56	3.04	3.71	4.45	5.28	6.08

(iv)

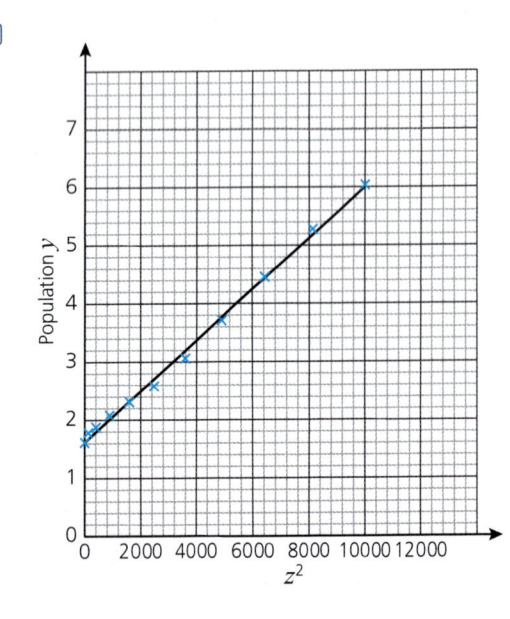

(v) $y = 0.000441z^2 + 1.62$
(vi) 5.60, 19.27
(vii) The first is very reliable as it is interpolation and the line is a very good fit. The second is very unreliable as it is extrapolation, well beyond the data range.

Chapter 6

Discussion point, page 132

They should ideally choose a random sample of customers. However, this will be difficult, so they could instead ask, for example, 1 in every 10 customers to fill in a questionnaire. They should do this over a period so that they sample customers who are watching different types of films.

Discussion points, page 140
- the expected frequencies
  The first figure in each cell in the table
- the contributions to the X^2 statistic
  The second figure in each cell in the table
- the degrees of freedom
  Next to df below the table
- the value of the X^2 statistic
  Next to X^2 below the table
- the p-value for the test
  Next to p below the table

The observed frequencies which is the third figure in each cell in the table.

Discussion point, page 147
The data are real. The model is just your theory.

Discussion point, page 147
One cannot be certain, but it is definitely possible.

Discussion point, page 157
The fit looks suspiciously good but see the text that follows.

Exercise 6.1
1. (i) Walk 78, Cycle 66, Bus 113, Car 73, Age 13 172, Age 16 158
   (iv) No, because, for instance, younger students might be less likely to be allowed by their parents to cycle.

2. (i)
	Pass	Fail
Less than 10 hours	21.31	9.69
At least 10 hours	33.69	15.31

   (ii)
	Pass	Fail
Less than 10 hours	3.2421	7.1327
At least 10 hours	2.0511	4.5125

3. $X^2 = 35.87$
   $v = 12$
   Reject H_0 at 5% level or above; association

4. $X^2 = 2.886$
   $v = 1$
   Accept H_0 at 5% level or below; independent

5. $X^2 = 0.955$
   $v = 1$
   Accept H_0 at 10% level or below; no association

6. $X^2 = 7.137$
   $v = 4$
   Accept H_0 at 10% level or below; independent

7. $X^2 = 10.38$
   $v = 1$
   Reject H_0 at 1% level (c.v. = 6.635): related

8. $X^2 = 13.27$
   $v = 6$
   Reject at 2.5% level or above: not independent

9. $X^2 = 11.354$
   $v = 4$
   Reject H_0 at 5% level (c.v. = 9.488): association. The cells with the largest value of $\frac{(f_0 - f_e)^2}{f_e}$ are medium/induction and long/induction so medium and long service seem to be associated, respectively, with more than and fewer than expected employees with induction-only training.

10. (i) $X^2 = 5.36$
    $v = 2$
    Reject H_0 at 10% level (c.v. 4.605): association
    (ii) Two degrees of freedom, since once the urban/none and urban/one values are fixed, all the other cell values follow from the row and column totals.
    (iii) It appears that fewer rural residents than expected read more than one newspaper.

11. $X^2 = 22.48$
    $v = 9$
    Reject H_0 at 5% level (c.v. = 16.92): association
    Considering the values of $\frac{(f_0 - f_e)^2}{f_e}$ for each cell, shows that rural areas seem to be associated with more reasonable and excellent and less poor or good air quality than expected.

12. H_0: no association, H_1: association
    $X^2 = 19.79$, c.v. = 16.81
    Reject H_0, seems to be association
    SE and Midlands have more short and fewer long lifespans than expected; 'rest' has fewer short and more long lifespans than expected.

13. (i) Some of the expected frequencies may be less than 5.
    (ii) H_0: no association, H_1: association
    (iii) $X^2 = 1.445$, $v = 2$, c.v. = 5.991. Accept H_0 not enough evidence to suggest association.
    (iv) Best to combine small and large businesses as these have more similarities than any other group.
    H_0: no association, H_1: association
    $X^2 = 0.0384$, $v = 1$, c.v. = 3.841. Accept H_0 not enough evidence to suggest association.

14 (i) 4.136, 5.091

(ii) Because some of the expected frequencies are less than 5.

(iii) Combine 'Under 20' and '20–39' and combine '40–59' and '60 or over'.

(iv) H_0: no association, H_1: association. $X^2 = 13.22$, $v = 2$, c.v. = 5.991. Reject H_0 there is enough evidence to suggest association.

(v)
Contribution to test statistic	Pop	Classical	Jazz
Under 40	4.060	0.077	3.375
40 and over	3.086	0.058	2.565

The values of 4.06 and 3.09 show that under 40s have a strong positive association with pop, whereas 40 and over have a strong negative association with pop. The values of 3.37 and 2.56 show that under 40s have a strong negative association with jazz, whereas 40 and over have a strong positive association with jazz. The observed frequencies for classical are much as expected.

Activity 6.2, page 156
Estimated $p = 0.0683$, $X^2 = 0.55$, $v = 4$, critical value = 9.488; accept H_0, this binomial model fits the data

Exercise 6.2
1
x	0	1	2	3	≥ 4
Exp	12.13	24.00	22.55	13.38	7.95

2
x	0	1	2	3	4	≥ 5
Exp	12.11	19.38	15.51	8.27	3.31	1.42

3 H_0: the distribution of the observations can be modelled by the Poisson (2) distribution. H_1: the distribution of the observations cannot be modelled by the Poisson (2) distribution. $X^2 = 14.887$, $v = 5$, significant

4 (i) $\bar{x} = 1.725$

H_0: the number of mistakes on a page can be modelled by the Poisson distribution. $X^2 = 36.3$, $v = 4$, significant

(ii) The mean rate may not be constant, for example, she may make more mistakes when she is tired. The mistakes might not be independent if, for example, some sections are about things she cannot spell.

5 (i) Binomial, $B\left(5, \frac{1}{4}\right)$.

(ii) H_0: the number of white flowers in each tray can be modelled by a binomial distribution, $B\left(5, \frac{1}{4}\right)$. H_1: the number of white flowers in each tray cannot be modelled by this distribution. $X^2 = 0.343$, $v = 2$, not significant

6 (i) 0.6

(ii) H_0: the distribution of the number of times travellers were satisfied with their journeys has a binomial distribution. H_1: the distribution of the number of times travellers were satisfied with their journeys does not have a binomial distribution. $X^2 = 4.84$, $v = 2$, significant

(iii) The sample must be random. This is unlikely to be the case if only those who have made exactly three journeys are sampled.

7 H_0: the students guessed the answers at random. H_1: the students did not guess the answers at random. $X^2 = 18.8$, $v = 4$, significant

8 (i) H_0: the size of rocks is distributed evenly on the scree slope. H_1: the size of rocks is not distributed evenly on the scree slope. $X^2 = 7.82$, $v = 2$, significant

(ii) The test shows that rocks of different sizes are not evenly distributed. Another, different test will be needed to determine whether the larger rocks are nearer the bottom of the slope.

9 (i) 3.303. Yes since the sample variance and mean are similar.

(iii) p-value > 0.05 so accept H_0 at 5% level: Poisson model may be appropriate or 3.303 < 9.488 so accept H_0 at 5% level: Poisson model may be appropriate

10 (i) Mean = 0.933, variance = 0.929

(ii) $p = 0.1333$
H_0: these data can be modelled by the binomial distribution. H_1: these data cannot be modelled by the binomial distribution. $X^2 = 0.28$, $v = 1$, not significant

(iii) Poisson, because of general spread of data in table and because mean ≈ variance.

11 (i) Several observed frequencies are too small. In order to have $f_e \geq 5$ in each class there would be only two classes. There are two constraints and so no degrees of freedom, therefore the χ^2 test cannot be used.

(ii) $\bar{x} = 0.92$

H_0: the occurrence of Morag's spelling mistakes may be modelled by the Poisson distribution.

H_1: the occurrence of Morag's spelling mistakes may not be modelled by the Poisson distribution.

$X^2 = 2.46$, $v = 1$, not significant

(iii) Spelling mistakes occur singly, randomly and independently. This could be realistic.

12 Reject H_0 because the test statistic is much larger than the critical value, 9.488, at the 5% significance level when $v = 4$.

13 (i)

No. of children	0	1	2	3	4	5+
f_e	246.6	345.2	241.7	112.8	39.5	14.2

(ii) H_0: Number of children per household can be modelled by the Poisson (1.40) distribution.

H_1: Number of children per household cannot be modelled by the Poisson (1.40) distribution.

$X^2 = 32.17$, $v = 5$, significant

14 (i)

	A	B	C	D	E	F	G	H
f_e	71	113	104	71.5	57	49	29.5	5
f_o	53	105	111	80	63	49	36	3

(ii) H_0: distribution of properties in Trumpton reflects the national distribution.

H_1: distribution of properties in Trumpton does not reflect the national distribution.

Conclusion: $v = 7$, $9.475 < 12.02$ so accept H_0

(iii) There is not enough evidence to reject H_0.

15 (i) H_0: shoplifting is equally likely to occur in all months.

H_1: shoplifting is more likely to occur in some months than others.

$X^2 = 14.28$, $v = 11$, not significant at 5% level.

(ii) $X^2 = \Sigma \dfrac{(f_o - f_e)^2}{f_e} = \dfrac{\Sigma(f_o^2 - 2f_o f_e + f_e^2)}{f_e}$

$= \dfrac{1}{f_e}\Sigma f_o^2 - 2\Sigma f_o + \Sigma f_e$

$= \dfrac{1}{f_e}\Sigma f_e^2 - \Sigma f_e$ because $\Sigma f_o = \Sigma f_e$

16 (i) H_0: the two dice used in the casino are fair

H_1: the two dice used in the casino are not fair.

(iii) Conclusion: $X^2 = 10.1$, $v = 11$, not significant so accept H_0, there is insufficient evidence to suggest that the dice are loaded.

17 (i) H_0: the distribution of the distances customers travel to the store is the same as at the manager's previous store.

H_1: the distribution of the distances customers travel to the store is not the same as at the manager's previous store.

$X^2 = 7.44$, $v = 2$, significant

There are more customers in the 5–10 miles category and fewer in the other two.

(ii) It is unlikely as all the customers were sampled at a similar time on a particular day.

18 $X^2 = 0.57$, $v = 4$, not significant.

Practice questions: Set 1 (page 165)

1 (i) Vertical sections through the weight on age scatter diagram show similar means (except perhaps for the very oldest patients). Spread is greatest for younger patients because there are more with very high weight. Vertical sections through the height on age scatter diagram show decreasing means from the twenties onwards. The spread decreases too.

(ii) (A) Positive skew (as the data points are more spread out above the mean).

(B) Little or no skew, though the small number of short patients would give slight negative skew.

(iii) Using the raw data, the mean weight is about 74 kg so accept 69–79 kg.

Using the raw data, the mean height is about 162 cm so accept 159–165 cm.

Mean height (about 5'4") strongly suggests that these are women.

Mean weight (just over 11 stone) sounds a little high for women, but it is consistent with recent figures in the United States.

(iv) The scatter diagrams for weight and age and for height and age show negative

341

correlation. Height and weight will be positively correlated, so 0.31.

(v) There is no suggestion that these individuals form a random sample. They may differ from the population in having a condition that has brought them to the clinic for treatment.

2 (i) No evidence of bivariate Normality.

(ii) $\Sigma D^2 = 90$, $r_s = 5/11 = 0.45$.

(iii) H_0: there is no association between age of female and age of male.
H_1: there is some association between age of female and age of male.

Critical value for $n = 10$, two-tailed 5% test is 0.6485.

The observed value is less than the critical value, and so not significant at the 5% level.

Insufficient evidence to suppose that there is any association between age of female and age of male.

3 (i) (A) $0.6^2 \times 0.4 = 0.144$
(B) $0.6^6 = 0.0467$
(C) $0.6^6 \times (1 - 0.6^6) = 0.0445$

(ii) Geometric with $p = 0.4$.
$E(X) = 2.5$

(iii) Esperanza expects to win $12 \times 0.4 = 4.8$ prizes.
The expected value of these prizes is $4.8 \times £27 = £129.60$.

4 (i) The elliptical data cloud suggests an underlying bivariate Normal distribution.

(ii) The pmcc has magnitude 0.708. It is clearly negative, so −0.708.

(iii) $y = 1.0569$.
This is an estimate of the mean value of y when $x = 25$; that is, an estimate of the mean body density for people with BMI 25.

(iv) Calculating x when $y = 1.08$ requires the regression line of x on y. That is quite different from the regression line of y on x.

5 (i) There are relatively few only children and middle born children when compared with first and last born children. This suggests that the majority of families have 2 children.

(ii) The 150 for first born and 90 for last born suggest that first born children may be more likely than last born children to go to university.

(iii) H_0: there is no association between birth order and subject studied at university.
H_1: there is an association between birth order and subject studied at university.

(iv) B9: = E2 * B6 / E6
B15: = (B2 − B9)^2 / B9

(v) Degrees of freedom 6.
5% critical value is 12.59.
Observed result is in the critical region. There is sufficient evidence to suppose that birth order is associated with subject studied at university.

(vi) 4.53: far more middle born children than expected (under H_0) study humanities.
2.24: fewer middle born children than expected (under H_0) study other subjects.

6 (i) Faulty pixels occur independently of one another and at a uniform average rate.

(ii) (A) 0.3012   (B) 0.9662

(iii) $P(Y = 0) = 0.3012 / 0.9662 = 0.3117$

(iv) $P(Y = 1) = 0.3741$, $P(Y = 2) = 0.2244$, $P(Y = 3) = 0.0898$

(v) $E(Y) = 1.092$
$E(Y^2) = 2.0798$ $Var(Y) = 0.8867$
$SD(Y) = 0.9417$

Answers

Chapter 7

Discussion point, page 171
$P(Y \cap C)$ = Probability tests positive and has the condition = 0.20.

$P(Y \cap C')$ = Probability tests positive and does not have the condition = 0.15.

$P(Y' \cap C)$ = Probability tests negative and has the condition = 0.05.

$P(Y' \cap C')$ = Probability tests negative and does not have the condition = 0.60.

Discussion point, page 172
The four numbers in the body of the table occur at the ends of the branches of the trees. Those in the margins do not appear.

The final answers would be the same, although the tree would look different.

Discussion point, page 174
When DNA is collected, the probability of two people having the same DNA profile is very small, but not zero. If only a partial DNA sample has been collected from a crime scene, then this probability could be rather larger. Let us suppose that the probability of two different people having the same partial profile as that found at a crime scene in London is only 1 in one million. The population of London is roughly 9 million. So there will be approximately 9 people who share this profile. So without any other evidence, the probability that the sample comes from a person who has this DNA profile is $\frac{1}{9}$.

Exercise 7.1
1. (i) 0.33
   (ii) 0.385
   (iii) 0.2
2. (i) 0.24
   (ii) 0.44
   (iii) 0.136
3. (i) $P(W) \times P(C) = 0.20 \times 0.17 = 0.034 \neq P(W \cap C) = 0.06$ so not independent

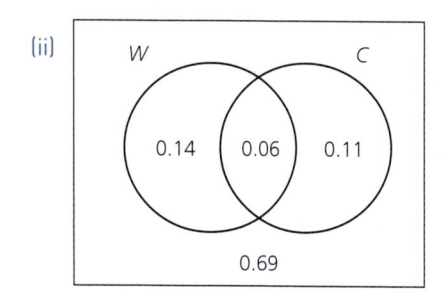

   (ii) Venn diagram with sets W and C: W only region 0.14, intersection 0.06, C only region 0.11, outside 0.69

   (iii) 0.353
   (iv) Children are more likely than adults to be able to speak Welsh.
4. (i) 0.033
   (ii) 0.545
5. (i) 0.05329
   (ii) 0.0650
   (iii) 0.9350
   (iv) It has a high false positive rate so it is not very effective unless combined with further testing.
6. (i) 0.07
   (ii) 0.0476
7. 0.6087
8. (i) 0.01465
   (ii) 0.662
9. (i) 0.025
   (ii) 0.4
10. (i) 0.1825
    (ii) 0.8

Chapter 8

Discussion point, page 181
It is reasonable since the wave heights are not predictable.

Discussion point, page 193
b, c, d, e

Discussion point, page 211
£150 is quite a large prize, but probably small in comparison to the total entry fees so it may be worth it if the model is very good. The model

343

should work for any number of runners and should be adjustable if the nature of the entry changes.

Exercise 8.1

1. (i) $k = \dfrac{2}{35}$

   (ii) [graph of f(x): line from (1, 2/35) to (6, 12/35)]

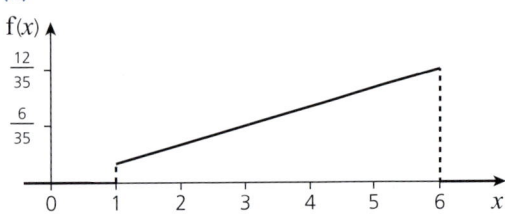

   (iii) $\dfrac{11}{35}$

   (iv) $\dfrac{1}{7}$

2. (i) $k = \dfrac{1}{12}$

   (ii) [graph of f(x): line from (0, 5/12) down to (4, 1/12)]

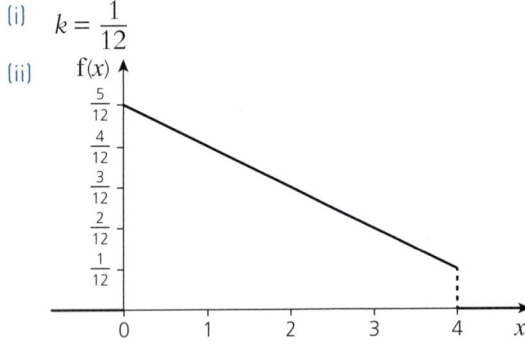

   (iii) 0.207

3. (i) $c = \dfrac{1}{8}$

   (ii) [graph of f(x): horizontal line at 1/8 from x = −3 to x = 5]

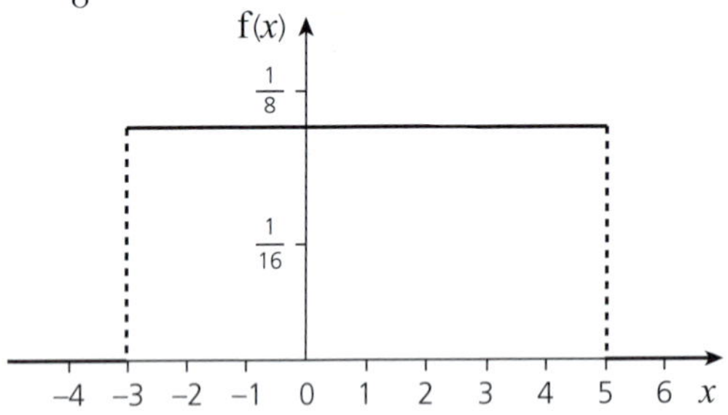

   (iii) $\dfrac{1}{4}$

   (iv) $\dfrac{3}{8}$

4. (i) $k = \dfrac{1}{4}$

   (ii) [graph of f(x): triangle peaking at (2, 1/2), from x = 0 to x = 4]

5. (i) $a = \dfrac{4}{81}$

   (ii) [graph of f(x): increasing curve from 0 to 3, reaching just above 1]

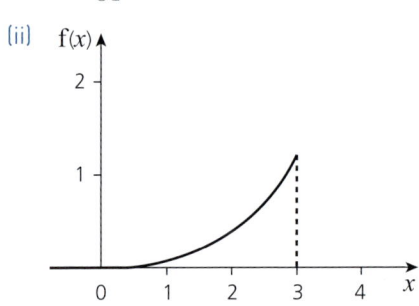

   (iii) $\dfrac{16}{81}$

6. (i) $k = 0.048$

   (ii) [graph of f(x): parabolic arch from x = 1 to x = 6, peak ≈ 0.3]

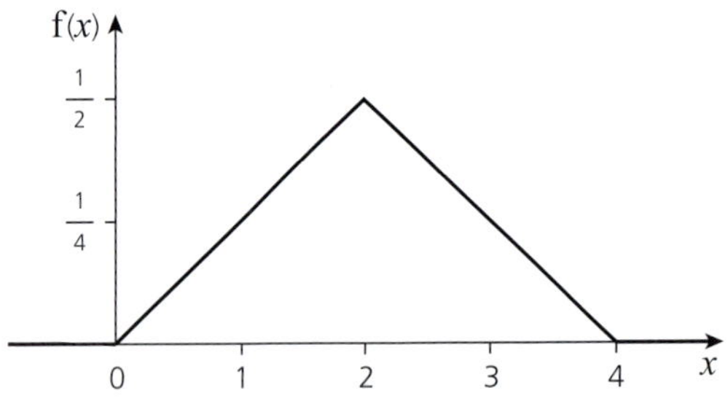

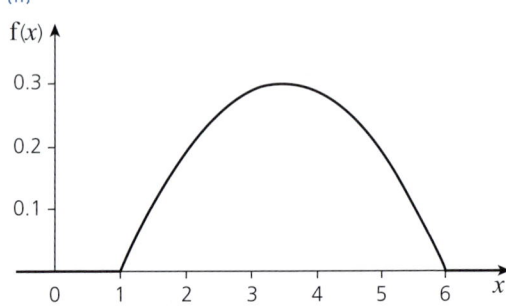

   (iii) 0.248

7. (i) $a = \dfrac{5}{12}$

   (ii) [graph of f(x): small arch from x = 1 to x = 2 reaching 3/12, then rectangle at 5/12 from x = 2 to x = 4]

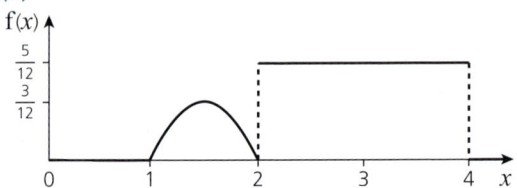

   (iii) 0.292

   (iv) $\dfrac{7}{12}$

8. (i) $k = \dfrac{2}{9}$

   (ii) 0.067

9. (i) $k = \dfrac{1}{100}$

   (ii) [graph of f(x): straight line from (0, 0.2) down to (10, 0)]
   Length of stay (hours)

(iii) $\dfrac{27}{32}$

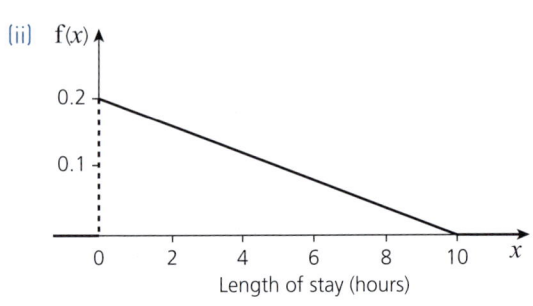

(iii) 19, 17, 28, 36
(iv) Yes
(v) Further information needed about the group 4–10 hours. It is possible that many of these stay all day so are part of a different distribution.

10 (i)

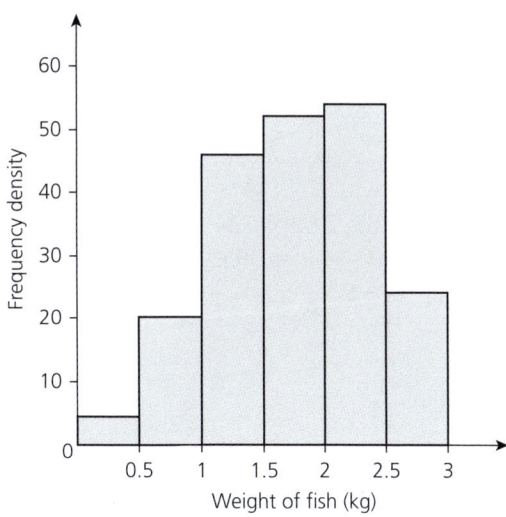

[Histogram of weight of fish (kg) vs frequency density]

Negative skew

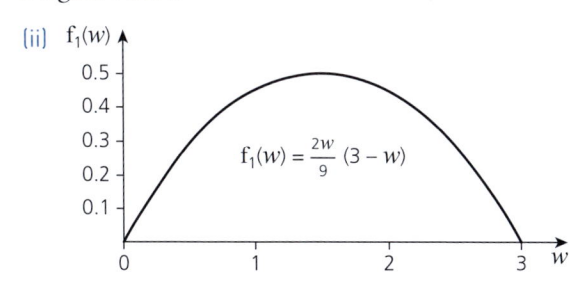

(ii) $f_1(w)$ graph with $f_1(w) = \frac{2w}{9}(3-w)$

$f_2(w)$ graph with $f_2(w) = \frac{10w^2}{81}(3-w^2)$

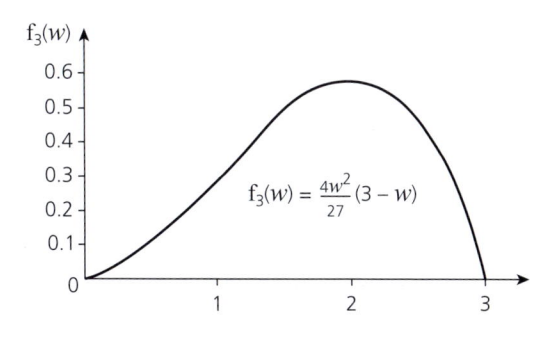

$f_3(w)$ graph with $f_3(w) = \frac{4w^2}{27}(3-w)$

$f_4(w)$ graph with $f_4(w) = \frac{4w}{27}(3-w)^2$

$f_3(w)$ matches the data most closely.
(iii) 1.62, 9.49, 20.14, 28.01, 27.55, 13.19
(iv) Model seems good.

11 (i) $a = 100$
(ii) 0.045
(iii) 0.36

12 0.803, 0.456

13 (i) 0, 0.1, 0.21, 0.12, 0.05, 0.02, 0
(ii) 0.1, 0.31, 0.33, 0.17, 0.07, 0.02
(iii) $k = \frac{1}{1728}$
(iv) 0.132, 0.275, 0.280, 0.201, 0.095, 0.016
(v) Model quite good. Both positively skewed.

Exercise 8.2

1 (i) 2.67
(ii) 0.89
(iii) 2.828

2 (i) 2
(ii) 2
(iii) 1.76

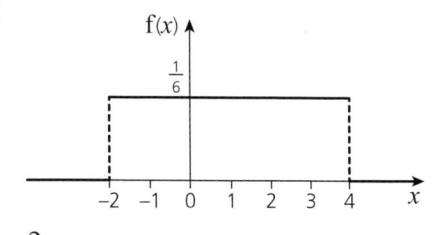

3 (i) [Graph of f(x), uniform at 1/6 from −2 to 4]

(ii) $\frac{2}{3}$
(iii) 1
(iv) $\frac{1}{2}$

4 (i) 0.6
(ii) 0.04

5 (i) 1.5
(ii) 0.45
(iii) 1.5
(iv) 1.5

(v)

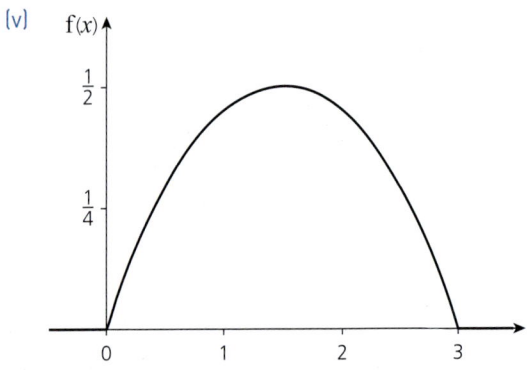

The graph is symmetrical and peaks when $x = 1.5$ thus E(X) = mode of X = median value of X = 1.5.

6 (i) $f(x) = \frac{1}{7}$ for $-2 \leq x \leq 5$
   (ii) 1.5
   (iii) 4.08
   (iv) $\frac{5}{7}$

7 (ii) 1.083, 0.326
   (iii) 0.5625

8 (i) $f(x) = \frac{1}{3}$ for $4 \leq x \leq 7$
   (ii) 5.5
   (iii) $\frac{3}{4}$
   (iv) 0.233

9 (i) $f(x) = \frac{1}{10}$ for $10 \leq x \leq 20$
   (ii) 15, 8.33
   (iii) (a) 57.7%   (b) 100%

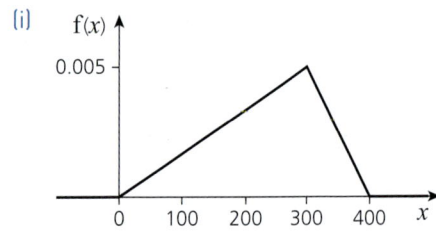

10 (i)
   (iii) $233\frac{1}{3}$ hours
   (iv) 7222.2
   (v) 0.083

11 (i) $k = 1.2 \times 10^8$
   (ii)
   (iii) The distribution is the sum of two smaller distributions, one of moderate candidates and the other of able ones.

   (iv) Yes, if the step size is small compared with the standard deviation.

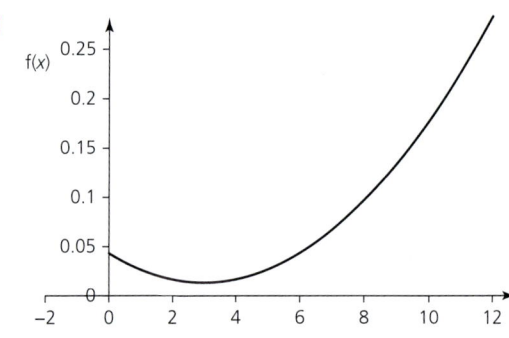

12 (i)
   (ii) 8.88, 2.88; 0.724
   (iii) $m^3 - 9m^2 + 39m - 450 = 0$

13 (i) $a = k$
   (ii) $\frac{1}{k}$
   (iii) $\frac{1}{k^2}$
   (iv) $\frac{\ln 2}{k}$
   (v) For example, the lifetime in hours of an electric light bulb.

14 (i) 200
   (ii) 0.082
   (iii) 0.139
   (iv) $k = 7.31$

15 (i) $a = 1.443$
   (ii)
   (iii) 1.443, 0.083
   (iv) 41.5%
   (v) 1.414

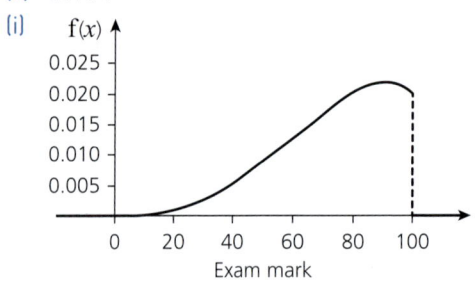

16 (i)
   The model suggests that these candidates were generally of high ability as a large proportion of them scored a high mark.
   (iii) 12.5%
   (iv) No; 91

Exercise 8.3

1. (i) $k = 0.2$
   (ii) f(x) graph: horizontal line at 0.2 from $x=0$ to $x=5$
   (iii) 2.5
   (iv) 7
2. (i) 0.8
   (ii) $0.\dot{6}$
   (iii) $0.02\dot{6}$
3. $0.8, 0.16, £8$
4. (i) 1.5
   (ii) 2.7
   (iii) 0.45
   (iv) 13.9
   (v) 0.45; both are the variance of Y.
5. (i) 0.6
   (ii) −3.4
   (iii) 0.2
   (iv) 0.64
6. (i) $3\frac{2}{3}$
   (ii) $66\frac{1}{6}$
   (iii) $14\frac{5}{6}, 66\frac{1}{6}$
7. (i) $f(x) = \frac{1}{6}$ for $2 \le x \le 8$
   (ii) $a = \frac{\sqrt{3}x^2}{4}$
   (iii) 0.352
   (iv) 12.12, 57.6
8. (i) $E(X) = 3.2$
   (ii) p.d.f. graph over Time (minutes) from 0 to 10

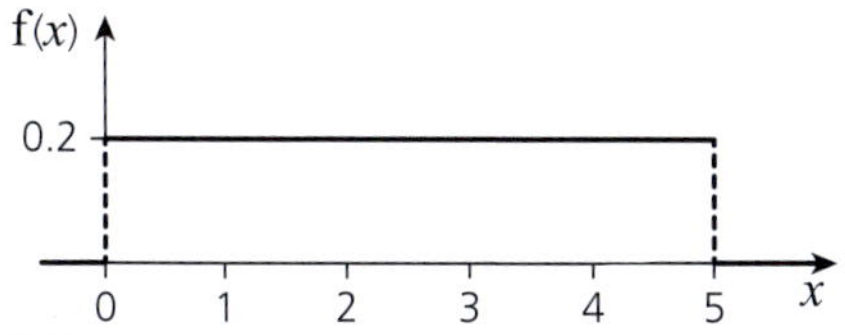

   The model implies that all of the doctor's appointments last between 2 and 10 minutes, the mean time being 5.2 minutes and the variance of the distribution being 2.56 minutes^2.
9. $k = \frac{1}{36}$, mean $= 3$, probability $= \frac{5}{32}$
10. (i) $f(t) = \begin{cases} 0.1 & \text{for } 0 \le t \le 10 \\ 0 & \text{otherwise} \end{cases}$

    mean $= 5$, variance $= 8\frac{1}{3}$

   (ii) f(x) triangular graph peaking at (10, 0.1), from 0 to 20
   (iii) $E(X) = 10, \text{Var}(X) = 16\frac{2}{3}$
   (iv) 0.18; because $T_1 \ge 7$ and $T_2 \ge 7$ is not the only way for $X \ge 14$. The latter inequality also includes other possibilities, such as waiting 9 minutes in the morning and 6 minutes in the evening.

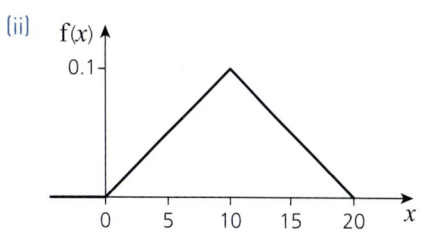

Exercise 8.4

1. (i) 2.5
   (ii) $F(x) = \begin{cases} 0 & \text{for } x < 0 \\ \frac{x}{5} & \text{for } 0 \le x \le 5 \\ 1 & \text{for } x > 5 \end{cases}$
   (iii) 0.4
2. (i) $k = \frac{2}{39}$
   (ii) f(u) graph from $u=5$ to $u=8$, rising from $\frac{10}{39}$ to $\frac{20}{39}$
   (iii) $F(u) = \begin{cases} 0 & \text{for } u < 5 \\ \frac{u^2}{39} - \frac{25}{39} & \text{for } 5 \le u \le 8 \\ 1 & \text{for } u > 8 \end{cases}$
   (iv) F(u) graph
3. (i) $c = \frac{1}{21}$
   (ii) $F(x) = \begin{cases} 0 & \text{for } x < 1 \\ \frac{x^3}{63} - \frac{1}{63} & \text{for } 1 \le x \le 4 \\ 1 & \text{for } x > 4 \end{cases}$
   (iii) 3.19
   (iv) 4
4. (i) $F(x) = \begin{cases} 0 & \text{for } x < 0 \\ 1 - \frac{1}{(1+x)^3} & \text{for } x \ge 0 \end{cases}$

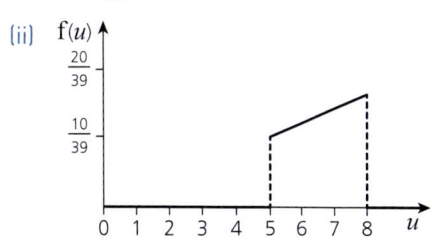

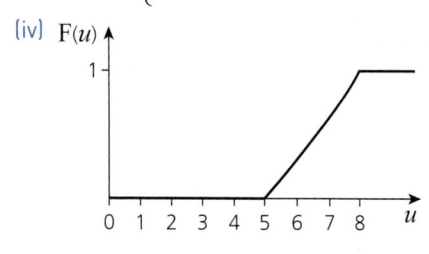

347

(ii) $x = 1$

5 (i) $\dfrac{1}{4}$

(ii) 0.134

(iii) $f(x) = 2 - 2x$ for $0 \le x \le 1$

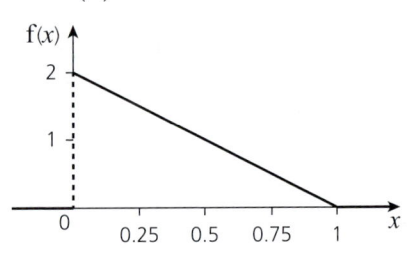

[graph of f(x): line from (0,2) to (1,0)]

6 $E(X) = \dfrac{3}{4}, \text{Var}(X) = \dfrac{19}{80}$

$F(x) = \begin{cases} 0 & \text{for } x < 0 \\ \dfrac{3x}{4} - \dfrac{x^3}{16} & \text{for } 0 \le x \le 2 \\ 1 & \text{for } x > 2 \end{cases}$

7 $\dfrac{3}{5}, 0.683$

8 (ii) $F(t) = \begin{cases} 0 & \text{for } t < 0 \\ \dfrac{t^3}{432} - \dfrac{t^4}{6912} & \text{for } 0 \le t \le 12 \\ 1 & \text{for } t > 12 \end{cases}$

(iv) 0.132

9 $F(x) = \dfrac{k}{2} - \dfrac{k \cos 2x}{2}$; 0.146

10 (i) (a) 0.3935 (b) 0.2231

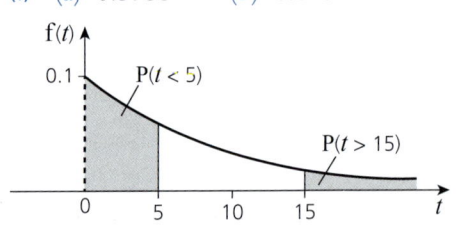

[graph of f(t) with P(t<5) and P(t>15) shaded]

(ii) $F(t) = 1 - e^{-0.1t}$; median $= 6.93$

(iii) 0.183

11 (ii) $1.25\left(1 - \dfrac{1}{m}\right) = \dfrac{1}{2}$

(iii) 0.495

(iv) $f(x) = \dfrac{1.25}{x^2}$ for $1 \le x \le 5$

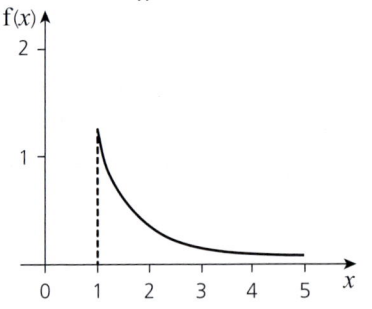

[graph of f(x)]

(v) $m = \dfrac{2b}{b+1}$, which is always less than 2

12 (i) $M = 3.568; 5.335$

(ii) $f(x) = \begin{cases} (x) = \dfrac{324}{x^5} & \text{for } x \ge 3 \\ 0 & \text{otherwise} \end{cases}$

(iii) $\dfrac{81}{256}$

13 $F(x) = \int f(t)\,dt$ and so $F'(x) = f(x)$.

Uniform distribution with mean value $\dfrac{a}{2}$.

$F(x) = 1 - \dfrac{(a-x)^2}{a^2}$ for $0 \le x \le a$.

Mean of sum of smaller parts $= a$

14 (i) (a) Validates p.d.f. form of Z.
      (b) Demonstrates that $E(Z) = 0$.
   (ii) (a) $E(Y) = 1$
       (b) $\text{Var}(Y) = 2$

Chapter 9

Exercise 9.1

1 (i) 0.8413
   (ii) 0.0548
   (iii) 0.7333

2 (i) 0.0548
   (ii) 0.6051
   (iii) 0.6816

3 (i) $4, 0.875$
   (ii) $1.5, 0.167$

(iii)

Main course	Dessert	Price
Fish and chips	Ice cream	£4
Fish and chips	Apple pie	£4.50
Fish and chips	Sponge pudding	£5
Bacon and eggs	Ice cream	£4.50
Bacon and eggs	Apple pie	£5
Bacon and eggs	Sponge pudding	£5.50
Pizza	Ice cream	£5
Pizza	Apple pie	£5.50
Pizza	Sponge pudding	£6
Steak and chips	Ice cream	£6.50
Steak and chips	Apple pie	£7
Steak and chips	Sponge pudding	£7.50

(iv) Mean of $T = 5.5$, variance $= 1.042$

4 (i) $N(90, 25)$
   (ii) $N(10, 25)$
   (iii) $N(-10, 25)$

5 0.196

6 (i) 0.0228

(ii) 56.45 minutes
(iii) 0.362
7 (i) 230 g, 10.2 g
  (ii) 0.1587
  (iii) 0.0787
8 5.92%
9 (i) 0.266
  (ii) No, people do not choose their spouses at random: the height of a husband and wife may not be independent.
10 0.151
11 (i) 0
   (ii) 0.0037
12 (i) 0.3533
   (ii) 60
   (iii) Using exact probability of 0.0521 gives 0.1482, using 0.05 gives 0.1426
13 (i) 0.29
   (ii) 4347
   (iii) Because the probability of scoring between 0 and 10 is about 0.99
   (iv) 0.0258
   (v) 113 or more
14 (i) (a) 0.025   (b) 0.242
   (ii) 130
   (iii) 0.161
   (iv) 0.03559

Exercise 9.2

1 (i) $N(5\mu, 25\sigma^2)$
  (ii) $N(5\mu, 5\sigma^2)$
2 (i) N(30, 15)
  (ii) N(100, 500)
  (iii) N(110, 205)
3 0.1946
4 0.0745
5 0.1377
6 (i) N(34, 30)
  (ii) N(−4, 30)
  (iii) N(24, 29)
7 (i) 0.316
  (ii) 0.316
8 (i) N(100, 26)
  (ii) N(295, 353)
  (iii) N(200, 122)
  (iv) N(−65, 377)
9 (i) 0.0827
  (ii) 0.3103
  (iii) 0.5
10 (i) 0.0827
   (ii) 0.1446
   (iii) 0.5

11 (i) N(7400, 28 900)
   (ii) N(1200, 27 700)
   (iii) $N(600a+1000b, 400a^2+900b^2)$
12 (i) 0.4546
   (ii) 93.491
13 0.9026
   Assume weights of participants are independent since told teams were chosen at random.
14 (i) N(2000, 1250)
   (ii) 1942
   (iii) 0.7373
15 (i) 14%
   (ii) 0.6
   (iii) 15 m
   (iv) 0.3043
16 (i) $S \sim N(600, 105.8)$; 0.0724
   (ii) 0.839
   (iii) 0.161
   (iv) $\mu = 30.54$ g
17 (i) N(80, 8)
   (ii) N(40n, 4n)
   (iii) 0.0207
   (iv) 0.0456
   Choice of limits is ±2 standard deviations from the mean and so will include 95% of piles that contain 25 pamphlets.
18 (i) 0.3341
   (ii) 0.1469
   (iii) 394.38 mm
   (iv) 0.9595
   (v) 0.1478

Exercise 9.3

1 (i) N(60, 8)
  (ii) N(300, 40)
  (iii) N(3000, 400)
2 (i) Cannot because the distribution of the parent population is unknown
  (ii) N(6000, 27 000)
  (iii) N(20 000, 90 000)
3 N(540, 270). Assume that the times are independent.
4 0.1030
5 0.9772
6 (i) 120
  (ii) 0.7977
  (iii) If the claim is true, the probability of a result as low or lower than this is 0.0000023. This suggests very strongly that the claim is wrong.
7 (i) 0.5945
  (ii) 200
8 $n = 80$

9 (i) 0.1367
  (ii) 0.2635
  (iii) 0.5176
10 (i) 0.2420
  (ii) 0.01343
11 (i) 1.6
  (ii) (a) 0.06227 (b) 0.0144 (c) 0.6515

Chapter 10

Discussion point, page 247
One cannot make any firm conclusions unless it is known that the sample is random.

Discussion point, page 247
It tells you that μ is about 101.2 but it does not tell you what 'about' means, i.e. how close to 101.2 it is reasonable to expect μ to be.

Exercise 10.1
2 (i) 1021.5
  (ii) 1.94
3 (ii) −3.00 to 4.58
  (iii) No evidence to suggest that there is any difference since the interval contains zero.
4 (ii) 0.054 to 0.818
  (iii) Since the interval does not contain zero, there is evidence to suggest that the absentee rate is less after the introduction of the scheme.
5 (i) 5.205
  (ii) 5.117, 5.293
6 (i) 47.7
  (ii) 34.7 to 60.7
  (iii) 27.3 to 68.1
7 (i) 0.9456
  (ii) £7790–£8810
8 (i) (a) 0.1685
      (b) 0.0207
  (ii) 163.8–166.6
  (iii) 385
9 (i) 6.83, 3.05
  (ii) 6.58, 7.08
10 (i) 5.71 to 7.49
   (ii) It is more likely that the short manuscript was written in the early form of the language.

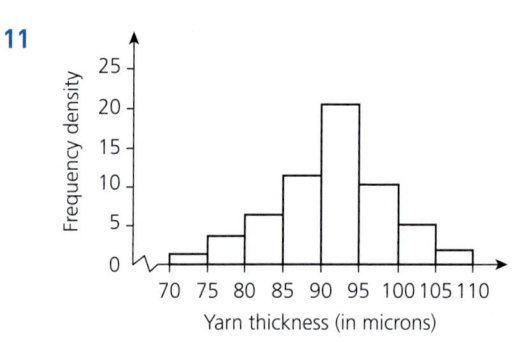

11

91.32, 7.41; 0.43; 90.5, 92.2

12 (i) Players' scores cannot be Normally distributed because symmetry would require negative scores.
   (ii) 11.79, 13.64
   (iii) It would reduce the width of the confidence interval but the interval would be centred in the same place.
   (iv) Approximately 102 500
13 (i) 0.00467
   (ii) 1.1128 to 1.1352
       You must assume that the data are from a random sample and that 0.00467 is an acceptable value for σ^2.
   (iii) μ is not a random variable so cannot have a probability attached to it. The correct interpretation is that 90% of all such intervals that could arise in repeated sampling will contain the population mean.
   (iv) It is not reasonable to suppose that the target is being met as 1.136 is not in the interval.
14 (i) 7.4, 4.05
   (ii) 7.64, 64.758
       This suggests that the mean is about right but that the variance is much too small.
   (iii) 6.316 to 8.964
   (iv) The confidence interval is only approximate because the distribution cannot be assumed to be Normal and because σ^2 is not known. The approximation is good because the sample is large enough to suggest that both the central limit theorem would apply, so that $\bar{X}$ can be assumed to be approximately Normal, and that s^2 could be used as an approximation for σ^2 without serious loss of accuracy.
15 (i) 3.768, 0.4268
   (ii) 3.644 to 3.892
   (iii) 90% of all such intervals that could arise in repeated sampling will contain the population mean.

(iv) N(0, 1)
(v) The sample is large enough to suggest that v could be used as a good approximation for σ^2 without serious loss of accuracy.

16 (i) 1.838 mm
(ii) 1.630 to 1.910
(iii) The coach's suspicious seem to be confirmed as 4 mm is not in the confidence interval.

17 0.484 to 1.016
Assume that the sample standard deviation is an acceptable approximation for σ. The aim has not been achieved as the interval contains values below 0.5.

Exercise 10.2

1 (i) $\sqrt{\dfrac{s^2}{n}} = \sqrt{\dfrac{148.84}{7}} = 4.61$

2 (i) 11.25

3 (i) 322.9, 79.54
(ii) 278.8–366.9

4 (i) 66, 17.15
(ii) 51.7–80.3
(iii) The distribution of the yield of all the fruit farmer's trees is Normal.
(iv) Number all the trees with different consecutive integers. Copy these integers on to separate pieces of paper; put these in a hat and pick out eight at random. The numbers chosen will identify the trees to be picked for the sample.

5 (i) 18.25, 3.72
(ii) 16.32–20.18
(iii) The distribution of lengths of sentences written by the accused man is Normal and the text represented by the sample sentences is representative of the general length of sentences he writes.
(iv) The sample mean lies just outside the particular 90% confidence limits provided by this sample but could well be inside those provided by other samples. Further, it is within the 95% confidence limits. So the evidence is not sufficient to declare him not guilty.

6 (i) Monday
(ii) The 23 weekdays
(iii) 629.7–661.9
(iv) True, this distribution is not a Normal one, but it may still be accurately modelled by one. $s = 37.24$ so the step size is small compared with the standard deviation. It is very common in statistics to make a Normal approximation to a discrete distribution and the results are usually very reliable.

7 (i) 63.6–72.0
(ii) Statistical: the distribution of tyre condemnation mileages is Normal and the 12 tyres tested in the sample are representative of the distribution. Practical: the tyres are tested under genuine working conditions.

8 (i) 21
(ii) The distribution is not Normal.
(iii) No because the confidence interval obtained would be too wide to be meaningful.
(iv) 45.0–66.3; the procedure will be valid provided that the distribution of life expectancies for this group is Normal.

9 (i) 0.633–0.647
(ii) 0.78, 0.160
(iii) 0.616–0.944
(iv) Large sample; no need to assume underlying Normality

10 (i) $1.9859 < \mu < 2.3202$
(ii) 12
(iii) The population of heights must be Normal and the sample must be random.

11 (i) Mean = 2.36, standard deviation = 3.06; $a = -0.557$, $b = 5.277$
Assumptions: journey times are a random sample; distribution of T is Normal.
(ii) Commuter's interpretation is wrong. It should be '90% of such confidence intervals should contain the true mean'.
(iii) Since the confidence interval contains zero, there is insufficient evidence to support the suspicion.
(iv) Confidence interval is likely to be narrow because of lower percentage-point for t value and lower standard error since sample size is large.

12 (i)

(ii) $0.616 < \mu < 0.804$
It is assumed that (1) the throws are independent, (2) that the sample size is large

enough for the estimate of σ^2 to be reliable enough to regard σ^2 as known and (3) that the sample size is large enough for the central limit theorem to indicate that $\bar{x}$ is Normally distributed.

(iii) 177. The standard deviation of the parent distribution is unknown and the distribution of R is not Normal.

(iv) The population is not Normal and the sample is small, therefore, neither the t distribution nor the central limit theorem can be used.

13 (i) The method must ensure that each club member has an equal chance of being chosen. Could put names in a hat and select at random or use the random number generator on a calculator.

(ii) Mean = 4.74, s^2 = 2.74

(iii) $3.56 < \mu < 5.92$
Background population is Normal.

(iv) By increasing the sample size; 13

14 (i) A random sample is one selected in such a way that all possible samples of the given size are equally likely.

(ii) All samples are possible so a sample of 'unusual' firms might be chosen. 'Biased' here means not representative of the population.

(iii) 8.748–9.552
The population is Normally distributed. 99% of all such intervals that could arise in repeated sample will contain the population mean.

15 (i) Because, on average, the confidence interval will not contain 55 mm in 1 in 20 batches.

(ii) Take a larger sample and construct a confidence interval based on this sample.

(iii) The Normal probability plot does not appear to show linearity.

(iv) $47.31 < \mu < 55.31$.

16 (i) $-0.29 < \mu < 1.72$

(ii) No, since the interval contains zero.

(iii) Assumptions: random sample of areas – could well have been;
Normally distributed differences in unemployment rates – not unreasonable.

17 (i) $-0.297 < \mu < 0.186$

(ii) Yes, since the interval contains zero.

(iii) Assumptions: random sample of races – apparently not since all the sprints on just one afternoon are taken;
Normally distributed differences in timings – not unreasonable.

18 (i) $1.84 < \mu < 14.16$

(ii) We do not know if the experimenter takes a random sample of the relevant population of rats. It seems plausible that the differences in the rats' times in the two conditions might be Normally distributed.

(iii) So that the effect of having learned to run the maze on the second trial affects each condition in the same way.

19 1.934–2.052, 9.373–10.551; 120, halved

Chapter 11

Exercise 11.1

1 (i) 0.9
  (ii) 1.9
  (iii) 1.645
  (iv) 1.9 > 1.645 so H_0 should be rejected.

2 (i) Because the sample is large so the central limit theorem applies.
  (ii) $H_0: \mu = 1.5$, $H_1: \mu < 1.5$
  (iii) 0.00142
  (iv) −1.968
  (v) −2.326
  (vi) −1.968 > −2.326 so H_0 should be accepted. There is insufficient evidence to suggest that the bags are underweight.

3 (i) This is the critical value for a 5% two-tailed test.
  (ii) $0.8796 < 2.3646$ so accept H_0.
  (iii) p-value $0.4082 > 0.05$ so accept H_0.

4 (i) $H_0: \mu = 0.155$; $H_1: \mu > 0.155$
    Where μ denotes the mean weight in kilograms of the population of onions of the new variety.
  (ii) $2.531 > 2.326$ so reject H_0. It is reasonable to conclude that the new variety has a higher mean weight.

5 $H_0: \mu = 47$, $H_1: \mu > 47$, $0.8185 < 1.645$ so accept H_0.

6 $H_0: \mu = 33.5$, $H_1: \mu < 33.5$, $-3.851 < -2.326$ so reject H_0. There is sufficient evidence to suggest that the mean weight has been reduced.

7 (i) $H_0: \mu = 18.6$, $H_1: \mu \neq 18.6$, Estimate of population standard deviation = 1.2438, $-1.46 < -1.645$ so accept H_0. There is insufficient evidence to suggest that the mean times have changed.

(ii) Alternative test is *t*-test. Critical value for $v = 29$ not given in tables but for $v = 25$ critical value is 1.725 so using this $-1.908 < -1.725$ so reject H_0. There is sufficient evidence to suggest that the mean times have changed.
Assumption is that the population of journey times is Normally distributed.

8 (i) $H_0: \mu = 72$ $H_1: \mu > 72$, $3.047 < 3.106$ so accept H_0. There is insufficient evidence to suggest that the batch has a higher than ideal rate.
(ii) Statistical: the distribution of drying rates is Normal and the sample is random.

9 (i) $H_0: \mu = 750\,g$, $H_1: \mu < 750\,g$
(ii) $t = -4.57$, significant
(iii) The distribution of weights in the shoal is Normal, this may be reasonable. The sample is random; this is certainly not the case since all the pollack came from one shoal. The masses are independent; this may not be true when all the fish are taken from one shoal and so are likely to be of the same age.

10 (i) The distribution of total points in a hand is Normal. This assumption is not fully justified because the distribution is not symmetrical about the mean; it is positively skewed. For example, you cannot have a hand with fewer than 0 points in it but you can get a hand with more than 20 points in it.
(ii) $H_0: \mu = 10$, $H_1: \mu < 10$
(iii) $t = -1.16$, not significant

11 (i) $H_0: \mu = 75$, $H_1: \mu \neq 75$
(ii) The population must be Normally distributed and the sample must be random
(iii) $t = 1.836$, not significant

12 (i) 0.1290
(ii) 0.4284
(iii) $t = 0.7026$, not significant

13 (i) $H_0: \mu = 14.0$, $H_1: \mu > 14.0$; $t = 2.8296$, significant
(ii) 14.197–15.763
(iii) The sample should be random, pigs should be similar (e.g. in initial weight), pigs should be kept under controlled conditions (e.g. in respect of exercise).

14 (i) $H_0: \mu = 9$, $H_1: \mu > 9$; $t = 3.51$, significant
Assume the population is Normally distributed and the sample is random.

15 (i) $H_0: \mu = 50$; $H_1: \mu < 50$, $-1.875 < -1.645$ so reject H_0. There is evidence to support the suspicion.
(ii) Maximum value = 49.7368
   (a) It should be accepted.
   (b) $N(49.9, 0.16)$
   (c) 0.8461
   (d) Conclusion should be to reject H_0 since $\mu < 50$, so probability of correct conclusion = 0.1539.

16 (i) $N(190, 5\frac{1}{3})$
(ii) The skulls in group B have greater mean lengths and so a one-tailed test is required.
(iii) 193.8
(iv) Sample mean = $194.3 > 193.8$ (or $1.809 > 1.645$) so reject H_0. There is evidence to support the belief that the skulls belong to group B.

Discussion point, page 293

There are several Wilcoxon tests; this one is for single samples, another for paired samples and a third is a 2 sample test. So the description as a single sample test distinguishes it from the others. The term 'signed rank test' says something about the nature of the test; it uses ranks and the test statistic distinguishes between ranks that can be assigned positive and negative ranks.

Discussion point, page 294

The null hypothesis is that the population median is 1.

The alternative hypothesis is that it is not 1 so a two-tailed test is required.

There are 3 values equal to the median so they are discarded, leaving a sample of size 12.

The value of W_- is 15 and the critical value for the test is 17.

So H_0 is rejected even though it is true. The wrong conclusion is reached.

The reason is that the distribution is not symmetrical so the test should not have been applied.

Exercise 11.2

1 (i) 25
(ii) $36 > 25$ so H_0 should be accepted.

2 (i) $n = 9$
(ii) 8

3. (iii) $8 \geq 8$ so H_0 should be rejected. There is sufficient evidence to suggest that the median is greater than 25.

3. (i) $W_- = 44$, $W_+ = 11$
   (ii) because $n = 10$ and $\frac{1}{2} \times 10 \times 11 = 55$
   (iii) $11 \geq 10$ so H_0 should be accepted. There is insufficient evidence to suggest that the median times have reduced.

4. $W = 19.5$, critical value $= 10$
   Accept H_0: no difference

5. $W = 166$, critical value $= 175$
   Reject H_0: score better
   She must have made the claim before she saw that year's scores were better than the borough average.

6. $W = 360$, critical value $= 336$ (Normal approximation)
   Accept H_0: watches not set fast

7. $W = 14$, critical value $= 19$
   Reject H_0: not correct

8. (i) A Wilcoxon signed rank test might be used when nothing is known about the distribution of the background population.
   Must assume symmetry (about the median).
   (ii) $H_0: m = 28.7$ $H_1: m > 28.7$ where m is the population median.
   $W_- = 18$, critical value $= 17$
   Result is not significant. Insufficient evidence to suggest that the median speed has increased.

9. (i) We have no information about the background population.
   (ii) Must assume symmetry (about the median).
   (iii) $H_0: m = 23$, $H_1: m < 23$ where m is the population median.
   $W_+ = 21$, critical value $= 17$
   Result is not significant. Insufficient evidence to suggest that the median number of days absent has been reduced.

10. (i) $W = 16$, critical value $= 13$
    Accept H_0: not greater
    The percentage of moisture in samples of grain is symmetrically distributed about its median level.
    (ii) $t = 1.933$, critical value $= 1.812$
    Reject H_0: greater
    The percentage of moisture in samples of grain is Normally distributed.
    (iii) The half of the data which is between the upper and lower quartiles is closely grouped around 3.4, there are long upper and lower quartile tails and the data is positively skewed. It is this odd sample distribution which produces a significant t statistic and an insignificant Wilcoxon statistic. It could be an erratic sample (only 11 items) or, if it is representative of the population, both Normal distribution and symmetry look unreasonable as assumptions.

11. There are 25 sets of ranks with sums less than or equal to 8 and $\frac{25}{512} = 0.0488 < 0.05$, but 33 sets of ranks with sums less than or equal to 9 and $\frac{33}{512} = 0.0645 > 0.05$.

12. (i) The distribution is likely to be skewed.
    (ii) $T = 6$
    (iii) (a) $T \leq 8$
         (b) $T \leq 3$
    (iv) There is some but not strong evidence against the claim.
    (v) $p = 0.0324$; good agreement

Chapter 12

Exercise 12.1

1. (i) = SUM(A2:J2)
   (ii) 0.2
   (iii) Not very good since it is based on only 10 trials.
   (iv) Use a much larger number of trials.

2. (i) = SUM(A2:H2)
   (ii) 0.25
   (iii) 0.144. This is rather less than the estimate, but since the estimate was based on only 20 trials, it is not likely to be very accurate.

3. (i) =RANDBETWEEN(1,4), =SUM(A2:F2)
   (ii) 0.55
   (iii) May not be very accurate since it is based on only 20 trials.
   (iv) Use a much larger number of trials.

4. (i) 0.75
   (ii) $\frac{1}{64}$
   (iii) Less because there are 64 possible outcomes and the higher two scores have to be equal. If the highest is 3, that only leaves one possibility {3, 3, 3} out of 64. If the highest is 6, that only leaves two possibilities {3, 6, 6} and {6, 6, 6}, etc.
   (iv) 0.24

5. (i) 0.6
   (ii) 0.0778

(iii) 0.76
(iv) Increase the number of trials.
(v) Add two more columns after column E for Saturday and Sunday and find the total for all 7 days.
(vi) =15*RAND()

6 (i) 5
(ii) 341.67
(iii) (a) 0.75 (b) 0.05 (c) 0.65

7 (i) 0.0912
(ii) =8*RAND()
(iii) =NORM.INV(RAND(),21,3)
(iv) 0.36

8 (i) Because the means of both Y and Z will be 250 and so, on average, half of the simulated values for each of Y and Z will be above 250 and half below.
(ii) =NORM.INV(RAND(),50,10)
(iii) $P(Y > 275) = 0.2$, $P(Z > 275) = 0.3$
(iv) Because far more trials than 10 would need to be carried out to provide evidence for such a statement.
(v) $P(Y > 275) = 0.1318$, $P(Z > 275) = 0.3618$

9 (i) With $n = 4$, the distribution of the sample mean is not Normal.
With $n = 15$, the distribution of the sample mean should be approaching Normal.
(ii) The probability plot for $n = 4$ is not very close to a straight line and also the p-value for the test is well below 0.01, which both again suggest that the distribution of the sample mean is not Normal.
The probability plot for $n = 15$ is very close to a straight line and also the p-value for the test is far above 0.10, which both again suggest that the distribution of the sample mean is very close to Normal.

10 (i) 0.5, $\frac{1}{12}$
(ii) 3, 0.5
(iii) 0.2397, 0.0786, 0.0169
(iv) 0.5, 0.25
(v) 3, 1.5
(vi) 0.3415, 0.1103
(vii) 0.2422, 0.0779, 0.0160. These three are all very close to the calculated probabilities.
(viii) 0.3433, 0.1086. Again, these two are all very close to the calculated probabilities.
(ix) Because the data are discrete, so a continuity correction is required.
(x) No, because the estimates from the spreadsheet are very close to the values from the Normal distribution.

11 (i) 0.0210
(ii) 0.2610
(iii) 0.2601

12 (i) 0.24
(ii) 0.35
(iii) 0.331
(iv) Because the value of n is only 5, so the central limit theorem does not apply.

Practice questions: Set 2 (page 319)

1 (i) $\mu = 2.4 \pm 2.2010 \times 1.3 / \sqrt{12}$; lower limit 1.57, upper limit 3.23.
(ii) The sample may be regarded as random. The data come from a Normal underlying population.
(iii) 95% of such confidence intervals contain the true but unknown value of the parameter.

2 (i) It would not be safe to assume an underlying Normal distribution.
(ii) The underlying distribution is symmetrical about its median. The sample may be regarded as random.
(iii) Null hypothesis: median is 5. Alternative hypothesis: median is not 5.
Sum of ranks for score below 5 is 31; sum of ranks for scores above 5 is 24.
Critical value for 5% two-sided test with a sample size of 10 is 8.
Since 24 > 8, there is insufficient evidence to reject the null hypothesis. That is, no reason to doubt that the median is 5.

3 (i) (a) $F(50) = 0.632$
(b) $F(30.4) - F(20.2) = 0.123$
(ii) $1 - e^{-0.02t} = 0.5 \Rightarrow t = \frac{\ln 0.5}{-0.02}$, 34.7 days
(iii) $f(t) = \frac{d(F(t))}{dt} = 0.02e^{-0.02t}$.
So this is an exponential distribution with $\lambda = 0.02$ and mean $\frac{1}{\lambda} = 50$.

[Alternatively: Original mean = $\int_0^\infty t \times 0.02 e^{-0.02t} dt = 50$]

An increase to 109.3 days shows the new medicine is likely to be beneficial.

4 (ii)

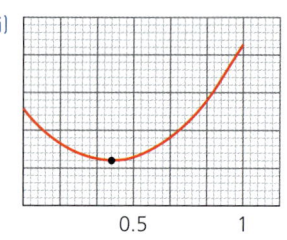

Low and high proportions are more common than middling proportions. That is, days tend to be mostly sunny or mostly cloudy rather than mixed.

(iii) $E(X) = 4/7$. $Var(X) = 3/7 - (4/7)^2 = 5/49$.

(iv) $E(Y) = 4/7$. $SD(Y) = (\sqrt{5})/35 \approx 0.0639$.

The distribution will be approximately Normal by the central limit theorem.

5 (i) These values look like clear errors (or outliers). It seems likely that the students concerned have measured the length of one arm.

(ii) The correlation shows that increases in height are closely associated with increases in arm length, but it does not show that they are approximately equal. The same correlation could apply if height was equal to 0.8 × arm length, for example.

(iii) The gradient (1.017) shows that a 1 cm increase in arm span is, on average, associated with just over a 1 cm increase in height. This supports the hypothesis.

However, the intercept (−3.989) indicates that the regression line does not pass through the origin. This casts some doubt on the hypothesis.

The gradient and intercept would vary from sample to sample so these two figures might be not significantly different from 1 and 0.

(iv) Null hypothesis: population mean difference is 0. Alternative hypothesis: population mean difference is not 0.

Test statistic: 1.268.

Critical value for a two-tailed z-test is 1.960.

Insufficient evidence to reject the null hypothesis. That is, no reason to doubt that, in the underlying population, height is equal to arm span on average.

(v) The sample size is large enough to use a Normal approximation to the distribution of the mean. So the test is not invalidated.

6 (i) The null hypothesis is that the underlying distribution is Normal. The alternative hypothesis is that the underlying distribution is not Normal.

Alpha is the significance level of the test (here 5%). The *p-value* is the probability, when the null hypothesis is true, of obtaining a result as extreme as, or more extreme than, the one observed.

The *p-value* is less than *Alpha* so the null hypothesis is rejected. That is, the test suggests that the underlying distribution is not Normal.

(ii) The *p-value* is (much) greater than *Alpha* so the null hypothesis would be accepted. That is, there would be no reason to suppose the distribution is non-Normal.

With such a large *p-value* the graph (a Normal probability plot) would be very nearly linear.

(iii) In the long run, 5% of samples will lead to the conclusion 'Reject null hypothesis'.

With a larger sample size, but still at the 5% level of significance, 5% of samples will lead to the conclusion 'Reject null hypothesis'.

A larger sample will make the test more sensitive to deviations from Normality.

Index

A
alternative hypothesis 277
associations 76
    non-linear 90, 104–5

B
Bayes' theorem 174–6
    key points 178
bimodal distribution 7
binomial distribution 45–6
    comparison with Poisson distribution 59–60
    expectation and variance 46–7
    goodness of fit test 152–6
    key points 72
bivariate data 12, 75
    see also correlation; regression

C
categorical (qualitative) data 8
causation 90
censuses 3
central limit theorem 240–2
    spreadsheet investigation 308–9
central tendency, measures of 11
    see also mean; median; mode
chi-squared (χ^2) distribution 135–7
    left-hand tail 156–8
chi-squared (χ^2) tests 148–9, 164
    for contingency tables 134–5, 138–40
    notation 137–8
    properties of 137
    using a spreadsheet 141
    using statistical software 140–1
class boundaries 182
cluster sampling 5
coefficient of determination 117, 124
conditional probability 173–4
    Bayes' theorem 174–6
    key points 178
    notation 170, 171
    screening tests 170–2
confidence intervals 247
    dice-throwing experiment 251–3
    key points 274–5
    known and estimated standard deviation 250
    paired samples 250–1
    and sample sizes 253–4
    t distribution 262–5
    theory of 247–9
    using statistical software 249
confidence levels 248
confidence limits 248
contingency tables 133–4
    chi-squared (χ^2) tests 134–5, 138–40
    and conditional probabilities 171–2
    degrees of freedom 136
    key points 164
continuity corrections 228, 242
continuous data 9
continuous random variables
    cumulative distribution function 209–16
    expectation and variance 190–2
    exponential distribution 198–9
    functions of, expectation and variance 203–6
    key points 220–1
    median 192, 194
    mode 193–4
    probability density 180–1
    probability density function 181–6
continuous uniform (rectangular) distribution 195–6
    key points 221
    mean and variance 197
    simulation of 305–6
controlled variables 76
correlation 76
    interpretation 90–2
    key points 113
    product moment correlation 79–89
    rank correlation 101–5
    scatter diagrams 77–9
critical ratios, hypothesis testing 279
critical regions, hypothesis testing 278
cumulative distribution function (c.d.f.) 209–11
    examples 213–16
    general results 212
    key points 221
    median 212
cumulative frequency curves 10

D
data collection 3
    sampling techniques 4–7
data description 7–9
data displays 9–10
data distributions 7
data processing 7
data types 8–9, 18
degrees of freedom 89, 148, 164, 260
    and chi-squared distribution 136
    for a contingency table 136
dependent variables 76, 115
deviation from the mean 12
differences of Normal variables 225–7, 231–3
differences of random variables 35–8
discrete data 9
discrete probability distributions
    binomial distribution 45–7, 60
    geometric distribution 67–70
    key points 72–3
    Poisson distribution 49–60
    uniform distribution 64–7
discrete random variables 20–1
    expectation and variance 26–35
    functions of, expectation and variance 203
    key points 42–3
    linear combinations 38
    notation and conditions for 22–3
    sums and differences of 35–8
discrete uniform distributions 64–7
    simulation of 304–5
distribution-free tests 158

E
effect sizes 91–2
errors, Type 1 and Type 2 277
estimates of parameters 3
expectation
    of the binomial distribution 46–7
    of a continuous random variable 190–2
    of a discrete random variable 27–30, 42–3
    of an exponential distribution 198
    of a function of a continuous random variable 203–6
    of a function of a discrete random variable 203
    general results 34, 205
    of a geometric distribution 69
    of a linear function of a random variable 33
    of a uniform distribution 65–7
expected frequencies of a Poisson distribution 50
exponential distribution 198–9
    key points 221
extrapolation 90–1, 119

F
factorials 50
false positives, false negatives 170–1
finite discrete random variables 21
frequency charts 9–10
    for discrete random variables 20
frequency of a variable 7
functions of a continuous random variable 203–6
functions of a discrete random variable 203

G
geometric distribution 67–70
    key points 73
geometric random variables 67
goodness of fit tests
    for a binomial distribution 152–6
    interpretation 158

Index

key points 164
    for a Normal distribution 265–8, 275
    for a Poisson distribution 149–52, 156–7
    for a uniform distribution 147–9
Gosset, William S. 262
grouped data 7

H

histograms 9–10
hypothesis testing 277
    key points 299–300
    large samples 280–1
    product moment correlation 85–9
    rank correlation 102–4
    using a spreadsheet 283
    using statistical software 279–80
    using the Normal distribution 277–81
    using the t distribution 281–3
    Wilcoxon signed rank test 289–96

I

independent variables 76, 115
infinite discrete random variables 21

K

Kalmogorov–Smirnov (Lilliefors) test 267–8

L

large samples, hypothesis testing 280–1
least squares regression
    key points 131
    random on non-random 115–20
    random on random 124–5
left-hand tail, chi-squared (χ^2) distribution 156–8
Lilliefors (Kalmogorov–Smirnov) test 267–8
linear combinations of random variables 38
    expectation and variance 38
    Normal distribution 233–5
linear functions of a random variable 33
    expectation and variance 33
location parameters 296

M

marginal totals, contingency tables 133
matched samples
    confidence intervals 250–1
    t distribution 264–5
mean 11–12, 19
    of a discrete random variable 27–30
    distribution of the sample mean 238–40
    of a Normal distribution 223
    of a Poisson distribution 53
    of the uniform (rectangular) distribution 197
    see also expectation
median 8

of a continuous random variable 192, 194
of a cumulative distribution function 212
mode 193–4
multivariate data sets 75

N

negative correlation 76, 77
non-linear association 90, 104–5
non-parametric tests 290
Normal distribution 223–5
    goodness of fit tests 261, 265–8, 275
    hypothesis testing 277–81, 299–300
    key points 243–4
    linear combinations of random variables 233–5
    modelling discrete variables 227–8
    notation 223
    simulation of 306–7
Normal probability plots 265–7
Normal variables, sums and differences of 225–7, 231–3
null hypothesis 277
numerical (quantitative) data 8–9
    displays 9–10
    summary measures 11

O

one-tailed tests 85, 149
    hypothesis testing 277, 278
    left-hand tail 156–8
opportunity sampling 6
outliers 8, 78

P

paired samples
    confidence intervals 250–1
    t distribution 264–5
parameters 3
parent population 3
Pearson, Karl 105
Pearson's product moment coefficient 81–4, 113
perfect correlation 76
planning 2
Poisson distribution 49–51
    comparison with binomial distribution 59–60
    conditions for 51
    examples 52
    goodness of fit test 149–52, 156–7
    key points 72
    mean and variance 53
    modelling with 52–5
    sum of two or more distributions 57–9
populations 3
positive correlation 76, 77
probabilities, use in hypothesis testing 278–9
probability density 180–1
probability density function (p.d.f.) 181–6
probability distributions 22–3

expectation and variance 26–30
problem-solving cycle 2, 18
product moment correlation coefficient 81–4
    interpretation 84–9
    key points 113
p-values 279, 280

Q

qualitative (categorical) data 8
quantitative (numerical) data 8–9
    displays 9–10
    summary measures 11
quartiles 8
quota sampling 6

R

random on non-random regression lines 115–20, 131
random on random regression lines 124–5, 131
random processes 3
random variables 7
rank correlation 101–2
    hypothesis testing 102–4
    key points 113
    when to use it 104–5
ranked data 8
    Wilcoxon signed rank test 289–92
rectangular (continuous uniform) distribution 195–6
    continuous 195–7, 221
    expectation and variance 197
    goodness of fit test 147–9
    key points 221
    simulation of 305–6
regression lines
    key points 131
    least squares regression (random on non-random) 115–20
    least squares regression (random on random) 124–5
residuals 116

S

sample sizes 253–4
sampling 3, 4, 18
sampling distribution (of the means) 238–40, 244
    central limit theorem 240–2
sampling error 3
sampling fraction 3
sampling frame 3
sampling techniques
    cluster sampling 5
    opportunity sampling 6
    quota sampling 6
    self-selected sampling 6
    simple random sampling 4
    stratified sampling 5
    systematic sampling 5–6

scatter diagrams 75
    interpretation 77–9
    non-linear association 90
    regression lines 115–20
screening tests
    Bayes' theorem 174–6
    conditional probability 170–2
self-selected sampling 6
set notation 170, 171
significance levels 279, 280
simulation 308
    and central limit theorem 308–9
    of continuous uniform distributions 305–6
    dice-throwing 302–3
    of discrete uniform distributions 304–5
    key points 318
    of Normal distributions 306–7
skew 7
small samples 259–61
Spearman, Charles 105
Spearman's rank correlation coefficient 101–2, 113
    hypothesis testing 102–4
spread, measures of 11
spreadsheets
    chi-squared tests 141
    dice-throwing simulation 252–3, 302–3
    expectation and variance of the binomial distribution 46–7
    goodness of fit test for a Poisson distribution 152
    hypothesis testing 88, 283
    investigation of central limit theorem 308–9
    least squares regression 120

product moment correlation 84
simulation of continuous uniform distributions 305–6
simulation of discrete uniform distributions 304–5
simulation of Normal distributions 306–7
standard deviation 11–13, 19, 28
    of a Normal distribution 223
standard error of the mean 239, 241
stratified sampling 5
Student's t test *see* t distribution
sums of Normal variables 225–7, 231–3
sums of Poisson distributions 57–9
sums of random variables 35–8
systematic sampling 5–6

T

t-distribution 261
    confidence intervals 262–5
    hypothesis testing 281–3, 300
    key points 275
    paired samples 264–5
    tests for Normality 265–8
test statistics, hypothesis testing 279
tree diagrams 172
two-tailed tests 85
    hypothesis testing 277
Type 1 errors 277
Type 2 errors 277

U

uniform distribution 64–5
    continuous 195–7, 221
    expectation and variance of 65–7

goodness of fit test 147–9
    key points 72
unimodal distribution 7

V

variables 7
    controlled 76
    dependent and independent 76, 115
variance 12, 19
    of the binomial distribution 46–7
    of a continuous random variable 190–2
    of a continuous uniform distribution 197
    of a discrete random variable 27–30, 42, 43
    of a discrete uniform distribution 65–7
    of an exponential distribution 199
    of a function of a continuous random variable 203–6
    of a function of a discrete random variable 203
    general results 34–5, 205
    of a geometric distribution 69
    of a Poisson distribution 53

W

Wilcoxon signed rank test (Wilcoxon single sample test) 289–92, 300
    examples 294–5
    formal procedure 292–3
    rationale for 293–4
    uses of 296

Y

y on x regression lines 117, 124